DIRECTORY OF
TOWN PLANS
IN BRITAIN

Published by the Automobile Association
Fanum House, Basingstoke, Hants RG21 2EA

Produced by the Publishing Division of the Automobile Association.

Maps in this book can be found in Thompson Local Directories.

Published by the Automobile Association, Fanum House, Basingstoke, Hampshire RG21 2EA.

Printed and bound by Graficromo SA, Spain.

ISBN 0 86145 400 6

AA Ref 59323

TO USE THIS BOOK

This book is divided into four colour-coded sections:

SOUTHERN ENGLAND   **LONDON**
CENTRAL ENGLAND AND WALES
NORTHERN ENGLAND AND SCOTLAND

Look for the town or airport you want in the complete index below. Use the colour coding to find the right section, then turn to the page number shown.

INDEX OF TOWNS AND AIRPORTS

Contents

Route Planning Maps   IV – XIII

Southern England ▨

London ▨

Central England and Wales ▨

Northern England and Scotland ▨

See opposite for how to use this book. For easy reference, a regional list of contents is also given at the start of each section, showing town and airport plans with page numbers and a regional location map.

INDEX OF TOWNS AND AIRPORTS

Cardigan

Bay

Aberdovey

Aberystwyth

Aberaeron

Tregaron

New Quay

Lampeter

Cardigan

Newcastle
Emlyn

Llandeilo

Strumble Head

Fishguard

Carmarthen

St Clears

Ammanford

St David's

Pontardulais

Ramsey
Island

Haverfordwest

Narberth

Llanelli

Skomer
Island

Milford
Haven

Neyland

Skokholm
Island

Pembroke

Tenby

Swansea

**Port
Talbot**

St Govan's Head

Port-Eynon

Porthca

B r

Lynton

Fo

Lundy

Ilfracombe

Lynmo

Morte Point

*Combe
Martin*

Braunton

Barnstable

E X M

Hartland Point

Bideford

South

*Great
Torrington*

Chulmleigh

Kilkhampton

Bude

Hatherleigh

Cred

Holsworthy

Okehampton

Tintagel

Launceston

D A R T M O O

Camelford

*Trevose
Head*

Padstow

B O D M I N

Tavistock

Ashburton

M O O R

Callington

Buckfastleigh

Wadebridge

Bodmin

Liskeard

Saltash

Totnes

Newquay

Lostwithiel

Plympton

Modbury

St Austell

Fowey

Looe

Plymouth

Truro

St Mawes

Dodman Point

Rame
Head

Kin

St Ives

Redruth

Camborne

Salcombe

Penzance

Hayle

Helston

Falmouth

Land's
End

Lizard

Lizard Point

IV

Isles of Scilly

TOWN PLANS IN GREATER & CENTRAL LONDON

1 Barking
2 Barkingside
3 Barnet
4 Battersea
5 Beckenham
6 Brentford
7 Brixton
8 Bromley
9 Carshalton
10 Coulsdon
11 Croydon
12 Dalston/Hackney
13 Ealing
14 East Ham
15 Edgware
16 Edmonton
17 Eltham
18 Enfield
19 Epsom
20 Finchley
21 Greenwich
22 Hammersmith
23 Hampstead
24 Harlesden
25 Harrow
26 Hayes
27 Heathrow Airport
28 Hendon
29 Holloway
30 Hornchurch
31 Hounslow
32 Ilford
33 Islington
34 Kingston
35 Lambeth/Bermondsey
36 Lewisham
37 Leyton
38 Leytonstone
39 London (Central)
40 Loughton
41 Mitcham
42 Orpington
43 Palmers Green
44 Peckham
45 Purley
46 Putney
47 Richmond
48 Romford
49 Southall
50 Stanmore
51 Stoke Newington
52 Stratford
53 Streatham
54 Surbiton
55 Sutton
56 Tottenham
57 Twickenham
58 Upminster
59 Uxbridge
60 Walthamstow
61 Wandsworth
62 Wembley
63 West Drayton
64 Whitechapel
65 Willesden
66 Wimbledon
67 Wood Green
68 Woolwich
69 Yiewsley

VII

Cape Wrath

Faraid Head

Whiten Head

Strathy Point

Dunnet Head

Stroma

Pentland Skerries

Duncansby Head

Durness

A838

Scrabster

Thurso

A836

Castletown

John O'Groats

Bettyhill

Melvich

A836

Halkirk

Noss Head

Handa

Tongue

A836

Laxford Bridge

A838

A894

Altnaharra

A836

Kinbrace

Latheron

Wick

A9

A882

A885

Point of Stoer

Unapool

A837

Rubha Coigeach

Summer Isles

Ledmore Junction

A835

Lairg

A839

Brora

Helmsdale

A9

Lochinver

Priest Island

Horse Island

Greenstone Point

Ullapool

A835

A837

A836

Bonar Bridge

Golspie

A839

Rubha Reidh

A832

Braemore Junction

Dornoch

A9

Longa

Gairloch

A832

A835

Tain

Tarbat Ness

Moray Firth

Rona

Kinlochewe

A832

Garve

Dingwall

Invergordon

Alness

Cromarty

Lossiemouth

Buckie

Cullen

Portsoy

Ba

Torridon

Shieldaig

A896

Achnasheen

A832

A890

A832

A835

A832

Nairn

Forres

A96

Elgin

A941

A98

A95

Inner Sound

aasay

Lochcarron

A896

A890

A862

Inverness

A96

Rothes

Charlestown of Aberlour

A941

Keith

A95

Scalpay

Kyle of Lochalsh

Stromeferry

A87

A890

Dornie

A831

A82

A833

Cannich

A831

Drumnadrochit

Dufftown

A920

Huntly

A96

ro

Kyleakin

A850

Shiel Bridge

A87

Invermoriston

A887

A82

Grantown-on-Spey

Carrbridge

A938

A95

Rhynie

A97

Sound of Sleat

A851

A87

Fort Augustus

A82

MONADHLIATH

MOUNTAINS

Boat of Garten

A939

Tomintoul

A944

Alford

A980

Mallaig

Invergarry

Aviemore

A93

Arisaig

A830

A861

A82

Kingussie

Newtonmore

Laggan

A86

A889

A9

Braemar

Ballater

Aboyne

Banch

of Arisaig

Kinlochmoidart

Spean Bridge

A86

Dalwhinnie

A9

Salen

A861

Corpach

Fort William

A82

Laurenc

Lochaline

A884

Glencoe

South Ballachulish

A828

Portnacroish

A861

A82

Blair Atholl

A924

Brechin

A933

Lismore

OF

rba

Kerrera

Connel

Oban

Taynuilt

Dalmally

A85

A828

Killin

A827

Aberfeldy

Dunkeld

A826

Pitlochry

Blairgowrie

A923

A93

Kirriemuir

A926

A94

Forfar

A932

XII

Luing

Kilmelford

A816

Inverarary

A83

Crianlarich

A85

Lochearnhead

Comrie

Crieff

Methven

Perth

A85

Errol

Coupar Angus

A923

A928

Dundee

Newport-on-Tay

Carnoustie

Monifieth

arba

Ford

Strachur

A821

Callander

Doune

Dunblane

Auchterarder

Auchtermuchty

Bridge of Earn

M90

Kinros

Cupar

Ladybank

St Andrews

Crail

Anstruthe

Fi

Southern England

AREA MAPS ARE INDICATED IN BOLD.

Alton

Locally grown hops and water from the Wey Spring were once the mainstay of the brewers of Alton, a town whose origins stretch back to Roman times. Modern Alton has two attractive parks and a fine modern sports centre which is in great demand from both the locals and those in the surrounding area. The Curtis Museum, founded in 1855, contains local records and natural history.

Petersfield's focal point is The Square, a centuries-old market place, and the town also boasts a number of late 16th-century buildings, dating from before its days as a coaching route staging post. This attractive market town's amenities include the Festival Hall, for opera, concerts and plays, a modern sports centre, and the Heath, which lies to the south and is good for boating, fishing and rambling.

Haslemere in summer re-echoes to the sounds of medieval and Elizabethan music — the speciality of the annual Haslemere Festival, which is one of the oldest in the country. Once dependent on its iron, cloth and leather industries, this is now a popular residential area, and a number of well-preserved old buildings survive, particularly around the High Street. For local organisations, the town's best feature is possibly its Educational Museum, which they use extensively for its archaeology, geology, zoology, and art.

Central Petersfield / **Central Haslemere**

LEGEND

Town Plan

- AA recommended route
- Restricted roads
- Other roads
- Buildings of interest — Court | P |
- Car parks — | P |
- Parks and open spaces

Area Plan

- A roads
- B roads
- Locations — Froxford ○
- Urban area

Street Index with Grid Reference

Alton

Ackender Road	A3-A2-B2
Albert Road	A1
Amery Hill	C3
Amery Street	C3
Anstey Lane	F4
Anstey Road	E3-E4-F4
Archery Rise	A1
Ashdell Road	D2-E2
Basingstoke Road	A3
Bennet Close	B4
Bingley Close	B4
Borovere Close	A1
Borovere Gardens	A1
Borovere Lane	A1-B1
Bow Street	B1
Brandon Close	A4
Buckingham Close	A3-A2

Butts Road	A1-B1-B2
Caker Stream Road	F2-F3
Chalcrafts	E4
Chauntsingers Road	C3-D3-D4
Chawton Park Road	A1
Church Street	C3
Churchill Close	B1
Crowley Drive	D2-D1
Curtis Road	E1
Dickers Lane	E2-E3-F3
Eastbrook Road	D4-E4
Goodyers	D1-E1-E2
Greenfields Avenue	A4-B4-C4
Grove Road	B1
High Street	B2-C2-C3
Huntsmead	E1
Kings Road	A2
Kingsland Road	B2-B3
Kings Mead	E4
Lansdowne Road	E4
Langham Road	A3-B3-B2
Lenten Street	B3-B2-C3
Littlefield Road	D4-E4-E3
Lower Turk Street	C2-D2
Market Square	B2-C2
Market Street	C3-C2
Mill Lane	E2-F2-F3
Morland Close	C1-D1
Mount Pleasant Road	B2-B1-C1
Netherfield Close	B4
New Barn Lane	C1-D1
New Odiham Road	A4-A3
Normandy Street	C3-D3-E3-E4
Northanger Close	B4
Nursery Road	D4-E4
Old Acre Road	B1-B2
Old Odiham Road	C3-C4
Orchard Lane	D2-D3
Paper Mill Lane	D3-E3-E2
Park Close Road	E4
Plevna Close	D4
Princess Drive	A3
Queens Road	A2-B2-B1
Rack Close	A2-B2
St Lawrence Road	C4-C3-D3
Sandringham Close	A3
Spicers	D1
Spitalfields Road	C4-D4
Spital Hatch	E2-F2
Station Road	E3
Stillions Close	D1
Tanhouse Lane	B3-C3
The Ridgeway	D1
Thorpe Gardens	A4
Tilney Close	A4

Tower Street	B1
Turk Street	C2
Upper Grove Road	B1
Vaughans	D1
Vicarage Hill	C3
Vicarage Road	C2
Victoria Road	D3-D4-E4
Wentworth Gardens	B4-A4
Westbrooke Road	B2-B3
Whitedown	A2-A1
Willoughby Close	A4
Wilsom Close	E2
Wilsom Road	E2-E1-F1
Windmill Hill	C2-C1-D1
Young's Road	D4

Petersfield

Barham Road	B2-C2
Bedford Road	A2
Bell Hill	A4-A3
Bell Hill Ridge	A4
Borough Grove	B1
Borough Road	A1-B1-B2
Buckingham Road	A2
Bucksmore Avenue	A3
Causeway	B1-C1
Chapel Street	B2
Charles Street	B2
College Street	C3-C2
Cranford Road	B1
Dragon Street	B2
Frenchmans Road	A3-A2-B2
Gloucester Road	A2
Grange Road	B1
Heath Road	C2
Heath Road West	C1-C2
Highfield Road	B3
High Street	B2-C2
Hylton Road	B2-C2-C1
Kimbers	B3
King George Avenue	B3-C3-B2-C2
Kingsfernsden Lane	C4
Lavant Street	B2
Love Lane	C3
Lynton Road	A3
Madeline Road	C3
Moggs Mead	C2
Monks Orchard	B4
Noreuil Road	A2
North Road	B3

Oaklands Road	A3
Osborne Road	B3
Penns Road	B3
Princes Road	A2
Queen's Road	A2
Ramshill	C3-C4
Readon Close	C3
Rushes Road	A3-A2
Sandringham Road	B3
Selbourne Close	B4-C4
Stafford Road	B4
Stanton Road	A3
Station Road	B2-B3-C3
Sussex Gardens	C2-C1
Sussex Road	C2-C1
Swan Street	B2
The Avenue	C2
The Borough	B2
The Square	B2
Tilmore Gardens	B4-C4
Tilmore Road	B4-B3
Tor Way	C3-C2
Weston Road	C2
Winchester Road	A2-A3
Winton Road	B3-B2
Woodbury Avenue	A3

Haslemere

Bartholomew Close	B4
Beech Road	B3-C3-C4
Bridge Road	B3
Bunch Lane	A3-A4-B4
Chatsworth Avenue	B4
Chestnut Avenue	B2-B3
Church Lane	B3-C3
Church Road	B3
Chiltern Close	A1
Collards Lane	C2
College Hill	B2
Courts Hill Road	A2-B2
Courts Mount Road	A2-B2
Denbigh Road	C1
Derby Road	A2-A3-B3
Field Way	B3
Grayswood Road	C3-C4
Great Gates Lane	C3
Halfmoon Hill	B2
Haste Hill	C1
Hazel Drive	A1
High Lane	B4-B3
High Street	B2-C2-C3

Higher Combe Road	C3
Hill Road	B2-B1-C1
Kemnal Park	C3
Kiln Fields	B4-B3
Kings Road	A2
Longdene Road	A1-A2
Lower Street	A2-B2
Midhurst Road	A1-B1-B2
Museum Hill	B2-C2
Old Haslemere Road	B1
Park Road	B2-B1
Parsons Close	B4
Parsons Green	B4
Path Fields Close	B3-C3
Pepperham Road	B4
Petworth Road	B2-C2-C1
Pine View Close	B4
Puckshot Way	B4-C4
Sandrock Street	B2
Scotland Close	A1
Scotlands Lane	A1-B1-C1
Shawbarn Road	C2
Shepherds Hill	B2
Stoatley Rise	A4
Tanners Lane	B2-B3
Tennysons Lane	C1
Uplands Close	C4
West Road	B2
Wey Hill	B2
Weycombe Road	B3-B4-C4
Weydown Road	A2-A3-A4-B4
Whitfield Road	B4

PETERSFIELD
Butser Ancient Farm, reconstructed to a prehistoric design, is one of the attractions of Queen Elizabeth Country Park — a serene area of countryside covering over 1,000 acres, which lies just three miles south of Petersfield on the A3.

Ashford

One of Britain's more unusual museums is that of the Intelligence Corps at Ashford's Templar Barracks — but those who only wish to investigate the secrets of this thriving market town might prefer to visit the Local History Museum or the Ashford Heritage Centre, which traces its bygones through to Roman times. Now an important industrial and commercial centre with good shops, Ashford also enjoys the facilities of the Stour Sports Centre and the greenery of Victoria Park.

Folkestone is a town of contrasts — between the gleaming modern ferries carrying holidaymakers to France and Belgium, and the narrow cobbled streets and old buildings which lie around its harbour. Flanked by 15th-century Martello towers on the clifftop is the Leas promenade, site of the Leas Cliff Hall (a major entertainment centre), and the New Metropolitan Arts Centre, which stages regular exhibitions. Visitors to the Leas can go by road or by lift — an unusual water-driven model has been in operation here since the 19th century.

Hythe Main terminus for the Romney, Hythe and Dymchurch Light Railway, which runs along the coast from here to Dungeness, Hythe is a peaceful, unspoiled resort. One of the Cinque Ports, its places of interest include the 17th-century Old Manor House and a parish church which has several 13th-century features.

Central Ashford

Central Hythe

LEGEND

Town Plan

AA Recommended roads	
Other roads	
Restricted roads	
Buildings of interest	Library
Car parks	P
Parks and open spaces	
One way streets	→

Area Plan

A roads	
B roads	
Locations	Lyminge
Urban area	

Street Index with Grid Reference

Folkstone

Alexandra Gardens	D2
Alexandra Street	F4
Archer Road	E4
Bayle Street	E2
Black Bull Road	D4-E4
Bolton Road	E4
Boscombe Road	D4
Bournemouth Road	C4-D4
Bouverie Place	D2
Bouverie Road West	A2-B2-C2
Bouverie Square	C2-D2
Bradstone Avenue	D3-D4
Bradstone Road	D3-E3
Bridge Street	F4
Broadfield Road	A4
Broadmead Road	C4-D4
Brockman Road	C3
Cambridge Gardens	E3
Canterbury Road	E4-F4
Castle Hill Avenue	B1-B2-B3-C3
Charlotte Street	E3
Cheriton Gardens	C2-C3
Cheriton Place	C2
Cheriton Road	A4-B4-C4-C3-D3-D2
Christ Church Road	C2-C3
Church Street	D2-E2
Claremont Road	C3
Clarence Street	E3
Clifton Crescent	A1-B1
Clifton Road	B1
Connaught Road	D3
Coolinge Road	C3-D3
Cornwallis Avenue	B4
Dawson Road	E4
Denmark Street	E4
Dover Road	E2-E3-F3-F4
Dudley Road	F3
Dyke Road	F2
Earls Avenue	A1-A2-A3
East Cliff	F2-F3
Eastfields	E4
Fern Bank Crescent	F3
Folly Road	F3
Foord Road	D3-D4
Foresters Way	D2-D3
Garden Road	D4
Gloucester Place	D2
Godwyn Road	A2-A3
Grace Hill	D3-D2-E2-E3
Grimston Avenue	A2-A3
Grimston Gardens	A2-A3
Grove Road	E3-F3
Guildhall Street	D2-D3
Harbour Approach Road	E1
Harbour Way	E2-E3
Harvey Street	E2-E3
Ingles Road	B2-C2
Jointon Road	A3-B3
Julian Road	B4
Kingsworth Gardens	B3-C3
Langhorne Gardens	B1
Linden Crescent	E4
London Street	E3-E4
Lower Sandgate Road	A1-B1-C1-D1-E1-E2
Manor Road	C2-C3
Marine Parade	D1-E1
Marine Terrace	E1
Martello Road	F3
Marten Road	A3-A4
Metropole Road East	A1-A2
Middleburg Square	C2-D2
Millfield	C2-D2
Morrison Road	F3-F4
North Street	E2-F2
Old High Street	E2
Oxford Terrace	D2
Pavilion Road	D4
Playdell Gardens	C1
Princess Street	F4
Queen Street	E3
Radnor Bridge Road	E3-F3-F2
Radnor Park Avenue	C4
Radnor Park Crescent	C4-D4
Radnor Park Road	C4-D4
Radnor Park West	B4-C4
Raventa Road	A4
Rendezvous Street	D2-E2
Road of Remembrance	D1-E1
Rossendale Road	F3
Ryland Place	F3
St John's Church Road	D4
St Johns Street	E3
St Michael's Street	E2-E3
Sandgate Road	A2-B2-B1-C1-C2-D2-D1-D2
Shakespeare Terrace	C1
Shellons Street	D2-D3
Shepway Close	D4-E4
Ship Street	D4
Shorncliffe Road	A4-A3-B3-C3
The Bayle	E2
The Durlocks	F2
The Leas	B1-C1-D1
The Parade	E2
The Tram Road	E2-F2-F3
Tontine Street	E2-E3
Trinity Crescent	A1-A2
Trinity Gardens	B2
Trinity Road	A2-B2-B3
Victoria Grove	D2-D3
Victoria Road	C4-D4
Walton Road	D4-E4
Wear Bay Road	F2
Westbourne Gardens	A2
West Terrace	D1-D2
Wiltie Gardens	C4
Wilton Road	B4

Ashford

Albert Road	B3-B4
Apsley Street	A2-B2
Bank Street	B2-B3
Belmore Park	A4
Blue Line Lane	B3-B4
Canterbury Road	B3-B4-C4
Castle Street	B2
Chart Road	A4
Church Road	B2
Dover Place	B1-C1
Eastern Avenue	A3
East Hill	A2
East Street	A2-A3
Elwick Road	B1-B2
Forge Lane	A3-B3
Gasworks Lane	A2
George Street	B1
Godington Road	A3-A2-B2
Hardinge Road	B3-C3
Hempstead Street	B3
High Street	B3-B2-C2
Inner Ring Road	B3
Kent Avenue	A3-B3
Kipling Road	A3
Mace Lane	C3
Magazine Road	A3-A4-B4-C4
Maidstone Road	A4
Milton Road	A3
New Street	A3-B3
Northbrook Lane	C1
North Street	B2-B3
Norwood Gardens	A3
Norwood Street	B2
Park Road	B3
Park Street	B3-C3
Quantock Drive	A4
Queen's Road	B4-C4
Queen Street	B2
Rooke Road	B4
Somerset Road	B3-C3
Station Road	B1-C2
Sussex Avenue	A4-B4-B3
Tannery Lane	C2
Tufton Street	B2
Vicarage Lane	B2-C2
Victoria Crescent	A1-B1
Victoria Road	A1-B1
Wall Road	B4
Wellesley Road	C2-C3
West Street	A2-A3

Hythe

Albert Lane	A2-B2
Albert Road	A2
Barrack Hill	A4
Bartholomew Street	B3
Boundary Road	A3
Brockhill Road	A4-B4
Castle Avenue	B4
Castle Road	B4
Chapel Street	B3
Churchill Court	A2
Church Road	B3-C3
Cinque Ports Avenue	A2-A3
Cobden Road	A2
Dental Street	B3-C3
Dymchurch Road	A3
Earlsfield Road	C2-C3
East Street	C3
Fairlight Avenue	A4
Fort Road	A3
Frampton Road	A3
Green Lane	A4
High Street	B3-C3
Hillcrest Road	B4
Hillside Street	B3
Ladies Walk (footpath)	B2
London Road	A4
Lower Black House Hill	C3
Lucy's Walk (footpath)	B2
Marine Parade	B2-C2
Military Road	A4-A3
Napier Gardens	B2
North Road	A4-B4-B3-C3
Ormonde Road	B2
Park Road	A2-B2
Portland Road	A3-B3
Prospect Road	B3-C3
Prince's Parade	C1-C2
Rampart Road	B3
Range Road	A2
St Leonard's Road	A2-A3-B3
St Nicholas Avenue	A3
Seaton Avenue	B4
Sir John Moore Avenue	A2-A4
South Road	B2-C2
Stade Street	B2-B3
Station Road	C3
Tanners Hill	C3-C4
Tanners Hill Gardens	C4
Tower Gardens	B2
Twiss Avenue	C3
Twiss Road	C2-C3
Victoria Road	B2
Wakefield Walk (footpath)	B2-C2
Wakefield Way	A2
West Parade	A2-B2
William Ditt Close	C3
Windmill Street	A2-B2

HYTHE
Running from Hythe to Dungeness Lighthouse, the 15-inch-gauge Romney, Hythe and Dymchurch Railway, with its 11 diminutive steam locomotives and one diesel, proudly claims the title of The Smallest Public Railway in the World.

Barnstaple

During the 18th century the wool trade created a prosperity in Barnstaple to which the town's elegant Georgian buildings testify. Queen Anne's Walk, a colonnade where merchants conducted business, is both a fine example of this period and a reminder that Barnstaple has always been a trading centre. This tradition continues as today it is one of the area's busiest market towns. Of the many picturesque shopping streets Butchers Row is particularly attractive.

Ilfracombe This is North Devon's well-established "Queen of the Coast". Originally a fishing harbour, Ilfracombe evolved in the 19th century – when enterprise was all – into one of the typical seaside resorts that mushroomed all over England. Here, terraces of large Victorian hotels and houses follow the contours of the hills down to the harbour and a welter of little coves. The town is also the main departure point for Lundy Island.

Bideford South-west of Barnstaple and Ilfracombe, Bideford too has always made its living by trading and the sea. Sir Richard Grenville, a Bideford man famous for his fight against the Spaniards in the Azores, gained a charter for the town from Elizabeth I and it prospered as a port and shipbuilding centre until the 18th century. A nautical air still pervades Bideford and the long, tree-lined quay is popular.

Central Bideford

Central Ilfracombe

LEGEND

Town Plan
- AA recommended route
- Restricted roads
- Other roads
- Buildings of interest — Station
- Car parks — P
- Parks and open spaces
- One way streets

Area Plan
- A roads
- B roads
- Locations — Patchole ○
- Urban area

Street Index with Grid Reference

Barnstaple

Abbey Road	A1-A2
Alexandra Road	C3
Allen Bank	F4
Ashleigh Crescent	D4-E4
Ashleigh Road	D4
Barbican Close	D4-E4
Barbican Lane	E4
Barbican Road	D4-E4
Barbican Terrace	D3-E3
Barum Arcade	C3
Bear Street	C3-C4
Bedford Street	D3
Belmont Road	B4
Belmont Terrace	B3-C3
Bevan Road	D4
Bicton Street	B4-C4
Boutport Street	B2-B3-C3-C2

Braunton Road	A1
Broadfield Road	E4-F4
Buller Road	D3
Bull Hill	A2
Butcher's Row	C2-C3
Byron Close	A3
Carlyle Avenue	A3-B3
Carrington Terrace	B3-B4
Castle Street	C1-C2
Charles Dart Crescent	B4-C4
Charles Street	B3
Clifford Street	D1
Coronation Street	B2-B3
Cross Street	C2
Derby Road	B4
Diamond Street	D2-D3
Fair View	A1-A2
Fort Street	C3-C4-D4
Fort Terrace	C3-D3
Gaydon Street	C3
George Street	B2-B3
Gloster Road	E4-F4
Goodleigh Road	C4
Granville Avenue	A3-B3
Green Lane	C4
Grosvenor Street	C4
Higher Church Street	D3
Higher Raleigh Road	A3
High Maudelin Street	B3
High Street	B2-C2
Hills View	C4
Holland Street	C1-C2
Joy Street	C2
King Edward Street	B3
Lethaby Road	B4
Litchdon Street	D2-D3-E3
Long Bridge	D2
Lower Raleigh Road	A3-A4
Magdalen Lawn	B3
Maiden Street	D2
Masefield Avenue	A3
Miller Crescent	C4
Mill Road	B1-B2
New Buildings	B3
Newport Road	E3-E4-F4
New Road	E3
Norfolk Terrace	F4
North Road	A2-A3-A4
North Walk	B1-B2
Park Lane	F4
Pathfield Lawn	A1-A2
Pilton Causeway	A2-B2
Pilton Lawn	A3
Pilton Street	A2
Portland Street	F4

Pottington Road	B1
Princes Street	B3
Priory Close	A2
Pulchrass Street	D3-D4
Queen Street	C3-D3
Raleigh Lawn	A3
Raleigh Road	A2-A3
Richmond Street	B4-C4
Riddel Avenue	A2-B2-B3
Rock Avenue	F4
Rock Gardens	F4
Rolle Street	B1-B2
St George's Road	A2-A3-A4
St Mary's Road	B4
Salem Street	D3
Signal Terrace	D1-E1
Silver Street	D3
South Walk	E3-F3
Sticklepath Terrace	D1-E1
Summerland Street	D3-D4
Sunflower Road	C4
Taw Vale	D2-D3-E3
The Rock	A2
The Square	D2
The Strand	C2-D2
Trinity Place	E3
Trinity Street	D3
Tuly Street	B2-C2
Vicarage Lawn	B3-C3
Vicrarage Street	B3-B4
Victoria Lawn	E4
Victoria Street	E4
Wells Street	C2-D2-D3
Yeo Vale Road	B2-B3

Bideford

Abbotsham Road	A2
Alexandra Terrace	A4
Allhalland Street	B2
Barnstaple Street	C2-C3
Bideford Bridge	B2-C2
Bridgeland Street	B3
Bridge Street	B2
Bull Hill	B1-B2
Buttgarden Street	B2
Chingswell Street	B3
Church Walk	B2
Clovelly Road	A1
Cold Harbour	B3
Cooper Street	B3
Copp's Close	A4

Coronation Road	A1
Elmdale Road	A4
Elm Grove	A3
Geneva Place	A1-A2
Glendale Terrace	A4
Grange Road	C2
Grenville Street	B2
Higher Gunstone	A2-B2-B3
High Street	A2-B2
Honestone Street	A2-B2
Hyfield Place	B2
Kingsley Road	A4-B4-B3
Kingsley Street	A3
Lime Grove	A3
Lower Gunstone	B3
Main Road	C3
Market Place	B2
Marland Terrace	A1
Meadowville Road	A4
Meddon Street	A1-A2-B2-B1
Mill Street	B2-B3
Milton Place	A2
Myrtle Gardens	A2-A3
Myrtle Grove	A3
New Road	B1-B2
Newton Road	A4-B4
Northam Road	A3-A4
Northdown Road	A3-B3
North Road	A3-B3
Northview Avenue	A4
Old Town	A2
Park Avenue	B3-B4
Park Lane	B4
Pitt Lane	A2-A3
Railway Terrace	C1-C2
Rectory Park	A2-A3
Rope Walk	B3
Silver Street	B3
The Quay	B2-B3-C3-C2
The Strand	B3
Torridge Hill	B1
Torridge Mount	C1
Torrington Lane	C1
Torrington Street	C1-C2
Victoria Gardens	A2-B2
Victoria Grove	A2-B2
Westcombe Lane	A3

Ilfracombe

Avenue Road	A3-B3
Belmont Road	A1-A2

Brookdale Avenue	A2-A3
Capstone Crescent	B4-C4
Castle Hill	C3
Church Hill	A2
Church Road	A2-A3
Comyn Hill	B1-C1
Fairlands	B2-C2-C1
Fernway	B1
Fore Street	B3-C3
Furze Hill Road	A2-A1-B1
Granville Road	A3-A4
Green Close Road	A3
Highfield Road	A2-B2-B3-C3
High Street	A2-A3-B2
Hillsborough Road	C3
Horne Park Road	A2-B2-B1
Horne Road	A2
Hostle Park Road	B3
Marine Drive	C3-C4
Market Street	B3
Marlborough Road	A2-B2
Mill Head	B3-B4
Montpellier Road	B3-C3
Northfield Road	A3
Osborne Road	A2
Oxford Grove	B3
Oxford Park	B3
Park Hill Road	B1-B2
Portland Street	B3-C3
Princess Avenue	B3-B2-C2
Promenade	B3-B4
Regent Place	A3
Richmond Road	A1
Riverdale Avenue	A3
Ropery Road	B4-C4
Runnacleave Road	A3
St Brannocks Park	A1
St Brannocks Park Road	A1-A2
St Brannocks Road	A1-A2
St James Place	B4-C4
Slade Road	A1
Springfield Road	B3
Station Road	A1-A2
The Quay	C4
Torrs Park	A3
Whittingham Road	C2-C3
Wilder Road	A2-A3
Worth Lane	C1-C2-C3

BARNSTAPLE
This ancient town stands on the Taw estuary and until the 19th century was an important port. The bridge across the river was originally built in the 1400s but has since been widened and extensively altered.

Basingstoke

Ever-expanding Basingstoke has seen a remarkable transformation in the last half-century, from quiet market town to major commercial and industrial centre, with a population of about 90,000. Rehousing for thousands of Londoners in the 1960s began the process, and easy access by road and rail to Heathrow Airport, Southampton Docks and London has made moving here an attractive proposition for large companies.

At the heart of the town is a large pedestrian shopping centre with good parking, a Sports Centre and a thriving theatre. Several specially created sports parks are in easy reach, and Mays Bounty, the local cricket ground, is regularly used by Hampshire for part of its County programme.

Basingstoke still boasts a number of older buildings, notably the 13th-century ruins of the Holy Ghost Chapel, which lie to the north of the railway station on the site of an ancient burial ground. St Michael's Parish Church dates mainly from the 16th century and has traces of Norman influence, although Second World War bombing destroyed most of the stained glass. The church also suffered damage in the Civil War from Cromwell's forces; two miles to the east of Basingstoke lie the ruins of Basing House, destroyed in 1645 by Parliamentary forces after a three-year resistance.

Central Basingstoke

Basingstoke Area

LEGEND

Town Plan

AA recommended route
Restricted roads
Other roads
Buildings of interest   Station
Car parks   **P**
Parks and open spaces
One way streets

Area Plan

A roads
B roads
Locations   Faccombe○
Urban area

Street Index with Grid Reference

Basingstoke

Abbey Road	C7-D7
Aldermaston Road	B8-C8-C7
Alencon Link	D4-D5
Alresford Road	C1-D1-D2
Armstrong Road	F5
Ashwood Way	B6
Attwood Close	B4
Basing View	D4-E4-E5-E4
Beech Way	A1-B1
Berkley Drive	A1-B1
Blackdam Way	E2-F2-F3-E3
Bounty Road	C4-C3-D3
Brahms Road	A1
Brighton Way	A1
Brighton Way	A2
Britten Road	A2-B2
Brunel Road	B6
Buckland Avenue	A6
Camrose Way	D2-D3
Carpenters Down	E7-E8-F8-F7
Cedar Way	A6
Chapel Hill	D5
Chineham Lane	D8-E8-E7
Chopin Close	A1-A2
Chuchill Way	D5-D4
Churchill Way East	E4-F4
Churchill Way West	A5-B5-C5-C4
Cliddesden Lane	A1
Cliddesden Road	B1-C1-C2-D2-D3
Cordale Road	C3
Coronation Road	E5
Cranbourne Lane	B2-B3
Crockford Lane	F7-F8
Cromwell Road	D5
Crossborough Hill	E3-E4
Culver Road	C3
Cumberland Avenue	A2
Darlington Road	D6
Deep Lane	B5-B4-C4
Doswell Way	E5
Eastrop Way	E4
Elizabeth Road	B3-B4
Elmwood Way	A6-A7-B7
Essex Road	C4
Fairfields Road	D3
Falkland Road	E7-F7
Faraday Road	F5-F6
Foyle Park	C3-C2-D2
Frescade Crescent	C3
Grafton Way	A5-B5-B4
Gresley Road	C2-D2-E2
Grove Road	C2-D2-E2
Hackwood Road	D4-D3-D2
Hamilton Close	B6-C6
Harlech Close	A5-A6
Hatch Warren Lane	A1-B1-B2
Hawthorne Way	A6
Hillary Road	C6-D6
Hill View Road	B3
Holbein Close	E2-E3
Houndmills Road	B5-B6-C6
Jays Close	B2-B1-C1-C2
Jefferson Road	E6
Jersey Close	E8-F8
Kelvin Hill	A3
Kingsclere Road	C6-C5-D5
Kingsclere Road	A7-B7
Kings Furlong	B3-B4

Brighton Way	A2
Britten Road	A2-B2
Brunel Road	B6
Buckland Avenue	A6
Camrose Way	D2-D3
Carpenters Down	E7-E8-F8-F7
Cedar Way	A6
Chapel Hill	D5
Chineham Lane	D8-E8-E7
Chopin Close	A1-A2
Chuchill Way	D5-D4
Churchill Way East	E4-F4
Churchill Way West	A5-B5-C5-C4
Cliddesden Lane	A1
Kingsmill Road	C2-C3
King's Road	A3-A4
Laburnum Way	A6
Lefroy Avenue	E5
Lilac Way	A6
Lister Road	B2-B3
Loggon Road	B2-C2
London Road	D4-E4-E3-F3
Lower Brook Street	B5-C5
Ludlow Close	A5-A6
Lydford Road	D5-E5
Lytton Road	E4
Madeira Close	F7
Maldive Road	F7
Mansfield Road	A3
Maple Crescent	D6
Merton Road	C6-D6
Millard Close	C6
Montserrat Road	E7-E8
Morley Road	B2-C2
Morse Road	B4
Neville Close	C2-D2
New Road	D4-D3
New Street	D4
Norn Hill	E5-E6
Oaklands Way	A6-A7
Oakridge Road	C6-D6-E6
Old Common Road	E3-F3
Old Worting Road	A5
Packenham Road	B4-C4-C3
Paddock Road	A3-A4
Pelton Road	C5
Penrith Road	C4
Pinkerton Road	A3
Popley Way	C7-D7-E7-F7-F6
Portacre Rise	B3-B4
Priestley Road	C7-C8
Queen Mary Avenue	D5-E5
Rankine Road	F6
Reading Road	F6-F7
Richmond Road	D5
Ringway East	F6-F5-F4-F3
Ringway North	B7-C7-D7-D6-E6
Ringway South	B3-C3-D3-E3-F3
Ringway West	B3-B4-B5-B6
Roman Road	A7
St Patrick's Road	A3-B3
St Peter's Road	A4
Sandy's Road	B3-B4
Sarum Hill	B4
Shakespeare Road	E7-E6-F6-F7
Sheppard Road	B2-C2
Sherborne Road	D7-D8
Shetland Road	E7-F7
Sherborne Road	C6-D6-D5

Shooters Way	E5-E6
Soper Grove	D5
Southern Road	D3
South Ham Road	B4
Stag Hill	A3
Station Approach	D5
Stocker Close	C2
Stratfield Road	D6-E6
Stravinsky Road	B1
Stukeley Road	B4-C4
Sullivan Road	A2-B2-B1
Swing Swang Lane	F5
Sycamore Way	B6-B7
Telford Road	B6
Tewkesbury Close	E7
The Harrow Way	A2-B2-C2
Timberlake Road	D4
Tintern Close	C7-D7
Upton Crescent	D6
Victoria Road	E6
Vivian Road	E6
Vyne Road	D5-D6
Wade Road	F5-F6
Wallis Road	D3
Warwick Road	A6
Wella Road	B3
Wessex Close	B3-C3
Western Way	A3-A4-B4
Willoughby Way	A5-A6
Winchester Road	A2-A3-B3-C3-C4-D4
Winchester Street	C4-E4
Winklebury Way	A6-A5-B5-B6
Worting Road	A5-A4-B4-C4

Basingstoke Central

Alencon Link	A3-B3-B4-C4-C3
Basing View	C3-C4
Beaconsfield Road	B1
Bounty Road	A2-A1-B1
Bramblys Drive	A2
Burgess Road	A4-B4
Castle Road	B1
Chapel Hill	A4-B4
Chequers Road	C2-C3
Churchill Way	A3-B3-C3
Churchill Way East	C3
Churchill Way West	A3
Church Square	B3
Church Street	B2-B3
Cliddesden Road	B1
Cordale Road	A1
Council Road	B1
Crossborough Hill	C1-C2
Doswell Way	C4
Eastfield Avenue	C2-C3
Eastrop Lane	C2-C3
Eastrop Way	C3
Essex Road	A3
Fairfields Road	B1
Flaxfield Road	A3-A2-B2
Frances Road	A2
Frescade Crescent	A1
Goat Lane	C3
Hackwood Road	C1-C2
Hardy Lane	A1-A2
Jubilee Road	B1-B2
Kingsclere Road	A4
London Road	C2
London Street	B2
Lower Brook Street	A3
Lytton Road	C2
Mortimer Lane	A3
New Road	B2-C2-C3
New Street	B2
Norn Hill	C4
Old Reading Road	C4
Penrith Road	A1-A2
Rayleigh Road	A3
Ringway South	C1
Rochford Road	A3
Sarum Hill	A3-A2-B2
Soper Grove	B4
Southend Road	A3
Southern Road	B2
Timberlake Road	A3-B3-C3
Victoria Street	B2
Vyne Road	B4
Wallis Road	B1
White Hart Lane	C2
Winchcombe Road	A2
Winchester Road	A1-A2-B2
Winchester Street	B2
Worting Road	A3
Wote Street	B2

BASINGSTOKE
Fanum House, headquarters of the AA, rises out of the Eastrop business area of town, which overlooks tranquil Eastrop Park.

Bath

This unique city combines Britain's most impressive collection of Roman relics with the country's finest Georgian townscape. Its attraction to Romans and fashionable 18th-century society alike was its mineral springs, which are still seen by thousands of tourists who visit the Roman Baths every year. They are now the centre-piece of a Roman museum, where exhibits give a vivid impression of life 2000 years ago. The adjacent Pump Room to which the waters were piped for drinking was a focal point of social life in 18th- and 19th-century Bath.

The Georgian age of elegence also saw the building of Bath's perfectly proportioned streets, terraces and crescents. The finest examples are Queen Square, the Circus, and Royal Crescent, all built of golden local stone. Overlooking the Avon from the west is the great tower of Bath Abbey – sometimes called the "Lantern of the West" because of its large and numerous windows.

Bath has much to delight the museum-lover. Near the abbey, in York Street, is the Burrows Toy Museum – a treasure-trove of playthings spanning two centuries. The Assembly Rooms in Bennett Street, very much a part of the social scene in Georgian Bath, are now the home of the Museum of Costume, and nearby, in Circus Mews, is the Carriage Museum, which vividly recalls coaching days.

Key to Town Plan and Area Plan

Town Plan

A A Recommended roads	
Other roads	
Restricted roads	
Buildings of interest	Library
Car Parks	P
Parks and open spaces	
Churches	†
One Way Streets	←

Area Plan

A roads	
B roads	
Locations	Box ○
Urban Area	

Street Index with Grid Reference

Central Bath

Ambury	C1-C2
Archway Street	E1-E2
Argyle Street	D3-D4
Avon Street	C2
Barton Street	C3
Bridge Street	C3-D3
Broadway	E2
Broad Street	C3-C4
Broad Quay	C1
Chapel Row	B3
Charles Street	B2-B3
Charlotte Street	B3-B4
Cheap Street	C3
Claverton Street	C1-D1
Corn Street	C2
Darlington Place	F2-F3
Dorchester Street	C1-D1
Duke Street	D2
Edward Street	E4
Ferry Lane	D2-E2
Gay Street	B4-C4-C3
George Street	B4-C4
George Street	F2-F3
Grand Parade	D3
Great Pulteney Street	D4-E4
Green Park	A2-B2
Green Park Road	B1-B2-C2-C1
Grove Street	D3-D4
Henrietta Gardens	E4
Henrietta Mews	D4-E4
Henrietta Street	D4
Henry Street	C2-D2
High Street	C3
Horseshoe Walk	F1
James Street West	A3-B3-B2-C2
John Street	B2
Kingsmead North	B2
Kingsmead Terrace	B2
Kingsmead West	B2
Laura Place	D3-D4
Lime Grove	E2-F2-F1
Lower Bristol Road	A2-A1-B1-C1
Lower Borough Walls	C2
Lower Oldfield Park	A1
Manvers Street	D1-D2
Marlborough Lane	A4
Midland Bridge Road	A2-B2-B3
Milk Street	B2
Milsom Street	C3-C4
Monmouth Place	B3
Monmouth Street	B3-C3
New Street	B2-B3-C3
New Bond Street	C3
New King Street	A3-B3
Nile Street	A3
Norfolk Crescent	A3
North Parade	D2
North Parade Road	D2-E2
Philip Street	C1-C2
Pierrepont Street	D2-D3
Princes Buildings	E1
Princes Street	B3
Pulteney Mews	E4
Pulteney Road	E1-E2-E3-E4
Queen Square	B3-B4-C4-C3
Quiet Street	C3
Raby Place	E4-E3-F3
Raby Villas	E4-F4
Rossiter Road	D1-E1
Royal Avenue	A4-B4
St Ann's Street	F3
St Jame's Parade	C2
St John's Road	D4
Sham Castle Lane	F4
Southgate	C1-C2
South Parade	D2
Spring Crescent	E2
Spring Gardens	D2
Stall Street	C2-C3
Stanhope Street	A3
Sutton Street	E4
Sydenham Buildings	A1-A2
Sydney Buildings	F1-F2-F3
Sydney Mews	E4-F4
Sydney Place	E4-F4
Sydney Road	F4
Sydney Wharf	F3-F4
The Circus	B4
Union Street	C3
Upper Borough Walls	C3
Upper Bristol Road	A4-A3-B3
Vane Street	E4
Walcot Street	C3-C4
Wells Road	A1-B1-C1
Westgate Buildings	C2-C3
Westgate Street	C3
York Street	C2-D2-D3

Trowbridge

Ashmead	B1
Ashton Street	C3
Avenue Road	A2
Bellefield Crescent	C4
Bond Street	A1-A2
Bradford Road	A2-A3
Bradley Road	A1-B1
British Row	B4
Brown Street	B2-C2
Bythesea Road	B2-B3
Castle Street	B2-B3
Charles Street	A4-B4
Cherry Gardens	B1-C1
Church Street	B3-C3
Clapendon Avenue	C2
Court Street	B2-B3
Cross Street	B4-C4
Delamare Road	C4
Drynham Road	C1
Duke Street	C3-C4
Dursley Road	B1-C1
Fore Street	B3
Francis Street	A4-B4
Frome Road	A1-B1
Fulford Road	C4
George Street	B4
Gloucester Road	A2
Haden Road	C1
Harford Street	C3
Hill Street	B3
Hilperton Road	C3-C4
Holbrook Lane	B1-C1
Innox Road	A3
Islington	C4
Jenkins Street	A4-B4
Linden Place	A3
Longfield Road	B2-C2
Lowmead	C4
Melton Road	B4
Mill Lane	B3
Mortimer Street	B2
New Road	B1-B2
Newtown	A2-B2
Orchard Road	B1-B2-C2-C1
Park Street	A2-A1-B1
Polebarn Road	C3
Prospect Place	B4-C4
River Way	A3-B3
Rock Road	A1
Roundstone Street	C3
Rutland Crescent	B1
St Thomas' Road	B4
Seymour Road	B4
Shails Lane	B3-B4
Silver Street	B3-C3
Southway	C4
Stallard Street	A2-A3-B3
Studley Rise	B1
The Hayle	C4
The Mount	C4
Timbrell Street	C4
Union Street	B3-B4-C4-C3
Waterwoks Road	A1-A2
Wesley Road	A2-B2
West Street	A2
West Ashton	C2-C3
Westbourne Gardens	A2-A3
Westbourne Road	A2
Westcroft Street	A4-B4
Wicker Hill	B3
Wingfield Road	A2

Bradford-on-Avon

Ashley Road	A4
Avon Close	C1
Bath Road	A3-A4-B4-B3
Berryfield Road	A4-B4
Bridge Street	B4
Christchurch Road	A4
Church Acre	A4
Church Street	A2-B2
Conigre Hill	A2-A3
Coppice Hill	B2-B3
Coronation Avenue	C3-C4
Greenland View	C1
Highfield Road	C3
Holt Road	B2-C2
Huntingdon Street	A3
Kingston Road	B2
Junction Road	B1
Market Street	A2-B2
Masons Lane	A3-B3
Mill Lane	B2
Mount Pleasant	B3
Newtown	A1-A2-B2
New Road	B3-C3
Palmer Drive	B4
Pound Lane	A1-B1
Priory Close	A3-B3
Priory Park	A3-B3
Regents Place	B1-C1
Rome Road	B1
St Margaret's Place	B1-B2
St Margaret's Street	B2-B1-C1
Silver Street	B2
Sladesbrook	B3-B4
Springfield	C2-C3
The Wilderness	A3
Upper Regents Park	B1-C1
White Hill	B2-B3
Whitehead Lane	B2-B3
Winsley Road	A3-A4
Woolley Drive	C3-C4
Woolley Street	C2-C3

11

Bexley / Dartford

The rural sights and sounds of Stone Lodge Farm Park and Farm Museum — just east of town off the A226 — make an unexpected contrast with the old River Darent market town of Dartford. Its main concerns for many years have been engineering and papermaking, and Dartford enjoys some excellent modern facilities such as the Arndale Centre and the Orchard theatre complex. A number of old buildings survive in the centre, the oldest being the Norman-towered parish church of Holy Trinity. There is also a local museum.

Bexleyheath was once known simply as Bexley New Town. This is the administrative centre for the Borough of Bexley. Modern development has brought the Broadway Shopping Centre and the swimming pool and solarium of the Crook Log Sports Centre. Out of doors, Danson Park, scene of the July Danson Show, was first designed by Capability Brown.

Gravesend Making a vital link with Essex through the Tilbury ferry service, Gravesend's prime position on the Thames Estuary has always been a major factor in its growth, and the recent restoration of the 1842 Royal Terrace Pier celebrates a long maritime tradition. Much of the town was destroyed by fire in the 18th century, but several older buildings still survive in the Promenade area, including 14th-century Milton Chantry, a former chapel.

Street Index with Grid Reference

Bournemouth

Albert Road	C3-D3
Avenue Road	B3-C3
Bath Road	D2-E2-E3-E4-F4
Beacon Road	C1
Bodorgan Road	C4
Bourne Avenue	B3-C3
Braidley Road	B3-B4
Branksome Wood Road	A4
Cambridge Road	A2-A3
Central Drive	B4
Chine Crescent	A1-A2
Chine Crescent Road	A1-A2
Christchurch Road	F4
Cotlands Road	F4
Cranbourne Road	B2-C2
Crescent Road	A3-B3
Dean Park Crescent	C4-D4
Dean Park Road	C4
Durley Chine Road	A1-A2
Durley Gardens	A1-A2
Durley Road	A1-A2-B1
East Overcliff Drive	E2-F2-F3
Exeter Crescent	C2
Exeter Lane	C2-D2
Exeter Park Road	C2-D2
Exeter Road	C2-D2
Fir Vale Road	D3-D4
Gervis Place	C3-D3
Gervis Road	E3-F3
Glenfern Road	D3-E3-E4
Grove Road	E3-F3
Hahnemann Road	A1-B1-B2
Hinton Road	D2-D3-E2
Holdenhurst Road	F4
Lansdowne Road	E4-F4
Lorne Park Road	E4
Madeira Road	D4-E4
Marlborough Road	A2
Meyrick Road	F3-F4
Norwich Avenue	A2-A3-B3
Norwich Avenue West	A3
Old Christchurch Road	D3-D4-E4-F4
Parsonage Road	D3-E3
Poole Hill	A2-B2
Poole Road	A2
Priory Road	C1-C2

Richmond Hill	C3-C4
Russell Cotes Road	E2
St Michael's Road	B2-B1-C1
St Peter's Road	D3-E3
St Stephen's Road	B3-B4-C4-C3
Stafford Road	E4
Suffolk Road	A3-B3
Surrey Road	A3
Terrace Road	B2-C2
The Triangle	B2-B3
Tregonwell Road	B2-C2-C1
Undercliffe Drive	D1-D2-E1-E2-F2
Upper Hinton Road	D2-D3-E2
Upper Norwich Road	A2-B2
Upper Terrace Road	B2-C2
Wessex Way	A3-A4-B4-C4-D4-E4
West Cliff Gardens	B1
West Cliff Promenade	B1-C1-D1-C1
West Cliff Road	A1-B1
Westhill Road	A2-B2-B1-C1
Westover Road	D2-D3
West Promenade	C1-D1
Wimborne Road	C4
Wootton Gardens	E3-E4
Yelverton Road	C3-D3

Christchurch

Albion Road	A4
Arcadia Road	A4
Arthur Road	B3
Avenue Road	A3-B3-B4
Avon Road West	A3-A4-B4
Bargates	B3
Barrack Road	A4-A3-B2-B3
Beaconsfield Road	B2-C3
Bridge Street	C2
Bronte Avenue	B4
Canberra Road	A4
Castle Street	B2-C2
Christchurch By-Pass	B2-C2-C3
Clarendon Road	A3-B3
Douglas Avenue	A2-B2
Endfield Road	A4
Fairfield	B3
Fairmile Road	A4-B4-B3
Flambard Avenue	B4
Gardner Road	A3-A4
Gleadowe Avenue	A2-B2
Grove Road East	A3-B3

Grove Road West	A3
High Street	B2
Iford Lane	A1
Jumpers Avenue	A4
Jumpers Road	A3-A4-B4
Kings Avenue	A2-B2
Manor Road	B2
Millhams Street	B2-C2
Mill Road	B3-B4
Portfield Road	A3-B3
Queens Avenue	B1
Quay Road	B1
St John's Road	A2
St Margarets Avenue	B1
Sopers Lane	B1-B2
South View Road	A1-B1
Stony Lane	C4-C3-C2
Stour Road	B3-B2-A1-A2
The Grove	A4
Tuckton Road	A1
Twynham Avenue	B2-B3
Walcott Avenue	A4-B4
Waterloo Place	C2
Wickfield Avenue	B1-B2
Wick Lane	A1-B1-B2
Willow Drive	A1-B1
Willow Way	A1-B1
Windsor Road	A3

Poole

Ballard Road	B1-C1
Church Street	A1
Dear Hay Lane	A2-B2
Denmark Road	C3
East Quay Road	B1
East Street	B1
Elizabeth Road	C3
Emerson Road	B1-B2
Esplanade	B3
Garland Road	C4
Green Road	B2-B1-C1
Heckford Road	C3-C4
High Street	A1-B1-B2
Hill Street	B2
Johns Road	C3-C4
Jolliffe Road	C4
Kingland Road	B2-C2
Kingston Road	C3-C4
Lagland Street	B1-B2

Longfleet Road	C3
Maple Road	C3-C4
Mount Pleasant Road	C2-C3
Newfoundland Drive	C1
New Orchard	A1-A2
North Street	B2
Old Orchard	B1
Parkstone Road	C3-C2
Perry Gardens	B1
Poole Bridge	A1
St Mary's Road	C3
Seldown Lane	C2-C3
Shaftesbury Road	C3
Skinner Street	B1
South Road	B2
Stanley Road	B1
Sterte Avenue	A4-B4
Sterte Road	B2-B3-B4
Stokes Avenue	B4-C4
Strand Street	A1-B1
Tatnam Road	B4-C4
The Quay	A1-B1
Towngate Bridge	B2-B3
West Quay Road	A1-A2-B2
West Street	A1-A2-B2
Wimborne Road	B3-C3-C4

LEGEND

Town Plan

AA Recommended route	
Other roads	
Restricted roads	
Buildings of interest	Town Hall
AA Centre	AA
Car Parks	P
Parks and open spaces	
One way streets	

Area Plan

A roads	
B roads	
Locations	Mudeford O
Urban area	

Bournemouth

Until the beginning of the 19th century the landscape on which Bournemouth stands was open heath. Its rise began when a scattering of holiday villas were built by innovative trend-setters at a time when the idea of seaside holidays was very new. Soon a complete village had taken shape. In the next 50 years Bournemouth had become a major resort and its population catapulted to nearly 59,000.

Today's holidaymakers can enjoy Bournemouth's natural advantages – miles of sandy beaches, a mild climate and beautiful setting, along with a tremendous variety of amenities. These include some of the best shopping in the south – with shops ranging from huge departmental stores to tiny specialist places. Entertainments range from variety shows and feature films to opera, and the music of the world-famous Bournemouth Symphony Orchestra.

Poole has virtually been engulfed by the suburbs of Bournemouth, but its enormous natural harbour is still an attraction in its own right. At Poole Quay, some 15th-century cellars have been converted into a Maritime Museum, where the town's association with the sea from prehistoric times until the early 20th century is illustrated, and the famous Poole Pottery nearby offers guided tours of its workshops.

Central Poole

STOKES AVENUE
TATNAM ROAD
STERTE AVENUE
ESPLANADE
STERTE ROAD
WIMBORNE ROAD
JOLLIFFE ROAD
GARLAND ROAD
KINGSTON ROAD

Holes Bay

N

P.O.
Poole Stadium
P

Coach & Lorry Park
P

HECKFORD RD
JOHN ST
MAPLE ROAD
ST MARY'S RD
SHAFTESBURY RD
ELIZABETH RD
DENMARK RD
LONGFLEET ROAD

Poole Station
P

TOWNGATE BR.

PARKSTONE ROAD
SELDOWN LANE
MOUNT PLEASANT RD

Poole Arts Centre
KINGLAND RD
KINGLAND RD
MOUNT PLEASANT

Pedestrians Only
NORTH ST
L.C.

Pedestrian Precinct 10.00-1800hrs Mon-Sat

Bus Station

Quay West Marina

RNLI Headquarters
DEAR HAY LANE
NEW ORCHARD
WEST STREET
HIGH STREET
SOUTH ST
LAGLAND STREET
EAST ST
SKINNER ST
GREEN ROAD
PERRY GDNS
EMERSON ROAD
NEWFOUNDLAND DRIVE

Arndale Shopping Centre

Dolphin Indoor Swimming Pool
P

Guildhall
Byngley House
ST CHURCH
HILL
OLD ORCHARD
STRAND ST
E QUAY
STANLEY RD
BALLARD

Scaplen's Court Museum
Fisheries Office
BR.
POOLE
Maritime Museum
Custom House
Rock and Gem Centre
Purbeck Pottery
Harbour Office
Aquarium
THE QUAY
Poole Pottery
Lifeboat Station Museum

Poole Harbour

Central Christchurch

THE GROVE RD
ALBION RD
ARCADIA RD
ENDFIELD ROAD
CANBERRA
WALCOTT A.
FLAMBARD AVE
BRONTE AVE
FAIRMILE
BURTON
STONY LANE

Christchurch Hospital
Cemetery

JUMPERS AVE
GARDNER RD
JUMPERS ROAD
AVON ROAD WEST
GROVE ROAD EAST
MILL ROAD
Fire Station

WINDSOR ROAD
BARRACK ROAD
GROVE ROAD WEST
PORTFIELD ROAD
CLARENDON RD

Junior School
Station
ARTHUR
FAIR-FIELD
BEACONSFIELD ROAD
CHRISTCHURCH BY-PASS

RIVER STOUR
RIVER AVON

GLEADOWE AVE
KINGS AVENUE
MANOR ROAD
STOUR ROAD
TWYNHAM AVE
BARGATES

Law Court
Police Station
P

DOUGLAS AVENUE
SOPERS LANE
Rec. Grnd.
HIGH ST
Shopping Centre
Town Hall

Twynham Comprehensive School
SOUTH VW
WICKFIELD AVE
Library
Theatre
P.O.
M. HAMSH
CASTLE ST
BRIDGE ST
WATER-LOO PL.

Tucktonia

WILLOW DRIVE
MARGARETS AVENUE
WK LA.
QUEENS AVE
Mus. & Art Gall.
Castle Ruins
Civic Offices

WILLOW WAY
Pontins Holiday Camp
Wick Ferry
Christchurch Priory and Church

River Stour
Christchurch Quay

IFORD LANE
TUCKTON ROAD
WICKLA
WICK LANE

Central Bournemouth

Meyrick Park

BRANKSOME WOOD ROAD
BRAIDLEY ROAD
CENTRAL DRIVE
BODORGAN ROAD
WIMBORNE ROAD
DEAN PARK ROAD
Horseshoe Common
WESSEX WAY
Police Station
P
COTLNDS ROAD
Fire Station

WESSEX WAY
SURREY ROAD
MADEIRA ROAD
LORNE PARK RD
STAFFORD ROAD
LANSDOWNE
HOLDENHURST RD
CHRISTCHURCH ROAD
Library

Town Hall
St Stephen's Church
ST STEPHEN'S ROAD
Hospital
BOURNE AVENUE
Town Hall
Upper Gardens
Railway Museum
YELVERTON ROAD
RICHMOND HILL
OLD CHRISTCHURCH ROAD
ST PETER'S RD
FIRVALE RD
GLENFERN ROAD
Synagogue
WOOTTON GARDENS
ST PETER'S ROAD
College
BATH ROAD
MEYRICK ROAD
GROVE ROAD

WESSEX WAY
NORWICH AVE WEST
CAMBRIDGE RD
CRESCENT RD
SUFFOLK ROAD
NORWICH AVE
The Bourne
AVENUE ROAD
ALBERT RD
PO
St Peter's Church
PARSONAGE ROAD
UPPER HINTON RD
GROVE ROAD

POOLE RD
UPPER NORWICH ROAD
THE TRIANGLE
POOLE HILL
Pedestrians & Buses only
GERVIS PLACE
Pedestrians & Buses only
HINTON ROAD
UPPER HINTON RD
Cinema
Ice Rink
WESTOVER ROAD
Cinemas
RUSSELL COTES RD
East Cliff
UNDERCLIFF DRIVE
EAST OVERCLIFF DRIVE

MARLBOROUGH ROAD
DURLEY ROAD
DURLEY CHINE ROAD
CHINE CRESCENT ROAD
WESTHILL
ST MICHAEL'S
TERRACE RD
UPP TERRACE ROAD
EXETER ROAD
EXETER CRES
EXETER LANE
EXETER PARK RD
Lower Gardens
Playhouse Theatre
Pavilion
Royal Bath Hotel
Rothesay Mus.

CHINE CRESCENT ROAD
HAHNEMANN ROAD
ST MICHAEL'S ROAD
CRANBORNE RD
TREGONWELL ROAD
Winter Gardens
PRIORY ROAD
Royal Exeter Hotel
BATH ROAD

WEST CLIFF ROAD
WESTHILL ROAD
BEACON ROAD
Conference Centre
WEST CLIFF PROMENADE
WEST PROMENADE
Pier Leisure Centre

WEST CLIFF GARDENS
WEST CLIFF GARDENS
Pedestrians only
Pier Theatre
Bournemouth Pier

N

BOURNEMOUTH
The pier, safe sea-bathing, golden sands facing south and sheltered by steep cliffs, and plenty of amenities for the holiday maker make Bournemouth one of the most popular resorts on the south coast of England.

15

Brighton

Dr Richard Russell, from nearby Lewes, created the resort of Brighton almost singlehandedly. And he did it not by building houses or hotels, but by writing a book. His book, which praised the health-giving properties of sea-bathing and sea air, soon came to the attention of George, then Prince Regent and one day to become King George IV. He stayed at Brighthelmstone – as it was then known –

in 1783 and again in 1784. In 1786 the Prince rented a villa on the Steine – a modest house that was eventually transformed into the astonishing Pavilion. By 1800 – its popularity assured by royal patronage – the resort was described in a contemporary directory as 'the most frequented and without exception one of the most fashionable towns in the kingdom'.

Perhaps the description does not quite fit today, but Brighton is a perennially popular seaside

resort, as well as a shopping centre, university town and cultural venue. The Pavilion still draws most crowds, of course. Its beginnings as a villa are entirely hidden in a riot of Near Eastern architectural motifs, largely the creation of John Nash. Brighton's great days as a Regency resort *par excellence* are preserved in the sweeping crescents and elegant terraces, buildings which help to make it one of the finest townscapes in the whole of Europe.

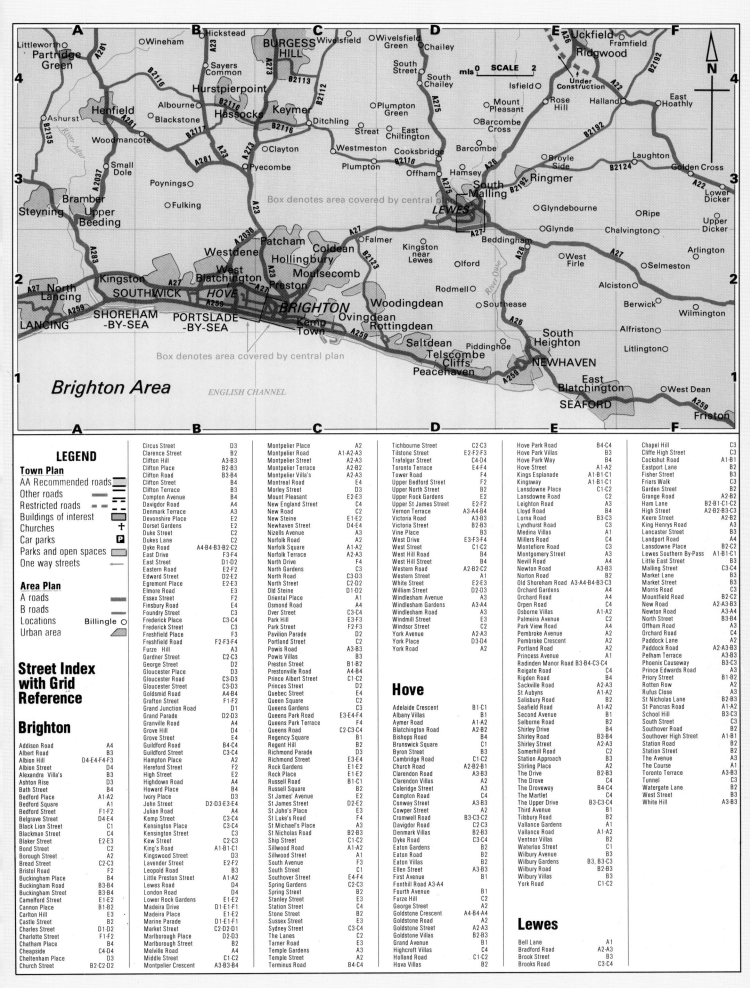

Brighton Area — ENGLISH CHANNEL

LEGEND

Town Plan

AA Recommended roads
Other roads
Restricted roads
Buildings of interest
Churches +
Car parks P
Parks and open spaces
One way streets

Area Plan

A roads
B roads
Locations   Billingle ○
Urban area

Street Index with Grid Reference

Brighton

Addison Road	A4
Albert Road	B3
Albion Hill	D4-E4-F4-F3
Albion Street	D4
Alexandra Villa's	B3
Ashton Rise	D3
Bath Street	B4
Bedford Place	A1-A2
Bedford Square	A1
Bedford Street	F1-F2
Belgrave Street	D4-E4
Black Lion Street	C1
Blackman Street	C4
Blaker Street	E2-E3
Bond Street	C2
Borough Street	A2
Bread Street	C2-C3
Bristol Road	F2
Buckingham Place	B4
Buckingham Road	B3-B4
Buckingham Street	B3-B4
Camelford Street	E1-E2
Cannon Place	B1-B2
Carlton Hill	E3
Castle Street	B2
Charles Street	D1-D2
Charlotte Street	F1-F2
Chatham Place	B4
Cheapside	C4-D4
Cheltenham Place	D3
Church Street	B2-C2-D2
Circus Street	D3
Clarence Street	B2
Clifton Hill	A3-B3
Clifton Place	B2-B3
Clifton Road	B3-B4
Clifton Street	B4
Clifton Terrace	B3
Compton Avenue	B4
Davigdor Road	A4
Denmark Terrace	A3
Devonshire Place	E2
Dorset Gardens	E2
Duke Street	C2
Dukes Lane	C2
Dyke Road	A4-B4-B3-B2-C2
East Drive	F3-F4
East Street	D1-D2
Eastern Road	E2-F2
Edward Street	D2-E2
Egremont Place	E2-E3
Elmore Road	E3
Essex Street	F2
Finsbury Road	E4
Foundry Street	C3
Frederick Place	C3-C4
Frederick Street	C3
Freshfield Place	F3
Freshfield Road	F2-F3-F4
Furze Hill	A3
Gardner Street	C2-C3
George Street	D2
Gloucester Place	D3
Gloucester Road	C3-D3
Gloucester Street	C3-D3
Goldsmid Road	A4-B4
Grafton Street	F1-F2
Grand Junction Road	D1
Grand Parade	D2-D3
Granville Road	A4
Grove Hill	D4
Grove Street	E4
Guildford Road	B4-C4
Guildford Street	C3-C4
Hampton Place	A2
Hereford Street	F2
High Street	E2
Highdown Road	A4
Howard Place	B4
Ivory Place	D4
John Street	D2-D3-E3-E4
Julian Road	A4
Kemp Street	C3-C4
Kensington Place	C3-C4
Kensington Street	C3
Kew Street	C2-C3
King's Road	A1-B1-C1
Kingswood Street	D3
Lavender Street	E2-F2
Leopold Road	A2
Little Preston Street	A1-A2
Lewes Road	D4
London Road	D4
Lower Rock Gardens	E1-E2
Madeira Drive	D1-E1-F1
Madeira Place	E1-E2
Marine Parade	D1-E1-F1
Market Street	C2-D2-D1
Marlborough Place	D2-D3
Marlborough Street	B2
Melville Road	A4
Middle Street	C1-C2
Montpelier Crescent	A3-B3-B4
Montpelier Place	A2
Montpelier Road	A1-A2-A3
Montpelier Terrace	A2-B2
Montpelier Villa's	A2-A3
Montreal Road	E4
Morley Street	D3
Mount Pleasant	E2-E3
New England Street	C4
New Road	C2
New Steine	E1-E2
Newhaven Street	D4-E4
Nizells Avenue	A3
Norfolk Road	A2
Norfolk Square	A1-A2
Norfolk Terrace	A2-A3
North Drive	F4
North Gardens	C3
North Road	C3-D3
North Street	C2-D2
Old Steine	D1-D2
Oriental Place	A1
Osmond Road	A4
Over Street	C3-C4
Park Hill	E3-F3
Park Street	F2-F3
Pavilion Parade	D2
Portland Street	C2
Powis Road	A3-B3
Powis Villas	B3
Preston Street	B1-B2
Prestonville Road	A4-B4
Prince Albert Street	C1-C2
Princes Street	D2
Quebec Street	E4
Queen Square	C2
Queens Gardens	C3
Queens Park Road	E3-E4-F3
Queens Park Terrace	F4
Queens Road	C2-C3-C4
Regency Square	B1
Regent Hill	B2
Richmond Parade	D3
Richmond Street	E3-E4
Rock Gardens	E1-E2
Rock Place	E1-E2
Russell Road	B1-C1
Russell Square	B2
St James' Avenue	E2
St James Street	D2-E2
St John's Place	E3
St Luke's Road	F4
St Michael's Place	A3
St Nicholas Road	B2-B3
Ship Street	C1-C2
Sillwood Road	A1-A2
Sillwood Street	A1
South Avenue	F3
South Street	C1
Southover Street	E4-F4
Spring Gardens	C2-C3
Spring Street	B2
Stanley Street	E3
Station Street	C4
Stone Street	B2
Sussex Street	E3
Sydney Street	C3-C4
The Lanes	C2
Tarner Road	E3
Temple Gardens	A3
Temple Street	A2
Terminus Road	B4-C4
Tichbourne Street	C2-C3
Tilstone Street	E2-F2-F3
Trafalgar Street	C4-D4
Toronto Terrace	E4-F4
Tower Road	F4
Upper Bedford Street	F2
Upper North Street	B2
Upper Rock Gardens	E2
Upper St James Street	E2-F2
Vernon Terrace	A3-A4-B4
Victoria Road	A3-B3
Victoria Street	B2-B3
Vine Place	B3
West Drive	E3-F3-F4
West Street	C1-C2
West Hill Road	B4
West Hill Street	B4
Western Road	A2-B2-C2
Western Street	A1
White Street	E2-E3
William Street	D2-D3
Windlesham Avenue	A3
Windlesham Gardens	A3-A4
Windlesham Road	A3
Windmill Street	E3
Windsor Street	C2
York Avenue	A2-A3
York Place	D3-D4
York Road	A2

Hove

Adelaide Crescent	B1-C1
Albany Villas	A1-A2
Aymer Road	A1-A2
Blatchington Road	A2-B2
Bishops Road	B4
Brunswick Square	C1
Byron Street	B3
Cambridge Road	C1-C2
Church Road	A2-B2-B1
Clarendon Road	A3-B3
Clarendon Villas	A2
Coleridge Street	A3
Compton Road	C4
Conway Street	A3-B3
Cowper Street	A2
Cromwell Road	B3-C3-C2
Davigdor Road	C2-C3
Denmark Villas	B2-B3
Dyke Road	C3-C4
Eaton Gardens	B2
Eaton Road	B2
Eaton Villas	B2
Ellen Street	A3
First Avenue	B1
Fonthill Road	A3-A4
Fourth Avenue	B1
Furze Hill	C2
George Street	A2
Goldstone Crescent	A4-B4-A4
Goldstone Road	A2
Goldstone Street	A2-A3
Goldstone Villas	B2-B3
Grand Avenue	B1
Highcroft Villas	C4
Holland Road	C1-C2
Hova Villas	B2
Hove Park Road	B4-C4
Hove Park Villas	B3
Hove Park Way	B4
Hove Street	A1-A2
Kings Esplanade	A1-B1-C1
Kingsway	A1-B1-C1
Lansdowne Place	C1-C2
Lansdowne Road	C2
Leighton Road	A3
Lloyd Road	B4
Lorna Road	B3-C3
Lyndhurst Road	C3
Medina Villas	A1
Millers Road	C4
Montefiore Road	C3
Montgomery Street	A3
Nevill Road	B4
Newton Road	A3-B3
Norton Road	B2
Old Shoreham Road	A3-A4-B4-B3-C3
Orchard Gardens	A4
Orchard Road	A4
Orpen Road	C4
Osborne Villas	A1-A2
Palmeira Avenue	C2
Park View Road	A4
Pembroke Avenue	A2
Pembroke Crescent	A2
Portland Road	A2
Princess Avenue	A1
Radinden Manor Road	B3-B4-C3-C4
Reigate Road	C4
Rigden Road	B4
Sackville Road	A2-A3
St Aubyns	A1-A2
Salisbury Road	B2
Seafield Road	A1-A2
Second Avenue	B1
Selborne Road	B2
Shirley Drive	C4
Shirley Road	B3-B4
Shirley Street	A2-A3
Somerhill Road	C2
Station Approach	B3
Stirling Place	A2
The Drive	B2-B3
The Drove	C4
The Droveway	B4-C4
The Martlet	C4
The Upper Drive	B3-C3-C4
Third Avenue	B1
Tilsbury Road	B2
Vallance Gardens	A1
Vallance Road	A1-A2
Ventnor Villas	B2
Waterloo Street	C1
Wilbury Avenue	B3
Wilbury Gardens	B3-B3-C3
Wilbury Road	B2-B3
Wilbury Villas	B3
York Road	C1-C2

Lewes

Bell Lane	A1
Bradford Road	A2-A3
Brook Street	B3
Brooks Road	C3-C4
Chapel Hill	C3
Cliffe High Street	C3
Cockshut Road	A1-B1
Eastport Lane	B2
Fisher Street	B3
Friars Walk	C3
Garden Street	B2
Grange Road	A2-B2
Ham Lane	B2-B1-C1-C2
High Street	A2-B2-B3-C3
Keere Street	A2-B2
King Henrys Road	A3
Lancaster Street	B3
Landport Road	A4
Lansdowne Place	A3
Lewes Southern By-Pass	A1-B1-C1
Little East Street	B3
Malling Street	C3-C4
Market Lane	B3
Market Street	B3
Morris Road	C3
Mountfield Road	B2-C2
New Road	A2-A3-B3
Newton Road	A3-A4
North Road	B3-B4
North Street	B2
Offham Road	A3
Orchard Road	C4
Paddock Lane	A2
Paddock Road	A2-A3-B3
Pelham Terrace	A3-B3
Phoenix Causeway	B3-C3
Prince Edwards Road	A3
Priory Street	B1-B2
Rotten Row	A2
Rufus Close	A3
St Nicholas Lane	B2-B3
St Pancras Road	A1-A2
School Hill	B3-C3
South Street	C3
Southover High Street	A1-B1
Station Road	B2
Station Street	B2
The Avenue	A3
The Course	A1
Toronto Terrace	A3-B3
Tunnel	C3
Watergate Lane	B2
West Street	B3
White Hill	A3-B3

Bristol

One of Britain's most historic seaports, Bristol retains many of its visible links with the past, despite terrible damage inflicted during bombing raids in World War II. Most imposing is the cathedral, founded as an abbey church in 1140. Perhaps even more famous than the cathedral is the Church of St Mary Redcliffe. Ranking among the finest churches in the country, it owes much of

its splendour to 14th- and 15th-century merchants who bestowed huge sums of money on it.

The merchant families brought wealth to the whole of Bristol, and their trading links with the world are continued in today's modern aerospace and technological industries. Much of the best of Bristol can be seen in the area of the Floating Harbour – an arm of the Avon. Several of the old warehouses have been converted into museums, galleries and exhibition centres. Among them are

genuinely picturesque old pubs, the best-known of which is the Llandoger Trow. It is a timbered 17th-century house, the finest of its kind in Bristol. Further up the same street – King Street – is the Theatre Royal, built in 1766 and the oldest theatre in the country. In Corn Street, the heart of the business area, is a magnificent 18th-century corn exchange. In front of it are the four pillars known as the 'nails', on which merchants used to make cash transactions, hence 'to pay on the nail'.

18

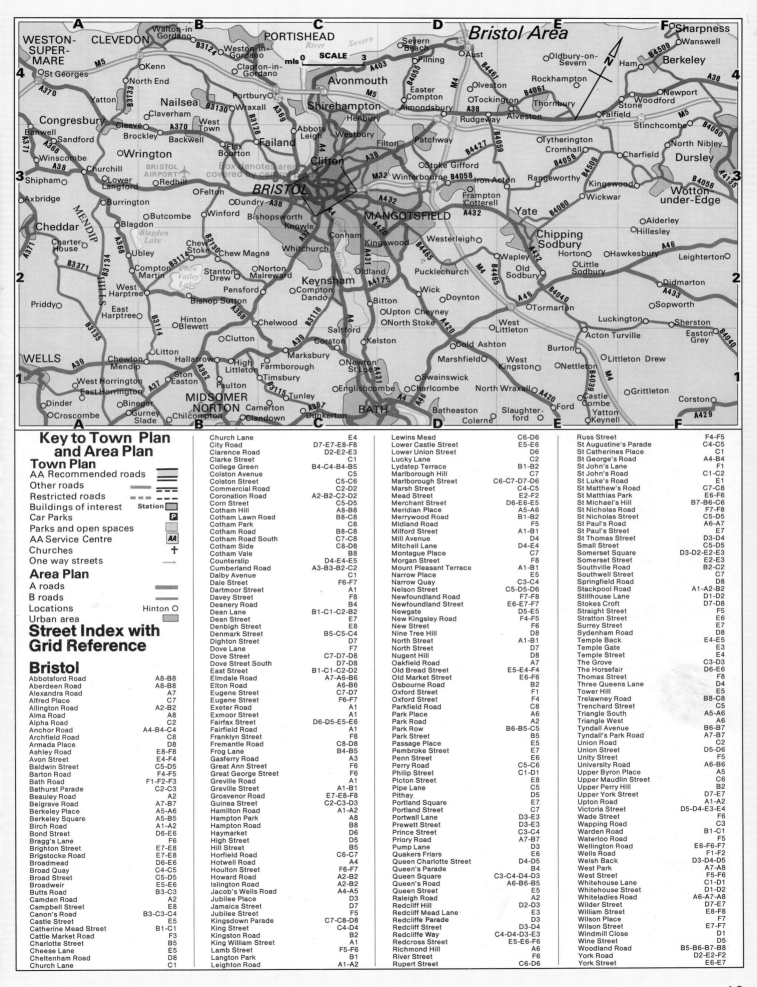

Key to Town Plan and Area Plan

Town Plan

AA Recommended roads	
Other roads	
Restricted roads	
Buildings of interest	Station
Car Parks	P
Parks and open spaces	
AA Service Centre	AA
Churches	+
One way streets	→

Area Plan

A roads	
B roads	
Locations	Hinton ○
Urban area	

Street Index with Grid Reference

Bristol

Abbotsford Road	A8-B8
Aberdeen Road	A7
Alexandra Road	A7
Alfred Place	C7
Allington Road	A2-B2
Alma Road	A8
Alpha Road	C2
Anchor Road	A4-B4-C4
Archfield Road	C8
Armada Place	D8
Ashley Road	E8-F8
Avon Street	E4-F4
Baldwin Street	C5-D5
Barton Road	F4-F5
Bath Road	F1-F2-F3
Bathurst Parade	C2-C3
Beauley Road	A2
Belgrave Road	A7-B7
Berkeley Place	A5-A6
Berkeley Square	A5-B5
Birch Road	A1-A2
Bond Street	D6-E6
Bragg's Lane	F6
Brighton Street	E7-E8
Brigstocke Road	E7-E8
Broadmead	D6-E6
Broad Quay	C4-C5
Broad Street	C5-D5
Broadweir	E5-E6
Butts Road	B3-C3
Camden Road	A2
Campbell Street	E8
Canon's Road	B3-C3-C4
Castle Street	E5
Catherine Mead Street	B1-C1
Cattle Market Road	F3
Charlotte Street	B5
Cheese Lane	E5
Cheltenham Road	D8
Church Lane	C1
Church Lane	E4
City Road	D7-E7-E8-F8
Clarence Road	D2-E2-E3
Clarke Street	C1
College Green	B4-C4-B4-B5
Colston Avenue	C5
Colston Street	C5-C6
Commercial Road	C2-D2
Coronation Road	A2-B2-C2-D2
Corn Street	C5-D5
Cotham Hill	A8-B8
Cotham Lawn Road	B8-C8
Cotham Park	C8
Cotham Road	B8-C8
Cotham Road South	C7-C8
Cotham Side	C8-D8
Cotham Vale	B8
Counterslip	D4-E4-E5
Cumberland Road	A3-B3-B2-C2
Dalby Avenue	C1
Dale Street	F6-F7
Dartmoor Street	A1
Davey Street	F8
Deanery Road	B4
Dean Lane	B1-C1-C2-B2
Dean Street	E7
Denbigh Street	E8
Denmark Street	B5-C5-C4
Dighton Street	D7
Dove Lane	F7
Dove Street	C7-D7-D8
Dove Street South	D7-D8
East Street	B1-C1-C2-D2
Elmdale Road	A7-A6-B6
Elton Road	A6-B6
Eugene Street	C7-D7
Eugene Street	F6-F7
Exeter Road	A1
Exmoor Street	A1
Fairfax Street	D6-D5-E5-E6
Fairfield Road	A1
Franklyn Street	F8
Fremantle Road	C8-D8
Frog Lane	B4-B5
Gasferry Road	A3
Great Ann Street	F6
Great George Street	F6
Greville Road	A1
Greville Street	A1-B1
Grosvenor Road	E7-E8-F8
Guinea Street	C2-C3-D3
Hamilton Road	A1-A2
Hampton Park	A8
Hampton Road	B8
Haymarket	D6
High Street	D5
Hill Street	B5
Horfield Road	C6-C7
Hotwell Road	A4
Houlton Street	F6-F7
Howard Road	A2-B2
Islington Road	A2-B2
Jacob's Wells Road	A4-A5
Jubilee Place	D3
Jamaica Street	D7
Jubilee Street	F5
Kingsdown Parade	C7-C8-D8
King Street	C4-D4
Kingston Road	B2
King William Street	A1
Lamb Street	F5-F6
Langton Park	B1
Leighton Road	A1-A2
Lewins Mead	C6-D6
Lower Castle Street	E5-E6
Lower Union Street	D6
Lucky Lane	C2
Lydstep Terrace	B1-B2
Marlborough Hill	C7
Marlborough Street	C6-C7-D7-D6
Marsh Street	C4-C5
Mead Street	E2-F2
Merchant Street	D6-E6-E5
Meridian Place	A5-A6
Merrywood Road	B1-B2
Midland Road	F5
Milford Street	A1-B1
Mill Avenue	D4
Mitchell Lane	D4-E4
Montague Place	C7
Morgan Street	F8
Mount Pleasant Terrace	A1-B1
Narrow Place	E5
Narrow Quay	C3-C4
Nelson Street	C5-D5-D6
Newfoundland Road	F7-F8
Newfoundland Street	E6-E7-F7
Newgate	D5-E5
New Kingsley Road	F4-F5
New Street	F6
Nine Tree Hill	D8
North Street	A1-B1
North Street	D7
Nugent Hill	D8
Oakfield Road	A7
Old Bread Street	E5-E4-F4
Old Market Street	E6-F6
Osbourne Road	B2
Oxford Street	F1
Oxford Street	F4
Parkfield Road	C8
Park Place	A6
Park Road	A2
Park Row	B6-B5-C5
Park Street	B5
Passage Place	E5
Pembroke Street	E7
Penn Street	E6
Perry Road	C5-C6
Philip Street	C1-D1
Picton Street	E8
Pipe Lane	C5
Pithay	D5
Portland Square	E7
Portland Street	C7
Portwall Lane	D3-E3
Prewett Street	D3-E3
Prince Street	C3-C4
Priory Road	A7-B7
Pump Lane	D3
Quakers Friars	E6
Queen Charlotte Street	D4-D5
Queen's Parade	B4
Queen Square	C3-C4-D4-D3
Queen's Road	A6-B6-B5
Queen Street	E5
Raleigh Road	A2
Redcliff Hill	D2-D3
Redcliff Mead Lane	E3
Redcliffe Parade	D3
Redcliff Street	D3-D4
Redcliffe Way	C4-D4-D3-E3
Redcross Street	E5-E6-F6
Richmond Hill	A6
River Street	F6
Rupert Street	C6-D6
Russ Street	F4-F5
St Augustine's Parade	C4-C5
St Catherines Place	C1
St George's Road	A4-B4
St John's Lane	F1
St John's Road	C1-C2
St Luke's Road	E1
St Matthew's Road	C7-C8
St Matthias Park	E6-F6
St Michael's Hill	B7-B6-C6
St Nicholas Road	F7-F8
St Nicholas Street	C5-D5
St Paul's Road	A6-A7
St Paul's Street	E7
St Thomas Street	D3-D4
Small Street	C5-D5
Somerset Square	D3-D2-E2-E3
Somerset Street	E2-E3
Southville Road	B2-C2
Southwell Street	C7
Springfield Road	D8
Stackpool Road	A1-A2-B2
Stillhouse Lane	D1-D2
Stokes Croft	D7-D8
Straight Street	F5
Stratton Street	E6
Surrey Street	E7
Sydenham Road	D8
Temple Back	E4-E5
Temple Gate	E3
Temple Street	E4
The Grove	C3-D3
The Horsefair	D6-E6
Thomas Street	E7
Three Queens Lane	D4
Tower Hill	E5
Trelawney Road	B8-C8
Trenchard Street	C5
Triangle South	A5-A6
Triangle West	A6
Tyndall Avenue	B6-B7
Tyndall's Park Road	A7-B7
Union Road	C2
Union Street	D5-D6
Unity Street	F5
University Road	A6-B6
Upper Byron Place	A5
Upper Maudlin Street	C6
Upper Perry Hill	B2
Upper York Street	D7-E7
Upton Road	A1-A2
Victoria Street	D5-D4-E3-E4
Wade Street	F6
Wapping Road	C3
Warden Road	B1-C1
Waterloo Road	F5
Wellington Road	E6-F6-F7
Wells Road	F1-F2
Welsh Back	D3-D4-D5
West Park	A7-A8
West Street	F5-F6
Whitehouse Lane	C1-D1
Whitehouse Street	D1-D2
Whiteladies Road	A6-A7-A8
Wilder Street	D7-E7
William Street	E8-E8-F8
Wilson Place	F7
Wilson Street	E7-F7
Windmill Close	D1
Wine Street	D5
Woodland Road	B5-B6-B7-B8
York Road	D2-E2-E2
York Street	E6-E7

19

Central Chichester

Chichester Area

0 SCALE 4
mls

Chichester

The graceful spire of Chichester Cathedral, consecrated in 1184, rises over the rooftops to the west of this city, which dates back to Roman times and is one of Britain's oldest. Notable among its 18th-century streets are the Pallants and the Pallant House, and at Fishbourne Priory nearby, visitors can admire the mosaics, formal garden and other remains of the largest Roman residence found in Britain.

Chichester today gives pleasure to thousands with its Festival Theatre and its harbour — thronged with sailing enthusiasts throughout the summer and with a variety of wild birds during the winter. Other attractions are the Open Air Museum and West Dean Gardens.

Bognor Regis was plain Bognor until 1929 when George V granted the suffix Regis after convalescing there. A former fishing village, it began its transformation into a seaside town in the 1790s, and is now a favourite destination for family holidays. Elegant Hotham Park House is worth a visit.

Littlehampton at the mouth of the River Arun was once a busy port for passengers and cargo going to France; today it is a popular target for holidaymakers, who come here for the good fishing, bathing and sailing. The local museum concentrates on marine subjects.

20

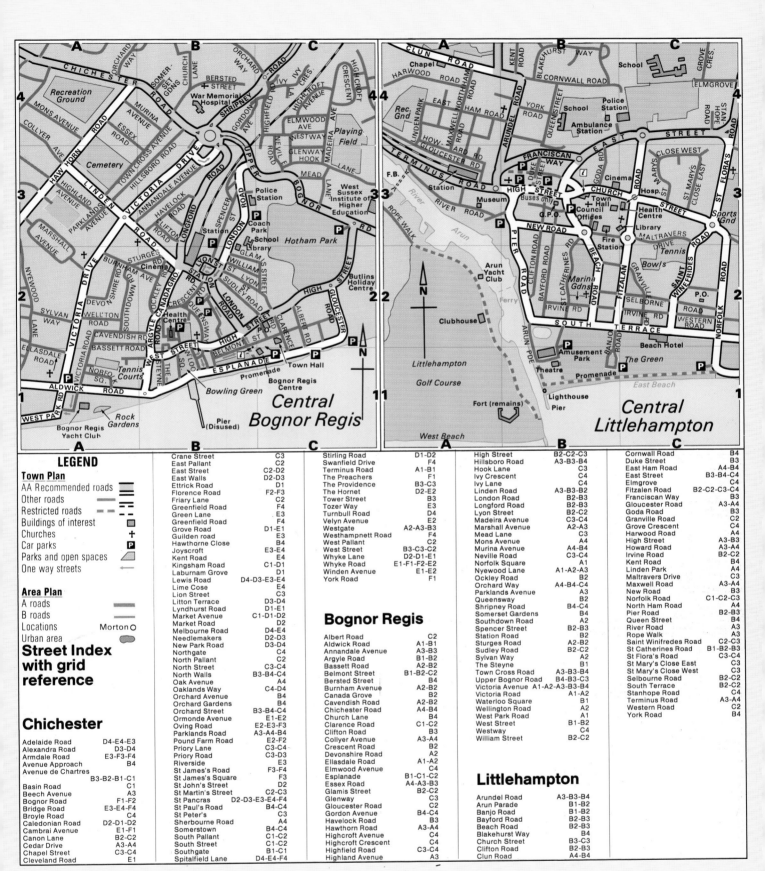

Central Bognor Regis

Central Littlehampton

LEGEND

Town Plan
AA Recommended roads
Other roads
Restricted roads
Buildings of interest
Churches
Car parks
Parks and open spaces
One way streets

Area Plan
A roads
B roads
Locations   Morton ○
Urban area

Street Index with grid reference

Chichester

Adelaide Road	D4-E4-E3
Alexandra Road	D3-D4
Armdale Road	E3-F3-F4
Avenue Approach	B4
Avenue de Chartres	B3-B2-B1-C1
Basin Road	C1
Beech Avenue	A3
Bognor Road	F1-F2
Bridge Road	E3-E4-F4
Broyle Road	C4
Caledonian Road	D2-D1-D2
Cambrai Avenue	E1-F1
Canon Lane	B2-C2
Cedar Drive	A3-A4
Chapel Street	C3-C4
Cleveland Road	E1
Crane Street	C3
East Pallant	C2
East Street	C2-D2
East Walls	D2-D3
Ettrick Road	D1
Florence Road	F2-F3
Friary Lane	C2
Greenfield Road	F4
Green Lane	E3
Greenfield Road	F4
Grove Road	D1-E1
Guilden road	E3
Hawthorne Close	B4
Joyscroft	E3-E4
Kent Road	E4
Kingsham Road	C1-D1
Laburnam Grove	D1
Lewis Road	D4-D3-E3-E4
Lime Cose	E4
Lion Street	C3
Litton Terrace	D3-D4
Lyndhurst Road	D1-E1
Market Avenue	C1-D1-D2
Market Road	D2
Melbourne Road	D4-E4
Needlemakers	D2-D3
New Park Road	D3-D4
Northgate	C4
North Pallant	C2
North Street	C3-C4
North Walls	B3-B4-C4
Oak Avenue	A4
Oaklands Way	C4-D4
Orchard Avenue	B4
Orchard Gardens	B4
Orchard Street	B3-B4-C4
Ormonde Avenue	E1-E2
Oving Road	E2-E3-F3
Parklands Road	A3-A4-B4
Pound Farm Road	E2-F2
Priory Lane	C3-C4
Priory Road	C3-D3
Riverside	E3
St James's Road	F3-F4
St James's Square	F3
St John's Street	D2
St Martin's Street	C2-C3
St Pancras	D2-D3-E3-E4-F4
St Paul's Road	B4-C4
St Peter's	C3
Sherbourne Road	A4
Somerstown	B4-C4
South Pallant	C1-C2
South Street	C1-C2
Southgate	B1-C1
Spitalfield Lane	D4-E4-F4
Stirling Road	D1-D2
Swanfield Drive	F4
Terminus Road	A1-B1
The Preachers	F1
The Providence	B3-C3
The Hornet	D2-E2
Tower Street	B3
Tozer Way	E3
Turnbull Road	D4
Velyn Avenue	E2
Westgate	A2-A3-B3
Westhampnett Road	F4
West Pallant	C2
West Street	B3-C3-C2
Whyke Lane	D2-D1-E1
Whyke Road	E1-F1-F2-E2
Winden Avenue	E1-E2
York Road	F1

Bognor Regis

Albert Road	C2
Aldwick Road	A1-B1
Annandale Avenue	A3-B3
Argyle Road	B1-B2
Bassett Road	A2-B2
Belmont Street	B1-B2-C2
Bersted Street	B4
Burnham Avenue	A2-B2
Canada Grove	B2
Cavendish Road	A2-B2
Chichester Road	A4-B4
Church Lane	B4
Clarence Road	C1-C2
Clifton Road	B3
Collyer Avenue	A3-A4
Crescent Road	B2
Devonshire Road	A2
Ellasdale Road	A1-A2
Elmwood Avenue	C4
Esplanade	B1-C1-C2
Essex Road	A4-A3-B3
Glamis Street	B2-C2
Glenway	C3
Gloucester Road	C2
Gordon Avenue	B4-C4
Havelock Road	B3
Hawthorn Road	A3-A4
Highcroft Avenue	C4
Highcroft Crescent	C4
Highfield Road	C3-C4
Highland Avenue	A3
High Street	B2-C2-C3
Hillsboro Road	A3-B3-B4
Hook Lane	C3
Ivy Crescent	C4
Ivy Lane	C4
Linden Road	A3-B3-B2
London Road	B2-B3
Longford Road	B2-B3
Lyon Street	B2-C2
Madeira Avenue	C3-C4
Marshall Avenue	A2-A3
Mead Lane	C3
Mons Avenue	A4
Murina Avenue	A4-B4
Neville Road	C3-C4
Norfolk Square	A1
Nyewood Lane	A1-A2-A3
Ockley Road	B2
Orchard Way	A4-B4-C4
Parklands Avenue	A3
Queensway	B2
Shripney Road	B4-C4
Somerset Gardens	B4
Southdown Road	A2
Spencer Street	B2-B3
Station Road	B2
Sturges Road	A2-B2
Sudley Road	B2-C2
Sylvan Way	A2
The Steyne	B1
Town Cross Road	A3-B3-B4
Upper Bognor Road	B4-B3-C3
Victoria Avenue	A1-A2-A3-B3-B4
Victoria Road	A1-A2
Waterloo Square	B1
Wellington Road	A2
West Park Road	A1
West Street	B1-B2
Westway	C4
William Street	B2-C2

Littlehampton

Arundel Road	A3-B3-B4
Arun Parade	B1-B2
Banjo Road	B1-B2
Bayford Road	B2-B3
Beach Road	B2-B3
Blakehurst Way	B4
Church Street	B3-C3
Clifton Road	B2-B3
Clun Road	A4-B4
Cornwall Road	B4
Duke Street	B3
East Ham Road	A4-B4
East Street	B3-B4-C4
Elmgrove	B4
Fitzalen Road	B2-C2-C3-C4
Franciscan Way	B3
Gloucester Road	A3-A4
Goda Road	B3
Granville Road	C2
Grove Crescent	C4
Harwood Road	A4
High Street	A3-B3
Howard Road	A3-A4
Irvine Road	B2-C2
Kent Road	B4
Linden Park	A4
Maltravers Drive	C3
Maxwell Road	A3-A4
New Road	B3
Norfolk Road	C1-C2-C3
North Ham Road	A4
Pier Road	B2-B3
Queen Street	B4
River Road	A3
Rope Walk	A3
Saint Winifredes Road	C2-C3
St Catherines Road	B1-B2-B3
St Flora's Road	C3-C4
St Mary's Close East	C3
St Mary's Close West	C3
Selborne Road	B2-C2
South Terrace	B2-C2
Stanhope Road	C4
Terminus Road	A3-A4
Western Road	C2
York Road	B4

CHICHESTER
Opened in 1962 under the direction of Sir Laurence (later Lord) Olivier, the Festival Theatre draws an annual audience of half a million to its wide range of music and drama, both during the summer festival and throughout the year.

Central Falmouth

Flushing Passenger Ferry

St Mawes Passenger Ferry

Penryn River

Inner Harbour

Falmouth Docks

Falmouth Station

FALMOUTH BAY

Central Penzance

MOUNT'S BAY

Cornish towns

Falmouth Twin fortresses, St. Mawes and Pendennis, guard the harbour entrance and serve as a reminder of Falmouth's once vital strategic importance. Lying in the sheltered waters of the Carrick Roads and provided with one of the world's largest natural harbours, Falmouth prospered on trade until the 19th century. Today the town is popular with holidaymakers.

St Ives is one of the few British towns with a style of painting named after it, for both artists and holidaymakers are drawn to the port, with its charming old quarter known as Down-Long. Regular exhibitions of local painting, sculpture and pottery are held, and the work of sculptor Barbara Hepworth, who spent much of her creative life here, is displayed in the Hepworth Gallery.

Penzance is the first and last town in Britain — it lies at the western extremity of Mounts Bay and basks in a temperate climate and sub-tropical vegetation. Places of interest include the ornate Egyptian House (now a National Trust shop), and steamers and helicopters go to the Scilly Isles.

Newquay Favourite haunt of surfboarders for its Fistral and Watergate beaches, Newquay has a 'Huer's House' where lookouts once warned fishermen of approaching shoals of pilchards. There are fine beaches for holidaymakers, such as Towan, Lusty Glaze and Great Western.

22

Central Newquay

Crantock

Trencreek

Newquay

Agar Road	C1
Atlantic Road	B2
Bank Street	B2-C2
Berry Road	C2
Bonython Road	E3
Carminow Way	E3
Chester Way	E2
Chynance Drive	B1-C1
Chyverton Close	B1
Cliff Road	C2-D2
Colvreath Road	D2
Crantock Street	B2
Dane Road	B3
East Street	C2
Edgcumbe Avenue	D2
Edgcumbe Gardens	D2
Eliot Gardens	D2
Esplanade Road	A2
Fairview Terrace	C2
Fernhill Road	B2
Fore Street	B2-B3
Gannel Road	B1
Glamis Road	E2
Hawkins Road	C1
Headland Road	B3
Headleigh Road	C1-D1
Henver Road	E2-E3
Higher Tower Road	B2
Hillgrove Road	D2-D3
Hope Terrace	B2
King Edward Crescent	B3
Lanhenvor Avenue	C1
Lawton Close	A2
Listry Road	C1
Lusty Glaze Road	E3
Manor Road	B2-C2
Mayfield Road	C1
Mount Wise	B2-B1-C1-C2
Narrowcliffe	D2-D3
North Quay Hill	B3
Pargolla Road	C2-D2-D1
Penpol Hill	A1
Pentire Avenue	A2
Pentire Crescent	A2
Pentire Road	A2-B2
Porth Way	E3
Praze Road	E3
Quarry Park Road	D1-D2
Rawley Lane	C1
Riverside Avenue	A2
St Annes Road	D2-E2
St Georges Road	B1-B2
St John's Road	B2
St Michael's Road	B2-C2
St Pirans Road	B2
St Thomas Road	C2-C1-D1
Station Parade	D2
Sweet Briar Crescent	D1
Tolcarne Road	D2

Tower Road	B2-B3
Trebarwith Crescent	C2
Tregunnel Hill	B1
Trelawney Road	C1
Treloggan Lane	D1
Trenance Avenue	C1
Trenance Lane	C1-D1
Trenance Road	C1-C2
Treninnick Hill	D1-A2-B2
Trethellan Hill	A1-E2-E1
Tretherras Road	D2
Trethewey Way	B1
Trevelveth Road	A1
Trevemper Road	C1-D1
Trevenson Road	E1-E2
Ulalia Road	D2
Whitegate Road	E2

St Ives

Albert Road	B4-B5
Back Road East	C5
Back Road West	C5
Bedford Road	B5
Bishops Road	B4-B5
Boskerris Road	A2-B2
Bullans Lane	B5
Carnellis Road	A5
Counthouse Lane	A2-A3
Fore Street	B5
Headland Road	B1-B2
Higher Stennack	A5
Laity Lane	A1
Menhyr Drive	A2-A3
Pannier Lane	A2-A3
Park Avenue	B5
Polmenr Drive	A1
Polwithen Drive	A1-A2
Porthia Road	A5
Porthrepta Road	A1-B1-B2
St Ives Road	A1-A2-A3
Steeple Lane	A3
Stennack Gardens	A5-B5
The Belyars	A4-B4
The Burrows	A5-B5
The Stennack	B5
The Warren	B4-B5
The Wharf	B5-C5
Treloyhan Park Road	A3-B3
Trelyon Avenue	A3-B3-B4
Trencrom Lane	A1
Trenwith Lane	A4-A5
Treverbyn Road	A5-B5
Valley Road	A2
Wheal Speed Road	A2

Central St Ives

23

Crawley

Crawley New Town, the only one of that generation of post-war new towns to be built south of London, has been grafted on to the old Crawley where many ancient buildings resolutely survive. However, the new town does have its own examples of good architecture, including the bandstand in Queens Square which came from nearby Gatwick Racecourse – now the site of Gatwick Airport.

This, London's second largest airport, is expected to increase its passenger handling capacity from 16 million to 25 million passengers a year in the 1990s on completion of a second terminal.

Horsham is another town that has suffered from a rash of modern development as a result of being within striking distance of the capital. However, one or two corners of the original centre reveal some interesting old buildings. One of these

is a 16th-century black-and-white timbered house containing the local museum. Here, a period Sussex kitchen, a blacksmith's forge and a wheelwright's shop can be seen.

East Grinstead The well-heeled residential housing of commuter-land radiates from this old market town that has retained a number of Tudor buildings along its High Street. Sackville College, the 17th-century almshouses founded by the 2nd Earl of Dorset, forms an attractive group.

Central Horsham

Central Horley

Key to Town Plan and Area Plan

Town Plan

A A Recommended roads
Other roads
Restricted roads
Buildings of interest — Mill
Car Parks — P
Parks and open spaces
A A Service Centre — AA

Area Plan

A roads
B roads
Locations — Lickey End○
Urban Area

Street Index with Grid Reference

Crawley

Aintree Road	F1
Albany Road	A4-A3-B3
Alpha Road	B3
Arden Road	E1-E2-F2
Ash Keys	D2
Ashfield Way	D3
Baker Close	C1
Barley Close	C2
Barrington Road	C1
Beeches	C2-D2
Beechside	D2
Bligh Close	E1
Brantridge Road	E1
Brewer Road	C2-D2-D1
Brighton Road	B1-C1-C2-C3
Broad Walk	C3
Brookside	E4
Brunel Place	D3
Buckman's Road	B4-C4-B4
Burwash Road	F2-F3
Caburn Heights	A1-B1
Chanctonbury Way	A1-B1-C1
Clayton Hill	A1-B1-B2
Clayton Road	D3-D4
College Road	C3
Coltash Road	F2
Cook Road	D1-E1
Crawley Avenue	A1-A2
Crosskeys	C3
Crossways	E4-F4
Darley Dale	A1-B1
Ditchling Hill	B1
Dovedale Crescent	A1
Downland Drive	A1-B1
Drake Road	D1
East Park	C3-C2-D2
Eastwood	E3

Epsom Road	F1
Ewhurst Road	A4-B4
Exchange Road	D4
Fisher Close	D1
Forester Road	D1
Friars Rookery	E4
Furnace Drive	E1-F1
Gales Drive	E4-F4
Gales Place	F4
Ginhams Road	A4
Goffs Lane	A3-A4
Goffs Park Road	B2-C2-C1
Greenacres	F2-F3
Hanover Close	E1
Haslett Avenue	C3-D3-E3-F3
Hawkins Road	D1
Hawth Avenue	D1-E1-E2-F2-F3
High Street	C3-C4
Hillside Close	A1-A2
Holmcroft	D2
Holmcroft Crescent	D2
Horsham Road	A1-A2-B2-B3
Hudson Road	D1
Hylands Close	F2
Ifield Road	A4-A3-B3-C3
Kilnmead	D4
Kingscote Hill	A1
Kites Close	B4
Leopold Road	B3
Livingstone Road	D1-E1
Loppets Road	E1
Lyndhurst Close	B2-C2
Malthouse Road	C1-C2
Malvern Road	B2
Mason Road	C1-D1
Meadowlands	A4-B4
Mitchell's Road	E4
Newlands Road	B2-B3
Newmarket Road	F1
North Road	F4
Northgate Avenue	D4-E4
Northgate Road	C4-D4
Oak Road	B3
Old Horsham Road	A1-A2
Orchard Street	C3-C4
Parkside	D3
Perryfield Road	B2-C2
Princess Road	B3
Priors Walk	E4
Queens Square	C3-D3
Queensway	D3-D4
Railey Road	D4
Ringwood Close	D1-D2-E2-E1
Robinson Road	C3
Russell Way	F3
Smalls Mead	B3-B4
Southgate Avenue	D1-D2-D3
Southgate Drive	C1-D1
Southgate Road	C1-C2
Spencer's Road	B3-C3
Spindle Way	E3
Springfield Road	B3-C3
Station Road	C3-D3
Station Way	D3-D3
Stonefield Close	C2
Sullington Hill	C1
Sunnymead	C4
Sylvan Road	F1
Telford Place	D3
The Boulevard	C4-D4
The Broadway	C3-C4

The Chase	F2
The Dingle	A4
The Glade	F1-F2
The Link	B4-C4
Theydon Close	F2
Three Bridges Road	D3-E3-E4-F4
Tilgate Drive	F1-F2-F3
Town Barn Road	B4
Town Mead	C4
Victoria Road	B3
Wakehurst Drive	C1
Waterlea	F2
Weald Drive	F1-F2
West Street	B2-B3-C3
Westfield Road	A3
West Green Drive	B4-B3-C3
Woodfield Road	D4

Horsham

Albion Way	A2-B2
Angus Road	B4
Arthur Street	C1
Bartellot Road	B1-B2
Bedford Road	A2
Bishopric	A3
Blunts Way	A3
Brighton Road	C1
Burford Road	C2-C3
Cambridge Road	C1-C2
Carfax	A2-B2
Cedar Close	A3
Clarence Road	C1-C2
Denne Parade	B1
Denne Road	A1-B1
Depot Road	C3
Devonshire Road	C2
East Street	B1
Foundry Lane	C3-C4
Gladstone Road	C3
Gorings Mead	C1
Hurst Avenue	B3-B4-C4
Hurst Close	B3-C3
Hurst Road	B4-B3-C3
Kempshott Road	A4
Livingstone Road	B1-C1
London Road	A2-B2
Market Square	A1-B1-B2
Mill Bay Lane	A1
Milnwood Road	A4
Moon Lane	C1
New Street	C1-C2
Newlands Road	A4
Norfolk Road	B2
North Parade	A3-A4-B4
North Street	B2-C2-C3
Oxford Road	C2
Park Street	B1-B2
Park Terrace West	B1-B2
Parkfield	B4
Percy Road	A3
Queen Street	B1-C1
Queenway	B1
Richmond Road	B4
Rushams Road	A2-A3
South Street	A1
Spencers Road	A3-A3
Springfield Crescent	A2-A3
Springfield Road	A2
Springfield Park Road	A2
Station Road	C2-C3

Swindon Road	A4
The Causeway	A1
Trafalgar Road	A3-A4
Victory Road	A3-A4
West Parade	A4
West Street	A2
Wimblehurst Road	B4
Winterton Court	C2

Horley

Albert Road	B3-B4
Avenue Gardens	C2
Balcombe Gardens	C2
Balcombe Road	B4-B3-C3-C2-C1
Bayhorne Lane	C1
Blundell Avenue	A4
Bremner Avenue	A4
Brighton Road	A2-A3-B3-B4
Castle Drive	C2
Charlesfield Road	A4
Chequers Drive	B4
Cheyne Walk	A2-B2
Church Road	A2-A3-B3
Court Lodge Road	A3
Crescent Way	A2-B2-B1
Fairfield Avenue	B1-B2
Grove Road	A4
Haroldslea Drive	A4
Hatchgate	C2
Hevers Avenue	A4-B4
High Street	B3
Horley Row	A4-B4
Langshott Road	C3-C4
Lee Street	A4
Limes Avenue	C2
London Road	A2-A1-B1
Longbridge Road	A2
Lumley Road	B3-B4
Manor Drive	A3
Massetts Road	A2-B2-B3
Michael Crescent	B1-B2
Oakwood Road	B3-B4
Oldfield Road	A2
Parkway	B3
Queens Road	B3
Ringley Avenue	B2-B3
Riverside	A1-B1
Russells Crescent	B2
Sangers Drive	A3
Silverlea Gardens	C2-C3
Smallfield Road	C3
Smallmead	C3
Southlands Avenue	A4-B4
Station Approach	B2
Station Road	B2-B3
The Avenue	A2
The Crescent	B1
The Drive	B1-B2
The Grove	B2-B3
The Meadway	C3-C4
The Ridgeway	B1
Upfield	B1-B2
Vicarage Lane	A3-A4
Victoria Road	A3-B3-B2-C2
Wheatfield Way	C3-C4
Wolverton Gardens	A2
Yattendon Road	B3

Central Margate

A · B · C

Winter Gardens

Lighthouse
The Harbour
FORT CRESCENT
FORT HILL
Pol. Sta.
Trinity Square
Zion Place
Caves
NORTHDOWN ROAD
Tudor House
KING STREET
The Bay
THE PARADE
HIGH STREET
HAWLEY ST
PARMKT ST
NEW ST
UNION ROW
P.O.
UNION CRES.
CECIL SQ.
CECIL PLACE
ADDINGTON ST
DANE HILL
DANE RD
Centre Precinct
Council Offices & Library
School
School for the Deaf
Casino Amusements
Clock Tower
MARINE DRIVE
MARINE GDNS
GROSVENOR HILL
MARINE TERRACE
Twin Cinema's & Squash Courts
Bembom Brothers Amusements Park
BELGRAVE ROAD
EATON ROAD
CHURCHFIELDS
HIGH STREET
MILL LA.
ST. ANNE TERR.
LAUS.
CHARSOT
Plaza Cinema
Fire Sta.
VICTORIA ROAD
COWPER ROAD
MILTON AVE.
CH. ST
ST PETER'S FOOTPATH
School
VICARAGE PLACE
QUEENS AVE.
VIC. CRES.
ST PETER'S RD
Margate Station
MARINE AVENUE
ST'RD
ALL SAINTS AVE
ALL SAINTS AVENUE
Golf Course
TIVOLI PARK
TIVOLI ROAD
Marlboro Road
BUCKINGHAM ROAD
RAMSGATE RD.
ALEXANDRA ROAD
CONNAUGHT ROAD
Swimming Pool
Hantsdown Park
Sports Centre
Thanet United F.C.
Tivoli Park
Tivoli Industrial Estate

Central Dover

GUSTON ROAD
Bleriot Memorial
UPPER ROAD
JUBILEE
To Eastern Docks
Terminal Building
AA Port Service Centre
TERMINAL BUILDING
Connaught Park
CONNAUGHT ROAD
CASTLE AVENUE
CASTLEMOUNT ROAD
School
Castle Walls
Dover Castle
St Mary's Church & The Pharos
Castle Walls
CASTLE HILL ROAD
Youth Hostel
SALISB ROAD
PARK AVE
GODWYNE RD
LEYBURNE RD
HAROLD ST
TASWELL STREET
VICTORIA PARK
LAURESTON PLACE
EAST CLIFF
MARINE PARADE
MAISON DIEU ROAD
Health Centre
Fire Sta.
Pol. College of Sta. Technology
Bus Sta.
WOOLCOMBER ST
Sports Centre & Swimming Pool
LADYWELL PK
Town Hall & Museum & Library
Pencester Gardens
CASTLE ST
RUSSELL ST
PENCESTER RD
Hosp.
BIGGIN ST
CANNON ST
YORK STREET
TOWN WALL ST
THE GATEWAY
Bureau de Change
Dover College
JEFF HAM
H.P.O.
Roman Painted House
LANC. RD
ALBANY PLACE
DURHAM HILL
CAMBRIDGE RD
Central Dover
FOLKESTONE ROAD
Priory Station
Cowgate Cemetery
SNAREGATE ST
WATERLOO CRESCENT
Wellington Basin
Prince of Wales Pier
CLARENDON PLACE
CLARENDON ROAD
MILITARY ROAD
NORTH Walls
CENTRE ROAD
Knight's Templars
AA Hire Services
AA
UNION STREET
Granville Basin
Terminal Building
Hovercraft Terminal
North Pier
Tidal Basin
Western Docks South Pier
SOUTH MILITARY ROAD
CITADEL ROAD
CHANNEL VIEW
LIMEKILN ST
THE VIADUCT
LORD WARDEN SQUARE
B.R. Car Ferry Reception Area
Marine Station
Admiralty Pier
Walls
Walls
Citadel H.M. Borstal

Central Canterbury

A · B · C

West Station
St John's Hospital
St Stephen's Rd
NEW RUTTINGTON LANE
NOTLEY STREET
ST DUNSTAN'S STREET
ROPER RD
STATION RD WEST
NORTH LANE
POUND LANE
ST RADIGUNDS STREET
NORTHGATE
UNION ST
MILITARY ROAD
ARTILLERY ST
ORCHARD ST
L.C.
Westgate Museum
Westgate Hall
Sidney Cooper Centre
Blackfriars Refectory
Marlowe's Th.
Weavers
BROAD ST
Amb Station
LINDEN GROVE
WHITEHALL ROAD
Westgate Gardens
ST PETER'S LA
ST PETER'S PLACE
Hospital
Black Griffin Lane
THE FRIARS
BEST LA
KING'S School
City Walls
OLD RUTTINGTON LANE
NORTH HOLMES RD
HAVELOCK ST
RHEIMS WAY
ST PETER'S GROVE
STOUR ST
HAWKS LA
P.O.
Art Gallery Library & Museums
Cathedral
Christ Church Gateway
Chequers of the Hope
PALACE ST
GUILDHALL
HIGH ST
MERCERY LA
SUN ST
BURGATE
Roman Pavement
ST MARGARET'S ST
MONASTERY ST
BROAD ST
Teacher's Training College
St Augustine's Abbey
Great Stour
Greyfriars
Poor Priests Hospital & Her. Centre
Queen Elizabeth's Guest Chamber
STOUR STREET
WATLING ST
ROSE LA
ST GEORGE'S ST
ST GEORGE'S PLACE
ST Augustine's College
LONGPORT
Mag. Ct.
IVY LANE
LOWER CHANTRY LA
Castle
Dane John
ST JOHN'S LA
ST MARY'S ST
ABC Cinema
UPP. BRIDGE ST
DOVER ST
Fire Station
RHODAUS TOWN
PIN HILL
CASTLE ROW
CASTLE ST
Police Station
NEW DOVER ROAD
OATEN HILL
COSSINGTON ROAD
STATION ROAD EAST
RHODAUS CLOSE
East Station
SIMMONDS ROAD
WINCHEAP
GORDON ROAD
YORK ROAD
VICTORIA RD
HEATON RD
MARTYR'S FIELD ROAD
LIME KILN ROAD
GUILDFORD ROAD
OXFORD ROAD
CAMBRIDGE ROAD
ZEALAND ROAD
NORMAN ROAD
NUNNERY ROAD
LANSDOWN ROAD
PROSPECT FIELDS
PUCKLE LANE
RAY- MOND AVE

Key to Town Plan and Area Plan

Town Plan

AA Recommended roads	▬▬
Restricted roads	▬ ▬ ▬
Other roads	▬▬
Buildings of interest	Art Gallery
Car Parks	P
Churches	†
Parks and open spaces	
One Way Streets	→

Area Plan

A roads	▬▬
B roads	▬▬
Locations	Womenswold ○
Urban area	

Street Index with Grid Reference

Margate

Addington Road	C3
Addington Street	C2-C3
Alexandra Road	B1-C1
All Saints Avenue	A2
Belgrave Road	B2
Buckingham Road	B1-C1
Cecil Square	B3
Cecil Street	B3-C3
Charlotte Square	C2
Churchfields	C2
Churchfields Place	B3-C3-C2
Church Street	C2
Connaught Road	C1
Cowper Road	C2
Dane Hill	C3-C4

Dover

Travellers tend to rush through Dover – it is one of the busiest passenger ports in England – and by so doing miss an exciting town with much of interest. Outstanding is the castle. Its huge fortifications have guarded the town since the 12th century, but within its walls are even older structures – a Saxon church and a Roman lighthouse called the Pharos. In the town itself, the town hall is housed within the walls of a 13th-century guest house called the Maison Dieu. The Roman Painted House in New Street consists of substantial remains of a Roman town house and include the best-preserved Roman wall paintings north of the Alps.

Canterbury is one of Britain's most historic towns. It is the seat of the Church in England, and has been so since St Augustine began his mission here in the 6th century. The cathedral is a priceless work of art containing many other works of art, including superb displays of medieval carving and stained glass. Ancient city walls – partly built on Roman foundations – still circle parts of the city, and a wealth of grand public buildings as well as charming private houses of many periods line the maze of lanes in the shadow of the cathedral.

Margate and **Ramsgate** both grew as commercial ports, but for many years they have specialised in catering for holidaymakers who like safe, sandy beaches and excellent facilities.

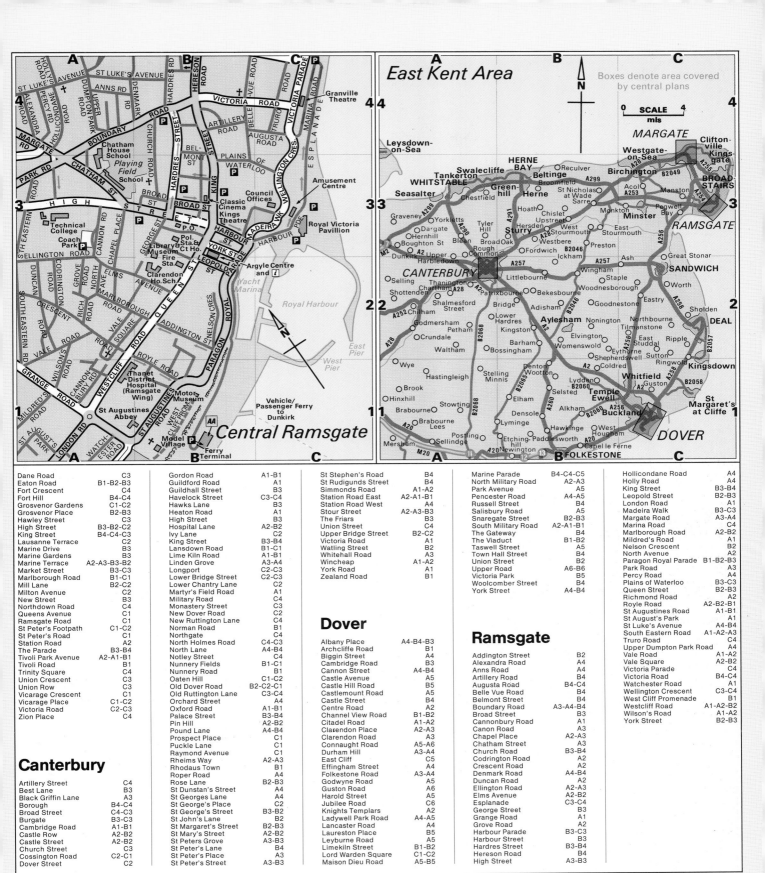

East Kent Area

Boxes denote area covered by central plans

SCALE 0 — 4 mls

Central Ramsgate

Dane Road	C3
Eaton Road	B1-B2-B3
Fort Crescent	C4
Fort Hill	B4-C4
Grosvenor Gardens	C1-C2
Grosvenor Place	B2-B3
Hawley Street	C3
High Street	B3-B2-C2
King Street	B4-C4-C3
Lausanne Terrace	C2
Marine Drive	B3
Marine Gardens	B3
Marine Terrace	A2-A3-B3-B2
Market Street	B3-C3
Marlborough Road	B1-C1
Mill Lane	B2-C2
Milton Avenue	C2
New Street	B3
Northdown Road	C4
Queens Avenue	C1
Ramsgate Road	C1
St Peter's Footpath	C1-C2
St Peter's Road	C1
Station Road	A2
The Parade	B3-B4
Tivoli Park Avenue	A2-A1-B1
Tivoli Road	B1
Trinity Square	C4
Union Crescent	C3
Union Row	C3
Vicarage Crescent	C1
Vicarage Place	C1-C2
Victoria Road	C2-C3
Zion Place	C4

Canterbury

Artillery Street	C4
Best Lane	B3
Black Griffin Lane	A3
Borough	B4-C4
Broad Street	C4-C3
Burgate	B3-C3
Cambridge Road	A1-B1
Castle Row	A2-B2
Castle Street	A2-B2
Church Street	C3
Cossington Road	C2-C1
Dover Street	C2
Gordon Road	A1-B1
Guildford Road	A1
Guildhall Street	B3
Havelock Street	C3-C4
Hawks Lane	B3
Heaton Road	A1
High Street	B3
Hospital Lane	A2-B2
Ivy Lane	C2
King Street	B3-B4
Lansdown Road	B1-C1
Lime Kiln Road	A1-B1
Linden Grove	A3-A4
Longport	C2-C3
Lower Bridge Street	C2-C3
Lower Chantry Lane	C2
Martyr's Field Road	A1
Military Road	C4
Monastery Street	C3
New Dover Road	C2
New Ruttington Lane	C4
Norman Road	C4
Northgate	C4
North Holmes Road	C4-C3
North Lane	A4-B4
Notley Street	C4
Nunnery Fields	B1-C1
Nunnery Road	B1
Oaten Hill	C2
Old Dover Road	B2-C2-C1
Old Ruttington Lane	C3-C4
Orchard Street	A4
Oxford Road	A1-B1
Palace Street	B3-B4
Pin Hill	A2-B2
Pound Lane	A4-B4
Prospect Place	C1
Puckle Lane	C1
Raymond Avenue	C1
Rheims Way	A2-A3
Rhodaus Town	B1
Roper Road	A4
Rose Lane	B2-B3
St Dunstan's Street	A4
St Georges Lane	A4
St George's Place	C2
St George's Street	B3-B2
St John's Lane	B2
St Margaret's Street	B2-B3
St Mary's Street	A2-B2
St Peters Grove	A3-B3
St Peter's Lane	B4
St Peter's Place	A3
St Peter's Street	A3-B3
St Stephen's Road	B4
St Rudigunds Street	B4
Simmonds Road	A1-A2
Station Road East	A2-A1-B1
Station Road West	A4
Stour Street	A2-A3-B3
The Friars	B3
Union Street	C4
Upper Bridge Street	B2-C2
Victoria Road	A1
Watling Street	B2
Whitehall Road	A3
Wincheap	A1-A2
York Road	A1
Zealand Road	B1

Dover

Albany Place	A4-B4-B3
Archcliffe Road	B1
Biggin Street	A4
Cambridge Road	B3
Cannon Street	A4-B4
Castle Avenue	A5
Castle Hill Road	B5
Castlemount Road	A5
Castle Street	B4
Centre Road	A2
Channel View Road	B1-B2
Citadel Road	A1-A2
Clarendon Place	A2-A3
Clarendon Road	A3
Connaught Road	A5-A6
Durham Hill	A3-A4
East Cliff	C5
Effingham Street	A4
Folkestone Road	A3-A4
Godwyne Road	A5
Guston Road	A6
Harold Street	A5
Jubilee Road	C6
Knights Templars	A2
Ladywell Park Road	A4-A5
Lancaster Road	A4
Laureston Place	B5
Leyburne Road	A5
Limekiln Street	B1-B2
Lord Warden Square	C1-C2
Maison Dieu Road	A5-B5
Marine Parade	B4-C4-C5
North Military Road	A2-A3
Park Avenue	A5
Pencester Road	A4-A5
Russell Street	B4
Salisbury Road	A5
Snaregate Street	B2-B3
South Military Road	A2-A1-B1
The Gateway	B4
The Viaduct	B1-B2
Taswell Street	A5
Town Hall Street	B4
Union Street	B2
Upper Road	A6-B6
Victoria Park	B5
Woolcomber Street	B4
York Street	A4-B4

Ramsgate

Addington Street	B2
Alexandra Road	A4
Anns Road	A4
Artillery Road	B4
Augusta Road	B4-C4
Belle Vue Road	B4
Belmont Street	B4
Boundary Road	A3-A4-B4
Broad Street	B3
Cannonbury Road	A1
Canon Road	A2
Chapel Place	A2-A3
Chatham Street	A3
Church Road	B3-B4
Codrington Road	A2
Crescent Road	A2
Denmark Road	A4-B4
Duncan Road	A2
Ellington Road	A2-A3
Elms Avenue	A2-B2
Esplanade	C3-C4
George Street	B3
Grange Road	A1
Grove Road	A2
Harbour Parade	B3-C3
Harbour Street	B3
Hardres Street	B3-B4
Hereson Road	B4
High Street	A3-B3
Hollicondane Road	A4
Holly Road	A4
King Street	B3-B4
Leopold Street	B2-B3
London Road	A1
Madeira Walk	B3-C3
Margate Road	A3-A4
Marina Road	B2
Marlborough Road	A2-B2
Mildred's Road	A1
Nelson Crescent	B2
North Avenue	A2
Paragon Royal Parade	B1-B2-B3
Park Road	A3
Percy Road	A4
Plains of Waterloo	B3-C3
Queen Street	B2-B3
Richmond Road	A2
Royle Road	A2-B2-B3
St Augustines Road	A1-B1
St August's Park	A4
St Luke's Avenue	A4-B4
South Eastern Road	A1-A2-A3
Truro Road	C4
Upper Dumpton Park Road	A1-A2
Vale Road	A1-A2
Vale Square	A2-B2
Victoria Parade	C4
Victoria Road	B4-C4
Watchester Road	A1
Wellington Crescent	C3-C4
West Cliff Promenade	B1
Westcliff Road	A1-A2-B2
Wilson's Road	A1-A2
York Street	B2-B3

DOVER

The famous White Cliffs of Dover provide exhilarating coastal walks with views out across the Channel. Paths to the north-east lead to Walmer and to the south-east, to Folkestone.

Central Eastbourne

Eastbourne Area

mls 0   **SCALE**   2

Eastbourne

Magnificent flower displays along the promenade combine with parks and gardens to provide a dazzling spectacle of colour from spring to autumn for this resort, which is one of the largest on the south coast and lies in the shelter of dramatic Beachy Head. Major sporting events take place throughout the year, including International and Championship tennis; on the cultural side, Eastbourne's Towner Art Gallery, Lifeboat Museum and Redoubt Fortress are all worth visiting. The town also offers good shopping and a wide choice of theatres and cinemas. For children, the imaginative Playcentre is designed with paddling pools, slides and big models of jungle animals.

Seaford boasts a three mile long promenade, which leads down to the seashore and to the Martello Tower (at the eastern end of the Esplanade) which houses the local museum. From Seaford Head a breathtaking view can be had of the coastline and the Seven Sisters, a line of cliffs stretching out along the shoreline. Between Cuckmere River and Seaford Head, a nature reserve supports a wide variety of plant and bird life.

Hailsham and ropemaking have gone together since the early 19th century, and another long-standing feature of the town is its cattle market, which has been operating on the same site since 1868.

Central Seaford

Central Hailsham

Key to Town Plan and Area Plan

Town Plan

A A Recommended roads
Other roads
Restricted roads
Buildings of interest
Car Parks
Parks and open spaces
One way streets

Area Plan

A roads
B roads
Locations   Ripe ○
Urban Area

Street Index with Grid Reference

Eastbourne

Arundel Road	B2-C2-C3
Ashburnham Road	B3-C3
Ashford Road	C2-D2
Astaire Avenue	D4
Avondale Road	D3
Baldwin Avenue	A3-A4
Beach Road	E3
Bedfordwell Road	C3-D3
Belmore Road	D2
Beverington Road	A4-B4
Blackwater Road	C1-D1
Bourne Street	D2
Burton Road	B3-B4
Carew Road	B3-C3
Carlisle Road	C1-D1
Cavendish Avenue	D2-D3
Cavendish Place	D1-D2
Channel View Road	E3-E4
Church Street	A2-B2
Churchdale Road	D4-E4
Cobbold Avenue	A4

Compton Drive	A1
Compton Place Road	B2-B1-C1
Devonshire Place	D1
Dittons Road	B2-C2
East Dean Road	A2
Eldon Road	A3-B3
Enys Road	C2-C3
Firle Road	D2-D3
Furness Road	C1
Gildredge Road	C1-C2
Grand Parade	D1
Green Street	C1-C2
Grove Road	C1-D1
Hardwick Road	C1-D1
Hartfield Road	C2-C3
High Street	B2
Hurst Road	B3-B4
Kinfauns Avenue	D4
King's Avenue	B3-B4
King's Drive	B4-C4-C3
Latimer Road	E2-E3-E4
Lewes Road	C3
Lismore Road	D1-D2
Longland Road	A2-A3
Lottbridge Drive	E4-F4
Meads Road	B1-C1
Mill Gap Road	C2-C3
Mill Road	A3
Milton Road	A3
Marine Parade	D1-D2-E2
Marison Road	A2-A3-B3
Moy Avenue	D3-D4
Myrtle Road	E4-F4
Northbourne Road	E4
Northiam Road	A3
Ocklynge Road	B2-B3
Paradise Drive	A1-B1-B2
Pashley Road	A1-A2
Prideaux Avenue	B3-C3
Prideaux Road	C3
Ringwood Road	D4-D3-E3
Rodmill Drive	B4
Rodmill Road	B3-B4
Roselands Avenue	D4-E4-E3
Royal Parade	E2-E3-F3-F4
St Anne's Road	B3-C3-C2
St Leonard's Road	C2-D2
St Phillip's Avenue	D3-D4-E4
Saffrons Road	B2-C2-C1
Seaside	D2-E2-E3-E4
Selwyn Road	B3-B2-C2
Sidley Road	E3-E4
South Street	C1
Southbourne Road	D4-E4
Southfields Road	C2
Stuart Avenue	A4
Summerdown Road	A1-A2
Susan's Road	D2
The Avenue	C2
The Goffs	B2
Trinity Trees	D1-D2
Upper Avenue	C2-D2-D3
Upperton Road	B2-C2
Vicarage Drive	A2
Vicarage Road	A2-B2
Victoria Drive	A2-A3-A4
Wartling Road	E4
Watts Lane	B3
Whitley Road	D3-E3
Willingdon Road	A4-B4-B3
Woodgate Road	D4-D3-E3

Seaford

Alfriston Road	B4-C4
Arundel Road	C3-C4
Avondale Road	A2-B2-A3
Blatchington Hill	A3
Blatchington Road	A2-A3
Bramber Road	B2-C2
Broad Street	A2-B2
Brooklyn Road	A2
Buckland Road	A4
Chichester Road	A2
Church Street	A2-A1-B1
Chyngton Road	C2
Claremont Road	A2
Cliff Close	C1
Cliff Road	C1
Clinton Place	A2
College Road	B1-C1
Cornfield Road	B2-B3
Corsica Close	C1-C2
Corsica Road	C1-C2
Cricketfield Road	B1-C1
Croft Lane	B2
Crooked Lane	B2
Dane Road	A1
Downs Road	B3-C3
Downsview Road	B3-C3
East Street	B2
East Albany Road	B3
Eastbourne Road	C4
Esher Close	A4
Esplanade	A1-B1-C1
Fitzgerald Avenue	C1-C2
Gildredge Road	B3
Glebe Drive	A3
Green Lane	A1
Grove Road	B2-B3
Hartfield Road	B3-C3-C4
Haven Brow	B4
Head Road	B3
Headland Avenue	C2-C3
Heathfield Road	C3-B3-B2-C2
High Street	B1-B2
Homefield Road	A3-A4
Kendale Road	A2-A3
Lions Place	C2
Lower Drive	A4
Marine Crescent	B1
Marison Road	B4-C4
Mason Road	A4
Middle Furlong	B2-B3
Milldown Road	B3
North Camp Lane	A4
North Way	A4
Pelham Road	A1
Ridgeway	B1
Ringmer Road	A3
Rose Walk	A4
Rother Road	C2-C3
St Peter's Road	A4
Salisbury Road	A2
Sandore Road	B4-C4
Saxon Lane	B1
Sherwood Road	A3-A4
Southdown Road	B3-C3-C2
Stafford Road	A2-A3-B3
Station Approach	A1-A2
Steyne Road	B1-B2-C2
Sutton Avenue	C2-C3

Sutton Drove	A3-B3-B4-C4
Sutton Road	A2-B2-B3-B4-C4
Sutton Park Road	A2-B2
Upper Belgrave Road	A3-A4
Upper Sherwood Road	A4-B4
Vale Road	A3-B3-B4
Valley Rise	A4
West Street	A1
West View	A1-B1

Hailsham

Archery Walk	B1
Battle Road	B3-B4-C4
Bayham Road	C1-C2
Bell Banks Road	B1-B2
Bowley Road	B1-C1
Clyde Park	C1-C2
Derwent Close	A3-A4
Diplocks Way	A1-A2
Ersham Road	A1
Ersham Way	A1
Forest View	A3
Garfield Road	B2
Geering Park	C1-C2
George Street	B2
Gordon Road	A1-A2
Greenwich Road	C2
Grovelands Road	A3
Harebeating Lane	C4
Harmers Hay Road	B4
Hawks Road	A4
Hawthylands Road	B4-C4
Hempstead Lane	A4
High Street	B2-B3
London Road	A4-A3-B3
Market Street	B1-B2
Marshfoot Lane	C2
Mill Road	B1-C1
Milland Road	A4-B4
Moore Park	C1-C2
North Street	B2-B3
St Mary's Avenue	C1-C2
Sandbanks Way	A1
South Road	A1-A2-B2
Station Road	B1-B2
Summerfields Avenue	A3
Summerheath Road	A2-A3-B3-B2
Sussex Avenue	A2-A3
Swan Road	B1-C1
The Avenue	A1-B1
The Drive	B1
The Gages	C2
The Lowlands	A4
The Holt	A1
The Stringwalk	B1
Vicarage Lane	B2-B3
Vicarage Road	B2-C2
Western Road	A2-A3
Windsor Road	A1
Woodpecker Drive	A3

Exeter

The cathedral is Exeter's greatest treasure. Founded in 1050, but rebuilt by the Normans during the 12th century and again at the end of the 13th century, it has many beautiful and outstanding features – especially the exquisite rib-vaulting of the nave. Most remarkable, perhaps, is the fact that it still stood after virtually everything around it was flattened during bombing raids in World War II.

There are still plenty of reminders of Old Exeter, which has been a city since Roman times. Roman and medieval walls encircle parts of the city; 14th-century underground passages can be explored; the Guildhall is 15th-century and one of the oldest municipal buildings in the country; and Sir Francis Drake is said to have met his explorer companions at Mol's Coffee House. Exeter is famous for its extensive Maritime Museum, with over 100 boats from all over the world. Other

museums include the Rougemont House and the Royal Albert Memorial Museum and Art Gallery.

Exmouth has a near-perfect position at the mouth of the Exe estuary. On one side it has expanses of sandy beach, on another a wide estuary alive with wildfowl and small boats, while inland is beautiful Devon countryside.

Newton Abbot lies on the River Teign. It is a busy market town and has been an important railway junction since the mid 19th century.

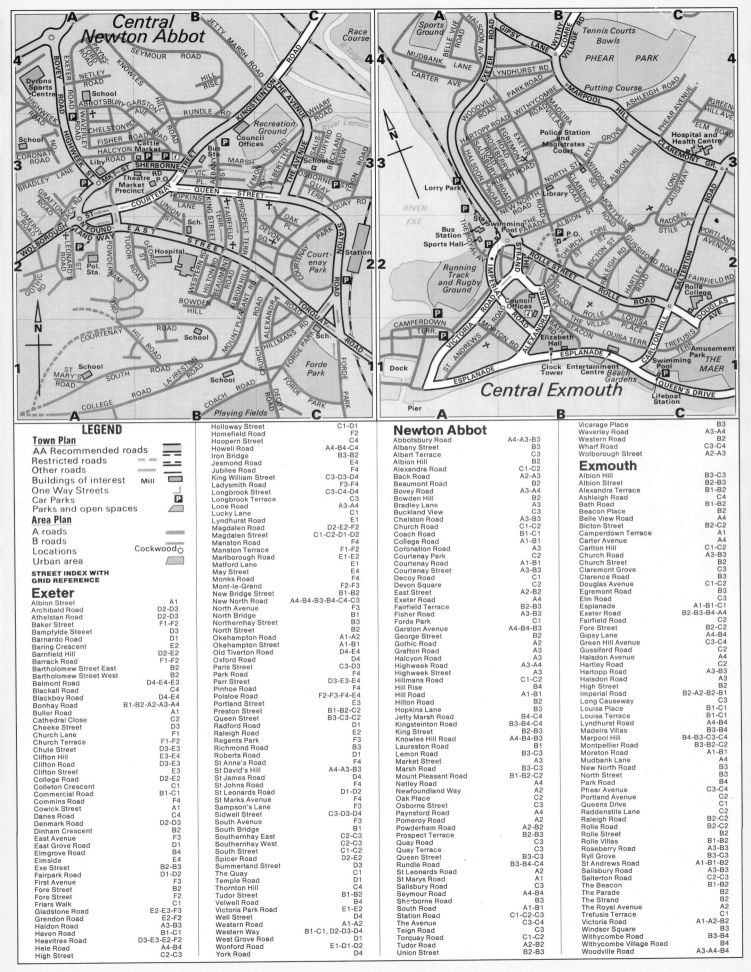

Central Newton Abbot

Central Exmouth

LEGEND

Town Plan
AA Recommended roads	
Restricted roads	
Other roads	
Buildings of interest	Mill
One Way Streets	
Car Parks	P
Parks and open spaces	

Area Plan
A roads	
B roads	
Locations	Cockwood
Urban area	

STREET INDEX WITH GRID REFERENCE

Exeter

Albion Street	A1
Archibald Road	D2-D3
Athelstan Road	D2-D3
Baker Street	F1-F2
Bampfylde Steeet	D3
Barnardo Road	D1
Baring Crescent	E2
Barnfield Hill	D2-E2
Barrack Road	F1-F2
Bartholomew Street East	B2
Bartholomew Street West	B2
Belmont Road	D4-E4-E3
Blackall Road	C4
Blackboy Road	D4-E4
Bonhay Road	B1-B2-A2-A3-A4
Buller Road	A1
Cathedral Close	C2
Cheeke Street	D3
Church Lane	F1
Church Terrace	F1-F2
Chute Street	D3-E3
Clifton Hill	E3-E4
Clifton Road	D3-E3
Clifton Street	E3
College Road	D2-E2
Colleton Crescent	C1
Commercial Road	B1-C1
Commins Road	F4
Cowick Street	A1
Danes Road	C4
Denmark Road	D2-D3
Dinham Crescent	B1
East Avenue	F2
East Grove Road	D1
Elmgrove Road	B4
Elmside	E4
Exe Street	B2-B3
Fairpark Road	D1-D2
First Avenue	F3
Fore Street	B2
Fore Street	C1
Friars Walk	F2
Gladstone Road	E2-E3-F3
Grendon Road	E2-F2
Haldon Road	A3-B3
Haven Road	B1-C1
Heavitree Road	D3-E3-E2-F2
Hele Road	A4-B4
High Street	C2-C3
Holloway Street	C1-D1
Homefield Road	F2
Hoopern Street	C4
Howell Road	A4-B4-C4
Iron Bridge	B3-B2
Jesmond Road	E4
Jubilee Road	F4
King William Street	C3-D3-D4
Ladysmith Road	F3-F4
Longbrook Street	C3-C4-D4
Longbrook Terrace	C3
Looe Road	A3-A4
Lucky Lane	C1
Lyndhurst Road	E1
Magdalen Road	D2-E2-F2
Magdalen Street	C1-C2-D1-D2
Manston Road	F4
Manston Terrace	F1-F2
Marlborough Road	E1-E2
Matford Lane	E1
May Street	E4
Monks Road	F4
Mont-le-Grand	F2-F3
New Bridge Street	B1-B2
New North Road	A4-B4-B3-B4-C4-C3
North Avenue	F3
North Bridge	B1
Northernhay Street	B3
North Street	B2
Okehampton Road	A1-A2
Okehampton Street	A1-B1
Old Tiverton Road	D4-E4
Oxford Road	D4
Paris Street	C3-D3
Park Road	F4
Parr Street	D3-E3-E4
Pinhoe Road	F4
Polsloe Road	F2-F3-F4-E4
Portland Street	E3
Preston Street	B1-B2-C2
Queen Street	B3-C3-C2
Radford Road	D1
Raleigh Road	E2
Regents Park	F3
Richmond Road	B3
Roberts Road	D1
St Anne's Road	F4
St David's Hill	A4-A3-B3
St James Road	D4
St Johns Road	D1-D2
St Leonards Road	D1-D2
St Marks Avenue	F4
Sampson's Lane	F3
Sidwell Street	C3-D3-D4
South Avenue	F3
South Bridge	B1
Southernhay East	C2-C3
Southernhay West	C2-C3
South Street	C1-C2
Spicer Road	D2-E2
Summerland Street	D3
The Quay	C1
Temple Road	D1
Thornton Hill	C4
Tudor Street	B1-B2
Velwell Road	B4
Victoria Park Road	E1-E2
Well Street	D4
Western Road	A1-A2
Western Way	B1-C1, D2-D3-D4
West Grove Road	D1
Wonford Road	E1-D1-D2
York Road	D4

Newton Abbot

Abbotsbury Road	A4-A3-B3
Albany Street	B3
Albert Terrace	C3
Albion Hill	B2
Alexandra Road	C1-C2
Back Road	A2-A3
Beaumont Road	B2
Bovey Road	A3-A4
Bowden Hill	B2
Bradley Lane	A3
Buckland View	C3
Chelston Road	A3-B3
Church Road	C1-C2
Coach Road	B1-C1
College Road	A1-B1
Coronation Road	A3
Courtenay Park	C2
Courtenay Road	A1-B1
Courtenay Street	A3-B3
Decoy Road	C1
Devon Square	C2
East Street	A2-B2
Exeter Road	A4
Fairfield Terrace	B2-B3
Fisher Road	A3-B3
Forde Park	C1
Garston Avenue	A4-B4-B3
George Street	B2
Gothic Road	A2
Grafton Road	A3
Halcyon Road	A3
Highweek Road	A3-A4
Highweek Street	A3
Hillmans Road	C1-C2
Hill Rise	B4
Hill Road	A1-B1
Hilton Road	B2
Hopkins Lane	B3
Jetty Marsh Road	B4-C4
Kingsteinton Road	B3-B4-C4
King Street	B2-B3
Knowles Hill Road	A4-B4-B3
Laureston Road	B1
Lemon Road	B3-C3
Market Street	A3
Marsh Road	B3-C3
Mount Pleasant Road	B1-B2-C2
Netley Road	A4
Newfoundland Way	A2
Oak Place	C2
Osborne Street	C3
Paynsford Road	A4
Pomeroy Road	A2
Powderham Road	A2-B2
Prospect Terrace	B2-B3
Quay Road	C3
Quay Terrace	C3
Queen Street	B3-C3
Rundle Road	B3-B4-C4
St Leonards Road	A2
St Marys Road	A1
Salisbury Road	C3
Seymour Road	A4-B4
Sherborne Road	B3
South Road	A1-B1
Station Road	C1-C2-C3
The Avenue	C3-C4
Teign Road	C3
Torquay Road	C1-C2
Tudor Road	A2-B2
Union Street	B2-B3
Vicarage Place	B3
Waverley Road	A3-A4
Western Road	B2
Wharf Road	C3-C4
Wolborough Street	A2-A3

Exmouth

Albion Hill	B3-C3
Albion Street	B2-B3
Alexandra Terrace	B1-B2
Ashleigh Road	C4
Bath Road	B1-B2
Beacon Place	B2
Belle View Road	A4
Bicton Street	B2-C2
Camperdown Terrace	A1
Carter Avenue	A4
Carlton Hill	C1-C2
Church Road	A3-B3
Church Street	B2
Claremont Grove	C3
Clarence Road	B3
Douglas Avenue	C1-C2
Egremont Road	B3
Elm Road	C3
Esplanade	A1-B1-C1
Exeter Road	B2-B3-B4-A4
Fairfield Road	C2
Fore Street	B2-C2
Gipsy Lane	A4-B4
Green Hill Avenue	C3-C4
Gussiford Road	C2
Halsdon Avenue	A4
Hartley Road	C2
Hartopp Road	A3-B3
Halsdon Road	A3
High Street	B2
Imperial Road	B2-A2-B2-B1
Long Causeway	C3
Louisa Place	B1-C1
Louisa Terrace	B1-C1
Lyndhurst Road	A4-B4
Madeira Villas	B3-B4
Marpool Hill	B4-B3-C3-C4
Montpellier Road	B3-B2-C2
Moreton Road	A1-B1
Mudbank Lane	A4
New North Road	B3
North Street	B3
Park Road	B4
Phear Avenue	C3-C4
Portland Avenue	C2
Queens Drive	C1
Raddenstile Lane	C2
Raleigh Road	B2-C2
Rolle Road	B2-C2
Rolle Street	B2
Rolle Villas	B1-B2
Roseberry Road	A3-B3
Ryll Grove	B3-C3
St Andrews Road	A1-B1-B2
Salisbury Road	A3-B3
Salterton Road	C2-C3
The Beacon	B1-B2
The Parade	B2
The Strand	B2
The Royal Avenue	A2
Trefusis Terrace	C1
Victoria Road	A1-A2-B2
Windsor Square	C1
Withycombe Road	B3-B4
Withycombe Village Road	B4
Woodville Road	A3-A4-B4

Fareham Area

A B3035 Wildern, Long Common, A3051, A334, Curdridge, Botley, A334, B3035
B Waltham Chase, Shirrell Heath, A333, Shedfield
C Soberton Heath, Newton, A32, Worlds End, Hundred Acres, North Boarhunt
Hedge End, Wickham, Curbridge, A333, Boarhunt, Southwick, A333
River Hamble, Lowford, Bursledon, A27, M27, Lower Swanwick, Burridge, Swanwick, Funtley, River Meon, A32, M27
Sarisbury, Park Gate, A27, Titchfield Park, Hill Park, Heathfield, FAREHAM, A27 Paulsgrove
A3051, Hamble, Locks Heath, A27, Titchfield Common, Titchfield, Box denotes area covered by central plan
Warsash, Southampton Water, B3334, Stubbington, B3385, B3334, A32, Elson, Hardway, Bridgemary, Portsmouth Harbour, Portchester
Calshot, Hill Head, Rowner, Brockhurst, Privett, GOSPORT, Portsea, Alverstoke
Lee-on-the-Solent, B3333, Box denotes area covered by central plan, Clayhall
THE SOLENT, Stokes Bay

SCALE 0—2 mls

Central Gosport

Ferrol Rd, Parham Rd, Alber St, Victoria St, Leonard Rd, FORTON ROAD, St Georges Barracks, Royal Clarence Yard, Weevil Lake, Weevil Lane, MUMBY ROAD, Jetty, School, Grove Avenue, Carlton Rd, Strathmore Rd, Peel Rd, Holly St, Oaks St, Prince of Wales Rd, Walpole Rd, St Georges Barracks, Services Rec. Gnd, North Cross St, Harbour Road, Yacht Marina, MUMBY ROAD, Avenue Road, Stoke Road, Jamaica Place, Spring Garden Lane, Woodnak, Nice Rd, Clarence Road, HIGH STREET, Mus., P.O., Town Lib. Hall, Pol. Sta., Shopping Precinct, SOUTH STREET, Court, Church Pa., Portsmouth Passenger Ferry, Bus Sta., South Street, Walpole Creek, Walpole Pk, Swimming Pool, TRINITY GREEN, Woodstock Road, Dock Road, THE ANCHORAGE, Willis Rd, Walpole Park, Boating Lake, ESPLANADE, Cranbourne Rd, Mayfield Road, Industrial Estate, Dolman, Old Road, Road, Hilton Rd, Haslar Lake, Haslar Road, Haslar Bridge, Haslar Rd, HMS Horne, Submarine Museum

Central Fareham

Inverness Ave, Frost Hole, Argyle Bal Cres, Argyle Cres, Cres Elgin Cres, Maylings Farm Road, Morshead Crescent, Mallory Crescent, School, Bruce Close, Norton Drive, Cemy, FURN OLD TURNPIKE, EAUX GDNS, MEAD WAY, SERPENTINE ROAD, WICKHAM ROAD, Fareham Industrial Park, STANDARD WAY, M27, Hospital, Wallington River, NORTH WALLINGTON, RIVERSIDE AVE, WALLINGTON, STANDARD WAY, Hamm ond Rd, Gudge Heath Lane, Argyle Cres, Beaufort Avenue, Miller Drive, Somervell Drive, Bentley Crescent, Oxford Close, Denbigh Drive, Chau Cer Cl, Arundel Drive, Baths, Park, Uplands Cres, Park Lane, College, School, Harrison Road, Southampton Road, Broadcut, Drift Road, Delme Drive, Wallington Shore Road, Seashill, Fort Wallington Industrial Estate, Military Road, Greenbanks Gdns, Water Side, Pinks Hill, Oak Road, Abbey Rd, Alan Grove, Marg Aritard, Beech Rd, Nicholas Crescent, Nicholas Crescent, Heath Lane, Leigh Road, The Drive, Gordon Road, Grove Road, Colenso Rd, Trinity Street, Osborn Road, P.O., Civic Offices, Library, Civic Way, HIGH STREET, WALLINGTON WAY, BRIDGEFOOT HILL, THE CAUSEWAY, THE RIDGEWAY, CAMS HILL, Blackbrook Road, Jonathan Rd, Blackbrook Park, Avenue, Blackbrook Drive, Maternity Home, Station, Fire Sta., Deryln Road, Court, Osborn Road, P.O., Shopping Centre, EAST STREET, PORTCHESTER ROAD, Southmead Rd, THE AVENUE, Justin Close, School, Technical College, School, Paxton Road, Ave Rd, Redlands Lane, WEST STREET, Kings Road, Queens Road, Western Rd, Bus Sta., Police Sta., Portland, Quay St, WESTERN WAY, EASTERN WAY, Recreation Ground, Deanes, Pk Rd, Mendips Road, Snowdon Drive, Longmynd Drive, Malvern Avenue, Bishopsfield, Westley Grove, Highfield Gr, St Annes Gr, St Michaels Gr, Walisdean Ave, School, Sports Centre Fareham Town F.C., Coombe, Alex Grove, Farm Ave Road, Mill Road, Fayre Rd, Belvoir Close, Elmhurst Rd, Holbrook, Low Quay Rd, Earls Rd, Hartland, Road

Fareham

Naval connections have long been a feature of this old market town. A large number of its residents work at the Naval Base in Portsmouth, naval training establishment HMS Collingwood stands on the town's outskirts, and its pre-19th century importance as a boat-building centre is being recaptured today with the manufacture of small sailing craft.

The trade is centred mainly around the Lower Quay on Fareham Creek (which flows virtually into the town centre), and buildings used as a hospital for French prisoners during the Napoleonic Wars can also be seen in this part of town. The High Street has retained a distinctly Georgian flavour; neighbouring West Street reflects Fareham's popularity as a shopping centre and has seen a good deal of development.

Gosport is another town whose trade has always been associated with the needs of the navy. Lying on the west side of Portsmouth Harbour and a major naval port since the 17th century, Gosport has probably the most extensive areas of military and naval housing in the country. HM Submarine Alliance, which houses a submarine museum, can be seen in Haslar Creek, and also of interest are Gosport Museum, 19th-century Fort Brockhurst, and the parish church, which dates from the 17th century and has an almost unchanged interior.

HM Submarine Alliance and Submarine Museum

Gosport's history as a submarine base goes back almost as far as submarines themselves, so this is a fitting home for the Royal Navy Submarine Museum and HM Submarine Alliance.

Submarines have come a long way since the days when a disgruntled Controller of the Navy said that "submariners should be hanged as pirates in wartime". In spite of early Admiralty misgivings, these sleek but lethal underwater travellers are the frontrunners of the Royal Navy today.

At the Submarine Museum in Gosport's Haslar Creek, visitors can see just how submarines have developed to become a crucial part of the modern fleet. Centrepiece of the museum is HM Submarine Alliance, which was intended for use in World War II but not ready in time to take part in any engagements. On her 'retirement' from service, she was presented to the Submarine Museum, and has been completely restored and raised up out of the water for easy access. Visitors enter through doors which have been cut in the pressure hull, and can walk right through the vessel. On the way, they are given a feel of the life and work of the submariners of World War II and they can also explore a more modern side to submarining, by looking at the new equipment which has been installed here. Guides are on hand to explain the functions of the various compartments, and to answer questions.

A recent arrival at the museum is HM Submarine Holland I — Britain's first submarine, newly salvaged from the seabed after the unlikely reprieve of sinking on her way to the breaker's yard. Named after her inventor John Philip Holland, she was launched in 1901, but has the porpoise-hull profile of the most up-to-date nuclear versions.

In the main body of the museum, models of all varieties of submarine are on display, coming right up to the advanced nuclear versions of today. Models featured in this section include HM Submarine Conqueror, while representing an earlier period in submarine development is the 1776 Turtle, built for American revolutionaries to launch an (unsuccessful) attack on Admiral Lord Howe's flagship in New York Harbour.

Visitors are advised to give themselves at least an hour and a half in order to do justice to all the museum has to offer, and to allow longer at busy times like the summer.

OPENING TIMES The Museum is open all year round, from 9.30am to 4.30pm, every day except Christmas Eve and Christmas Day.

TO GET THERE See town plan **Gosport**, grid squares B1 and C1. Cross Haslar Bridge and then turn left off Haslar Road. From here follow signs to the Submarine Museum.

Farnborough

Dick Turpin is said to have been associated with Farnborough's Tumbledown Dick inn and the Ship Inn was once used by patrons of illegal prize fights — but today the town is synonymous with the high technology of aeronautical research, and with the army. This is the scene of the biennial Farnborough Air Show, and the town's growth really began in the mid-19th century, when large numbers of military personnel were moved into the area.

Aldershot is the appropriate home of the Wellington Monument, which was moved here from London's Hyde Park Corner in 1885. It stands near the 19th-century Royal Garrison Church — another symbol of Aldershot's military importance since the Army arrived here in 1885 and instigated the town's expansion. Every two years in June the Army Display is held in the Rushmoor Arena and in 1969, the Army combined with the council to found the Stainforth Ski Centre.

Camberley is mainly a residential town, close to the Royal Staff College and the Royal Military Academy at Sandhurst.

Farnham is the home of the thriving Redgrave Theatre, and its cultural life is also served by the Maltings, an Adult Education and community centre. Much of Farnham's character as an 18th-century market town has been retained, and the castle dates back to the 12th century.

Key to Town Plan and Area Plan

Town Plan

AA Recommended roads
Other roads
Restricted roads
Buildings of interest — Cinema
Car Parks — P
Parks and open spaces
One Way Streets

Area Plan

A roads
B roads
Locations — Elstead○
Urban area

Street Index with Grid Reference

Farnborough

Abbey Way	B3-C3
Albert Road	B1-C1
Alexandra Road	B1
Avenue Road	C1-C2-C3
Boundary Road	B1-C1
Cabrol Road	A4
Canterbury Road	C1
Carlyon Close	C3
Cedar Road	B2-C2
Chalfont Drive	C1
Chingford Avenue	C4
Church Avenue	B1-B2-C2-C3-B3
Clockhouse Road	A3-B3
Eastmead	B2-B3
Elles Road	A1-A2
Elmgrove Road	A3-A4
Farnborough Road	B1-B2-B3-B4
Green School Lane	B4-C4
Highgate Lane	B4-C4
Highview Road	A3-A4
Hilder Gardens	C1-C2
Invincible Road	A2
Kingsmead	B2-B3
Meudon Avenue	A2-B2
Monks Close	C3
Northmead	A3
Oak Road	B2
Orchard Road	A3
Pierfondes Avenue	A4
Pinehurst Avenue	A2-B2
Pirbright Road	B1-C1
Prospect Road	A4
Queensmead	B2-B3
Rectory Road	B3-C3
St Michaels Mews	C3
Salisbury Road	B1-B2-B3
Solatron Road	A2-A3
Station Approach	B4
Station Road	A3-A4
Sycamore Road	B1-C1
The Crescent	B2-C2
Union Street	A4-B4
Victoria Road	A3-B3
Virginia Gardens	C1
Waverley Road	C2
West Heath Road	A4
Westmead	A2-B2-B3-A3-B3
Wymering Court	C2

Camberley

Abbetts Lane	A1
Bath Road	B4-C4
Beech Avenue	C1
Belmont Road	A1
Brackendale Road	B2-C2-C1
Bridge Road	A1
Charles Street	B4
Chillingham Way	A1-A2
College Road	A4-B4
Firlands Avenue	B3-C3-C2
Firwood Drive	A2-B2-B3
Forest Hills	A2
France Hill Drive	A2-A3
Frimley Road	A1-A2
Garfield Road	B2
Goddards Lane	A1
Gordon Avenue	A1-A2
Gordon Road	A2-B2-B3
Grace Reynolds Walk	B3-B4-C4
Grand Avenue	B3-B4
Hartford Rise	C4
Heathcote Road	C3

Heatherdale Road	B2-B1-C1
Heatherley Road	A2-A3
Heath Rise	C1
Heathway	C2-C3
Heathway Close	C2
High Street	B4-C4-C3
Kingsclear Park	B1-B2
Kingsley Avenue	B1-C1
Kings Ride	C4
Knoll Road	C3-C4
Krooner Road	A1
Linkway	A1
London Road	A3-A4-B4-C4
Middle Gordon Road	B3-C3
Obelisk Way	B4
Park Avenue	B1-C1
Park Lane	B3
Park Road	A1-B1-B2-C2-C3
Park Street	B2-B3-B4
Parkway	A1-B1
Pembroke Road	B3-C3
Pine Avenue	C1
Pine Mount Road	C1
Portesbury Road	C3
Princes Way	B3-C3
St Mary's Road	B3
Seaton Road	A2
Southern Road	B3
Southwell Park Road	A3-B3
Tekels Avenue	B2-C2-C1-C2
Th Avenue	A2-A3
The Square	B3
Upper Gordon Road	C3
Valroy Close	C4
Watchetts Road	A1
West Road	C3
Woodlands Road	A2-A3
York Road	C4

Farnham

Abbey Street	B3
Abbots Ride	C1
Adams Park Road	C4
Alfred Road	B2
Arthur Road	A2-B2
Beavers Road	A4
Bridgefield	C3
Broomleaf Road	C2-C3
Castle Hill	A4-B4
Castle Street	B4
College Garden	A3-A4
Darvills Lane	B3-C3
Dogflud Way	B4-C4
Downing Street	B3
East Street	B4-C4
Falkner Road	A4
Farnham By-pass	A2-B2-B3-C3
Firgrove Hill	B1-B2-B3
Great Austins	B1-C1
Hale Road	C4
High Park Road	B4
Holland Close	C1
Lancaster Avenue	B1
Little Austins Road	C1
Long Bridge	B3
Long Garden Walk	A4-B4
Longley Road	C2
Lynch Road	C2
Mavins Road	B1
Mead Lane	A3
Menin Way	C1-C2
Morley Road	B1-B2-C2
Old Farnham Lane	B1
Park Row	B4
Potters Gate	A3-A4
Red Lion Lane	A2-A3-B3
Ridgway Hill Road	A1
Ridgway Road	A1-B1
Ryle Road	A1-A2
St George's Road	B2
St James's Avenue	C4
St John's Road	A1
Saxon Croft	B2-B3
Searle Road	A1-B1
Sheephouse	A1-B1
South Street	B3-B4
Station Hill	B2-B3
Station Road	B2-B3-B2-B3
Stoke Hills	C4
Stoneyfields	C1
Summer Road	C4
The Borough	B3-B4
The Close	C1
The Fairfield	B3-C3
The Hart	A3-A4
Tilford Road	B2-C2-C1
Trafalgar Court	A2-B2
Trebor Avenue	B1-B2
Union Road	B3
Upper Church Lane	A3-B3
Upper Way	A1
Waverley Lane	B2-C2
Wessex Place	B2
West Street	A3-B3-B4
Weydon Hill Road	A1-A2
Weydon Lane	A2
Weydon Mill Lane	A2
Woolmead	B4

Wykham Road	B4
York Road	B1-B2

Aldershot

Alamein Road	B4-C4
Albert Road	C3
Alexandra Road	A2-A3-B3
Alison Way	A3
Anzio Close	B4
Arthur Road	C3
Avondale Road	A2
Ayling Hill	
Ayling Lane	A2-A1-B1
Badajos Road	A4
Barrack Road	A4-A3-B3-B4
Birchett Road	B3
Boxalls Lane	B1-C1
Bridge Road	B1-B2-C2
Brockenhurst Road	C2
Cambridge Road	A2-A3
Campbell Road	B4
Cargate Avenue	B2-B3
Cargate Grove	B2
Cargate Hill	A2-B2-B3
Cassino Close	B4-C4
Cavendish Mews	B2
Cavendish Road	C2
Church Lane East	B2-C2
Church Lane West	A2-B2
Church Street	A2-A3
Cranmore Lane	A1-A2
Crimea Road	C4
Edward Street	A3-B3
Eggars Hill	B1-B2
Elms Road	B3
Falaise Close	B4-C4
Gordon Road	B3
Grosvenor Road	B2-B3
Gun Hill	B4
Halimote Road	B2-B3
Highfield Avenue	C1-C2
Highfield Gardens	C1
High Street	B4-C4-C3
Hillside Road	B1
Hospital Hill	A4-B4
Kilnway	C1
Kings Road	A2
Kingsway	A2
Laburnum Road	B3
Lime Street	A3
Lysons Road	B2-B3
Manor Road	B2
Middle Hill	B4
Northbrook Road	C2
Old Brickfield Road	C1
Ordnance Road	C4
Perowne Street	B3
Pickford Street	B4-C4-C3
Queens Road	A2-A3-B3
Redan Hill	C3-C4
Rock Gardens	A2
Rowhill Avenue	A2-A1-B1
St Georges Road	C2-C3
St Josephs Road	B2-C2-C3
St Michaels Road	C2-C3
Salerno Crescent	B4
Sandford Road	A2
Southmead Road	C2
Station Road	B4-B3-C3
Stovolds Way	A1
The Grove	B3
Upper Elms Road	B3
Victoria Road	B3-C3-C4
Wellington Avenue	A3-A4-B4
Wellington Street	B3-B4
Weybourne Road	B1
Willems Avenue	A4
Windsor Way	C3
Winton Road	B2
York Crescent	A2
York Road	A2-A3

FARNHAM
Attractive shops and houses line the broad thoroughfare of Castle Street, which is overlooked by the castle itself. Founded in the 12th century, this was once the seat of the bishops of Winchester and of Guildford.

Guildford

Guildford's impressive modern redbrick Anglican cathedral, consecrated in 1961, looks down on the county town of Surrey from its hill-top setting on the outskirts. Nearby are the differently-styled modern buildings of the University of Surrey. Another example of modern architecture is the Yvonne Arnaud Theatre, which opened in 1958 on the banks of the River Wey. Despite being a busy

modern shopping centre the town retains many old buildings and its steep, partly-cobbled High Street has an unchanging Georgian character. Most prominent is the Guildhall with its hexagonal bell-turret and gilded clock overhanging the pavement. All that remains of the city's castle, just off the High Street, is the 12th-century keep built by Henry II, but close by the Castle Museum has a comprehensive range of local antiquities.

Godalming An important staging post on the

London to Portsmouth road in stagecoach days, this attractive North Downs town still has several old coaching inns as well as a number of other 16th-century buildings. Local artefacts can be found in the Borough Museum.

Woking A residential and commuter town on the disused Basingtoke Canal, Woking developed as a direct result of the arrival of the railway in the 1830s. Its most distinctive feature is its large Mosque, built in 1889.

Central Godalming

Guildford Area

SCALE

mls

LEGEND

Town Plan
AA recommended route
Restricted roads
Other roads
Buildings of interest   Station ▣
Car parks   ℗
Parks and open spaces
One way streets

Area Plan
A roads
B roads
Locations   Fairlands ○
Urban area

Street Index with Grid Reference

Guildford

Abbot Road	C1
Addison Road	E2-F2-F1
Albury Road	F2-F3
Aldersey Road	F2-F3
Alexandra Terrace	D3
Artillery Road	B4-C4
Artillery Terrace	C4
Austen Road	E3-F3-F2
Baillie Road	E2-E3
Bedford Road	B2
Bridge Street	B2-B3
Bright Hill	D2
Brodie Road	D2
Buryfields	B1
Bury Street	B1-B2
Castle Hill	C1
Castle Street	C2
Chapel Street	C2
Chertsey Street	C3
Cheselden Road	D2-D3
Chesham Road	E2-E3
Church Road	B3-B4-C4
Clandon Road	D4-E4
Cline Road	E2-F2
College Road	B3-C3
Copper Road	E2
Cranley Road	E4-F4
Cross Lanes	E4-F4-F3-F2
Dapdune Road	B4-C4
Dene Road	D3
Denzil Road	A2-A3

Drummond Road	B4-C4
Eagle Road	C4
Eastgate Gardens	D3
Epsom Road	D3-E3-F3
Falcon Road	C4
Farnham Road	A2-B2
Flower Walk	B1
Foxenden Road	D4
Friary Bridge	A2-B2
Friary Street	B2
George Road	B4-C4
Guildford Park Avenue	A3
Guildford Park Road	A3
Harvey Road	D2-E2-E3
Haydon Place	C3
High Street	B2-C2-D2-D3
Hillier Road	F4
Jenner Road	D2-D3
Laundry Road	B3
Lawn Road	B1
Leapale Lane	C3
Leapale Road	C3
Leas Road	B2
London Road	D3-D4-E4
Lower Edgeborough Road	
	E4-E3-F3
Ludlow Road	A2
Maori Road	F4-F3
Mareschel Road	A1-A2
Margaret Road	B3-B4
Markenfield Road	B4-C4
Market Street	C2
Martyr Road	C3
Mary Road	B3-B4
Millbrook	B2-C2-C1
Millmead	B1-B2
Millmead Terrace	B1
Mount Pleasant	B1-B2
Mountside	A1
Nightingale Road	D4
North Street	C2-C3
Onslow Road	C4-D4
Onslow Street	B3
Park Road	C4
Park Street	B2
Pewley Bank	D2-E2-E1
Pewley Hill	C2-D2-D1-E1
Pewley Way	D2-E2-E1-F1
Portsmouth Road	B1-B2
Poyle Road	D1
Quarry Street	C2-B3-C3
Queens Road	C4-D4
Rupert Road	A3
Sandfield Terrace	C3
Semaphore Road	D1-D2
South Hill	C2-C1-D1
Springfield Road	D4
Stoke Fields	C4
Stoke Road	C4
Sydenham Road	C2-D2-D3
Sydney Road	E3-F3-E2
Testard Road	A2
The Bars	C3
The Mount	A1-B1-B2
Tunsgate	C2
Upper Edgeborough Road	F2-F3
Upperton Road	A2
Walnut Treet Close	B2-B3-A3-A4
Ward Street	C3
Warren Road	E3-E2-F2
Waterden Road	D3-E3

Watford Close	F4
Wherwell Road	B4
Woodbridge Road	B4-B3-C3-C2
Wodeland Avenue	A1-A2-B2
York Road	B3-C3-C4-D3-D4

Woking

Abbey Road	A3
Arthurs Bridge Road	A3-B4
Ashwood Road	D2-E2
Beaufort Road	F4
Beta Road	F4
Birch Hill	A1
Boundary Road	B4
Bracken Close	D2
Brewery Road	B3-C3-C4
Brooklyn	B1-C1
Broomhill Lane	C4
Broomhill Road	C4
Bulbeggars Lane	A3
Bury Lane	A3-A4
Bylands	D1
Cavendish Road	A1-B1
Cawsey Way	C3
Cherry Street	B2
Chertsey Road	C3-D3-D4
Chobham Road	C4
Church Close	B4
Church Hill	B3-B4
Church Street	C2-C3
Church Street East	C3-D3
Cleardown	E1-E2
Coley Avenue	D2-D3
College Lane	A1
College Road	F4
Commercial Way	C3
Constitution Hill	C1
Courteney Road	D4-E4
Elm Road	A2-A1
East Hill	F3-F4
Fairview Avenue	C1-C2
Ferndale Road	C4
Frailey Hill	B1
Goldsworth Road	A1-A2-B2-C2
Guildford Road	B1-C1-C2
Heathfield Road	E2
Heathside Crescent	C2-D2-D3
Heathside Gardens	D2
Heathside Park Road	C2-D2-E2
Heathside Road	C1-D1-E1
Heathside Road	E2
High Street	A3-B4
High Street	C3
Hill Close	A4
Hill View Road	C2-D2
Hockering Gardens	E2
Hockering Road	E2-F2
Hopfields	B2
Horsell Moor	A3-B3-C3
Horsell Park	B3-B4-C4
Horsell Park Close	B3-B4
Horsell Vale	B4-C4
Ivy Lane	E2-F2
Kent Road	F4
Kings Road	E4
Kings Way	A1-A2-B2
Kirby Road	A3
Knowl Hill	F1-F2

Lavender Road	F3
Lych Way	B4
Lytton Road	E3-F3
Mabel Street	A2-B2
Manor Road	A4
Maybury Hill	E4-F4-F3-F2
Maybury Road	D3-D4-E4
Mayhurst Avenue	F4
Meadway Drive	A4
Midhope Road	B1
Mount Hermon Road	B1-C1
North Road	D4-E4
Oaks Road	B2-B3
Ockenden Road	D1-D2
Old Malt Way	B3
Old Woking road	F1-F2-F3
Omega Road	A4
Onslow Crescent	D3-E3
Oriental Road	C2-C3-D2-D3-E3-E4
Ormonde Road	A3-A4
Pares Close	A4-B4
Park Drive	C1-C2
Park Road	D3-E3-E2-F2
Parley Drive	A1-A2
Pembroke Road	E2-E3-E4
Pollard Road	F4
Poole Road	B2-C2
Poplar Grove	C1
Port Road	D3-D4
Princes Road	A4
Rosehill Avenue	A4
Royal Oak Road	A1
St Johns Road	A1
St Marys Road	A3
St Pauls Road	E3
Sandy Lane	F2-F3-F4
Sandy Way	F3
School Road	D4
Shaftesbury Road	E3-F3
Silversmiths Way	A2
South Close	A4
Stanley Road	D3
Station Approach	C2-C3-D3
Station Road	C2
The Broadway	D3
The Grove	C4-D4
The Ridge	E3-F3
Trigg's Close	A1
Trigg's Lane	A1
Vale Farm Road	B2-B3-C3
Victoria Way	C2-C3-C4-D4
Waldens Park Road	A3
Waldens Road	A3
Walton Road	D3-D4-E4
Well Lane	A3
Wendella Close	D1
West Hill Road	B1
White Rose Lane	D2-D1-E1-F1
Winnington Way	A1-A2
Wilson Way	B4
Wolsey Way	C3
York Road	B1-B2-C2

Godalming

Borough Road	B3-B4
Braemar Close	A1-A2
Bridge Road	B3-C3-C4
Bridge Street	B3

Brighton Road	B3-B2-C2-C1
Busbridge Lane	A2-B2-B1
Carlos Street	B2
Catteshal Lane	B3-C3-C2-C3
Chalk Road	B4-C4
Charterhouse Road	B4
Church Street	B3
Croft Road	B2
Crownpits Lane	B1-C1
Dean Road	A4
Deanery Road	B4
Duncombe Road	B1
Filmer Grove	B4
Frith Hill Road	B4
Great George Street	B3
Grosvenor Road	B1-C1
Grove Road	A2
Hallam Road	C4
Hare Lane	B3
High Street	B3
Holloway Hill	A2
Latimer Road	B2
Llanaway Road	C4
Marshall Road	C4
Meadrow	C4
Mill Lane	A3
Mint Street	A3-B3
Moss Lane	B3
Nightingale Road	B4-C4
Oakdene Road	B1
Ockford Road	A2-A3-B2-B3
Park Road	B1
Peperharow Road	A4-B4
Pullman Lane	A1
Queen Street	B3-B2
Ramsden Road	A1-B1-B2
Shackstead Lane	A2-A1-B1
South Hill	C2-C3
South Street	B2-B3
Station Approach	A3
Summerhouse Road	A2-B2
The Avenue	C1
The Burys	B3
The Close	C1
The Drive	C1
The Fairway	C1
Town End Street	B2-C2
Tuesley Lane	A2-A1-B1
Valley View	A2
Westbrook Road	A3
Wharf Street	B3-C3
Wolseley Road	C4

Central Hastings

Hastings Area

mls 0   SCALE   4

Hastings

Overlooking the beach of this popular resort are the remains of a castle established by William the Conqueror; Battle Abbey, the actual site of the great conflict of 1066, lies to the north of the town on the A2100. The Hastings Embroidery, which was commissioned in 1966 to commemorate the battle's 900th anniversary and depicts 81 memorable events in British history, can be seen at the Town Hall.

Rich in historical associations, Hastings also has a historic Old Town — a pleasant jumble of ancient buildings and narrow streets, and site of the local fish market and Fisherman's Museum. Theatres, pubs and amusement areas fill the main resort, which has all the amenities expected of a major holiday centre.

Bexhill offers the entertainment facilities of the De La Warr Pavilion, which overlooks the sands, and a good range of outdoor activities can be enjoyed in nearby Egerton Park. Manor Gardens, in the older part of the town, contains the Manor Costume Museum and the ruins of the manor house.

Rye is an atmospheric town of cobbled streets and half-timbered houses. A gang of smugglers had its headquarters at the 15th-century Mermaid Inn, and other places of interest include the Baddings Tower Museum, the Rye Town Model and the old harbour, which is now a nature reserve.

Central Bexhill

Central Rye

Key to Town Plan and Area Plan

Town Plan
AA Recommended roads
Restricted roads
Other roads
Buildings of interest — Castle
Car Parks — P
Churches — +
Parks and open spaces
One Way Streets

Area Plan
A roads
B roads
Locations — Kingston O
Urban area

Street Index with Grid Reference

Hastings

Amherst Road	B4
All Saints Street	F2-F3
Bembrook Road	F4
Bethune Way	D4
Bohemia Road	A3-A2-B2
Braybrooke Road	B3-C3-C4-D4
Brook Street	C3-D3
Cambridge Road	B2-C2
Carlisle Parade	C2
Castlehill Road	D2-E2-E3
Castle Street	D2
Collier Road	E3-E4-F4
Cornwallis Gardens	B3-B2
Cornwallis Street	C3-D3
Cornwallis Terrace	B3-C3
Courthouse Street	E2
Croft Road	E4-F4-F3-E3
Crown Lane	F2
Denmark Place	C2-D2
Devonshire Road	C3
Dorset Place	B2
Earl Street	C3

East Parade	E2
East Street	E2
Emmanuel Road	E4
Eversfield Place	A1
Falaise Road	A2
George Street	D2-E2
Harold Place	C2
Havelock Road	C2
High Street	E2-F2-F3
Hill Street	E2
Hillyglen Close	B3
Hopsgarden Close	B3-B4
Linton Road	B4-B3
Lower Park Road	C4-D4
Mann Street	C3-D3
Marine Parade	D2-E2
Middle Street	C2
Milward Crescent	D3
Milward Road	D3-D4-E4
Nelson Road	D4
Pelham Arcade	D2
Pelham Place	D2
Plynlimmon Road	E3-E4
Priory Avenue	B4-C4-C3
Priory Close	C4
Priory Road	E3-E4-F4
Priory Street	C2
Prospect Place	B2
Queens Road	C2-D2-D3-D4
Robertson Street	B2-C2
Rock-a-Nore Road	F2
St Helens Road	D4
St Margaret's Road	A2
St Mary's Terrace	E3-E4
South Terrace	C3-D3
Stanley Road	B3-C3-C4
Station Road	C2-C3
Stonefield Road	D3-D4
Tackleway	F2-F3
The Coppice	B4-C4
The Bourne	E2-F2
Vicarage Road	E4
Waterworks Road	D4
Wellington Place	C2-D2
Wellington Road	D3-D2-E2
Wellington Square	D2
White Rock	B1-B2
White Rock Road	A2-B2
Whitefriars Road	E4
Winterbourne Close	A3-A4
Wykeham Road	B4-B3-C3

Bexhill

Albany Road	A1
Albert Road	A1
Amherst Road	A2-A3
Ashdown Road	C2
Bancroft Road	A4
Barrack Road	A3-B4
Beaconsfield Road	B4
Bedford Avenue	C2-C1
Beeching Road	A3
Belle Hill	B3
Bolebrook Road	C2-C1
Brassey Road	B1
Buckhurst Road	A2-B2
Cantelupe Road	B1-C1-C2
Channel View	B1
Chantry Avenue	B4-C4
Chantry Lane	B4-B3
Chelsea Close	C2
Chepbourne Road	A3
Church Street	B3
Churchvale Road	B4-C4
Clifford Road	B2
Cornwall Road	A2-A1
Cranfield Road	B2
Crowmere Avenue	B4
De la Warr Parade	B1-C1
De la Warr Road	C3
Devonshire Road	A1-B1
Dorset Road	C2-C3
Dorset Road South	C2-C1
Eversley Road	B1
Fairmount Road	C3-C4
Hastings Road	C4-C3
High Street	B3
Hillside Road	A4
Inchgates Close	B4-C4
Jameson Road	B2-C2
King Offa Way	A3-B3-C3
Knole Road	B1-C1
Larkhill	A3-B3
Linden Road	A1
Links Drive	C2
Lionel Road	C1
London Road	A4-A3-A2
Magdalen Road	B2-C2
Manor Road	C2-C3
Marina	A1-B1
Middlesex Road	C1
Millfield Rise	A3-B3
New Park Avenue	A3-B3-B2
Old Manor Close	C2-C3
Park Road	A1-A2
Parkhurst Road	A1
Reginald Road	A2
Rotherfield Avenue	B2
St Andrew's Road	A4-B4

St Davids Avenue	A4-B4
St George's Road	A4-B4
St Leonard's Road	B2-B1
St Peters Crescent	B4-C4
Sackville Road	A2-A1
Salisbury Road	A3
Sea Road	B1-B2
Station Road	A2-B2
Terminus Road	A2
The Colonade	A1
Upper Sea Road	B2-B3
Victoria Road	A2
West Parade	A1
Western Road	A2
Wickham Avenue	A2
Wilton Road	B1
Windsor Road	A3-A2

Rye

Church Square	B2
Cinque Ports Street	A2-B2-B3
Conduit Road	B3-B2
Cyprus Place	A2
Deadmans Lane	B4
Eagle Road	B3
East Street	B2
Ferry Road	A2
Fishmarket Road	B2-B3
High Street	B2
Hillyfield	B4
Kings Avenue	C3-C4
Landgate	B3
Lion Street	B2
Love Lane	A4-B4
Market Road	B2
Mermaid Street	A2-B2
Military Road	B4-C4
New Road	B3-C3
North Salts	C4
Rope Walk	B3
Rye Harbour Road	B1-C1
Rye Hill	B4
South Undercliff	B1-B2
Strand	A2
The Grove	B4-B3
The Mint	A2-B2
The Quay	A2
Tillingham Avenue	A2-A3
Tower Street	B3
Watchbell Street	B2
West Street	B2
Winchelsea Road	A1-A2
Wish Street	A2

HASTINGS
Although the harbour of this one-time Cinque Port silted up centuries ago, fishing boats are still winched up on the shingle beach, and fishermen's net-drying huts at the foot of the cliff railway are a distinctive feature.

Isle of Wight

Most visitors to the island arrive at Ryde so its streets are always busy throughout the summer months. During the 19th century it was turned from a small village into a fashionable holiday resort which is as popular as ever today; sandy beaches, a pier with an electric railway, a boating lake and pleasant gardens are its main attractions.

Sandown lies at the centre of Sandown Bay on the south-east side of the island and as the largest resort, its holiday facilities are numerous. The Museum of Isle of Wight Geology houses, among other exhibits, over 5000 fossils from the island.

Shanklin Here attractions range from the excitement of the pier to the seclusion of Hope Beach. The old village has thatched cottages festooned with roses, and the natural gorge called Shanklin Chine has lovely gardens and a waterfall.

Newport, capital of the island, occupies a conveniently central position. Just south-west of the town is the 12th-century Carisbrooke Castle where Charles I was imprisoned for a year before his execution in London. Other places of interest include the Roman Villa in Cypress Road.

Cowes is the headquarters of the Royal Yacht Squadron and Cowes Week, held during the first week of August, is *the* fashionable event of the yachting calendar. The club house stands on the site of a castle built by Henry VIII.

Central Ryde

Central Sandown

LEGEND

Town Plan

AA recommended route	
Restricted roads	
Other roads	
Buildings of interest	Cinema
Car parks	P
Parks and open spaces	

Area Plan

A roads	
B roads	
Locations	Wootton ○
Urban area	
Hovercraft	(H)
Hydrofoil	(Hf)
Passenger Ferry	(P)
Vehicle Ferry	(V)

Street Index
Cowes

Adelaide Grove	A1-B1
Albany Road	C2
Albert Street	A4-B4
Alexandra Road	A4
Alfred Street	A1
Arctic Road	A2-A3-B3
Baring Road	C4
Beckford Road	B3
Belleview Road	A3-A4
Bridge Road	B2-B3
Cambridge Road	C1-C2
Castle Hill	C4
Castle Road	C4
Castle Street	B2-B1-B2-C2
Church Road	B4-C4
Clarence Road	A1-B1
Consort Road	B3
Coronation Road	A4
Cross Street	B3
Denmark Road	B3-B4-B3
Esplanade	C2
Fellows Road	A3
Ferry Road	B1-B2
Granville Road	B4
Gordon Road	B3
Hefford Road	C1
High Street	B3-C3-C4
Kings Road	A1-B1
Maresfield Road	C2
Market Hill	C3-C4
Medina Road	B2-B3
Mill Hill	B3
Mill Hill Road	A3-B3
Moorgreen Road	A4-B4
Newport Road	A2-A3-B3
Oaktree Way	B1
Old Road	C1-C2
Osborne Road	A1-B1
Parade	C4
Park Road	A4-B4
Pelham Road	A2-B2
Queens Road	C4
St Faiths Road	A2-A3
St Mary's Road	B3-B4
St Thomas' Road	C1
Seaview Road	A4
Stephenson Road	A3
Sun Hill	C3-C4
Sylvan Avenue	B1-C1
Tennyson Road	A2
Terminus Road	B4-C4-C3
The Grove	C4
Thetis Road	A2-B2
Upper Moorgreen Road	A2
Victoria Road	A3-B3-B4
Ward Avenue	B4
Well Road	B1-B2
Westhill Road	B3
Yarborough Road	A1
York Avenue	B1
York Street	B2-B3

Newport

Albert Street	B2
Ash Road	C2-C3
Avondale Road	B2-C2
Barton Road	C3
Blackhouse Lane	C4
Caesars Road	A3
Carisbrooke Road	A2-A3
Castle Hold	B3
Castle Road	A1-A2
Chapel Street	B2-B3
Church Litten	B2-B3
Clarence Road	B2-C2
Clifford Street	A3
College Road	C1
Crocker Street	B3
Cypress Road	B1-C1
Drill Hall Road	A3
East Street	C3
Elm Grove	A1-B1
Fairlee Road	C3-C4
Field Place	A2-A3
Furlongs	C2-C3
Hearn Street	A3-B3
Hillside	C4
High Street	B3-C3
Holyrood Street	B3-B4
Home Meade	C2
Hunny Hill	B4
Linden Road	B3
Lugley Street	B3
Medina Avenue	B2-C2-C1
Melbourne Street	A1-A2
Mill Street	A3-B3
Milne Way	B1
Mount Pleasant Road	B1-B2
Nelson Road	A1-A2
New Street	B2-B3
Portland Street	A2
Prospect Road	C2-C3
Pyle Street	B3-C3
Quay Street	B3-C3
Queens Road	B1
Riverway	B2
Robin Hood Street	B3-B4
St James Street	B3-B4
St Johns Road	B1-B2
Sea Street	B4-C4-C3
Seaclose Quay	C4

Shide Road	B1-C1
South Street	B3-C3
Staplers Road	C3-C4
Sylvan Drive	A4-B4
Terrace Road	B2
The Quay	C4
Trafalgar Road	A2-B2
Union Street	B2
Upper St James Street	B2-B3
Victoria Road	C4
Water Gate Road	B1
Westminster Lane	A3
West Street	B2-B3
Whitepit Lane	A1-B1
Wilver Road	A2-A3
Winston Road	A1
Worsley Road	A4-B4
York Road	B2

Ryde

Adelaide Place	A4
Albert Street	A3
Alexandra Road	A1
Alfred Road	A3
Appley Rise	B1-C1
Argyle Street	A4-B4
Arthur Street	A4
Augusta Road	B4-C4
Barfield	B3
Bellvue Road	B2-C2-C3
Belvedere Street	B3
Benett Street	A2-B2
Castle Street	C3
Church Avenue	C3-C4
Cross Street	B3
Daniel Street	A2-B2
Dover Street	B3-C3-C2
East Hill Road	A1-B1-C1
East Street	C2
Esplanade	C1-C2-C3
George Street	B3-C3
Green Street	A3-B3-B4
High Park Road	A1
High Street	A2
High Street	A3-B3-B4
John Street	B4
Lind Street	B4
Longmead Road	A3
Lower Highland Road	A1-A2
Melville Street	B2-B3
Monkton Street	A2-B2-C2
Nelson Place	C3
Nelson Street	B3-C3
North Walk	C1
Park Road	B1-B2-B3
Pell Lane	A4
Pellhurst Road	A4-B4
Player Street	A3-B3
Preston Place	A3-A4
Prince Street	A3
Quarry Road	A2-A3
Queen's Road	B4
Ratcliffe Avenue	A4
Reed Street	A2
Riboleau Street	A3-B3
Rink Road	B1-B2
St Johns Avenue	A1
St Johns Hill	A1-A2
St Johns Road	A2-A3
St Johns Wood Road	A2-A1-B1
St Thomas Street	B4-C4-C3

Sandcroft Avenue	A3
School Street	A2
Simeon Street	C1-C2
Spencer Road	B4-C4
Star Street	B3
Strand	B1-C1-C2
Surrey Street	A2
Swanmore Road	A3-A4
Trinity Street	B2-C2
Union Road	B3-C3
Union Street	B3-C3
Victoria Street	B4
Victoria Road	A3-B3
Warwick Street	B3
Weeks Road	A3
Well Street	B4-C4
Westfield Park	B4-C4
West Hill Road	A1-B1
West Street	A4-B4
Westwood Road	B4
Winton Street	B2
Wood Street	B2-B3

Sandown

Albert Road	B3
Avenue Road	A4-B4-C4-C3
Beachfield Road	B1-B2
Broadway	A4-B4-B3-B2-B1
Brownlow Road	A4
Carter Street	B3-B4
Central Way	A3
Cox's Green	A3
Crescent Road	C4
Cross Street	B4
Culver Road	C3-C4
Downsview Chalets	A3-A4
Esplanade	B2-B3-C3
Fairmead	A1
Fairview Crescent	A1
Fitzroy Street	B2-B3
Fort Mews	B4
Fort Street	B4-C4
Foxes Close	A4
Gordon Close	A3
Grafton Street	B2B-B3
Grove Road	A3-B3
High Street	B2-B3-C3
Hill Street	A2-B2
Jeals Lane	A3-A4
Lake Green Road	A4
Lake Hill	B1
Leed Street	A2-B2-B3
Medeway	A1
Melville Street	B2
New Street	B2
Nunnwell Street	A2-B2
Parsonage Road	A4
Perowne Way	A2-A3-A4
Pier Street	B2
Queens Road	B4
Ranelagh Road	B1
Roseway	A1
Royal Crescent	B2
St Johns Crescent	B4
St Johns Road	B2
Station Avenue	A2-A3-B3
Station Approach	A2
Station Lane	A2-A3-B3
Talbot Road	B1
The Fairway	A3-A2-A1-B1
The Mall	B1
Victoria Road	B3-C3

Vinings Road	B4
Winchester Park Road	A3-B3
York Road	B3

Shanklin

Albert Road	B2
Alexandra Road	B2-C2
Arthurs Hill	B3-B4
Atherley Road	B3
Avenue Road	B3
Beatrice Avenue	B3-C3
Brook Road	B2
Carter Avenue	A2-B2-B3
Chatsworth Avenue	A1
Chine Avenue	B1-C1-C2
Church Road	B1-C1-B1
Clarence Gardens	B4-C4
Clarence Road	B3-B4
Clarendon Road	B3-C3
Collingwood Road	A2-B2
Crescent Road	B3-C3
Culver Road	B4-C4
Donnington Drive	A3-A4
Duncroft Gardens	A3-B3
Esplanade	C2-C3-C4
Everton Road	C2
Florence Road	B1
Furzehill Road	B1-B2
Garfield Road	A2-B2
Grange Road	B2
Green Lane	A3-A4-B4
Hatherton Road	B2
High Street	B1-B2
Highfield Road	B1
Hope Road	B3-C3
Howard Road	B4-C4
Hyde Lane	A2-A3
Hyde Road	A3-B3
Landguard Road	B2-B3
Landguard Manor Road	A4-A3-B3
Luccombe Road	C1
Northcliffe Gardens	C4
North Road	B2-B3
Oaklyn Gardens	B4
Orchard Road	A1-A2
Osborne Road	C2
Palmerston Road	B2-C2
Park Road	C2-C3
Pomona Road	B1
Popham Road	C1
Priory Road	C1
Prospect Road	B2
Queens Road	B3-B2-C2
Regent Street	B2-B3
St Boniface Cliffe Road	B4-C4
St Georges Road	B2-B3
St Johns Road	B3
St Martins Avenue	B4-C4
St Pauls Avenue	B3
St Pauls Crescent	B3
Sandown Road	B4
Sibden Road	A1-A2-B2
Spring Gardens	B3
Victoria Avenue	A1-B1-B2
Western Road	B2
Westhill Drive	A1
Westhill Road	A1, B1
Wilton Road	B2
Wilton Park Road	B3-B4
Witbank Gardens	A4-B4

41

Maidstone

County town of Kent, Maidstone has long been a place of importance. The ruins of the 14th-century Archbishop's Palace overlook the River Medway, and Allington Castle dates from the 13th century. Maidstone Museum and Art Gallery explores the town's extensive history; also of interest is the Tyrwhitt-Drake Museum of Carriages, housed in the Palace stables.

Rochester Medieval walls enclose the Norman castle and cathedral of this attractive and historic town, but its quaint old shops, inns and tea shops give it a distinctly Victorian flavour. Charles Dickens spent much of his life in the area and featured Rochester in his novels: justly proud of its associations with the great man, the town boasts an award-winning Charles Dickens Centre.

Gillingham has been associated with the nearby Royal Naval Dockyard since Tudor times and it

continues the tradition with the Royal Naval Barracks and the Royal School of Military Engineering, both situated in the Brompton area.

Chatham Home of the Royal Naval Dockyard since the 16th century, Chatham today is dominated by the office tower block which crowns the Pentagon Centre, a shopping and entertainments complex. Pleasant riverside gardens have been laid out on the site of the old Gun Wharf, and the Medway Heritage Centre is in Dock Road.

Central Chatham · *Central Gillingham*

LEGEND

Town Plan

AA Recommended roads	
Restricted roads	
Other roads	
Buildings of interest	Station ■
Churches	†
Parks and open spaces	
Car Parks	P
One Way Streets	↳

Area Plan

A roads	
B roads	
Locations	Muckingford ○
Urban area	

Street Index with Grid Reference

Maidstone

Allen Street	C4
Bank Street	B2
Barker Road	A1-B1
Bishops Way	B1-B2
Boxley Road	B4-C4
Brewer Street	B3-C3
Broadway	A1-B1-B2
Brunswick Street	C1
Buckland Hill	A3
Buckland Road	A2-A3
Charles Street	A1
Church Street	C2-C3
College Avenue	B1
College Road	B1
County Road	B4-B3-C3-C4
Earl Street	B2-B3
Fairmeadow	B2-B3
Foley Street	C4
Foster Street	B1-C1
Gabriel's Hill	B2-C2
Hart Street	A1
Hastings Road	C1
Hedley Street	C3-C4
High Street	B2
Holland Road	C3-C4
James Street	C4
Kingsley Road	C1
King Street	B2-C2
Knightrider Street	B1-C1
Lower Stone Street	C1-C2
Market Buildings	B2
Market Street	B2-B3
Marsham Street	C2
Medway Street	B2
Melville Road	C1
Mill Street	B1-B2
Mote Road	C1
Museum Street	B2-B3
Padsole Lane	C1
Palace Avenue	B1-B2-C2
Priory Road	B1
Pudding Lane	B2
Queen Anne Road	C2
Reginald Road	A1
Rocky Hill	A1-A2
Romney Place	C1
St Faith's Street	B3
St Peter's Street	A2-A3
Sandling Road	B4
Station Road	B3
Terrace Road	A1-A2
Tufton Street	C3
Union Street	B3-C3
Upper Stone Street	C1
Waterlow Road	C4
Week Street	B2-B3
Well Road	B4-C4
Wheeler Street	C3-C4
Wyatt Street	C2-C3

Rochester

Bardell Terrace	B2-C2
Blue Boar Lane	B3
Boley Hill	A3
Castle Hill	A3-A4
Cazeneuve Street	B2
City Way	B2-B1-C1
Corporation Street	A4-B4-B3-B2
Crow Lane	B2-B3
Delce Road	B1-B2
Dunnings Lane	A2-B2
East Row	B2
Esplanade	A2-A3-A4
Ethelbert Avenue	A1
Foord Street	B1
Furrells Road	B2-C2
Gashouse Road	B4
Gordon Terrace	A1-A2
High Street	A4-A3-B3-B2-C2
Hoopers Road	A1-B1
James Street	B1
John Street	B2-B1-A1-B1
King Edward Road	A2
King Street	B2
Lockington Grove	A2-B2
Longley Road	A1-B1
Love Lane	A2-A3
Maidstone Road	A1-A2-B2
New Road	B1-C1
Rochester Avenue	A1-B1
Rochester Bridge	A4
Roebuck Road	A1-A2
St Margaret's Street	A1-A2-A3
South Avenue	A1
The Terrace	B2
Victoria Street	B2
Vines Lane	A3-A2-B2
Watts Avenue	A1-A2

Gillingham

Adelaide Road	B1-B2
Albany Road	C1-C2
Arden Street	A4
Balmoral Road	B2-B3-C3
Barnsole Road	C1-C2-C3
Belmont Road	A2
Beresford Road	C2-B2-C2
Borough Road	B1-C1
Brasenose Avenue	C2
Britton Farm Street	A3-A4
Brompton Road	A4
Burnt Oak Terrace	B4
Byron Road	A1-B1
Canterbury Street	A3-A2-B2-B1
Carlton Avenue	C2
College Avenue	A2
Copenhagen Road	A2-B2
Coulman Street	C2
Cross Street	A4-B4
Duncan Road	B2-B3
Ferndale Road	C3
Franklin Road	B3-C3
Frederick Road	A1-A2
Gardiner Street	B3-B4
Gillingham Road	B2-B3-C3
Gordon Road	C3
Gorst Street	B2-B3
Granville Road	A3-B3
Green Street	A3-B3
High Street	A3-B3
Ingram Road	C3-C4
James Street	A3-B3-B4
Jeffrey Street	A3-B3
Junction Road	C1
Kingswood Road	B3-B4
Khyber Road	A4
Livingstone Road	C2-C3
Lock Street	A3
Marlborough Road	A2-A3-A4
May Road	A2
Mill Street	A1-B1
Montgomery Road	B1-C1-C2-C3
Napier Road	B2-B1-C1
Nelson Road	C1
Oxford Road	C1
Paget Street	A3
Park Avenue	C1
Parr Avenue	B4-C4
Railway Street	B3-C3
Randolph Road	B3
Richmond Street	B4
Rock Avenue	B1-B2
St George's Road	A4-B4
Saunders Street	A4-B4
Saxton Street	A2-A3
Seaview Road	B1-B2
Skinner Street	A3-A4
Stafford Street	A2
Stopford Road	B1
Sturdee Avenue	C2
Trafalgar Street	A2-B2
Vicarage Road	A2
Victoria Street	B3-B4
Windmill Road	A1-B1-B2
Windsor Road	B3-C3
York Avenue	A1-A2

Chatham

Albany Terrace	A3
Albert Street	B1-C1
Best Street	B3
Boundary Road	A2-A3
Brisbane Road	C1-C2
Bryant Street	B2
Buller Road	B1
Castle Road	C1
Chalk Pit Hill	B1-B2
Charter Street	B1
Chatham Hill	C2
Clover Street	B3
Corkwell Street	A1
Cross Street	B3-C3
Dale Street	A1-A2
Dock Road	B4
Eldon Street	C3
Fort Pitt Hill	A3
Fort Pitt Street	A2-A3
Gladstone Road	A1
Glencoe Road	B1-C1
Grosvenor Avenue	A1
Hartington Street	B2-C2
Herbert Street	B2-C2
High Street	A3-B3-C3
Hills Terrace	A2
Holcombe Road	B1-B2
Ingle Road	B1
Jenkins Dale	B2
Lester Road	C2
Luton Road	C2
Magpie Hall Road	C1-C2
Maidstone Road	A3-A2-B2-B1-A1
Manor Road	A3
Medway Street	A3-A4-B4
Military Road	B3-B4
Mills Terrace	C2
Mount Road	B1-B2
Neville Road	A1
New Road	B3-B2-C2
New Road Avenue	A3-B3
New Street	C1
Old Road	A3-B3-B2
Ordnance Street	A1-A2-A3
Ordnance Terrace	A3
Otway Street	C1-C2
Otway Terrace	C2
Pagitt Street	A1
Palmerston Road	B1
Perry Street	A1-A2
Purbeck Road	A1
Railway Street	A3-B3
Redvers Road	B1
Rochester Street	A1-A2
Salisbury Road	C2
Singapore Drive	C4
Skinner Street	B2
Southill Road	B1
Sturla Road	C1-C2
Sydney Street	B2-C2-C1
Symons Avenue	B1-C1
The Brook	B4-B3-C3
The Paddock	B3
Upbury Way	C2-C3
White Road	B1

Newbury

Racegoers flock to Newbury's racecourse all the year round, but in the 15th century this principal town of West Berkshire was better known for broadcloth than for betting. The cloth manufacturing era is recalled in the Newbury District Museum, which is appropriately housed in the former Cloth Hall and lies near to the area known as the Wharf. A number of well preserved 17th- and 18th-century buildings can be seen here, including the 18th-century Granary.

Other places of interest include St. Nicholas' Church, built in the 16th century in the Perpendicular style.

Hungerford still retains a flavour of its years as a staging point on the Bath Road, notably in the Bear Inn and in the 17th- and 18th-century shops and houses of the High Street.

Two miles to the north west lies Littlecote House, a charming Tudor manor which features 'Frontier City' (an authentic Wild West town), and excavations of a Roman villa in its grounds.

Thatcham has also kept several buildings from the 17th and 18th centuries in the midst of its industrial and residential expansion. Notable are two interesting old coaching inns, the King's Head and the White Hart. An early 14th-century chapel at the eastern end of town has been converted into an antiques shop.

Newbury Area

SCALE
0 — 4
mls

Box denotes area covered by central plan

Box denotes area covered by central plan

Key to Town Plan and Area Plan

Town Plan

AA Recommended roads	
Restricted roads	
Other roads	
Buildings of interest	Station
Car Parks	P
Parks and open spaces	
One Way Street	→

Area Plan

A roads	
B roads	
Locations	Bradfield ○
Urban area	

Street Index with Grid Reference

Newbury

Amberley Close	B4
Andover Road	B1-C1
Argyle Road	B1-C1
Arnhem Road	E2
Avon Way	F4
Bartholomew Street	C1-C2
Bath Road	A4-B4-B3-C3
Bear Lane	C2
Berkeley Road	B2
Blenheim Road	B2
Bone Lane	D2-E2
Boundary Road	D1-D2
Bridge Street	C2
Brummell Road	A4
Catherine Road	C1
Chalford Road	A2
Cheap Street	C2
Cherry Close	C4
Chestnut Crescent	C4-D4
Cleveland Grove	B3
Clifton Road	A2
Craven Road	A2-B2-C2
Cresswell Road	F4
Croft Lane	B3-B4
Curling Way	E4-F4
Digby Road	A4
Enborne Grove	A1-B1
Enborne Place	A1
Enborne Road	A1-B1
Faraday Road	D3-D4

Gaywood Drive	F4
Gloucester Road	A2-B2
Gordon Road	D2
Green Lane	A1-A2
Greenham Road	C2-C1-D1
Hambridge Road	D2-E2-F2
Hawthorn Road	C4-D4
Hedgeway	E4-F4
Highfield Avenue	C2
Hill Road	A3-A4
Howard Road	C1-D1
Hutton Close	D4
Jubilee Road	D1
Kennet Road	B2
Kersey Crescent	A4
Kings Road	D2
Link Road	C1
London Road	C3-C4-D4-D3-E3-F3
Maple Crescent	C4
Market Place	C2
Market Street	C2
Mill Lane	D2
Moor Lane	C2
Newport Road	D3-D4-E4
Northbrook Street	C2-C3
Northcroft Lane	B3-C3-C2
Oakley Road	F4
Oxford Road	B4-C4
Oxford Street	C3-C4
Park Street	C3
Park Way	C3
Pelican Lane	C4
Pembroke Road	C3
Pound Street	B1-C1
Queen's Road	D1
Racecourse Road	D1
Railway Road	D1-D2
Rectory Close	B1
Redfield Court	F3-F4
Remembrance Road	A1
Rockingham Road	B1-B2
Russell Road	A2-B2
St George's Avenue	A1-B1
St John's Road	C1
St Mary's Road	D3-D4
St Michael's Road	B1-C1
Sandleford Link	C1-D1
Shaw Road	D4
Skyllings	E3-E4
Speen Lane	A4-B4
Stanley Road	D1
Station Road	C1
Strawberry Hill	B3-C3
The Wharf	C2
Tudor Road	C1
Turnpike Road	E4-F4
Walton Way	E4

Western Avenue	B4-C4-D4
Westgate Road	A1
West Mills	B2-C2
West Street	C3
Wharf Road	C2
Winchcombe Road	C2
York Road	D1

Hungerford

Atherton Crescent	B1-B2
Atherton Road	B2
Bath Road	C4
Bourne Vale	A1-A2
Bridge Street	B4
Bulpit Lane	B1-C1
Canal Walk	B4
Charnham Street	A4-B4-C4
Chilton Way	A2
Church Street	A3-B3
Church Way	A3-A2-B2-B1
Clark Gardens	B1-C1
Everland Road	B3-C3
Fairview Road	B1-B2-B3
Faulknor Square	B4-C4
High Street	B1-B2-B3-B4
Hillside Road	B1
Homefield Way	A1-A2
Honeyfields	A2-B2
Lancaster Way	B1
Macklin Close	B2-C2
Moores Place	A2
Morley Close	B1-B2
North View Heights	B3-C3-C2
Park Street	B3-C3
Parsonage Lane	A3
Priory Avenue	B1-C1
Priory Close	B1
Priory Road	B1
Prospect Road	B2-B3
Salisbury Road	A1-B1
Sanden Close	A1
Sarum Way	B1
Smitham Bridge Road	A2-A3
South View	B2-C2
Station Road	C3
Tarrant's Hill	B1
The Croft	A3-B3
The Forge	B4-C4
Uplands	A2

Thatcham

Alexander Road	C1
Bath Road	A3-A2-B2
Beechwalk	C1
Beverley Close	A2-A3

Bluecoats	B2
Blyth Avenue	C1
Bowling Green Road	A4
Brown Close	A3-B3
Chapel Street	B2-C2
Chesterton Road	B4
Church Gate	B2
Coombe Court	C2
Coopers Crescent	A3
Crowfield Drive	A2
Dunstan Road	C3
Eliot Close	B4
Elms Avenue	C2
Exmoor Road	A1-B1-B2
Fyling Dales	A1
Goldsmith Close	B4
Green Lane	B2
Hartmead Road	C2
Hartshill Road	C2-C3
Heath Lane	A4-B4
High Street	B2
Ilkley Way	A1
Lamb Close	A4
Lancaster Close	A3-A4
Lower Way	A2-B2
Masefield Road	B3-B4
Marsh Road	C3
Mount Road	C3
Northfield Road	A3-A4
North Way	A4
Oaktree Road	C1
Park Avenue	B3-C3-C2
Park Lane	B2-B3-B4
Parkside Road	B4
Rosedale Gardens	A1
St Johns Road	A2
St Marks Close	A2
Sagecroft Road	A4-B4-B3
Shakespeare Road	A3-A4
Spurcroft Road	B1-C1
Station Road	B2-C2-C1
Stoney Lane	C1-C2
The Broadway	B2
The Frances	B2-B3
The Grove	B3
The Haywards	B3-C3-C2
The Henrys	B3-B2-C2
The Moors	A2-A1-B1
The Waverleys	B3
Victor Road	C1-C2
Vincent Road	C3
Westfield Road	A4

45

Plymouth

Ships, sailors and the sea permeate every aspect of Plymouth's life and history. Its superb natural harbour – Plymouth Sound – has ensured its importance as a port, yachting centre and naval base (latterly at Devonport) over many centuries. Sir Francis Drake is undoubtedly the city's most famous sailor. His statue stands on the Hoe – where he really did play bowls before tackling the

Spanish Armada. Also on the Hoe are Smeaton's Tower, which once formed the upper part of the third Eddystone Lighthouse, and the impressive Royal Naval War Memorial. Just east of the Hoe is the Royal Citadel, an imposing fortress built in 1666 by order of Charles II. North is Sutton Harbour, perhaps the most atmospheric part of Plymouth. Here fishing boats bob up and down in a harbour whose quays are lined with attractive old houses, inns and warehouses. One of the memorials on

Mayflower Quay just outside the harbour commemorates the sailing of the *Mayflower* from here in 1620. Plymouth's shopping centre is one of the finest of its kind, and was built after the old centre was badly damaged in World War II. Nearby is the 200ft-high tower of the impressive modern Civic Centre. Some buildings escaped destruction, including the Elizabethan House and the 500-year-old Prysten House. Next door is St Andrew's Church, with stained glass by John Piper.

SCALE
0 mls 2

N

Key to Town Plan and Area Plan

Town Plan

AA Recommended roads
Other roads
Restricted roads
Buildings of interest
Car Parks   P
Parks and open spaces
One way streets

Area Plan

A roads
B roads
Locations   Sandplace O
Urban area

Street Index with Grid Reference

Plymouth

47

Central Portsmouth

Portsmouth

Richard the Lionheart first recognised the strategic importance of Portsea Island and subsequently ordered the first docks, and later the town of Portsmouth, to be built. Over the centuries, succeeding monarchs improved the defences and extended the docks which now cover some 300 acres – as befits Britain's premier naval base. Of the defensive fortifications, Fort Widley and the Round Tower are the best preserved remains. Two famous ships rest in Portsmouth; *HMS Victory* and the *Mary Rose.* The former, Lord Nelson's flagship, has been fully restored and the adjacent Royal Naval museum houses numerous relics of Trafalgar. The *Mary Rose,* built by Henry VIII, lay on the sea bed off Southsea until she was spectacularly raised in 1982. She has now been put on display and there is an exhibition in Southsea Castle of artefacts that have been recovered from her. Portsmouth suffered greatly from bombing in World War II and the centre has been almost completely rebuilt. However, the old town, clustered around the harbour mouth, escaped severe damage and, now restored, forms an attractive and fashionable area of the city.

Southsea, Portsmouth's near neighbour, developed in the 19th century as an elegant seaside resort with fine houses and terraces, an esplanade and an extensive seafront common.

Central Havant (map)

Portsmouth Area (map)

LEGEND

Town Plan
- AA recommended route
- Restricted roads
- Other roads
- Buildings of interest — Station
- Car parks — P
- Parks and open spaces
- One way streets

Area Plan
- A roads
- B roads
- Locations — O Lovedean
- Urban area

Street Index with grid reference

Portsmouth

Admiralty Road	B7-B8
Albany Road	E4
Albert Grove	E4-F4
Albert Road	E4-F4
Alfred Road	C7-D7-D8
Allens Road	F3
Alver Road	F8
Anglesea Road	C6-C7
Ariel Road	F7
Arundel Street	D7-E7-F7
Aukland Road	D3-E3-E2
Bailey's Road	E5-E6
Beach Road	E2
Bellvue Terrace	C4
Belmont Street	D5
Bembridge Crescent	F2-F3
Blackfriars Road	E6
Boulton Road	F4
Bradford Road	E6-F6
Bramble Road	F5
Britain Street	B6
Broad Street	A5-A4-B4
Burnaby Road	C6
Cambridge Road	C5-C6
Campbell Road	E4-F4-F5
Canal Walk	E6-E7
Castle Avenue	D2-D3
Castle Road	C4-D4-D5
Cecil Place	C4
Charles Street	E7-D8
Charlotte Street	D8
Chelsea Road	F4
Chetwynd Road	F4-F5
Church Path	E8
Church Street	E8
Clarence Esplanade	
	C3-C2-D2-E2-E1-F1
Clarence Parade	C3-D3-D2-E2
Clarence Road	E2-E3
Clarendon Road	D3-E3-E2-F2
Clarendon Street	E8-F8
Clive Road	F7-F8
Cobourg Street	F7
College Street	B6-B7
Collingwood Road	E4-E3-F3
Commercial Road	D6-D7-D8
Cornwallis Crescent	E8
Cottage Grove	D5-E5
Crasswell Road	D7-E7
Cross Street	B7-B8
Cumberland Street	B8-C8
Curzon Howe Road	B7
Darlington Road	F4
Duisburg Way	C3-C4
Duncan Road	E3-F3-F4
East Street	A5-B5
Edinburgh Road	C7-D7
Eldon Street	D5
Elm Grove	D5-D4-E4
Elphinstone Road	D3-D4
Exmouth Road	E3-E4
Fawcett Road	F4-F5-F6
Flathouse Road	C8-D8
Florence Road	E2
Fraser Road	E5-E6
Fratton Road	F6-F7-F8
Gains Road	F3
Garnier Street	F7
Goodwood Road	F4
Granada Road	F2
Green Road	D5
Greetham Street	D6-E6
Grosvenor Street	D5-D6
Grove Road North	E5
Grove Road South	D4-E4
Gun Wharf Road	B5-B6
Hampshire Terrace	C5-C6
Harold Road	F4
Havant Street	B7
Havelock Road	E5-F5
High Street	B4-B5-C5
Holbrook Road	E7-F7-E8
Hudson Road	E5
Hyde Park Road	D6-E6
Inglis Road	F4
Isambard Brunel Road	D6-D7
Jessie Road	F5
Jubilee Terrace	C4-C5
Kenilworth Road	F2
Kent Road	C4-D4
Kent Street	B7
King Street	B7-C7
King Street	C5-D5
King's Road	C5-D5
King's Terrace	C5
Lake Road	D8-E8
Landport Terrace	C5
Lawrence Road	F4-F5

Lawson Road	F5
Lennox Road South	E2-E3
Livingstone Road	E5-F5
Lorne Road	F5
Lowcay Road	F3
Malvern Road	E2-E3
Manners Road	F5-F6
Margate Road	E5
Marion Road	F2
Market Way	D8
Marmion Road	D4-D3-E3
Merton Road	D4-E4
Middle Street	D5-D6
Montgomerie Road	E6-E5-F5
Museum Road	C5
Napier Road	E3-F3-F4
Nelson Road	D4-E4-E3
Newcombe Road	F7
Norfolk Street	D5
North Street	C7-C8
Northam Street	E7
North Church Road	E8-F8
Olinda Street	F8
Orchard Road	F6
Osborne Road	C3-D3
Outram Road	E4-E5
Oxford Road	F4
Pain's Road	E5
Palmerston Road	D3
Paradise Street	D7-D8
Park Road	B6-C6
Park Street	C5-D5
Parkstone Avenue	F2-F3
Pelham Road	D4-D5
Pembroke Road	B4-C4
Penhale Road	F7
Penny Street	B4-B5
Percy Road	F5
Pier Road	C3-C4
Portland Road	D3-D4
Prince George Street	B7-C7
Queen's Crescent	D4
Queen Street	B7
Raglan Street	E6
Railway View	D7-E7
Richmond Place	C6-C7
Rivers Street	E6
Rugby Road	F6
St Andrew's Road	E4-E5-E6
St David's Road	E5
St Edward's Road	C4
St George's Road	B6-B5-C5
St Georges Way	B6-B7-C7
St Helen's Parade	F2
St James's Road	D5-D6
St Mary's Road	F8
St Nicholas' Street	B4-B5
St Paul's Road	C5-C6
St Ronans Road	F2-F3
St Simons Road	E2-F2
Sackville Street	D5
Sansted Road	E5-F5
Shaftesbury Road	D3-D4
Somers Road	D5-E5-E6

Somers Road North	E6-F6-F7
South Parade	E2-F2
Southsea Terrace	C4
Stanhope Road	D7
Stanley Street	D3-E3
Station Street	D7
Stone Street	C4-C5
Sussex Road	D4
The Hard	B6-B7
The Retreat	D4
Thomas's Street	B4-B5-C5
Unicorn Road	C8-D8
Victoria Avenue	C4
Victoria Grove	E4-F4
Victoria Road North	E4-E5-F5-F6
Victoria Road South	E3-E4
Villiers Road	D3-E3
Walmer Road	F6
Warblington Street	B5
Waverley Road	F2-F3-F4
Welch Road	F3
Western Parade	C3-C4
White Hart Road	B4-B5
Whitwell Road	F2
Wimbledon Park Road	E3-F3
Winston Churchill Avenue	
	C6-D6-E6
Wisborough Road	F3
Woodpath	D4
Worthing Road	E2
Yarborough Road	D4-D5
York Street	C7-C8
Yorke Street	C5-D5

Havant

Barncroft Way	A3-A4
Bedhampton Way	B4
Beechworth Road	C2
Bellair Road	C2
Blendworth Crescent	A4-B4
Brockhampton Lane	A1-A2-B2
Brockhampton Road	A1-A2
Brookside Road	A1
Boundary Way	A2
Catherington Way	B4
Civic Centre Road	B3
Connaught Road	C2
Cross Way	A2
Crossland Drive	C4
Dunhurst Close	C4
East Street	B2-C2
Eastern Road	B3-C3
Elm Lane	B2
Elmleigh Road	B3
Emsworth Road	C2
Fairfield Road	B2-C2-C3
Fair Oak Drive	B4
Fraser Road	A3
Grove Road	B1-C1
Havant By-Pass	A1-B1-C1
Hipley Road	C4

James Road	A3
Juniper Square	B1-C1
Kingsworthy Road	B4
Leigh Road	B3-B4-C4
Lockerley Road	C4
Lower Grove Road	C1
Lymbourn Road	C1-C2
Manor Close	B2-C2
Market Parade	B2
Mavis Crescent	B3
Medstead Road	B4
Montgomery Road	C2
New Lane	C3-C4
New Road	A3-B3
North Close	C1
North Street	B2
Oaklands Road	C2
Orchard Road	C1
Park Road North	B2-B3
Park Road South	B1-B2
Park Way	A2-B2
Petersfield Road	B3-B4
Prince George Street	B2
Priorsdean Crescent	A4
Ranelagh Road	A2
Russell Road	B3
St Albans Road	C4
Slindon Gardens	B1
Solent Road	A1-B1
Soberton Road	A4
South Close	C1
South Street	B1-B2
Staunton Road	A2-A3
Stockheath Lane	A3-A4
Stroudwood Road	C4
The Drive	B4
The Pallant	B2-C2
Timsbury Crescent	A3-A4
Wade Court Road	C1-C2
Waterloo Road	B2-C2
Wendover Road	A3-B3
West Street	A2-B2
Western Road	A2
Woolgreen Avenue	A3-A4

Central Reading

LEGEND

Town Plan
AA recommended route
Restricted roads
Other roads
Buildings of interest   School
Car parks   P
Parks and open spaces
One way streets

Area Plan
A roads
B roads
Locations   Wilsden ○
Urban area

Reading

Shopping and light industry first spring to mind when thinking of Reading, but the town actually has a long and important history. Its rise to significance began in 1121 when Henry I founded an abbey here which became the third most important in England. However, after the Dissolution of the Monasteries, only a few ruins were left. Reading also used to be one of the major centres of the medieval cloth trade, but, already declining in the early 17th century, this source of income was reduced still further as a result of Civil War disturbances.

A fascinating collection of all types of farm implements and domestic equipment can be found in the extremely comprehensive Museum of English Rural Life, situated in the University Campus at Whiteknights Park. The town's own museum has major displays about nearby Silchester – the powerful Roman town of *Calleva*.

Henley-on-Thames, famous for its annual rowing regatta, is a lovely old town, well-provided with old coaching inns, Georgian façades and numerous listed buildings.

Wokingham has been a market town for centuries and over the years has been known for its silk industry and its bell-foundry. Half-timbered gabled houses can be seen in the town centre, although modern development surrounds it.

Central Henley on Thames

Streets and places:
SIMMONS RD, LUKER AVE, RUPERT CL., CRISP RD, CRISP ROAD, BADGEMORE LA., KING'S ROAD, MOUNT VIEW, BMOUNT VIEW, Kenton Theatre, REMENHAM LANE, School, Friar Park, HOP GARDENS, Townlands Hospital, YORK RD, KING'S CL., Regal Cinema, BELL STREET, NEW STREET, Brewery, Henley Rowing Club, RIVERSIDE, RIVER, Regatta Headquarters, Leander Club, S.O.D.C., Police Station, HART STREET, MKT. PL., WHITE HILL, WEST STREET, Fire Station, DUKE ST., THAMES SIDE, Henley Bridge Cricket Gnd, GRAVEL HILL, Town Hall & Library, South Oxfordshire Technical College, FRIDAY ST., GREYS ROAD, General Post Office, Squash Club, RIVER TER., THAMES, ANCASTLE GRN, PARADISE RD, DEANFIELD AVE, Tel. Exch., GREYS, Sch., ALBERT RD, QUEEN STREET, STATION RD, MEADOW RD, Mill Meadows Recreation Ground, Youth Centre, College Annexe, NORMAN AVE, READING, Sta., Recreation Ground, GREYS HILL, HAMILTON AVE, VICARAGE ROAD, ST MARK'S RD, READING ROAD, UPTON CL., PARK ROAD, GRANGE RD, GROVE RD, GAINSBOROUGH HILL, THE CLOSE, Sacred Heart Catholic School, Henley Trinity Junior School, ST MARK'S ROAD, ANDREW'S ROAD, St Mary's School, PO, WALTON AVE

Central Wokingham

Streets and places:
MATHEWSGREEN ROAD, TWYFORD ROAD, BELL FOUNDRY LANE, WARREN HOUSE ROAD, Cantley Recr. Grnd, SEWELL AVE, MARKS RD, CANTLEY CR, MARTINS DRIVE, BELL RD, WARREN HOUSE ROAD, KEEPHATCH RD, School, CLIFTON ROAD, COPSE DR., JUBILEE AVE, MILTON RD, BENNING WY, ASHRIDGE RD, CRUTCHLEY RD, BUDGES RD, READING, HOLT LANE, Joel Park, Girls School, WILTSHIRE ROAD, SARUM CRES, NORREYS AVENUE, HUGHES RD, School, School, ARTHUR DRIVE, GLEBELANDS RD, CLARE AVE, NORREYS AVENUE, ELISABETH ROAD, BARRETT CR., OXFORD ROAD, School, Pol. Sta., SHUTE END, RECTORY ROAD, ROSE ST, LONDON ROAD, MURRAY ROAD, School, STATION RD, BROAD ST, Library, PEACH ST, School, Sta., PARK, PO, W. COTT RD, St Crispins Sch., Wokingham Hospital, Council Offices, WELLINGTON ROAD, DENMARK ROAD, Town Hall, EASTHAMPSTEAD, School, MEADOW RD, Council Offices, ELMS ROAD, HOWARD RD, STURGES ROAD, Sch., BARKHAM ROAD, Sports Grnd, MOLLY MILLARS LANE, LANGBORO' RD, MURDOCH RD, OAKLANDS DR., Cricket Ground, CAREY RD, SOUTH DRIVE, GIPSY LANE, HOLMES CRES., Football Ground, FINCHAMPSTEAD, FISH PONDS RD, EASTHEATH AVE, S. LANDS ROAD, GIPSY LANE

Reading Area

SCALE 0 — 4 mls

Blewbury, Aston Tirrold, North Stoke, Ipsden, Bix, Middle Assendon, Mill End, Medmenham, Bisham, Cookham Rise, Cookham, Moulsford, Stoke Row, Highmoor Cross, Lower Assendon, Remenham, Aston, Hurley, Cookham Dean, Compton, South Stoke, Checkendon, Shepherd's Green, Rotherfield Greys, Remenham Hill, Hurley Bottom, Littlewick Green, MAIDENHEAD, Bray, Aldworth, Woodcote, Rotherfield Peppard, HENLEY-ON-THAMES, Cockpole Green, Knowl Hill, Woodlands Park, Streatley, Goring, Cray's Pond, Sonning Common, Harpsden, Warren Row, Wargrave, Hare Hatch, White Waltham, Holyport, Fifield, Lower Basildon, Cane End, Whitchurch Hill, Kidmore End, Binfield Heath, Lower Shiplake, Shiplake, Waltham St. Lawrence, Ashampstead, Whitchurch, Tokers Green, Dunsden Green, Play Hatch, Charvil, Twyford, Shurlock Row, Paley Street, Pangbourne, Purley, Emmer Green, Sonning, Whistley Green, Hurst, Hampstead Norreys, Upper Basildon, Tidmarsh, Sulham, Caversham, Woodley, Warfield, Winkfield, Hermitage, Frilsham, Bradfield, North Street, Calcot, READING, A4 Southcote, Winnersh, Sindlesham, Winkfield Row, Binfield, Newell Green, North Ascot, Stanford Dingley, Southend, Engelfield, Theale, Whitley, Wokingham, Popeswood, Bracknell, Cold Ash, Bucklebury, Chapel Row, Sheffield Bottom, Burghfield, Three Mile Cross, Shinfield, Arborfield, Barkham, Upper Bucklebury, Beenham, Sulhamstead, Burghfield Hill, Grazeley, Spencers Wood, Arborfield Cross, Arborfield Garrison, Crowthorne, Thatcham, Midgham, Aldermaston Wharf, Ufton Nervet, Burghfield Common, Wokefield Park, Farley Hill, Woolhampton, Padworth, Aldermaston, Mortimer, Swallowfield, Finchampstead, Sandhurst, Brimpton, Wasing, Stratfield Mortimer, Beech Hill, Riseley, Crookham, Headley, Ashford Hill, Heath End, Tadley, Aldermaston Soke, Pamber Heath, Mortimer West End, Silchester, Owlsmoor

Box denotes area covered by central plan

READING
Whiteknights, which consists of 300 acres of landscaped parkland, provides Reading's modern university with an incomparable campus setting and includes a conservation area and a biological reserve for research purposes.

Central Reigate/Redhill

Box denotes area covered by central plan

Box denotes area covered by central plan

REIGATE

REDHILL

Reigate Area

mls 0   SCALE   2

Reigate/Redhill

One of the earliest public libraries in the country can be found in Reigate's parish church of St. Mary Magdalen. The library dates from 1701; the church goes back as far as the 12th century. Industry and commerce are changing the face of the area, especially in Redhill, but Reigate has kept a number of open spaces, such as Reigate Park (the site of a former priory), Reigate Heath (where an 18th-century windmill has been converted into a church) and Earlswood Common.

Dorking lies at the foot of Box Hill, a popular beauty spot today and at least as far back as the early 1800s, when Jane Austen featured it in her novel *Emma*.

Modernisation has done little to erode the charm of the town, where weeping willows surround the attractive Mill Pond. Overlooking the High Street is the gabled White Horse Inn, reminiscent of coaching days.

Leatherhead's Thorndyke Theatre has been entertaining the area since the 1960s, and the town is also known for its Royal School for the Blind, which was founded here in the late 18th century. With a museum that traces the history of the region, and a parish church which dates mainly from the 12th to the 15th centuries, Leatherhead today is the home of several industrial research establishments.

52

Central Dorking

Central Leatherhead

Key to Town Plan and Area Plan

Town Plan

A A Recommended roads	
Other roads	
Restricted roads	
Buildings of interest	Theatre
Car Parks	P
Parks and open spaces	
Churches	

Area Plan

A roads	
B roads	
Locations	Leigh O
Urban Area	

Street Index with Grid Reference

Redhill/Reigate

Albert Road North	A3
Albert Road South	A3
Albion Road	C1
Alders Road	B3-B4-C4
Alma Road	B3-B4-C4
Althorne Road	F1
Bancroft Road	B2
Batts Hill	D4-E4-E3
Baxter Avenue	E3
Beaufort Road	A3
Beech Road	A4
Bell Street	B1-B2
Belmont Road	C1
Beverley Heights	B4
Blackborough Road	C1-C2-D2
Blackstone Hill	D2
Blanford Road	C1-D1-D2
Brambletye Park Road	F1
Brightlands Road	C3-C4
Brighton Road	E1-F1-F2
Brokes Crescent	B4
Brokes Road	A4-B4
Brook Road	F1-F2
Brooklands Way	E4
Buckhurst Close	E4
Carlton Road	D4, E4-F4
Chart Lane	B2-C2-C1
Chartway	B2-B3
Church Street	B2
Cockshot Road	C1
Colebrook Road	E4
Coniston Way	D3-E3
Cornfield Road	C1
Crakell Road	C1

Cromwell Road	E3-F3
Cronkshill	C1-D1
Croydon Road	B2-B3-C3-C4
Danes Hill	E3-E4
Deerings Road	C2-C3
Doods Road	C2-D3
Doods Way	D3
Doods Park Road	C3-C2-D2
Doran Drive	D2-D3
Earlsbrook Road	F1
Elm Road	E2
Eversfield Road	C2
Fairfax Avenue	E3
Fairlawn Drive	D1-E1
Fengates Road	E2
Frenches Road	F4
Furzefield Road	C1
Garlands Road	E1-E2-F2
Gatton Road	C4
Gatton Park Road	D4
Glovers Road	B1-C1
Green Lane	A2
Green Lane	D4-E4
Green Way	D4-E4
Grove Hill Road	E2-F2
Hardwicke Road	A2-A3
Hatchlands Road	D2-E2-E3
High Street	A2-B2
High Street	F2-F3
Highlands Road	D3
High Trees Road	C1-D1
Holmesdale Road	B3-C3
Hooley Lane	E1-F1
Hurstleigh Drive	E4-F4
Ladbroke Road	F3-F4
Lesbourne Road	B1
Linkfield Lane	E3-E4-F4
Linkfield Street	E2-E3
London Road	A2-A3-B3
London Road	F3-F4
Lymden Gardens	B1
Madeira Walk	D3
Manor Road	A3-A4
Mill Street	E1
Monks Walk	B2
Nash Drive	F4
North Street	E3
Nutley Lane	A2-A3
Oak Road	C3
Oakdene Road	E2
Oaks Road	C3-D3
Oakway	D1
Oxford Road	E3
Park Lane	A1-A2
Park Road	E3-E4
Parkgate Road	B1
Pilgrims Way	A3-A4
Prince Way	E3
Queensway	F3
Raglan Close	C4
Raglan Road	B4-C4
Ranelagh Road	E2
Redstone Hill	F2-F3
Redstone Hollow	F1-F2
Reigate Road	B2-C2-D2
Reigate Hill Road	B3-B4
Ridgeway Road	E2
Ringley Park Avenue	D1-D2
Ringley Park Road	C2-D2
Rushworth Road	B3
St Albans Road	A3-A4

St John's Road	F1
St Mary's Road	B1-C1
Sandpit Road	E1
Smoke Lane	C1
Somers Road	A3-B3
Station Road	E3-F3
The Cedars	C2-D2
The Chase	D1-D2
The Close	B2
The Cutting	E1
The Way	D3
Timperley Gardens	D4-E4
Upper Bridge Road	E2
Victoria Road	F1
Warren Road	B3-C3
Warwick Road	E3-F3
Waterlow Road	C1-D1
West Street	A2
Whitepost Hill	D2-E2
Windermere Way	D3
Windmill Drive	D4
Windmill Way	D4
Woodcrest Walk	D4
Woodlands Road	E1
Wray Lane	D4
Wray Common Road	C3-D3-D2
Wrayfield Avenue	C3
Wray Park Road	B3-C3-C4
Yorke Road	A3-B3

Dorking

Ansell Road	B2-B3
Ashcombe Road	A3-A4-B4
Beresford Road	B2
Calvert Road	B4
Chalkpit Road	A3
Chalkpit Terrace	A3-A4
Chart Lane	C1-C2
Church Street	A2-B2
Cold Harbour Lane	A1
Croft Avenue	B4
Curtis Road	A2-A3
Deepdene Avenue	C1-C2-C3-C4
Deepdene Drive	C2-C3
Deepdene Gardens	B3-C3-C2
Deepdene Park Road	C3
Deepdene Vale	C3-C4
Dene Street	B2
Fairfield Road	B3-B4
Glebe Road	A2
Hampstead Lane	A1
Hampstead Road	A1-B1
Hart Road	B3
Heath Hill	B2-B3
High Street	B2-B3-C3
Hill Rise	A4
Horsham Road	A1-B1
Keppel Road	A4-B4
Ladygate Road	B4-C4
Lincoln Road	B4
London Road	B3-B4-C4-B4
Marlborough Road	B2
Mill Lane	B2-B3
Moores Road	B3-B2-C2
North Street	B2
Nower Road	A1-A2
Park Way	A3
Pixham Lane	C4

Ranmore Road	A3-A4
Reigate Road	C3
Rose Hill	B1-B2
Rothes Road	B3
St Paul's Road East	B2
St Paul's Road West	A1-B1
South Drive	C3
South Street	A1-B1-B2-A2-B2
South Terrace	B1
Spital Way	C3
Station Approach	B4-C4
Station Road	A2-A3
Upper Rose Hill	B1
Vincents Lane	A1-A2
West Street	A2-B2
West Bank	A1
Westcott Road	A2
Yew Tree Road	A4-B4

Leatherhead

Belmont Road	A2-B2
Bridge Street	A2-B2
Church Road	C2-C3
Church Street	B2
Cobham Road	A1
Copthorne Road	C4
Dorking Road	B2-B1-C1
Elm Close	C1
Elm Drive	C1
Elm Road	B2-C2
Elmer Cottages	A1
Emlyn Lane	B2
Epsom Road	C3
Fairfield Road	B3
Garlands Road	C3-C4
Guildford Road	A1-A2
High Street	B2-B3-C2
Highlands Road	C2
Kingston Avenue	B3-B4
Kingston Road	B3-B4
Leret Way	B3-C3
Levett Road	C4
Linden Gardens	C4
Linden Pit Path	C3-C4
Linden Road	B3-C3
Mill Lane	A2
Minchin Close	B2
Oaks Close	B3-B4
Park Rise	B3
Poplar Avenue	C2
Poplar Road	C2-C3
Randalls Road	A4-A3-B3
St John's Avenue	B3-B4-C4
St Mary's Road	C1
St Nicholas Hill	C1-C2
Station Road	A3-B3
The Crescent	B2-C2
The Withies	C4
Thorncroft Drive	B1-C1
Upper Fairfield Road	B3
Waterway Road	A2-A3
Windfield	C3

53

Salisbury

Its attractive site where the waters of the Avon and Nadder meet, its beautiful cathedral and its unspoilt centre put Salisbury among England's finest cities. In 1220 the people of the original settlement at Old Sarum, two miles to the north, moved down to the plain and laid the first stone of the cathedral. Within 38 years its was completed and the result is a superb example of Early English architecture.

The cloisters are the largest in England and the spire the tallest in Britain. All the houses within the Cathedral Close were built for cathedral functionaries, and although many have Georgian façades, most date back to the 13th century. Mompesson House is one of the handsome mansions here and as it belongs to the National Trust, its equally fine interior can be seen. Another building houses the Museum of the Duke of Edinburgh's Royal Regiment. At one time, relations

between the clergy and the citizens of Salisbury were not always harmonious, so the former built a protective wall around the Close.

The streets of the modern city follow the medieval grid pattern of squares, or 'chequers', and the tightly-packed houses provide a very pleasing townscape. Salisbury was granted its first charter in 1227 and flourished as a market and wool centre; there is still a twice-weekly market in the spacious square.

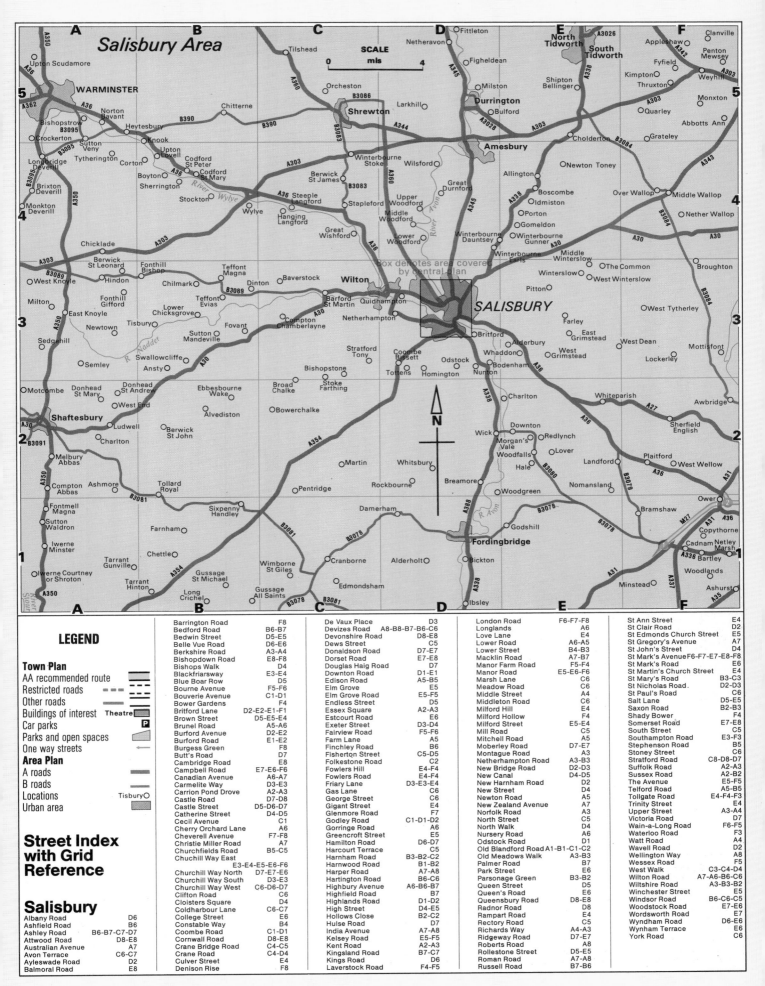

Salisbury Area

LEGEND

Town Plan
- AA recommended route
- Restricted roads
- Other roads
- Buildings of interest — Theatre
- Car parks — P
- Parks and open spaces
- One way streets

Area Plan
- A roads
- B roads
- Locations — Tisbury
- Urban area

Street Index with Grid Reference

Salisbury

Albany Road	D6
Ashfield Road	B6
Ashley Road	B6-B7-C7-D7
Attwood Road	D8-E8
Australian Avenue	A7
Avon Terrace	C6-C7
Ayleswade Road	D2
Balmoral Road	E8
Barrington Road	F8
Bedford Road	B6-B7
Bedwin Street	D5-E5
Belle Vue Road	D6-E6
Berkshire Road	A3-A4
Bishopdown Road	E8-F8
Bishops Walk	D4
Blackfriarsway	E3-E4
Blue Boar Row	D5
Bourne Avenue	F5-F6
Bouverie Avenue	C1-D1
Bower Gardens	F4
Britford Lane	D2-E2-E1-F1
Brown Street	D5-E5-E4
Brunel Road	A5-A6
Burford Avenue	D2-E2
Burford Road	E1-E2
Burgess Green	F8
Butt's Road	D7
Cambridge Road	E8
Campbell Road	E7-E6-F6
Canadian Avenue	A6-A7
Carmelite Way	D3-E3
Carrion Pond Drove	A2-A3
Castle Road	D7-D8
Castle Street	D5-D6-D7
Catherine Street	D4-D5
Cecil Avenue	C1
Cherry Orchard Lane	A6
Cheverell Avenue	F7-F8
Christie Miller Road	A7
Churchfields Road	B5-C5
Chuchill Way East	E3-E4-E5-E6-F6
Churchill Way North	D7-E7-E6
Churchill Way South	D3-E3
Churchill Way West	C6-D6-D7
Clifton Road	C6
Cloisters Square	D4
Coldharbour Lane	C6-C7
College Street	E6
Constable Way	B4
Coombe Road	C1-D1
Cornwall Road	D8-E8
Crane Bridge Road	C4-C5
Crane Road	C4-D4
Culver Street	E4
Denison Rise	F8

De Vaux Place	D3
Devizes Road	A8-B8-B7-B6-C6
Devonshire Road	D8-E8
Dews Street	C5
Donaldson Road	D7-E7
Dorset Road	E7-E8
Douglas Haig Road	D7
Downton Road	D1-E1
Edison Road	A5-B5
Elm Grove	D5
Elm Grove Road	E5-F5
Endless Street	D5
Essex Square	A2-A3
Estcourt Road	E6
Exeter Street	D3-D4
Fairview Road	F5-F6
Farm Lane	A5
Finchley Road	B6
Fisherton Street	C5-D5
Folkestone Road	C2
Fowlers Hill	E4-F4
Fowlers Road	E4-F4
Friary Lane	D3-E3-E4
Gas Lane	C6
George Street	C6
Gigant Street	E4
Glenmore Road	F7
Godley Road	C1-D1-D2
Gorringe Road	A6
Greencroft Street	E5
Hamilton Road	D6-D7
Harcourt Terrace	C5
Harnham Road	B3-B2-C2
Harnwood Road	B1-B2
Harper Road	A7-A8
Hartington Road	B6-C6
Highbury Avenue	A6-B6-B7
Highfield Road	B7
Highlands Road	D1-D2
High Street	D4-E5
Hollows Close	B2-C2
Hulse Road	D7
India Avenue	A7-A8
Kelsey Road	E5-F5
Kent Road	A2-A3
Kingsland Road	B7-C7
Kings Road	D6
Laverstock Road	F4-F5

London Road	F6-F7-F8
Longlands	A6
Love Lane	E4
Lower Road	A6-A5
Lower Street	B4-B3
Macklin Road	A7-B7
Manor Farm Road	F5-F4
Manor Road	E5-E6-F6
Marsh Lane	C6
Meadow Road	C6
Middle Street	A4
Middleton Road	C6
Milford Hill	E4
Milford Hollow	E4
Milford Street	E5-E4
Mill Road	C5
Mitchell Road	A5
Moberley Road	D7-E7
Montague Road	A3
Netherhampton Road	A3-B3
New Bridge Road	D2-D3
New Canal	D4-D5
New Harnham Road	D2
New Street	D4
Newton Road	A5
New Zealand Avenue	A7
Norfolk Road	A3
North Street	C5
North Walk	D4
Nursery Road	A6
Odstock Road	D1
Old Blandford Road	A1-B1-C1-C2
Old Meadows Walk	A3-B3
Palmer Road	B7
Park Street	E6
Parsonage Green	B3-B2
Queen Street	D5
Queen's Road	E6
Queensbury Road	D8-E8
Radnor Road	E4
Rampart Road	E4
Rectory Road	C5
Richards Way	A4-A3
Ridgeway Road	D7-E7
Roberts Road	A8
Rollestone Street	D5-E5
Roman Road	A7-A8
Russell Road	B7-B6

St Ann Street	E4
St Clair Road	D2
St Edmonds Church Street	E5
St Gregory's Avenue	A7
St John's Street	D4
St Mark's Avenue	F6-F7-E7-E8-F8
St Mark's Road	E6
St Martin's Church Street	E4
St Mary's Road	B3-C3
St Nicholas Road	D2-D3
St Paul's Road	C6
Salt Lane	D5-E5
Saxon Road	B2-B3
Shady Bower	F4
Somerset Road	E7-E8
South Street	C5
Southampton Road	E3-F3
Stephenson Road	B5
Stoney Street	C6
Stratford Road	C8-D8-D7
Suffolk Road	A2-A3
Sussex Road	A2-B2
The Avenue	E5-F5
Telford Road	A5-B5
Tollgate Road	E4-F4-F3
Trinity Street	E4
Upper Street	A3-A4
Victoria Road	D7
Wain-a-Long Road	F6-F5
Waterloo Road	F3
Watt Road	A4
Wavell Road	D2
Wellington Way	A8
Wessex Road	F5
West Walk	C3-C4-D4
Wilton Road	A7-A6-B6-C6
Wiltshire Road	A3-B3-B2
Winchester Street	E5
Windsor Road	B6-C6-C5
Woodstock Road	E7-E6
Wordsworth Road	E7
Wyndham Road	D6-E6
Wynham Terrace	E6
York Road	C6

Slough

The town is something of a non-starter as far as architectural beauty or historical interest is concerned. However, it is a good shopping centre and has plenty of sports and leisure facilities.

Windsor The distinctive outline of the castle's towers and battlements above the Thames completely dominates the town. First built by the Normans to guard the approaches to London, it has been altered and added to at different times by various kings, but Henry III and Edward III contributed most to its present haphazard shape. The State Apartments are magnificent, as is St George's Chapel, with its superb fan-vaulted ceiling. Queen Mary's Dolls' House is an exquisite model house of the 1920s, complete down to the last detail. The town itself, squeezed between the castle walls and the river, has several attractive streets graced with fine buildings. One 17th-century colonnaded building by Sir Christopher Wren contains a small museum of local interest, and a recent new attraction is the Madame Tussaud's Royalty and Railways Exhibition.

Maidenhead used to be an important stage-post on the London to Bath road and is now a prosperous Thameside residential town. Oldfield House, near the ancient bridge designed by Brunel, contains the Henry Reitlinger Bequest Museum, specialising in glass and ceramics.

56

A | **B** | **C**

Central Windsor — Eton, The Brocas, River Thames, Windsor Castle, Riverside Station, Broad Water, Datchet Road, Frogmore Drive

Central Maidenhead — Industrial Estate, Braywick Playing Fields, Maidenhead Golf Course

---

LEGEND

Town Plan
- AA recommended route
- Restricted roads
- Other roads
- Buildings of interest — Station
- Car parks — P
- Parks and open spaces
- One way streets
Area Plan
- A roads
- B roads
- Locations — Hightown○
- Urban area

Street Index with Grid Reference

Slough

Albert Street	C1-D1-E1
Aldin Avenue	E2-F2
Alexandra Road	B1-B2
Alpha Street	D1-E1-E2
Arthur Road	B2
Bath Road	A3-B3-C3
Baylis Road	B4-C4
Beechwood Gardens	C2
Belgrave Road	D4
Benson Close	E4
Bourne Road	A2
Bradley Road	B4-C4
Broadmark Road	F4
Brunel Way	D3
Burlington Avenue	C2-C3
Chalvey Park	C2

Chalvey Road East	B2-C2-C1
Chalvey Road West	B2
Church Street	A2-B2
Church Street	D1-D2
Cippenham Lane	A2-A3
Clifton Road	F2
Clive Court	A2-B2-B1
College Avenue	C1
Conegar Court	C3
Diamond Road	E3-F3-F2
Dolphin Road	F2
Ellis Avenue	B3-C3
Everard Avenue	B3-B2-C2
Farnham Road	A3-A4
Fleetwood Road	D4
Gilliat Road	C4
Glentworth Place	A3
Greys Road	D4
Harewood Place	E1
Hatfield Road	E1-E2
Hazlemere Road	F4
Hencroft Street	D1-D2
Henry Road	B2-B3
Herschel Street	D2-E2
High Street	D2-E2
High Street Chalvey	A2-A1-B1-B2
Hillside	B2
King Edward Street	B2
Kings Road	C1
Ladbroke Road	A1
Landsdowne Avenue	C3
Lascelles Road	F1
Ledgers Road	B1-B2-B3
Little Down Road	D4
London Road	F1-F2
Martin Road	B1
Mere Road	D1
Merton Road	E1
Mill Street	D4
Montem Lane	A3-B3-B2
Osborne Street	D1-D2
Park Street	D1-D2
Petersfield Avenue	E4-E3-F3
Pitts Road	A4
Princes Street	F2
Queens Road	D4
Ragstone Road	B1-C1
Richmond Crescent	E3
St John's Road	E4-F4
St Lawrence Way	E1
St Paul's Avenue	D4-E4-F4
Salt Hill Avenue	A3-A4
Salt Hill Drive	A4
Salt Hill Way	A4-B4
Shackleton Road	C4

Seymour Road	A2
Spackmans Way	A1
Stoke Gardens	C4-D4
Stoke Road	D3-D4
Stoke Poges Lane	B3-C3-C4
Stratford Road	E2-E3
Sussex Place	E2-F2-F1
The Crescent	B2-C2
The Green	A2-A1-B1
The Grove	E1-E2
Tuns Lane	A1-A2-A3
Upton Park	C1-D1
Upton Road	E1
Uxbridge Road	E2-F2-F3
Vale Grove	C1-D1
Wellesley Road	E3
Wellington Street	D3-E3-E2-F2
Wexham Road	E2-E3-F3-F4
White Hart Road	A1-B1
Windmill Road	A3-A4
Windsor Road	C1-C2-D2-D3
Woodland Avenue	B4
Yew Tree Road	E1-E2-F2

Maidenhead

Australia Avenue	B4
Bad Godesberg Way	B3
Bell Street	B2
Belmont Road	A3-A4
Blackamoor Lane	C3-C4
Boyn Valley Road	A1-A2
Braywick Road	B1-B2
Bridge Avenue	C2-C3
Bridge Road	C3
Bridge Street	B3-C3
Broadway	B2
Castle Hill	A2
Cedars Road	C2-C3
Clare Road	A1-A2
Clivemont Road	A4-B4
College Avenue	A3
College Road	A2-A3
Cookham Road	B3-B4
Cordwallis Road	A3-A4-B2
Cordwallis Street	A4
Court Lands	B1
Crauford Rise	A3
Denmark Street	A4
Depot Road	B1-B2-C2
Forlease Road	C2-C3
Frascati Way	B2

Grassy Lane	A3
Grenfell Place	A3
Grenfell Road	A2-B2
Gringer Hill	A4
High Street	B2-B3
High Town	A2-B2
Holman Leaze	B3-C3
Keble Road	A3
Kennet Road	B3
King's Grove	A3
King Street	B2
Ludlow Road	A1
Marlow Road	A3-B3
Norfolk Road	A3-B3
North Dean	B4
North Road	A2
Park Street	B2
Queen Street	B2-B3
Ray Mill Road West	B4-C4
Rushington Avenue	B1
St Cloud Way	B3-C3
St Ives Road	B2-B3
St Luke's Road	A3-B3-B4
Shoppenhangers Road	A1-B1
South Road	A2
Stafferton Way	B1-C1
The Crescent	A3
Vicarage Road	A3-A4-B4
West Street	B2
Windrush Way	B3-B4
York Road	B2-C2

Windsor

Adelaide Square	B2-C2
Albany Road	B2
Albert Road	C1
Albert Street	A3
Alexandra Road	B2-B3
Alma Road	B3-A3-A2-A1-B1
Arthur Road	A3-B3
Balmoral Gardens	B1
Barry Avenue	A4-B4
Beaumont Road	B2
Bexley Street	A3
Bolton Avenue	B1
Bolton Crescent	B1
Brocas Street	B4
Brook Street	C2
Bulkeley Avenue	A1
Castle Hill	C3
Clarence Crescent	B3

Clarence Road	A3-B3
College Crescent	A1-A2
Dagmar Road	B2
Datchet Road	B4-C4
Devereux Road	B2
Dorset Road	B2-B3
Duke Street	A3-A4
Elm Road	A1
Fountain Gardens	B1-C1
Florence Avenue	B2
Frances Road	B1-B2-C2
Frogmore Drive	C3
Goslar Way	A2
Goswell Road	B3-B4
Green Lane	A2
Grove Road	B2
High Street	B4
High Street	B3-C3
King's Road	C1-C2
Osborne Road	A2-B2-B1-C1
Oxford Road	A3
Park Street	C3
Peascod Street	B3
Princess Avenue	A1
Queens Road	A2-B2
River Street	B4
Royal Mews	C3
Russell Street	B2
St Albans Street	C3
St Leonard's Road	A1-B1-B2
St Mark's Road	A2-B2
Sheet Street	C2-C3
Springfield Road	A1-A2
Stovell Road	A4
Temple Road	B2
Thames Street	B3-B4-C4
The Long Walk	C1-C2-C3
Trinity Place	B2-B3
Vansittart Road	A2-A3-A4
Victoria Street	B3-C3
Ward Royal	B3
York Avenue	A1-A2
York Road	A2

SLOUGH
Salt Hill Park in the centre of Slough features a bowling green, tennis courts and a children's play area, as well as pleasant walks through landscaped gardens. This is one of several recreational areas scattered throughout the town.

Southampton

In the days of the great ocean-going liners, Southampton was Britain's premier passenger port. Today container traffic is more important, but cruise liners still berth there. A unique double tide caused by the Solent waters, and protection from the open sea by the Isle of Wight, has meant that Southampton has always been a superb and important port. Like many great cities it was devastated by bombing raids during World War II. However, enough survives to make the city a fascinating place to explore. Outstanding are the town walls, which stand to their original height in some places, especially along Western Esplanade. The main landward entrance to the walled town was the Bargate – a superb medieval gateway with a Guildhall (now a museum) on its upper floor. The best place to appreciate old Southampton is in and around St Michael's Square. Here is St Michael's Church, oldest in the city and founded in 1070. Opposite is Tudor House Museum, a lovely gabled building housing much of interest. Down Bugle Street are old houses, with the town walls, pierced by the 13th-century West Gate, away to the right. At the corner of Bugle Street is the Wool House Maritime Museum, contained in a 14th-century warehouse. On the quayside is God's House Tower, part of the town's defences and now an archaeological museum.

Key to Town Plan and Area Plan

Town Plan

A.A. Recommended roads
Other roads
Restricted roads
Buildings of interest — Cinema
A A Service Centre — AA
Car Parks — P
Parks and open spaces
One way streets

Area Plan

A roads
B roads
Locations — Ower O
Urban Area

SOUTHAMPTON
Although liners still use Southampton's docks which handled all the great ocean-going passenger ships before the age of air travel replaced sea travel, the port is chiefly used by commercial traffic today.

Key to Town Plan and Area Plan

Town Plan

AA Recommended roads	
Restricted roads	
Other roads	
Buildings of interest	Station
One Way Streets	←
Parks and open spaces	
Car Parks	P

Area Plan

A roads	
B roads	
Urban area	

STREET INDEX - with grid reference

Staines

Avenue Road	A1-A2
Beehive Road	D1
Billet Road	E4
Birch Green	D3-D4
Boleyn Close	B1
Bowes Road	B1
Bremer Road	E4
Bridge Street	B2-B3
Broad Acre	E1
Budebury Road	D1-E1
Cherry Orchard	D2-E2
Chertsey Lane	B2-B1-C1
Chestnut Manor Close	F2
Church Street	B3-B2-C2
Clarence Street	B2-C2
Colinbridge Close	B2
Coopers Close	C1
Cotswold Close	E2
Cumberland Street	A1-A2
Drakes Avenue	D2
Edgell Road	D1
Elmsleigh Road	C2
Fairfield Avenue	D3-D4
Fairways	E1
Farm Close	B1
Farmers Road	B2
Farnell Road	E4
George Street	D3
Georgian Close	F3
Goodman Place	C2
Gordon Close	F1
Goring Road	A1-B1
Greenlands Road	E2-E3
Gresham Road	C1-D1-D2-E2-F2
High Street	C2-C3

Staines

The old and the new exist surprisingly happily together in Staines, a flourishing township which pre-dates the Domesday Survey of 1086.

Set in the Surrey countryside, Staines has attracted many new industries. But as well as signs of prosperity like the popular modern shopping centre, the town has a good number of churches and other features to mark its long history, including graceful Staines Bridge, opened in 1832. The London Stone nearby was put in place in 1285 and now marks the Surrey-Berkshire border.

Chertsey has been a boatbuilding centre for many years, and its attractive position on the River Thames appeals both to boating enthusiasts and to commuters working in London and nearby towns. Central to all river activity is handsome Chertsey Bridge. Alongside the water lies the 150-acre open space of Chertsey Meads and Orchard Gardens (site of the ancient Abbey fishponds), while just upstream, Salter river steamers ply their trade.

The local museum has good collections of costumes and porcelain, along with interesting examples of tiles uncovered during the excavation of the original Abbey site. Various sports and recreation facilities are to be found in the town, and visitors can survey a fine view of the surrounding countryside from the top of St Anne's Hill. Lying to the north, it rises to 240ft (73m).

Hythe Road	A1-A2	Plover Close	C4
Island Close	A3	Priory Green	F2
Kestral Avenue	C3-C4	Prospect Close	C1-D1
Kingfisher Drive	C3	Railway Terrace	A1
Kingston Road		Raleigh Court	E2-E3
	D3-D2-E2-F2-F1	Richmond Crescent	
Knowle Green	E1-F1		C1-C2-D2-D1
Knowle Park	F1	Richmond Road	C1-D1-D2
Laleham Road	C1-D1	River Park Avenue	A2
Lammas Drive	A3-B3	Riverside Drive	B1-C1
Langley Road	D1	Robin Way	C3-C4
Lark Avenue	C4	Rosefield Road	E2-E3
Leacroft	E2-F2-F3	Sianash Crescent	F1
Leacroft Close	F3	Sidney Road	D3-E3
London Road		Silverdale Court	F2
	C3-D3-E3-E4-F4	South Street	C1-C2-D2-C3
Manor Place	F2	Staines By-Pass	
Market Square	B2		C4-D4-E4-E3-F3
Mathews Lane	D2-D3	Stanwell Moor Road	E4
Meadow Court	A4-B4	Stanwell New Road	E4
Meadow Lane	D3	Thames Street	C1-C2
Mill Mead	C3	The Causeway	A2
Moor Lane	A4-B4-B3	The Fernery	B1
Moremede Crescent		The Hythe	B1-B2
	C3-C4-D4-D3	Thorpe Road	A1-A2
Murdoch Close	D1	Tilley Lane	C2
Mustard Mill Road		Vicarage Road	A4-A3-B3
	B4-B3-C3	Victoria Road	B4
Norris Road	C3	Wapshott Road	B1
Pinewood Drive	E2	Waters Drive	C4-C3-D3

Wendover Road	A1	Hanworth Lane	A1-A2
Wraysbury Road	A3-B3	Herrings Lane	A4-B4
Wyatt Road	D1-E1	Herriot Road	A3-A2-B2-B3
		Highfield Road	B1
Chertsey		Horsell Court	C2-C3
Abbey Gardens	B4	King Street	A2-B2
Abbey Road	C2-C3	Laburnum Road	B1
Alwyns Lane	A4-B4	London Street	B3-C3
Barker Road	A2	Longbourne Way	A4
Black Smith Lane	B3	Masonic Hall Road	A4
Bramley Close	C1	Meadhurst Lane	C2
Bridge Road	C3	Mead Lane	C2
Chaeside Gardens	C3	North Grove	A4
Charles Street	A2	Paddocks Way	C2
Colonel's Lane	B4	Pound Road	C2-C3
Cowley Avenue	A2-A3	Pretoria Road	A1-A2
Cowley Lane	A2-A3	Pyrcroft Road	A2-A3
Drill Hall Road	B3-C3	Queen Street	B1-B2
Eastworth Road		Railway Approach	A2
	A2-B2-B1-C1	Riversdell Close	A3
Fairway	B2-C2	Roakes Avenue	C1
Fordwater Road	C1-C2	St Ann's Road	A4
Fox Lane North	A2	Staines Lane	A4-B4
Free Prae Road	B2-C2	Station Road	A2-B2-B1
Galsworthy Road	B3	Stepgates	C2
Gogmore Lane	A3-B3	Victory Road	B2
Grove Road	A4	Wheatash Road	C1
Guildford Road	A1-A2	Wier Road	C2-C3
Guildford Street	A2-A3-B3	Willow Walk	C3
Hamilton Close	A1	Windsor Street	B3-B4

CHERTSEY
Designed by James Paine and completed in 1785, the graceful arches and ashlar stonework of the Bridge overlook the serenity of Chertsey meads and a bustle of activity from boatyards, riverside pubs and river traffic.

Swindon Area

Swindon

Brunel's decision in 1841 to build the Great Western Railway's workshops here transformed Swindon from an agricultural village into a major industrial centre. The surviving buildings of the original railway village have been restored.

Regrettably the fortunes of the BR Engineering Ltd locomotive and other workshops (the heart of the Great Western system and renowned for

locomotives such as the King George V) have declined considerably and even face complete closure — but modern Swindon has seen a remarkable revival. Plans were made in the 1950s to reduce the town's dependence on one industry, and with the combination of development aid and improved road access via the M4, Swindon has seen the arrival of a wide range of manufacturing industries and a near doubling of its population, to 150,000. Aptly chosen for the relocation of

the British Rail's Western Region Headquarters from Paddington, the town now boasts a modern shopping complex, a regional theatre and the impressive Oasis Leisure Centre, while an illustrious past is recalled in the Great Western Railway Museum.

Outside Swindon are 19th-century Lydiard Mansion, standing in 150 acres of parkland, the leisure facilities of Coate Water, and a museum on naturalist and writer Richard Jeffries.

Central Swindon

Goddard Avenue	C1	Maidstone Road	C2	Prospect Place	D1-D2	Thurlestone Road	F2
Graham Street	D5-D4-E4	Manchester Road	C4-D4-E4	Quarry Road	D1	Union Street	D2
Great Western Way	A5-B5-C5	Manton Street	A5	Queen's Drive	E4-F4-F3	Upham Road	E2-F2
Grosvenor Road	A1-A2	Maxwell Street	B3	Radnor Street	B2	Victoria Road	D1-D2-D3
Groves Street	A4	Merton Street	D4	Redcliffe Street	A3-A3	Walcot Road	E2-F2
Groundwell Road	D3-E3	Milford Street	C4	Regent Street	C3-D3	Westcott Place	A2-A3-B3
Hawkins Street	A4-A5	Milton Road	B3-C3	Rodbourne Road	A3-A4-A5	Whitehouse Road	C5-D5
Hawksworth Way	B5-C5	Morris Street	A4-A5	Sheppard Street	C4	William Street	A2-B2
High Street	E1	Morse Street	C2-C3	Shrivenham Road	E4-F4-F5	Wood Street	D1-E1
Hughes Street	A5	Newburn Crescent	A2-A3	South Street	D2	Woodside Avenue	F2
Hunt Street	D2	Newcastle Street	E3-E4	Southampton Street	E3	Wootton Bassett Road	A2
Hythe Road	C1-C2	Newcom Drive	A5-B5	South View Avenue	F2-F3	York Road	E3-E4
Iffley Road	A5	Newport Street	D1-E1	Spring Gardens	D3-D4		
Islington Street	D3	North Street	D2	Stafford Street	C2		
Jennings Street	A4	Okus Road	A1-B1-C1	Stanier Street	C2-C3		
Kent Road	C1-C2	Old Mill Lane	E1	Station Road	C4-D4-D5		
King William Street	D1	Park Lane	A3-B3	Sunnyside Avenue	A1-A2		
Kingshill Road	A2-B2-B1-C1	Parklands Road	E2-F2	Swindon Road	D2		
Lansdown Road	C1-D1	Pembroke Street	C2-D2	Tennyson Street	B3-C3		
Lennox Drive	F3	Plymouth Street	E3	Tithe Barn Crescent	A1		
London Street	B4-C4	Prince's Street	D3-D4	The Mall	C1		
Lorne Street	B3	Prospect Hill	D2	The Parade	C3-C4		

SWINDON
Making waves at the Oasis Leisure Centre 'free-shaped' pool — under the biggest glazed dome in Britain, the water drops away gradually from inches-deep for paddling to a portholed diving area, and is fringed with tropical shrubs.

LEGEND

Town Plan

AA Recommended roads	
Other roads	
Restricted roads	
Buildings of interest	Theatre
One Way Streets	
Parks and open spaces	

Area Plan

A roads	
B roads	
Locations	Ham
Urban area	

Street Index with Grid Reference

Taunton

Taunton

The hub of Somerset, surrounded by the rolling, wooded Quantocks and the Blackdown Hills, Taunton lies on the River Tone in the fertile Vale of Taunton Dene. Famous for its thriving local cider industry, the town is also a lively commercial and agricultural centre whose livestock market rivals Exeter's as the most important in the West Country. In the past it was a major centre of the wool trade.

As befits a county town, Taunton is the headquarters of Somerset's entertaining and successful cricket team. It also offers National Hunt racing, has no fewer than three public schools and, somewhat improbably, the British Telecom Museum where antique telephone equipment is kept. There has been a castle in the town since Norman times: now it is home for the Somerset County and Military Museums.

Bridgwater, an industrial centre, was a busy port until Bristol overshadowed it. Twice a day a bore – a great tidal wave – surges up the River Parrett from Bridgwater Bay; the times are posted on the bridge in the town centre for those who want to see it.

In 1695 the rebel Duke of Monmouth is reputed to have surveyed the field before the Battle of Sedgemoor from the town's church tower. Dating from the 14th century, the Church of St Mary has some particularly fine Jacobean screenwork.

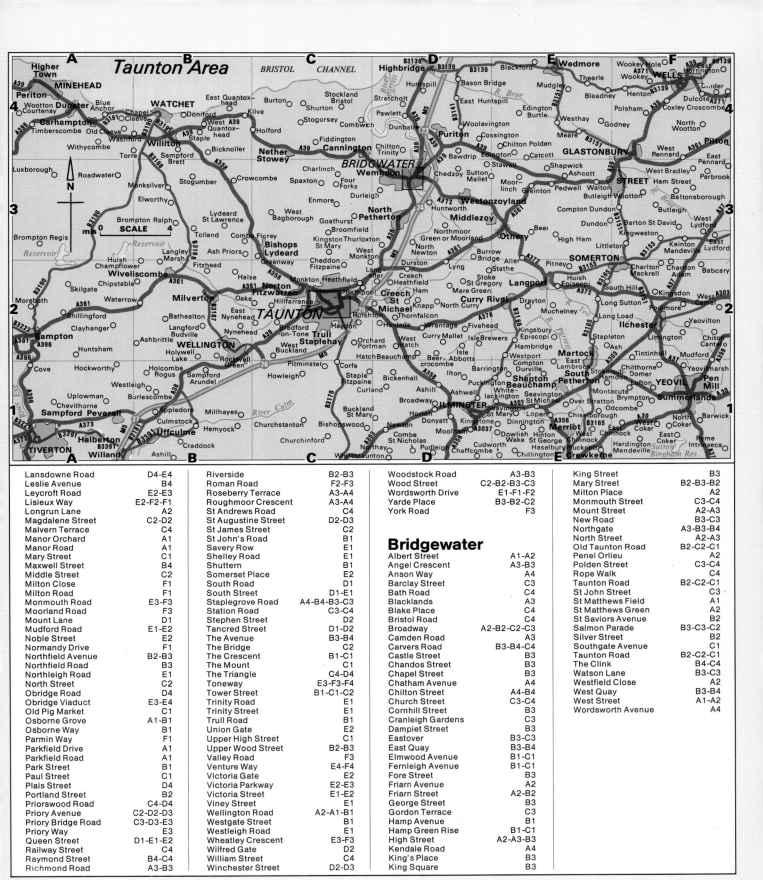

Taunton Area

(Map showing the Taunton area with grid references A–F across top and 1–4 down sides, including towns: Higher Town, Minehead, Periton, Dunster, Watchet, Williton, Carhampton, Timbercombe, Withycombe, Luxborough, Roadwater, Monksilver, Elworthy, Brompton Ralph, Brompton Regis, Morebath, Skilgate, Chipstable, Waterrow, Wiveliscombe, Milverton, Bampton, Shillingford, Clayhanger, Huntsham, Ashbrittle, Bathealton, Langford Budville, Nynehead, Wellington, Holywell Lake, Rockwell Green, Sampford Arundel, Holcombe Rogus, Burlescombe, Westleigh, Uplowman, Chevithorne, Sampford Peverell, Tiverton, Halberton, Willand, Uffculme, Craddock, Ashill, Culmstock, Hemyock, Millhayes, Churchstanton, Churchinford, Bishopswood, Buckland St Mary, Combe St Nicholas, Whitestaunton, Chard, Nether Stowey, Bridgwater, Highbridge, Wedmore, Wells, Glastonbury, Street, Somerton, Langport, Ilchester, Yeovil, Martock, Ilminster, Crewkerne, and many others)

Street Index

Lansdowne Road	D4-E4	Riverside	B2-B3
Leslie Avenue	B4	Roman Road	F2-F3
Leycroft Road	E2-E3	Roseberry Terrace	A3-A4
Lisieux Way	E2-F2-F1	Roughmoor Crescent	A3-A4
Longrun Lane	A2	St Andrews Road	C4
Magdalene Street	C2-D2	St Augustine Street	D2-D3
Malvern Terrace	C4	St James Street	C2
Manor Orchard	A1	St John's Road	B1
Manor Road	A1	Savery Row	E1
Mary Street	C1	Shelley Road	E1
Maxwell Street	B4	Shuttern	B1
Middle Street	C2	Somerset Place	E2
Milton Close	F1	South Road	D1
Milton Road	F1	South Street	D1-E1
Monmouth Road	E3-F3	Staplegrove Road	A4-B4-B3-C3
Moorland Road	F3	Station Road	C3-C4
Mount Lane	D1	Stephen Street	D2
Mudford Road	E1-E2	Tancred Street	D1-D2
Noble Street	E2	The Avenue	B3-B4
Normandy Drive	F1	The Bridge	C2
Northfield Avenue	B2-B3	The Crescent	B1-C1
Northfield Road	B3	The Mount	C2
Northleigh Road	E1	The Triangle	C4-D4
North Street	C2	Toneway	E3-F3-F4
Obridge Road	D4	Tower Street	B1-C1-C2
Obridge Viaduct	E3-E4	Trinity Road	E1
Old Pig Market	C1	Trinity Street	E1
Osborne Grove	A1-B1	Trull Road	B1
Osborne Way	B1	Union Gate	E2
Parmin Way	F1	Upper High Street	C1
Parkfield Drive	A1	Upper Wood Street	B2-B3
Parkfield Road	A1	Valley Road	F3
Park Street	B1	Venture Way	E4-F4
Paul Street	C1	Victoria Gate	E2
Plais Street	D4	Victoria Parkway	E2-E3
Portland Street	B2	Victoria Street	E1-E2
Priorswood Road	C4-D4	Viney Street	E1
Priory Avenue	C2-D2-D3	Wellington Road	A2-A1-B1
Priory Bridge Road	C3-D3-E3	Westgate Street	B1
Priory Way	E3	Westleigh Road	E1
Queen Street	D1-E1-E2	Wheatley Crescent	E3-F3
Railway Street	C4	Wilfred Gate	D2
Raymond Street	B4-C4	William Street	C4
Richmond Road	A3-B3	Winchester Street	D2-D3

Woodstock Road	A3-B3	King Street	B3
Wood Street	C2-B2-B3-C3	Mary Street	B2-B3-B2
Wordsworth Drive	E1-F1-F2	Milton Place	A2
Yarde Place	B3-B2-C2	Monmouth Street	C3-C4
York Road	F3	Mount Street	A2-A3
		New Road	B3-C3
Bridgewater		Northgate	A3-B3-B4
		North Street	A2-A3
Albert Street	A1-A2	Old Taunton Road	B2-C2-C1
Angel Crescent	A3-B3	Penel Orlieu	A2
Anson Way	A4	Polden Street	C3-C4
Barclay Street	C3	Rope Walk	C4
Bath Road	C4	Taunton Road	B2-C2-C1
Blacklands	A3	St John Street	C3
Blake Place	C4	St Matthews Field	A1
Bristol Road	C4	St Matthews Green	A2
Broadway	A2-B2-C2-C3	St Saviors Avenue	B2
Camden Road	A3	Salmon Parade	B3-C3-C2
Carvers Road	B3-B4-C4	Silver Street	B2
Castle Street	B3	Southgate Avenue	C1
Chandos Street	B3	Taunton Road	B2-C2-C1
Chapel Street	B3	The Clink	B4-C4
Chatham Avenue	A4	Watson Lane	B3-C3
Chilton Street	A4-B4	Westfield Close	A2
Church Street	C3-C4	West Quay	B3-B4
Cornhill Street	B3	West Street	A1-A2
Cranleigh Gardens	C3	Wordsworth Avenue	A4
Dampiet Street	B3		
Eastover	B3-C3		
East Quay	B3-B4		
Elmwood Avenue	B1-C1		
Fernleigh Avenue	B1-C1		
Fore Street	B3		
Friarn Avenue	A2		
Friarn Street	A2-B2		
George Street	B3		
Gordon Terrace	C3		
Hamp Avenue	B1		
Hamp Green Rise	B1-C1		
High Street	A2-A3-B3		
Kendale Road	A4		
King's Place	B3		
King Square	B3		

TAUNTON
Taunton School, an attractive rambling building in Staplegrove Road, is one of the town's three public schools for boys. This is the largest of the three in terms of numbers of pupils and is inter-denominational.

Torquay

With its sparkling houses, colourful gardens and sub-tropical plants set among the limestone crags of the steep hillside, Torquay has the air of a resort on the French Riviera – an impression strengthened by the superb views of sea and coast from Marine Drive, the 'corniche' road that sweeps around the rocky headland. Torquay is undoubtedly the Queen of the Devon coast, a resort carefully planned in the early 19th century to cater for the wealthy and discriminating visitor. It had begun to be popular with naval officers' families during the Napoleonic wars when no one could travel to the continent, and this burgeoning popularity was exploited by the Palk family through two generations. Sir Robert Palk, who had made his fortune in India, inherited from a friend an estate which included Torquay, and he and his descendants set about transforming it into the spacious, well-planned town we see today. Among the numerous amenities, Aqualand is particularly interesting.

Paignton, set on the huge sweep of Tor Bay south of Torquay, continues the range of holiday amenities and has good, sandy beaches.

Brixham, which lies a little further down the coast, falls into two parts – the old village on the hill slopes – and the fishing village half a mile below. Less commercialised than its neighbours, it is popular with holidaymakers.

Tunbridge Wells

Dudley, Lord North, set this spa town on the road to fame in the 17th century, when he pronounced on the restorative properties of its Chalybeate Spring. Tunbridge Wells became a fashionable resort under the patronage of Queen Henrietta Maria, wife of Charles I, and later under that of Queen Victoria. It was awarded the title of 'Royal' Tunbridge Wells in 1909.

Today the Chalybeate Spring can still be sampled in the delightful setting of the Pantiles, an elegant precinct started in 1700 and lined with picturesque shops and inns. Fine examples of 19th-century architecture can also be seen in the Mount Pleasant and Mount Ephraim areas, where exclusive Victorian housing estates were built. The Museum and Art Gallery features examples of the wooden souvenir ware which has been produced by the town for over 200 years.

Sevenoaks is a residential town with an old-established Grammar School. Nearby Knole, a fine manor house set in an extensive deer park, was the birthplace of Vita Sackville-West.

Tonbridge has the remains of the Norman castle built here to guard the crossing of the River Medway. Part of the 11th-century wall and the gatehouse, added in the 13th century, are still intact, and stand in attractive gardens. The Angel Centre offers sports, music and drama.

Key to Town Plan and Area Plan

Town Plan

AA Recommended roads	▬▬
Restricted roads	▬ ▬ ▬
Other roads	▬▬
Buildings of interest	Museum
Car Parks	P
Parks and open spaces	
One way streets	←

Area Plan

A roads	▬▬
B roads	▬▬
Locations	Godstone ○
Urban area	

Street Index with Grid Reference

Tunbridge Wells

Albert Cottages	E4
Albert Street	D4-E4
Arundel Road	D1-E1
Bayhall Road	F2
Beech Street	E4
Beulah Road	E4
Bishops Down	A2-B2
Bishops Down Park Road	A4-A3-B3-B4-A4
Bishops Down Road	A2-A3-B3-B2
Boyne Park	B4-C4-C3
Brunswick Terrace	D1
Buckingham Road	D1-D2
Calverley Park	D3-E3-E2
Calverley Park Crescent	D3-E3
Calverley Park Gardens	E3-F3
Calverley Road	D3-E3
Calverley Street	D3-E3-E4
Cambridge Street	E2
Camden Hill	E1-E2
Camden Park	F1-E1-E2-F2
Camden Road	D3-D4-E4
Carlton Crescent	E3-F3
Carlton Road	E3-E4
Castle Road	C1-C2-C3
Chapel Place	C1
Church Road	C3-D3
Claremont Gardens	E1
Claremont Road	D1-E1-E2
Clarence Road	C2-C3
Court Road	A4-B4
Crescent Road	D3-E3
Cromwell Road	F2
Culverden Street	C4-D4
Dale Street	E4
Dudley Road	C3-D3
Earl's Road	B4
Eden Road	C1-D1
Ely Lane	D3-D4
Eridge Road	B1-C1
Farmcombe Lane	D1
Farmcombe Road	D1-E1
Ferndale Road	E4-F4
Fir Tree Road	B2
Frog Lane	C1-D1
Garden Road	E4
Garden Street	D3-E3
Golding Street	D3-D4
Goods Station Road	D4-E4
Grecian Road	D1
Grosvenor Park	D4
Grosvenor Road	D3-D4
Grove Hill Gardens	D1-D2-E2
Grove Hill Road	D2-E2
Hanover Road	C4-D4
Henley Close	F4
High Street	E1-F1
Hollyshaw Close	C1-D1-D2
Hungershall Park	A1-B1
Hurstwood Lane	A3-B3
Inner London Road	C2-C3
Kingswood Road	F2-F3
Kirkdale Road	D4-E4
Lake Road	A4
Langton Road	A2
Lansdowne Road	E3-E4
Lime Hill Road	C3-D3
Little Mount Sion	C1-D1
London Road	C1-C2-C3-C4
Lonsdale Gardens	C2-D2
Madeira Park	D1
Major York's Road	A2-B2-B1-C1
Manor Close	A3
Manor Park	A2-A3
Mayfield Road	B4
Molyneux Park Road	A4-B4-B3-C3
Monson Road	D3
Mount Edgecombe Road	C2
Mount Ephraim	B2-B3-C3-C4
Mount Ephraim Road	C4-D4-D3
Mount Pleasant Avenue	D2-D3
Mount Pleasant Road	D2-D3
Mount Sion	C1-D1
Nevill Park	A2
Nevill Street	C1
Norfolk Road	D1
North Park Street	E2-F2
Oakdale Road	B4
Oakfield Court Road	E2
Pembury Road	E3-F3
Poona Road	E1-E2
Princes Street	E2-F2
Prospect Road	E2-E3
Rock Villa Road	C4-D4
Royal Chase	B4-C4
St James's Road	E4-F4
Sandrock Road	E4-F4
Shandon Close	F3
Somerville Gardens	C3-C4
Stone Street	E4
The Chase	C1
The Pantiles	C1
Tunnel Road	D4
Upper Grosvenor Road	D4
Vale Avenue	C2-D2
Vale Road	C2-D2
Varney Street	D3-D4
Victoria Road	D4-E4
Warberry Close	A4
Warwick Park	C1
Windmill Street	F2
Wood Street	E4
York Road	C3-D3

Sevenoaks

Argyle Road	B2
Ashley Close	B4
Ashley Road	B3-B4
Avenue Road	C3
Bayham Road	C4
Bethel Road	C4
Bosville Drive	A4
Bosville Road	A4
Bourchier Close	B1
Bradbourne Park Road	A4-B4
Bradbourne Road	C4
Buckhurst Lane	B2-C2
Carrick Drive	B4
Chart Way	C3
Clarendon Road	A3-A2-B2
Clenches Farm Lane	A1
Clenches Farm Road	A1
Corden Road	C4
Courtwood Drive	A3
Crownfields	B2
Dartford Road	C3-C4
Eardley Road	A3-B3-B2
Garylock Drive	A1
Granville Road	A3-B3-B2
Hartsland Road	C4
Hall Lane	C4
High Street	B2-C2-C3
Hitchen Hatch Lane	A3-A4-B4-C4-C3
Holly Bush Lane	C3-C4
Holyoake Terrace	A3
Hunsdon Drive	C4
Kippington Road	A1-A2-A3-A4
Knole Lane	B1-C1
Knole Way	C2
Linden Chase	B4-C4
Little Court Road	A3-A4
London Road	A3-A4, B1-B2
Merlewood	B4
Mount Harry Road	A4-B4-C4
Oak Hill Road	A4-A3-A2-A1-B1
Oak Lane	A1-B1
Park Lane	C3
Pembroke Road	B2
Pendennis Road	B4
Plymouth Drive	C2-C3
Plymouth Park	C2-C3
Pound Lane	C3
Rectory Lane	B1
Redlands	A3
Rockdale Road	B1
Rosefields	A3
St Botolphs Road	A3-B3-C3
St Johns Hill	C3
Seal Hollow	C3
South Park	A2-B2
The Dene	B1
The Drive	B2-B3
The Glade	B4
Tonbridge Road	B1-C1-B1-B2
Tubs Hill	B2-B3
Valley Drive	B1-B2
Victoria Road	B2
Vine Avenue	B3-C3
Vine Court Road	C3-C4
Warren Court	C2
Woodside Road	B4
Yoemans Meadow	A1

Tonbridge

Albert Road	A1-B1
Angel Lane	B2
Avebury Avenue	A2-B2
Bank Street	B3
Barden Road	A2-B2
Bordyke	B4
Botany Street	B3
Bradford Street	B2
Brook Street	A1-B1
Caistor Road	A1-A2
Cannon Lane	C4
Castle Street	B3
Chichester Road	A1
Church Lane	B3
Church Street	B3
Cromer Street	A1-A2
Deakin Leas	C1
Douglas Road	A1-B1
Drayton Road	C1
Dry Hill	A4-B4
East Street	B3-B4
Garden Road	B4-C4
Goldsmid Road	C1-C2
Hadlow Road	A3-A4
Havelock Road	A3
Hawden Road	C2
Hectorage Road	C4
High Street	B2-B3-B4
Kendall Drive	B4
Kings Road	C1
Lansdowne Road	A4-B4
Lavender Hill	B2-B1-C1
Lionel Road	A1
London Road	A4-B4
Lyons Crescent	B3
Mabledon Road	A1
Meadow Road	A1
Medway Wharf Road	B3-C3
Mill Crescent	B4
Mill Lane	B4-C4
Morley Road	C2-C3
Mountfield Park	C1
Nelson Avenue	A1-A2
New Wharf	A3-B3
Northcote Road	A2
Pembury Road	B1-C1
Portman Park	B4
Postern Lane	C4
Preston Street	A1-A2
Priory Road	B1-B2-C2
Priory Street	B1-B2
Quarry Hill Road	B1-B2
River Lawn Road	B2
Rose Street	C2
Royal Avenue	C1-C2
St Marys Road	B1
St Stephens Street	C2
Sovereign Way	B1
Springwell Road	A3
Stafford Road	A1
Sussex Road	A3-A4
The Crescent	B1
The Drive	B4-C4
The Grove	A3-B3
The Slade	A1-B1
Tulip Tree Close	C3
Vale Road	B2-C2-C3, C3-C4
Walters Farm Road	C3
Waterloo Road	B1-B2
Woodfield Road	B1

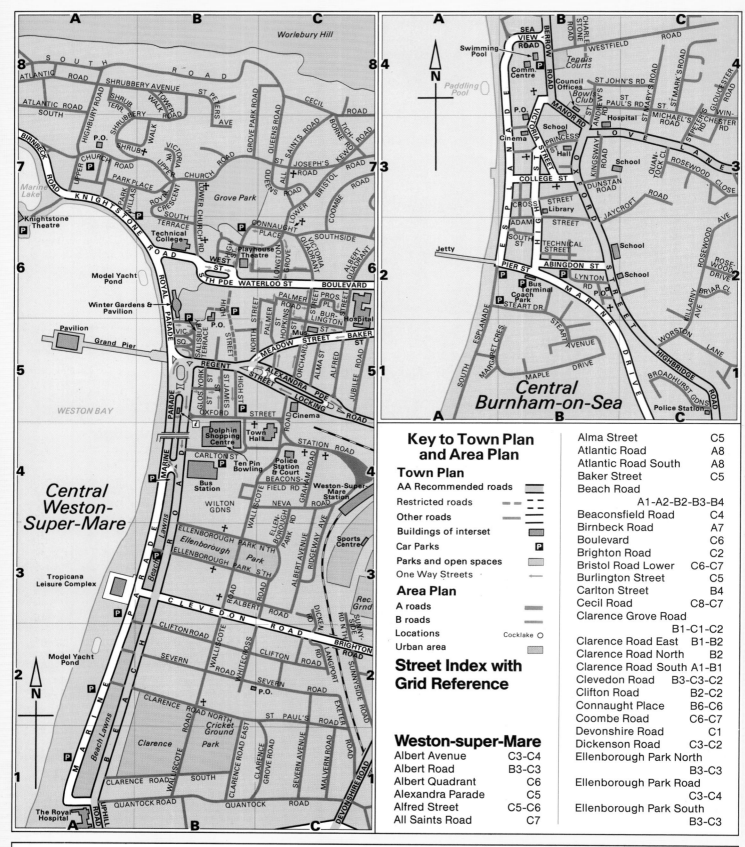

Key to Town Plan and Area Plan

Town Plan

AA Recommended roads	
Restricted roads	
Other roads	
Buildings of interset	
Car Parks	P
Parks and open spaces	
One Way Streets	←

Area Plan

A roads	
B roads	
Locations	Cocklake ○
Urban area	

Street Index with Grid Reference

Weston-super-Mare

Albert Avenue	C3-C4
Albert Road	B3-C3
Albert Quadrant	C6
Alexandra Parade	C5
Alfred Street	C5-C6
All Saints Road	C7
Alma Street	C5
Atlantic Road	A8
Atlantic Road South	A8
Baker Street	C5
Beach Road	A1-A2-B2-B3-B4
Beaconsfield Road	C4
Birnbeck Road	A7
Boulevard	C6
Brighton Road	C2
Bristol Road Lower	C6-C7
Burlington Street	C5
Carlton Street	B4
Cecil Road	C8-C7
Clarence Grove Road	B1-C1-C2
Clarence Road East	B1-B2
Clarence Road North	B2
Clarence Road South	A1-B1
Clevedon Road	B3-C3-C2
Clifton Road	B2-C2
Connaught Place	B6-C6
Coombe Road	C6-C7
Devonshire Road	C1
Dickenson Road	C3-C2
Ellenborough Park North	B3-C3
Ellenborough Park Road	C3-C4
Ellenborough Park South	B3-C3

Weston-Super-Mare

Elegant piers, promenades and hotels mark Weston-Super-Mare's 19th-century transformation into a flourishing seaside resort. At one time nothing more than a small fishing village, the town now boasts several attractive parks and gardens, and near the beach are numerous entertainment and leisure centres.

Havens for children are the Winter Garden Complex and Tropicana, both equipped with water slides, swimming pools and solaria. Madeira Cove attracts visitors to its Marine Lake, aquarium and model village, and Knightstone Island nearby provides further entertainments.

The High Street has been turned into a pedestrian area for easy shopping, and tucked away down a cobbled street is the Woodspring Museum full of nostalgic memories of a town which still retains its character and charm.

Burnham-on-Sea enjoys two local breweries, responsible for supplying the real ales which are exclusive to the pubs in this area. Developed into a resort as early as the 18th century, Burnham-on-Sea also offers many other amenities, including a mild Somerset climate, acres of sandy beaches, a Leisure Park and a pier which was built in 1856 as a terminal for passing steamers and the railway. Live entertainment can be seen at Princess Hall.

Weston-Super-Mare Area

WESTON-SUPER-MARE

Box denotes area covered by central plan

BURNHAM-ON-SEA

Box denotes area covered by central plan

Exeter Road	C2-C1	Royal Crescent	B7	Whitecross Road	B2-C2-C3
Gloucester Street	B5	Royal Parade	B6-B5	Wilton Gardens	B4
Graham Road	C4	St James Street	B5	York Street	B5
Grove Park Road	B7-B8-C8	St Joseph's Road	C7		
Highbury Road	A7-A8	St Paul's Road	C2-C1		
High Street	B6-B5	St Peter's Avenue	B8-B7		
Hopkin Street	C5-C6	Salisbury Terrace	B5	**Burnham-on-Sea**	
Jubilee Road	C5	Severn Avenue	C1-C2	Abingdon Street	B2
Kew Road	C7	Severn Road	B2-C2	Adam Street	B2-B3
Knightstone Road	A7-A6-B6	Shrubbery Avenue	A8-B8	Berrow Road	B4
Langport Road	C2	Shrubbery Road	A7-B7-B8	Briar Close	C2
Locking Road	C5-C4	Shrubbery Terrace	A8	Broadhurst Gardens	C1
Longton Grove	C6	Shrubbery Walk	A7-B7	Charlestone Road	B4
Lower Church Road	B7-B6	South Parade	B6	College Street	B3
Malvern Road	C1	South Road	A8-B8	Cross Street	B3
Marine Parade		Southside	C6	Dunstan Road	B3
	A1-A2-A3-B3-B4-B5	South Terrace	B7-B6	Esplanade	A2-B2-B3-B4
Meadow Street	B5-C5	Station Road	C4	Gloucester Road	C4
Neva Road	B4-C4	Sunnyside Road	C2	Highbridge Road	C1
North Street	B5-C5-C6	Sunnyside Road North		High Street	B2-B3
Orchard Street	C5-C6		C3-C2	Jaycroft Road	B2-B3-C3
Oxford Street	B5-C5	Tichbourne Road	C7	Kilarny Avenue	C1-C2
Palmer Road	C6	Tower Walk	B8	Kingsway Road	B3
Palmer Street	C5-C6	Upper Church Road	A7-B7	Love Lane	B3-C3
Park Place	A7-B7	Victoria Park	B7	Lynton Road	B2
Park Villas	A7	Victoria Square	B5	Manor Road	B4-B3
Prospect Place	C6	Victoria Quadrant	C6	Maple Drive	B1
Quantock Road	A1-B1-C1	Walliscote Road		Margaret Crescent	A1-B1
Queens Road	C7-C8		B1-B2-B3-B4-C4-C5	Marine Drive	B2-B1-C1
Regent Street	B5-C5	Waterloo Street	B6-C6	Oxford Street	B3-B2-C2-C1
Ridgeway Avenue	C3-C4	West Street	B6		

Pier Street	B2
Princess Street	B3
Quantock Close	C3
Rosewood Avenue	C2-C3
Rosewood Close	C3
Rosewood Drive	C2
St Andrew's Road	B3-B4
St John's Road	B4-C4
St Marks Road	C4
St Mary's Road	C3-C4
St Michael's Road	C4-C3
St Paul's Road	B4-C4
St Peter's Road	C3-C4
Sea View Road	B4
South Esplanade	A1-A2
South Street	B2
Steart Avenue	B2-B1
Steart Drive	A2-B2
Technical Street	B2
Victoria Street	B4-B3
Westfield Road	B4-C4
Winchester Road	C4-C3
Worston Lane	C1

WESTON-SUPER-MARE
The piers and good beaches of Weston-Super-Mare attract over three million visitors a year, and town spectaculars such as the aircraft displays of Great Weston Air Day and the summer carnival are another powerful draw.

71

Central Dorchester

**Map labels (Central Dorchester):**
POUNDBURY ROAD, West Mills Road, THE GROVE, GLYDE PATH ROAD, Dorchester Prison, FRIARY, FROME TERR., Dorchester, County Hall & Crown Court, Library, COLLITON, NORTH SQ, ICHARD, Council Offices, Museum, Central Dorchester, BRIDPORT ROAD, AA, HIGH WEST ST, HIGH EAST ST, LONDON RD, Princes Street, DURNGATE ST, ST, FLEET, HIGH ST, CORNWALL ROAD, County Hospital, Cinema, P.O., TRINITY STREET, SOUTH ST, CHARLES ST, ACLAND, WAY, ALL SAINTS ROAD, St Helens Road, ALBERT RD, Borough Gdns, WEST WALKS, WOLLASTON ROAD, ICEN, Hospital, ALBERT RD, VICTORIA ROAD, LINDEN AVE, DAMERS, GREAT WESTERN RD, SOUTH WALKS ROAD, WAY, Cattle Market, Dorchester West Station, FAIRFIELD RD, WEYMOUTH AVENUE, PRINCE OF, YORK RD, LANCASTER ROAD, COBURG ROAD, Dorchester South Station, WALES, CULLIFORD ROAD, Police H.Q., ROAD, QUEENS AVE, Maumbury Rings, ASHLEY ROAD, CROMWELL ROAD, ALFRED ROAD, ROTHESAY ROAD, MONMOUTH, MONMOUTH ROAD, School, Cemy, MAUMBURY ROAD, SOUTH COURT AVE, Playing Fields, School

Central Bridport

**Map labels (Central Bridport):**
PARSONAGE ROAD, BROADMEAD AVE, ROAD, CLAREMONT ROAD, Northmills Trading Estate, CONEYGAR, BEAUMONT AVE, ST SWITHIN'S, NORTH MILLS, VICTORIA, OSBOURNE ROAD, CONEYGAR ROAD, FULBROOKS LANE, Brit, GROVE, CONEYGAR LANE, HARDY ST, FULBROOKS CLOSE, ALLINGTON, River, DELAPRE GDNS, Health Centre, Bridport General Hospital, Council Offices, Police Station, WEST ALLINGTON, CHARDSMEAD, Mag. Court, Port Bredy Hospital, SPARACRE GDNS, ANDREWS GDNS, KENWYN ROAD, WEST STREET, VICTORIA, NORTH, P.O., RAX LANE, SEA ROAD NORTH, Bus Sta., Youth Hostel, TANNER, ST MICHAEL'S LA., ROPE WALKS, EAST STREET, Library, EAST ROAD, Sch., Town Hall, Museum & Art Gallery, GUNDRY LA., PRIORY LANE, Palace Cinema, FOLLY MILL LANE, KINGS, School, EAST RD, Central Bridport, PRINCESS ROAD, ALEXANDRA ROAD, Playing Field, CHURCH ST, Fire Sta., River Simene, SOUTH, River Asker, CROCK LANE, ELIZ. AVE, Football Gnd, PASTURE WAY, NORDONS, SLADES GR.

Central Weymouth

**Map labels (Central Weymouth):**
HANOVER RD, ALEXANDRA RD, NORTH, Weymouth District Hospital, MELCOMBE, DORCHESTER ROAD, Eye Infirmary, CARLTON ROAD NTH, KIRKLETON AVE, GLENDINNING, WESTERHALL RD, GREENHILL, Greenhill Gardens, Greenhill Terrace, CARLTON ROAD, RADIPOLE, GRANGE ROAD, Brunswick Terrace, CASSIOBURY ROAD, CHARLES ST, PENNY ST, LENNOX, WILLIAM, PARK DRIVE, WALPOLE, BROWNLOW, School, Pier Bandstand, RANELAGH, CHELMSFORD, DERBY, VICTORIA, CRESCENT, Weymouth Bay, L.C., Weymouth Station, KING STREET, ESPLANADE, Jubilee Clock, RSPB Information Centre, Bus Sta., QUEEN ST, GLOUCESTER, MEWS, Projected, BATH ST, PARK ST, GEO. ST, ROYAL TERRACE, Radipole Lake, WESLEY'S, Cinema, Bowling Greens, PARK ROAD, ABBOTSBURY ROAD, WESTHAM ROAD, George III Statue, STAVORDALE ROAD, EMBANKMENT BR., Library, Museum, School, Car Ferry Terminal, WESTWAY ROAD, COMMERCIAL ROAD, LOWER BOND, BOND, Harbour, P.O. LOWER, ST MARY ST, ST ALBAN ST, ST ALBAN ST, ST NICHOLAS ST, ST THOMAS ST, ST KT, Harbour Station, Court, Backwater, MAIDEN ST, EAST ST, ESPLANADE, Nothe Fort, Weymouth F.C., CUSTOM HOUSE QUAY, Guildhall, NORTH QUAY, TOWN BR., TRINITY ROAD, PDE, NOTHE WALK, Nothe Gardens, HIGH ST, Trinity Terrace, Municipal Offices, BARRACK ROAD, HOPE ST, HOPFORD ST, NEWBERRY, Newtons Cove, LOVE LANE, RODWELL, FRANCHISE, LEONARD'S, SPRING, OAKLEY, NEWBD, NEWTONS, Portwey Hospital, WYKE RD, PORTWAY CL., SPRING, ORION ST, MAYCROFT, AVENUE, RODWELL RD, KEMP AVE, STON, SPRING, Newtons Cove

---

Key to Town Plan and Area Plan

Town Plan
- AA Recommended roads
- Restricted roads
- Other roads
- Buildings of interest
- Churches †
- Car Parks P
- Parks and open spaces
- One Way Streets ←

Area Plan
- A roads
- B roads
- Locations — Piddletown ○
- Urban area

Street Index with Grid Reference

Weymouth

Abbotsbury Road	A3
Alexandra Road	A6
Avenue Road	B5-B6
Barrack Road	B2-C2
Bath Street	A4
Bond Street	B3
Brownlow Street	A5-B5
Brunswick Terrace	B5-B6-C6
Carlton Road North	A6
Carlton Road South	A6-B6
Cassiobury Road	A5-A6-B6
Charles Street	A5
Chelmsford Street	A5-B5
Commercial Road	A4-A3-A2
Crescent Street	B4-B5

Weymouth

King George III favoured the ancient port of Weymouth and as a result the town acquired a certain fashionable status as a resort in the late 18th century. Still popular with holidaymakers, it offers good bathing, fishing and golf, and it is also a busy Channel Islands ferry port. Georgian houses – many of which have been turned into guest houses – overlook the broad esplanade, but near the harbour older buildings line narrow, picturesque streets and alleyways. One of the 17th-century houses in Trinity Street has been restored and refurnished in contemporary style, and another place of interest is the museum in Westham Road.

Dorchester is essentially still the busy market town Thomas Hardy featured in many of his novels. He was born at nearby Higher Bockhampton and several of his personal possessions are displayed in the Dorset County Museum in Dorchester. A series of fires in the 17th and 18th centuries left the town rather short of historic buildings, although St Peter's Church, which dates back to the 1400s, survived, as did the Old Shire Hall – scene of the trial of the Tolpuddle Martyrs in 1834.

Bridport's wide pavements used to be called 'ropewalks' because new ropes were laid out on them for twisting and drying. The 750-year-old industry continues to this day, and relics of the old trade are kept in the museum in South Street.

West Dorset Area

Box denotes area covered by central plan

Box denotes area covered by central plan

Box denotes area covered by central plan

SCALE
mls
0   4

ISLE OF PORTLAND

Portland Bill

WEYMOUTH
Little has changed along the town's seafront since George III first came to the resort in the late 18th century to try out a new-fangled contraption called a bathing machine. A statue of the King stands on the esplanade.

73

Key to Town Plan and Area Plan

Town Plan

AA Recommended roads	▬▬
Other roads	▬▬
Restricted roads	▬ ▬
Buildings of interest	Station ▬
Churches	+
Car Parks	P
Parks and open spaces	▬
One Way Streets	→

Area Plan

A roads	▬▬
B roads	▬▬
Locations	Bonkle○
Urban area	⬭

Street Index with Grid Reference

Winchester

Alresford Road	E3-F3-F4
Andover Road	B4
Avenue Road	A2-A3
Bar End Road	F1
Baring Road	F3
Beggars Lane	E3-E4
Blue Ball Hill	E3
Broadway	D2-E2
Brook Street	D3
Canon Street	C1-D1
Canute Road	F2-F1
Cheriton Road	A2
Chesil Street	E2-F2-E1-F1
Christchurch Road	B1
City Road	B3-C3
Clifton Hill	B2
Clifton Road	A3-A2-B2
Clifton Terrace	B2-B3
Colebrook Street	D2-E2
College Street	D1-E1
College Walk	E1
Cranworth Road	A4
Cross Street	B2-C2-C3
Culver Road	D1
Domun Road	E1-F1
Durngate	D4-E4
Eastgate Street	D3-E3-E2
East Hill	F1-F2
Ebden Road	E4
Edgar Road	C1
Elm Road	A2-A3
Fairfield Road	A3-A4
Firmstone Road	F4
Friarsgate	D3-E3
Garbett Road	F4
Gladstone Road	B3
Gordon Road	C4
Great Minster Street	C2
Guildhall	D2
Hatherley Road	A4
Highcliffe Road	F1-F2
High Street	C2-D2

Winchester

King Alfred designated Winchester capital of England, a status it retained until after the Norman Conquest. Although gradually eclipsed by London, the city maintained close links with the Crown until the reign of Charles II.

Tucked away unobtrusively in the heart of Winchester is the impressive cathedral which encompasses Norman, and all the later Gothic styles of architecture. William of Wykeham was a bishop here in the 14th century and it was he who founded Winchester College, one of the oldest and most famous public schools in England. The buildings lie just outside the peaceful, shady Close where Pilgrims' Hall can be visited. Nearby are the Bishop's Palace and remains of Wolvesley Castle, one of Winchester's two Norman castles. Of the other, only the Great Hall, just outside the Westgate, survives. Here hangs the massive circle of oak claimed to be King Arthur's Round Table.

The streets of the city, which cover a remarkably small area, are lined with many charming old buildings of different periods. A walk along the pedestrianised High Street takes you past the former Guildhall – now a bank – and the old Butter Cross, into the Broadway where a statue of King Alfred stands near the River Itchen. A delightful path follows the river alongside the remnants of the old city walls.

Winchester Area

WINCHESTER
Standing on the site of the old Hall of Court in the Broadway is the city's Guildhall. Built in 1873, its style was influenced by Northampton Town Hall. It is now a centre for culture and the arts.

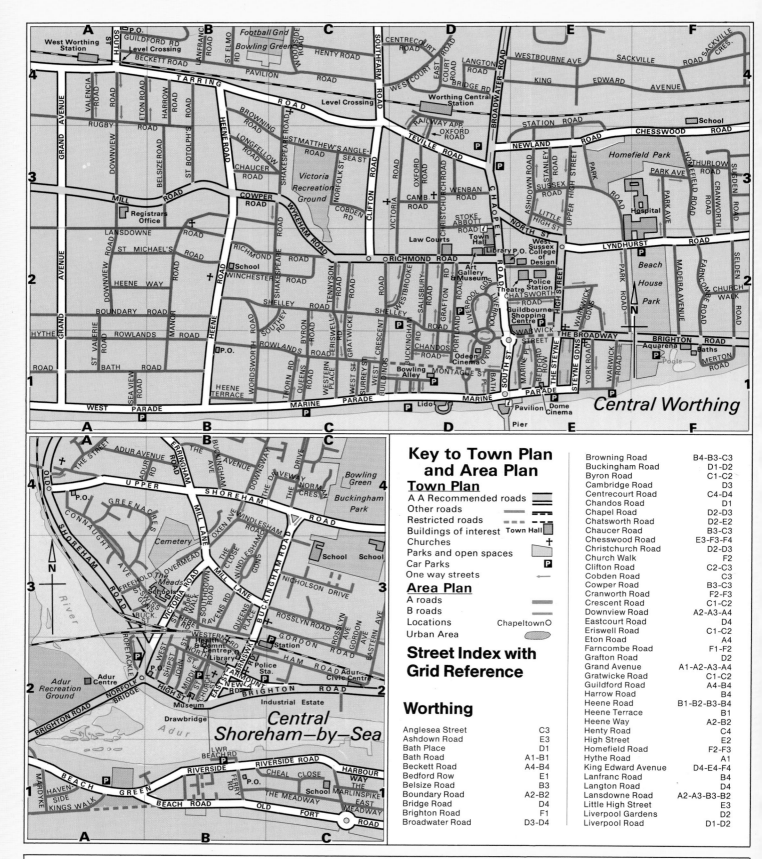

Central Worthing

Key to Town Plan and Area Plan

Town Plan
A A Recommended roads	
Other roads	
Restricted roads	
Buildings of interest	Town Hall
Churches	+
Parks and open spaces	
Car Parks	P
One way streets	←

Area Plan
A roads	
B roads	
Locations	ChapeltownO
Urban Area	

Street Index with Grid Reference

Worthing

Anglesea Street	C3
Ashdown Road	E3
Bath Place	D1
Bath Road	A1–B1
Beckett Road	A4–B4
Bedford Row	E1
Belsize Road	B3
Boundary Road	A2–B2
Bridge Road	D4
Brighton Road	F1
Broadwater Road	D3–D4

Browning Road	B4–B3–C3
Buckingham Road	D1–D2
Byron Road	C1–C2
Cambridge Road	D3
Centrecourt Road	C4–D4
Chandos Road	D1
Chapel Road	D2–D3
Chatsworth Road	D2–E2
Chaucer Road	B3–C3
Chesswood Road	E3–F3–F4
Christchurch Road	D2–D3
Church Walk	F2
Clifton Road	C2–C3
Cobden Road	C3
Cowper Road	B3–C3
Cranworth Road	F2–F3
Crescent Road	C1–C2
Downview Road	A2–A3–A4
Eastcourt Road	D4
Eriswell Road	C1–C2
Eton Road	A4
Farncombe Road	F1–F2
Grafton Road	D2
Grand Avenue	A1–A2–A3–A4
Gratwicke Road	C1–C2
Guildford Road	A4–B4
Harrow Road	B4
Heene Road	B1–B2–B3–B4
Heene Terrace	B1
Heene Way	A2–B2
Henty Road	C4
High Street	E2
Homefield Road	F2–F3
Hythe Road	A1
King Edward Avenue	D4–E4–F4
Langton Road	D4
Lanfranc Road	B4
Lansdowne Road	A2–A3–B3–B2
Little High Street	E3
Liverpool Gardens	D2
Liverpool Road	D1–D2

Central Shoreham-by-Sea

Worthing

A mecca for bowls devotees, Worthing hosts both national and international competitions on the excellent greens at Beach House Park. Golf and sailing are popular pastimes, and more than adequate facilities exist for other sports.

Worthing became a fashionable resort in the 18th century and today it offers the visitor a pleasant mixture of Victorian buildings and areas of modern development: this is one of the major shopping centres of West Sussex, and several pleasant precincts and covered centres have been built. Brooklands Pleasure Park and a good range of shows in the summer season are another draw for visitors. Worthing Museum and Art Gallery has collections of costumes and toys as well as items of local interest, and exhibitions of arts and crafts are held here regularly. At Tarring, one mile from the town centre, a group of 15th-century cottages has been restored and now houses the Sussex Folklore Museum.

Shoreham has been the site of a port since Roman times, and by the early 14th century it had become a major shipbuilding town. Lying at the mouth of the River Adur, it still keeps up a thriving maritime life in the shape of a busy harbour and several yachting and sailing clubs. The Marlipins Museum, which explores the history of the area, concentrates on Shoreham's nautical connections.

Map labels (Worthing Area):

Coldwaltham · Watersfield · West Burton · Bury · Amberley · Houghton · North Stoke · South Stoke · Burpham · Wepham · Warningcamp · ARUNDEL · Poling · Lyminster · Wick · LITTLEHAMPTON · Rustington · East Preston · Angmering-on-Sea · Ferring · Angmering · Patching · Clapham · High Salvington · Durrington · Salvington · Broadwater · West Tarring · Goring-by-Sea · West Worthing · East Worthing · WORTHING · Findon Valley · Findon · North End · Washington · Heath Common · Wiston · Storrington · Cootham · Rackham · Abingworth · Ashington · B2133 · Steyning · Bramber · Upper Beeding · Small Dole · Henfield · Ashurst · SHOREHAM AIRPORT · Sompting · Lancing · Old Shoreham · SHOREHAM-BY-SEA · Kingston-by-Sea · SOUTHWICK · PORTSLADE-BY-SEA · HOVE · Aldrington · West Blatchington · Portslade Village · Hangleton · Mile Oak · Westdene · Pyecombe · Poynings · Fulking · Edburton · Woodmancote · Blackstone · Albourne · Hurstpierpoint · Hurst Wickham

Box denotes area covered by central plan

ENGLISH CHANNEL

SCALE 0 — 2 mls

Worthing Area

Longfellow Road	B3-C3	Stoke Abbott Road	D3	Beach Road	A1-B1	Riverside	B1
Lyndhurst Road	E2-F2	Sugden Road	F2-F3	Brighton Road	A1-A2, B2-C2	Riverside Road	B1-C1
Madeira Avenue	F1-F2	Surrey Street	C1	Brunswick Road	B2	Ropetackle	A2-A3
Manor Road	B1-B2	Sussex Road	E3	Buckingham Avenue	B4	Rope Walk	B3
Marine Parade	B1-C1-D1-E1	Tarring Road	A4-B4-C4-C3	Buckingham Road	B3-C3-C4	Rosslyn Avenue	C2-C3
Marine Place	E1	Tennyson Road	C2	Buckingham Street	A3-B3	Rosslyn Road	C3
Merton Road	F1	Teville Road	C4-D4-D3	Cheal Close	B1-C1	Ship Street	B2
Mill Road	A3-B3	The Broadway	E1	Church Street	B2	Southdown Road	B3
Montague Street	C1-D1	The Steyne	E1	Connaught Avenue	A3-A4	Swiss Gardens	A3-B3
Newland Road	D3-E3	Thorn Road	C1	Downsway	B4-C4	Tarmount Lane	B2
Norfolk Street	C3	Thurlow Road	F3	East Meadway	C1	The Avenue	B4
North Street	D3-E3-E2	Upper High Street	E2-E3	East Street	B2	The Close	B3
Oxford Road	D3-D4	Valencia Road	A4	Eastern Avenue	C2-C3	The Drive	C4
Park Avenue	F2-F3	Victoria Road	D2-D3	Erringham Road	B4	The Driveway	C4
Park Road	E1-E2-E3	Warwick Gardens	E2	Ferry Road	B1	The Marlinspike	C1
Pavilion Road	B4-C4	Warwick Road	E1	Freehold Street	A3	The Meadway	B1-C1
Portland Road	D1-D2	Warwick Street	E1	Gordon Avenue	B3-C3-C2	The Street	A4
Queens Road	C1	Wenban Road	D3	Gordon Road	B3-C3-C2	Upper Shoreham Road	A4-B4-C4
Railway Approach	D3-D4	West Buildings	C1	Greenacres	A4-B4-A4-A3	Victoria Road	A2-B2-B3
Richmond Road	B2-C2-D2	West Parade	A1-B1	Ham Road	B2-C2	West Street	B2-B3
Rowlands Road	A1-B1-C1	West Street	C1	Harbour Way	C1	Western Road	B2-B3
Rugby Road	A4-B4-B3	Westbourne Avenue	D4-E4	Havenside	A1	Windlesham Gardens	B3-B4
St Boltolph's Road	B3-B4	Westbrooke	C2-D2	Hebe Road	B3	Windlesham Road	B4-C4-C3
St Elmo Road	B4	Westcourt Road	C4-D4	High Street	B2		
St Mathew's Road	C3	Western Place	C1	John Street	B2		
St Michael's Road	A2-B2	Winchester Road	B2-C2	Kings Walk	A1		
St Valerie Road	A1-A2	Woodside Road	C4	Lower Beach Road	B1		
Sackville Crescent	F4	Wordsworth Road	B1-B2	Mardyke	A1		
Sackville Road	E4-F4	Wykeham Road	C2-C3	Middle Street	B2		
Salisbury Road	D2	York Road	E1	Mill Lane	B3-B4		
Sea View Road	A1			New Road	B2		
Seldon Road	F1-F2			Nicholas Drive	C3		
Shakespeare Road	C2-C3-C4			Norfolk Bridge	A2		
Shelley Road	B2-C2-D2-D1			Norman Crescent	C4		
South Street	A4	**Shoreham**		North Street	B2		
South Street	D1-E1			Old Fort Road	B1-C1		
Southey Road	B2-C2	Adur Avenue	A4-B4	Old Shoreham Road	A4-A3-A2-B2		
Southfarm Road	C4	Adur Road	A4-B4	Overmead	B3		
Stanley Road	E3	Beach Green	A1-B1	Oxen Avenue	B3-B4		
Station Road	D3-E3-E4-E3			Queens Place	B3		
Steyne Gardens	E1			Ravens Road	B3		

WORTHING
The Marine Parade and West Pier — now the largest town in West Sussex, Worthing was a small fishing village until Princess Amelia, youngest daughter of George III, set a new trend by holidaying here in 1798.

Yeovil

Home of the Westland helicopter and aircraft factory — as a result of which it suffered bomb damage in the Second World War — and six miles south of the Fleet Air Museum at Yeovilton, the market town of Yeovil is also known for its more homely glovemaking. There is a fine 14th-century church, and a collection of firearms and local interest items at Hendford Manor.

Sherborne Full of medieval buildings built in the golden Ham Hill stone, Sherborne has a magnificent, mainly 15th-century, abbey church. Of the town's two public schools, the 1550 boys' school occupies some of the abbey buildings, and the abbey gatehouse has a museum.

East of the town are two castles: a Norman structure which was partly destroyed after the Civil War, and the 'new' castle, a fine Elizabethan house built and occupied by Sir Walter Raleigh, and full of treasures.

Chard was the scene of one of Judge Jeffreys' Bloody Assizes, held in the courthouse (built 1590) here after the Monmouth Rebellion of 1685. The town's grammar school was founded in 1671, the Choughs Hotel is Elizabethan and the porticoed Town Hall dates back to 1834. All stand in the main street, from which streams flow north to the Bristol Channel and south to the English Channel — at 400ft (122m), this is the county's highest town.

78

Key to Town Plan and Area Plan

Town Plan

AA Recommended roads	
Restricted roads	
Other roads	
Buildings of interest	Library
Car Parks	P
Parks and open spaces	
Churches	†

Area Plan

A roads	
B roads	
Locations	Terry's Green ○
Urban area	

Street Index

Yeovil

Addlewell Lane	D1-D2
Beer Street	B2
Brunswick Street	C1-D1
Carisbrooke Gardens	B3
Clarence Street	C3
Crofton Avenue	D4-E4
Crofton Park	D4
Cromwell Road	F4
Earle Street	D3-E3
Eastland Road	E3-E4
Eastville	E3-E4
Goldcroft	D3-D4
Gordon Road	E4
Grass Royal	E4-F4
Grove Avenue	B3-B4
Hendford	C1-C2
Hendford Hill	B1-C1
High Street	C2-D2
Horsey Lane	B2-B1-C1
Huish	B3-C3
Ilchester Road	C4
King Street	D4-E4
Kingston	C3-C4
Legion Road	A4
Linden Road	A3-B3
Lysander Road	A1
Manor Road	C2
Market Street	D3
Matthews Road	E4-F4
Middle Street	D2-E2-E3
Mill Lane	D2
Mitchelmore Road	E4
Mount Pleasant	E4
Newton Road	E3-E2-F2-F1
North Lane	C3-D3
Old Station Road	E2
Orchard Street	B2-B3
Osborne Road	E2
Park Gardens	C3
Park Road	C3
Park Street	D1-D2
Penn Hill	D1-D2
Petters Way	C2
Preston Grove	A3-B3
Preston Road	A4-B4-C4
Princes Street	C3
Reckleford	C3-D3-E3
Richmond Road	B2-B3
Roping Road	C4-D4
St Andrews Road	A3-A4
St Michael's Avenue	F4
St Michael's Road	F4
St Thomas Cross	E4
Salthouse Lane	C2-C3
Seaton Road	A2-B2-B1
Sherborne Road	E3-F3-F4
South Street	C2-D2
Southville	E3-E4
South Western Terrace	E2
Sparrow Road	C4-D4
Stars Lane	D2-E2
Summerlands	A4
Summerleaze Park	A4
Swallowcliffe Gardens	C3-C4
The Avenue	D3-D4
The Park	B4-B3-C3
Vicarage Walk	D3
West Hendford	A1-B1-B2-C2
West Park	B3
West Street	B2-B3
Westfield Road	A4
Westland Road	A1-A2-B2
Westville	E4
Willow Road	B4

Chard

Ash Grove	A4-B4
Auckland Way	C1
Bath Street	A2-B2
Beckington Crescent	B1-C1
Bewley Court	A3
Boden Street	B2
Bonfire Close	A1
Bradfield Way	B2-C2-C1
Bubwith Road	C1-C2
Cedar Close	A4
Church Street	B1-B2
Combe Street	A3-B3-B2
Crimchard	A3-A4
Culverhayes	B1
Druids Walk	B4
Duck Lane	A2-B2
Dwelly Close	B2
East Street	C3
Elder Close	B4
Elm Street	B4
Fore Street	B2-B3
Forton Road	B1-C1
Furnham Road	C3-C4
Furzehill	C4
Glynswood	A4-B4-C4
Harvey Road	C1-C2
Helliers Close	A3
Helliers Road	A2-A3
High Street	A2-B2
Holyrood Street	B2
King Alfred Drive	B1
Larch Avenue	A4
Lordlease Lane	C1
Mill Lane	B2
Millfield	B2-C2
Mintons	A1
Mintons Orchard	A1
Montague Way	B1
Oak End Way	B4
Old Town	B2
Pine Avenue	B4
Ravensmead	B4
St Mary's Close	B1
Silver Street	B2-B3
Summerfields Road	A2-A1-B1

Tapstone Road	C3
Tatworth Road	B1
Thordun Park Drive	B4-C4
Touchstone Lane	A4
Victoria Avenue	C3-C4
Zembard Lane	A3-B3

Sherborne

Abbey Road	A2-B2-B3
Acreman Street	A2-A3
Back Lane	A3
Blackberry Lane	A4
Bristol Road	A4-B4
Cheap Street	B2-B3
Coldharbour	B4-C4
Coombe Road	A4
Digby Road	B1-B2
East Mill Lane	C2
Gas House Hill	B1
Green Hill	A3-B3-B4
Halfmoon Street	B2
Harbour Road	B4-C4
Harbour Way	B4
Hill House Close	C4
Horse Castle	A1-A2
Hospital Road	A3
Hound Street	B3
Kings Crescent	B4
Kings Road	A4-B4
Kitt Hill	A3
Long Street	B2-C2-C3
Ludbourne Road	B2-C2
Marston Road	A3-A4
New Road	B1-C1-C2-C3
Newell	B2
Newland	B3-C3
North Road	B3-B4
Oborne Road	C3
Ottery Lane	A1
Priestlands	A4
Richmond Green	A2-A3
Richmond Road	A2
St Swithins Road	B2-B3
South Street	B1-B2
The Avenue	C3-C4-B4-C4
The Green	A3-B3
Tinneys Lane	C3
Trendle Street	A2-B2
Westbury	A1-A2-B2
Wingfield Road	A1-A2
Wootton Grove	B4

SHERBORNE
The 'new' castle was built by Sir Walter Raleigh in 1594, and is said to be the place where a servant, horrified at the sight of smoke rising from his newfangled tobacco pipe, promptly doused him with ale to 'put out the fire'.

Post House Hotel

Airport Service Station

Gatwick Penta Hotel

Gatwick Moat House Hotel

River Mole

SITE FOR NEW NORTH TERMINAL (OPEN 1987)

Police Station

Control Barrier

General Aviation Terminal

N

Cargo Terminal

Barrier (Maintenance Vehicles only)

Cyclists only

Permit Holders Only

Road restricted to authorised vehicles

Petrol Station

BAA STAFF CAR PARK

M23 SPUR

AA 63

STAFF CAR PARK

BAA Head Office

Tourist information centre

Spectator Area

SATELLITE

Gatwick Airport Station

Terminal Building

Gatwick Hilton Hotel

Entrance and Exit

PIER 2

Terminal Entrance

3

2

1

COACH PARK

MULTI-STOREY CAR PARKS

PIER 1

Cargo Terminal No2

LONG TERM CAR PARK

RUNWAY

RUNWAY

PERIMETER

ROAD

MAINTENANCE AREA

Control Barrier

Scale

yds 0   220   440
mtrs 0   200   400

Emergency Gate

Gatwick Concorde Hotel

Helicopter Base

INDUSTRIAL ESTATE

A23

INDUSTRIAL EST

Gatwick Airport

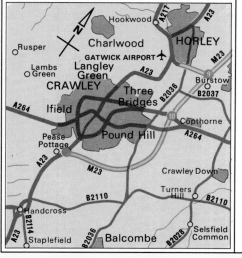

Hookwood

Rusper

Charlwood

HORLEY

GATWICK AIRPORT ✈

Lambs Green

Langley Green

CRAWLEY

Three Bridges

Burstow

Copthorne

Ifield

Pease Pottage

Pound Hill

Crawley Down

Handcross

Turners Hill

Staplefield

Balcombe

Selsfield Common

Gatwick is London's second busiest airport, coming second only to Heathrow. Well situated near the new town of Crawley, West Sussex, for easy access via the A23 and M23 London to Brighton motorway, it also has its own adjoining British Rail mainline railway station. Fast 15-minute frequency trains make a link 24 hours a day between Victoria Station and Gatwick, and a link is also provided to the capital by a Green Line Coach service. Coach connections to Heathrow and Luton, are available.

Lying on the edge of the North Downs, this has been the site of an airport since 1936. It was taken over by the Air Ministry, which established a training school for RAF pilots on the site in 1937. Wartime saw Gatwick's expansion into an RAF station of major importance, so much so that it had to be extended to take in the nearby racecourse. After the war, it went over to commercial use, but was only opened as an international airport in 1958, after extensive modernisation. At that time, it was hailed as the most advanced airport in Europe, with its linking of road, rail and air facilities.

Today this busy air traffic centre is used by most major airlines and by charter services of other airline companies, as well as being open in case of need to aircraft diverted from Heathrow. Passengers travelling between the two airports of Gatwick and Heathrow can also enjoy the service of rapid helicopter flights from one to the other. This helicopter airlink is run daily and takes only about quarter of an hour.

A spectators' viewing area, signposted through the International Arrivals section, allows visitors to watch the ever-changing panorama of an important international airport in action. A small fee is charged for this. The viewing area is open daily until dusk, and includes car parking facilities. Three linked multi-storey car parks and an open air car park are also provided for travellers and other visitors to the airport.

Several bars and eating places catering for different tastes have been established within the airport, and can be found on the 'catering level' above the international arrivals hall.

London

AREA MAPS ARE INDICATED IN BOLD.

Barking

A flourishing fishing industry operating from the Town Quay was the mainstay of Barking until well into the 19th century, when the coming of the railways and easy access to the east coast ports brought about its decline. The area has since undergone a good deal of industrial development but Barking still has a number of pleasant parks, notably Barking Park, which has a miniature railway and a large open air swimming pool. Still to be seen are the remains of Barking Abbey (founded in the 7th century and focus of the original settlement), Eastbury House, which dates from the 16th century, and the 13th-century Parish Church of St Margaret, where Captain Cook, the explorer, was married in 1762.

East Ham's Central Park is the scene of the colourful Town Show staged by the Borough of Newham each year. Dating back to Roman times, this ancient parish saw heavy development during the late 19th century, when most of the local industry was centred around the nearby docks.

Stratford Controversial new productions are the speciality of the Victorian Theatre Royal, a local landmark near the modern shopping centre. Site of a Roman fording of the River Lea, Stratford also has the Passmore Edwards Museum, which was built to house the collections of the Essex Field Club and now deals with local history and archaeology.

Key to Town Plan and Area Plan

Town Plan

AA Recommended roads	▬▬
Other roads	▭▭
Restricted roads	- - -
Buildings of interest	School ▢
Churches	✝
Car Parks	P
Parks and open spaces	▢
BR and	
Underground Stations	⊕
One way streets	←

Area Plan

A roads	▬▬
B roads	▬▬
Stations	Woodside ⊕
Borough boundary	- - -

Street Index with Grid Reference

Barking

Abbey Road	A3-A2-B2-B1
Aldersey Gardens	C4-D4
Alfreds Gardens	D1-E1
Bamford Road	B4
Barking By-Pass	D1-E1-F1-F2
Beccles Drive	E4
Blake Avenue	E2-F2
Boundary Road	B1-C1
Broadway	B2
Buller Road	D3-D4
Cecil Avenue	C3-C4
Charlton Crescent	E1-F1
Church Road	B4
Clare Gardens	F4
Cowbridge Lane	A3-B3
Cranbourne Road	C2-D2
Cranleigh Gardens	C4
Dawson Avenue	E3-F3
Denham Way	E2
Devon Road	D2-E2
Digby Road	E3
Eastbury Square	E2
East Street	B2-B3-C3
Edgefield Avenue	F3-F4
Eldred Road	D2
Essex Road	C3-D3-D2
Faircross Avenue	B4-C4
Fanshawe Avenue	B4-C4
Felton Road	D1-E1
Fresh Wharf Road	A1-B1
Gascoigne Road	B2-B1-C1
George Street	B3
Glenny Road	B4-C4
Gordon Road	D2
Greatfields Road	D1-D2
Harpour Road	B4
Harrow Road	D2-E2
Harts Lane	A4-B4-B3
Hertford Road	A2-A3
Highbridge Road	A1-A2
Howard Road	C1-C2-D2
Hulse Avenue	D4-E4-E3
Hurstbourne Gardens	D4-E4
Jackson Road	D1-D2
James Street	B3
Keith Road	D1
Kennedy Road	D1-D2
Keir Hardie Way	F3
King Edwards Road	C2-C1-D1
Lambourne Road	E2-E3
Lancaster Avenue	D2-D3
Levett Road	D4
Linton Road	B3
London Road	A2-A3-B3
Longbridge Road	C3-C4-D4
Loxford Road	A4-B4
Lyndhurst Gardens	D4-E4
Manor Road	E4-F4
Maybury Road	F1
Meadow Road	F3
Melford Avenue	E4
Melish Court	E1-E2
Morley Road	C2-D2
Movers Lane	D1-D2
Netherfield Gardens	C4-D4-D3
Norfolk Road	D3
North Street	B2-B3
Oakley Avenue	F4
Park Avenue	B4-C4
Perth Road	C1-D1
Priory Road	C3
Queens Road	B3-B4
Ripple Road	B3-C3-C2-D2-E2-F2
River Road	D1-E1
Rosslyn Road	D3-C4-D4
St Annes	B2-C2-C1
St Awdrys Road	C3-C2-D2
St Erkenwald Road	C2-C3
St Johns Road	D1-E1
St Margarets	C2
St Marys	C1
St Pauls Road	B2-C2
Sandringham Drive	E4
Salisbury Avenue	C3-D3-D4-E4
Sherwood Gardens	C4-C3-D3
Shirley Gardens	D4-E4
Sisley Road	E2-F2
Somerby Road	C3-C4
Sparsholt Road	D2-E2-E1
Strathfield Gardens	C4-D4
Stratton Drive	E4-F4
Sterry Road	E2
Suffolk Road	C3-D3-D2
Sunningdale Avenue	C2-C3
Surrey Road	D2-D3
Sutton Road	D1-E1
Tanner Street	B4
The Drive	E4-F4
The Shaftesburys	B1-C1
Thornhill Gardens	E3
Thorpe Road	C3

Town Quay	A2-B2
Tresham Road	E3
Upney Lane	E4-E3-F3-F2
Victoria Road	A4-B4
Wakering Road	B4-B3-C3
Wedderburn Road	D2
West Bank	A2
Westbury Road	C2
Westrow Drive	E4-F4
Wheelers Cross	C1
Whiting Avenue	A3-B3
Wilmington Gardens	C4-D4-D3-E3-E4

Stratford

Abbey Lane	A1
Abbey Road	B1
Aileen Walk	C2
Albert Square	C4
Aldworth Road	B2
Alma Street	A4-B4
Angel Lane	B3
Ash Road	C4
Atherton Road	C3-C4
Bridge Road	A2-B2-B1
Bridge Terrace	A2-B2
Broadway	B2-B3
Burford Road	A2-B2-B1
Buxton Road	B4-C4
Caistor Park Road	C1
Carnarvon Road	C3-C4
Carpenters Road	A1-A2
Cedars Road	C3
Chandos Road	A4-B4
Chant Street	B2
Chobham Road	A4-B4
Church Street	B1-C1
Cruickshank Road	C4
David Street	C2
Densham Road	B1-B2-C2
Devenay Road	C2
Earlham Grove	C4
Evesham Road	C2
Fairland Road	C3
Farringdon Road	B2-C2
Forest Lane	B4-C4
Francis Street	B4
Geere Road	C1-C2
Glenavon Road	B3-C3-C2
Gibbins Road	A2
Great Eastern Road	A2-A3-B3
Grove Crescent Road	B3
Gurney Road	B4-C4
Ham Park Road	C2-C3
Harberson Road	C1
Hartland Road	C2
Heaton Place	A4
Henniker Road	A4-B4
High Street	A1-A2
Idmiston Road	C4
John Street	C1
Jupp Road	A2
Jupp Road West	A1-A2
Keogh Road	B3-C3-C4
Leyton Road	A4-A3-B3
Leytonstone Road	B4

Livingstone Road	A1
Louise Road	C3-C4
McGrath Road	C3-C4
Major Road	A4
Maneby Grove	B3
Maneby Street	B3-C3
Manor Road	C1
Maryland Park	B4
Maryland Road	B4
Maryland Street	B4
Meath Road	C1
Mortham Street	B1
New Plaistow Road	B1-C1
Paul Street	B1-B2
Plaistow Road	C1
Portway	C2
Richford Road	C1-C2
Rokeby Street	B1-B2
Romford Road	B3-C3
St James Road	C4
Sandal Street	B1
Skiers Street	B1
Stephen's Road	B1-C1
Tavistock Road	C3
Temple Mill Lane	A4
Tennyson Road	B2-B3
The Green	C3
The Grove	B3
Union Street	A1
Vaughan Road	C3
Vicarage Lane	C2-C3
Victoria Street	B2
Waddington Road	B3-B4
Waddington Street	B3-B4
Warton Road	A1
Water Lane	B4-B3-C3
West Ham Lane	B1-B2
Willis Road	C1
Windmill Lane	B3
Wise Road	A1

East Ham

Aintree Avenue	A2-A3
Altmore Avenue	C2-C3-C4
Arthur Road	C1
Barking Road	A2-B2-C2
Bartle Avenue	B1-B2
Basil Avenue	A1
Bedford Road	C2-C3
Bendish Road	B4
Bridge Road	C4
Burgess Road	B4-C4
Caledon Road	B3-C3
Campbell Road	B2-B3
Caulfield Road	B3-C3
Central Park Road	A1-B1-B2
Cheltenham Gardens	A1
Clements Road	B4-C4
Colvin Road	A4-B4-B3
Cotswold Gardens	A1
Ernald Avenue	A2-A1-B1
Eversleigh Road	A4
Flanders Road	B1-C1
Friars Road	A2-A3
Geoffrey Gardens	A1

Gillett Avenue	A1-A2
Grangewood Street	A3
Grosvenor Road	A3
Haldane Road	A1
Hall Road	C2-C3
Harrow Road	B3-B4
Hartley Avenue	A2-A3
Heigham Road	A4-B4
Henniker Gardens	A1
Henry Road	B2
High Street North	B2-B3-B4
High Street South	B1-B2
Hockley Avenue	A1-A2
Holme Road	B3
Howard Road	C1
Katherine Road	A2-A3-A4
Kempton Road	B3-C3
Keppel Road	B4-B3-C3-C2
Kimberley Avenue	A1-A2
Ladysmith Avenue	A1-A2
Lathom Road	B4-C4
Latimer Avenue	C2-C3
Lawrence Road	A4-B4
Lloyd Road	B2-C2
Mafeking Avenue	A1-A2
Malvern Road	A3
Market Street	B1-C1
Melbourne Road	C1-C2
Milton Avenue	A4-B4
Montpelier Gardens	A1
Napier Road	C1-C2
Navarre Road	B2
Nelson Street	B2-C2
Norfolk Road	C2-C3
Oakfield Road	A3-B3
Outram Road	A3-A4-B4
Phashet Grove	A4
Poulett Road	B2-C2
Pulleyns Avenue	A1-B1
Rancliffe Road	A1-B1
St Barts Road	B2
St Bernards Road	A2-A3
St Johns Road	A2-B2
Shoebury Road	C4
Sibley Grove	B4
Skeffington Road	B3-C3
Southend Road	B4-C4
Southchurch Road	B1-C1
Spencer Road	A3-A4
Stamford Road	A3-B3
Streatfield Avenue	C2-C3
Talbot Road	C1-C2
Thorpe Road	B3-C3
Tilbury Road	B1-C1
Victoria Avenue	A4
Wakefield Street	A3-B3
Wellington Road	C1-C2
Winter Avenue	B2-B3

Barnet

Immortalised as the Cockney rhyming slang for 'hair', Barnet Fair started in the Middle Ages and is still held every year in September at Brent Lodge Farm, Mays Lane.

This was a fashionable residential area as early as the 18th century, and after the extension of the main line and underground railways in the late 19th and early 20th centuries, it developed into an important London borough. Long before this, its position on the Great North Road had made Barnet a popular staging post for coaches, and the High Street probably dates back to the 15th century. The Barnet Museum in Wood Street has an interesting local history collection.

Edgware lies on the line of Watling Street, the major Roman road which is roughly paralleled by the M1. Now mostly residential, Edgware was also at one time an important staging post. Several old buildings in the High Street date from that period, notably the White Hart, a 17th-century inn which has retained its covered wagon-way.

Finchley kept its country air until the late 19th century when it was heavily built on. The Bishop of London owned an extensive estate in this area during the 14th century, and despite intensive modernisation, Finchley still has several interesting quarters. The old parish church is in the Church End area.

BARNET
The Parish Church of St James, Friern Barnet, on the eastern side of the borough. Although part of London, Barnet reaches out into open country and still has distinct village communities.

Key to Town Plan

AA Recommended roads
Other roads
Restricted roads
Buildings of interest   Hospital
Car Parks
Parks and open spaces
One Way Streets
Stations

Key to Area Plan

A roads
B roads
Locations   Newton○
Urban area
Borough boundary

STREET INDEX- with grid reference

Bromley

Aldermary Road	C3-C4
Aylesbury Road	B3-C1
Babbacombe Road	C4
Beaconsfield Road	F1
Beckenham Lane	A3-B3
Beechfield Road	E2-E3
Bickley Road	F2-F3
Bird-in-Hand Lane	F2
Bishop Avenue	C4
Blyth Road	B3-B4
Brackenhill Road	B3
Bromley Avenue	A4-B4
Bromley Gardens	B2
Bromley Road	A3
Canon Road	E2-F2

Cedar Road	E3
Celtic Avenue	A1
Chistlehurst Road	F3
Church Road	A2
Church Road	B2-B3-C3
Clarence Road	F1-F2
College Road	C3-C4
Crescent Road	C4
Cromwell Road	C1
Cumberland Road	A1-B1
Durham Avenue	B1
Durham Road	B1
East Street	C3
Elmfield Road	C1-C2
Ethelbert Road	C2
Farnaby Road	A4-A3-B3
Farwig Lane	B4-C4
Forde Avenue	D2
Freelands Road	D3-D4
Freelds Grove	D4
Glanville Road	D1-E1
Glassmill Lane	B2
Glebe Road	C4
Godwin Road	E1
Grasmere Road	B4
Green Close	A2
Gundolph Road	E1
Hammelton Road	B4-C4
Harwood Avenue	C3-D3
Hawes Road	C4-C4
Hayes Road	C1
Henville Road	D3-D4
High Street	B3-C3-C2-C1
Highland Road	B3-B4
Hill Brow	F3-F4
Hillside Road	B2
Holligrave Road	C4
Holwood Road	C2
Homefield Road	D3-D4
Homesdale Road	E1-F1-F2
Horley Road	C4-D4
Kingswood Road	A1-A2
Landowne Road	C4-D4

Bromley

Birthplace of H G Wells, Bromley is thought by some to be one of the most favoured residential areas to the south of London. It has an abundance of trees and parks, and even in the centre, Queens Garden and Church House Gardens form quiet oases. In spite of development this century, Bromley has kept many of its older buildings, Bromley Palace and Bromley College

among them. The house in which H G Wells was born no longer stands, but a plaque marks its site in the High Street. At Norman Park, Bromley also boasts an excellent all-weather running track.

Beckenham Development in the 1920s and 1930s left few of the older buildings standing except in a small area near the High Street, but Beckenham's tree-lined roads and numerous parks are compensation for this. Kelsey Park, in the town centre, is a beautiful expanse of woods, lawns,

flowers and a stream.

Orpington's history can be traced back to the Stone Age, but ironically it was the last of the major areas of the borough to be developed. When it came, in the 1930s and later, development included such innovations as The Walnuts, a town centre shopping precinct, Civic Centre and sports hall. Reminders of the town's past still survive, and the London Borough of Bromley Priory Museum, in Church Hill, has interesting exhibits.

Central London

Key to Town Plan

Town Plan

- AA Recommended roads
- Restricted roads
- Other roads
- Buildings of interest — Cinema ▣
- Car Parks — P
- Churches — †
- Parks and open spaces
- Underground Stations — ⊖
- One Way Streets — →

Street Index with Grid Reference

Central London

Street	Grid
Abingdon Street	G3-G4
Adams Row	D6-E6
Albany Road	K1-L1
Albemarle Street	E6-E5-F5-F6
Alberta Street	J2
Albion Street	C6
Aldridge Street	L2
Alderney Street	E2-F2-F1
Aldford Street	D5-D6
Aldgate Street	J7-K7-K6
Aldwych	H6-H7-I7
Allsop Place	C8-D8
Alsey Street	C2
Amelia Street	J2-K2
Appold Street	L8-L9
Argyll Street	E7-F7
Ashmill Street	B8-C8
Astell Street	C1-C2
Atterbury Street	G2
Aylesford Street	G1
Baker Street	C8-D8-D7
Balcombe Street	C8
Baldwins Gardens	I8
Balfour Street	K2-K3
Bankside	J6-K6
Banner Street	K9
Barbican	K9
Basil Street	C3-C4
Basinghall Street	K7-K8
Bath Terrace	K3-K4
Baylis Road	I4
Bayswater Road	A6-B6-C6
Beauchamp Place	C3
Beak Street	F6
Bear Lane	J5
Beaufort Street	A1-B1
Bedford Avenue	G8
Bedford Place	G8
Bedford Square	F8-G8
Bedford Walk	G9
Beech Street	J8-K8
Belgrave Place	D3
Belgrave Road	E3-E2-F2
Belgrave Square	D3-D4
Bell Street	B8-C8
Bell Yard	I7
Belvedere Street	H4-H5
Berkeley Square	E6
Berkeley Street	C7-D7
Berkeley Street	E5-E6
Berners Street	F7-F8
Berwick Street	F6-F7
Birdcage Walk	F4-G4
Bishopsgate	L7-L8
Blackfriars Bridge	J6
Blackfriars Road	J4-J5
Black Prince Road	H2-I2
Blandford Street	D7
Blomfield Road	A8
Bloomsbury Street	G7-G8
Bloomsbury Way	G8-H8
Bolsover Street	E8-E9
Bolton Street	E5
Borough High Street	K4-K5-J5
Borough Road	J4-K4
Boswell Street	H8
Bourdon Street	E6
Bourne Street	D2
Bouverie Street	I7
Bowling Green Lane	I9
Bow Street	H7
Braganza Street	J1-J2
Brandon Street	K2-K3
Bray Place	C2
Bressenden Place	E3-F3
Brewer Street	F6
Brick Street	E5
Bridge Street	G4-H4
Britten Street	B1-C1
Broadley Street	B8
Broadwick Street	F6-F7
Brompton Road	C2-B2-B3-C3-C4
Brook Drive	I3-J3
Brook Street	D6-E6-E7
Browning Street	K2
Brown Street	C7
Brunswick Square	G9-H9
Bruton Lane	E6
Bruton Street	E6
Bryanston Square	C7
Buckingham Gate	E3-E4-F4-F3
Buckingham Palace Road	E2-E3
Bunhill Row	K8-K9
Cadiz Street	K1-K2
Cadogan Gardens	C2-D2
Cadogan Lane	D3
Cadogan Place	D3
Cadogan Square	C2-C3
Cadogan Street	C2
Cale Street	B1-B2-C2
Calthorpe Street	H9-I9
Cambridge Street	E2-F2-F1
Cannon Street	J7-K7-K6-L6
Cardigan Street	I1-I2
Carey Street	H7-I7
Carlisle Lane	I3-I4
Carlisle Place	F3
Carlyle Square	B1
Carnaby Street	F6-F7
Carter Lane	J7-K7
Carter Road	J1-K1
Castle Lane	F3-F4
Cathcart Road	A1
Cavendish Square	E7
Caxton Street	F4
Chancery Lane	I7-I8
Chandos Place	G6
Chandos Street	E7-E8
Chapel Street	D4-E4
Chapel Street	B7-B8-C8
Charing Cross Road	G6-G7
Charles Street	E5-E6
Charles II Street	F5-F6-G6
Charlotte Street	F8
Charlwood Street	F1-F2
Charter Road	J1
Charterhouse Street	J8
Chatham Street	K3-L3
Cheapside	K7
Chelsea Bridge Road	D2-D1-E1
Chelsea Manor Street	C1
Chelsea Square	C1
Chesham Place	D3
Chester Row	D2
Chester Square	D3-E3-E2
Chester Street	D3-D4-E4-E3
Chester Terrace	A6-A7
Chilworth Street	A7
Chiswell Street	K8-L8
Christchurch Street	C1
Church Street	B8
Churchill Gardens Road	E1-F1
City Road	K9-L9-L8
Clabon Mews	C2-C3
Clarendon Street	E2-F2
Clarges Street	E5
Claverton Street	F1
Clayton Street	I1
Clerkenwell Road	I8-I9-J9
Cleveland Square	A6
Cleveland Street	E9-E8-F8
Cleveland Terrace	A7
Clifford Street	E6-F6
Clifton Gardens	A8
Clifton Street	L8-L9
Clink Street	K5-K6
Clipstone Street	E8-F8
Cock Lane	J8
Coin Street	I5
Coleman Street	K7-K8
Cole Street	K4
Compton Street	J9
Conduit Street	E6-F6
Congreve Street	L2-L3
Connaught Street	B6-B7-C7-C6
Constitution Hill	E4-F4
Conway Street	E8-F8
Cook's Road	J1
Copperfield Street	J5-K5
Cork Street	E6-F6
Cornhill	K7-L7
Cornwall Road	I4-I5
Cosser Street	I3
County Street	K3
Courtenay Street	I1-I2
Courtfield Road	A2
Covent Garden	G6-H6-H7
Coventry Street	F6-G6
Cowan Street	L1
Cowcross Street	J8
Crampton Street	J2-K2
Cranley Gardens	A2-A1-B1
Craven Hill	A6
Craven Terrace	A6
Crawford Street	C7-C8-D8
Cresswell Place	A1-A2
Cromwell Road	A2-A3-B3
Cullcross Street	D6
Cumberland Market	E2-E1-F1
Curtain Road	L9
Curzon Street	D5-E5-E6
Dante Road	J2-J3
Darwin Street	L3
Date Street	K2
Davies Street	E6-E7
Dawes Street	L2
Deacon Way	K3
Dean Street	F7
Decima Street	L4
Delaune Street	J1-J2
Denbigh Street	F1-F2
Devere Gardens	A3-A4
Deverell Street	K3-L3
Devonshire Street	D8-E8
Doddington Grove	J1
Dolben Street	J5
Dolphin Square	F1
Dorset Street	C7-C8-D8
Doughty Street	H9
Douglas Street	F2-G2
Dovehouse Street	B1
Dover Street	E5-E6
Downing Street	G5
Draycott Avenue	C2
Draycott Place	C2
Drayton Gardens	A1-A2
Drummond Street	E9-F9
Dufferin Street	K9
Duke Street	D7
Durham Street	H1
Dury Lane	G7-H7
Eastbourne Terrace	A7
East Castle Street	F7
Eastcheap	L6
East Street	K2-L2
Eaton Place	D3
Eaton Square	D3-E3
Eaton Terrace	D2
Eccleston Place	E2-E3
Eccleston Square	E2
Eccleston Street	E3
Ebury Bridge Road	D1-E1-E2
Ebury Street	D2-E2-E3
Edgware Road	A8-B8-B7-C7-C6
Egerton Terrace	C3
Eldon Street	L8
Elizabeth Street	D3-D2-E2
Elliots Row	J2
Elm Park Gardens	A1-B1
Elm Park Road	A1-B1
Elsted Street	L2
Elvaston Place	A3
Elystan Place	C2
Elystan Street	B2-C2
Emerson Street	K5-K6
Endell Street	G7-H7
Ennismore Gardens	B3-B4
Epworth Street	L9
Erasmus Street	G2
Euston Road	E9-F9
Evelyn Gardens	A1-B1
Ewer Street	J5
Exhibition Road	B3-B4
Exmouth Market	I9
Falmouth Road	K3-K4
Fann Street	J8-J9-K9-K8
Faringdon Road	I9
Farm Street	D6-E6
Farringdon Road	I8-J8
Farringdon Street	J7-J8
Fenchurch Street	L6-L7
Fielding Street	K1
Finsbury Circus	L8
Finsbury Square	L8-L9
First Street	C2-C3
Fisherton Street	A9-B9-B8
Fitzalen Street	I8
Fitzroy Street	F8-F9
Fleet Street	I7-J7
Fleming Road	J1
Flint Street	L2
Flood Street	C1
Floral Street	G6-G7-H7
Foley Street	E8-F8
Fore Street	K8
Foulis Terrace	B8-B9
Frampton Street	B8-B9
Frazer Street	I4
Frith Street	G7
Fulham Road	A1-B1-B2
Gee Street	C7-D7
George Street	C7-D7
Gerrard Street	G6
Gilbert Road	I2-I3-J3
Gilbert Street	D7-D8-E8
Gillingham Street	E2-F2-F3
Gilston Road	A1
Giltspur Street	J7-J8
Glasshouse Walk	H2
Glebe Place	B1
Gloucester Place	C9-C8-C7-D7
Gloucester Road	A2-A3
Gloucester Square	B6-B7
Gloucester Street	E1-F1-F2
Gloucester Terrace	A6-A7
Goodge Street	F8
Golden Lane	K8-K9
Gordon Square	F9-G9
Gordon Street	F9
Gossfield Street	E8-F8
Goswell Road	J8-J9
Gough Street	H9-I9
Gower Street	F9-F8-G8
Gracechurch Street	L6-L7
Grafton Way	F9
Gray's Inn Road	H9-I9-I8
Great Castle Street	E7-F7
Great Cumberland Place	C6-C7
Great Dover Street	K4-K3-L3
Great George Street	G4
Great Guildford Street	J5-K5
Great Marlborough Street	F7
Great Ormond Street	H8-H9
Great Peter Street	F3-G3
Great Portland Street	E7-E8-E9
Great Russel Street	F7-F8-G8
Great Smith Street	G3-G4
Great Suffolk Street	J4-J5
Great Titchfield Street	E8-E7-F7
Greek Street	G7
Greencoat Place	F3
Green Street	D6
Gresham Street	K7
Greville Street	I8
Greycoat Street	F3
Grosvenor Gardens	E3
Grosvenor Place	D4-E4-E3
Grosvenor Road	E1-F1-G1
Grosvenor Square	D6-E6
Grosvenor Street	D6-E6
Guildford Street	G9-H9
Guy Street	L4
Halkin Street	D4
Hallam Street	E8
Hall Place	A8-B8
Hamilton Place	D4-D5-E5-E4
Hanover Square	E7
Hans Crescent	C3-C4
Hans Place	C3
Hans Road	C3
Harewood Avenue	C8-C9
Harley Ford Road	H1
Harley Street	D8-E8-E7
Harper Road	K3-K4
Harriet Walk	C4-D4-D3
Harrington Gardens	A2
Hasker Street	C2-C3
Hatfields	I5-J5
Hatton Garden	I8
Hayle Street	I8
Haymarket	F6-G6-G5
Hay's Mews	E5-E6
Henrietta Place	E7
Hercules Road	I3-I4
Hertford Street	D5-E5
High Holborn	G7-H7-H8-I8
Hill Street	E5-E6
Holbein Place	D2
Holborn	H8-I8
Holborn Circus	I8
Holborn Viaduct	I8-J8-J7
Holland Street	J5-J6
Hollywood Road	A1
Holyoake Road	J2-J3
Hopton Street	J5-J6
Horseferry Road	F3-G3
Horse Guards Road	G4-G5
House Street	E8-F8
Howick Place	F3
Howland Street	F8
Hugh Street	E2
Huntley Street	F8-F9
Hyde Park Crescent	B7
Hyde Park Gate	A3-A4
Hyde Park Square	B6
Hyde Park Street	B6-B7
Innfields	H7-I7
Ivor Place	C8-C9
Ixworth Place	B2-C2
James Street	D7
James Street	F6
Jermyn Street	F5-F6
Jockey's Fields	H8
John Adams Street	G6-H6
John Islip Street	G2-G3
John Street	F6
John Street	J9
Jubilee Place	C1-C2
Kempsford Road	I2-J2
Kennington Lane	I2-J2
Kennington Park	I1-J1
Kennington Park Road	I1-J1-J2
Kennington Road	I1-I2-I3
Kensington Road	A4-B4
King Charles Street	G4
King James Street	J4
Kingsgate Street	L1-L2
Kingly Street	F6-F7
King's Road	B1-C1-C2-D2-D3-E3
King Street	F5
Kingsway	H7-H8
King William Street	K7-L7-L6
Kipling Street	L4-L5
Knightsbridge	B4-C4-D4
Lambeth Bridge	G3-H3
Lambeth High Street	H2-H3
Lambeth Palace Road	H3-H4
Lambeth Road	H3-I3-I4-J4
Lambeth Walk	H2
Lanark Gate	A9
Lancaster Gate	A6
Langham Place	E7-E8
Langle Lane	H1
Lant Street	K4
Larcom Street	K2
Launceston Place	A3
Lavington Street	J5
Lawn Lane	H1
Law Street	L3-L4
Leadenhall Street	L7
Leather Lane	I8-I9
Leather Market Street	L4
Leicester Square	G6
Leinster Gardens	A6-A7
Lennox Gardens	C3
Leonard Street	L9
Lincoln's	H7-H8
Lisle Street	G6
Lisson Grove	B8-C8
Liverpool Grove	K1-K2
Lodge Road	B9
Lollard Street	H3-I3-I2
Lombard Street	K7-L7
London Bridge	L5-L6
London Road	J2-J3
London Wall	K8-L8-L7
Long Acre	G6-G7-H7
Longford Street	E9
Long Lane	J8
Long Lane	K4-L4
Lorrimore Road	J1
Lower Belgrave Street	E3
Lower Marsh	I4
Lower Sloane Street	D2
Lower Thames Street	L6
Lowndes Square	D4
Lowndes Street	D3
Ludgate Hill	J7
Lupus Street	E1-F1
Lyall Street	D3
Maddox Street	E6-E7
Maida Avenue	A8
Maiden Lane	G6-H6
Malet Street	F9-G8-G9
Manciple Street	K4-L4
Manresa Road	B1
Manor Place	J1-J2-K2
Marchmont Street	G9
Marcia Road	L2
Margaret Street	E7-F7
Markham Street	C1-C2
Marshall Street	F6-F7
Marshalsea Road	K4-K5
Marsham Street	G2-G3
Marylebone High Street	D7-D8
Marylebone Lane	D7-E7
Marylebone Road	B8-C8-D8-D9-E9
Mecklenburgh Square	H9
Medway Street	F3
Melton Street	F9
Merrow Street	K1-L1-L2
Methley Street	I1-I2
Milk Street	K7
Millbank	G2-G3
Mint Street	J4
Monk Street	G3
Monmouth Street	G6-G7
Montague Place	G8
Montagu Street	C7
Montpelier Street	C3-C4
Moorfields	K8
Moore Street	C2-C3
Moorgate	K7-K8-L8
Morecambe Street	K2
Moreton Place	F2
Mortimer Street	E7-F7-F8
Morley Street	I4
Morpeth Street	F3
Motcomb Street	D3-D4
Mount Row	E6
Munton Road	K3
Museum Street	G7-G8
Neal Street	G7
New Bond Street	E6-E7
New Bridge Street	J6-J7
New Cavendish Street	D8-E8-F8
New Change	K7
New Compton Street	G7
New Kent Road	J3-K3-K4
Newcomen Street	K5-L5
Newgate Street	J7
Newington Butts	J2-J3
Newington Causeway	J3-J4-K4
New North Street	G7-G8
Newman Street	F7-F8
New Oxford Street	G7-G8
Newton Street	H7-H8
Nine Elms Lane	G1
Norfolk Crescent	B7-C7
Norfolk Square	B7
North Carriage Drive	B6-C6
North Gower Street	F9
Northington Street	H9-I9
Northumberland Avenue	G5-H5
North Row	D6
Old Bailey	J7
Old Bond Street	E6-E5-F5
Old Broad Street	L7-L8
Old Brompton Road	A1-A2-B2
Old Compton Street	F6-G6-G7
Old Marylebone Road	B7-C7-C8
Old Park Lane	D5-E5
Old Pye Street	F3
Old Street	J9-K9-L9
Olney Road	J1-K1
Onslow Gardens	A2-B2
Onslow Square	B2
Oswin Street	G3
Ontario Street	J3-J4
Orb Street	K2
Orchardson Street	B8-B9
Orchard Street	D7
Outer Circle	C9-D9-D8-D9-E9
Oval Way	H1
Oxford Street	D6-D7-E7-F7
Paddington Street	D8
Page Street	G3
Pages Walk	L3
Palace Gate	A3-A4
Palace Street	E4-F4-F3
Pall Mall	F5-G5
Pardoner Street	L4
Paris Garden	J5
Park Crescent	E8-E9
Park Lane	C6-D6-D5-D6
Park Road	B9-C9
Park Street	J5-J6
Parry Street	G1-H1
Paul Street	L9
Pavilion Road	C4-C3-D3-D2
Pearman Street	I4
Pelham Crescent	B2
Pelham Street	B2
Penfold Street	B8
Penrose Street	K1-J1-K1-K2
Penton Place	J2-K2
Piccadilly	E4-E5-F5-F6
Pilgrimage Street	K4
Pimlico Road	D2-E2
Pocock Street	J4-J5
Poland Street	F7
Pond Place	B2
Ponsonby Place	G2
Pont Street	C3-D3
Porchester Terrace	A6
Portland Place	E8
Portland Street	K2-K1-L1
Portman Square	D7
Portman Street	D6-D7
Portugal Street	H7
Poultry	K7
Praed Street	A7-B7
Prince's Gardens	B3-B4
Queens Gardens	A6
Queen's Gate	A3-A4
Queens Gate Gardens	A3
Queen's Gate Terrace	A3
Queen Square	G8-G9-H9-H8
Queen Victoria Street	J7-J6-K6-K7
Radnor Walk	C1
Randolph Avenue	A8-A9
Rathbone Place	F7-F8
Rawlings Street	C2
Redburn Street	C1
Redcross Way	K5
Red Lion Street	H8
Reeves Mews	D6
Regency Street	G2-G3
Regent Street	E7-F7-F6-F5-G6
Renfrew Road	J2-J3
Rivington Street	L9
Rochester Row	F2-F3
Rockingham Street	J3-K3
Rodney Road	K3-K2-L2
Roland Gardens	A1-A2
Romilly Street	G6-G7
Rossmore Road	B8-B9-C9
Roupell Street	I5-J5
Royal Avenue	C1-C2
Royal Hospital Road	C1-D1-D2
Royal Street	H4-I4
Rupert Street	F6-G6
Russell Square	G8-G9
Rutland Gate	B4-B3-C3
St George's Drive	E2-F2-F1
St George's Road	I4-I3-J3
St George's Square	F1-G1
St George Street	E6-E7
St Giles High Street	G7
St James Square	F5
St James's Road	K1
St James's Street	E5-F5
St John Street	J8-J9
St Leonard's Terrace	C1-D1-D2
St Martin's Lane	G6
St Mary Axe	L7
St Michael's Street	B7
St Thomas Street	K5-L5
Saffron Hill	I8-I9
Salisbury Street	B8
Sancroft Street	H2-I2
Savile Row	E6-F6
Savoy Place	H6
Scritton Street	L9
Sekforde Street	J9
Seymour Place	C7-C8
Seymour Street	C6-C7
Seymour Walk	A1
Shaftesbury Avenue	F6-G6-G7
Shelton Street	G7
Shepherd Street	E5
Shoe Lane	I7-J7
Sidney Street	B2-B1-C1
Silk Street	K8
Skinner Street	I9-J9
Sloane Avenue	C2
Sloane Gardens	D2
Sloane Street	C4-C3-D3-D2
Smith Square	G3
Smith Street	C1
Snows Fields	L5
Soho Square	G7
Southampton Row	H8
South Audley Street	D5-D6
South Carriage Drive	B4-C4-D4
South Eaton Place	D2-D3
South Parade	B1-B2
South Terrace	B2-B3
Southwark Bridge	K6
Southwark Bridge Road	J3-J4-K4-K5
Southwark Street	J5-K5
Stag Place	F3-F4
Stamford Street	I5-J5
Stanhope Gardens	A2
Stanhope Terrace	B6
Stannary Street	I1
Star Street	B7
Stead Street	K2
Store Street	F8-G8
Strand	G5-G6-H6-H7
Sturgeon Road	J1
Sumner Place	B2
Sumner Street	J5-K5
Sun Street	L8
Surrey Square	K2
Sussex Gardens	A6-B6-B7
Sussex Place	B6-B7
Sussex Street	E2-F2
Sutherland Street	E1-E2
Sutherland Walk	K1
Tabard Street	K4-L4-L3
Tabernacle Street	L9
Tachbrook Street	F2
Tavistock Square	G9
Tavistock Street	H6-H7
Tedworth Square	C1
Temple Avenue	I6-I7
The Boltons	A1-A2
The Cut	I4-I5-J5
The Little Boltons	A1
The Mall	F4-F5-G5
Theobald's Road	H8-I8
The Vale	A1
Threadneedle Street	K7-L7
Throgmorton Street	K7-L7
Thurloe Place	B2-B3
Thurloe Square	B2-B3
Thurloe Street	L1-L2
Tite Street	C1-D1
Tooley Street	L5
Torrington Place	F8-F9-E9
Tottenham Court Road	F9-F8-G8-G7
Trafalgar Square	G5-G6
Tregunter Road	A1
Trevor Place	C4
Tufton Street	G3
Tudor Street	I7-J7
Turks Row	D1-D2
Turnmill Street	I9-I8-J8
Tyers Street	H2
Ufford Street	I4-J4
Union Street	J5-K5
Upper Brook Street	D6
Upper Grosvenor Street	D6
Upper Ground	I5-I6-J6
Upper Thames Street	J6-K6-L6
Vauxhall Bridge	G1-H1
Vauxhall Bridge Road	E3-F3-F2-G2
Vauxhall Street	H2-H1-I1
Vauxhall Walk	H2
Vere Street	E7
Victoria Embankment	H5-H6-I6-I7
Victoria Road	A3-A4
Victoria Street	E3-F3-F4-G4
Vincent Square	F2-F3
Vincent Street	F2-G2
Walnut Tree Walk	I3
Walton Street	C2-C3
Walworth Road	J3-K3-K2-K1
Wardour Street	F6-F7
Warren Street	E9
Warrington Crescent	A8-A9
Warwick Avenue	A8
Warwick Square	F2
Warwick Street	F6
Warwick Way	E2-F2
Waterloo Bridge	H6-H5-I5
Waterloo Road	I5-I4-J4
Watling Street	K7
Webber Street	I4-I4
Welbeck Street	D7-D7-E7
Wells Street	F7-F8
Westbourne Terrace	A7-A6-B6
Westcott Road	J1
West Square	J3
Westway	A7-A8-B8
Wetherby Gardens	A2
Weymouth Street	D8-E8
Whitcomb Street	G6
Whitecross Street	K8-K9
Whitefriars Street	I7
Whitehall	G4-G5-H5
Whitehall Place	H5
Whiteheads Grove	C2
Whitfield Street	F8-F9
Wigmore Street	D7-E7
Wild Street	H7
Willow Place	F2-F3
Wilson Street	L8
Wilton Crescent	D4
Wilton Place	D4
Wilton Road	E3-F3-F2
Wimpole Street	D8-E8-E7
Winchester Street	E2-E1-F1
Wincott Street	I2
Woburn Place	G9
Woolers Street	K2-L2-L1-K1
Worship Street	L9
Yeomans Row	C3
York Gate	D9
York Road	H4-H5-I5
York Street	C8
York Terrace	D8-D9

London

History, tradition, culture, commerce, grandeur and beauty are just a few of the ingredients that make up England's magical capital. London's history begins in the 1st century when the Romans bridged the Thames in order to reach Colchester. An important city rapidly developed and right up until the 16th century London stayed more or less within the limits of the original Roman walls. However, from the 1600s onwards the city grew at an amazing rate, and even the Great Fire of 1666 – to which we owe the creation of the present St Paul's Cathedral and many other churches designed by Wren – did not halt expansion. The Thames winds through the heart of London and along its banks stand some of the city's most famous landmarks. Just by Westminster Bridge are the Houses of Parliament, easily distinguished by the clock-tower affectionately known the world over as Big Ben. Originally Westminster Palace, Charles Barry designed the present Gothic building, and much of its lavish decoration is the work of Augustus Pugin. Downstream, past the new complex of buildings including the Festival Hall and the National Theatre, is St Paul's Cathedral. Despite surrounding office blocks, the majesty of its enormous dome is not diminished. Next comes Tower Bridge and the Tower of London which, in its time, has been royal residence, prison, stronghold and place of execution.

However, London is not by any means all grand and famous buildings. Another of its many facets is its variety of shops. These range from the luxurious, prestigious Knightsbridge stores, led by Harrods, to the dozens of street markets, each with their own unique character. Covent Garden, Billingsgate, Smithfield and Petticoat Lane have become household names, but traders sell their wares throughout the city, and specialist shops steeped in tradition cater for individual tastes.

Yet another contrasting aspect of London is its parks and gardens. Best-known of these are the Royal parks. St James's, Green Park, Regent's Park – home of the London Zoo – and Hyde Park are all welcome havens from the busy streets. Past kings and queens were responsible for these green spaces and, in turn, their palaces add grace and splendour to the city. Buckingham Palace with its daily Changing of the Guard – just one of the ceremonies that flourish in London – takes pride of place, but St James's Palace and Kensington Palace deserve no less attention.

No account of London is complete without mentioning its superb theatres, concert halls, galleries and museums. As a cultural centre the capital plays host to the world's greatest performers and gives space to some of its greatest treasures.

Theatres, Concert Halls and Cinemas
A Guide to Entertainments in the Centre of London

THEATRES AND CONCERT HALLS

1 **Adelphi**, The Strand, WC2. Tel: 836 7611
2 **Albery**, St Martin's Lane, WC2. Tel: 836 3878
3 **Aldwych**, Aldwych, WC2. Tel: 836 6404
4 **Ambassadors**, West Street, WC2. Tel: 836 1171
5 **Apollo**, Shaftesbury Avenue, W1. Tel: 437 2663
6 **Apollo** (Victoria), Wilton Road, SW1. Tel: 828 8665 (Not on plan)
7 **Arts** (Theatre Club), Gt Newport Street, WC2. Tel: 836 3334
8 **Astoria**, Charing Cross Road, WC2. Tel: 734 4291
9 **Barbican Centre**, Silk Street, EC2. Tel: 628 8795 (Not on plan)
10 **Cambridge**, Earlham Street, WC2. Tel: 836 6056
11 **Coliseum**, St Martin's Lane, WC2. Tel: 836 3161
12 **Comedy**, Panton Street, SW1. Tel: 830 2578
13 **Criterion**, Piccadilly, W1. Tel: 9303216
14 **Drury Lane, Theatre Royal**, Catherine Street, WC2. Tel: 836 8108
15 **Duchess**, Catherine Street, WC2. Tel: 836 8243
16 **Duke of York's**, St Martin's Lane, WC2. Tel: 836 5122
17 **Fortune**, Russell Street, WC2. Tel: 836 2238
18 **Garrick**, Charing Cross Road, WC2. Tel: 836 4601
19 **Globe**, Shaftesbury Avenue, W1. Tel: 437 1592
20 **Haymarket, Theatre Royal**, Haymarket, SW1. Tel: 930 9832
21 **Her Majesty's**, Haymarket, SW1. Tel: 930 6606
22 **Jeanetta Cochrane**, Theobalds Road, WC1. Tel: 242 7040.
23 **Lyric**, Shaftesbury Avenue, W1. Tel: 437 3686
24 **Mayfair**, Berkeley Street, W1. Tel: 629 3036
25 **Mermaid**, Puddle Dock, EC4. Tel: 236 5568 (Not on plan)
26 **National Theatre**, South Bank, SE1. Tel: 928 2252
27 **New London**, Parker Street, WC2. Tel: 405 0072
28 **Old Vic**, Waterloo Road, SE1. Tel: 928 7616
29 **Palace**, Shaftesbury Avenue, W1. Tel: 437 6834
30 **Palladium**, Argyll Street, W1. Tel: 437 7373
31 **Phoenix**, Charing Cross Road, WC2. Tel: 836 2294
32 **Piccadilly**, Denman Street, W1. Tel: 437 4506
33 **Prince Edward**, Old Compton Street, W1. Tel: 930 6877
34 **Prince of Wales**, Coventry Street, W1. Tel: 930 8681
35 **Queen Elizabeth Hall**, South Bank, SE1. Tel: 928 3191
36 **Queen's**, Shaftesbury Avenue, W1. Tel: 734 1166
37 **Royal Court**, Sloane Square, SW1. Tel: 730 1745 (Not on plan)
38 **Royal Festival Hall**, South Bank, SE1. Tel: 928 3191
39 **Royal Opera House**, Covent Garden, WC2. Tel: 240 1066
40 **Royalty**, Portugal Street, WC2. Tel: 405 8004
41 **St Martin's**, West Street, WC2. Tel: 836 1443
42 **Sadler's Wells**, Roseberry Avenue, EC1. Tel: 278 8916 (Not on plan)
43 **Savoy**, Strand, WC2. Tel: 836 8888
44 **Shaftesbury**, Shaftesbury Avenue, WC2. Tel: 836 6596
45 **Strand**, Aldwych, WC2. Tel: 836 2660
46 **Vanbrugh**, Malet Street, WC1. Tel: 580 7982 (Not on plan)
47 **Vaudeville**, Strand, WC2. Tel: 836 9988
48 **Victoria Palace**, Victoria Street, SW1. Tel: 834 1317 (Not on plan)
49 **Warehouse**, (Donmar), Earlham Street, WC2. Tel: 836 1071
50 **Westminster**, Palace Street, SW1. Tel: 834 0283 (Not on plan)
51 **Whitehall**, Whitehall, SW1. Tel: 930 7765
52 **Wigmore Hall**, Wigmore Street, W1. Tel: 935 2141
53 **Wyndhams**, Charing Cross Road, WC2. Tel: 836 3028.
54 **Young Vic**, The Cut, SE1. Tel: 928 6363

CINEMAS

1 **ABC 1 & 2**, Shaftesbury Avenue, WC2. Tel: 836 8861
2 **Academy 1, 2 & 3**, Oxford Street, W1. Tel: 437 2981
3 **Biograph**, Wilton Road, SW1. Tel: 834 1624 (Not on plan)
4 **Cinecenta**, Panton Street, SW1. Tel: 930 0631
5 **Cinecenta**, Piccadilly, W1. Tel: 437 3561
6 **Classic**, Charing Cross Road, WC2. Tel: 930 6915
7 **Classic Complex**, Haymarket, SW1. Tel: 839 1527
8 **Classic, 1, 2, 3, 4 & 5**, Oxford Street, W1. Tel: 636 0310
9 **Classic**, Shaftesbury Avenue, W1. Tel: 734 5414
10 **Classic Complex**, Tottenham Court Road, W1. Tel: 636 6148
11 **Curzon**, Curzon Street, W1. Tel: 499 3737
12 **Dominion**, Tottenham Court Road, W1. Tel: 580 9562
13 **Empire**, Leicester Square, WC2. Tel: 437 1234
14 **Eros**, Piccadilly Circus, W1. Tel: 437 3839
15 **Filmcenta**, Charing Cross Road, WC2. Tel: 437 4815
16 **Gate 2**, Brunswick Square, WC1. Tel: 837 8402 (Not on plan)
17 **Gate, Mayfair**, Mayfair Hotel, Stratton Street, W1. Tel: 493 2031
18 **Institution of Contemporary Arts**, Carlton House Terrace SW1. Tel: 930 6393
19 **Leicester Square Theatre**, Leicester Square, WC2. Tel: 930 5252
20 **Lumiere**, St Martin's Lane, WC2. Tel: 836 0691 (Not on plan)
21 **Minema**, Knightsbridge, SW1. Tel: 235 6225 (Not on plan)
22 **Moulin Cinema Complex**, Gt Windmill Street, W1. Tel: 437 1653
23 **National Film Theatre**, South Bank, SE1. Tel: 928 3232
24 **Odeon**, Haymarket, SW1. Tel: 930 2738
25 **Odeon**, Leicester Square, WC2. Tel: 930 6111
26 **Odeon**, Marble Arch, W2. Tel: 723 2011 (Not on plan)
27 **Plaza, 1, 2, 3 & 4**, Regent Street, W1. Tel: 437 1234
28 **Prince Charles**, Leicester Place, WC2. Tel: 437 8181
29 **Scene, 1, 2, 3 & 4**, Swiss Centre, Leicester Square, WC2. Tel: 439 4470
30 **Sherlock Holmes Centa**, Baker Street, W1. Tel: 935 2772
31 **Studio 1, 2, 3 & 4**, Oxford Street, W1. Tel: 437 3300
32 **Times Centa 1 & 2**, Chiltern Court, Baker Street, NW1. Tel: 935 9772
33 **Warner West End, 1, 2, 3 & 4**, Cranbourn Street, WC2. Tel: 439 0791

Key

Parking	P
One Way Street	●—●
Cinema	●
Theatre	●
Underground	⊖

Key to Town Plan and Area Plan

Town Plan

AA Recommended roads	
Other roads	
Restricted roads	
Buildings of interest	School
One Way Streets	←
Car parks	P
Parks and open spaces	

Area Plan

A roads	
B roads	
Stations	Grove Hill ●
Borough boundary	

Street Index with Grid Reference

Croydon

Aberdeen Road	B2–B3
Addiscombe Grove	C5
Altre Road	C4–C5
Barclay Road	B4–C4
Bedford Park	B6
Bedford Place	B6–C6
Beech House Road	B4–C4
Birdhurst Avenue	C2–C3
Birdhurst Gardens	C3
Birdhurst Rise	C2
Birdhurst Road	C2
Blake Road	C5–C6
Bramley Hill	A2–A3–B3
Brighton Road	B1–B2
Cedar Road	C6
Chatsworth Road	C3–C4
Cherry Orchard Road	C5–C6
Church Road	A4–A5
Church Street	A5
Clarendon Road	A6
College Road	B5–C5
Colson Road	C5–C6
Coombe Road	B3–C3
Cranmer Road	A4
Croham Road	B2–C2–C1
Cross Road	C6–C7
Crown Hill	A5–B5
Dean Road	C2
Derby Road	A6
Dering Place	A2–B2
Dering Road	B2–B3
Dingwall Road	B6–C6–C5
Dornton Road	C1
Drover's Road	B1
Drummond Road	A5
Duppas Hill Terrace	A3–A4
Edbridge Road	B3–B4
Eden Road	B3–C3
Elmwood Road	A8
Fairfield Road	C4–C5
Friends Road	B4–C4
Frith Road	A5
George Street	B5–C5
Gladstone Road	C8
Gloucester Road	C7–C8
Haling Park Road	A1–A2
Haling Road	B1–C1
Hartley Road	A8
Hathaway Road	A7–A8
Hazledene Road	C5
Heathfield Road	B2–B3
High Street	B3–B4–B5
Howley Road	A4
Hurst Road	C2
Junction Road	B1–C1
Katharine Street	B4
Keeley Road	A5
Keens Road	B3
Kidderminster Road	A7–A8
Lansdowne Road	B6–C6–C7

Croydon

Lofty office blocks piercing the south London skyline, one of the largest shopping centres in south-east England and modern developments like the Whitgift Centre and Fairfields Hall (an arts and exhibitions complex containing the Ashcroft Theatre) characterise modern Croydon — but it still has numerous features recalling its prosperity in earlier times. The Archbishops'

Palace (now a girls' school) was occupied by the Archbishops of Canterbury until the 18th century. The oldest shop in the town can be seen in South End, a 16th- to 17th-century building with an overhanging upper storey. Wrencote, in the High Street, is a fine example of an 18th-century town house. Other places of interest include the 16th-century Whitgift Hospital (an almshouse) the Flemish style 19th-century Town Hall, and the Parish Church of St John the Baptist, rebuilt in

1867 — after a fire — by Sir Gilbert Scott, in the original 15th-century style.

Purley grew rapidly after the end of the 18th century. There are good shopping facilities and the Village Green on the Webb Estate has been designated a conservation area.

Coulsdon Beautiful Farthing Downs and Happy Valley (where nature trails can be followed) lie close by. The Church of St John the Evangelist is a fine example of 13th-century architecture.

Laud Street	A3-A4-B4	Sydenham Road	B6-B7-C7-C8
Lennard Road	A7	Tamworth Road	A5-A6
Leslie Grove	C7	Tanfield Road	A3
Lodge Road	A8	Tavistock Road	B6-B7
London Road	A6-A7	Temple Road	B3-C3-B3
Lower Coombe Street	A3-B3	The Waldrons	A3
Mead Place	A6	Thornhill Road	B8
Milton Avenue	C7-C8	Union Road	B1-C1
Milton Road	C7-C8	Upland Road	A3
Mint Walk	B4	Violet Lane	A1-A2-A3
Montague Road	A7	Waddon New Road	A5-A6
Moreton Road	C1-C2	Waldronhyst	A2
Mulgrave Road	B3-C3	Wandle Road	A4-B4-B3
North End	A6-A5-B5	Warham Road	A2-B2
Nottingham Road	A2-B2	Water Tower Hill	C3
Nova Road	A7	Wellesley Road	B5-B6-B7
Oakfield Road	A6-A7-B7	West Street	A3-B3
Old Palace Road	A4-A5	Windmill Road	A8-B8
Old Town	A3-A4	Whitehorse Road	B7-B8
Oval Road	C6	Whitgift Avenue	A1-B1-B2
Park Lane	B3-B4-B5	Woburn Road	B7
Park Street	B5	Woodstock Road	B4-C4
Parker Road	B3		
Parsons Mead	A6-A7		
Pitlake	A6		
Poplar Walk	A6-B6		
Queen Street	A3-B3		
Roman Way	A5-A6		

Coulsdon

St James's Park	A8	Bramley Avenue	A3
St James's Walk	A7-A8-B8-B7-C7	Brighton Road	A1-B1-B2-A2-A3-B3-B4-C4
St Peter's Road	B3-B2-C2-B2	Byron Avenue	C2-C3
St Peter's Street	C1-C2	Chaldon Way	B1
St Saviour's Road	A8	Chipstead Valley Road	A2-A3-B3
Selsdon Road	B2-B1-C1	Coulsdon Court Road	C1-C2
Scarbrook Road	A4-B4	Coulsdon Rise	B1-C1
South Bridge Place	A3	Coulsdon Road	C1-C2-C3
South Bridge Road	A3-B3-B2	Deepfield Way	B2-C2
South End	B2-B3	Downs Road	B1
South Park Hill Road	C2-C3	Fairdene Road	A1-B1
Stanhope Road	C3-C4	Grove Wood Hill	A4-B4
Stanton Road	A7-B7	Hartley Down	C3-C4
Station Road	A6-B6-B7	Hartley Old Road	C3-C4
Surrey Street	A5-B5-B4	Hartley Way	C3
Sussex Road	C1	Howard Road	A3-A4
		Julien Road	A3
		Lion Green Road	A2

Malcolm Road	A3-B3	Glenn Avenue	C3
Marlpit Avenue	B1	Godstone Road	B2-C2-C1
Marlpit Lane	B2-B1-C1	Graham Road	B1
Petersfield Crescent	B3-C3	Grasmere Road	C3
Portnall Road	A2	Grovelands Road	A1
Reddown Road	A1-B1-B2	Hereward Avenue	B3-B4
Redlands	B2	High Street	B2-B3-C3
Rutherwick Rise	C1-C2	Higher Drive	B1
South Drive	B3-B4	Highfield Road	A4-B4
Southwood Avenue	A3	Hill Road	A2
Station Approach	B2-B3	Lansdowne Road	A1-B1-B2
Stoats Nest Road	C3-C4	Monahan Avenue	A2-A3-A2
Stoats Nest Village	B3-C3	Montpelier Road	C4
Stoney Field Road	C1	More Close	B3
The Avenue	A3-B3	Northwood Avenue	B1-C1
The Chase	A4-B4	Olden Lane	B1-C1
The Drive	B4-C4	Pampisford Road	B3-B4-C4
The Grove	B3-B4	Plough Lane	A3-A4
The Ridge	B4	Purley Hill	C2
The Vale	B4-C4	Purley Knoll	A3-B3-B2
Ullswater Crescent	B2-C2	Purley Park Road	C4
Warwick Road	A4-B4	Purley Rise	A1-A2-B2
Windermere Road	B3-B4-C4	Purley Road	B2
Woodcote Grove Road	A3-A4-B4	Purley Vale	C1
Woodhatch Spinney	B2-C2	Purley Way	B3-B4
Woodmansterne Road	A3	Russell Green Close	B4
		Russell Hill	A4-A3-B3-B4

Purley

Banstead Road	B3	Selcroft Road	C2-C3
Beaumont Road	B1	Warren Road	C2-C3
Box Ridge Avenue	A2	Whytecliffe Road	B2-B3-C3-C4
Brighton Road	A1-A2-B2-B3-C3-C4	Woodcote Valley Road	A2-A3-B3
Cliff End	C1-C2	Woodcrest Road	A1
Dale Road	C1-C2	Wyvern Road	B4-C4
Downlands Road	A1		
Downs Court Road	C1-C2		
Elm Road	C1		
Foxley Gardens	C1		
Foxley Hill Road	B1-B2-C2		
Foxley Lane	A3-B3		
Friends Road	C2		
Furze Hill	A3		
Furze Lane	A3		

CROYDON
Beyond the gleaming blue glass of St Crispins House, the extensive Fairfield Halls complex offers concerts for music-lovers, with drama at the Ashcroft Theatre and exhibitions at the Arnhem Gallery.

Ealing

The Ealing Comedies, cinema classics of the 1940s and 1950s were made in studios overlooking Ealing Green — studios which have now been taken over by the BBC for the production of television films. Ealing is a pleasantly leafy London suburb. Fine shopping facilities can be found in the Broadway area and buildings of interest include the fine Victorian Town Hall, and the former Pitshanger

Manor, in Walpole Park, which has become the central library.

Southall has been known for its cattle market since the late 17th century, and this still takes place every Wednesday, close to the High Street. In recent years the Southall area has become the home of numerous Commonwealth immigrants, and it now has a distinctive Asian character of its own, particularly in the main Broadway shopping area. Southall Manor, standing on the Green, dates

originally from the 16th century.

Hammersmith is seen by most of those who pass through as a vista of roof tops — the view from the flyover built to ease congestion where traffic from the Great West Road and Hammersmith Bridge meet with the many vehicles entering and leaving Central London. Hammersmith is also the site of the Lyric Theatre, known for its pre-West End productions; the BBC TV Studios lie a short distance to the north.

STREET INDEX WITH
GRID REFERENCE
EALING

Adelaide Road	A1
Albany Road	B4
Alexandria Road	A3-B3
Amherst Avenue	C4
Amherst Road	C4
Arden Road	C3
Argyle Road	A4-B4-B3
Arlington Road	E1
Ascott Avenue	E1
Beaconsfield Road	C1-D1
Bedford Road	B2-B3
Blakesley Avenue	D4
Blandford Road	D1-E1
Bonchurch Road	A1-B1
Bond Street	D3
Bradley Gardens	B4-C4
Bridge Road	A4
Broadway	A2
Broomfield Road	B2
Broughton Road	B2-B3
Brownlow Road	A2
Cairn Avenue	D1
Carew Road	C1
Carlton Gardens	C3-C4
Carlton Road	C3-C4-D4
Castlebar Road	C4-D4
Cavendish Avenue	A4
Chapel Road	B2
Churchfield Road	B2-C2
Coldershaw Road	A1-A2
Colebrooke Avenue	B4
College Road	B4
Connaught Road	B2-B3
Courtfield Gardens	A4
Craven Avenue	C3
Craven Road	C3
Creffield Road	F3
Croft Gardens	A1
Crosslands Avenue	F1

Culmington Road	C1-C2
Delamere Road	E1-F1
Denbigh Road	B3-B4-C4
Denmark Road	B3-C3
Disraeli Road	D1-D2
Drayton Avennue	A3-B3
Drayton Gardens	A3
Drayton Green	A3-A4
Drayton Grove	A3-A4
Drayton Road	A3-A4-B3
Drayton Green Road	B2-B3
Dudley Gardens	B1
Eaton Rise	D4
Elers Road	C1
Elgar Avenue	F1
Elm Avenue	F1
Elm Crescent	E1-F1
Elmgrove Road	E1-F1
Felix Road	A3
Florence Road	E2-E3
Freeland Road	F3
Glenfield Road	F1
Gordon Road	B3-C3-D3
Grange Park	E1-E2-F2
Grange Road	D2-E2-F2-F3
Green Man Lane	A2-A3
Grosvenor Road	A1-A2
Grove Place	D2-D3
Grove Road	D2
Gunnersbury Avenue	F1-F2
Hamilton Road	E3-F3
Hanger Lane	F2-F3-F4
Hartington Road	B2-B3
Hastings Road	B3-C3
Haven Green	D4-E3-E4
Haven Green West Side Road	D3-D4
Haven Lane	E4
Hazelwood Close	E1
Hessel Road	A1-B1
High Street	D3
Inglis Road	F3
Kenilworth Road	E1-E2
Kerrison Place	D2-E1
Kerrison Road	E1
Kingsdown Avenue	B1-C1
Kirchen Road	B2-B3
Lammas Park	D1
Lammas Park Gardens	C1-D1
Lavington Road	B1-B2-C1
Leeland Terrace	A2
Leighton Road	A1-B1
Leopold Road	E1
Liverpool Road	E1
Longfield Avenue	D3
Longfield Road	D3-D4
Loveday Road	B1-B2
Lyncroft Gardens	C1
Lynton Avenue	A4
Madeley Road	E4-F4
Manor Road	A3-B3
Mattock Lane	B2-C2-D2
Melbourne Avenue	C2
Mortimer Road	C4
Mountfield Road	E4
Mount Park Crescent	D4
New Broadway	D3
Northcote Avenue	E3
North Common Road	E3-F3
Northfield Avenue	B1-B2
Northfield Road	B1
Oaklands Road	A1
Oxford Road	E2-E3

Park Place	D1-D2
Park Road	D4
Ranelagh Road	D1-E1
Rathgar Avenue	B1-C1-C2
Regina Road	A1-A2
Richmond Road	E1
St James's Avenue	A1-A2
St Kilda Road	A1
St Leonard's Road	C3-C4
St Mary's Road	D1
Seaford Road	A2-B1-B2
Seward Road	A1
Singapore Road	A2
Somerset Road	B2-C1-C2
Spring Bridge	D3
Sunnyside Road	D1
Sutherland Avenue	B4
Sutherland Road	A4-B4
Sydney Road	A1-A2-B1
Talbot Road	A2-A3
The Avenue	B3-B4
The Bridge	E3
The Broadway	D3-E3
The Common	E2-E3-F2
The Green	D2
The Grove	D2-D3
The Mall	E3
The Park	E3
Uxbridge Road	A2-B2-C2-C3
Uxbridge Road	E3-F2-F3
Waldeck Road	B4-C4
Waldemar Avenue	C1
Walpole Close	C1
Warwick Dene	E2-F2
Warwick Road	D1-E1-E2
Webster Gardens	D2-E2
Westbury Road	E4
Western Road	D3-E2-E3
Westfield Road	A1-A2-B1
Windsor Road	E2-E3
Woodville Gardens	E4-F4
Woodville Road	E4

SOUTHALL

Abbotts Road	B2-B3
Alexandra Rod	B3-B4
Alma Road	A4
Avenue Road	B2-C2-C3
Balfour Road	A1
Beaconsfield Road	A1-A2-B2
Beresford Road	A3-A4
Berwick Avenue	A4
Bridge Road	B2-C2
Burns Avenue	C4
Carlyle Avenue	B4-C4
Cherry Avenue	A3
Clarence Street	A1
Crescent Road	B2
Dane Road	B3-B4
Delamere Road	A4
Dudley Road	A1
East Avenue	A4
Featherstone Road	A1-B1
Featherstone Terrace	B1
Greenford Avenue	B3-B4
Gregory Road	C1
Grosvenor Road	A4
Hamborough Road	A2-A3-B3
Hammond Road	B1
Hanson Gardens	B2
Hartington Road	A1-A2
Havelock Road	B1-C1
High Street	B3

Hilary Road	C1
Hortus Road	B2
Hunt Road	C1
King Street	B1
Kingsley Avenue	C3-C4
Kingston Place	B2
Lady Margaret Road	C3-C4
Lancaster Road	B3-B4
Livingstone Road	A4
Lowden Road	A4-B4
Montague Waye	A1-B1
Norman Avenue	B4
North Avenue	B4-C4
North Road	C3-C4
Northcote Avenue	B3-B4
Orchard Avenue	B3
Osterley Park Road	B1
Oswald Road	B3
Palgrave Avenue	C4
Park Avenue	B2-C2
Park View Road	A1-A2
Queen's Road	C4
Ranelagh Road	A3-A4
Ruskin Road	A4
St Georges Avenue	B3-B4
St Johns Road	A1-B1
St Joseph's Drive	B3
Saxon Road	B3-B4
Scott's Road	A1
Shackleton Road	B4-C4
South Avenue	B4
South Road	B2-B3-C3
Southbridge Way	B2
Stanley Road	A4
Sussex Road	A1
The Broadway	A4-B3-C3
The Green	B1-B2
The Straight Road	A2-B2
Townsend Road	A3
Trinity Road	A3
Tudor Road	A4
Villiers Road	C2-C3
Waltham Road	A1
West Avenue	B4
West End Road	A3
Western Road	A1-B1
White Street	A2
Windsor Road	B1-C1
Woodlands Road	A3-A4

HAMMERSMITH

Adeney Close	C1
Adie Road	B4
Agate Road	B4
Aldensley Road	A4
Angel Walk	B2-B3
Arundel Terrace	A1
Atwood Road	A3-A4
Augustine Road	C4
Averill Street	C1
Aynhoe Road	C4
Banim Street	A3-A4
Batoum Gardens	B4
Beadon Road	B3
Beryl Road	B2-C2
Biscay Road	B2-C2
Blacks Road	B3
Blythe Road	C4
Boileau Road	A4
Brackenbury Road	A4
Bridge Avenue	A2-A3-B3
Brook Green	B4-C3-C4
Bute Gardens	B3-C3

Butterwick	B2-B3
Caithness Road	C4
Cambridge Grove	A3
Cardross Street	A4
Carthew Road	A4
Castlenau	A1
Ceylon Road	C4
Chancellor's Road	B2
Clavering Avenue	A1
Claxton Grove	C1-C2
Colet Gardens	C2-C3
Colwith Road	B1-C1
Crisp Road	B2
Dalling Road	A3-A4
Dewhurst Road	B4
Distillery Road	B1-B2
Dunsany Road	C4
Everington Street	C1
Faroe Road	C4
Fulham Palace Road	B1-B2-C1
Gastein Road	C1
Girdlers Road	C3-C4
Glentham Road	A1
Glenthorne Road	A3-B3
Great Church Lane	C2
Great West Road	A2
Greyhound Road	C1
Hammersmith Bridge	A2
Hammersmith Grove	B3-B4
Hammersmith Road	B3-C3
Hammersmith Bridge Road	B2-B3
Iffley Road	A4
King Street	A3-B3
Larnach Road	C1
Leamore Street	A3
Lena Gardens	B4
Lilian Road	A1
Lochaline Street	B1
Lonsdale Road	A1
Lurgan Avenue	C1
Luxemburg Gardens	C3-C4
Macbeth Street	A2-A3
Manbrae Road	B1
Mall Road	A2
Margravine Gardens	C2
Margravine Road	C1-C2
Masbro' Road	C4
Merthya Terrace	A1
Nasmyth Street	A3
Nella Road	B1-C1
Nigel Playfair Avenue	A2-A3
Overstone Road	B3-B4
Paddenswick Road	A4
Parfrey Street	B1-C1
Queen Caroline Street	B2-B3
Rannoch Road	B1
Raynham Road	A4
Redan Street	C4
River View Gardens	A1
Rosedew Road	B1-C1
Rowan Road	C3
St Dunstan's Road	C2
Shepherd's Bush Road	B3-B4
Shortlands	C2-C3
Sterndale Road	B4-C4
Studland Street	A3
Southerton Road	B3-B4
Tabor Road	A4
Talgarth	B2-C2
Upper Mall	A2
Winslow Road	B1
Yeldham Road	B2-C2

15

Central Enfield

Enfield Area

LEGEND

Town Plan
AA Recommended roads
Other roads
Restricted roads
Buildings of interest — Library
Churches — †
Car parks — P
Parks and open spaces
One way streets — ←

Area Plan
A roads
B roads
Urban area

Street Index with Grid Reference

Enfield

Abbots Crescent	B3
Aldersbrook Avenue	D3-E3
Apple Grove	E2
Armfield Road	D4
Baker Street	D2-D3-D4-E4
Baynes Close	F4
Bell Road	D4
Beresford Gardens	E1
Bertram Road	F1
Bicknoller Road	E4
Buckingham Close	E3-E4
Burleigh Road	E1
Bycullah Avenue	B2-B3
Bycullah Road	B2-B3
Canonbury Road	D4-E4
Carisbrooke Close	E4
Carnarvon Avenue	E2-E3
Caterhatch Lane	E4-F4-F3
Cecil Avenue	E1
Cecil Road	C2-C1-D1
Chailey Avenue	E3
Chalkwell Park Avenue	D1
Chapel Street	C2
Chase Court Gardens	B2-B3
Chase Green Avenue	B3-C3-C2
Chase Ridings	A2-A3
Chase Side	C2-C3-C4
Chase Side Avenue	C3
Cheviot Close	D3
Churchbury Lane	D2-D3-D4-E4
Churchbury Road	D3
Church Lane	D2
Church Street	C2-C1-D1-D2
Clive Road	F1
College Close	D3-D4
Connaught Avenue	E2-E3
Crescent Road	B1
Cross Road	E1
Culloden Road	B2-B3
Donkey Lane	F3
Drapers Road	A3-A4
Dunraven Drive	A3
Eastbury Avenue	E4
Eaton Road	E1-E2
Elizabeth Avenue	B2
Essex Road	D1
Fairview Road	A4
Falmer Road	E1
Farr Road	D4
Fillebrook Avenue	E3
Fir Tree Walk	D2
Florence Avenue	B2-C2
Florence Drive	B2-C2
Fotheringham Road	E1
Fyfield Road	D2
Gentlemans Road	C2
Glebe Avenue	B2
Gordon Hill	B4-C4
Gordon Road	C4-C3-D3
Graeme Road	D3-E3
Halifax Road	C3-D3
Halstead Road	E1
Hardyway	A4
Heene Road	C3-C4-D4
Hedge Hill	B4
Holtwhites Hill	A4-B4-B3-C3
Holt Whites Way	C3
Hunters Way	A4
Inverness Avenue	E4
Kenilworth Crescent	D4-E4

Enfield

Built in the 17th century to bring fresh water from Hertford to London, the attractive New River waterway still winds through the centre of Enfield, separating the Town Park from the Golf Course. Although this residential town on the edge of the Green Belt saw a good deal of expansion when the railways arrived in the 19th century, much of the older part has survived.

Near the 12th- to 14th-century parish church are Holly Walk and Gentleman's Row, which has a number of picturesque old cottages, including one where 19th-century essayist Charles Lamb would often stay with his sister Mary. They later rented a house close by in Chase Side.

Forty Hall, at nearby Forty Hill, dates from the 17th century and has a local history museum.

Edmonton's parish church has some Norman features, and Charles Lamb is buried in the churchyard. Edmonton itself is a residential area with modern shopping facilities centred around the open air market and pedestrian precinct at Edmonton Green.

Palmers Green became a fashionable residential suburb during the early part of the present century, and is the home of the Intimate Theatre, which stages many pre-West End productions. The attractive Broomfield Park (being restored) contains a museum of local history.

Edmonton

Palmers Green

ENFIELD
Lamb's Cottage in Gentleman's Row — Charles Lamb and his sister Mary came to Enfield to stay with friends in 1825 and liked it so much that they made repeated visits back and eventually decided to settle here.

Central Dalston/Hackney

Central Stoke Newington

Key to Town Plan and Area Plan

Town Plan

AA Recommended roads	
Other roads	
Restricted roads	
Buildings of interest	Hospital
Car Parks	P
Parks and open spaces	
Churches	†
One way streets	→

Area Plan

A roads	
B roads	
Stations	New Cross
Borough Boundary	

Street Index with Grid Reference

Dalston/Hackney

Alvington Crescent	B3
Amhurst Road	C4-C3-D3-E3-E2
Andre Street	D4
Anton Street	D3-D4
Arcola Street	B4
Arundel Grove	A3
Balls Pond Road	A2-B2
Barrett's Grove	A4-B4
Beechwood Road	B1-B2
Belgrade Road	A4-B4
Belsham Street	F2
Bodney Road	D3-D4
Boleyn Road	A3-A2-B2
Brenthouse Road	E1-F1-F2
Brett Road	E3
Brickbeck Road	B2-B3
Buckingham Road	A1
Burder Road	A2
Cecilia Road	C3-C4
Chatham Place	F2
Churchill Walk	F3-F4
Clapton Square	E4-F4
Clarence Place	E4
Clarence Road	E3-E4
Colverstone Crescent	B2-B3-C3
Cowper Road	A4
Cresset Road	F2
Crossway	A3-B3
Culford Road	A1-A2
Dalston Lane	B2-C2-C3-D3-E3
Darnley Road	E1-E2-F2
De Beavoir Road	A1
Downs Park Road	B3-C3-C4-D4-E4
Dunn Street	B3-B4
Eleanor Road	D2-D1-E1
Ellingfort Road	E1
Elrington Road	C1-C2
Elsdale Street	F1-F2
Elton Place	A3
Engleford Road	A1-B1
Fasset Road	C2-D2
Fasset Square	C2
Ferncliffe Road	C3-C4
Forest Road	B1-C1-D1
Frampton Park Road	F1-F2
Gayhurst Road	C1-D1
Glenarm Road	F4
Gillette Street	A3-B3
Goulton Road	E4-F4
Graham Road	C2-D2
Green Wood Road	D1-D2-D3
Hertford Road	A1
Hindrey Road	E3-E4
Holly Street	B1
Horton Road	D2-E2-E1
Kenmure Road	E3
King Henry Street	A3
King Henry's Walk	A2-A3
Kingsland High Street	B2-B3-B4
Kingsland Road	B1-B2
Kingsbury Road	A2
Landsdowne Drive	D1-D2
Laurel Street	B2-C2
Lentham Road	C1
Lesbia Road	F4
Loddiges Road	E1-F1
London Lane	E1
Lower Clapton Road	E3-E4-F4
Malvern Road	C1-D1
Mapleden Road	C1-D1
Mare Street	E1-E2-E3
Martello Street	E1

Hackney / Dalston

Not so long ago this was a rural area on the west bank of the River Lea. Although most of its open land was swallowed up by development in the 19th century, pleasant spaces still remain in Hackney Downs, in the north, and London Fields, in the south, and attractive parks have been created.

The only old building of note is the ancient tower of St Augustine's Church, probably dating from the 13th century. This is a good area for street markets, one of the largest being in Saturdays, along busy Kingsland Road.

Stoke Newington was once the home of *Robinson Crusoe* author Daniel Defoe, and his house can still be seen in Stoke Newington Church Street — one of a number of reminders of the past to be found in this area. This old Saxon settlement became a fashionable residential area during the 19th century, but was extensively rebuilt following bomb damage in World War II. The Old Church of St Mary makes a picturesque scene at one corner of pleasantly landscaped Clissold Park.

Whitechapel was the scene of the notoriously grisly Jack the Ripper murders in the late 19th century. Famous also for its markets, which include Petticoat Lane (Middlesex Street), it has been a stopping point for immigrants since the 18th century. The National Museum of Labour History can be seen at nearby Limehouse Town Hall.

Central Whitechapel

Hackney/Tower Hamlets Area

Mathias Road	A4	Brighton Road	A1
Mead Place	F1-F2	Brodia Road	A2-A3
Median Road	F4	Brooke Road	B2-B3-C3
Mehetabel Road	F3	Cazenove Road	B4-C4
Mildmay Road	A3	Chesholme Road	A2
Miller Avenue	B4	Clapton Way	C1
Montague Road	C3	Darville Road	B2
Morning Lane	E2-F2	Defoe road	A2-A3
Mountford Road	C3	Downs Road	C1
Navarino Road	D1-D2-D3	Dumont Road	A3
Palatine Road	A4-B4	Durlston Road	C3-C4
Paragon Road	E2-F2	Dynevor Road	A2-A3
Parkholme Road	C1-C2	Evering Road	B1-B2-C2
Pellerin Road	A3-A4	Farleigh Road	B1
Pembury Road	D3-D4-E4	Filey Avenue	B4-C4
Ponsford Street	F2-F3	Foulden Road	B1-C1
Powerscroft Road	F4	Fountayne Road	C3-C4
Prince George Road	A4-B4	Garnham Street	B3
Princess May Road	A4-B4	Geldeston Road	C3
Queensbridge Road	C1-C2	Hollar Road	B2
Ram Place	F2	Jenner Road	B3-C3-C2
Ramsgate Street	B2	Kersley Road	A2-A3
Reading Lane	E1-E2	Kynaston Road	A2-A3
Retreat Place	F2	Kyverdale Road	B3-B4-C4-B4
Richmond Road	B1-C1-D1-E1	Lavers Road	A2
Ridley Road	B2-C2-C3	Leswin Road	B1-B2
Ritson Road	C2	Listria Park	A4
Roseberry Place	B1-B2	Manor Road	A4-B4
St Jude Street	A3	Manse Road	B1-C1
St Marks Rise	B2-B3	Maury Road	C2-C3
St Phillips Road	C1-C2	Nevill Road	A1-A2
St Thomas Place	F1	Norcott Road	C2-C3
Sandringham Road	B3-C3-D3	Northwold Road	B3-C3
Seal Street	B4	Old Field Road	A1-A2-A3
Shacklewell Lane	B3-B4-C4	Osbaldeston Road	C3-C4
Shacklewell Street	B4-C4	Rectory Road	B3-B2-C2-C1
Shellness Road	E4	Rendlesham Road	C1-C2
Sigdon Road	D3	Stamford Terrace	B3
Sladen Place	E4	Stamford Hill	B3-B4
Somerford Grove	B4	Stoke Newington Church Street	A3-B3
Spenser Grove	A4	Stoke Newington Common	B3-C3
Spurstone Terrace	D3	Stoke Newington High Street	A2-B2-B3
Stamford Road	A1-B1	Stoke Newington Road	A1
Stoke Newington Road	B3-B4	Sydner Road	B1-C1
Sutton Place	F3	Tyssen Road	B2
Sylvester Road	E2	Victorian Grove	A2
Tilia Road	E4	Victorian Road	A1
Tolsford Road	E3	Walford Road	A1
Tottenham Road	A2-A1-B1	Windus Road	B4
Trumans Road	A3-B3	Yorkshire Close	A2
Urswich Road	F3-F4		
Vallette Street	E2		
Wayland Avenue	D3		
Well Street	F1		
Wilman Grove	D1		
Wilton Way	C2-D2-E2		
Wordsworth Road	A4		

Stoke Newington

Alconbury Road	C3
Alkham Road	B3-B4
Amhurst Road	B1-C1
Batley Road	B2
Bayston Road	C2
Beatty Road	A1
Belfast Road	B4
Benthall Road	C2-C3
Bouverie Road	A3

Whitechapel

Adler Street	C2
Aldgate High Street	B1-B2
Alie Street	B1-C1-C2
Appolo Street	A3-A4
Artillery Lane	A3-B3
Back Church Lane	C1
Bacon Street	C4
Batty Street	C1
Bell Lane	B2-B3
Bethnal Green Road	B4-C4
Bevis Marks	A2
Bishopsgate	A2-A3
Boyd Street	C1
Braham Street	B1-B2-C2
Brick Lane	C2-C3-C4
Brune Street	B3

Brushfield Street	A3-B3
Bury Road	A2
Buxton Street	C3-C4
Calvin Street	B4
Cheshire Street	C4
Chicksand Street	C3
Christian Street	C1
Clifton Street	A3-A4
Cobb Street	B2
Commercial Road	C1-C2
Commercial Street	B2-B3-B4
Crosswall	A1-B1
Curtain Road	A4
Cutler Street	A2
Dukes Place	A1-A2
East Tenter Street	B1
Ellen Street	C1
Fairclough Street	C1
Fashion Street	B3
Fenchurch Street	A1
Folgate Street	B3-B4
Fournier Street	B3
Goulston Street	B2
Gowers Walk	C1-C2
Gravel Lane	B2
Greatorex Street	C2-C3
Greenfield Road	C1-C2
Grey Eagle Street	B3-B4
Hanbury Street	B3-C3-B3
Harrow Place	A2-B2
Hart Street	A1
Hearn Street	A4
Heneage Street	C3
High Street	B4
Houndsditch	A2-B2-B1-A2
Jewry Street	A1-B1
Lamb Street	B3
Leadenhall Street	A1
Leman Street	B1-C1
Lime Street	A1
Liverpool Street	A2-A3
Lloyds Avenue	A1
Mansell Street	B1
Mark Lane	A1
Middlesex Street	A3-A2-B2
Mincing Lane	A1
Minories	B1
Mitre Street	A1-A2
Montague Street	C2-C3
North Tenter Street	B1
Norton Folgate	A3-A4-B4
Old Castle Street	B2
Pedley Street	C4
Pinchin Street	C1
Pindar Street	A4
Plumbers Row	C2
Porsoken Street	B1
Prescot Street	B1-C1
Princelet Street	C3
Quaker Street	B4-C4
Redchurch Street	B4-C4
St Botolph Street	B2
St Mary Axe	A2
Sclater Street	B4-C4
Scrutton Street	A4
Shoreditch	B4
South Tenter Street	B1
Spital Square	A3-B3
Spital Street	C3-C4
Toynbee Street	B2-B3
Underwood Road	C3

Wentworth Street	B2-C2
West Tentor Street	B1
Wheeler Street	B4
Whitechapel High Street	B2
Whitechapel Road	C2
White's Row	B3
Wilks Street	B3
Wilson Street	A4
Woodseer Street	C3
Worship Street	A4

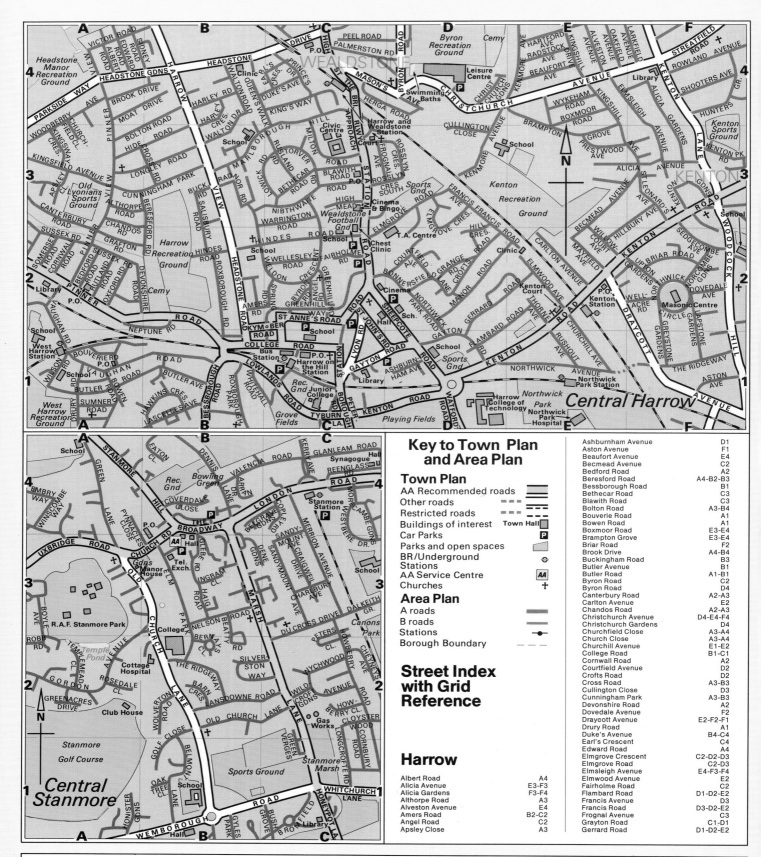

Key to Town Plan and Area Plan

Town Plan

AA Recommended roads	
Other roads	
Restricted roads	
Buildings of interest	Town Hall
Car Parks	P
Parks and open spaces	
BR/Underground Stations	
AA Service Centre	AA
Churches	†

Area Plan

A roads	
B roads	
Stations	
Borough Boundary	

Street Index with Grid Reference

Harrow

Harrow

Sheridan, Byron, Anthony Trollope and Sir Winston Churchill all spent time in Harrow — as pupils at the historic public school, which was founded in 1572. During term time, the present-day pupils are recognisable by their distinctive uniform, and tail coats are still worn by members of the Upper School. The school itself has been modernised to some extent over the years, but a number of ancient buildings still remain, notably the 17th-century schoolroom.

Expanded and developed between the two World Wars, modern Harrow is home of a number of industrial concerns, including the Kodak film and photographic paper factory and the Northern European Office of Hitachi Electronics.

St Mary's Church is of Norman origin but was greatly restored by Sir George Gilbert Scott during the mid-19th century. Headstone Manor, which dates back to the 14th century, has an impressive restored Tithe Barn which is open to the public.

Stanmore Marconi Space and Defence Systems is one of the occupants of Stanmore's main industrial estate, and as well as such modern innovations, the area still has some older buildings, including fine 18th-century houses on Stanmore Hill. St Lawrence's Church, also 18th-century, is noted for its painted walls and ceiling.

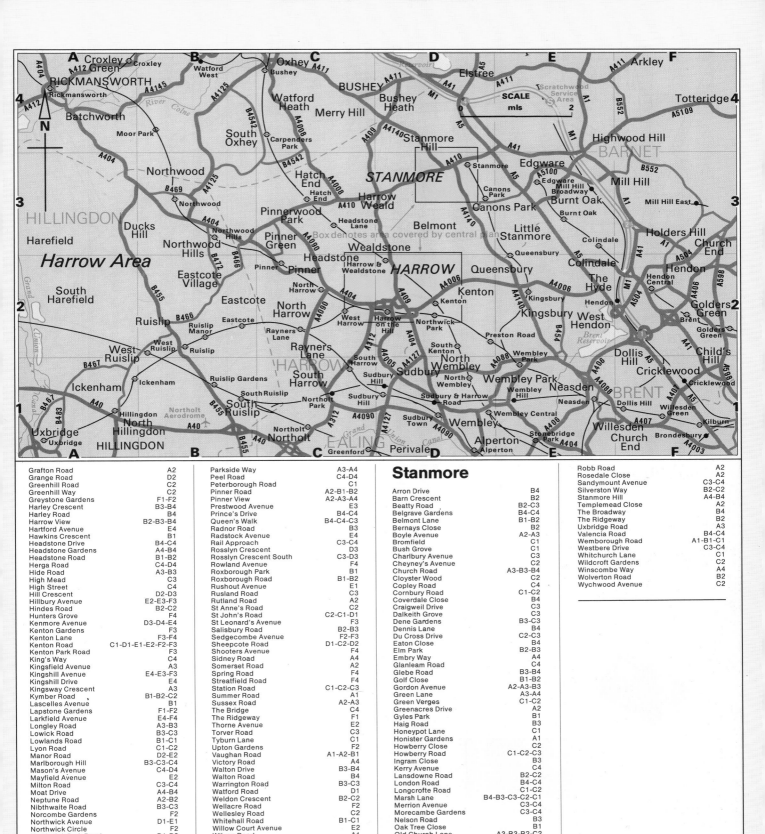

Grafton Road	A2	
Grange Road	D2	
Greenhill Road	C2	
Greenhill Way	C2	
Greystone Gardens	F1-F2	
Harley Crescent	B3-B4	
Harley Road	B4	
Harrow View	B2-B3-B4	
Hartford Avenue	E4	
Hawkins Crescent	B1	
Headstone Drive	B4-C4	
Headstone Gardens	A4-B4	
Headstone Road	B1-B2	
Herga Road	C4-D4	
Hide Road	A3-B3	
High Mead	C3	
High Street	C4	
Hill Crescent	D2-D3	
Hillbury Avenue	E2-E3-F3	
Hindes Road	B2-C2	
Hunters Grove	F4	
Kenmore Avenue	D3-D4-E4	
Kenton Gardens	F3	
Kenton Lane	F3-F4	
Kenton Road	C1-D1-E1-E2-F2-F3	
Kenton Park Road	F3	
King's Way	C4	
Kingsfield Avenue	A3	
Kingshill Avenue	E4-E3-F3	
Kingshill Drive	E4	
Kingsway Crescent	A3	
Kymber Road	B1-B2-C2	
Lascelles Avenue	B1	
Lapstone Gardens	F1-F2	
Larkfield Avenue	E4-F4	
Longley Road	A3-B3	
Lowick Road	B3-C3	
Lowlands Road	B1-C1	
Lyon Road	C1-C2	
Manor Road	D2-E2	
Marlborough Hill	B3-C3-C4	
Mason's Avenue	C4-D4	
Mayfield Avenue	E2	
Milton Road	C3-C4	
Moat Drive	A4-B4	
Neptune Road	A2-B2	
Nibthwaite Road	B3-C3	
Norcombe Gardens	F2	
Northwick Avenue	D1-E1	
Northwick Circle	F2	
Northwick Park Road	D1-D2	
Oakfield Avenue	E4	
Oxford Road	A2	
Palmerston Road	C4-D4	

Parkside Way	A3-A4	
Peel Road	C4-D4	
Peterborough Road	C1	
Pinner Road	A2-B1-B2	
Pinner View	A2-A3-A4	
Prestwood Avenue	E3	
Prince's Drive	B4-C4	
Queen's Walk	B4-C4-C3	
Radnor Road	B3	
Radstock Avenue	E4	
Rail Approach	C3-C4	
Rosslyn Crescent	D3	
Rosslyn Crescent South	C3-D3	
Rowland Avenue	F4	
Roxborough Park	B1	
Roxborough Road	B1-B2	
Rushout Avenue	E1	
Rusland Road	C3	
Rutland Road	A2	
St Anne's Road	C2	
St John's Road	C2-C1-D1	
St Leonard's Avenue	F3	
Salisbury Road	B2-B3	
Sedgecombe Avenue	F2-F3	
Sheepcote Road	D1-C2-D2	
Shooters Avenue	F4	
Sidney Road	A2	
Somerset Road	A2	
Spring Road	F4	
Streatfield Road	F4	
Station Road	C1-C2-C3	
Summer Road	A1	
Sussex Road	A2-A3	
The Bridge	C4	
The Ridgeway	F1	
Thorne Avenue	E2	
Torver Road	C3	
Tyburn Lane	C1	
Upton Gardens	F2	
Vaughan Road	A1-A2-B1	
Victory Road	A4	
Walton Drive	B3-B4	
Walton Road	B4	
Warrington Road	B3-C3	
Watford Road	D1	
Weldon Crescent	B2-C2	
Wellacre Road	F2	
Wellesley Road	C2	
Whitehall Road	B1-C1	
Willow Court Avenue	E2	
Wilson Road	A1	
Woodberry Avenue	A3-A4	
Woodcock Hill	F1-F2-F3	
Wykeham Road	E4	

Stanmore

Arron Drive	B4	
Barn Crescent	B2	
Beatty Road	B2-C3	
Belgrave Gardens	B4-C4	
Belmont Lane	B1-B2	
Bernays Close	B2	
Boyle Avenue	A2-A3	
Bromfield	C1	
Bush Grove	C1	
Charlbury Avenue	C3	
Cheyney's Avenue	C2	
Church Road	A3-B3-B4	
Cloyster Wood	C2	
Copley Road	C4	
Cornbury Road	C1-C2	
Coverdale Close	B4	
Craigweil Drive	C3	
Dalkeith Grove	C3	
Dene Gardens	B3-C3	
Dennis Lane	B4	
Du Cross Drive	C2-C3	
Eaton Close	B4	
Elm Park	B2-B3	
Embry Way	A4	
Glanleam Road	C4	
Glebe Road	B3-B4	
Golf Close	B1-B2	
Gordon Avenue	A2-A3-B3	
Green Lane	A3-A4	
Green Verges	C1-C2	
Greenacres Drive	A2	
Gyles Park	B1	
Haig Road	B3	
Honeypot Lane	C1	
Honister Gardens	A1	
Howberry Close	C2	
Howberry Road	C1-C2-C3	
Ingram Close	B3	
Kerry Avenue	C4	
Lansdowne Road	B2-C2	
London Road	B4-C4	
Longcrofte Road	C1-C2	
Marsh Lane	B4-B3-C3-C2-C1	
Merrion Avenue	C3-C4	
Morecambe Gardens	C3-C4	
Nelson Road	B3	
Oak Tree Close	B1	
Old Church Lane	A3-B3-B2-C2	
Peters Close	C2-C3	
Pynnacles Close	A4-A3-B3	
Reenglass Road	C4	

Robb Road	A2	
Rosedale Close	A2	
Sandymount Avenue	C3-C4	
Silverston Way	B2-C2	
Stanmore Hill	A4-B4	
Templemead Close	A2	
The Broadway	B4	
The Ridgeway	B2	
Uxbridge Road	A3	
Valencia Road	B4-C4	
Wemborough Road	A1-B1-C1	
Westbere Drive	C3-C4	
Whitchurch Lane	C1	
Wildcroft Gardens	C2	
Winscombe Way	A4	
Wolverton Road	B2	
Wychwood Avenue	C2	

HARROW
The Old School building, Harrow School, whose 1572 founder John Lyon drew up an elaborate pupils' reading list of Latin and Greek — but no English — books, and stipulated that no girls be received into the school.

Key to Town Plan and Area Plan

Town Plan

AA Recommended roads
Other roads
Restricted roads
Buildings of interset   School
Car Parks   P
Parks and open spaces
One Way Streets
Underground stations

Area Plan

A roads   A406
B roads   B552
Borough boundary
BR and underground stations   Kensal

Street Index with Grid Reference

Hendon

Alba Gardens	F2
Alderton Crescent	C4
Algernon Road	B4-B3
Allington Road	C3-C4
Audley Road	B3-B4
Beaufort Gardens	D3
Bell Lane	F4
Bertram Road	B3-B4
Beverley Gardens	F1-F2
Brent Green	E4
Brent Street	E4-E3-F3
Brent Terrace	C1
Brent Park Road	B2-C2
Brent View Road	A3
Brentfield Gardens	E2-E1
Central Circus	C4-D4
Cheyne Walk	C4-D4-D3
Claremont Road	D2
Coles Green Road	A1
Cool Oak Lane	A2-A3
Crespigny Road	C3-C4
Dallas Road	B3-B2
Daniel Place	C3-C3
Danescroft Avenue	F3-F4
Danescroft Gardens	F3-F4
Dartmouth Road	B3-B4
Dehar Crescent	A2
Denehurst Gardens	D4
Edware Road	B1
Elliot Road	C3
Elm Close	E3
Elmcroft Crescent	E1-F1
Elm Park Gardens	E3-E4
Elms Avenue	E3-E4
Esmar Crescent	A2
Faber Gardens	B4
Fairfield Avenue	C3
Foscote Road	C3-C4
Garrick Road	A4
Golders Gardens	F1
Golders Green Road	F3-F2-F1
Golders Manor Drive	E2-F2
Golders Rise	E4
Graham Road	B4-B3-C3
Green Lane	E3-E4-F4
Green Walk	F4
Haley Road	D2-E2
Hamilton Road	E1
Haslemere Avenue	E3-E2
Heathfield Gardens	A2
Hendon Way	C4-C3-D3-D2-E2-E1
Heriot Road	D4-E4
Highfield Avenue	E1-E2-F2
Highfield Gardens	E2-F2
Highfield Road	F2
Holmbrook Drive	F4
Holmdale Gardens	E4-F4
Holmfield Avenue	F4
Irving Way	A4
Layfield Close	C2
Layfield Crescent	B2-C2
Layfield Road	B2-C2
Limes Avenue	F1
Malcolm Crescent	B4
Marriots Close	A4-A3
Mayfield Gardens	E3
Montagu Road	B4
Montpellier Rise	E1-F1
Mount Road	B3
Neeld Crescent	C4
Nicoll Place	C2-C3

Hendon

The magnificent RAF Museum is situated here, next to Hendon Aerodrome (once famous for its air displays) which is also the site of the Battle of Britain and Bomber Command Museum. People flock to Hendon for these — and for the vast regional shopping centre at Brent Cross. Other local landmarks are the Metropolitan Police Training College and the Church Farm House Museum.

But Hendon is probably best known to the world for its closeness to the M1 Motorway, which has its southern terminal close by, near to the Staples Corner Junction on the North Circular road.

Hampstead Artists, poets and politicians have made their homes in Hampstead, where the celebrated Heath stretches for 800 acres of grass and woodland. Fine 17th- to 19th-century houses can be found in the 'village', and the stylish shops of Heath Street and Hampstead High Street add to the colourful atmosphere.

Outstanding buildings open to the public are Keats House (1815), home of the poet John Keats, Fenton House, which is a fine late 17th-century building, and Kenwood House, remodelled in about 1765 by Robert Adam and visited for its paintings and open-air concerts. Noted pubs of Hampstead include the Old Bull and Bush (the original for the music-hall song), the Flask, the Spaniards and Jack Straw's Castle.

Central Hampstead

GOLDERS GREEN · GOLDERS GREEN · HIGHGATE · WEST END · SWISS COTTAGE · CAMDEN TOWN

North Circular Road	A1-B1-C1-D1-D2-E2-E3-F3-F4
Oakfield Court	E2
Park Road	A3-B3-C3-D3
Park View Gardens	E3-E4
Perryfield Way	A3
Prayle Grove	D1-E1
Priestley Way	A1-B1
Prince Charles Drive	C2-D2
Princes Park Avenue	F2-F3
Queens Gardens	E4
Queens Road	D4-E4
Queens Way	D4-E4
Renter's Avenue	D3-D2
Riverside	B2
Rose Mead	A3-A2
Rundell Crescent	C4
Russel Gardens	F2
Russel Road	A4
St Davids Place	B3-B2
St Marys Road	F1-F2
Sandringham Road	E1-F1
Seelig Avenue	A2
Sevington Road	B3-C3-C4
Shirehall Close	E3
Shirehall Gardens	E3
Shirehall Grove	E2-F2-F3
Shirehall Lane	E2-E3
Shirehall Park	E2-E3
Spalding Road	D2
Station Road	A3-A4-B4
Stuart Avenue	A2
Sturgess Avenue	B2-C2
Sydney Grove	D4
Talbot Crescent	B4
Templehof Avenue	C1-D1
The Broadway	A4-A3-A2-B2-B1
The Crest	E4
The Drive	F2-F1
The Grove	F1
Tilling Road	C1-D1-D2
Tyrrel Way	A3
Verulam Court	A2
Vicarage Road	B3
Vivian Avenue	B4-C4
Warner Close	A3
Waterbrook Lane	E4
Waterloo Road	C4
Watford Way	E4
West Avenue	E4
Western Avenue	E2-F2
Whitefield Avenue	D2
Wilberforce Road	A3-A4
Woodlands	F3-F4

Woodlands Close	F3-F4
Woodville Road	E1-F1
Woodward Avenue	B4
Woolmead Avenue	A2
Wykeham Road	D4

Hampstead

Achilles Road	A1-A2
Admirals Walk	C3-D3
Agincourt Road	F2
Ajax Road	A2
Akenside Road	D1
Aldred Road	A1
Alvanley Gardens	B1
Ardwick Road	A3
Arkwright Road	C1-D1-D2
Belsize Avenue	E1
Balsize Lane	E1
Bracknell Gardens	B2
Branch Hill	C4-C3
Briardale Gardens	A4-A3
Broomsleigh Street	A1
Burgess Hill	A3
Burnard Road	A2
Cannon Hill	B1-B2
Cannon Lane	D4-D3
Cannon Place	D3-D4
Carlingford Road	D2-E2
Chesterford Gardens	C2
Christchurch Hill	D3-E3
Church Row	C2
Clorane Gardens	A3
Constantine Road	F2
Crediton Hill	B1
Cressy Road	F2
Daleham Gardens	D1
Denning Road	D3-E3
Dennington Park Road	A1-B1
Downshire Hill	E2-E3
Downside Crescent	F1
East Heath Road	C4-D4-E4-E3-F3
Eklon Grove	E2
Ellerdale Road	C2-D1-D2
Fawley Road	B1
Ferncroft Avenue	A3-B3
Finchley Road	A4-A3-A2-B2-B1-C1
Fitzjohns Avenue	D2-D1
Flask Walk	D3
Fleet Road	F2-F1
Fortune Green Road	A3-A2-A1
Frognal	C3-C2-C1
Frognal Close	C2

Frognal Gardens	C2-C3
Frognal Lane	B1-B2-C2
Frognal Way	B4
Gainsborough Gardens	D3-E3
Garnett Road	F1
Gayton Crescent	D3
Gayton Road	D2-D3
Glenloch Road	E1-F1
Greenaway Gardens	B2
Hampstead Grove	C3-C4
Hampstead Hill Gardens	E1
Hampstead High Street	D2-E2
Haverstock Hill	E1-F1
Heath Drive	B2-B3
Heath Street	C4-D4-D3-D2
Heath Hurst Road	E2
Heathside	D3
Hermitage Gardens	A4
Hermitage Lane	A4
Hillfield Court	E1-F1
Hillfield Road	A1-A2
Holford Road	D4-D3
Holly Hill	C3-D3
Holly Walk	C2-C3
Hollycroft Avenue	A4-A3-B3
Holmdale Road	A1
Honeybourne Road	B1
Hewitt Road	F1
Ingham Road	A2
Inglewood Road	A1-B1
Keats Grove	E2
Kemplay Road	D2-E2
Kidderpore Avenue	A3-A2-B2
Kidderpore Gardens	B2-B3
Langland Gardens	C1-C2
Lawn Road	F1
Lindfield Gardens	C1-C2
Lithos Road	C1
Lower Terrace	C3-C4
Lymington Road	B1-C1
Lyncroft Gardens	A1-A2-B2
Lyndhurst Gardens	D1-E1
Lyndhurst Grove	E1
Lyndhurst Road	D1-E1-E2
Lyndhurst Terrace	D1
Mackeson Road	F2
Maresfield Gardens	D1
Mill Lane	A1
Narcissus Road	A1
Nassington Road	F2-F3
Netherhall Gardens	C1-D1
New End	D3
New End Walk	D3
North End Way	C4

Nutley Terrace	D1
Oak Hill Avenue	B2-B3
Oakhill Park	C3
Oakhill Park Mews	C3
Ornan Road	E1
Pandora Road	A1
Parkhill Road	F1
Parliament Hill	E2-E3
Parsifal Road	A2
Pattisons Lane	A3-A4-B4
Perceval Avenue	E1
Perrins Walk	C2-D2
Pilgrims Lane	E2-E3
Platts Lane	A3-A4-B4
Pond Street	E2-F2
Prince Arthur Road	D2
Ranulf Road	A3
Redington Gardens	B3
Redington Road	B4-B3-B2-C2
Rosecroft Avenue	A4-B4-B3
Rosslyn Hill	E2-E1
Rowland Hill Street	E1-F1
Solent Road	A1
South End Lane	E3-E2-F2
South Hill Park	F2-F3
Spaniards Road	C4-D4
Sumatra Road	A1
Tanza Road	F3
Templewood Avenue	B3-B4
Templewood Gardens	B3
Thurlow Road	D1-D2-E2
Tudor Close	E1
Ulysses Road	A1
Upper Park Road	F1
Wedderburn Road	D1-E1
Weech Road	A2
Well Road	D3-D4
Well Walk	D3
West Cottages	A1
West End Lane	A1-B1
West Heath Close	A4-B4
West Heath Gardens	A4
West Heath Road	A4-B4-C4
Willoughby Road	D2-D3
Willow Road	D3-E3
Windmill Hill	C3

HAMPSTEAD
John Keats wrote *Ode to a Nightingale* while living at Wentworth Place (now Keats House) from 1818 to 1820. Books, letters and other mementoes of the poet and his fianceé, Fanny Brawne, can be seen here.

23

Key to Town Plan and Area Plan

Town Plan

AA Recommended roads	
Other roads	
Restricted roads	
Buildings of interest	Cinema
Car Parks	P
Parks and open spaces	
Churches	†

Area Plan

A roads	
B roads	
Stations	Brockley
Borough Boundary	

Street Index with Grid Reference

Ilford

Ilford

Situated seven miles from London, Ilford is developing into a light industrial town with expanding industrial estates and a development programme to pedestrianise several important shopping streets. Valentines Park provides 130 acres of recreation area and includes peaceful havens such as the Old English Garden, the Rosary Terrace and Bishops Walk, as well as an ornamental pond and a lake. Set within the grounds of the park is one of the oldest buildings in the borough, Valentines House, which was built at the end of the 17th century.

Loughton's prominent Lopping Hall was built in 1884 by the City of London, after protests by local woodsmen about the lopping rights of the townspeople, and is now used for various community functions. Even today, the woodlands of Epping Forest dominate the town: Loughton stretches along its south-easterly side, and is bordered by the Rover Roding to the east. Interesting older buildings in the area include Loughton Hall and partly 16th-century Alderton Hall.

Barkingside is growing steadily due to recent business and housing developments and has a pleasant shopping area, various recreation grounds and the Redbridge Sports Centre. Fairlop Plain, just north of the town, is used for football, sailing and flying model aeroplanes.

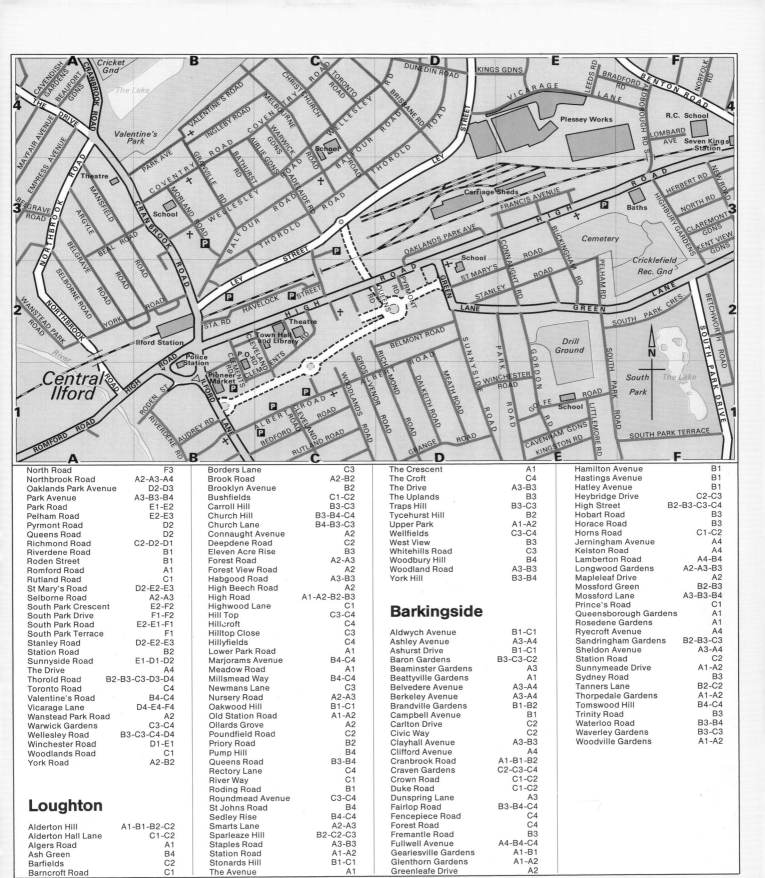

North Road	F3	Borders Lane	C3	The Crescent	A1	Hamilton Avenue	B1

North Road F3
Northbrook Road A2-A3-A4
Oaklands Park Avenue D2-D3
Park Avenue A3-B3-B4
Park Road E1-E2
Pelham Road E2-E3
Pyrmont Road D2
Queens Road D2
Richmond Road C2-D2-D1
Riverdene Road B1
Roden Street B1
Romford Road A1
Rutland Road C1
St Mary's Road D2-E2-E3
Selborne Road A2-A3
South Park Crescent E2-F2
South Park Drive F1-F2
South Park Road E2-E1-F1
South Park Terrace F1
Stanley Road D2-E2-E3
Station Road B2
Sunnyside Road E1-D1-D2
The Drive A4
Thorold Road B2-B3-C3-D3-D4
Toronto Road C4
Valentine's Road B4-C4
Vicarage Lane D4-E4-F4
Wanstead Park Road A2
Warwick Gardens C3-C4
Wellesley Road B3-C3-C4-D4
Winchester Road D1-E1
Woodlands Road C1
York Road A2-B2

Loughton

Alderton Hill A1-B1-B2-C2
Alderton Hall Lane C1-C2
Algers Road A1
Ash Green B4
Barfields C2
Barncroft Road C1

Borders Lane C3
Brook Road A2-B2
Brooklyn Avenue B2
Bushfields C1-C2
Carroll Hill B3-C3
Church Hill B3-B4-C4
Church Lane B4-B3-C3
Connaught Avenue A2
Deepdene Road C2
Eleven Acre Rise B3
Forest Road A2-A3
Forest View Road A2
Habgood Road A3-B3
High Beech Road A2
High Road A1-A2-B2-B3
Highwood Lane C1
Hill Top C3-C4
Hillcroft C4
Hilltop Close C3
Hillyfields C4
Lower Park Road A1
Marjorams Avenue B4-C4
Meadow Road A1
Millsmead Way B4-C4
Newmans Lane C3
Nursery Road A2-A3
Oakwood Hill B1-C1
Old Station Road A1-A2
Ollards Grove A2
Poundfield Road C2
Priory Road B2
Pump Hill B4
Queens Road B3-B4
Rectory Lane C4
River Way C1
Roding Road B1
Roundmead Avenue C3-C4
St Johns Road B4
Sedley Rise B4-C4
Smarts Lane A2-A3
Sparleaze Hill B2-C2-C3
Staples Road A3-B3
Station Road A1-A2
Stonards Hill B1-C1
The Avenue A1

The Crescent A1
The Croft C4
The Drive A3-B3
The Uplands B3
Traps Hill B3-C3-C4
Tycehurst Hill B2
Upper Park A1-A2
Wellfields C3-C4
West View B3
Whitehills Road C3
Woodbury Hill B4
Woodland Road A3-B3
York Hill B3-B4

Barkingside

Aldwych Avenue B1-C1
Ashley Avenue A3-A4
Ashurst Drive B1-C1
Baron Gardens B3-C3-C2
Beaminster Gardens A3
Beattyville Gardens A1
Belvedere Avenue A3-A4
Berkeley Avenue A3-A4
Brandville Gardens B1-B2
Campbell Avenue B1
Carlton Drive C2
Civic Way C2
Clayhall Avenue A3-B3
Clifford Avenue A4
Cranbrook Road A1-B1-B2
Craven Gardens C2-C3-C4
Crown Road C1-C2
Duke Road C1-C2
Dunspring Lane A3
Fairlop Road B3-B4-C4
Fencepiece Road C4
Forest Road C4
Fremantle Road B3
Fullwell Avenue A4-B4-C4
Geariesville Gardens A1-B1
Glenthorn Gardens A1-A2
Greenleafe Drive A2

Hamilton Avenue B1
Hastings Avenue B1
Hatley Avenue B1
Heybridge Drive C2-C3
High Street B2-B3-C3-C4
Hobart Road B3
Horace Road B3
Horns Road C1-C2
Jerningham Avenue A4
Kelston Road A4
Lamberton Road A4-B4
Longwood Gardens A2-A3-B3
Mapleaf Drive A2
Mossford Green B2-B3
Mossford Lane A3-B3-B4
Prince's Road C1
Queensborough Gardens A1
Rosedene Gardens A1
Ryecroft Avenue A4
Sandringham Gardens B2-B3-C3
Sheldon Avenue A3-A4
Station Road C2
Sunnymeade Drive A1-A2
Sydney Road B3
Tanners Lane B2-C2
Thorpedale Gardens A1-A2
Tomswood Hill B4-C4
Trinity Road B3
Waterloo Road B3-B4
Waverley Gardens B3-C3
Woodville Gardens A1-A2

ILFORD
A resplendent turn-of-the-century Town Hall epitomises the confidence felt by those who fostered Ilford's expansion — one of them guaranteed season ticket sales worth £10,000 when a station opened here in 1889.

Islington

Taverns and amusements made Islington a fashionable residential area and place of entertainment during the 18th century. Its theatrical traditions are carried on today by Sadler's Wells Theatre, dating from the 17th century and now home of the Sadler's Wells Royal Ballet Company. Cannonbury Tower is a much restored former manor house which is now in use as

a theatre, and also worth a visit are the antique shops and market stalls of Camden Passage.

Wood Green has become synonymous in North London with Shopping City, an extensive complex which was officially opened in 1981, and also houses the New River Sports Centre. Once a rural hamlet, Wood Green is now the administrative centre for the London Borough of Haringey.

Holloway is noted for the Sobell Sports Centre, said to be the largest in the country. The

Arsenal Football Club is another feature of the local landscape.

Tottenham Rivalling its nearby neighbours Tottenham Hotspur Football Club has its ground here — probably the most widely known aspect of this part-industrial, mainly residential area, which was once an agricultural community on the River Lea. There are several pleasant parks, and Bruce Castle Park has a local museum in a partly-Elizabethan building.

LEGEND

Town Plan

AA Recommended roads	
Other roads	
Restricted roads	
Buildings of interest	College
Car Parks	P
Parks and open spaces	
Churches	†
BR and Underground Stations	⊖

Area Plan

A roads	
B roads	
Stations	Stamford Hill ●
Borough Boundary	

STREET INDEX WITH GRID REFERENCE

WOOD GREEN

Acacia Road	C4
Alexandra Road	B2
Bedford Road	A4
Bounds Green Road	A4-B4
Braemar Avenue	A4
Brook Road	B3
Buckingham Road	A4
Burghley Road	B2
Bury Road	B2-C2
Carlingford Road	C1
Church Lane	A1
Claredon Road	A2-B2
Cobham Road	C2
Coburg Road	B4
Cranbrook Park	A1-A2
Cross Lane	C3
Darwin Road	A4
Dorset Road	C4
Dunbar Road	B4
Ewart Grove	B4
Falkland Road	B1-C1
Farrant Avenue	B3-C3
Frobisher Road	B1-C1
Gathorne Road	B3
Gladstone Avenue	B3-C3
Glebe Road	A1
Green Lanes	C1-C2
Hampden Road	A1-B1
Hawke Park Road	C2
Hewitt Avenue	C2-C3
High Road	B4-B3-B2-C2
High Street	A1
Hillfield Avenue	A1
Hornsey Park Road	B2-B3
King's Road	B4
Langham Road	C1-C2
Lausanne Road	B1
Leith Road	C4
Lordship Lane	B3-C3-C4-C3
Lymington Avenue	B2-B3-C3
Lyttle Road	B2
Malvern Road	B2
Mannock Road	C2
Mayes Road	A3-B3

Meads Road	C2
Morley Avenue	B3-C3
Moselle Avenue	B3-C3
Park Avenue	A4
Park Ridings	B2-B3
Parkland Road	B3
Pelham Road	B3
Pellatt Grove	B4-C4
Perth Road	C4
Progress Way	C4
Raleigh Road	B1
Ravenstone Road	B2
Russell Avenue	C2-C3
Salisbury Road	B1
Selbourne Road	A4-B4
Sirdar Road	C2
Solway Road	C4
Stanmore Road	C1
Station Road	A4-A3-B3
Stirling Road	C4
Sydney Road	B1
The Avenue	B2
The Sandlings	B3-B2-C2
Tottenham Lane	A1
Trinity Road	A4-B4
Turnpike Lane	A1-B1-B2
Vincent Road	C3
Waldeck Road	C1
Watsons Road	B4
West Beech Road	B2-C2
Westbury Avenue	C2
Western Road	A2-A3
West Green Road	C1
White Hart Lane	B4-C4
Whymark Avenue	B2-C2
Wightman Road	B1
Willingdon Road	C2
Willoughby Road	B2-B1-C1
Winkfield Road	C3-C4

TOTTENHAM

Adams Road	A4
Antill Road	B1-B2-C2
Arnold Road	B2-B3
Ashby Road	B1
Ashley Road	C2-C3
Beaconsfield Road	A1-A2
Bedford Road	A1-A2
Braemar Road	A1
Broad Lane	B1-C1-C2
Broadwater Road	A4
Bruce Grove	A4-B4
Brunswick Road	A1
Buller Road	C3
Carew Road	C4
Chandos Road	A4
Chester Road	A3
Chestnut Road	B3-C3
Clyde Circus	A2
Clyde Road	A2-B2
Cunningham Road	B2-C2-C1
Dongola Road	A2-A3
Dowsett Road	B4-C4
Drayton Road	A3-A4
Elmhurst Road	A4-B4
Fairbanks Road	B2-B3
Fairbourne Road	A3
Farley Road	C2
Ferry Lane	B2
Forster Road	B3
Fountayne Road	C1
Greenfield Road	A1
Greyhound Road	A2-A3-B3
Griffin Road	A4

Grove Park Road	A1-A2
Hale Road	C2-C3
Hanover Road	B1-B2
Havelock Road	C4
High Road	B1-B2-B3-B4
Holcombe Road	B3-C3
Jansons Road	A2
Kimberley Road	C3-C4
Kirkton Road	A1
Kitchener Road	A2-A3
Ladysmith Road	B3-B4
Lawrence Road	A1-A2
Linley Road	A4
Lordsmead Road	A4
Mafeking Road	C4
Markfield Road	C1
Mitchley Road	B3-C3
Monument Way	B2-C2-C3
Morrison Avenue	A3
Mount Pleasant Road	A2-A3-A4
Napier Road	A3
Newlyn Road	B4
Page Green Terrace	B1
Park View Road	C3-C4
Pembury Road	B4
Phillip Lane	A2-B2
Portland Road	B1
Poynton Road	C4
Radley Road	A4
Ranelagh Road	A3
Rangemoor Road	B1
Reed Road	B3-B4
Roseberry Avenue	C4
Roslyn Road	A1
St Loy's Road	A3-B3
Scales Road	B3-C3
Seaford Road	A1
Seymour Avenue	B4-C4
Sherringham Avenue	B4-C4
Southey Road	A1
Sperling Road	A4-A3-B3
Springfield Road	B2-C2
Stamford Road	C1
Station Road	C2
Steele Road	A3-B3
Talbot Road	B1-B2
Tamar Way	B3-C3
Thackeray Avenue	C4
The Avenue	A3-A4-B4
The Hale	C2-C3
Tynemouth Road	B2-C2
Wakefield Road	B1
Westerfield Road	B1
West Green Road	A1-B1
Willan Road	A3-A4
Wimbourne Road	A4
Winchelsea Road	A2-A3-B3
Woodside Gardens	A3-A4-B4

HOLLOWAY

Alexandra Road	A3-A4
Ambler Road	C3-C4
Andover Road	A4-B4
Annette Road	B2
Arvon Road	C1
Ashburton Grove	B2-C2
Aubert Park	C2
Avenell Road	C2-C3
Axminster Road	A3-B3
Battledean Road	C1
Beacon Hill	A1
Benwell Road	B2-B1-C1
Berriman Road	B3
Biddestone Road	A2-B2
Birnham Road	A4-B4
Blackstock Road	C4
Bracey Street	A4
Briset Way	B4
Bryantwood Road	C1
Caledonian Road	A2-A1-B1
Camden Road	A1-A2
Cardozo Road	A1
Citizen Road	B2-B3
Clifton Terrace	B4
Corker Way	B3-B4
Cornwallis Road	A3-A4
Drayton Park	C1-C2-C3
Dunford Raod	B2
Durham Road	B4
Eburne Road	A3
Eden Grove	B1
Elfort Road	C2-C3
Fieldway Crescent	C1
Finsbury Park Road	C4
Fonthill Road	B4-C4
Freegrove Road	A1
Georges Road	B1
Gillespie Road	C3
Hatley Road	B4
Hertslet Road	A3-A2-B2
Highbury Crescent	C1
Highbury Hill	C2-C3
Hillmarton Road	A1-B1
Holloway Road	A3-A2-B2-B1-C1
Hornsey Road	A4-A3-B3-B2-B1
Horsell Road	C1
Isledon Road	B3-C3-C4
Jackson Road	B2
Kingsdown Road	A4
Landseer Road	A3-A4
Lennox Road	B4
Lister Mews	B2
Liverpool Road	B1-C1
Loraine Road	B2
Lowman Road	B2
Manor Gardens	A3
Mayton Street	A3-B3
Medina Road	B3
Mingard Walk	A3-B3-B4
Moray Road	B4
Morgan Road	C1
Monsell Road	C3
Newington Barrow Way	B3-B4
Parkhurst Road	A1-A2
Penn Road	A1-A2
Plimsoll Road	C3-C4
Queens Drive	C4
Queensland Road	B2-C2
Quemerford Road	B1-B2
Rock Street	C4

Roden Street	A2-B2-B3
Romilly Road	C3-C4
Ronalds Road	C1
Roth Walk	B4
St Thomas's Road	C3-C4
Salterton Road	A3
Seven Sisters Road	A2-A3-B3-B4-C4
Stavordale Road	C2
Stock Orchard Crescent	B1
Sussex Way	A4-A3-B3
Tabley Road	A2
Thane Villas	B3
Tollington Park	A4-B4
Tollington Road	B2-B3
Tollington Way	A3-A4
Tufnell Park Road	A2-A3
Warlters Road	A2
Wells Terrace	B4-C4
Whistler Street	C1-C2
Widdenham Road	A2-B2-B1
Wilberforce Road	C4
Windsor Road	A3
Witherington Road	C1
Wray Crescent	A4
Yonge Park	B3

ISLINGTON

Almeida Street	B3
Amwell Street	A1
Baldwin Terrace	C2
Barford Street	B3
Barnsbury Park	A4-B4
Barnsbury Road	A2-A3
Barnsbury Square	A4
Barnsbury Street	A4-A3
Belitha Villas	A4
Baron Street	A1-A2
Bewdley Street	A4-B4
Bishop Street	C3
Braes Street	C4
Britannia Row	C3
Brooksbury Street	A4-B4
Burgh Street	C2
Camden Walk	B2
Canonbury Villas	C4
Canonbury Road	C4
Central Street	C1
Chadwell Street	B1
Chapel Market	A2-B2
Charlotte Terrace	A2-A3
City Garden Row	C1-C2
City Road	B1-C1
Clare Square	A1
Cloudesley Place	A2-B2
Cloudesley Road	A2-A3
Cloudesley Square	A3-B3
Cloudesley Street	A2-A3
Colebrooke Row	B1-B2-B3
College Cross	B4
Copenhagen Street	A2-A3
Cross Street	B3-C3
Cruden Street	C2-C3
Culpepper Street	A2
Dagmar Terrace	B3-C3
Danbury Street	B2
Devonia Street	B2-C2
Dewey Road	A2
Donegal Street	A1-A2
Duncan Street	B2
Duncan Terrace	B1-B2
Elia Street	B2-B1-C1
Essex Road	B2-B3-C3-C4
Florence Street	B3-B4
Friend Street	B1
Frome Street	C2
Gerrard Road	B2-C2
Gibson Square	B3
Goswell Road	B1-C1
Graham Street	C1-C2
Grant Street	A2
Green Man Street	C3-C4
Hall Street	C1
Halton Road	C3-C4
Hawes Street	B4-C4
Hemingford Road	A3-A4
High Street	B2
Islington Park Street	B4
Liverpool Road	B2-B3-B4
Lloyd Street	A1
Lofting Road	A4-B4
Lonsdale Square	A3-A4
Masons Place	C1
Milner Square	B3-B4
Moon Street	B3
Moreland Street	C1
Myddleton Square	A1-B1
New North Road	C4
Noel Road	B2-C2
Offord Road	A4
Packington Square	C2-C3
Packington Street	C3
Parkfield Street	B2
Penton Street	A1-A2
Pentonville Road	A1-B1
Percy Circus	A1
Percy Street	A1
Pleasant Place	C3-C4
Popham Street	C3
Prebend Street	C3
Raleigh Street	C2-C3
Rawstorne Street	B1
Rheidol Terrace	C2
Richmond Avenue	A3-B3
Richmond Crescent	A3
Ripplevale Grove	A3-A4
River Place	C4
River Street	A1
St John Street	B1
St Peters Street	B3-C3-C2
Sebbon Street	B4-C4
Stonefield Street	A3
Sudeley Street	B1-C1-C2
Theberton Street	B3
Thornhill Road	A3-A4
Upper Street	B2-B3-B4
Vincent Terrace	B2-C2
Wakley Street	B1
Wenlock Street	C1-C2
Wharf Road	C1-C2
White Lion Street	A2-B2

Kingston upon Thames Area

Central Kingston upon Thames

Kingston

Seven Saxon kings — at least — were crowned where the coronation stone now stands, near the Guildhall in the centre of town. Kingston kept up its connections with royalty, and they reached a peak in 1927 when George V confirmed its status as a Royal Borough.

Hampton Court, Kew Gardens and Richmond Park are all nearby. A number of ancient buildings can be seen in the High Street, and the Kingston Heritage Centre in Fairfield West is well worth a visit. A pleasant Thames-side setting, an extensive open-air market, the recently completed Eden Walk shopping precinct and a variety of old-established shops ensure Kingston's continued popularity.

Surbiton was chosen in preference to Kingston for the first local railway station in the 19th century, and rapidly grew in importance. A pleasant residential suburb, it has good entertainment facilities at the Assembly Rooms and the popular Surrey Grass Court Tennis Championships are held at Surbiton Lawn Tennis Club each year.

Epsom was already popular as a 'dormitory' town in the 18th century. Towards the end of that century, horse racing became popular on Epsom Downs, and the first Oaks was run here in 1779, followed by the first Derby in 1780. Modern Epsom is still mainly residential.

28

LEGEND

Town Plan

AA recommended route
Restricted roads
Other roads
Buildings of interest
Car parks   **P**
Parks and open spaces

Area Plan

A roads
B roads
Locations   Ockham o
Urban area

Street Index with Grid Reference

Kingston Upon Thames

Acre Road	B4-C4
Albert Road	C2-C3
Alexandra Road	D4-E4
Alfred Road	C1
Arundel Road	F2-F3
Athelstan Road	C1-D1
Beechcroft Avenue	F2-F3
Beresford Road	C4-D4
Birkenhead Avenue	C3-D3
Blenheim Gardens	E4
Bonner Hill Road	D2-E2
Brook Gardens	F3-F4
Brook Street	B2
Brunswick Road	D4-E4
Burritt Road	D2-E2
Cambridge Road	D3-D2-E2
Canbury Park Road	C3-D3-D4
Cardinal Crescent	F3
Caversham Road	C2-C3
Charter Road	E2-F2
Chatham Road	D3
Chesham Road	D3
Church Grove	A3
Church Road	C2-C3-D3
Clarence Avenue	F2
Clarence Street	A3-B3
Clifton Road	D3-D4

Cobham Road	D3
Coombe Lane West	E3-F3
Coombe Rise	F3-F4
Coombe Road	D3-E3
Cranbury Avenue	C3-C4-D4
Craven Road	C4-D4
Cromwell Road	B3-C3
Dagmar Road	D4
Dawson Road	C1-D1-D2-C2
Deacon Road	C3-C4-D4
Denmark Road	B1-C1
Dickerage Lane	F1-F2
Dickerage Road	F2-F3
Douglas Road	E1-E2
Down Hall Road	B3
Ernest Road	E2
Eastbury Road	B4
East Road	B4-C4
Eden Street	B2-B3
Elm Crescent	C3-C4
Elm Grove	C3
Elm Road	C3-C4-D4
Elton Road	D4
Fairfield East	C2-C3
Fairfield Place	C1
Fairfield Road	B2-C2
Fairfield South	C2
Fairfield West	B2-B3-C3
Fife Road	B3
Fleetwood Road	F1-F2
Galsworthy Road	E3-E4
Gibbon Road	B4-C4
Glamorgan Road	A4
Gloucester Road	E2-E3
Gordon Road	C3-D3
Grange Road	B2-B1-C1
Grove Crescent	B1
Grove Lane	B1-C1
Hampden Road	E1-E2
Hampton Court Road	A3
Hawks Road	C2-D2
High Street	A3
High Street	A1-A2-B2
Homersham Road	E3
Kenley Road	E3-F3-F2
King Henry's Road	E1-E2-F2
Kings Road	B4-C4
Kingston Hill	D3-D4-E4
Kingston Road	E2-E1-F1
Knights Park	B1-B2
Linden Grove	D2
London Road	B3-C3-D3
Lower Ham Road	B3-B4
Lower Teddington Road	A3-A4
Lowther Road	C4-D4
Manor Gate	D3-E3
Mill Place	C2
Mill Street	C1-C2
Milner Road	B1
Neville Road	E2-E3
Norbiton Avenue	E2-E3
Orchard Road	B2
Park Road	D3-D4
Park Street	A3
Penrhyn Road	B1-B2
Piper Road	D2
Porchester Road	E2-F2
Portland Road	B1-C1
Portsmouth Road	A1-B1
Princes Road	D4
Queens Road	E4

Revell Road	E3-F3
Richmond Park Road	B4-C4
Richmond Road	B3-B4
Rosebery Road	E2
Rowells Road	D2
St James's Road	B2
St Johns Road	A3
Seymour Road	A3-A4
Somerset Road	D2
Springfield Road	B1
Station Road	A4
Station Road	D3
Surbiton Road	B1
Thames Side	B3
Thames Street	B2-B3
The Bittoms	B1-B2
The Triangle	F2
Union Street	B2-B3
Upper Teddington Road	A3-A4
Victoria Road	C2-C3
Villiers Road	C1-C2
Vincent Road	D2-E2
Waters Road	E2
Willingham Way	D2
Willoughby Road	D3-D4
Wolsey Close	F3-F4
Wolverton Avenue	E3-E4
Woodbines Avenue	B1
Wood Street	B3
York Road	D4

Surbiton

Adelaide Road	B2-B3
Akerman Road	A1-A2
Alfred Road	C4
Anglesea Road	A4-B4-B3
Arlington Road	B1
Avenue Elmers	C2-B2-B3
Balaclava Road	A1
Beaufort Road	B3-B4
Berrylands Road	C2
Brighton Road	A1-A2
Britannia Road	C1
Browns Road	C1
Burney Avenue	C3
Cadogan Road	A3-A2-B2
Catherine Road	A3-B3
Cheyne Hill	C3-C4
Church Hill Road	B2
Claremont Road	B2-B3
Cleaveland Road	A2
Corkran Road	B1
Cottage Grove	A1-A2
Cranes Drive	C3
Cranes Park	B3-C3-C2
Cranes Park Avenue	B3-C3-C4
Cranes Park Crescent	C3
Electric Parade	A1
Eversley Road	C3
Ewell Road	C1-C2
Fasset Road	B3-B4
Geneva Road	C4
Glenbuck Road	B1-B2
Grove Crescent	B4
Grove Lane	B4-C4
Grove Road	A3-B3-B2

Guildford Avenue	C3
Howard Road	C1-C2
Ivy Place	C1
King Charles Road	C1-C2
Lamberts Road	C2
Langley Road	C1
Lingfield Avenue	B4-C4
Lovelace Gardens	A1-B1
Lovelace Road	A1-B1
Lower Marsh Lane	C4
Maple Road	A2-B2-B3
Minniedale	C3
North Road	A2-B2
Oakhill	B1
Oakhill Crescent	C1
Oakhill Grove	B1
Oakhill Road	B1-C1
Palace Road	A3-B3
Paragon Grove	C2
Parklands	C2
Park Road	C2
Penrhyn Road	B4
Portland Road	B4-C4
Portsmouth Road	A2-A3-A4
Riverside Close	A4-B4
St Andrews Square	A2
St James' Road	A2-B2
St Leonards Road	A3-A2-B2
St Marks Hill	B2-C2
Seething Wells Lane	A1-A2
South Bank	B2-C2
South Terrace	B2-C2
Springfield Road	B4
Surbiton Crescent	B3-B4
Surbiton Hill Park	C2
Surbiton Hill Road	B3-C3-C2
Surbiton Road	B3-B4
The Crescent	B2-B3
The Mall	A2
Upper Brighton Road	A1-B1
Uxbridge Road	A3-B3
Victoria Avenue	A1
Victoria Road	A1-B1-B2
Villiers Avenue	C2-C3-C4
Walpole Road	B1
Westfield Road	A2

Epsom

Albert Road	C1-C2
Almond Road	B4
Andrews Close	C1
Ashley Avenue	A1-B1
Ashley Road	B1-B2
Blenheim Road	B4
Burnet Grove	A2
Chase Road	B3
Church Road	C1-C2-C3
Church Street	B2-C2-C1
College Road	C1
Depot Road	B2-C2
Downside	C1
Downs Road	C1
East Street	B2-B3-C3
East Way	A4
Felstead Road	B4
Gosfield Road	A2-A3

Grove Avenue	C2
Grove Road	C1-C2
Hamilton Close	A3-A4
Hawthorne Place	C2-C3
Hazon Way	B2-A2-A3-B3
Heathcote Road	B1
High Street	A2-B2
Hook Road	A4-B4-B3-B2
Horsley Close	A2-B2
Horton Hill	A4
Hurst Road	A4
Kendor Avenue	A4
Kiln Lane	C3-C4
Lintons Lane	C3
Long Mead Road	B4
Lower Court Road	A4
Manor Green Road	A4
Middle Lane	C3-C4
Miles Road	B3-B4-B3
Mill Road	C2-C3
Pikes Hill	C2
Pitt Road	C1
Pound Lane	A4-B4
Rosebank	A1
St Martins Avenue	C1
South Street	A1-A2
Station Approach	A2-B2
Stone's Road	C3-C4
Temple Road	A4-B4-A3-B3
The Grove	C1-C2
The Parade	B2-B1-C1
Upper Court Road	A4
Upper High Street	B2-C2
Victoria Place	C3
Waterloo Road	B2-B3
West Hill	A2
West Hill Avenue	A3
West Street	A1-A2
Wheelers Lane	A2
Woodcote Close	A1-B1-A1
Worple Road	B1-C1

Lambeth

Lambeth/Bermondsey A memory of other times for Lambeth can be found in Cherry Gardens Pier, which juts into the Thames at Bermondsey Wall East and recalls the days when this was a resort area (spa waters were found here in the 18th century). Some 13 Victorian churches can be found in the borough, and two places of interest are the Imperial War Museum and the Cuming Museum, which displays local archaeological finds. The Oval is the home of Surrey County Cricket Club.

Streatham Cinemas, dance halls, theatres, a bowling alley, an ice-rink and a swimming pool made Streatham a major entertainment centre for south London after the Second World War, and to some extent it still has that role. It first became popular with city merchants after the Great Fire because of its pleasant rural setting, and later on, spa waters were discovered on Streatham Common, which still has 36 acres of land.

Brixton The present site was a wasteland until suburban development reached it in the early 19th century. The large Italianate houses of St Johns Crescent are typical of the period.

Peckham was covered with market gardens and pasture until the 19th century. It still enjoys the 64 acres of Peckham Rye Common and the sports facilities of Peckham Rye Park. The house at No 2 Woods Road, Peckham, dates back to about 1690.

Key to Town Plan and Area Plan

Town Plan
One way streets
AA Recommended roads
Restricted roads
Other roads
Buildings of interest   Hall
Churches
Car parks   P
Parks and open spaces
BR and Underground stations

Area Plan
A roads
B roads
Borough boundary
Stations   Waterloo

STREET INDEX WITH GRID REFERENCE

LAMBETH

Street	Ref
Abbey Street	F4
Albany Road	E1-F1-F2
Alberta Street	A1-A2-A3
Albert Embankment	E2-F2
Aldbridge Street	D2
Amelia Street	A2
Atterbury Street	D3-D4
Bath Terrace	B4-C4
Baylis Road	F4
Bermondsey Street	C4
Blackfriars Road	C4
Black Prince Road	C4-D4-E4
Borough Road	C2-C1-D1
Branganza Street	D2
Brandon Street	A4
Bridge Street	C3-D3
Brook Drive	D2-E2
Browning Street	B1-B2
Cardigan Street	B3-B4
Carlisle Lane	E2-E3
Chatham Street	B1-C1
Clayton Street	F1-F2
Cobourg Street	D4-E4
Cole Street	E2-F2
Congreve Street	C1
Cooks Road	B3
Cosser Street	D3
Country Street	B1-B2
Courtenay Street	E1-F1
Cowan Street	D2
Crampton Street	C2-C3
Dante Road	E2-E3
Darwin Street	E2
Dawes Street	D3
Deacon Way	E4-F4-F3
Decima Street	C1
De Laune Street	E3
Deverell Street	C1
Doddington Grove	F4
Druid Street	F2-F3
Dunton Road	

Street	Ref
Durham Street	B1
East Street	D2-E2-F2
Elliots Row	C3
Elsted Street	E2
Falmouth Road	D3-E3-E4
Fitzalan Street	D3
Fleming Road	C1-D1
Flint Street	E2
Frazer Street	B4-C4
Gilbert Road	C2-C3
Glasshouse Walk	A1-A2-B2
Grange Road	F3
Grange Walk	F3-F4
Gray Street	C4
Great Dover Street	D4-E4-E3
Great Peter Street	A3
Great Suffolk Street	D4
Guy Street	E4
Harleyford Road	A1-B1
Harper Road	D3-D4
Hayles Street	C3
Hercules Road	B3-B4
Heygate Street	D2-D3
Holyoake Road	C2-C3
John Islip Street	A2-A3
Jonathan Street	B2
Kempstead Road	C2
Kennington Butts	C2-D2-D3
Kennington Lane	A1-B1-C1-C2
Kennington Park Road	C1-C2
Kennington Road	B3-C3-C2-C1
King Charles Street	A4
King James Street	C4-D4
Kinglake Street	E1-F1-F2
Kipling Street	E4
Lambeth Bridge	A3
Lambeth High Street	A2-B2-B3-B3
Lambeth Palace Road	A3-B3-B4
Lambeth Road	A3-B3-C3-C4
Lambeth Walk	B2-B3
Lant Street	D4
Law Street	E3-E4
Leather Market Street	E4-F4
Lollard Street	C4-D4
London Road	C4-C3-D3
Long Lane	E4-F4

Street	Ref
Lorrimore Road	D1
Lynton Road	F2
Lower Marsh	B4
Manciple Street	E4
Manor Place	D1-D2
Marcia Road	F2
Marshalsea Road	D4
Merrow Street	D1-E1-E2
Methley Street	C1
Millbank	A2-A3-A4
Mina Road	F1-F2
Mint Street	D4
Montford Place	B1
Morley Street	C4
Morecambe Street	D2-E2
Munton Road	D3-E3
Neate Street	E1-F1
Newington Causeway	D3-D4
New Kent Road	D3-E3
Nine Elms Lane	A1
Old Kent Road	E3-E2-F2-F1
Olney Road	D1
Ontaria Street	D3-D4
Oswin Street	C3
Oval Way	B1
Page Street	A3
Pages Walk	E3-F3
Pardoner Street	E4
Parry Street	A1
Pearman Street	C4
Penrose Street	D1-D2
Penton Place	C2-D2-D1
Pilgrimage Street	E4
Pocock Street	C4-D4
Portland Street	E1-E2
Renfrew Road	C2-C3
Riley Road	F4
Rockingham Street	D3
Rodney Road	D3-D2-E2
Rothsay Street	E3-E4
Royal Street	B4
St Georges Circus	C4
St Georges Road	C4-C3-D3
Sandcroft Street	B2-C2
Smith Square	A3
Southwark Bridge	D3-D4
Spa Road	F3
Stannary Street	C1
Stead Street	E2
Sturgeon Road	D1
Surrey Row	C4-D4
Surrey Square	E2-F2
Sutherland Walk	D1
Tabard Street	E3-E4
Tanner Street	F4
Thurlow Street	E1-E2
Tooley Street	F4
Tower Bridge Road	E3-F3-F4
Trafalgar Avenue	F1
Trinity Street	D4-E4
Tyers Street	B2
Ufford Street	C4
Vauxhall Bridge	A1
Vauxhall Street	B1-B2
Vauxhall Walk	A2-B2
Victoria Embankment	A4
Walnut Tree Walk	C3
Walworth Road	D1-D2-D3
Wandsworth Street	A1
Waterloo Road	B4-C4
Webber Street	C4-D4
Westcott Road	C1-D1
Westminster Bridge	A4-B4

Street	Ref
Westminster Bridge Road	B4-C4
Weston Street	E3-E4
Westmorland Road	D1-E1
West Square	C3
Willow Walk	F2-F3
Wooler Street	E2
York Road	B4

BRIXTON

Street	Ref
Acre Lane	A2-B2-B3
Allard Street	A3
Appach Road	B1
Arlingford Road	C1
Atlantic Road	B3-C3
Ballater Road	A2-A3
Bankton Road	C2
Barnwell Road	C1-C2
Barrington Road	C4
Baytree Road	A2-B2
Bellefields Road	B4
Bonham Road	A1-A2
Branksome Road	A1-A2
Brighton Terrace	A3-B3
Brixton Hill	A1-B1-B2
Brixton Road	B3-B4-C4
Brixton Station Road	B3-C3-C4
Brixton Water Lane	B1-C1
Canterbury Crescent	B4-C4
Chantrey Road	A4-B4
Chaucer Road	C1-C2
Coldharbour Lane	A4-B4
Combermere Road	A4-B4
Concannon Road	A2-A3
Corrance Road	A2-A3
Crownstone Road	B1
Dalberg Road	B2-C2-C1
Dalyell Road	A4-B4
Dol Street	A3
Dray Gardens	B1
Ducie Street	A3
Dulwich Road	C1
Eaton Road	C2
Effra Parade	C1-C2
Effra Road	B2-B1-C1
Electric Avenue	B3-C3
Ferndale Road	A3-B3
Fyfield Road	C4
Gateley Road	B4
Glen Street	A3
Gresham Road	B4-C4-C3
Hargwyne Street	A4
Haycroft Road	A4
Hayter Road	A2-B2-B1
Horsford Road	A2-A1-B1
Hubert Grove	A3-A4
Jelf Road	C2
Josephine Avenue	B1
Kellet Road	B2-C2-C3
Kett Gardens	C2
Lambert Road	A1-B1
Landor Road	A4
Marcus Garvey Way	C2-C3
Mayall Road	B2
Medwin Street	A3
Mervan Road	B2-C2
Mordaunt Street	A4
Morval Road	B1-C1
Nealden Road	A4
Nursery Road	B3-B4
Porden Road	B2
Probert Road	C2
Pulross Road	A4-B4
Raeburn Street	A2-A3

Street	Ref
Railton Road	C2-C3
Rattray Road	B2-C2-C1
Rushcroft Road	B3-C3
St James's Crescent	C4
St John's Crescent	B4-C4
St Mathew's Road	B1-B2
St Matts Road	B2
St Saviour's Road	A1-B1
Santley Street	A3
Saltoun Road	B2-B3-C3
Somerleyton Road	C2-C3
Spenser Road	C1
Stainsfield Road	A4-B4
Stockwell Avenue	B4
Stockwell Park	B4
Stockwell Road	B4
Strathleven Road	A1
Sudbourne Road	A2-B2
Talma Road	C2
Tintern Street	A3
Torrens Road	A1-A2
Trelawn Road	B1-C1
Trent Road	A1-B1
Trinity Gardens	A3-B3-B2
Tunstall Street	B3
Western Road	C4
Wiltshire Road	C4
Winslade Road	A1
Winterwell Road	A1

PECKHAM

Street	Ref
Adys Road	A1
Alpha Street	B2
Amott Road	A1-B1
Ansty Road	B1-B2
Assylum Road	C4
Barforth Road	C1
Bath Close	C4
Bellenden Road	A1-A2-A3-A4
Birch Lane	B2-B3
Blackpool Road	A3
Blenheim Grove	A2-A3-B3
Bournemouth Road	B3
Brayards Road	B2-C2-C3
Burchell Road	C3-C4
Carden Road	C1
Carlton Grove	C4
Caulfield Road	C3
Cerise Road	B3
Chadwick Road	A2-B2
Choumert Grove	A3-A2-B2
Choumert Road	A2-B2
Cicely Road	B3
Clayton Road	B2
Consort Road	B4-B3-C3-C2-C1
Copeland Road	B2
Cossal Walk	C3-C4
Costa Street	A2
Crews Road	C2-C3
Danby Street	A2
Denman Road	A3
Dewar Street	B1
East Dulwich Road	B1
Ellery Road	C2
Elm Grove	A3-B3
Fenwick Road	B1
Firbank Road	C3
Gatonby Street	A4
Goldsmith Road	B4
Gordon Road	C2-C3
Gowlett Road	A1-B1
Grummant Road	A4
Hanover Park	B3

Street	Ref
Harders Road	B3-C3
Heaton Road	B2
Highshore Road	A3
Hinckley Road	A1-B1
Holly Grove	A3-B3
Hollydale Road	C3
Howden Street	A1-A2
Keston Road	A1
King's Grove	C4
Kimberley Avenue	C2
Kinsale Road	B1
Kirkwood Road	C2
Lanvanor Road	C2-C3
Lindon Grove	C1
Lisford Street	A4
Lugard Road	C3-C4
Lyndhurst Way	A2-A3-B2
Lyndhurst Grove	A3
Marmont Road	B4
Marsden Road	A1
Maxted Road	A1-A2
McDermott Road	A2-B2
Melon Road	A4
Moncrieff Street	B3
Montpelier Road	C4
Mushchamp Road	A1
Nigel Road	B2
Nunhead Crescent	B1
Nunhead Green	C1-C2
Nunhead Grove	C1
Nunhead Lane	B1-C1
Nutbrook Street	A1-B1
Oglander Road	A1-A2
Old James Street	C1
Ondine Road	A1
Ophir Terrace	A3
Peckham High Street	A4-B4
Peckham Hill Street	A4-B4
Peckham Road	A4
Peckham Rye	B1-B2
Philip Road	B2
Pilkington Road	B2-C2
Queens Road	B4-C4
Raul Road	B3
Redham Street	A2
Relf Road	B1-B2
Rye Lane	A4-A3-B3-B2
Sand Street	A2
Scylla Road	B1-C1
Stanbury Road	C3
Sternhall Lane	B2
Sumner Road	A4
Sunwell Street	C3
Tresco	C2
Waghorn Street	A2-A1-B1
Whorlton Road	B2
Wingfield Street	A2
Wivenroe Close	A2
Woods Road	C4

STREATHAM

Street	Ref
Abbotswood Road	A3-A4
Adare Walk	B1
Albert Carr Gardens	A1
Aldrington Road	A1-A2
Ambleside Avenue	A2-B2
Amesbury Avenue	B4-C4
Angles Road	B2-C2
Ashlake Road	B2
Babbington Road	A1-B1-B2
Barcombe Avenue	B4-C4
Becmead Avenue	A3-B3
Bedford Hill	A3

Street	Ref
Blairderry Road	B4
Bournevale Road	B2
Broadway	B1-B2
Conifer Gardens	C3
Conyers Road	A1
Cricklade Avenue	B4-C4
Culverhouse Gardens	A1
De Montfort Road	B4
Dingley Lane	A4-B4
Downton Avenue	C4
Drewstead Road	A4-B4
Eardley Road	A1
Eliora Road	B1
Fairmile Avenue	A1
Farnan Road	B1
Farm Avenue	B2-B3
Faygate Road	C4
Garrad's Road	A2-A3
Gleneagle Road	A1-B1
Gleneldon Road	B2-C2
Gracefield Gardens	B3-C3
Grasmere Road	C1-C2-C3
Hailsham Avenue	C4
Hambro Road	A1-B1
Harborough Road	C2
Hillhouse Road	C1
Hoadley Road	A3-A4
Hopton Road	B1-A1
Keymer Road	C4
Kingscourt Road	B3
Leigham Avenue	A3-B3
Leigham Court Road	B4-C4-C3
Leithcote Gardens	C2-C3
Lewin Road	B1
Madeira Road	B1-B2-C2
Minehead Road	C1
Mitcham Lane	A1-A2-B2
Mountearl Gardens	C3-C4
Mount Ephraim Lane	A3-B3
Mount Ephraim Road	A4-B4-B3
Mount Nod Road	C3
Natal Road	A1-B1
Norfolk House Road	B3
Oakdale Road	B2-B1-C1
Ockley Road	B2-B3
Pendennis Road	B3-C3-C2
Pinfold Road	B2-B3
Polworth Road	B1-C1
Prentis Road	A2-B2
Riggindale Road	A1-A2
Romeyn Road	C3
Rosedene Road	C3
Rutford Road	B1
Rydal Road	A2
Shrubbery Road	B2
Stanhope Road	B2
Steep Hill	B3
Sternhold Avenue	A4-B4
Streatham Common North	B1-C1
Streatham High Road	B1-B2-B3-B4
Steatham Hill	B4
Sunnyhill Road	B2-C2
Thirlmere Road	B2
Tooting Bec Gardens	A2-B2
Tooting Bec Road	A2
Valley Road	C1-C2-C3
Valleyfield Road	C1-C2
Wellfield Road	B2
Westcote Road	A1
Woodbourne Avenue	A3-B3
Woodfield Avenue	A3-A4
Woodleigh Gardens	B3

Lewisham

This is a popular destination for south-east Londoners, who come for the good shopping and leisure facilities. Most of these can be found in the Riverside Centre, which also offers the sports facilities of the Lewisham Leisure Centre, and, for social functions, the Riverdale Hall.

Greenwich lies at the heart of Britain's maritime traditions. The Royal Naval College and the National Maritime Museum provide a fascinating insight into the seafaring past. Open to visitors on Greenwich pier is Gypsy Moth IV, the boat in which Sir Francis Chichester sailed singlehanded round the world in 1966. Cutty Sark, a 19th-century clipper, is in dry dock nearby.

The Greenwich Meridian, source of Greenwich Mean Time, can be seen outside the Old Royal Observatory (now a museum) which stands in the extensive and beautiful grounds of Greenwich Park.

The Greenwich Festival takes place each June at various venues throughout the Borough, and offers some 200 events featuring international artists.

Woolwich The South-East London Aquatic Centre, in the Dockyard, offers facilities for most water sports. The Rotunda houses the Museum of Artillery.

Eltham is notable as the birthplace of Bob Hope — and for the restored 14th-century Eltham Palace. The Great Hall was built originally by Edward IV, during the 15th century.

LEGEND

Town Plan
AA recommended route
Restricted roads
Other roads
Buildings of interest   P.O.
Car parks   P
Parks and open spaces
One way streets

Area Plan
A roads
B roads
Stations   Vauxhall

Street Index with Grid Reference

Greenwich

Ashburnham Grove	A2-B2
Ashburnham Place	A2-B2
Bardsley Lane	A3-B3
Blackheath Hill	A1-B1
Blackheath Road	A1
Blissett Street	A1-B1-B2
Brand Street	B2
Burney Street	B2-B3
Cade Road	C1
Catherine Grove	A1-A2
Circus Street	B2
Claremont Street	B3-A3
Clavell Street	B3
Copperas Street	A3
Crane Street	C4
Creek Bridge	A3
Creek Road	A3-B3
Creekside	A3
Croom's Hill	B3-B2-C2-C1
Dartmouth Hill	B1
Devonshire Drive	A1-A2
Diamond Terrace	B1-C1
Dutton Street	A3
Egerton Drive	A1-A2
General Wolfe Road	C1
Gloucester Circus	B2
Greenwich Church Street	B3-B4
Greenwich High Road	A2-B2-B3
Greenwich South Street	A1-B1-B2
Guildford Grove	A1
Haddo Street	A3-B3
Horseferry Place	A4-B4-B3
Hyde Vale	B2-B1-C1
John Penn Street	A1
King George Street	B2-C2
King William Walk	B4-B3-C3
Langdale Road	A2
Lewisham Road	A1
Lindsell Street	A1-B1
Maidstone Hill	B1
Nelson Road	B3
Norman Road	A2-A3
Norway Street	A3-A4
Old Woolwich Road	C4
Park Row	C3-C4
Point Close	B1
Point Hill	B1-B2
Prior Street	B2
Randall Place	B3
Rangers Square	C1
Romney Road	B3-C3-C4
Roan Street	A3-B3
Royal Hill	B2
Shooters Hill Road	B1-C1
Sparta Street	A1
Stockwell Street	B3
Straits Mouth	B3-B2
Tarves Way	A3
Thames Street	A4-B4-B3
The Avenue	C2-C3
The Stowage	A3
Trafalgar Road	C4
West Grove	B1-C1
Westgrove Lane	B1
Winforton Street	B1

Woolwich

Anglesea Road	C2-C3
Artillery Place	A2-B2-B3
Belson Road	A3
Beresford Street	B4-C4-C3
Bloomfield Road	C1-C2
Borgard Road	A3
Brookhill Road	B1-B2-C2-C3
Burrage Place	C2
Burrage Road	C1-C2-C3
Calderwood Street	B3
Cambridge Row	C1
Church Street	A4
Circular Way	A1
Conduit Road	C2
Crescent Road	C2
Dale Road	C1
Eglinton Road	B1-C1
Elmdene Road	C1-C2
Ferry Approach	B4
Frances Street	A2-A3-A4
Frederick Place	C2
Grand Depot Road	B2
Green Hill	A1-A2
Green Hill Terrace	A2
Green's End	C3
Ha-Ha Road	A1-B1
Hare Street	B4
Herbert Road	C1
Hill Reach	A2
John Wilson Street	B2-B3-B4

Kingsman Street	A4-A3-B3
Lord Warwick Street	A4
Macbean Street	B3-B4-C4
Market Hill	B4
Market Street	B3
Nightingale Place	B1
Nightingale Vale	B1
Ogilby Street	A3
Plumstead Common Road	C1
Plumstead Road	C4
Powis Street	B4-B3-C3
Rectory Place	B3
Repository Road	A1-A2
Ridout Street	A3
Rush Grove Street	A2-A3
St Mary Street	A3-A4-B4
Samuel Street	A3
Sandy Hill Road	C1-C2
Spray Street	C3
Thomas Street	B3-C3
Vincent Road	C2
Warren Lane	B4-C4-C3
Wellington Street	B3
Willenhall Road	B2-C2-C1
Woolwich Common	B1
Woolwich High Street	A4-B4
Woolwich New Road	B1-B2-B3-C3
Wrottesley Road	C1

Lewisham

Albion Way	B3
Algernon Road	A2-A3-A4
Beacon Road	C1
Belmont Grove	C3-C4
Belmont Hill	B3-C3
Belmont Park	C3
Blessington Road	C3
Bonfield Road	B3-C3
Boyne Road	B4-C4-C3
Brookbank Road	A3
Campshill Road	B1-B2
Caterham Road	B4-C4
Clarendon Rise	B2-B3
College Park Close	B2
Connington Road	B4
Cornmill Lane	A4
Courthill Road	B2-B1-C1
Cressingham Road	B4
Dermody Road	B2-C2
Eastdown Park	C2
Eliot Park	B4
Ellerdale Street	A3-A4
Elmira Street	A3-A4
Elswick Road	A4
Embleton Road	A2-A3
Ennersdale Road	B1-C1
Ermine Road	A2-A3
Fordyce Road	B1
Gillian Street	A2
Gilmore Road	B3-C3-C2
Granville Park	B4-C4
Halesworth Road	A4
Hither Green Lane	B2-B1-C1
Jerrard Street	A4
Knowles Hill Crescent	C1
Ladycroft Road	A3-A4
Ladywell Road	A4

Leahurst Road	C1-C2
Lee Bridge	B3
Lee High Road	B3-C3-C2
Legge Street	A2-B2
Lewis Grove	B3
Lewisham High Street	A1-A2-B2-B3-B4
Lewisham Hill	A1-B1
Lewisham Park	A1-B1
Lewisham Road	B4
Limes Grove	B2
Littlewood Road	B1
Loampit Vale	A4-B4
Longbridge Way	B2
Longhurst Road	C1
Malyons Road	A1-A2
Manor Park	C1-C2
Marischal Road	B3-C3
Marsala Road	A2-A3
Mercator Road	C3
Middleton Way	C3
Molesworth Street	B3-B4
Morley Road	B2
Murillo Road	C2
Nightingale Grove	C1
Northbrook Road	C2
Oakcroft Road	B4-C4
Pascoe Road	C1-C2
Radford Road	B1
Rennel Street	B3-B4
Romborough Way	A1-B1
Ryecroft Road	B1
St Swithun's Road	C1
Saxton Close	C3
Slaithwaite Road	B2
Thornford Road	B1
Thurston Road	A4
Vian Street	A4
Vicars Hill	A2
Weardale Road	C2
Wearside Road	A2
Whitburn Road	A2-B2
Wisteria Road	C2

Eltham

Admiral Seymour Road	A3-B3-B4
Appleton Road	A4
Arbroath Road	A4-B4
Archery Road	B1-B2
Arsenal Road	B4
Balcaskie Road	B2
Beechill Road	B2
Berryhill	C3
Bexley Road	C1-C2
Blunts Road	B1-B2
Bournbank Road	A4
Congreve Road	B3-B4
Court Road	B1
Court Yard	A1-B1
Craigton Road	B3
Crookston Road	B4-C4
Dairsie Road	B4-C4
Dickson Road	A4
Dobell Road	B2
Downman Road	A4
Dumbreck Road	B3-C3-B4
Dunvegan Road	B3-C3
Earlshall Road	B3-C3

Elderslie Road	C1-C2
Elibank Road	B3-C3
Elizabeth Terrace	B1
Elston Close	B2
Eltham High Street	B1-C1
Eltham Hill	A2-A1-B1
Eltham Park Gardens	C3
Foots Cray Road	C1
Froissart Road	A2
Glenesk Road	C2-C3-C4
Glenhouse Road	B2-C2
Glenlea Road	B2-C2-C3
Glenlyon Road	C2
Glenshiel Road	C2
Glenure Road	C2
Gourock Road	B2-C2
Granby Road	B4
Grangehill Road	B3-B4
Green Acres	B1-C1
Greenholm Road	C1-C2
Greenvale Road	B3-C3
Keynsham Road	A2
Kidbrooke Lane	A3
Kingsground	A1
Kingsholm Gardens	A3-A4
Kings Orchard	A1
Lassa Road	A2-B2
Lilburne Road	A2
Lovelace Green	B4
Maudsley Road	B4
Moira Road	B3-B4
North Park	B1-C1
Oakways	C1
Passey Place	B1
Prince John Road	A2
Prince Rupert Road	A3-B3-B4
Rancliffe Gardens	A4
Rochester Way	A4-A3-A4-B4-C4
Ross Way	A4
Sherrard Road	A2-B2
Shrapnel Road	B4
Southend Close	B1
Southend Crescent	C1
Strongbow Crescent	B2
Strongbow Road	B2
Tattersall Close	A2
Tilt Yard Approach	A1-B1
Wendover Road	B4
Well Hall Road	B1-B2-B3-A3-A4-B4
Westhorne Avenue	A3
Westmount Road	B4-B3-C3-C2-C1
Whynates Road	A4
Woodington Road	B1-C1

Richmond

Red deer and fallow deer roam Richmond Park's 2,500 acres of woodland and common, and Richmond itself has kept a village-like atmosphere in spite of a great deal of development over the last two centuries. Around the Green, antique and curio shops can be found nestling among the narrow lanes and alleyways of a bygone age. Richmond's other great attraction is the river: this has been a fashionable residential area for several hundred years, due to its pleasant Thames-side location and its proximity to Hampton Court Palace.

Twickenham Regular international matches are played during the season at this home of Rugby Union Football. Places of interest include Marble Hill House, a Palladian villa set in pleasant parkland, the Orleans House Gallery, which has paintings of local scenes, and the nearby Royal Botanic Gardens at Kew.

Hounslow Gunpowder and swords were the pride of Hounslow in the 17th century; three hundred years later, the area is mainly residential, with good shopping and leisure facilities.

Brentford's modern urban appearance belies its numerous places of interest. Gunnersbury Park has a local history museum, and St George's Church, in the High Street, houses a collection of musical instruments. A museum of steam engines can be seen at Kew Bridge Pumping Station.

Key to Town Plan and Area Plan

Town Plan

AA Recommended roads	
Other roads	
Restricted roads	
Buildings of interest	
Churches	Church
Car Parks	P
Parks and open spaces	
AA Service Centre	AA

Area Plan

A roads	
B roads	
Locations	Honley O
Urban area	

Richmond

Albert Road	C2-C3
Alton Road	C3
Audley Road	C2
Avalon Terrace	C3-C4
Beaumont Avenue	C4
Bridge Street	A1-A2
Cambridge Road	A1
Cardigan Road	B1
Castle Gate	C4
Cedar Terrace	C4
Chester Avenue	C1
Chislehurst Road	B1
Church Road	B3-B2-C2-C1
Clevedon Road	A1
Cresswell Road	A1
Crofton Terrace	C4
Dunstable Road	B3-C3
Dynevor Road	B2
Ellerker Gardens	B1
Eton Street	B2-B3
Evelyn Road	B4
Friars Lane	A2
Friars Stile Road	B1-C1
George Street	A2-A3
Greenside	A2-A3
Grosvenor Road	B2
Halford Road	B2
Hill Street	A2
Houblon Road	C2-C3
Jocelyn Road	B4-C4
Kew Foot Road	B4
Kew Road	B3-C4-C4
Kings Road	C1-C2-C3
Lancaster Park	B1-B2
Larkfield Road	B3-C3
Lower Mortlake Road	B4-C4
Maid of Honour Road	A3-A2
Marchmont Road	C1-C2
Marlborough Road	C1
Montague Road	B1
Mount Ararat Road	B2-B1-C1
Onslow Avenue	B1-B2
Onslow Road	B1-C1

Pagoda Avenue	C4
Paradise Road	B2
Park Hill	C1
Park Lane	A3-B3
Park Road	C1
Parkshot	A3-B3-B4
Pembroke Villas	A3
Petersham Road	A2-A1-B1
Portland Terrace	A3
Princes Road	C2-C3
Queens Rise	C1
Queens Road	C1
Red Lion Street	A2-B2
Richmond Hill	A1-B1
Richmond Road	A1
Royston Road	B2-C2
Selwyn Avenue	C4
Sheendale Road	C4
Sheen Park	C3
Sheen Road	B3-B2-B3-C3
Sheen Vale	C4
Spring Grove Road	C2
Sydney Road	B3
The Hermitage	A2-B2
The Orange Tree	A4-B4
The Quadrant	A3-B3
The Vineyard	A1-B1-B2
Townshend Road	C3
Townshend Terrace	C3
Twickenham Road	A3-A4
Water Lane	A2
Worple Way	C3

Twickenham

Amyand Park Road	C3-C4
Arragon Road	C2
Bell Lane	C2
Chertsey Road	A3-A4-B3-B4-C4
Chudleigh Road	A3-B3
Chuch Street	C2
Clifden Road	B2
Cole Park Road	B3-C3-B3-B4
Colne Road	A1-A2
Copthall Gardens	B2
Court Way	A3-B3
Craneford Way	A2-A3-B3
Cross Deep	B1-B2
Edwin Road	A2
Egerton Road	A3
Erncroft Way	B3-B4
Fulwood Gardens	B4
Glebeside	B4
Godstone Road	C3-C4
Gould Road	A2
Grange Avenue	A1
Grosvenor Road	B2
Grotto Road	B1
Grove Avenue	B2
Hampton Road	A1
Heathfield North	A3-B3
Heathfield South	A3-B3
Heath Gardens	A1-B1
Heath Road	A1-A2-B2
Hill View Road	B4
Holly Road	B2
Holmes Road	B1
Kenley Road	C4
King Street	B2-C2
Latham Road	B3
Laurel Avenue	A2-B2
Lebanon Park	C2
Lime Grove	B3

Lion Road	A2-B2
London Road	B4-B3-B2-C2
Marble Hill Gardens	C3
Marlow Crescent	B4
May Road	A1-A2
Oak Lane	C2-C3
Orchard Road	C4
Popes Avenue	A1
Popes Grove	A1-B1
Queens Road	B2
Radnor Road	B1-B2
Richmond Road	C2-C3
Rugby Road	A4
St Margaret's Road	C4
Saville Road	B1
Sherland Road	B2
Sidney Road	C4
Sion Road	C2
Station Road	B2
Strafford Road	C2-C3
The Avenue	A4
The Embankment	C1-C2
The Green	A1
Upper Grotto Road	A1-B1
Walpole Road	A1
Whitton Road	A3-A4-A3-B3
York Street	C2

Brentford

Albany Road	B2
Augustus Close	A1-B1
Avenue Road	A3-A4
Boston Manor Road	A1-A2-A3
Braemar Road	B2-B3
Brentford High Street	A1-B1-B2-C2-C3
Brent Lea	A1
Brent Road	A2
Brent Way	A1
Brentwick Gardens	B4-C4
Brook Lane North	A3-B3
Brook Road South	B2-B3
Burford Road	B3-C3
Carlyle Road	A4
Carville Crescent	B4-C4-B4
Challis Road	A4-B4
Chestnut Avenue	B4
Church Walk	A2
Clayponds Avenue	B4
Clayponds Gardens	B4
Clayponds Lane	C3
Clayton Crescent	A4-B4
Clifden Road	A2-B2-B3
Darwin Road	A4-B4
Dock Road	B1
Ealing Park Gardens	A4
Ealing Road	B4-B3-B2
Eastbourne Road	A3-A4
Enfield Road	A3-A4
Ferry Lane	B2
Glenhurst Road	A2-A3
Green Dragon Lane	C3
Hamilton Road	A2-A3-B3
Justin Close	B1
Lateward Road	B2
Layton Road	B3
Lionel Road	C4
Murray Road	A4
Netley Road	B3-C3
New Road	B3
North Road	C2-C3
Orchard Road	A2-A3
Pottery Road	C2-C3

Somerset Road	A2
Springvale Avenue	B4
The Butts	A2
Upper Butts	A2
Walnut Tree Road	B2-C2
Windmill Road	A2-A3-A4
Whitstile Road	A4-B4
York Road	A3

Hounslow

Albion Road	A1-A2-B2
Alexandra Road	B3
Argyle Avenue	B1
Balfour Road	B3
Bath Road	A3-B3-B2
Bell Road	B2
Bulstrode Avenue	A3-B3
Bulstrode Road	A3-B3
Chapel Road	B2-C2
Cromwell Road	A2-A1-B1
Cross Lances Road	B2
Dean Road	B1
Denbigh Road	B4-C4
Dene Avenue	A3
Ellerdine Road	C1-C2
Ellington Road	B3-C3
Great West Road	A4-B4
Greencroft Road	A4
Gresham Road	C4
Grove Road	A2-B2
Hanworth Road	A1-B1-B2-B3-C2-C3
Harte Road	A3-A4
Heath Road	B2-C2
Hibernia Gardens	B1-B2
Hibernia Road	A2-B2-B3
High Street	B2-B3-C3
Inwood Avenue	C2-C3
Inwood Road	B2-C2-C3
Kingsley Avenue	C4
Kingsley Road	B4-C4-C3
Lampton Avenue	A4
Lampton Road	B3-B4
Lyncroft Gardens	C1-C2
Maswell Park Road	B1-C1-C2
Millwood Road	C1
Myrtle Road	C3
North Drive	C3-C4
Park Road	B1-C1
Parkside Road	B1
Pears Road	C3
Queenswood Avenue	A4
Rosebery Road	C1
Roseville Avenue	A1
St Aubyns Avenue	A1
St Stephens Road	B1
Spring Grove Crescent	C4
Spring Grove Road	B4-C4
Staines Road	A2-B2
Stanley Road	C2
Station Road	B1-B2
Sutton Lane	A3-A4
Taunton Avenue	C3
The Drive	C3-C4
Tiverton Road	C3-C4
Victoria Avenue	A1
Wellington Road North	A2-A3
Wellington Road South	A1-A2
Wesley Avenue	A3-A4
Whitton Dene	B1-C1
Whitton Road	B1-B2
Worton Way	C3-C4
Yew Tree Walk	A1

Romford

Reputed to have some of the finest shopping facilities on the east side of London, Romford mixes the ancient with the modern in its high streets and traffic areas. Centrepiece of all shopping is Romford Market, where traders have been setting up stall three times a week for the past 700 years.

The oldest-founded building still standing in Romford is thought to be St Edward's Church, which was rebuilt in 1850 and has some interesting monuments. The Golden Lion survives as a fine example of an old coaching inn.

Hornchurch A bull's head and horns hung over the east window of St Andrew's Church gave Hornchurch its name — thought to be the only example in the country to be used instead of the traditional east end cross. Also unique to the church is the tomb of Thomas Witherings, 17th-century organiser of the postal system.

Modern shops line the High Street, which was once known as Pelt Street: Hornchurch was famous for its leather goods in the 13th century. The Queens Theatre stages concerts and professional repertory performances of a high standard.

Upminster's windmill was constructed in 1803 and has remained in excellent condition. Other buildings of interest include Upminster Hall and 15th-century Upminster Tithe Barn.

LEGEND

Town Plan
AA Recommended roads
Other roads
Restricted roads
Buildings of interest   Cinema
Car Parks
Parks and open spaces

Area Plan
A roads
B roads
Stations   Forest Bridge
Borough Boundary

STREET INDEX WITH GRID REFERENCE

ROMFORD

Ainsley Avenue	A1
Albert Road	E1-E2
Albion Close	C1-C2
Angel Way	C3
Beech Street	B4
Boundary Road	F1-F2
Brentwood Road	E1-F1-F2
Bridge Close	D1
Brooklands Road	B4-C4-C3
Burlington Avenue	A1-A2
Carlisle Road	F2
Carlton Road	E3-F3-F4
Cedar Road	A4-B4
Cherry Street	B3
Church Lane	D4
Claremont Road	F1
Clifton Road	F1
Como Street	B3-C3-C4
Cotleigh Road	C1-C2
Cottons Approach	C2-C3
Craigdale Road	E1
Cromer Road	A2-A1-B1
Derby Avenue	A1
Douglas Road	E1-F1
Drummond Road	B3-B4
Dunton Road	C4
Eastbury Road	B1-B2
Eastern Avenue	A4
Eastern Road	D2-E2-E3
Erroll Road	E4
Esher Avenue	A1-A2
Exchange Street	D2-D3
George Street	E1-E2
Gilbert Road	E4
Glenwood Drive	F3-F4
Globe Road	F1
Granger Way	F1-F2
Hearn Road	E2
Heath Park Road	F3

High Street	C3-D3
Honiton Road	B1-B2-C2
Ingrave Road	C4
Jubilee Avenue	A2
Junction Road	E3-E4
Kensington Road	B1-B2
Kimberley Avenue	A1
King Edward Road	E1-E2
Kings Road	F2
Kingsmead Avenue	D2-D1-E1
Kingston Road	E4
Knighton Road	B1-B2
Knightsbridge Gardens	C2-C3
Kyme Road	E1
Lennox Close	E1
Lessington Avenue	A1
Linden Street	C3-C4
Lodge Avenue	F3-F4
London Road	A2-B2-C2
Lonsdale Avenue	A1-A2
Main Road	D4-E4
Malvern Road	F1
Manor Road	F2-F3
Maple Street	B4
Market Link	D3-D4
Market Place	D3
Marks Road	B2-B3-C3
Mawney Road	A4-A3-B3-C3
Medora Road	B4-C4
Mercury Gardens	D3-E3
Mildmay Road	A3-B3
Milton Road	F2
Norfolk Road	B1-B2
North Street	C4-C3-D3
Oak Street	A3
Oldchurch Road	C1-D1
Olive Street	C3
Palm Road	A3-B3
Park Drive	C4-D4
Park Lane	F1
Park End Road	D4
Pretoria Road	A2-A3-A4
Princes Road	F2-F3
Poplar Street	A4-B4
Queen Street	C1-C2
Randall Road	E1-E2
Recreation Avenue	A2-B2
Regarth Avenue	D1
Richards Avenue	B2
Richmond Road	E1
St Andrews Road	C2
St Edwards Way	C2-C3-C4-D4
Shaftesbury Road	E2-F2
Shakespeare Road	E2-F2
Sherringham Avenue	A1-B1
Sims Close	E3-E4
South Street	D3-D2-D1-E1
Spring Gardens	A2
Stanley Avenue	F3-F4
Stockland Road	B1-C1
The Avenue	C4
The Mews	D3
The Ridgeway	F4
Thurloe Gardens	D1-E1
Victoria Road	D2-E2-E3-F3
Vine Street	C2
Waterloo Gardens	B3
Waterloo Road	C2-C1-D1
Western Road	D2-D3-E3
Wheatsheaf Road	E1
Willow Street	B3-B4
Yew Tree Gardens	C2-C3

HORNCHURCH

Abbs Cross Gardens	A2-B2-C2
Abbs Cross Road	A1-A2-A3
Alma Avenue	C1
Austral Drive	A3
Bedford Gardens	A1-A2
Belmont Road	A1
Berther Road	B4
Beulah Road	C4
Bevan Way	C1
Beverley Gardens	C4
Billet Lane	B3-B4
Boscombe Avenue	A3-A4
Bruce Avenue	A2-B2
Burnway	B4-C4-C3
Butts Green Road	B4
Cedar Road	A1
Chepstow Avenue	C1
Clement Way	C1
Cromer Road	A4-B4
Devonshire Road	A2-B2
Elmhurst Drive	A3-A4
Fairkytes Avenue	A3-B3
Glamis Drive	C3
Glanville Drive	C2-C3
Glebeway	B4-B3-C3
Grey Tower Avenue	A3
Goodwood Avenue	C1
Grosvenor Drive	A3-A4
Hacton Lane	C1-C2
Herbert Road	C4
High Street	A3-B3-B2-C2
Highfield Road	C2
Hillview Avenue	A4-B4
Hornchurch Road	A3
Keithway	B3-B4
Kempton Avenue	C1
Kenilworth Gardens	A1-B1
Kenley Gardens	C2
Keswick Avenue	A3-B3
Lambourne Gardens	B1-B2
Linkway	B3-C3
Lyndhurst Drive	A3-A4
Mansfield Gardens	A1-A2
Mavis Grove	B2
Maybush Road	C4
Mill Park Avenue	B1-B2
North Street	B3-B4
Osborne Drive	A4-B4
Patricia Drive	C3
Plumpton Avenue	C1
Priors Park	A1
Ravenscourt Drive	C1
Ravenscourt Grove	B1-C1-C2
Ringwood Avenue	A2
St Georges Avenue	C4
Shirley Gardens	A1-A2
Standen Avenue	B1-C1
Stanley Road	A2-B2
Station Lane	B1-B2
Suttons Avenue	A1-A2
Suttons Lane	B1
The Avenue	A2-B2
Upminster Road	C2
Urban Avenue	A1
Victor Gardens	B2-B3
Warriner Avenue	B1-B2
Wayside Avenue	A1-A2-B1
Westland Avenue	B3-C3-C2
Windsor Road	A4
Wingletye Lane	C2-C3
Woodall Crescent	C3

UPMINSTER

Acacia Drive	A1-A2
Argyle Gardens	C1-C2-C3
Ashburnham Gardens	B4-C4
Ashleigh Gardens	C1-C2
Beech Avenue	B1-B2
Benets Road	A4
Berkley Close	A4-B4-B5
Berkley Drive	A4-A3
Boundary Road	A2-A3
Brackendale Gardens	C1
Branfill Road	B3
Bridge Avenue	A2-A3
Brookdale Avenue	A2
Cedar Avenue	A1-A2
Cedar Gardens	C2
Champion Road	B3
Claremont Gardens	C4
Coniston Avenue	B1-C1
Corbets Tey Road	B1-B2-B3
Courtenay Gardens	C4
Cranborne Gardens	B3
Cranston Park Avenue	B1-C1
Derham Gardens	C2
Deyncourt Gardens	C4
Elm Avenue	B1-B2
Engayne Gardens	B4
Fairfield Avenue	C1-C2
Frimley Avenue	A4
Gaynes Court	A1-B1
Gaynes Road	B3
Gaynes Park Road	A1-B1
Grosvenor Gardens	C4
Hall Lane	B4-C4
Hedingham Road	A4
Highview Gardens	A3-B3
Hornminster Glen	A3-A4
Howard Road	B3-C3
Ingrebourne Gardens	C4
Leasway	B1-B2
Little Gaynes	B1
Little Gaynes Lane	A1-B1
Lime Avenue	A1
Maple Avenue	A1-A2
Meadow Way	B1-B2
Melstock Avenue	B1
New Place Gardens	C2-C3
Norfolk Road	A2-A3
Oak Avenue	A2-A1-B1
Park Drive	B1-C1
Roxburgh Avenue	C1-C2
Rushmere Avenue	C1-C2
St Lawrence Road	B3-C3
St Mary's Lane	A3-B3-C3
Somerset Gardens	A4
Southview Drive	A2-B2
Springfield Gardens	B2-C2
Station Road	B3
Stewarts Avenue	A2-B2
Sunnyside Gardens	B2-C2
Sycamore Avenue	A1-A2
The Grove	A1
The Shrubbery	B2-C2
Tudor Gardens	C2-C3
Upminster Road	A3
Waldegrave Gardens	B4

Sutton

Pleasant parks and modern shopping facilities are the chief attractions of Sutton, a residential area which was extensively developed in the 19th century. Recreation is catered for by the Westcroft Sports and Leisure Centre.

Wimbledon was a popular place for duelling in the 19th century, and it is still the site of hard fought contests — between the cream of the world's tennis players, who come here annually for the Lawn Tennis Championships, held at the end of June. The Lawn Tennis Museum can be visited in the grounds of the All England Tennis Club.

Wimbledon grew up around 16th-century Wimbledon House and has now become a pleasant residential area. The Wimbledon Theatre, in the Broadway, is popular for its Christmas pantomime, and the Polka Children's Theatre is based nearby. Wimbledon Common (scene of the duels) lies to the west and covers some 1,100 acres. An interesting restored windmill can be seen here.

Mitcham's cricket green is one of England's oldest pitches, in constant use since 1707.

Carshalton's attractive open spaces are enhanced by the River Wandle, which flows through the town and forms a pond near the centre. All Saints Church has 12th- and 13th-century features, and Little Holland, at Carshalton Beeches, has work by local craftsman Frank Dickenson.

Central Mitcham

Central Carshalton

LEGEND

Town Plan

AA recommended route
Restricted roads
Other roads
Buildings of interest — Hall ▪
Car parks — P
Parks and open spaces

Area Plan

A roads
B roads

Street Index with Grid Reference

Sutton

Abbots Road	A4
Albert Road	F1-F2
Alberta Avenue	A2-A3
Alfred Road	F1-F2
Bealah Road	B3-C3
Beauchamp Road	B3-C3
Benhill Avenue	D3-E3-F3
Benhill Road	F3-F4
Benhill Wood Road	E3-E4
Bourne Way	A2-B2
Bridge Road	D1
Brighton Road	D1-E1
Brunswick Road	E3-E4
Burgess Road	C3
Burnell Road	D4-E4
Bushey Lane	C4
Bushey Road	C4 D4
Camden Gardens	C1-C2
Camden Road	C2-D2
Carlisle Road	A2-A1-B1
Carshalton Road	D1-E1-E2-F2
Cedar Road	F1
Chaucer Gardens	C4
Cheam Road	A1-B1-C1-D1
Clarence Road	C3-C2-D2
Clyde Road	D1
Collingwood Road	B4-C4-C3-C2
Constance Road	E4
Cressingham Grove	E4
Crown Road	C3-C4-D4
Cumnor Road	E1-F1
Dale Road	A3
Eaton Road	F1
Elmbrook Road	A4-B4
Erskine Road	F4
Fairholme Road	A1

Frederick Road	A3-B3
Gandergreen Lane	A4-B4-B3-B2-B1
Gibson Road	D2
Greyhound Road	E2-F2
Grove Road	C1-D1
Haddon Road	C3-D3
High Street	D4-D3-D2
Hillcroome Road	F1
Hilldale Road	A3-B3
Jeffs Road	A3-A4
Landseer Road	B1
Langley Park Road	E2-E1-F1
Lenham Road	D3-E3-E2
Lewis Road	D4
Lind Road	F2-F3
Litchfield Road	E3
Lodge Place	D3
Lower Road	F3
Manor Lane	E3
Manor Place	D3
Manor Park Road	E2
Marshall's Road	D3-D4
Milford Grove	E4
Milton Road	B4-C4
Montpelier Road	F3
Morland Road	E1-F1
Myrtle Road	E2-E3
Norman Road	B2-B3
Oakhill Road	E4-F4
Oliver Road	F3
Orchard Road	C3
Palmerston Road	F2-F3
Parkhurst Road	F4
Princess Street	F4
Quarry Rise	A1
Quarry Park Road	A1-A2
Reading Road	F1-F2
Revell Road	A1
Robin Hood Lane	B2-C2-D2
Ruthered Close	F1
St Albans Road	A3-A4
St Barnabas Road	F2-F3
St Dunstan's Hill	A4
St James' Avenue	B3-B2-C2
St James' Road	B3-C2-C1
St Nicholas Way	D1-D2-D3-D4
Sherwood Park Road	C1-C2
Sunningdale Road	E1
Sutton Court Road	E1
Sutton Park Road	D1
Sydney Road	B3-C3-C4
Tate Road	F3-F4
Thicket Crescent	F3-F4
Thicket Road	F3-F4
Throwley Way	D4-D3-D2-E2-E1
Vale Road	C4-D4
Vernon Road	F2
Vicarage Road	C4
Victoria Road	F1-F2
Warwick Road	E2-E3
Wellesley Road	E1
West Street	D2
Western Road	B1-B2-C2
Westfield Road	A4
West Mead Road	F3
William Road	F2-F3

Mitcham

Acacia Road	C3
Albert Road	B2

Anne's Gardens	B2
Ashtree Avenue	A3
Baker Lane	C2-C3
Barnard Road	C3
Biggin Avenue	B4
Bond Road	A3-B3-B4
Bramcote Avenue	B1
Cedars Avenue	C1-C2
Church Hill	A2
Church Road	A2
Collingwood Road	A3-A2
Commonside East	B2-C2
Commonside West	B2-C2-C1
Cranmer Road	B1-C1
Cricket Green	B1-B2
Croydon Road	C1
Dalton Avenue	A2-A3
De'Arn Gardens	A3
Eastfield Road	C3-C4
Edmund Road	A2
Eveline Road	B4
Feltham Road	B4-B3-C3
Fernlea Road	C4
Frimley Gardens	A2
Galston Road	C2-C3
Glebe Avenue	A3
Glebe Path	B2
Graham Avenue	C4
Graham Road	C4
Grove Road	C2-C3
Heyford Road	A3-A4
King George VI Avenue	B1-C1
Lammas Avenue	C3
Langdale Avenue	B2
Lavender Avenue	A4-B4
Lewis Road	A3
Lock's Lane	B4-C4-C3
London Road	A1-B1-B2-B3-B4
Love Lane	A2-B2-B3
Lower Green	A2-B2
Lower Green West	A2-B2
Madeira Road	B1-C1
Miles Road	A2
Mitcham Park	A1-B1
Morden Road	A1
Mortimer Road	B4
Mount Road	A4
Ormerod Gardens	C4
Portland Road	A3
Priestley Road	C3-C4
Raleigh Gardens	B3
Rialto Road	C3-C4
Rodney Road	A2-A3
Rose Avenue	B4
St Mark's Road	B3-C3
Sadler Close	B3
Sandy Lane	C4
Sister's Mead	B4
Spencer Road	C2-C3
Streatham Road	B4-C4
Taffy's How	A3-B3
Tonstall Road	B3
Upper Green East	B3
Upper Green West	B3
Western Road	A4-A3-B3
Whitford Gardens	B2

Wimbledon

Alan Road	B3-B4
Alexandra Road	C2-C3
Alwyne Road	C2-C3

Arthur Road	B4-C4
Belvedere Avenue	B3
Belvedere Drive	B3
Belvedere Grove	B3
Berkeley Place	A1-A2
Beulah Road	C1
Burghley Road	A4-B4
Church Hill	C3
Church Road	A3-B3-B4
Clifton Road	A2
Compton Road	C2-C3
Darlaston Road	A1-B1
Denmark Avenue	B1
Denmark Road	A1-A2
Dundonald Road	C1
Edge Hill	A1
Elm Grove	B1
Glendale Drive	C3
Graham Road	C1
Hartfield Crescent	C1-C2
Hartfield Road	C1-C2
High Street	A3-B3
Highbury Road	B3
Hillside	A1-A2
Homefield Road	A3-B3
Home Park Road	C4
Lake Road	C3-C4
Lancaster Gardens	B3-B4
Lancaster Road	A3-B3
Lauriston Road	A2
Leeward Gardens	B3-C3
Leopold Road	C3-C4
Lingfield Road	A3-A2-B2
Malcolm Road	B2
Mansel Road	B2-C2
Margin Drive	A4
Marryat Road	A3-A4-B4
Murray Road	A2-B2
Parkside	A4-A3
Parkside Avenue	A4
Parkside Gardens	A3-A4
Peek Crescent	A3-A4
Raymond Road	B2
Ridge Way	A1-A2-B2-B3
Ridgeway Place	A2-B2-B1
St Aubyns Avenue	C3
St George's Road	C1-C2
St John's Road	A1-B1-B2
St Mary's Road	B4-B3-C3
South Side Common	A2-A3
Spencer Hill	B1-B2
Sunnyside	B2
Tabor Grove	B1-B2
The Downs	A1
The Grange	A2-A3
Thornton Hill	A1-B1
Thornton Road	A1-A2
Welford Place	B4
Wimbledon Hill Road	B3-B2-C2
Woodside	C2-C3
Worple Road	A1-B1-B2-C2

Carshalton

Albert Road	A2
Alma Road	B2-B3
Ashcombe Road	C2
Banstead Road	B1-B2
Barrow Hedges Way	B1
Beeches Avenue	B1
Benhill Road	A3-A4
Beynon Road	B2-C2
Blakehall Road	C1

Brookfield Avenue	A4-B4
Browning Avenue	B3-B4
Byron Avenue	A3
Byron Gardens	A4
Cambridge Road	B2
Carshalton Grove	A2-A3
Carshalton Road	A2-B2
Carshalton Park Road	B1-C1-C2-C3
Calburn Way	A4
Coldridge Avenue	B3-B4
Colston Avenue	B3-B4
Crichton Road	B1-C1
Croft Road	A3-B3
Denmark Road	C4
Downside Road	A2-A3-B3
Eaton Road	A1-A2
Erskine Road	A4-B4
Fairview Road	A2-B2
Florian Avenue	A3-A4
Gauntlett Road	A2
Gordon Road	B1-C1
Grosvenor Road	C1-C2
Harrow Road	B1-B2
Hawthorn Road	A2-B2
High Street	C3
Highfield Road	B2-B3
Hill Road	B1
Hillcroome Road	A1-A2
Kayemoor Road	A1
King's Lane	A2
Kingsley Avenue	A3-A4
Mayfield Road	A1
Mead Crescent	B4
Meadow Road	A3-B3
Mill Lane	C3-C4
Milton Avenue	A4-A3-B3
North Street	C3-C4
Orchard Way	A3-A4
Oxford Road	B1-B2
Paget Avenue	A4
Park Hill	B1-B2
Pound Street	B2-B3-C3
Prior Avenue	A1-B1
Ringstead Road	A2-A3
Rossdale	B3
Ruskin Road	C2-C3
St Barnabas Road	A2-A3
Salisbury Road	C1-C2
Shirley Avenue	A4-B4
Shorts Road	B2-B3
Sussex Road	B1-C1
Sutton Grove	A2-A3
Talbot Road	C2-C3
The Park	C2
The Ridgway	A1-A2
The Square	C3
Upland Road	A1
Wales Avenue	B2
Warnham Court Road	C1
Waterloo Road	A3
Waverley Road	B1
West Street	B4-C4-C3
West Street Lane	C3
Westmead Road	A3-B3
Willis Avenue	A1-B1
Woodfields Avenue	C1
Wrythe Lane	B4

Key to Town Plan and Area Plan

Town Plan
AA Recommended roads
Restricted roads
Other roads
Buildings of interest   Library
Car Parks
Parks and open spaces
One Way Streets

Area Plan
A roads
B roads
Urban area
Stations
BR and Underground Stations

Street Index with Grid Reference

Uxbridge

Ashley Road	A1
Austin Way	A2-B2
Bakers Road	B3
Bawtree Road	B4
Belmont Close	C4
Belmont Road	B3-B4-C4
Braybourne Close	B4
Bridge Road	B1-B2
Cambridge Road	B4-C4
Chiltern View Road	B1-C1
Chippendale Waye	C3
Church Lane	A1
Cleveland Road	C1
Cornwall Road	B4-C4
Cotswold Close	B2
Cowley Mill Road	A1-B1
Cowley Road	B1-B2
Cross Street	B2-B3
Culvert Lane	A1
Derby Road	B1
Eskdale Road	A1
Fairfield Road	B4-C4
Frays Waye	A2
George Street	B3-C3
Glebe Road	A1-B1
Harefield Road	B3-B4
High Street	B4-B3-C3-C2
Hillingdon Road	B2-C2-C1
Hinton Road	B2
Honey Croft Hill	C3
How's Road	B2
Iffley Close	C3
Jackson Road	C3
Lancaster Road	B3-B4
Longbridge Way	A1
Manor Waye	C1-C2
Mead Road	B4-C4
Montague Road	C3
Myddleton Road	B2
Newtown Road	A4
New Windsor Street	B2-B3
Norfolk Road	C4
Nursery Waye	C2
Orchard Waye	C1
Oxford Road	A4-B4-B3
Park Road	C2-C3-C4
Press Road	B4
Redford Way	B3

Uxbridge

The defence of London and south-east England was planned in an Uxbridge underground control room in World War II, and the headquarters of No 11 Corps Fighter Command was located here. RAF associations go back to 1917, when the Armament and Gunnery School of the Royal Flying Corps was established, although today the RAF Station is mainly concerned with administration.

Shortly before the arrival of the RAF, the opening of the Metropolitan and Great Western Railways had sparked off the expansion of this former market centre and staging post into a thriving suburb. It now has modern shopping precincts and sports facilities, including an artificial ski slope and a big open air swimming pool in Park Road.

Hayes has good shopping and also enjoys the leisure facilities of the modern Alfred Beck Centre, where concerts and drama can be staged.

West Drayton is a busy suburb lying close to the M4 Motorway and Heathrow Airport. But the West Drayton Green area has been preserved and recalls the town's peaceful origins. The Grand Union Canal runs through it and is popular with boating and fishing enthusiasts.

Yiewsley was once a brick-making town, but has become a London suburb. Few buildings remain from before the 19th century.

Uxbridge Area

Riverside Way	A2-A3
Rockingham Road	A2-A3
St Andrews Road	C2-C3
St John's Road	A1-A2
Tachbrook Road	B1
The Greenway	B1-C1
Thompson Road	C3
Trumper Way	B2-B3
Turnpike Lane	C1
Villier Street	B1-C1
Vine Street	B2-B3
Walford Road	B1-C1
Wallingford Road	A1
Waterloo Road	A1-A2
Wellham Road	B2
Westcott Way	B1
Whitehall Road	B2-B1-C1
Willow Avenue	A4
York Road	B3-C3

Hayes

Albert Road	B1
Austin Road	B2
Avondale Drive	C4
Bilton Way	C2-C3
Birch Way	C4
Blyth Road	A2-A1-B1-B2
Botwell Common Road	A3
Botwell Lane	A4-A3-B3-B2
Bourne Avenue	A1
Central Avenue	B3-B4
Chalfont Road	C2
Cherry Grove	C3-C4
Church Road	A4-B4-B3
Clarendon Road	B1-B2
Clayton Road	A2-B2
Coldharbour Lane	B3-B4-C4
Compton Road	A4
Cotmans Close	C4
Cross Way	C3
Dallas Terrace	C1
Dawley Road	A1-A2
Drenon Square	B4
East Avenue	B3-B4

East Holme	B4
East Walk	C3
Fairdale Gardens	B3-C3
Fairey Avenue	B1
Fifth Avenue	B4
First Avenue	B3
Forris Avenue	A3-A4
Freeman's Lane	A4
Glebe Road	B3
Golden Crescent	A3-B3
Gordon Crescent	C1
Halsway	C3-C4-C3
Harold Avenue	C1
Hermon Grove	C3-C4
Hitherbroom Road	C4
Hughes Road	C4
Hunters Grove	B3-C3
Hyde Way	B1
Keith Road	A1-B1
Lannock Road	A3-B3
Little Road	C2
Longmead Road	A4-B4
Marlow Gardens	A1
Minet Drive	B3-C3
Minet Gardens	C3
Moray Avenue	A3-A4
Mount Road	B3-C3
Neild Road	B3-B3
Nestles Avenue	B1-C1
North Hyde Road	A1-B1-C1
Orchard Road	B4
Pasedena Close	C3
Printing House Lane	A2-A3
Pump Lane	B3-B2-C2
Rostrever Gardens	A3
Rowan Place	B4
St Anselms Road	B2
Sandown Crescent	B1
Showers Way	C3-C4
Silverdale Gardens	C3
Silverdale Road	C2-B2
Station Road	B1-B2
Third Avenue	B3
Townfield Road	B4
Townfield Square	B4
Trevor Road	A2
Viveash Close	B1
West Avenue	B4

Western View	B2
West Walk	C3
Windsor Gardens	A1

West Drayton/ Yiewsley

Acacia Avenue	C3
Albert Road	B3
Apple Tree Avenue	C4
Ash Grove	C4
Avenue Close	A1
Bagley Close	B1
Bell Close Road	B2
Bentinck Road	A3-B3
Brandville Road	B2
Brooklyn Way	A1
Caroline Close	A1
Castle Avenue	B3-B4-C4
Chestnut Avenue	C3-C4
Church Road	A1-B1
Colham Mill Road	A2
Colham Road	B3
Cowley Peachey	A4
Drayton Gardens	A1-B1-B2
Edgar Road	B3
Fairfield Road	B3
Fairway Avenue	A2
Falling Lane	B4-C4
Ferrers Avenue	A1
Frays Avenue	A1-A2
Frays Close	A1
Furzeham Road	B2
Gordon Road	B4
Harmondsworth Road	B1
Heather Lane	B4
High Street	A4
Hornbill Close	A4
Horton Bridge Road	C2
Horton Close	C2
Horton Lane	C2-C3
Horton Road	B3-C3-C2
Kings Road	B1-C1
Kingston Avenue	C4
Kingston Lane	B1-B2-C2

Lawn Avenue	A2
Leacroft Close	B4
Lime Avenue	C4
Maple Avenue	B3
Money Lane	A1
Moorfield Road	A4
Mulberry Crescent	C1
North Road	C1
Oak Avenue	C1
Old Farm Road	A1
Otterfield Road	B3-B4
Padcroft Road	A3
Pear Tree Avenue	C4
Pinewood Avenue	C4
Poplar Avenue	C3-C4
Porters Way	B1-C1
Providence Road	B3-C3
Queens Road	B1
Rickard Close	A1
Royal Lane	C4
Ryeland Close	B4
St Stephens Road	A3-B3
South Road	C1
Station Road	B2-A2-B2-B1
Sunray Avenue	A2
Swan Road	A1-A2-B2
Sycamore Close	C3
Tavistock Road	A2-A3
The Green	A1
Thornton Avenue	B1-C1
Trout Road	A3
Warwick Road	B2
West Drayton Park Avenue	B1
West Drayton Road	C4
West Road	C1
Whitehorn Avenue	B3-C3
Wimpole Road	A3
Winnock Road	A3
Yew Avenue	B3-B4-C4
Yiewsley	B2-B3

Walthamstow

Greyhound racing at Walthamstow Stadium and a seemingly endless street market — said to be the longest in Britain — are two of the top attractions of Walthamstow, an area of dramatic transformations. Covered in forest before the 15th century, it prospered as a country retreat for London's rich in the 18th and saw even greater prosperity with the industrialisation of the 19th,

culminating in the development of Britain's first internal combustion engine car, the Bremer Car, on display at Walthamstow Museum. Little of the old town has survived but Walthamstow Village has many noteworthy buildings and is now a conservation area. Among the few remaining 18th-century houses are the Clockhouse, in Wood Street, and the Water House, home of the William Morris Gallery.

Leyton was a rural retreat for wealthy London merchants, who built their mansions here in the

18th century. Few reminders of this prosperous past withstood severe wartime bombing.

Leytonstone grew up on the Roman route from Epping Forest to London, and became a 'dormitory' town with the development of the railway system. Its growth continued with extensive development and also extensive demolition, so that little of the past remains. The early 19th-century terraced houses in Browning Street are the best examples of the old town.

LEGEND

Town Plan

AA Recommended roads	
Restricted roads	
Other roads	
Car Parks	P
Buildings of interest	Station
Parks and open spaces	
Churches	+

Area Plan

A roads	
B roads	
Stations	
Borough Boundary	

STREET INDEX WITH GRID REFERENCE

WALTHAMSTOW

Addison Road	F1
Albert Road	C1-D1
Arkley Crescent	B1
Attlee Terrace	E3-F3
Aubrey Road	E2-E3-E4
Baldis Road	D4
Barrett Road	F1-F2
Bedford Road	D4
Bemsted Road	C4
Beulah Road	E1-F1
Blackhorse Lane	A4
Blackhorse Road	A2-A3
Blenheim Road	A4
Borwick Avenue	C4
Bromley Road	E4
Brookdale Road	D2-D3
Brookfield Road	E4
Browns Road	D3
Brunner Road	B1
Brunswick Street	F1
Bunyan Road	A4
Buxton Road	B2-B3
Byron Road	E3-E4
Cairo Road	D3-E3-E2
Campbell Road	C3
Canning Road	B4
Carisbrooke Road	A2-B2
Cedar Avenue	D1
Century Road	A4-B4
Chandos Avenue	E4
Chatham Road	B4
Chewton Road	A2-A3
Chingford Road	E4
Church Hill	D2-E2
Church Hill Road	E2-F2-F3
Church Lane	E2-F2
Clacton Road	A1
Cleveland Park Avenue	D2-D3
Cleveland Park Crescent	D2-D3
Clifton Avenue	A4
Colebrook Road	C2
Coleridge Road	B3-C3-C4
Coppermill Lane	A1-A2
Cornwallis Road	A3
Cottenham Road	C3
Countess Road	C4
Diana Road	D4
East Avenue	E1-E2
Eastfield Road	D2-D3
Eden Road	E1
Edinburgh Road	C1
Eldon Road	C2
Elmsdale Road	B3-C3
Erskine Road	C2-C3
Essex Close	A3
Exeter Road	C1
Exmouth Road	B1-C1
Falmer Road	E3-E4
Farnborough Avenue	A4
Folkestone Road	E3
Forest Road	A4-B4-C4-D4-E4-F4
First Avenue	D1-E1
Frederick Street	A1
Gainsford Road	B3-C3
Gaywood Road	D4
Glen Road	C1
Glenthorne Road	A2
Gosport Road	B1-B2
Grange Road	B1
Greenleaf Road	C4-C3-D3
Grosvenor Rise East	E1-F1
Hatherley Road	C3-D3
Hawthorn Road	D4
Hazlewood Road	E4
Hervey Park Road	B3-B4
Higham Hill Road	B4
High Street	A2-B2-C2-D2
Hoe Street	D1-D2-D3-D4-E4
Holmes Avenue	C4
Hove Avenue	B1
Howard Road	E2-E3-E4
Hurst Road	E3-E4
Ickworth Park Road	B4
Jewel Road	D3-D4
Kenilworth Avenue	E4
King Edward Road	A4
Leo Road	D1
Leucha Road	A1
Linden Road	C2
Lime Street	A3
Longfield Avenue	A3
Lorne Road	C1
Luton Road	B4
Lynmouth Road	A1
Mansfield Road	B2-B3-C3
Marlowe Road	F2-F3
Maude Road	A2
Maude Terrace	A2
Maynard Road	F1
Melbourne Road	B3
Melford Road	B2
Melville Road	C3-C4
Mersey Road	C4
Milton Road	D3-E3
Mission Grove	A2-B2
Netley Road	B1-C1
Northcote Road	A2-B2-B3
Orford Road	D1-E1-F1-F2
Palmerston Road	B2-B3-B4
Park Road	C1
Pasquier Road	B4
Pearl Road	D4
Pembar Avenue	A4
Pembroke Road	E1
Pretoria Avenue	A2
Priory Avenue	D1
Prospect Hill	E2-F2-F3
Queen Elizabeth Road	A4-B4
Ravenswood Road	F1
Rectory Road	E2-E3
Renness Road	B4
Ritchings Avenue	A3-A4
Roma Road	B4
Rosebank Grove	C4
Ruby Road	D4
Russell Road	B4-C4-C3
St James Path	B2
St James Street	A1-B1
St Mary Road	D2-E2
Seaford Road	E3
Second Avenue	A4
Selborne Road	B2-C2-D2
Shernhall Street	F1-F2-F3-F4
Somers Road	B2-C2-D3
Southcote Road	A2
South Grove	B1
Spruce Hills Road	F4
Stainforth Road	D2
Station Road	A1
Storey Road	C2
Suffolk Park Road	A3-B3
Summit Road	F2
Tavistock Avenue	A4
Tenby Road	A2
The Drive	E2-E3-F3
The Links	A3
Third Avenue	D1-E1
Tower Hamlets Road	D3-D4
Turner Road	F3
Valentin Road	F2
Vernon Road	C1
Vestry Road	E1-E2
Walpole Road	B3
Warner Road	A3-B3

LEYTON

Abbot's Park Road	B2-C2
Addison Road	A2
Albert Road	D2
Auckland Road	E1
Barclay Road	A2
Beaumont Road	C2-C1
Belgrave Road	C2
Belmont Park Road	B1-B2
Beulah Road	A2
Brewster Road	C1-C2
Brisbane Road	D1-E1
Byron Road	C1
Calderon Road	E2-F2
Canterbury Road	B2
Carnarvon Road	A2
Capworth Street	B2-B1-C1
Chesterfield Road	B2
Church Road	D1
Clarendon Road	B1
Claude Road	C2-D2
Clyde Place	C1
Colchester Road	B2-C2
Copeland Road	A1-B1
Crowfield Road	F1-F2
Dawlish Road	D1-D2
Downsell Road	F2
Dunedin Road	E1-E2
Dunton Road	B1
Eden Road	A1-A2
Elm Road	D2-E2
Ely Road	B2
Epsom Road	B2
Essex Road	A2-B2
Farmer Road	C1-C2
First Avenue	A1
Francis Road	D1-D2-E2
Fraser Road	A2-B2
Frith Road	F2
Goldsmith Road	C1-D1
Grange Park Road	C1-D1
Granville Road	A1-B1
Griggs Road	B2
Grosvenor Park Road	A1
Grove Green Road	C1
Grove Road	A1-A2
Hainault Road	C2
High Road Leyton	B1-B2-C2-C1-D1-E1-E2-F2
Hoe Street	A1-B1
Huxley Road	D2-E2-E1
James Lane	A1
Knott's Green Road	B1-B2
Lea Bridge Road	A2-B2-B1
Leigh Road	C2
Leslie Road	F2
Leyton Green Road	B2
Lindley Road	D1-D2
Livingstone Road	B1
Wellington Road	B3-B4
West Avenue	E1-E2
West Avenue Road	E2
Westbury Road	C2-C3
William Morris Close	C4
Wingfield Road	E1
Winns Terrace	D4
Wolsey Avenue	C4
Woodbury Road	E2
Woodville Road	B2
Lyndhurst Drive	C2
Lyttelton Road	E1-E2
Matlock Road	B2
Maynard Road	A2
Melbourne Road	B1-C1
Merton Road	A2-B2
Millais Road	F2
Morley Road	C2-D2
Murchison Road	C2-D2-D1
Newport Road	D2
Norlington Road	C2
Nottingham Road	B2
Oliver Road	D1-E1
Orford Road	A1-A2
Park Road	C1
Pembroke Road	A1
Rawley Road	C1-D1
Rosedene Terrace	D1
Ruckholt Road	E2-E1-F1
Second Avenue	A1
Shernhall Street	A2
St Georges Road	E2
St Mary's Road	D2-E2
Scotts Road	C2-D2
Sedgewick Road	D1-D2
Shernall Street	A2
Skeltons Lane	C1-C2
Stewart Road	F2
Temple Mills Lane	F1
Third Avenue	A1
Tyndall Road	D1-D2
Vicarage Road	C1-D1
Warren Road	A1
West Avenue	A1
Westdown Road	F2
Windsor Road	D1-E1
Whitney Road	B1-C1
York Road	E1-E2

LEYTONSTONE

Acacia Road	D2
Arundel Close	F2
Ashbridge Road	A1
Aylmer Road	B2
Barclay Road	C1-C2
Beacontree Road	B2
Blenheim Road	F2
Borthwick Road	F1-F2
Browning Road	B2
Burghley Road	C1
Bush Road	B2
Bushwood	C2
Cambridge Road	A2
Cannhall Road	E2-F2-F1
Cary Road	E2
Cathall Road	D1-E1
Chadwick Road	A1-A2
Cheneys Road	E2
Chichester Road	E2
Church Lane	B1-C1
Cobden Road	D2-D1-E1
Colworth Road	A1-B1
Crownfield Road	F1
Cruickshank Road	F2
Davies Lane	C2
Dyers Hall Road	C1
Dyson Road	A1
Edith Road	F1
Elsham Road	E1-E2
Esther Road	A1-B1
Fairlop Road	B1-C1
Ferndale Road	C2
Fillebrook Road	B1-C1
Fladgate Road	A1
Forest Glade	A1
Gainsborough Road	B1-B2
Grove Green Road	C1
Grove Road	B2
Gurney Road	F2
Granleigh Road	D1
Harold Road	C2
Harrow Road	D2-E2-E1
Harvey Road	C1-C2-D2
High Road Leytonstone	B2-B1-C1-D1-E1-F1-F2
Holly Road	A2
Hollydown Way	D1-E1
Janson Road	F2
King's Road	B1
Kingsdown Road	E1-E2
Kirkdale Road	B1
Langthorne Road	E1-F1
Lemna Road	C1
Leyton Way	A2-A1-B1
Lister Road	C1-C2
Lonsdale Road	A2
Malvern Road	D2
Maple Road	A1
Marchant Road	D1
Matcham Road	D2-E2
Mayville Road	B1
Melford Road	C1
Michael Road	C1-C2
Montague Road	C2-D2
Mornington Road	B2-C2
Napier Road	E1-E2
Newcomen Road	D2
New Wanstead	A2
Norman Road	C1-D1
Poppleton Road	A1-B1
Preston Road	A1
Queen's Road	B1
Ramsay Road	E2-F2
Ranelagh Road	E1-E2-F2
Sansome Road	D2
Selby Road	E1-E2
Short Road	C1-D1
South Birkbeck Road	E1
Southwell Grove	D1
Stanmore Road	B2-C2
Steele Road	E1-F1-F2
Vernon Road	C1
Wadley Road	A1
Wallwood Road	B1
Whipps Cross Road	A1-A2
Wingfield Road	F1
Woodlands Road	C1-D1
Woodford Road	D2-E2
Woodhouse Road	D2-E2
Woodville Road	B2-C2
Worsley Road	E1-E2

Wandsworth

Oscar Wilde and Great Train Robber Ronald Biggs both spent time in Wandsworth, as inmates of the prison which is one of its best-known features. This is an industrialised area which grew when the railways arrived in the 19th century.

Battersea boasts two great landmarks for Londoners: its park and its power station. Battersea Park was opened in 1853 under royal command, and has since undergone a number of improvements and innovations, including the Festival of Britain Gardens, designed by Sir Osbert Lanchester and John Piper, and established in 1951. The power station dominates the London skyline with its four distinctive chimneys. Designed by Sir Giles Scot and first used in 1937, it is no longer operating but may become the centrepiece of a proposed leisure park. Battersea's Old Town Hall has been converted into an Arts Centre and many theatrical and musical productions are staged there.

Putney gives an overall impression of being distinctly Victorian and Edwardian. It grew into a fashionable London suburb during the 18th century, and continued to undergo a good deal of development right up until the 1920s, but since then has seen relatively little change. Putney Bridge has been the starting point for the University Boat Race since 1845.

Central Putney

Central Battersea

Street Index with with grid reference

Wandsworth

Acris Street	E2-E3
All Farthing Lane	D1-E1
Alma Road	D4-E4-E3
Amerland Road	A2-A1-B1
Armoury Way	B3-C3-D3
Barmouth Road	E1
Baylin Road	C2-D2
Birdhurst Road	E3-E4
Broomhill Road	B2
Buckhold Road	B1-C1-C2-C3
Cicada Road	E2-F2
Coleford Road	D3-E3
Crieff Road	E1-F1
Cromford Road	B2-B3
Dault Road	E1-E2
Dempster Road	E3-E4
Dighton Road	D3-E3-E4
East Hill	D2-D3-E3
Ebner Street	D3-D4
Eglantine Road	D2-E2
Elsynge Road	F3
Fairfield Street	C4-D4-D3
Fawe Park Road	A4-B4
Frognore	B3-C3
Fullerton Road	D3-E3
Galveston Road	A2-A3
Garratt Lane	C2-C1-D1
Geraldine Road	E1-E2-E3
Haldon Road	A2-B2-B1
Harbut Road	F4
Heathfield Road	E1-F1
Herndon Road	D3-E3-E2
Hill Road	A1-B1
Huguenot Place	E3-F3
Iron Mill Road	D1
Jessica Road	E2-F2
Lebanon Road	B2
Limes Gardens	B1
Longstaff Road	C1
Manchester Road	A3
Mapleton Crescent	C1-C2
Mapleton Road	C1-D1
Marcilly Road	F3
Melody Road	E1-E2-E3
Melrose Road	A1-B1
Merton Road	B1-B2
Mexfield Road	A2-A3
Neville Gill Close	C1-C2
Northfields	B4
North Passage	B4
Oakhill Road	A3-B3
Osiers Road	B4-C4
Pentland Street	D1-E1
Podmore Road	D4-E4
Point Pleasant	
Putney Bridge Road	A4-B4-B3
Quarry Road	E2-F2
Richmond Road	A2-A3
Ringford Road	A2-B2
Rosehill Road	E2
St Ann's Crescent	D2-E2-E1

St Ann's Hill	D2-D1-E1
St Ann's Park Road	E1
St John's Hill	E3-F3-F4
St John's Hill Grove	F4
Santos Road	B2-B3
Schubert Road	A2-A3
Sispara Gardens	A1
Southfields Road	B1-B2
Spencer Park	F2-F3
Sudlow Road	B4-B3-C3
Swanage Road	E1-F1
Tonsley Hill	D3
Tonsley Place	D3
Trefoil Road	E2-F2
Trinity Road	E4-E3-F3-F2-F1
Valonia Gardens	A2
Vermont Road	D1
Viewfield Road	A1-A2
Wandsworth Common North Side	F3
Wandsworth Common West Side	F1-F2
Wandsworth High Street	B2-B3-B3-C3-C2-D2
West Hill	A2-A2-B3
West Hill Road	B1
Westover Road	E1-F1
Wimbledon Park Road	B1
Windmill Road	F1-F2
York Road	C3-D3-D4-E4

Putney

Ashlone Road	A4-B4
Atney Road	C2-C3
Bangalore Street	A3-B3
Bemish Road	B3
Biggs Row	B1
Cambalt Road	B3-B4
Campion Road	A2
Carlton Drive	B1-C1-C2
Carmalt Gardens	A2
Castello Avenue	A1-A2
Charlwood Road	B2-B3
Chartfield Avenue	A1-B1
Chelverton Road	B2-B3
Clarendon Drive	A3-B3
Colinette Road	A2-A3
Cortis Road	A1
Dealtry Road	A2
Deddar Road	C3
Disraeli Road	B2-C2
Dryburgh Road	A3
Egliston Road	A3
Enmore Road	A2
Erpingham Road	A3-A4
Felsham Road	A3-B3-C3
Festing Road	B4
Fulham High Street	C4
Genoa Avenue	A1-A2
Gwendolin Road	B1-B2
Hazlewell Road	A2-B2
Holroyd Road	A2
Horne Way	A4
Hotham Road	A3-B3
Howard Lane	A2-B2
Keswick Road	C1
Lacy Road	B3
Landford Road	A3
Larpent Avenue	A1-A2
Lower Richmond Road	A4-B4-B3

Lytton Grove	B1-C1
Mercier Road	C1-C2
Montserratt Road	B3-C3-C2
New Kings Road	C4
Norroy Road	B2
Oxford Road	C2
Pentlow Street	A4
Portinscale Road	C1
Putney Bridge	C3-C4
Putney Bridge Approach	C4
Putney Bridge Road	C2-C3
Putney High Street	B2-B3-C3
Putney Hill	B1-B2
Rayners Road	B1-B2
Rotherwood Road	B4
St John's Avenue	B2-C2-C1
St Simons Avenue	A1-A2
Sefton Street	A4
The Embankment	B4-B3-C3
Upper Richmond Road	A3-A2-B2-C2-C1
Wadham Road	C2
Weiss Road	B3
Werter Road	B2-C2
Westleigh Avenue	A1-B1

Battersea

Afghan Street	B3
Albert Bridge Road	C4
Balfern Street	B3-B4
Barnard Road	B1
Battersea Bridge Road	B4-C4
Battersea High Street	A4-B4-B3
Battersea Park Road	B3-B4-C4
Battersea Rise	A1-B1-C1
Baynmaer Road	C4
Bolingbroke Grove	B1
Bullen Street	B3-B4
Burns Road	C3
Cabul Road	B3
Cairns Road	B1
Cambridge Road	B4-C4
Clapham Common North Side	C1
Clapham Common West Side	C1
Comyn Road	B1
Culvert Road	C3-C4
Eccles Road	C1-C2
Edna Street	B4
Eland Road	C2-C3
Elsey Road	C2
Elspeth Road	C1-C2
Elsynge Road	A1
Este Road	B2-B3
Eversleigh Road	C2-C3
Falcon Road	B2-B3
Fownes Street	B2
Frere Street	B3
Glycena Road	C2
Grant Road	A2-B2
Grayshott Road	C2-C3
Gwynne Road	A3-B3
Harbut Road	A1
Hope Street	A2
Ingrave Street	A3-B3-B2
Kersley Street	C4
Knowsley Road	C3
Latchmere Road	C2-C3-C4

Lavender Gardens	C1-C2
Lavender Hill	B2-C2
Lavender Sweep	C1-B1-B2-C2
Lavender Walk	C1-C2
Leathwaite Road	C1
Lombard Road	A3-A4
Maysoule Road	A2
Meyrick Road	A2-B2
Mossby Road	B2
Mysore Road	C1-C2
Orbel Street	B4
Parkham Street	B4
Petworth Street	B4-C4
Plough Road	A1-A2
Prince of Wales Drive	B4-C4
Reform Street	C3-C4
St John's Hill	A1-B1-B2
St John's Hill Grove	A1
St John's Road	B1-B2
Sheepcote Lane	C3
Shellgate Road	B1-C1
Shuttleworth Road	B4
Simpson Street	B3
Sisters Avenue	C1-C2
Spencer Road	A1
Surrey Lane	B4
Thirsk Road	C1-C2
Thomas Baines Road	A2
Vardens Road	A1
Vicarage Crescent	A4-B4
Webbs Road	C1
Westbridge Road	A4-B4
Winstanley Road	A2-B2
Yelverton Road	A3
York Road	A2-B2-B3

LEGEND

Town Plan

AA Recommended roads

Other roads

Restricted roads

Buildings of interest — Cinema

Churches

Car Parks

Parks and open spaces

Area Plan

A roads

B roads

Stations — Mitcham

Borough Boundary

Key to Town Plan and Area Plan

Town Plan

AA Recommended roads	
Other roads	
Restricted roads	
Buildings of interest	Library ▣
Churches	†
Car Parks	₱
Parks and open spaces	
BR and Underground Stations	⊖

Area Plan

A roads	
B roads	

Street Index with Grid Reference

Central Wembley

Allendale Road	A1-A2
Ashness Gardens	A1
Aspen Drive	A4
Babbington Rise	F1
Bassingham Road	C1
Beaumont Avenue	B2-B3-C3
Beechcroft Gardens	D3-E3-E4
Berkhamstead Avenue	E1
Bleheim Gardens	D4
Bridgewater Road	B2-B1
Brook Avenue	E4-F4
Byron Road	C4
Camden Crescent	A4
Castleton Avenue	C3-D3-D4
Cecil Avenue	D1-D2
Central Road	A2-B2
Chalkhill Road	F4
Chaplin Road	B1-C1
Charter House Avenue	B3-B2-C2
Chatsworth Avenue	E2-E1
Chestnut Grove	A2
Clarendon Gardens	C3-D3
Clifton Avenue	E1
Copeland Avenue	C2
Copeland Road	D1
Crawford Avenue	C2
Dagma Avenue	D2-E2
Dalmeny Close	B1
Danethorpe Road	C1
Dean Court	B4
District Road	A2-B2
Ealing Road	C1-D1
Eastcote Avenue	A2-A1
East Court	B4
East Lane	A4-B4-C4-D4-E4
Elm Road	D2
Elms Lane	A4-A3
Elton Avenue	B2
Empire Way Drive	E2-E3-F3-F4
Engineers Way	E3-F3
Eton Avenue	A2-A3-B3-C3
Fairview Avenue	C1
Farm Avenue	B1
Fernwood Avenue	B1
First Way	F2-F3
Forty Avenue	E4-F4
Forty Close	E4
Forty Lane	F4
Gauntlet Court	A3-A2
Georgian Court	F1
Grand Avenue	E2-E1-F1
Greengate	A1
Grendon Gardens	F4
Harrowdene Road	C2-C3-C4
Harrow Road	A3-A2-B2-C2, E2-E1-F1
Heights Avenue	A2-A1
Highfield Avenue	D4-E4
High Road	C2-D2-E2
High Street	E3
Hillcroft Crescent	E3
Hill Road	A4
Hillside Avenue	E3
Holland Road	C1
Holt Road	A4-B4
Homefield Road	A3
Jesmond Avenue	E1
Keswick Gardens	C2-D2
Kingsway	D3
Lancelot Avenue	C3
Lancelot Crescent	C3
Lancelot Road	C2
Lantern Close	C2
Lea Garden	D2
Lincoln Road	C1
Linden Avenue	E2

Wembley

Scene of FA and Rugby League Cup Finals, the 1948 Olympic Games, the 1966 World Cup Finals, countless concerts, public appearances and events such as the open air Mass during the 1982 Papal visit, Wembley Stadium is the chief claim to fame for this residential and industrial area.

Originally designed as a centrepiece for the British Empire Exhibition of 1924, the stadium complex includes Wembley Arena, used for horse shows and ice spectaculars, a national squash centre and a modern hotel. Nearby stands the Wembley Conference Centre, opened in 1976, which also provides facilities for exhibitions and concerts. Wembley itself began as a rural district centred around Wembley Park, but saw extensive development after the opening of the London to Birmingham railway in the mid-19th century.

Harlesden Animal shows, handicrafts, music and drama take over Roundwood Park in the north every year, for the annual Brent show. A village until the late 19th century, Harlesden grew when railway yards and sidings were established here and several major industrial companies arrived.

Willesden is another area which has undergone a good deal of housing and industrial development since the mid-19th century, when Willesden Junction was built. Places of interest include St Mary's Church, which is of Norman origin.

Linthorpe Avenue	B1
Llandover Road	C4-C3
London Road	D2-D1
Lonsdale Avenue	D1-D2
Lyon Park Avenue	D1
Manor Drive	E3
Meadow Way	C3
Milford Gardens	C2
Mostyn Avenue	E2
Napier Road	C2-C1
Neeld Crescent	E1-E2-F2
Nettleden Avenue	E1
Newlands Close	B1
North Church Road	E1
North End Road	F4-F3
North South	F1
Norton Road	C1
Oakington Avenue	E4
Oakington Manor Drive	E2-F2-F1
Oakwood Crescent	A1
Oldborough Road	B4
Olympic Way	F4-F3
Orchard Gate	A1-B1
Park Chase	E3
Park Court	D2
Park Lane	D2-D3-E3
Park Road	D1
Pasture Close	A4
Pasture Road	A4
Peel Road	C4
Pembroke Road	C3-C4
Perrin Road	A3
Petts Grove Avenue	B2
Preston Road	D4
Princes Court	D2
Queenscourt	D3
Ranelagh Road	C1
Rosemead Avenue	D2
Rosslyn Crescent	D3-D4
Rountree Road	A2
Royal Route	E2
Rugby Avenue	A2-B2-B3-C3
Rupert Avenue	D1-D2
Rustic Place	C3
St Augustines Avenue	D4
St John's Road	C3-C2-D2
St Michael's Avenue	F1
Saunderton Road	A2-B2
Scarle Road	C1
South Way	E2-F2
Stapenhill Road	A4
Station Approach	B2-B1-A1
Station Crescent	A2-A1
Station Grove	D1-D2
Stilecroft Gardens	A4
Sudbury Avenue	C2-C3-C4
Sudbury Crescent	A2
Swinderby Road	C1
Sylvester Road	B2-C2
Talbot Road	C1
The Chine	B2
The Close	D1
The Croft	B2
The Dell	B2-A2
The Dene	D3
The Fairway	B4-A4-B4
The Glen	C3
Thurlby Road	C1
Thurlow Gardens	C2
Tokyngton Avenue	E1
Tudor Court	F1
Turton Road	C2-D2

Victoria Avenue	F1-F2
Victoria Court	F1
Vivian Avenue	E2-E1-F1
Watford Road	A4-A3-A2
Waverley Avenue	E1
Wellgarth	A1
Wembley Hill Road	D4-D3-E3-E2
Wembley Park	E3-E4
West Court	B4
Whitton Avenue East	A1-B1
Windsor Crescent	F4
Woodcroft	A1
Woodfield Avenue	B4-B3
Wyld Way	F1

Willesden

Aberdeen Road	A4
Acland Road	B3
Agave Road	C4
Alexandra Avenue	B1
All Souls Avenue	B1
Alverstone Road	C1-C2
Anson Road	B4-C4
Beaconsfield Road	A3
Belton Road	A3
Bertie Road	A2-A3
Bleneheim Gardens	C3
Brondesbury Park	B2-C2
Bryan Avenue	B1-B2
Burnley Road	A4-A3-B3
Chamberlayne Road	C1-D1
Chambers Lane	B1-B2
Chandos Road	C3
Chaplin Road	A3-B3
Chapter Road	A3-B3
Chatsworth Road	C2
Churchill Road	B2-B3
Clement Close	C1
Colin Road	C3
Cooper Road	A3-A4
Cranhurst Road	C3
Cullingworth Road	B3-B4
Dawson Road	C4
Dean Road	C2
Denzil Road	A3
Dewsbury Road	A4-B4
Dicey Avenue	C4
Dobree Avenue	B1
Donnington Road	A1-B1
Doyle Gardens	A1
Dudden Hill Lane	A3-A4
Ellesmere Road	A4-B4
Fleetwood Road	A4-B4
Gardener Avenue	C4
Gary Close	B3-B4
Geary Road	A4-B4
Glebe Road	A3
Gowan Road	B2
Grosvenor Gardens	C3
Grove Road	C2-C3
Hamilton Road	A4
Hanover Road	C1
Harlesden Road	A1-A2-B2
Hawthorn Road	A2-B2
Helena Road	B4
High Road	A3-A2-B2-C2
Huddlestone Road	B2-B3
Ivy Road	C4
James Avenue	C4

Jeymer Avenue	B3-C3
Kendal Road	A4-B4
Kenneth Crescent	B3-C3
Kings Road	A2-B2
Lancaster Road	A4
Lechmere Road	B2-B3
Linacre Road	B2-B3
Litchfield Gardens	A2
Lydford Road	C2
Maybury Gardens	A2-B2
Melrose Avenue	B4-C4-C3
Milverton Road	C1-C2
Mount Pleasant Road	C1
Mulgrave Road	A4
Normandy Road	A4
North Park Avenue	B3-C3-C2
Olive Road	C4
Oman Avenue	C4
Park Avenue	B3-B4
Parkfield Road	A2-B2
Peter Avenue	B1-B2
Pound Lane	A2-A3
Riffel Road	C3-C4
Robson Avenue	A1-A2
Rowdon Avenue	B1-B2
Rutland Park	C2
St Paul's Avenue	B3-C3-C2
Sandringham Road	B2-B3
Sherrick Green Road	B3-B4
Sidmouth Road	B1-C1-C2
Sneyd Road	C4
Stanley Gardens	C3
Station Parade	C3
Staverton Road	C1-C2-B2
Strode Road	A2-A3
Tower Road	A2
Uffington Road	A1-B1
Villiers Road	B2-B3-A3
Walm Lane	C2-C3
Willesden Lane	B2
Windsor Road	B3
Wren Avenue	C4

Harlesden

Acton Lane	A2-A3-A2-B2
Alric Avenue	A4
Ambleside Road	B4-C4
Avenue Road	B2
Bishops Way	A4
Bramston Road	C2
Branshill Road	B2
Brentfield Road	A4
Brownlow Road	B4
Bruce Road	A4
Buckingham Road	B2-C2
Burns Road	B3-B4
Casselden Road	A4
Cecil Road	A3
Chadwick Road	B4-C4-C3
Charlton Road	B3
Church Road	A4-B4
Connaught Road	A3-B3-B2
Craven Park	A3-A4
Crownhill Road	B3-C3
Cunard Road	A1
Denbigh Close	A4
Drayton Road	B4-B3-C3
Fairlight Avenue	A2
Fortune Gate	B3-B4

Fry Road	C3-C4
Furness Road	C2
Goodson Road	B4
Greenhill Park	A3-B3
Greenhill Road	A3
Guilsborough Close	A4
Harlesden Gardens	B3-C3-C2
Harlesden Road	C2-C3
Harley Road	A3-A2-B2
Hazeldean Road	A4
High Street	B3-B2-C2-C1
Hillside	A4
Holly Close	B2
Knatchbull Road	A3-A4
Leghorn Road	C2
Leopold Road	B4
Letchford Gardens	C1
Longstone Avenue	C3-C4
Manor Park Road	B2-B3
Marian Way	B4
Minet Avenue	A2-A2-B2
Mordaunt Road	A3
Nicoll Road	B2-B3
Night Road	B2-C2
Old Park Lane	A1-B1-B2
Palermo Road	C2
Park Parade	B2-C2
Park Road	A3
Redfern Road	B4
Ridley Road	C2
Roundwood Road	B4-C4
Rucklidge Avenue	C2
St Albans Road	A3
St Mary's Rod	B3-B4
St Johns Avenue	B3-B4
Scrubbs Lane	C1
Sellons Avenue	C2-C3
Shakespeare Crescent	A3-A4
Springwell Avenue	C2-C3
Stonebridge Park	A4
Stracey Road	A3
Tubbs Road	B2-C2
Tunley Rod	A4-B4
Wendover Road	B2
West Ella Road	A4-B4
West Inman Road	A4-B4
Winchelsea Road	A3
Wrottesley Road	C2

Heathrow Airport

Biggest and busiest airport in the United Kingdom, handling more international traffic than any other airport in the world, Heathrow broke its own records on 31 August 1980, when 112,880 passengers passed through. 1983 saw a total of 26,749,200 travellers, assisted by the 45,000-strong staff of the British Airports Authority and the 74 airline companies from 68 countries which operate scheduled services from the airport. Aircraft go to over 90 countries, and Heathrow's No 1 runway, 2.42 miles (3.9km) in length, is the longest used by civilian aircraft in the United Kingdom.

It all began when the site was transferred from the Air Ministry to the Ministry of Civil Aviation on 1 January 1946. On 31 May 1946, it opened as London (Heathrow) Airport, superseding the Airport of London at Croydon, established in 1928. This resulted in the operation of direct services between the United Kingdom and the United States of America. On 16 December 1955, the first three permanent buildings were opened by the Queen, and all three passenger terminals are now interlinked by pedestrian subways with moving walkways. The terminals are situated in the central area of the airport, and are also linked to the M4. A fourth terminal is under construction on the south-eastern side of the airport.

Terminal 1 is used by United Kingdom and Irish airlines for domestic and European flights, and for British Airways flights to and from certain destinations in North America. Terminal 2 is used

by other European airlines except for the Irish airlines. Terminal 3 is the one used by intercontinental airlines going to Africa, America, Asia and Australia.

In 1966, the newly appointed British Airways Authority took over the responsibility for both Heathrow and the second airport at Gatwick (the two are linked by a frequent daily helicopter service). Direct rail access came in 1977 when the Underground's Piccadilly Line was extended and in the same year, Heathrow Central Station opened.

Today the Queens Building Roof Gardens and viewing gallery allow visitors to admire the aircraft and to watch the airport at work. There is a small admission charge for this.

Visitors who have come to the Queens Building Roof Gardens can also take refreshments there, at one of the many restaurants to be found throughout the airport. All three passenger terminals have licensed restaurants where full meals are served, and there are also grill bars providing hot meals. Light refreshments can also be bought.

Multi-storey car parks are sited at each of the passenger terminals for short term car parking. Heathrow also has long term car parks, situated on the northern perimeter road. A free coach carries passengers between the long term car parks and the terminals. During the night (from midnight to 6am), passengers wanting this service can contact the coach base on the special direct line telephones which are in use at the pick-up points.

Central England and Wales

AREA MAPS ARE INDICATED IN BOLD.

Basildon

'Pussiewillow's Clock' bursting into life at 15-minute intervals and the bronze 'Mother and Child' statue are two of the attractions of bustling Basildon, a town which has developed considerably over the last 50 years. Major companies are attracted to its expanding industrial estates, and as well as the vast Eastgate shopping precinct, it still has several interesting old buildings dotted about.

Rayleigh has kept much of its old world charm, even though some development has taken place within the town. Several of the original buildings still stand in the town centre, alongside bright modern shops, while evidence of a long and interesting history can be seen in Crown Hill's 17th-century Dutch Cottage and the Old Windmill — complete with fan tails and sails this is now used as an exhibition centre.

Tilbury saw the beginning of great changes in 1886, when the now extensive Docks were opened. A massive grain terminal and mill were also constructed on the site, which has become one of the largest container ports in Europe and serves major shipping companies. The pretty parish church at East Tilbury overlooks Coalhouse Fort, whose gun emplacements and granite walls provide the background for the Borough Park. Tilbury Fort stands not far from West Tilbury.

Key to Town Plan and Area Plan

Town Plan

AA Recommended roads	═══
Other roads	═══
Restricted roads	───
Buildings of interest	Station ▨
Churches	✝
Car Parks	P
Parks and open spaces	⬭

Area Plan

A roads	▦
B roads	═══
Locations	Nevendon ○
Urban area	⬭

Street Index

Basildon

Rayleigh

Tilbury

3

LEGEND

Town Plan
AA recommended route	
Restricted roads	
Other roads	
Buildings of interest	Theatre □
Car parks	P
Parks and open spaces	▲
One way streets	←

Area Plan
A roads	
B roads	
Locations	Kingston ○
Urban area	

Street Index with Grid Reference

Bedford

Adelaide Square	C4
Albany Road	E2-E3
Alexandra Place	B3-C3
Alexandra Road	B3-C3-C2
Allhallows	C3
Ampthill Road	D1
Ampthill Street	D1
Ashburnham Road	B2-B3-B4
Battison Street	C2
Bedeseley Lane	D2
Beverley Crescent	A4
Bower Street	F2-F3-F4
Brace Street	C3
Bradgate Road	F4
Brereton Road	C3
Bromham Road	A4-B4-C4-C3
Bushmead Avenue	F2-F3-F4
Campbell Road	F4
Cardington Road	D1-D2-E2-E1-F1
Castle Lane	D2-D3
Castle Road	E3-F3
Cauldwell Place	C1
Cauldwell Street	C1-D1-D2
Chaucer Road	A4
Commercial Road	C2
Conduit Road	B3-B4
Costin Street	C2-C3
Coventry Road	A1-A2-A3
Cromwell Road	A2
Cutcliffe Grove	A3-A4
Dame Alice Street	C3-D3
De Parys Avenue	D4
Duck Mill Lane	D2
Duke Street	D3
Dunville Road	A2-A3
Dynevor Road	B4
Fairfax Road	A2
Fenlake Road	F1
Ford End Road	A1-A2-B2
Foster Hill Road	D4
Gadsby Street	D3
Gibbons Road	B3
Glebe Road	E4
Goldington Avenue	F4
Goldington Road	E4-F4
Grafton Road	B2-B3
Gratton Road	A2-A3

Bedford

John Bunyan's *Pilgrim's Progress* was written in the unlikely setting of the County Gaol, where he spent 12 years on a charge of holding illegal religious meetings. Most of his life was spent in this area, and the town remembers him by a museum in his former Meeting House and by his statue on St Peter's Green. The Bunyan Centre, opened in 1974, is a popular venue for sports and also has a small theatre and a concert hall. Other places to visit in this county town of Bedfordshire are the Bedford Museum and the Cecil Higgins Art Gallery, which stands on the spot once occupied by Bedford Castle and has a collection of ceramics and glass. The parks and gardens which line the banks of the Great Ouse are a powerful attraction, as is the modern Harpur Shopping Centre, which stands on the site of a former school and has the original Victorian facade incorporated into the new design.

Biggleswade Barges on the River Ivel once carried local produce to London's markets, and Biggleswade itself has been a busy market town since the 16th century. A former staging post for coaches on the Great North Road, it is now chiefly concerned with light industry. A fine classical Town Hall and some charming half-timbered houses can be seen in the Market Square area. The Shuttleworth Collection of cars and cycles is one mile north-west, at Old Warden Aerodrome.

Greyfriars	B4-C4-C3	Preston Road	A3	Woburn Road	B3
Greyfriars Street	C3	Princes Street	C4-D4	**Biggleswade**	
Grove Place	E3	Priory Street	C3	Anne Street	B3
Hassett Street	C3	Queen Street	C4	Ash Road	B4
Harpur Street	D2-D3-D4	Raleigh Street	A1	Ashley Gardens	C4
Havelock Street	A1-A2	Rays Close	D1-E1	Auckland Road	C3
High Street	D2-D3	River Street	C2-C3	Back Street	A2-B2
Horne Lane	C2-D2	Roise Street	C3-C4	Banks Road	C4
Howard Avenue	A2	Rope Walk	D1-E1	Birch Road	A4-B4
Howard Street	D3	Rothsay Gardens	E3-E4	Blunham Road	A1
Howbury Street	F2-F3-F4	Rothsay Place	E3	Bond Lane	A2
Hurst Grove	A2-A3-A4	Rothsay Road	E2-E3	Broad Mead	B1-C1
Iddesleigh Road	A2	Rutland Road	B2-B3	Brunt's Lane	A3
Kempston Road	C1	St Cuthbert's Street	E3-E4	Cedar Avenue	A4
Kimbolton Road	E4	St John's Street	D1	Chestnut Lane	B2-B3
Kingsbrook Road	E1	St Loyes Street	C3-D3	Church Street	A2-B2
Kings Place	C1	St Mary's Street	D2	Coppice Mead	B1-C1
Kingsway	D1	St Paul's Square	D2	Crab Lane	B2
Landsdowne Road	B4	St Peter's Street	D3-D4-E4	Dark Lane	A3
Lawrence Street	A1	Shakespeare Road	A4-B4	Dells Lane	B1-B2
Lime Street	D3	Sidney Road	A4	Drove Road	C1-C2-C3-C4
Linden Road	B4	Silver Street	D3	Eaglefarm Road	C1-C2
Longholme Way	E1-F1	Spencer Road	A4	East Walk	C3-C4
Lurke Street	D3-E3	Tavistock Street	C4-D4	Edward Road	B3-C3
Maitland Street	C2	The Broadway	D3-D4	Elm Road	C1
Marlborough Road	A1-A2	The Crescent	C4	Fairfield Road	A4
Melbourne Street	D1	The Embankment	D2-E2-F2	Furzenhall Road	B4
Midland Road	B2-C2-C3-D3	The Grove	E3-E4	Glebe Road	C3
Mill Street	D3-E3	Union Street	B4-C4	Havelock Road	B3-B4
Milton Road	A4	Warwick Avenue	B4-C4	High Street	A2-B2
Nelson Street	A1	Waterloo Road	E2-E3-F3	Hitchin Street	A1-A2
Newnham Road	E2-E3	Wellington Street	D4	Hitchmeads Road	C2-C3
Newnham Street	E3	Westbourne Road	A1-A2	Holme Crescent	A1
Pembroke Street	F2-F3	Western Street	C2	Laburnham Road	C3-C4
Prebend Street	B2-C2-C1	Winifred Road	A3		

Lawnside	B3-C3
Lawrence Road	B3-C3
Lime Tree Walk	B4-C4-C3
Lindsell Crescent	B3-B4
London Road	B2-C2-C1
Market Place	A2
Mead End	B2-B1-C1
Mill Lane	A1
Palace Street	A2
Playfield Close	C1
Potton Road	B4-C4
Redman Gardens	A4
Rose Lane	B2-B3
Rowan Crescent	C3-C4
St Andrews Street	A2
St John's Street	A3-A4-B4-B3
Saffron Court	A1-B1
Saffron Road	A1-A2
Shortmead Street	A2-A3-A4
South View	A1
Spring Close	C3
Station Road	A2
Stoneland Avenue	B4-C4
Sun Street	A4-A3-B3
Teal Road	A1-A2
The Avenue	C2-C3
The Baulk	B2-C2
The Dells	B2
The Grove	B1-C1
West Walk	C3
Willsheres Road	A4-B4
Windsor Terrace	A3-B3
Winston Crescent	B4

BEDFORD
Overlooking the River Great Ouse, the 1813 Town Bridge replaced an older version which incorporated the Town Gaol into its structure. A model of the gaol is on display in the Bunyan Museum in Mill Street.

Birmingham

It is very difficult to visualise Birmingham as it was before it began the growth which eventually made it the second-largest city in England. When the Romans were in Britain it was little more than a staging post on Icknield Street. Throughout medieval times it was a sleepy agricultural centre in the middle of a heavily-forested region. Timbered houses clustered together round a green that was

eventually to be called the Bull Ring. But by the 16th century, although still a tiny and unimportant village by today's standards, it had begun to gain a reputation as a manufacturing centre. Tens of thousands of sword blades were made here during the Civil War. Throughout the 18th century more and more land was built on. In 1770 the Birmingham Canal was completed, making trade very much easier and increasing the town's development dramatically. All of that pales into near

insignificance compared with what happened in the 19th century. Birmingham was not represented in Parliament until 1832 and had no town council until 1838. Yet by 1889 it had already been made a city, and after only another 20 years it had become the second largest city in England. Many of Birmingham's most imposing public buildings date from the 19th century, when the city was growing so rapidly. Surprisingly, the city has more miles of waterway than Venice.

Key to Town Plan and Area Plan

Town Plan

AA Recommended roads

Restricted roads

Other roads

Buildings of interest — Station

AA Service Centre — AA

Car Parks — P

Parks and open spaces

One Way Streets

Area Plan

A roads

B roads

Locations — Meer End ○

Street Index with Grid Reference

Birmingham

Adelaide Street	F1
Albert Street	E4-E5-F5
Albion Street	A6
Alcester Street	F1
Allison Street	E3
Aston Road	E8-F8-F7
Aston Street	E6-E7-F7
Augusta Street	A7-A8
Bagot Street	E8
Barford Street	E1-E2-F2
Barr Street	B8
Bartholomew Street	F4-F5
Barwick Street	C5-D5
Bath Row	A1-A2-B2
Bath Street	D7
Bell Barn Road	B1
Bennett's Hill	C4-C5
Berkley Street	A3-B3
Birchall Street	F1-F2
Bishop Street	E1
Bishopsgate Street	A2
Blews Street	E8
Blucher Street	C2-C3
Bordesley Street	E4-F4-F3
Bow Street	C2
Bradford Street	E3-E2-F2
Branston Street	A8-B8-B7
Brewery Street	E8
Bridge Street	B3-B4
Bristol Street	C1-D1-D2-C2
Broad Street	A2-A3-A4-B4
Bromsgrove Street	D1-D2-E2
Brook Street	B6
Brunel Street	C3-C4
Buckingham Street	B8-C8
Bull Ring	E3
Bull Street	D5-E5-E4
Cambridge Street	A4-B4-B5

Camden Street	A5-A6
Cannon Street	D4
Caroline Street	B6-B7
Carrs Street	E4
Cecil Street	D8
Chapel Street	E5-E6
Charles Henry Street	F1
Charlotte Street	B5-B6
Cheapside	F1-F2
Cherry Street	D4-D5
Church Street	C6-C5-D5
Clement Street	A5
Cliveland Street	D7-D8-E8
Colmore Circus	D5-D6
Colmore Row	C4-C5-D5
Commercial Street	B2-B3-C3
Constitution Hill	B7-C7
Cornwall Street	C5-C6
Corporation Street	D4-D5-E5-E6-E7-E8
Coventry Street	E3-F3
Cox Street	B7
Cregoe Street	B1-B2
Cumberland Street	A3
Curzon Street	F5
Dale End	E4-E5
Dartmouth Middleway	F7-F8
Digbeth	E3-F3
Dudley Street	D3
Duke Street	F6
Edgbaston Street	D3-E3
Edmund Street	C5-D5
Edward Street	A5
Ellis Street	C2-C3
Essex Street	D2
Fazeley Street	E5-E4-F4
Fleet Street	B5
Floodgate Street	F3
Fox Street	F5
Frederick Street	A6-A7
Gas Street	A3-B3
George Road	A1
George Street	A5-B5-B6
Gooch Street North	D1-D2
Gosta Green	F7
Gough Street	C3
Graham Street	A6-B6
Grant Street	C1
Granville Street	A3-A2-B2
Great Charles St Queensway	B5-C5-C6
Great Colmore Street	B1-C1-D1
Great Hampton Row	C7-C8
Great Hampton Street	A8-B8
Grosvenor Street	F5-F6
Hall Street	B7-B8
Hampton Street	C7-C8
Hanley Street	D7-D8
Helena Street	A5
Heneage Street	F7
Henrietta Street	C7-D7
High Street	D4-E4
High Street Deritend	F2-F3
Hill Street	C4-C3-D3
Hinckley Street	D3
Hockley Street	A8-B8
Holland Street	B5
Holliday Street	A2-B2-B3-C3-C4
Holloway Circus	C2-C3-D3-D2
Holloway Head	B2-C2
Holt Street	F7-F8
Hospital Street	C7-C8
Howard Street	B7-C7-C8
Hurst Street	D3-D2-E2-E1

Hylton Street	A8
Inge Street	D2
Irving Street	C2-D2
Islington Middleway	A1
James Street	B6
James Watt Queensway	E5-E6
Jennens Road	E5-F5-F6
John Bright Street	C3-C4
Kent Street	D1-D2
Kenyon Street	B7
King Edward's Place	A4
King Edward's Road	A4-A5
Kingston Row	A4
Ladywell Walk	D2-D3
Lancaster Circus	E6-E7
Lawrence Street	F6-F7
Lee Bank Middleway	A1-B1
Legge Lane	A6
Lionel Street	B5-C5-C6
Lister Street	F7-F8
Livery Street	B7-C7-C6-D6-D5
Lombard Street	F1-F2
Louisa Street	A5
Love Lane	F8
Loveday Street	D7
Lower Darwin Street	F1
Lower Essex Street	D2-D1-E1
Lower Loveday Street	D7
Lower Tower Street	D8
Ludgate Hill	B6-C6
Macdonald Street	E1-F1
Marshall Street	C2
Mary Street	B7
Mary Ann Street	C6-C7
Masshouse Circus	E5
Meriden Street	E3-F3
Milk Street	F3
Moat Lane	E3
Molland Street	E8
Moor Street Queensway	E4-E5
Moseley Street	E2-F2-F1
Mott Street	B8-C8-C7
Navigation Street	C3-C4
New Street	C4-D4
New Bartholomew Street	F4
New Canal Street	F4-F5
Newhall Hill	A5-A6
Newhall Street	B6-B5-C5
New Summer Street	E5
Newton Street	E5
New Town Row	D8-E8-E7
Northampton Street	A8
Northwood Street	B6-B7
Old Square	D5-E5
Oozells Street	A3-A4
Oozells Street North	A3-A4
Oxford Street	F3-F4
Oxygen Street	F7-F8
Paradise Circus	B4-B5
Paradise Street	C4
Park Street	E3-E4
Pershore Street	D3-D2-E2
Pickford Street	F4
Pinfold Street	C4
Pitsford Street	A8
Price Street	D7-E7
Princip Street	D7-E7-E8
Printing House Street	D6
Priory Queensway	E5
Rea Street	E2-F2-F3
Rea Street South	E1-F1-F2
Regent Place	A7-B7

Rickman Drive	C1
Royal Mail Street	C3
St Chad's Circus	C7-C6-D6
St Chad's Queensway	D6-D7-E7
St George's Street	C8
St Martin's Circus	D3-D4-E4-E3
St Martin's Place	A4
St Paul's Square	B7-B6-C6
St Peter's Place	A4
Sand Pits Parade	A5
Severn Street	C3
Shadwell Street	D6-D7
Sheepcote Street	A3
Sherlock Street	D1-E1-E2
Smallbrook Queensway	C3-D3
Snow Hill	D5-D6
Snow Hill Queensway	D6
Spencer Street	A8-A7-B7
Staniforth Street	E7-E8
Station Approach	D3
Station Street	D3
Steelhouse Lane	D6-E6
Stephenson Street	C4-D4
Stoke Street	A2-A3
Suffolk Street Queensway	B4-C4-C3
Summer Row	A5-B5
Summer Lane	C7-D7-D8
Sutton Street	C2
Temple Row	C5-D5
Temple Street	D4-D5
Tenby Street	A6-A7
Tenby Street North	A7
Tennant Street	A2-A3
Thorpe Street	D2-D3
Tower Street	C8-D8
Trent Street	F3-F4
Union Street	D4
Upper Dean Street	D3-E3
Upper Gough Street	B2-C2-C3
Vesey Street	D7-E7
Vittoria Street	A6-A7
Vyse Street	A7-A8
Ward Street	D8
Warford Street	B8
Warstone Lane	A7-B7
Water Street	C6
Waterloo Street	C4-C5-D5
Weaman Street	D6
Wheeley's Lane	A1-B1-B2
Wheeley's Road	A1
Whittall Street	D6-E6
William Street	A2
William Street North	C8-D8
Woodcock Street	F6-F7
Wrentham Street	D1-E1
Wynn Street	C1

7

Brentwood area

Harlow Home of the country's first pedestrianised shopping centre and first all-purpose Sportcentre (embracing athletic and football clubs and a dry ski-slope), Harlow is the site of one of Britain's earliest 'New Towns'. Careful planning has produced a tasteful integration of housing, industrial estates and parks around the centre, and the Playhouse has a popular theatre. The ancient settlement of Old Harlow stands side by side with the new, and the Harlow Museum, set in a fine Georgian house with pleasantly landscaped grounds, has exhibits connected with the history of the area.

Brentwood Thermos Ltd and the Ford Motor Co are two of the major companies attracted to this former market town in recent years. It also enjoys modern shopping facilities and has a number of parks and stretches of woodland, while lying within easy reach of two country parks (Weald to the north-west and Thorndon to the south-east). The 'Old House' Arts and Community Centre provides a home for local societies and clubs, in premises dating back to Tudor times.

Epping is linked to London by main line and underground railways, but still enjoys the magnificent 600-acre expanse of Epping Forest which stretches south from the town and makes a peaceful haven from the area's busy main roads.

Central Epping (map, left)

Central Brentwood (map, right)

LEGEND

Town Plan

- AA recommended route
- Restricted roads
- Other roads
- Buildings of interest — Library ▢
- Car parks — P
- Parks and open spaces ◣

Area Plan

- A roads
- B roads
- Locations — Yardley ○

Street Index with Grid Reference

Brentwood

Alfred Road	B2-B3
Avenue Road	B1
Bardswell Close	A3
Brentwood Place	B4
Burland Road	B4
Chase Road	A1-A2
Copperfield Gardens	A4
Coptfield Road	B2-B3
Cornsland	B1-B2-B1-C1
Crescent Road	A1
Cromwell Road	B2-B3
Crown Street	A2
Downsland Drive	A2
Eastern Road	B1
Geary Drive	A4
Gerrard Crescent	A2
Gresham Road	B1-B2
Hart Street	A3-B3
Hartswood Road	C1
Highland Avenue	B4
High Street	A3-B3
Hills Chace	B1
Ingrave Road	B3-C3-C2
King Edward Road	B1
King's Chase	A2
King's Road	A2-B2-B1
London Road	A2-A3
Mayfield Gardens	A3-A4
Middleton Hall Lane	C2-C3-C4
Milton Road	A1
Mount Crescent	B1-C1
North Road	B3-B4
North Road Avenue	B3
Ongar Road	A4-B4-B3
Park Road	A3-B3
Priests Lane	C2
Primrose Hill	B2
Queen's Road	B2-B3
Rose Bank	B2
Rose Valley	B1-B2
St Francis Way	A3
St James's Road	A1
St Thomas Road	B3
Sawyer's Hall Lane	B4-C4-C3
Service Road	B3
Seven Arches Road	C1-C2
Shenfield Cross	C4
Shenfield Road	B3-C3-C4
The Chase	B2-C2
The Vale	A3-A4
Tower Hill	A3
Tree Tops	B4
Victoria Road	A1
Vine Way	A3-A4
Warley Hill	A1-B1
Warley Mount Road	B1
Weald Road	A3
Westbury Drive	A2
Westbury Road	A2
Western Avenue	B3-B4
Western Road	A3-B3

Harlow

Altham Grove	E4-F4
Arkwrights	F2
Ashtree Field	A4-B4
Broadfield	D2-E2
Burnt Mill	B4-C4
Canons Brook	A2
Canons Gate	A3
Coates Street	C1-C2
College Gate	C1
Collins Meadow	A1-B1
Common Fields	E3
Cross Street	C2
East Gate	C2
East Walk	C2
Elizabeth Way	A3-A4-B4-C4-D4
Fifth Avenue	C4-D4-D3-C3
First Avenue	C3-D3-E3-F3
Fold Croft	A2-A3
Fourth Avenue	A2-B2-C2-C3
Glebelands	F3-F4
Great Plumtree	F3-F4
Greenhills	D1-E1-E2
Halling Hill	E3-F3
Hammarskjold Road	C3
Hamstel Road	B3-B2-C2
Harberts Road	B1-B2
Hare Street	B1-C1
Hare Street Springs	B1
Haydens Road	B2-C2-C1
Heliens Road	A2-A1-B1
Herons Wood	B4
Hobtoe Road	A2-A3
Hodings Road	A2-A3-B3-C3
Home Close	E3
Howard Way	F1-F2-F3-F4
Linkway	C2
Little Grove Field	B1-B2
Long Ley	F1
Luther King Road	C1
Maddox Avenue	D3-D2-E2-E1-F1
Manston Road	E1
Market Square	C2
Minchen Wood	F2-F3
Monkswick Road	E3-E2-F2-F1
Morley Grove	C3
Mowbray Road	F4
Morthbrooks	B1-C1
North Gate	C2
Old House Croft	E3
Park Lane	D3-D4
Park Mead	B3
Parsonage Leys	E1
Pitmans Field	E2-F2
Post Office Road	C2
Pypers Hatch	F1-F2
Ram Gorse	A3-B3-A3-A4
Rectory Wood	B3-C3
River Mill	B4-C4
Ryecroft	A1
School Lane	D4-E4-E3-E2
Second Avenue	D1-E1
Sharpecroft	B1
Slackesbury Hatch	A1-B1
South Gate	C1
Spring Hills	A3
Stantons	A2
Terminus Street	C2
The Dashes	D2-D3-E3
The Downs	E1
The Drive	E2-E3
The Hides	D2-D3
The Hornbeams	B4-C4
The Stow	B4-C4
Third Avenue	C1-D1
Tunmeade	F1-F2
Upper Park	A2-A3-B3-B2
Upper Stonyfield	B1-B2
Velizy Avenue	C2-D2-D1
Vicarage Wood	F2
Wedhey	B2
West Gate	C2
White Waits	E1-E2
Wooding Grove	A2

Epping

Albany Court	A3-B3
Ambleside	B2-B1-C1
Amesbury Road	B1
Ashlyns Road	A2-A3
Bakers Lane	A2-B2-B3
Beaconfield Avenue	A4-B4
Beaconfield Road	A3-B3-B4
Beaconfield Way	B3-B4
Beulah Road	B4
Bower Hill	C1
Bury Road	A1
Buttercross Lane	B3
Centre Drive	B1
Chapel Road	A2
Church Hill	B3-B4
Clover Leas	A3
Coronation Hill	A3
Crows Road	A2-B2
Egg Hall	B4-C4
Fairfield Road	C4
Granville Road	C4
Hartland Road	B2
Hemnall Street	A1-B1-B2-B3
High Street	A1-B1-B2-B3
Homefield Close	B3
Ingels Mead	A3-B3
Kendal Avenue	B2-C2-C1
Lime Road	A2
Lincolns Field	A3-B3
Lindsey Street	A4-B4
Lower Bury Lane	A1
Lower Swaines	A2-A3
Lynceley Grange	A3
Madells	A1-B1
Maltings Lane	B4-C4
Meadow Road	A4-B4
Nicholl Road	B1-B2
Oak Road	A2
Ongar Road	C4
Rahn Road	B1
Ravensmere	B2-C2
Rayfield	B3
Regent Road	A2
St John's Road	A3-A2-B2
Severns Field	B3-B4
Shaftesbury Road	A3-A4-B4
Station Road	B2-B1-C1
Stonard's Hill	C3
Theydon Grove	B3-C3
Theydon Place	A1-B1
Thornwood Road	C4
Tidy's Lane	C4
Tower Road	A1-A2
Upper Swaines	A2
Wheelers	B3

BRENTWOOD
The Essex Regimental Chapel at Warley is a reminder of longstanding military links — Warley Barracks was once the Depot of the Essex Regiment, and the Essex HQ of the Royal Anglian Regiment is still in the area.

Burton upon Trent

Beer has been brewed here since medieval times and is still prevalent in the town, even though the number of breweries has diminished. The Bass Museum traces the history of the local brewing industry, and other places of interest include the Meadowside Centre, with its fine facilities for sports and the arts. Interesting old buildings can be seen, especially around Horninglow Street, and the Market Hall (now the new shopping centre) dates from the 19th century.

Loughborough Forty-seven locally-made bells ring out from the Queens Park Carillon Tower every Sunday during the summer, and many of Britain's churches have bells from Loughborough's John Taylor Foundry. A busy market and university town situated on the River Stour, Loughborough is also known for its colleges of technology and physical education. Its facilities include a modern Leisure Centre, and amongst local places of interest are the Parish Church of All Saints, dating from the 14th century, the much-restored Old Rectory, and Loughborough Central Station, where steam trains operate most weekends.

Ashby-de-la-Zouch Soap, crisp and biscuit making are the chief present-day concerns of this pleasant market town. The remains of the 15th-century castle are preserved near the centre of the town.

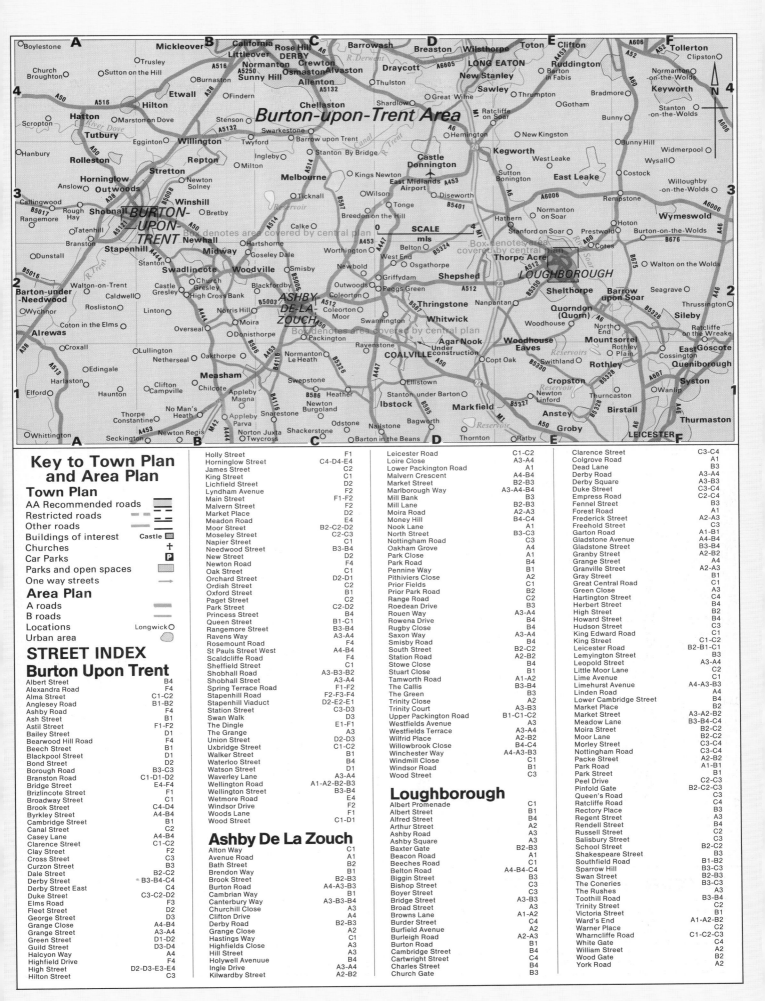

Key to Town Plan and Area Plan

Town Plan

AA Recommended roads
Restricted roads
Other roads
Buildings of interest — Castle
Churches
Car Parks
Parks and open spaces
One way streets

Area Plan

A roads
B roads
Locations — Longwick
Urban area

STREET INDEX

Burton Upon Trent

Albert Street	B4
Alexandra Road	F4
Alma Street	C1-C2
Anglesey Road	B1-B2
Ashby Road	F4
Ash Street	B1
Astil Street	F1-F2
Bailey Street	D1
Bearwood Hill Road	F4
Beech Street	B1
Blackpool Street	D1
Bond Street	D2
Borough Road	B3-C3
Branston Road	C1-D1-D2
Bridge Street	E4-F4
Brizlincote Street	F1
Broadway Street	C1
Brook Street	C4-D4
Byrkley Street	A4-B4
Cambridge Street	B1
Canal Street	C2
Casey Lane	A4-B4
Clarence Street	C1-C2
Clay Street	F2
Cross Street	C3
Curzon Street	B3
Dale Street	B2-C2
Derby Street	B3-B4-C4
Derby Street East	C4
Duke Street	C3-C2-D2
Elms Road	F3
Fleet Street	D2
George Street	D3
Grange Close	A4-B4
Grange Street	A3-A4
Green Street	D1-D2
Guild Street	D3-D4
Halcyon Way	A4
Highfield Drive	F4
High Street	D2-D3-E3-E4
Hilton Street	C3
Holly Street	F1
Horninglow Street	C4-D4-E4
James Street	C2
King Street	C1
Lichfield Street	D2
Lyndham Avenue	F2
Main Street	F1-F2
Malvern Street	C2
Market Place	D2
Meadon Road	E4
Moor Street	B2-C2-D2
Moseley Street	C2-C3
Napier Street	C1
Needwood Street	B3-B4
New Street	D2
Newton Road	F4
Oak Street	C1
Orchard Street	D2-D1
Ordish Street	C2
Oxford Street	B1
Paget Street	C2
Park Street	C2-D2
Princess Street	B4
Queen Street	B1-C1
Rangemore Street	B3-B4
Ravens Way	A3-A4
Rosemount Road	F4
St Pauls Street West	A4-B4
Scaldcliffe Road	F4
Sheffield Street	C1
Shobhall Road	A3-B3-B2
Shobhall Street	A3-A4
Spring Terrace Road	F1-F2
Stapenhill Road	F2-F3-F4
Stapenhill Viaduct	D2-E2-E1
Station Street	C3-D3
Swan Walk	C2
The Dingle	E1-F1
The Grange	A3
Union Street	D2-D3
Uxbridge Street	C1-C2
Walker Street	B1
Waterloo Street	B4
Watson Street	D1
Waverley Lane	A3-A4
Wellington Road	A1-A2-B2-B3
Wellington Street	B3-B4
Wetmore Road	E4
Windsor Drive	F2
Woods Lane	F1
Wood Street	C1-D1

Ashby De La Zouch

Alton Way	C1
Avenue Road	A1
Bath Street	B2
Brendon Way	B1
Brook Street	B2-B3
Burton Road	A4-A3-B3
Cambrian Way	B1
Canterbury Way	A3-B3-B4
Churchill Close	A3
Clifton Drive	A4
Derby Road	B2
Grange Close	A2
Hastings Way	C1
Highfields Close	A3
Hill Street	A3
Holywell Avenuue	B4
Ingle Drive	A3-A4
Kilwardby Street	A2-B2
Leicester Road	C1-C2
Loire Close	A3-A4
Lower Packington Road	A1
Malvern Crescent	A4-B4
Market Street	B2-B3
Marlborough Way	A3-A4-B4
Mill Bank	B3
Mill Lane	B2-B3
Moira Road	A2-A3
Money Hill	B4-C4
Nook Lane	A1
North Street	B3-C3
Nottingham Road	C3
Oakham Grove	A4
Park Close	A1
Park Road	B4
Pennine Way	B1
Pithiviers Close	A2
Prior Fields	C1
Prior Park Road	B2
Range Road	C2
Roedean Drive	B3
Rouen Way	A3-A4
Rowena Drive	B4
Rugby Close	B4
Saxon Way	A3-A4
Smisby Road	B4
South Street	B2-C2
Station Road	A2-B2
Stowe Close	B4
Stuart Close	B1
Tamworth Road	A1-A2
The Callis	B3-B4
The Green	B3
Trinity Close	A2
Trinity Court	A3-B3
Upper Packington Road	B1-C1-C2
Westfields Avenue	A3
Westfields Terrace	A3-A4
Wilfrid Place	B4-C4
Willowbrook Close	A4-A3-B3
Winchester Way	A4-A3-B3
Windmill Close	C1
Windsor Road	B1
Wood Street	C3

Loughborough

Albert Promenade	C1
Albert Street	B1
Alfred Street	B4
Arthur Street	A2
Ashby Road	A3
Ashby Square	A3
Baxter Gate	B2-B3
Beacon Road	A1
Beeches Road	C1
Belton Road	A4-B4-C4
Biggin Street	B3
Bishop Street	C3
Boyer Street	C3
Bridge Street	A3-B3
Broad Street	A3
Browns Lane	A1-A2
Burder Street	C4
Burfield Avenue	A2
Burleigh Road	A2-A3
Burton Road	B1
Cambridge Street	B4
Cartwright Street	C4
Charles Street	B4
Church Gate	B3
Clarence Street	C3-C4
Colgrove Road	A1
Dead Lane	B3
Derby Road	A3-A4
Derby Square	A3-B3
Duke Street	C3-C4
Empress Road	C2-C4
Fennel Street	B3
Forest Road	A1
Frederick Street	A2-A3
Freehold Street	C3
Garton Road	A1-B1
Gladstone Avenue	A4-B4
Gladstone Street	B3-B4
Granby Street	A2-B2
Grange Street	A4
Granville Street	A2-A3
Gray Street	B1
Great Central Road	C1
Green Close	A3
Hartington Street	C4
Herbert Street	B4
High Street	B2
Howard Street	B4
Hudson Street	C3
King Edward Road	C1
King Street	C1-C2
Leicester Road	B2-B1-C1
Lemyngton Street	B3
Leopold Street	A3-A4
Little Moor Lane	C2
Lime Avenue	C1
Limehurst Avenue	A4-A3-B3
Linden Road	A4
Lower Cambridge Street	B4
Market Place	B2
Market Street	A3-A2-B2
Meadow Lane	B3-B4-C4
Moira Street	B2-C2
Moor Lane	B2-C2
Morley Street	C3-C4
Nottingham Road	C3-C4
Packe Street	A2-B2
Park Road	A1-B1
Park Street	B1
Peel Drive	C2-C3
Pinfold Gate	B2-C2-C3
Queen's Road	C3
Ratcliffe Road	C4
Rectory Place	B3
Regent Street	A3
Rendell Street	B4
Russell Street	C2
Salisbury Street	C3
School Street	B2-C2
Shakespeare Street	B3
Southfield Road	B1-B2
Sparrow Hill	B3-C3
Swan Street	B2-B3
The Coneries	B3-C3
The Rushes	A3
Toothill Road	B3-B4
Trinity Street	C2
Victoria Street	B1
Ward's End	A1-A2-B2
Warner Place	A2
Wharncliffe Road	C1-C2-C3
White Gate	C4
William Street	A2
Wood Gate	B2
York Road	A2

Key to Town Plan and Area Plan

Town Plan

AA Recommended roads	
Restricted roads	
Other roads	
Buildings of interest	Theatre
Car Parks	P
One Way Streets	→
Parks and open spaces	

Area Plan

A roads	
B roads	
Locations	Prickwillow ○
Urban area	

Street Index with Grid Reference

Bury St Edmunds

Bury St Edmunds

This is one of the architectural gems of East Anglia with its streets of Georgian and earlier houses on the Norman grid pattern. The Norman Abbey ruins are set in attractive grounds with a magnificent gateway, and the cathedral church of St Edmunds-bury is adjacent to a massive Norman tower. Also worth seeing are the Guildhall (13th-century and later), the Athenaeum, the colonnaded Corn Exchange (1862) and the 1711 Pentecostal Church. Moyses Hall and Borough Museum goes back to the 12th century and the rebuilt Market Cross and Art Gallery to the 17th. Angel Corner has a fine display of clocks and watches, and St Mary's Church holds Mary Tudor's tomb.

Newmarket Headquarters of British horse racing, breeding and training for nearly 400 years, this is the home of the Jockey Club (founded 1750), the National Stud and the National Horseracing Museum. The racecourse has the world's longest 'straight'.

Thetford was once a Saxon cathedral city and seat of early kings. London overspill sparked off expansion in the 1960s, but Georgian and medieval buildings can still be seen in the town, as well as a Norman castle mound, 12th-century priory remains and Iron Age earthworks. *Rights of Man* author Thomas Paine was born here in 1737. The 15th-century Ancient House offers local history exhibits and the Museum of Childhood Treasures.

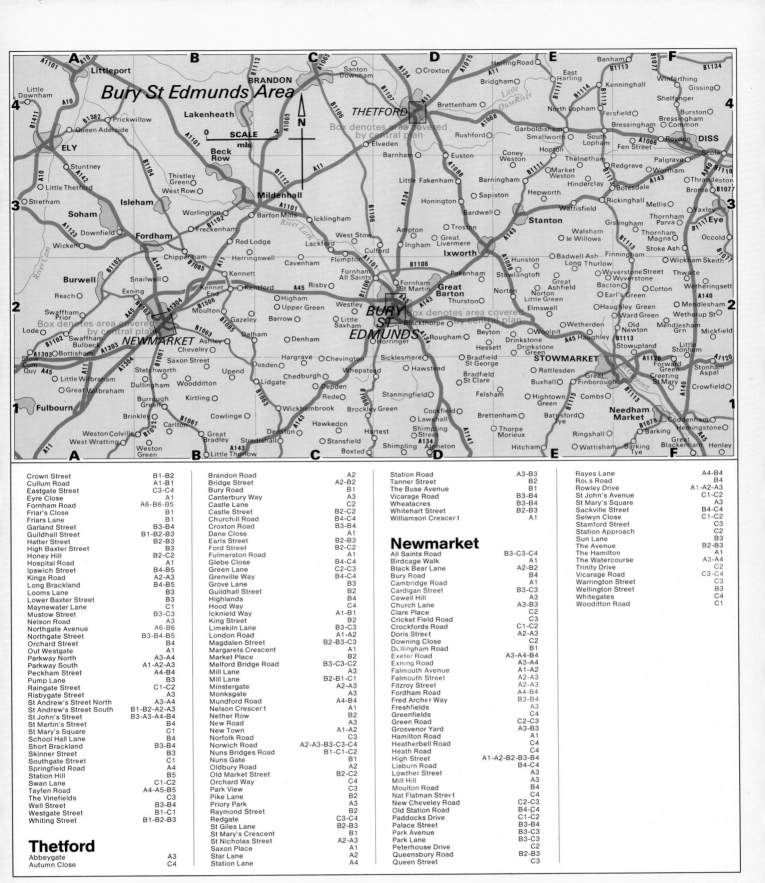

Bury St Edmunds

Street	Grid
Crown Street	B1-B2
Cullum Road	A1-B1
Eastgate Street	C3-C4
Eyre Close	A1
Fornham Road	A6-B6-B5
Friar's Close	B1
Friars Lane	C1
Garland Street	B3-B4
Guildhall Street	B1-B2-B3
Hatter Street	B2-B3
High Baxter Street	B3
Honey Hill	B2-C2
Hospital Road	A1
Ipswich Street	B4-B5
Kings Road	A2-A3
Long Brackland	B4-B5
Looms Lane	B3
Lower Baxter Street	B3
Maynewater Lane	C1
Mustow Street	B3-C3
Nelson Road	A3
Northgate Avenue	A6-B6
Northgate Street	B3-B4-B5
Orchard Street	B4
Out Westgate	A1
Parkway North	A3-A4
Parkway South	A1-A2-A3
Peckham Street	A4-B4
Pump Lane	B3
Raingate Street	C1-C2
Risbygate Street	A3
St Andrew's Street North	A3-A4
St Andrew's Street South	B1-B2-A2-A3
St John's Street	B3-A3-A4-B4
St Martin's Street	B4
St Mary's Square	C1
School Hall Lane	B4
Short Brackland	B3-B4
Skinner Street	B3
Southgate Street	C1
Springfield Road	A4
Station Hill	B5
Swan Lane	C1-C2
Tayfen Road	A4-A5-B5
The Vinefields	C3
Well Street	B3-B4
Westgate Street	B1-C1
Whiting Street	B1-B2-B3

Thetford

Street	Grid
Abbeygate	A3
Autumn Close	C4
Brandon Road	A2
Bridge Street	A2-B2
Bury Road	B1
Canterbury Way	A3
Castle Lane	C2
Castle Street	B2-C2
Churchill Road	B4-C4
Croxton Road	B3-B4
Dane Close	A1
Earls Street	B2-B3
Ford Street	B2-C2
Fulmerston Road	A1
Glebe Close	B4-C4
Green Lane	C2-C3
Grenville Way	B4-C4
Grove Lane	B3
Guildhall Street	B2
Highlands	B4
Hood Way	C4
Icknield Way	A1-B1
King Street	B2
Limekiln Lane	B3-C3
London Road	A1-A2
Magdalen Street	B2-B3-C3
Margarets Crescent	A1
Market Place	B2
Melford Bridge Road	B3-C3-C2
Mill Lane	A3
Mill Lane	B2-B1-C1
Minstergate	A2-A3
Monksgate	A3
Mundford Road	A4-B4
Nelson Crescent	A1
Nether Row	B2
New Road	A3
New Town	A1-A2
Norfolk Road	C3
Norwich Road	A2-A3-B3-C3-C4
Nuns Bridges Road	B1-C1-C2
Nuns Gate	B1
Oldbury Road	A2
Old Market Street	B2-C2
Orchard Way	C4
Park View	C3
Pike Lane	B2
Priory Park	B2
Raymond Street	B2
Redgate	C3-C4
St Giles Lane	B2-B3
St Mary's Crescent	B1
St Nicholas Street	A2-A3
Saxon Place	A1
Star Lane	A2
Station Lane	A4
Station Road	A3-B3
Tanner Street	B2
The Buse Avenue	B1
Vicarage Road	B3-B4
Wheatacres	B3-B4
Whitehart Street	B2-B3
Williamson Crescent	A1

Newmarket

Street	Grid
All Saints Road	B3-C3-C4
Birdcage Walk	A1
Black Bear Lane	A2-B2
Bury Road	B4
Cambridge Road	A1
Cardigan Street	B3-C3
Cewell Hill	A3
Church Lane	A3-B3
Clare Place	C2
Cricket Field Road	C3
Crockfords Road	C1-C2
Doris Street	A2-A3
Downing Close	C2
Dullingham Road	B1
Exeter Road	A3-A4-B4
Exning Road	A3-A4
Falmouth Avenue	A1-A2
Falmouth Street	A2-A3
Fitzroy Street	A2-A3
Fordham Road	A4-B4
Fred Archer Way	B3-B4
Freshfields	A3
Greenfields	C4
Green Road	C2-C3
Grosvenor Yard	A3-B3
Hamilton Road	A1
Heatherbell Road	C4
Heath Road	C4
High Street	A1-A2-B2-B3-B4
Lisburn Road	B4-C4
Lowther Street	A3
Mill Hill	A3
Moulton Road	B4
Nat Flatman Street	C4
New Cheveley Road	C2-C3
Old Station Road	B4-C4
Paddocks Drive	C1-C2
Palace Street	B3-B4
Park Avenue	B3-C3
Park Lane	B3-C3
Peterhouse Drive	C2
Queensbury Road	B2-B3
Queen Street	C3
Rayes Lane	A4-B4
Rous Road	B4
Rowley Drive	A1-A2-A3
St John's Avenue	C1-C2
St Mary's Square	A3
Sackville Street	B4-C4
Selwyn Close	C1-C2
Stamford Street	C3
Station Approach	C2
Sun Lane	B3
The Avenue	B2-B3
The Hamilton	A1
The Watercourse	A3-A4
Trinity Drive	C2
Vicarage Road	C3-C4
Warrington Street	C3
Wellington Street	B3
Whitegates	C4
Wooditton Road	C1

BURY ST EDMUNDS
Overlooked by Moyses Hall, market stalls still crowd the Cornhill and Buttermarket twice a week, and have been a feature of the town for several centuries.

Cambridge

Few views in England, perhaps even in Europe, are as memorable as that from Cambridge's Backs towards the colleges. Dominating the scene, in every sense, is King's College Chapel. One of the finest Gothic buildings anywhere, it was built in three stages from 1446 to 1515.

No one would dispute that the chapel is Cambridge's masterpiece, but there are dozens of

buildings here that would be the finest in any other town or city. Most are colleges, or are attached to colleges, and it is the university which permeates every aspect of Cambridge's landscape and life. In all there are 33 university colleges in the city, and nearly all have buildings and features of great interest. Cambridge's oldest church is St Bene't's, with a Saxon tower; its most famous is the Church of the Holy Sepulchre, one of only four round churches of its kind.

Huntingdon and *Ely* are both within easy driving distance of Cambridge. Oliver Cromwell and Samuel Pepys were pupils at Huntingdon Grammar School. The building is now a Cromwell museum. Ely also has strong Cromwellian connections – he and his family lived here for ten years. Ely's outstanding feature is the cathedral, a Norman foundation crowned by a stately octagonal lantern tower which contains the Stained Glass Museum.

Key to Town Plan and Area Plan

Town Plan

AA Recommended roads	▬▬
Restricted roads	▬ ▬ ▬
Other roads	▬▬
Buildings of interest	College ▨
Car Parks	℗
Parks and open spaces	◩
One Way Streets	←

Area Plan

A roads	▬▬
B roads	▬▬
Locations	Haslingfield ○
Urban area	▨

Street Index with Grid Reference

Cambridge

Adam and Eve Street	F1-F2
Adams Road	A2-A3
Auckland Road	F3
Aylestone Road	F4
Belvoir Road	F4
Benet Street	C1-C2-D2
Bridge Street	C3-D3
Broad Street	F1
Brunswick Terrace	F3
Brunswick Walk	F3
Burleigh Street	F2
Castle Street	C4
Chesterton Lane	C4-D4
City Road	F2
Clarendon Street	E1-E2
Clarkson Road	A3-A4
Corn Exchange Street	D1-D2
Cranmer Road	A1
De Freville Avenue	F4
Downing Street	D1
Drummer Street	D2-E2
Earl Street	E2
East Road	F1-F2
Eden Street	F2
Elm Street	E2-F2
Emmanuel Road	E2
Emmanuel Street	D1-D2-E2
Fair Street	F2-F3
Fitzroy Street	F2
Gold Street	F2
Grange Road	A1-A2-A3-A4
Green Street	C2-D2-D3
Hershel Road	A2
Hobston Street	D2-D3
James Street	F2-F3
Jesus Lane	D3-E3
John Street	F2
Kimberley Road	F4
King's Parade	C1-C2
King Street	D3-E3
Lady Margaret Road	B4
Lower Park Street	D3-D4
Madingley Road	A4-B4
Magdalene Street	C4
Maids Causeway	E3-F3
Malcolm Street	D3
Manor Street	D3-E3
Market Street	D2
Melbourne Place	E1-E2-F2
Mill Lane	C1
Mill Road	F1
Napier Street	F2-F3
Newmarket Road	F3
New Park Street	D4
New Square	E2-F2
Northampton Street	B4-C4
Orchard Street	E2-F2
Paradise Street	F2
Parker Street	E1-E2
Park Parade	D4
Parkside	E1-F1
Park Street	D3
Park Terrace	E1
Parsonage Street	F3
Pembroke Street	C1-D1
Pound Hill	B4-C4
Prospect Row	F1-F2
Queens Road	B1-B2-B3-B4
St Andrew's Street	D2-D1-E1
St John's Lane	D4
St John's Street	C3-D3
St Peter's Street	B4-C4
Short Street	E2-E3
Sidney Street	D2-D3
Silver Street	B1-C1
Tennis Court Road	D1
Thompson's Lane	C3-C4-D4
Trinity Street	C2-C3
Victoria Avenue	E3-E4
Victoria Street	E2
Warkworth Terrace	F1
West Road	A1-B1
Willis Road	F1

Huntingdon

Ambury Hill	B3
Ambury Road	A2-A3-B3-B4
American Lane	B3-B4-C4
Avenue Road	B3
Bevan Close	B4-C4
Brampton Road	A2
Brookside	B2-B3
California Road	B4-C4
Castle Hill	B1
Castle Moat Road	B1-B2
Chequers Way	B2
Clayton's Way	C3-C4
Coldhams North	C4
Coldhams South	C4
Coronation Avenue	C3-C4
Cowper Road	B3
Coxon's Close	B4
Cromwell Walk	A3-B3
Cross Street	C3
Driver's Avenue	C3-C4
East Street	C3
Ermine Street	A3
Euston Street	B2-C2
Ferrars Road	A2
George Street	A2
Great Northern Street	A3
Hartford Road	B2-C2-C3
High Street	B3
Horse Common Lane	B3
Huntingdon Bypass	A2-A1-B1-C1
Ingram Street	B2-C2
Lammas Gardens	A3-B3
Market Square	B2
Mayfield Road	C4
Merritt Street	A3
Mill Common	B1
North Street	C3
Nursery Road	B3-B2-C2
Orchard Lane	B2-C2
Primrose Lane	B3-C3
Princes Street	B2
Priory Grove	B3
Priory Lane	B3
Priory Road	B3
Queens Drive	C3-C4
Riverside Road	C2
St Germain Street	B2
St John's Street	A2-A3
St Mary's Street	B1-B2
St Peters Road	A3-A4
St Sayer Street	A3
South Street	C3
Swallowbush Road	A4-B4
The Avenue	C1
Temple Close	C2
Walden Road	A2-B2-B1
West Street	C3

Ely

Annesdale	C1
Archery Crescent	C4
Back Hill	B1-C1
Barton Road	A1-B1
Barton Square	B1-B2
Brays Lane	C3-C4
Broad Street	C1-C2-C3
Butchers Row	B3
Chapel Street	A3-A4-B4
Chequers Lane	B3
Church Lane	A2-A3
Cromwell Road	A2-A3
Downham Road	A3-A4
Egremont Street	a4-B4
Fore Hill	C3
High Street	B3-C3
Jubilee Terrace	C1
Lynn Road	B3-B4
Market Place	C3
Market Street	B3-C3
Minster Place	B2-B3
Needham Crescent	C4
New Barn Road	C4
Newnham Street	B3-B4-C4
Nutholt Lane	B4
Palace Green	A3-B3
Parade Lane	A1-A2
Prickwillow Road	C4
St Mary's Street	A2-A3-B3
Ship Lane	C2
Silver Street	A2-B2
Station Road	B2
The Gallery	B2
The Range	A2
The Vineyards	C3
Victoria Street	C1
West Fen Road	A3

CAMBRIDGE
Behind the gracious university college buildings beautiful lawns and gardens known as the Backs sweep down to the River Cam which, spanned by little bridges and shaded by willows, provides an idyllic setting for punting.

Chelmsford

Important since Roman times, this county town of Essex has undergone a good deal of expansion and development in recent years, providing it with good shopping and leisure facilities. Older buildings are concentrated in the Tindal Street area, notably the Shire Hall and the Cathedral, which dates from the 15th century. The cattle market (now on a modern site) has been going since Elizabethan days, and other places of interest include the Chelmsford and Essex Museum, which also houses the Museum of the Essex Regiment.

Braintree has been concerned with textile making since the early Middle Ages, and still keeps up the connection with the Courtaulds Group, associated with the area since the 19th century.

Maldon has retained a fascinating old quarter around All Saints Church, at the top of the High Street. A river port which has seen some industrialisation, it remains popular with holidaymakers for its position at the junction of the Blackwater and Chelmer rivers, and offers good facilities for boating along the river banks.

Witham's recent Town Development Scheme has brought expansion, incorporating housing estates, offices and factories for this ancient town on the River Brain. It has nevertheless retained some fine Georgian buildings, and several old coaching inns can be seen in the main street.

LEGEND

Town Plan

AA recommended route
Restricted roads
Other roads
Buildings of interest — Theatre
Car parks — P
Parks and open spaces
One way streets — →

Area Plan

A roads
B roads
Locations — Notley○
Urban area

Street Index with Grid Reference

Chelmsford

Anchor Street	C1
Andrews Place	A3
Arbour Lane	F4-F3
Ash Tree Crescent	A3-A2
Baddow Road	D1-E1
Baker Street	B1
Beeches Road	A3-A2
Bellmead	C2-D2
Bilton Way	A2-A1
Bishops Road	C4-D4
Boswells Avenue	E3-E2
Bradford Street	B1
Broomfield Road	C4
Byron Road	F2-F1
Cedar Avenue	B4-C4
Cottage Place	D3
Coval Avenue	B3
Coval Lane	B3-C3
Crompton Street	A1
Duke Street	C4-C3-D3
Elgin Avenue	B3
Fairfield Road	C3
Glebe Road	C4
Goldlay Road	D1
Grove Road	C1-D1
Haig Court	B1
Hall Street	D1
Hart Street	B1
High Street	D3-D2
Hill Crescent	F2
Hill Road	F2
Hill View Road	E4-F4
Legg Street	D3
Lower Anchor Street	B1-C1

Marconi Road	C4-D4
Market Road	C3-D3
Mildmay Road	D1
Mill Road	C3-C4-D4
Moulsham Street	C1-D1-D2
Navigation Road	E2
New London Road	B1-C1-D1-D2
New Street	D3-D4
New Writtle Street	B1-C1
Old Court Road	F3
Parklands Drive	E3-F3-F4
Park Road	C3
Parkway	B3-C3-C2-D2-D1-E1
Primrose Hill	B4
Prykes Drive	B3-B2
Queen Street	C1
Queens Road	E2-F2-F3
Railway Street	C4-C3
Rainsford Lane	A2-A3-B3-B4
Rainsford Road	A4-B4
Regina Road	E3-E4
Riverside	E3
Roman Road	D1
Sandford Road	F3
Seymour Street	B2-B1
Shelley Road	F2
Shrublands Close	E3
South Primrose Hill	A4-B4
Springfield Park Avenue	F2
Springfield Park Road	F2
Springfield Road	D2-E2-E3-F3-F4
Tindal Street	D3-D2
Townfield Street	C4-D4
Trinity Road	E3-F3-F2
Tudor Avenue	B4-B3
Upper Bridge Road	B1
Viaduct Road	B3-C3
Victoria Road	C3-D3-E3
Victoria Road South	C2-C3
Waterloo Lane	D3
Weight Road	E3-E2
Wharf Road	E2
Wheatfield Way	A4-B4
Wolsey Road	B1-B2

Maldon

Acacia Drive	A3-A2
Beacon Hill	A3-A4
Beeleigh Road	A4-B4
Browning Road	B1
Butt Lane	B3-C3
Cherry Garden Road	A3
Church Street	C2-C3
Colleridge Road	B1
Cromwell Hill	B4
Cromwell Lane	B4
Cross Road	B1-B2
Dorset Road	A2-A1
Downs Road	C3
Dykes Chase	A4
Essex Road	A2-A1
Fambridge Road	B3-B2-B1
Fitches Crescent	C2
Fullbridge	B4
Gate Street	B3-B4
Gloucester Avenue	A1-A2
Granger Avenue	A2-B2
Highlands Drive	A3-A4

High Street	B3
Jersey Road	C1
King Street	B2
Lodge Road	A4
London Road	A4-A3-B3
Longfellow Road	B1
Longship Way	A1
Manse Chase	B2
Market Hill	B3-B4
Meadway	C1
Mill Road	B2-C2-C3-B3
Milton Road	A3
Mount Pleasant	A3
Mundon Road	B2-B1-C1
Norfolk Road	A2
North Street	C3
Orchard Road	A3-A2
Park Drive	C2-C1
Park Road	B2
Plume Avenue	A2
Queens Avenue	B2
Queen Street	B2
St Giles Crescent	A3
St Peter's Avenue	A2-A3
Saxon Way	C1
Shakespeare Drive	B1
Spital Road	A2-A3-B3
Station Road	B4-C4
Suffolk Road	A2
The Causeway	B4-C4
The Quay	C3-C2
Tennyson Road	B1
Tenterfield Road	B3
Victoria Road	C3
Viking Road	A1-A2
Volwycke Avenue	A1-B1
Wantz Chase	B2
Wantz Road	B2-B3
Warwick Crescent	B2
Warwick Drive	B2
Washington Road	A2-B2
Wellington Road	A3
Wentworth Meadows	A3-A2
West Chase	A4
Wordsworth Avenue	B1

Witham

Abercorn Way	C3
Albert Road	B4
Allectus Way	A1
Armond Road	A3-B3
Avenue Road	B4-B3-C4-C3
Barnardiston Way	A4
Barwell Way	C3-C2
Bellfield Road	B4
Blackwater Lane	C1
Blunts Hall Road	A2
Brain Road	A4
Braintree Road	B4
Bridge Street	B1-B2
Chelmer Road	A3-B3
Chippingdell	A4-B4
Chipping Hill	A4-B4
Church Street	B4
Colchester Road	C3-C4
Collingwood Road	B3
Crittal Road	C4
Cromwell Way	A3

Cuppers Close	A2
Cut Throat Lane	B4-C4
Dengie Close	B1
Easton Road	B4
Elizabeth Avenue	B1-C1
Guithavon Road	A2-B2
Guithavon Street	B3-B2
Guithavon Valley	B3
Hatfield Road	A1-B1
Highfields Road	A4-A3
Howbridge Road	B1
King Edward Way	A1
Laurence Avenue	B1-C1
Luard Way	B1
Maidment Crescent	B1
Maldon Road	B2-C2-C1
Malyan Road	B1
Mersey Road	A3
Millbridge Road	A2
Mill Lane	C1
Newland Street	B2-B3-C3
Pattison Close	B1
Pelly Avenue	B1
Perry Road	C2
Pinkham Drive	B1
Pitt Avenue	C1
Powers Hall End	A4
Saxon Drive	A4
Spa Road	A4-A3-A2
Spinks Lane	A2-A1-B1
Station Road	B4-C4
Stepfield	C3
Stourton Road	A3-A4
The Avenue	B3-C3
The Grove	C3
The Paddocks	B3-C3

Braintree

Acorn Avenue	A2
Albert Road	C3
Aetheric Road	A3-A4
Bank Street	B3
Beadon Drive	C1
Blackwater Way	C4
Bocking End	B3-B4
Bradford Street	B4-C4
Brunel Road	C1
Buckwoods Road	B1
Bunyan Road	A3-B3-B4
Challis Lane	B1-C1
Clare Road	A3
Clydesdale Road	A3
Coggershall Road	B3-C3
Coldnailhurst Avenue	A4
College Road	A3
Coronation Avenue	B2
Courtauld Road	B4-C4-C3
Duggers Lane	C2-C1
East Street	C3
Fairfield Road	B3
George Road	A3
Giffins Close	A2-B2
Gilchrist Way	A4
Godlings Way	A2-B2
Grenville Road	A3
Harold Road	A3
High Street	A2-A3-B3
Hillside Gardens	B1-B2-C2

Hunnable Road	A3
John English Avenue	A4
John Ray Street	C4-C3
Julien Court Road	C4
Kenworthy Road	A2-B2
Lister Road	B1
Lodge Road	B1
London Road	A1-A2
Manor Street	B3-C3
Market Place	B3
Marlborough Road	C4
Marshalls Road	A2-A1
Mill Hill	C2
Mount Road	C3
Newnham Close	A2-A3
New Street	B3
Newton Road	B1
Nine Acres	C1
Notley Road	B2-B1
Orchard Drive	C1
Panefield Avenue	A4
Peartree Close	C2
Peel Crescent	A3
Railway Street	B2
Rayne Road	A3-B3
Rifle Hill	B2
Rosehill	C2
Rosemary Avenue	A4-B4
St John Avenue	B2
St Michaels Road	B3
St Peters in the Fields	B4
St Peters Walk	B3
Sandpit Road	B3
Saunders Avenue	C1
Skitts Hill	C1-C2
South Street	B3-B2-C2
Station Approach	B2-C2
Stephenson Road	B1-C1
Strawberry Close	C1
Sunnyside	A3-A4
Sycamore Grove	A2
The Avenue	B3
The Ridgeway	C1-C2
Tabor Avenue	A4
Telford Road	B1
Valley Road	C4
Victoria Street	B3-B3
Walnut Grove	A2
Woodfield Road	B3-C3

Central Chesterfield

Chesterfield Area

Chesterfield

Known as the Gateway to the Peak because of its proximity to the Derbyshire Peak District, Chesterfield became industrialised in the 18th and 19th centuries and attracted the interest of locomotive designer George Stephenson, who became involved in local industry before his death in 1848. Modern Chesterfield's new buildings have been carefully integrated with the picturesque

half-timbered shops and houses to be found near the middle of town. Old shop fronts have been preserved in the 'Pavements' shopping centre, (where the Peacock Information and Heritage Centre is housed in a 16th-century building), but quaintest feature of the town must be the crooked spire of the 14th-century Church of Our Lady and All Saints. This strange phenomenon has never been satisfactorily explained, but may be due to the use of unseasoned timber, and the effect of the

sun on the lead cladding.

Dronfield is a residential market town lying on the eastern slopes of the Pennines. Its oldest quarter has been designated a Conservation Area, and includes the 14th-century Parish Church of St John the Baptist and the 18th-century Manor House, which is now the County Library.

Bolsover Set in a district of coalmining and farming, Bolsover boasts a hilltop castle with Norman features, restored in the 17th century.

Central Dronfield (map A / B / C, grid 4 3 2 1)

Hospital · Holmley Bank · Sycamore Ave · Hawthorne Ave · Rec Grnd · School · Marsh Avenue · Fairview Road · Alma Cres · Holmley Lane · Cecil Road · Elm Tree Cres · Hilldr · Crescent · Snape Hill · Cecil Road · Snape Hill Crescent · Thirlmere Drive · Snape Hill · Holborn · Hartington Rd · Local Shopping Centre · Stonelow Rd · The Avenue · Playing Fields · Park Estate Ave · Sheffield Road · Chesterfield Road · Health Centre · Soaper Lane · High Street · Library · Civic Hall · Church St · Dronfield Station · Sports Centre · Shopping Centre · P.O. · School · Cally White La · Mill Lane · Summerwood Place · Stubley · Hollow · Stubley Lane · Wreakes Lane · Unstone · Dronfield By-Pass · West St · Victoria St · Manor Cres · Gosforth Grn · Gosforth Cres · Beechw'd Road · Searnater La · Ford Cl · Moonpenny Way · Cher Ave · School · Gomersal Lane · Netherdene Road · Caldey Rd · Scarsdale Rd · Cross Lr · Quoit La · Hallows · Cemetery Road · Fire Station · Gos-forth Dr · Gosforth By-Pass · Crofton Rise · Garth Way · Curzon Av · Cavend'sh Rise · Hillside Ave · Hollins Spring Ave · Pembroke Rise · Playing Fields · Holbein Close · Hogarth Rise · Gainsboro Road

Central Bolsover (map A / B / C, grid 4 3 2 1)

Springett Cres · Cundy Road · Rec Grnd · Quarry Rd · Hyndley Rd · Hyndley Road · Houfton Road · Shuttlewood Road · Bank Cl · Stratton Road · Oxcroft Lane · Welbeck Road · Davey Court · Haldane Crescent · New St · Lime Kiln Fields Road · Police Station · Old Hill · Hill Top · Council Offices · Long-lands · Long-lands · Steel Lane · Sports Ground · Station Road · Hides Grn · Council Offices · Castle · War Memorial · Mkt Town End · Welbeck Road · Schools · Clinic · Orchard Close · Cherry Tree Close · Sandhills Road · Laburn Close · Ham Close · School · Castle St · Hall · Fire Sta · P.O. · Library · Cotton St · Hornscroft Road · The Paddock · Moor Lane · Portland Crescent · Huntington Ave · Moorfield Square · Baths · Castle Lane · Rutland Ave · High Street · Recreation Ground · Portland Avenue · Smithson Ave · Moorfield Avenue · New Station Road · Bainbridge · School · Highfield Rd · Vale Cl · Ridgedale Rd · Searson Ave · Langwith Road · Morven Ave · Moorfield Square · Cavendish Road · Dumbles · Greenaway Dr · Valley Rd · Live Valley Rd

LEGEND

Town Plan

AA recommended route	▬▬▬
Restricted roads	-----
Other roads	▬▬
Buildings of interest	Castle
Car parks	P
Parks and open spaces	◢

Area Plan

A roads	▬▬
B roads	▬▬
Locations	Foolow ○
Urban area	Bramp ◢

STREET INDEX

CHESTERFIELD

Abercrombie Street	D4-E4
Albion Road	C3-D3
Alexandra Road West	C3
Alma Street West	B2
Ashgate Road	A4
Ashgate Valley Road	A4
Baden Powell Road	D1
Bank Street	B3-B2
Barker Fold	A2-A3
Barker Lane	A2
Beetwell Street	E2
Boythorpe Avenue	B1-C1-D1
Boythorpe Mount	C1
Boythorpe Road	C1-C2
Brewery Street	E3-E4-F4-F3
Brimington Road	F4
Broad Pavement	E3
Brockwell Lane	B4
Brookbank Avenue	A4
Brooklyn Drive	A4
Burlington Street	E3
Catherine Street	B2
Cavendish Street	E3
Central Avenue	B1
Charles Street	B2
Chatsworth Road	A1-A2-B2-C2
Chester Street	B4-B3-B2
Church Lane	E2
Church Way	E3-E2
Clarence Road	D3
Clifton Street	A3-B3
Cobden Road	C4
Compton Street	C4-C3
Corporation Street	F3
Cross Street	C4-D4
Derby Road	F1
Devonshire Street	E3-F3
Dixons Road	D3
Dock Walk	B1-C1-C2
Durrant Road	E3-F3
Elder Way	E3
Eyre Street	F2-F3
Factory Street	A1
Fairfield Road	C4
Felkin Street	F3
Foljambe Road	C3
Franklyn Road	A4
Goldwell Hill	B4
Goyt Side Road	A1-B1
Gladstone Road	C4
Glumangate	E3
Hall Road	A3-A4
Hasland Road	F1
Hawkesley Avenue	A4
Heathfield Avenue	A3-A4
High Street	D2-E2-E3
Hipper Street	E2
Hipper Street South	E1
Hipper Street West	B2
Holbeck Close	F4
Hollis Lane	F2
Holmebank East	A4-B4
Holmebank West	A4-B4
Holywell Street	E3
Hope Street	B3
Infirmary Road	F4
John Street	B3
Knifesmithgate	E3
Lordsmill Street	E2-F2-F1
Lower Grove Road	C3
Low Pavement	D2-E2
Malkin Street	F3
Malvern Road	B4
Marchwood Close	C4
Market Place	B2
Markham Road	C2-D2-E2
Marsden Street	D3-D4
Mill Lane	A1
New Beetwell Street	D2-E2
Newbold Road	D4-E4
New Square	D2
New Street	D1
Oakley Avenue	B4-C4
Old Road	A1-A2
Packers Row	E3-E2
Park Road	D1-D2
Queen Street	D4
Rose Hill	D3
Rose Hill East	D3
Rose Hill West	D3
Rutland Road	D4
Saltergate	C4-C3-D3-E3
School Lane	B2
Shaftesbury Avenue	A3-A4
Sheffield Road	E4
Sidney Street	A2-B2-B3
Soresby Street	D3
South Place	E2
South Street	E2
Spa Lane	F2
Spencer Street	D4
Springbank Road	C3
Springbank Avenue	A3-B3-B2
St Margarets Drive	C3-C4-D4
St Marks Road	A2-A3
St Mary's Gate	E2-F2-F3
Station Road	F2-F3
Stephenson Place	E3
Sterland Street	B2-B3
Sycamore Avenue	B1
Tapton Lane	F3
Tennyson Avenue	D3-D4
Vernon Road	A3-A2-B2
Vicar Lane	E2
Welfare Avenue	A2-A3
Wheatbridge Road	B2-C2
West Bars	C2-D2
West Street	C4

DRONFIELD

Alma Crescent	B4
Alexandra Road	C3
Beechwood Road	A2
Caldey Road	B1
Callywhite Lane	C2
Cavendish Rise	A1-B1
Cecil Avenue	A3
Cecil Road	B4-C3
Cemetery Road	C1
Chesterfield Road	B2-C2-C1
Church Street	B2
Crofton Rise	A2-A1
Cross Lane	C1
Curzon Avenue	A1-B1
Derwent Road	C4
Elm Tree Crescent	B4-C4
Fairview Road	B4
Fanshaw Road	C3-C4

Farwater Lane	A2-B2
Fletcher Avenue	B2-B1-C1
Ford Close	A2-B2
Gainsborough Road	A1
Garth Way	A1
Green Lane	C2-C3-C4
Gomersal Lane	B1
Gosforth Crescent	A2
Gosforth Drive	A2
Gosforth Green	A2
Gosforth Lane	A2-A1-B1
Hallows Lane	C1
Hartington Road	C3
Hawthorne Avenue	B4-C4
High Street	B2
Hillside Avenue	B1
Hogarth Rise	A1
Holbein Close	A1
Holborn Avenue	B3-B2-C2
Hollins Spring Avenue	B1-C1
Holmley Bank	B4
Holmley Lane	B4-C4
Lea Road	B2-C2
Manor Crescent	A2
Marsh Avenue	C4
Mill Lane	C2
Moonpenny Way	B2-B1
Moorgate Crescent	C1
Netherdene Road	B1
Park Estate Avenue	C3
Pembroke Rise	B1
Princess Road	C3-C2
Quoit Green	C1
Scarsdale Road	C1
School Lane	C2-C1
Sheffield Road	A4-B4-B3
Snape Hill	B3
Snape Hill Crescent	B3-B4-C4-C3
Snape Hill Drive	C4
Snape Hill Lane	B3-C3-C4
Soaper Lane	B2-B3
Stonelow Road	C3
Stubley Hollow	A4
Stubley Lane	A3
Summerfield Road	C4
Summerwood Place	A3
Sycamore Avenue	B4-C4
The Avenue	C3
Thirlmere Drive	B3
Unstone-Dronfield By-pass	A4-A3-A2-A1
Victoria Street	A2-A3
West Street	A3
Wreakes Lane	A4-A3-A2-B2

BOLSOVER

Bainbridge Road	A1
Bank Close	B4
Castle Lane	A2
Castle Street	B2
Cavendish Road	C1
Cherry Tree Close	C2
Cotton Street	B2
Cundy Road	A4
Davey Court	A4
Dumbles Road	A1
Greenaway Drive	A1
Haldane Crescent	A4
Hides Green	B3
High Street	A2-B2
Highield Road	A1-B1
Hill Top	A4
Hornscroft Road	B2
Houfton Road	A4-A3
Huntingdon Crescent	C2
Hyndley Road	A4-A3
Laburnam Close	C2
Langwith Road	B1-C1
Lime Kiln Fields Road	A4-B4
Longlands	B3-C3
Market Place	B2
Moor Lane	B2-C2
Moorfield Avenue	C1
Moorfield Square	C2-C1
Morven Avenue	C1
New Street	A4
New Station Road	A2-B1
Old Hill	A3
Orchard Close	C2
Oxcroft Lane	B4-B3-B2
Portland Avenue	C2-C1
Portland Crescent	C1
Quarry Road	B4
Ridgedale Road	A1-B1
Rutland Avenue	A2
Sandhills Road	C2
Searson Avenue	A1-B1
Shuttlewood Road	A4
Smithson Avenue	C2
Springfield Crescent	A4
Station Road	A3-B3
Steel Lane	C3
Stratton Road	B3-B4
The Paddock	C2
Town End	B2
Vale Close	A1
Valley Road	A1-B1
Welbeck Road	B2-B3

CHESTERFIELD
Octagonal in plan, the crooked spire of the Church of Our Lady and All Saints stands 228ft high. Its original position in relation to the building has been marked by brass studs in the church floor.

Key to Town Plan and Area Plan

Town Plan

AA Recommended roads
Restricted roads
Other roads
Buildings of interest   Theatre
One Way Streets
Car Parks   P
Parks and open spaces
Churches   +

Area Plan

A roads
B roads
Locations   RowhedgeO
Urban area

STREET INDEX WITH GRID REFERENCE

COLCHESTER

Albert Road	C4-D4
Alexandra Road	C1
Ashley Gardens	A2
Balkerne Hill	C3
Balkerne Lane	C2-D2
Balkerne Pass	C2
Beaconsfield Avenue	C1
Beverley Road	B1-B2
Bristol Road	F4
Burlington Road	C1
Butt Road	C1
Cambridge Road	B1
Carlisle Road	F4
Castle Road	E3-E4
Causton Road	C4-D4
Chapel Street	D1
Church Street	C2-D2
Colchester By-Pass	A4-B4
Creffield Road	B1-C1
Cromwell Road	E1
Crouch Street	C2
Crowhurst Road	C2
Culver Street East	D2-E2
Culver Street West	D2
East Hill	F4

East Stockwell Street	D3
Fairfax Road	E1
Flagstaff Road	D1
Golden Noble Hill	F1
Guildford Road	F3-F4
Headgate	C2-D2
Head Street	D2
High Street	D3-D2-E2-E3-F3
Hospital Road	B1-B2-C1
Inglis Road	B1
Lexden Road	A2-B2
Lincoln Way	F3-F4
Long Wyre Street	E2
Lucas Road	E1
Magdalen Street	E1-F1
Maidenburgh Street	D3-D3
Maldon Road	B1-C1
Manor Road	B2-C2
Mercers Way	D4
Mersea Road	E1
Military Road	E1-F1
Mill Street	F1
New Kiln Road	A2-A3
Northgate Street	D3
North Hill	C3-D3
North Station Road	C4
Nunn's Road	D3
Oaks Drive	B2
Osborne Street	D2-E2
Oxford Road	B1-B2
Pappillon Road	B2-C2
Priory Street	E2-F2-F3
Queens Road	A1-B1
Queen Street	E2
Rawstron Road	C2
Roddam Close	A1
Roman Road	E3-E4
Rosebery Avenue	F2-F3
Ryegate Road	D3-E3
St Albans Road	B2
St Botolph's Street	E2
St John's Street	D2
St Peter's Street	D3-D4
Sheepen Road	C3-B4-C4
Sherwell Road	D2
Sir Isaacs Walk	D2
Sleigh Court	A2
Smythies Avenue	F2-F3
South Street	C1-D1
Southway	C1-C2-D2-D1-E1
Sussex Road	A2-A3
The Avenue	A1
Victoria Road	A1
Vineyard Street	D2-E2
Water Lane	A4

Wellesley Road	C1-C2
West Lodge Road	A1-A2
West Stockwell Street	D3
West Street	C1-D1
West Way	C3-C4
Winnock Road	F1
Worcester Road	E4-F4

CLACTON

Agate Road	A1-A2
Agincourt Road	A4
Alton Park Road	C3
Alton Road	A1-A2
Anchor Road	A3
Astley Road	A4
Beach Road	B1-B2
Beaumont Avenue	C4
Berkeley Road	C4
Cambridge Road	B3-B4
Carnarvon Road	B1-B2-B3
Carrs Road	A4
Chapman Road	B2
Church Road	B1-C1
College Road	C2
Coppins Road	A4-B4
Croft Road	A4-B4
Crossfield Road	B3
Dudley Road	A4-B4
Edith Road	A1-A2
Ellis Road	A2
Ford Road	A3-A4
Granville Road	B2-C2
Harold Road	B1-B2
Harrow Road	B3-C3
Hayes Road	A2-A3
High Street	B2
Holland Road	B2-C2
Jackson Road	A2
Key Road	B3-B4
London Road	B4-C4
Marine Parade East	B1-C1
Marine Parade West	A1
Melbourne Road	B4
Meredith Road	B3
Old Road	A2-A3-B3-B4-C4
Olivers Road	B4
Orwell Road	B1-B2
Oxford Crescent	C3-C4
Oxford Road	B3-C3-C4
Page Road	B3
Pallister Road	B1-B2
Park Road	A3
Penfold Road	A1-A2
Pier Avenue	A2-A2-A3
Rosemary Road	A2-B2

St Albans Road	C1-C2
St Andrews Road	B3
St Anne's Road	B4
St Osyth Road	A3-A4
Severn Road	C3-C4
Skelmersdale Road	B2-B3-C2
Station Road	A2-B2-B3
Tewkesbury Road	C3-C4
The Grove	B2
Thomas Road	B4
Thornbury Road	C3-C4
Thoroughgood Road	C1-C2-C3
Tower Road	A1-A2
Vicarage Gardens	A2
Victoria Road	C1-C2
Victory Road	A4
Vista Road	C1-C2-C3
Walton Road	C2
Warwick Road	A3-A4-B4
Wash Lane	A2
Wellesley Road	A2-B2-B3-C3-C4
West Avenue	A2-A3

HARWICH

Albemarle Street	B3-B4
Albert Street	B3
Ashley Road	A2
Barrack Lane	B3-C3
Church Street	B4
Cliff Road	B2
Fern Lea Road	B3
Fronks Road	A1-A2
George Street	B3-B4
Gordon Road	A1
Grafton Road	B3
Harbour Crescent	B3-C3
Highfield Avenue	A1-A2
High Street	B2
Hill Road	B2
Ingestre Street	B3
King Georges Avenue	A2
King's Quay Street	B4-C4
King's Way	B2
Lee Road	A2-B2
Lime Avenue	A1-A2
Main Road	A2-B2-B3
Marine Parade	A1-A2-B2
Pattricks Lane	A2
Portland Avenue	A2-B2
Seafield Road	A1
Shaftesbury Avenue	A2
Stour Road	B3
The Drive	A1
West Street	B4
Wick Lane	A1

Colchester

The oldest recorded town in England, Colchester was also a Roman capital and the great walls built by the invaders stand to this day. Remains of one of their massive gateways, Balkerne Gate, have also survived. Colchester's Norman castle keep, the largest in Britain, retains an air of dark medieval menace, although it now houses nothing more sinister than the Colchester and Essex Museum

where many Roman antiquities can be seen. Colchester's proximity to the continent led to the arrival of Flemish refugees during the 16th century, and they revived the cloth trade that had flourished here in the Middle Ages. Many of their attractive gabled and colour-washed houses line West Stockwell Street, known as the Dutch Quarter. In contrast, much of the town centre has been turned into a modern shopping precinct.

Clacton On Sea was suddenly transformed

from a quiet little village into 'the seaside' with the arrival of the railway during the 1870s. The pier, an essential ingredient for such resorts, was erected in 1873, although since rebuilt several times, and seven years later the Pavilion was added.

Harwich, departure point for continental ferries and busy yachting centre, has been a port since medieval times. The 180ft-diameter fort known as the Redoubt was built in 1808 as a defence against Napoleonic invasion.

COLCHESTER
The castle keep, all that remains of Colchester's great fortress that once stretched from the High Street to the north wall of the town, was built round the masonry platform of the Roman Temple of Claudius.

Coventry

Few British towns were as battered by the Blitz as Coventry. A raid in November 1940 flattened most of the city and left the lovely cathedral church a gaunt shell with only the tower and spire still standing. Rebuilding started almost immediately. Symbolising the creation of the new from the ashes of the old is Sir Basil Spence's cathedral, completed in 1962 beside the bombed ruins.

A few medieval buildings have survived intact in the city. St Mary's Guildhall is a finely restored 14th-century building with an attractive minstrels' gallery. Whitefriars Monastery now serves as a local museum. The Herbert Art Gallery and Museum has several collections. Coventry is an important manufacturing centre – most notably for cars – and it is also a university city with the fine campus of the University of Warwick some four miles from the centre.

Nuneaton is an industrial town to the north of Coventry with two distinguished old churches – St Nicholas' and St Mary's. Like Coventry it was badly damaged in the war and its centre has been rebuilt.

Rugby was no more than a sleepy market town until the arrival of the railway. Of course it did have the famous Rugby School, founded in 1567 and one of the country's foremost educational establishments. The railway brought industry – still the town's mainstay.

22

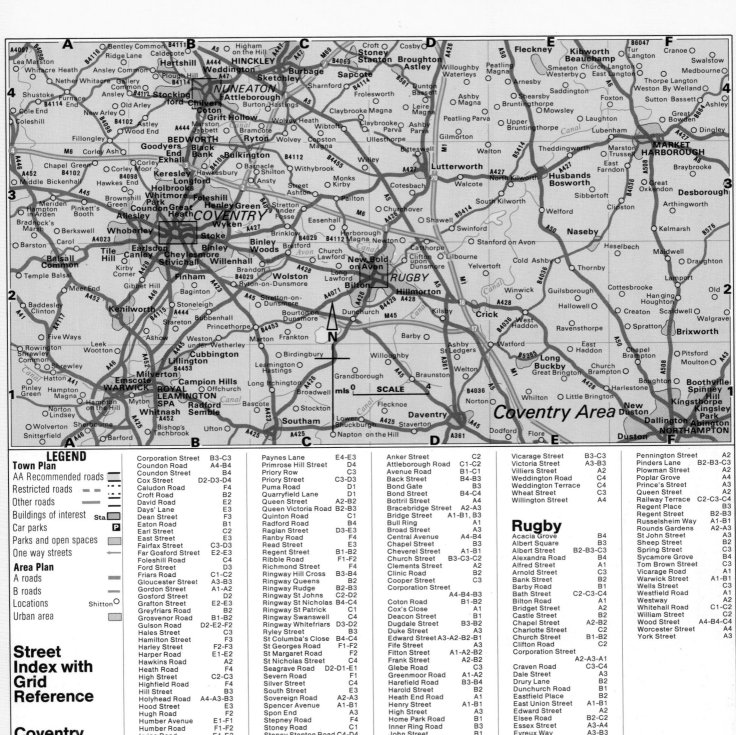

LEGEND

Town Plan

AA Recommended roads	
Restricted roads	
Other roads	
Buildings of interest	Sta.
Car parks	P
Parks and open spaces	
One way streets	

Area Plan

A roads	
B roads	
Locations	Shitton
Urban area	

Street Index with Grid Reference

Coventry

Abbotts Lane	B4
Acacia Avenue	D1-E1
Albany Road	A1-A2
Albert Street	D4-E4
Alfred Road	E4-F4
All Saints Lane	E3
Alma Street	D3-E3
Augustus Road	E4-F4
Barras Lane	A3-B3-B4
Bayley Lane	C3
Bedford Street	A2
Berkeley Road North	A1
Berry Street	E4
Binley Road	E3-F3-F2
Bishop Street	C3-C4
Bolingbroke Road	F1
Bond Street	B3
Botanor Road	E2
Bramble Street	E2-E3
Brighton Street	F3-F4
Britannia Street	E3-F3
Broadway	A1
Broomfield Road	A2
Butts Road	A3-A2-B2
Canterbury Street	D4-D3-E3
Chandos Street	F3
Charterhouse Road	E2
Chester Street	A4
Clifton Street	D4-E4
Colchester Road	E4
Collingwood Road	A2
Cornwall Road	E1
Coronation Road	E4-F4

Corporation Street	B3-C3
Coundon Road	A4-B4
Coundon Street	B4
Cox Street	D2-D3-D4
Caludon Road	F4
Croft Road	B2
David Road	E2
Days' Lane	E3
Dean Street	F3
Eaton Road	B1
Earl Street	C2
East Street	E3
Fairfax Street	C3-D3
Far Gosford Street	E2-E3
Foleshill Road	C4
Ford Street	D3
Friars Road	C1-C2
Gloucester Street	A3-B3
Gordon Street	A1-A2
Gosford Street	D2
Grafton Street	E2-E3
Greyfriars Road	B2
Grosvenor Road	B2
Gulson Road	D2-E2-F2
Hales Street	C3
Hamilton Street	F3
Harley Street	F2-F3
Harper Road	E1-E2
Hawkins Road	A2
Heath Road	F4
High Street	C2-C3
Highfield Road	F4
Hill Street	B3
Holyhead Road	A4-A3-B3
Hood Street	E3
Hugh Road	F2
Humber Avenue	E1-F1
Humber Road	F1-F2
Irving Road	E1-E2
Jesmond Road	E4
Jordan Well	D2
King Edward Road	E3
King Richard Street	F3
King William Street	D4-E4
Kingsway	F2-F3
Lamb Street	B4-C4
Lansdowne Street	E3-F3
Leicester Row	C4
Little Park Street	C2
London Road	D1-D2
Lower Ford Street	D3-E3
Lower Spon Street	B3
Manor Road	C2
Meadow Street	A2-B2
Melville Road	A3
Meriden Street	A3-A4-B4
Michaelmas Road	B1-C1
Middlesborough Road	B4
Mile Lane	C1-D1
Minster Road	A3
Monks Road	E2
Mowbray Street	F3
Much Park Street	D2
New Union Street	C2
Nicholls Street	D3
Northfield Road	E2-F2
Northumberland Road	A3-A4
Orwell Road	E1-F1
Oxford Street	E3
Park Road	C1
Park Side	C2-D2-D1

Paynes Lane	E4-E3
Primrose Hill Street	D4
Priory Row	C3
Priory Street	C3-D3
Puma Road	D1
Quarryfield Lane	D1
Queen Street	A2-B2
Queen Victoria Road	B2-B3
Quinton Road	C1
Radford Road	B4
Raglan Street	D3-E3
Ranby Road	F4
Read Street	E4
Regent Street	B1-B2
Ribble Road	F1-F2
Richmond Street	F4
Ringway Hill Cross	B3-B4
Ringway Queens	B2
Ringway Rudge	B2-B3
Ringway St Johns	C2-D2
Ringway St Nicholas	B4-C4
Ringway St Patrick	C1
Ringway Swanswell	C4
Ringway Whitefriars	D3-D2
Ryley Street	B3
St Columba's Close	B4-C4
St Georges Road	F1-F2
St Margaret Road	F2
St Nicholas Street	C4
Seagrave Road	D2-D1-E1
Severn Road	F1
Silver Street	C4
South Street	E3
Sovereign Road	A2-A3
Spencer Avenue	A1-B1
Spon End	A3
Stepney Road	F4
Stoney Road	C1
Stoney Stanton Road	C4-D4
Strathmore Avenue	E4
Swan Lane	F3-F4
Swanswell Street	C4
Terry Road	E2-E1-F1
Thackhall Street	F4
Tower Street	C4
Upper Spon Street	A3-B3
Upper Well Street	B4-B3-C3
Upper York Street	B2
Vecqueray Street	E2
Vernon Street	E4
Victoria Street	D4
Villiers Street	F3
Vine Street	D4-D3
Walsgrave	F3
Warwick Road	B1-B2-C2
Waverley Road	A3
Welland Road	E1-F1
West Street	E3
Westminster Road	B2-B1
Weston Street	D4
White Street	D4
Windsor Street	A2-A3
Winifrid Avenue	A1
Yardley Street	D4-E4

Nuneaton

Abbey Green	A4
Abbey Street	A4-A3-B3
Alexandra Street	A3
Amos Avenue	A1

Anker Street	C2
Attleborough Road	C1-C2
Avenue Road	B1-C1
Back Street	B4-B3
Bond Gate	B3
Bond Street	B4-C4
Bottril Street	A4
Bracebridge Street	A2-A3
Bridge Street	A1-B1, B3
Bull Ring	A1
Broad Street	A4
Central Avenue	A4-B4
Chapel Street	B3
Cheverel Street	A1-B1
Church Street	B3-C3-C2
Clements Street	A2
Clinic Road	B2
Cooper Street	C3
Corporation Street	A4-B4-B3
Coton Road	B1-B2
Cox's Close	A1
Deacon Street	B1
Dugdale Street	B3-B2
Duke Street	A1
Edward Street	A3-A2-B2-B1
Fife Street	A3
Fitton Street	A1-A2-B2
Frank Street	A2-B2
Glebe Road	C3
Greenmoor Road	A1-A2
Harefield Road	B3-B4
Harold Street	B2
Heath End Road	A1
Henry Street	A1-B1
High Street	A3
Home Park Road	B1
Inner Ring Road	B1
John Street	B1
King Edward Road	C2-C3
Kingsway	A3
Leicester Road	B3-C3-C4
Lister Street	C2
Manor Court Road	A4
Marlborough Road	A2-A3
Market Place	B3
Meadow Street	A4
Midland Road	A4
Milford Street	A1
Mill Street	B3
Mill Walk	B3
Mount Street	A3
Newdegate Street	B3
New Town Road	A4-B4
Norman Avenue	A2-A3
Oaston Road	C3-C4
Old Hinckley Road	C4
Orchard Street	C3
Park Street	C2
Prince's Avenue	A2
Queen's Road	A3-B3
Regent Street	B2
Ringway	A3-B3-B2
Riversley Road	B2
Rose Lane	B2
Roxanne	A3-A4
St Nicholas Road	A4
Sandon Road	A4
Seymour Road	C2
Simon Close	C1
Stewart Street	A1-B1-B2
Trent Road	C3-C4

Vicarage Street	B3-C3
Victoria Street	A3-B3
Villiers Street	A2
Weddington Road	C4
Weddington Terrace	C4
Wheat Street	C3
Willington Street	A4

Rugby

Acacia Grove	B4
Albert Square	B3
Albert Street	B2-B3-C3
Alexandra Road	B4
Alfred Street	A1
Arnold Street	C3
Bank Street	B2
Barby Road	B4
Bath Street	C2-C3-C4
Bilton Road	A1
Bridget Street	A2
Castle Street	B2
Chapel Street	A2-B2
Charlotte Street	B2
Church Street	B1-B2
Clifton Road	B1
Corporation Street	A2-A3-A1
Craven Road	C3-C4
Dale Street	A3
Drury Lane	B2
Dunchurch Road	B1
Eastfield Place	B2
East Union Street	A1-B1
Edward Street	A2
Elsee Road	B2-C2
Essex Street	A3-A4
Evreux Way	A3-B3
Firs Drive	A1
Frederick Street	A1
Gas Street	B2
Graham Road	C4
Grosvenor Road	C2-C3
High Street	B2
Hill Street	A3
Hillmorton Road	C1
Holbrook Avenue	B3
Horton Crescent	B1-C1
Hunters Lane	A4
James Street	B3-C3
Kew Road	B3
Kimberley Road	C4
King Street	B3
King Edward Road	B3-B4
Lancaster Road	A4-B4
Lawford Road	A1-A2
Lawrence Sherriff Street	B1-B2
Little Church Street	B1-B2
Lodge Road	B4
Lower Hillmorton Road	C2
Manor Road	B3-B4-C4
Maple Grove	A1
Market Street	C3
Mertons Drive	A1
Moultrie Road	C1-C2
Murray Road	C2-C3-C4
Newbold Road	A4-A3
North Street	B2-B3
Oliver Street	A2-A3
Park Road	B3-B4

Pennington Street	A2
Pinders Lane	B2-B3-C3
Plowman Street	A2
Poplar Grove	A4
Prince's Street	A3
Queen Street	A2
Railway Terrace	C2-C3-C4
Regent Place	A2
Regent Street	B2-B3
Russelsheim Way	A1-B1
Rounds Gardens	A2-A3
St John Street	A3
Sheep Street	B2
Spring Street	C3
Sycamore Grove	B4
Tom Brown Street	C3
Vicarage Road	A1
Warwick Street	A1-B1
Wells Street	C3
Westfield Road	A2
Westway	A2
Whitehall Road	C1-C2
William Street	B2
Wood Street	A4-B4-C4
Worcester Street	A4
York Street	A3

Derby

Present-day Derby, designated a city in 1977, is a product of the Industrial Revolution. During the 19th century the Midland Railway made its headquarters in the ancient country town, bringing with it prosperity and considerable new building. Around the old Market Place stand the Guildhall, which is now used as a concert hall, the Market Hall, and the façade of the old Assembly Rooms which burnt down in 1963. Later Rolls-Royce established its car manufacturing works here and one of the company's founders, Sir Henry Royce, is commemorated in the Arboretum, laid out by Joseph Loudon. Rolls-Royce aero engines can be seen in the Industrial Museum, appropriately housed in England's first silk mill, set up in 1717 on the banks of the Derwent.

Despite this strong industrial influence, for many people Derby means only one thing – porcelain. The Royal Crown Derby Porcelain Company produced work of such excellence that George III granted it the right to use the Crown insignia. A museum on the premises houses a treasure-trove of Crown Derby.

Derby's cathedral, All Saint's, was built during Henry VIII's reign but, except for its 178ft-high pinnacled tower, was rebuilt in 1725 by James Gibb. The tomb of Bess of Hardwick, who died in 1607, can be seen inside.

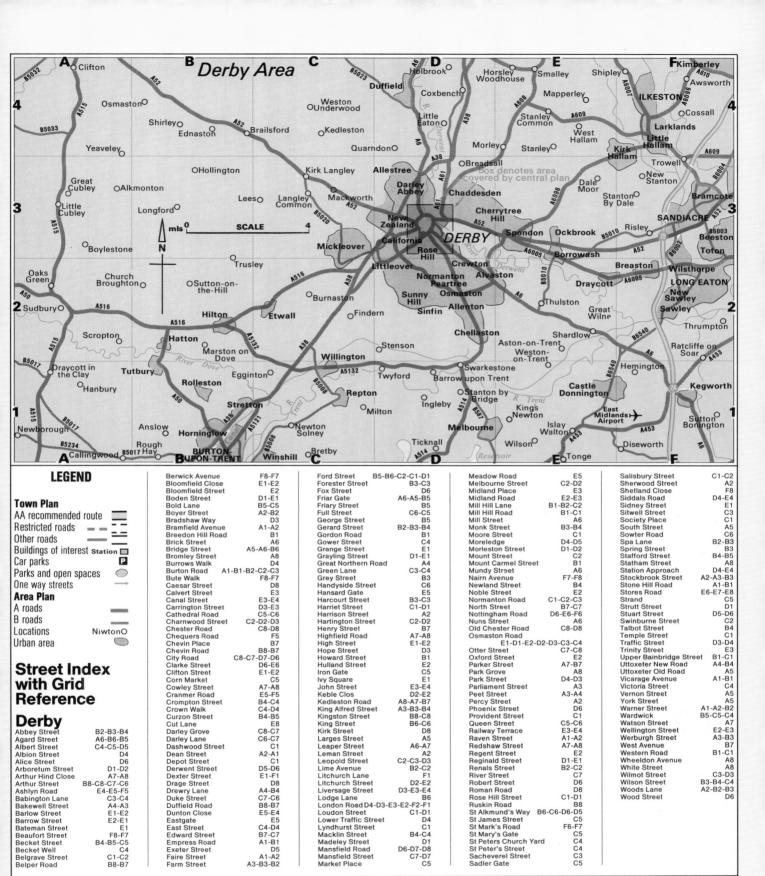

Derby Area

(Area map with grid references A–F horizontally and 1–4 vertically)

Map locations include: Clifton, Osmaston, Shirley, Ednaston, Brailsford, Weston Underwood, Kedleston, Quarndon, Duffield, Holbrook, Horsley Woodhouse, Smalley, Shipley, Kimberley, Awsworth, Coxbench, Little Eaton, Mapperley, Ilkeston, Cossall, Stanley Common, West Hallam, Larklands, Little Hallam, Yeaveley, Great Cubley, Alkmonton, Longford, Lees, Langley Common, Mackworth, Hollington, Kirk Langley, Allestree, Breadsall, Darley Abbey, Chaddesden, Morley, Stanley, Kirk Hallam, Trowell, New Stanton, Dale Moor, Stanton By Dale, Bramcote, Little Cubley, Boylestone, New Zealand, Derby, Cherrytree Hill, Spondon, Ockbrook, Risley, Sandiacre, Beeston, Oaks Green, Church Broughton, Trusley, Mickleover, California, Rose Hill, Littleover, Crewton, Alvaston, Borrowash, Breaston, Draycott, Long Eaton, New Sawley, Wilsthorpe, Toton, Sudbury, Scropton, Hilton, Etwall, Burnaston, Findern, Sunny Hill, Normanton, Peartree, Osmaston, Sinfin, Allenton, Thulston, Great Wilne, Shardlow, Sawley, Thrumpton, Hatton, Marston on Dove, Tutbury, Hanbury, Draycott in the Clay, Rolleston, Egginton, Willington, Stenson, Twyford, Chellaston, Aston-on-Trent, Weston-on-Trent, Swarkestone, Barrow upon Trent, Hemington, Ratcliffe on Soar, Kegworth, Stretton, Newton Solney, Repton, Milton, Ingleby, Stanton by Bridge, King's Newton, Castle Donnington, East Midlands Airport, Sutton Bonington, Newborough, Anslow, Horninglow, Rough Hay, Burton-upon-Trent, Winshill, Bretby, Ticknall, Melbourne, Wilson, Islay Walton, Diseworth, Tonge, Callingwood, Reservoir

Box denotes area covered by central plan

SCALE mls 0 — 4   N

LEGEND

Town Plan
- AA recommended route
- Restricted roads
- Other roads
- Buildings of interest — Station
- Car parks — P
- Parks and open spaces
- One way streets

Area Plan
- A roads
- B roads
- Locations — Niwton○
- Urban area

Street Index with Grid Reference

Derby

Street	Grid
Abbey Street	B2-B3-B4
Agard Street	A6-B6-B5
Albert Street	C4-C5-D5
Albion Street	D4
Alice Street	D6
Arboretum Street	D1-D2
Arthur Hind Close	A7-A8
Arthur Street	B8-C8-C7-C6
Ashlyn Road	E4-E5-F5
Babington Lane	C3-C4
Bakewell Street	A4-A3
Barlow Street	E1-E2
Barrow Street	E2-E1
Bateman Street	E1
Beaufort Street	F8-F7
Becket Street	B4-B5-C5
Becket Well	C4
Belgrave Street	C1-C2
Belper Road	B8-B7
Berwick Avenue	F8-F7
Bloomfield Close	E1-E2
Bloomfield Street	E2
Boden Street	D1-E1
Bold Lane	B5-C5
Boyer Street	A2-B2
Bradshaw Way	D3
Bramfield Avenue	A1-A2
Breedon Hill Road	B1
Brick Street	A6
Bridge Street	A5-A6-B6
Bromley Street	A8
Burrows Walk	B8-B7
Burton Road	A1-B1-B2-C2-C3
Bute Walk	F8-F7
Caesar Street	D8
Calvert Street	E3
Canal Street	E3-E4
Carrington Street	D3-E3
Cathedral Road	C5-C6
Charnwood Street	C2-D2-D3
Chester Road	C8-D8
Chequers Road	F5
Chevin Place	B7
Chevin Road	B8-B7
City Road	C8-C7-D7-D6
Clarke Street	D6-E6
Clifton Street	E1-E2
Corn Market	C5
Cowley Street	A7-A8
Cranmer Road	E5-F5
Crompton Street	B4-C4
Crown Walk	C4-D4
Curzon Street	B4-B5
Cut Lane	E8
Darley Grove	C8-C7
Darley Lane	C6-C7
Dashwood Street	C1
Dean Street	A2-A1
Depot Street	C1
Derwent Street	D5-D6
Dexter Street	E1-F1
Drage Street	D8
Drewry Lane	A4-B4
Duke Street	C7-C6
Duffield Road	B8-B7
Dunton Close	E5-E4
Eastgate	E5
East Street	C4-D4
Edward Street	B7-C7
Empress Road	A1-B1
Exeter Street	D5
Faire Street	A1-A2
Farm Street	A3-B3-B2
Ford Street	B5-B6-C2-C1-D1
Forester Street	B3-C3
Fox Street	D6
Friar Gate	A6-A5-B5
Friary Street	B5
Full Street	C6-C5
George Street	B5
Gerard Street	B2-B3-B4
Gordon Road	B1
Gower Street	C4
Grange Street	E1
Grayling Street	D1-E1
Great Northern Road	A4
Green Lane	C3-C4
Grey Street	B3
Handyside Street	C6
Hansard Gate	E5
Harcourt Street	B3-C3
Harriet Street	C1-D1
Harrison Street	A2
Hartington Street	C2-D2
Henry Street	B7
Highfield Road	A7-A8
High Street	E1-E2
Hope Street	D3
Howard Street	B1
Hulland Street	E2
Iron Gate	C5
Ivy Square	E1
John Street	E3-E4
Keble Clos	D2-E2
Kedleston Road	A8-A7-B7
King Alfred Street	A3-B3-B4
Kingston Street	B8-C8
King Street	B6-C6
Kirk Street	D8
Larges Street	A5
Leaper Street	A6-A7
Leman Street	A2
Leopold Street	C2-C3-D3
Lime Avenue	B2-C2
Litchurch Lane	F1
Litchurch Street	D2-E2
Liversage Street	D3-E3-E4
Lodge Lane	B6
London Road	D4-D3-E3-E2-F2-F1
Loudon Street	C1-D1
Lower Traffic Street	D4
Lyndhurst Street	C1
Macklin Street	B4-C4
Madeley Street	D1
Mansfield Road	D6-D7-D8
Mansfield Street	C7-D7
Market Place	C5
Meadow Road	E5
Melbourne Street	C2-D2
Midland Place	E3
Midland Road	E2-E3
Mill Hill Lane	B1-B2-C2
Mill Hill Road	B1-C1
Mill Street	A6
Monk Street	B3-B4
Moore Street	C1
Moreledge	D4-D5
Morleston Street	D1-D2
Mount Street	C2
Mount Carmel Street	B1
Mundy Street	A6
Nairn Avenue	F7-F8
Newland Street	B4
Noble Street	E2
Normanton Road	C1-C2-C3
North Street	B7-C7
Nottingham Road	D6-E6-F6
Nuns Street	A6
Old Chester Road	C8-D8
Osmaston Road	E1-D1-E2-D2-D3-C3-C4
Otter Street	C7-C8
Oxford Street	E2
Parker Street	A7-B7
Park Grove	A8
Park Street	D4-D3
Parliament Street	A3
Peet Street	A3-A4
Percy Street	A2
Phoenix Street	D6
Provident Street	C1
Queen Street	C5-C6
Railway Terrace	E3-E4
Raven Street	A1-A2
Redshaw Street	A7-A8
Regent Street	E2
Reginald Street	D1-E1
Renals Street	B2-C2
River Street	C7
Robert Street	D6
Roman Road	D8
Rose Hill Street	C1-D1
Ruskin Road	B8
St Alkmund's Way	B6-C6-D6-D5
St James Street	C5
St Mark's Road	F6-F7
St Mary's Gate	C5
St Peters Church Yard	C4
St Peter's Street	C4
Sacheverel Street	C3
Sadler Gate	C5
Salisbury Street	C1-C2
Sherwood Street	A2
Shetland Close	F8
Siddals Road	D4-E4
Sidney Street	E1
Sitwell Street	C3
Society Place	C1
South Street	A5
Sowter Road	C6
Spa Lane	B2-B3
Spring Street	B3
Stafford Street	B4-B5
Statham Street	A8
Station Approach	D4-E4
Stockbrook Street	A2-A3-B3
Stone Hill Road	A1-B1
Stores Road	E6-E7-E8
Strand	C5
Strutt Street	D1
Stuart Street	D5-D6
Swinburne Street	C2
Talbot Street	B4
Temple Street	C1
Traffic Street	D3-D4
Trinity Street	D3
Upper Bainbridge Street	B1-C1
Uttoxeter New Road	A4-B4
Uttoxeter Old Road	A5
Vicarage Avenue	A1-B1
Victoria Street	C4
Vernon Street	A5
Warner Street	A1-A2-B2
Wardwick	B5-C5-C4
Watson Street	A7
Wellington Street	E2-E3
Werburgh Street	A3-B3
West Avenue	B7
Western Road	B1-C1
Wheeldon Avenue	A8
White Street	A8
Wilmot Street	C3-D3
Wilson Street	B3-B4-C4
Woods Lane	A2-B2-B3
Wood Street	D6

DERBY

The 1907 Silver Ghost, one of Rolls Royce's first cars, was produced just before the company moved its factory to Derby. Cars were their sole product until World War I when the first aero engine was designed.

Dudley

The imposing remains of the castle which dominates the skyline bear witness to Dudley's importance as far back as medieval times, and later on it was again important as the capital of the 'Black Country' industrial region. Dudley is now the site of the open-air Black Country Museum, where numerous old buildings have been re-assembled to create a typical Black Country village, complete with examples of working industries and period transport. Other places of interest include Dudley Zoo, situated below the castle, where a fine selection of wild animals and reptiles are displayed in the unusual setting of the old limestone workings and the castle moat.

Halesowen's Leasowes Estate was once the home of 18th-century poet William Shenstone. The finely landscaped grounds were allowed to fall into disuse after his death, but are being restored to their former glory.

Stourbridge Crystal glass is the glittering attraction of this modernised market town, which has a number of glass factories open to visitors. The Broadfield House Glass Museum at nearby Kingswinford traces the evolution of the industry, and looks in particular at local firms such as Richardson's, Stevens and Williams, and Thomas Webb. Techniques of glassmaking and glassblowing are also featured here.

LEGEND

Town Plan

AA Recommended roads	
Other roads	
Restricted roads	
Buildings of interest	Library
Churches	+
Car parks	P
Parks and open spaces	P
One way streets	←

Area Plan

A roads	
B roads	
Locations	Longford ○
Urban area	

Street Index with Grid Reference

Dudley

Abberley Street	C1-C2
Angel Street	B1
Ashenhurst Road	A1-A2
Aston Road	B1
Bath Street	D1
Bean Road	E1
Beechwood Road	F3
Birmingham Road	F3-F4
Birmingham Street	D3-E3
Bishop's Close	F1
Blackacre Road	E1
Blower's Green Road	B1-C1
Bourne Street	E3
Brewery Street	F2
Brooke Street	C1
Bull Street	A1
Caroline Street	E2-F2
Castle Hill	D3-E3
Castle Street	D3
Castle View	B3-B4
Charlotte Street	B1-B2
Churchfield Street	C1
Church Street	D1-D2
Claughton Road	E2-E3
Cleveland Street	B1-B2
Constitution Hill	D1
Corbyn Road	A1

Corporation Road	F3
Court Passage	D2-D3
Cross Street	C2
Dando Road	E1
Dibdale Road	A4
Dixon's Green	E1-F1
Dock Lane	B2
Dudley's Row	D2-E2
East Street	F1
Ednam Road	C3-D3
Edward Street	B2-B3
Field Road	F3
Firs Street	E2
Fishers Street	D3
Flood Street	D1-D2
Gervase Drive	D4
Grange Road	A2-A3-B3
Greystone Street	B2-C2
Grove Street	F1
Hall Street	D2-E2
Hazel Road	C4
Hellier Street	C1
Highfield Road	F2-F3
Highland Road	A4
High Street	C2-D2
High View Street	F2
Hillcrest Road	F2-F3
Himley Road	A3-B3
Himley Street	A2
Hope Street	C1
The Inhedge	C2-C3
Junction Street	B1
Kings Street	C1-C2-D2
Lloyd Street	E1
London Heights	A4
Market Place	D2-D3
Marmion Grove	A1
Martin Hill Street	D1
Maughan Street	A2-B2
Nelson Road	B2-B3
New Mill Street	D2
New Street	D3
North Street	E2
Oakeywell Street	D1-D2
Occupation Street	A3-A4
Owen Street	F1
Oxford Street	B2
Paganel Drive	D4
Parkway Road	A3
Parson Street	C3
Peel Street	E1-F1
Pelham Drive	A3-A4
Porters Field	E3
Porter Street	E2
Price Street	F2
Priory Close	B4-C4
Priory Road	C4-C3-D3
Priory Street	C2-C3-D3
Prospect Row	D1-E1
Queens Cross	B1
Russsels Hall Road	A1
Russel Street	A2-B2
St James's Road	B3-C3
St James's Terrace	A4
St John's Road	E2-F2
Salop Street	A4-B4-B3
School Street	B3
Shaw Road	C1-D1
Shirley Road	F1
Stafford Street	B3-B2-C2
Stepping Stone	B2-C2

Stone Street	D2-D3
Stourbridge Road	A1-B1
Swancote Road	A1-B1
The Broadway	B4-C4-D4-D3
The Parade	B3-B4-C4
Terry Street	E2
Tetnall Street	D1
Tipton Road	E4-F4
Tower Street	D3
Trindle Road	E2-E3
Trinity Road	C3
Turner Street	B1-B2
Vauxhall Street	E1
Vicar Street	C2-D2-C1-D1
Waddam's Pool	E2-E1
Waterloo Street	E1
Watson's Green Road	E2-E3-F3-F2
Wellington Road	B1-B2
Westley Street	B1
West Street	A3
Whitehall Drive	A3-A4
Wolverhampton Street	B3-C3-C2-D2
Wolverton Road	E2-E3-F3

Halesowen

Albert Road	A1-A2
Alexandra Road	A2-A3
Andrew Road	B2
Attwood Street	A3-A4
Belbroughton Road	A1
Birmingham Road	B2-C2-B3-C3
Blackberry Lane	A1-B1-B2
Blakedown Road	A1
Bloomfield Street North	A3-A4
Broadway Avenue	A1-B1-C1
Bromsgrove Road	C2-C3
Bundle Hill	A2-B2
Carol Crescent	A4
Chadbury Road	C2
Chaple Street	A2
Cherry Orchard Avenue	A4
Cherry Street	A4
Church Croft	B2-B3
Cobham Road	C2-C3
Cranmoor Crescent	A4-B4
Cross Street	A1-A2
Dogkennel Lane	B2-B1-C1
Downing Street	B4
Dudley Road	C3-C4
Elizabeth Road	A1-A2
Fairfield Road	B1
Forge Lane	C3-C4
Furnace Hill	B4-C4
Furnace Lane	B3-B4
Grange Crescent	C2
Grange Road	C1-C2
Greenbush Drive	A4
Hagley Road	A1-B1-B2
Halesmere Way	C2
Hales Road	B3
Hawne Lane	A4
Hereward Rise	C4

Highfield Lane	A2-B2
High Street	B2-B3
Hill Street	A2
Honey Bourne Road	C2
Instone Road	A1-A2
Iverley Road	C2-C3
Kenswick Drive	A1-B1
King Street	B3
Loughton Grove	A3
Madresfield Drive	B1
Manor Way	A1-B1-C1
Melbourne Road	B4
Mount Street	B1
Mucklow Hill	C3
Newfield Crescent	B4
New Road	B3-C3
Old Hawne Lane	A4-B4-B3
Overbury Close	C1
Pershore Road	A1
Pool Street	B2
Prospect Road	C3-C4
Quarry Lane	A1
Queens Way	B2-C2
Red Leasowes Road	A1-A2
Richmond Street	A3-B3
Slims Gate	A3-B3
Somors Road	C3-C4
Stourbridge Road	A3-B3
Summer Hill	B2
Sunbury Road	A3
Tenter Fields	C2-C3
Wallwell	A2
Waxland Road	B1
Whitehall Road	C3
Whittingham Road	A4-B4
Windsor Road	A2-A3
Woodman Close	C1-C2
Woodridge Road	A4
Wytnall Road	A1-B1

Stourbridge

Albert Street	A3
Bath Road	B3
Baylie Street	A2-B2
Belbroughton Road	A1
Birmingham Street	B3-C3
Bowling Green Road	A3
Bradley Road	A4-B4
Bredon Road	B4-C4
Bridgnorth Road	A3-A4
Brook Street	A2-A3
Canal Street	A4-B4
Cathcart Road	A2-A3
Cecil Street	A3
Church Road	C1
Church Street	C2
Clark Street	A2
Cleveland Street	A2
Clifton Street	A2-A3
Colshaw Road	A1-A2
Corser Road	C4
Cotswold Road	C4
Enville Street	A3-B3
Farland Road	B1
Field Lane	B1-C1

Glasshouse Hill	C1
Glebe Lane	A2
Grampian Road	B4-C4
Greenfield Avenue	A2-A3-B3-B2
Green Street	A3-B3
Hagley Road	B2-C2-C1
Hall Street	B1-C1
Hanbury Hill	B2
Heath Lane	B2-B1-C1
Heath Street	A2
High Street	B3-B4
Hill Street	A2-B2
Ibstock Drive	C2
Junction Road	C2
Lawn Street	A2
Lickey Road	C4
Lion Street	A3-B3
Love Lane	B1
Lower High Street	B4-B3
Lowndes Road	A3-A4
Mamble Road	A3
Mill Race Lane	B4
Mill Street	B3-B4
New Road	B2-B3
Norton Road	A1
Old Wharf Road	A4-B4
Pargeter Street	A2-B2
Parkfield Road	C2-C3
Penfield Road	B4-C4
Porlock Road	B4
Priory Road	C1
Prospect Hill	B2
Queens Road	B3-B4
Red Hill	C1-C2
Robins Close	B1
St Johns Road	B4-B3-C3
Severn Road	A1
Scafell Road	C4
Scotts Road	A4-A3-B3
Stamford Road	C3-C4
Stanley Road	A1-B1
South Avenue	A2
South Road	A2
Union Street	B2-C2
Western Road	A3
West Street	A3
Wheeler Street	A3
Witton Street	A1-A2
Worcester Street	B2

27

Central Cheltenham

Central Gloucester

Gloucester

Gloucester's chief asset is its beautiful Norman cathedral. Originally an abbey, the building did not become a cathedral until the reign of Henry VIII and the lovely cloisters enclosing a delightful garden epitomise the tranquil beauty of medieval monastic architecture. The city's four main thoroughfares still follow the cruciform pattern of the original Roman roads built when *Glevum* guarded the

lowest Severn crossing. Since those days Gloucester has been an important inland port and today it is one of the country's major commercial and engineering centres.

Tewkesbury Black-and-white timbered buildings and ancient pubs with crooked roofs and curious names, such as *The Ancient Grudge,* lean haphazardly against each other in Tewkesbury's narrow streets. Rising above them all is the vast and beautiful abbey church, saved from destruction

in the Dissolution of the Monastries by the townsfolk who bought it from Henry VIII.

Cheltenham Elegant Regency architecture arranged in squares, avenues and crescents is Cheltenham's hallmark. The whole town was purpose-built around the medicinal springs discovered in the 18th century and, under Royal patronage, it became one of the country's most fashionable spas. The composer Gustav Holst was born here and his home is now a museum.

Gloucester/Cheltenham Area

SCALE
0   4
mls

Box denotes area covered by central plan

Box denotes area covered by central plan

LEGEND

Town Plan
AA recommended route
Restricted roads
Other roads
Buildings of interest   Station ▪
Car parks   P
Parks and open spaces
One way streets ←

Area Plan
A roads
B roads
Locations   Beedon ○
Urban area

Street Index with Grid Reference

Gloucester

Albion Street	B1-C1
Alexandra Road	F4
Alvin Street	D4-E4-E3
Archdeacon Street	B3-B4-C4
Arthur Street	D1
Barton Street	D2-D1-E1
Black Dog Way	D3
Brunswick Road	C1-C2-D2
Brunswick Square	C1
Bruton Way	D3-D2-E2-E1
Bull Lane	C2-C3
Clarence Street	D2
Commercial Road	B2
Cromwell Street	D1
Derby Road	F1
Eastgate Street	C2-D2
Great Western Road	E3-F3-F2
Hare Lane	C3-D3-D4
Heathville Road	F4

Henry Road	E4
Henry Street	E4
Honyatt Road	E4-F4
Ladybellgate	B2-C2
Llanthony Road	A1-B1
London Road	D3-E3-E4-F4
Longsmith Street	B2-C2
Lower Westgate Street	A4
Market Parade	D2-D3
Millbrook Street	F1
Nettleton Road	D1-D2-E2
Northgate Street	C2-C3-D3
Oxford Road	E4
Oxford Street	E3-E4
Park Street	C3-D3-D4
Park Road	C1-D1-E1
Parliament Street	C1
Pitt Street	C3-C4
Quay Street	B3
Russell Street	D2
St Catherine Street	C4-D4
St John's Lane	C3
St Mary's Street	C4
St Michael's Square	C1
St Oswald's Road	B4-C4
Severn Road	A1-A2-B2
Sherborne Street	D4-E4
Skinner Street	D2-E2
Station Road	D2
Southgate Street	B1-C1-C2
The Quay	B2-B3
Wellington Street	D1
Westgate Street	B3-C3-C2
Widden Street	E1-F1
Worcester Street	D3-D4

Cheltenham

Albert Road	E4
Albion Street	D2-D3
All Saints Road	E3-E4
Alstone Croft	A3-A4
Alstone Lane	A3
Ambrose Street	C3
Andover Road	A1-B1
Arle Avenue	A4-B4
Arle Road	A4
Bath Parade	D1-D2

Bath Road	C1-C2-D2
Bath Street	D2
Battledown Approach	F2
Bayshill Road	B2-C2
Bennington Street	D2
Berkeley Street	C4
Brunswick Street	C4
Carlton Street	E2
Central Drive	D4
Christchurch Road	A1-A2
Clarence Road	D4
Clarence Square	D4
Clarence Street	C3
Cleeve View Road	F3-F4
Clyde Crescent	F4
College Road	D1-D2
College Baths Road	D1
Douro Road	A2-B2-B1
Dunalley Street	C4
Eldon Road	E3-F3
Evesham Road	D4
Fairview Road	D3-E3
Gloucester Road	A3-A4-B4
Great Western Road	B3
Grosvenor Street	D2
Grove Street	B3-B4
Hale's Road	E1-E2-F2-F3
Hatherley Road	A1
Haywoods Road	F1
Henrietta Street	C3-C4
Hewlett Road	D2-E2-E3-F3
High Street	B4-C4-C3, D3-D2
Imperial Square	C2
Keynsham Road	D1-E1
King's Road	E2-F2
King Alfred Way	E1-F1
Knapp Road	B3-C3
Landsdown Crescent	A1-B1
Lansdown Road	A1-B1
Lansdown Parade Road	A1-A2
Leighton Road	E2
London Road	D2-E2-E1
Lypiatt Road	B1
Malvern Road	A3-A2-B2
Market Street	B3-B4
Marle Hill Parade	C4-D4
Mersey Road	F3-F4
Millbrook Street	A4-A3-B3
Milsom Street	C4
Monson Avenue	C1
Montpellier Parade	C4-D4
Montpellier Spa Road	C1-C2
Montpellier Street	B1-B2-C2
Montpellier Terrace	B1-C1

Montpellier Walk	B1-B2-C2
New Street	B3-C3
North Place	D3-D4
North Street	C3-D3
Old Bath Road	E1
Oriel Road	C2
Overton Road	A2-A3-B3-B2
Overton Park Road	B2-B3
Parabola Road	B1-B2
Pittville Circus	E4
Pittville Circus Road	E4-E3-F3
Portland Street	D3-D4
Prestbury Road	D4-E4
Prince's Street	E2
Queen's Road	A1
Regent Street	C2-C3-D3
Rodney Road	C2-D2
Royal Crescent	C2-C3
Royal Well Road	C2-C3
St George's Place	C2-C3
St George's Road	A3-B3-B2-C2
St Georges Street	C3-C4
St James's Square	C3
St James's Street	D2
St Luke's Road	C1-D1
St Margarets Road	C4-D4-D3
St Paul's Lane	C4
St Paul's Road	C4-D4
St Pauls Street South	C4
St Stephen's Road	A1
Sandford Road	C1-D1
Sandford Mill Road	E1
Selkirk Street	D4-E4-E3
Severn Road	F4
Sherborne Place	D3
Sherborne Street	D3-D4
Suffolk Parade	C1
Suffolk Road	B1-C1
Suffolk Square	B4-C4
Swindon Road	B4
Swindon Street	B4
Sydenham Road North	E2
Sydenham Villas Road	E1-E2
Tewkesbury Road	B4
The Promenade	C2-C3
Trafalgar Street	C1-C2
Townsend Street	B4
Vittoria Walk	C1-C2
Wellington Road	D4-E4
Wellington Square	D4
Wellington Street	C2-D2
Western Road	A3-B3
Whaddon Road	E4-F4
Winchcombe Street	D3-D4
Wymans Road	F4

GLOUCESTER
Gloucester Cathedral, one of the Britain's finest buildings, is a splendid example of Norman architecture. The beautiful stained-glass east window is a memorial to local men who fought at Crécy in 1346.

Hertford area

Bishop's Stortford still has a medieval street pattern. A crossing point of the River Lea in Roman times, its centre is dominated by modern buildings and pedestrianised shopping, but the town's oldest monument stands only a few hundred yards away — the remains of Waytemore Castle, which dates back to the 11th century.

Hertford A skilful blend of old and new distinguishes Hertford, which is set in some of Hertfordshire's most attractive countryside. The Quaker Meeting House is the oldest of its type still in use in the world, and stands alongside newer developments like the Castle Hall exhibition and entertainments complex. Even the modern shopping precinct, sited by the picturesque River Lea, complements the character of the town and indeed has given it a new lease of life.

Saffron Walden takes its name from saffron, an extract from the crocus which was once grown commercially here and is the celebrated symbol of the town, representing its prosperity over the centuries. This prosperity left numerous fine old buildings of unusual style and completeness: Myddylton Place and the Sun Inn are good 15th-century buildings, and the mile-long brick-built maze on the Common is the oldest of its type in the country. Today's town is built up on a well-preserved medieval street plan.

Central Hertford

Central Saffron Walden

Key to Town Plan and Area Plan.

Town Plan

AA Recommended roads
Other roads
Restricted roads
Buildings of interest   Theatre
Churches
Car Parks
Parks and open spaces
One Way Streets

Area Plan

A roads
B roads
Locations   Broomfield
Urban area

Street Index with Grid Reference

Bishop's Stortford

Adderley Road	C2-C3
All Saints Close	E3
Alpha Place	C4
Anchor Street	D1-D2
Apton Court	B2
Apton Fields	B1
Apton Road	B1-B2-C2-C3
Avenue Road	E1
Barrett Lane	C3
Bartholomew Road	B1-C1
Basbow Lane	B1
Bells Hill	B3
Bridge Street	C3
Castle Street	C1-C2
Causeway Link Road	C3-C4
Chantry Road	B4
Cherry Gardens	E4
Chestnut Close	B2
Church Manor	E4-F4
Church Street	C3
Council Road	F2
Crescent Road	D1-E1-D1
Crown Terrace	D2
Dane Street	D2-D3
Dell Lane	C2-D2
Dolphin Way	D4-E4
Dunmow Road	D2-E2-E3-F3-F2
East Road	F2
Edens Close	F3
Elm Grove	E3-F3
Firlands	B1
Foxley Drive	E3-E4
Gilbey Avenue	E1
Grange Road	D2-E2

Great Hadham Road	A1-A2
Hadham Road	A3-A4-B4-B3-B4-C4
Half Acres	B4-C4
Haymeads Avenue	F2
High Street	C3
Hillside Avenue	E2
Hockerhill Street	D2-D3
Jervis Road	B1-C1
King Street	B3-B4
Kingsbridge Road	E3-D3-D4-E4
Kingsmead Road	D4-E4
Limes Crescent	E3
London Road	D1-D2
Manor Road	E2-E3
Market Square	C3
Maze Green Road	A3-A4
Middle Row	B2
Nails Lane	C2
Newbury Close	B3-B4
Newtown Road	B2-C2
North Street	C3-C4
North Terrace	C4
Northgate End	B1-C1
Nursery Close	C1
Nursery Road	C1
Oak Street	B1
Pine Grove	E1
Plaw Hatch Close	F4
Pleasant Road	B4
Portland Place	C2
Portland Road	C2
Potter Street	C3
Regency Close	B3
Riverside	C2-C3
Sandoe Road	E3
Scott Road	A1-B1
Sidney Terrace	B1-C1
South Street	C1-C2-C3
Stanstead Road	D2-D3-E3-E4
Station Road	C2-D2
Stort Road	B1
Stortford Hall Park	E4-F4-F3-F2
The Causeway	C3-D3
The Common	B1
The Stewarts	A2-B2-B1
Thornfield Road	B3-B4
Trinity Close	C1
Trinity Street	C1
Urban Road	F2
Ward Crescent	A1
Warwick Road	D1-E1-E2-F2
Water Lane	C3-C4
Waytemore Road	A1
Wentworth Drive	A1-A2
West Road	B1
Westfield Close	A4-B4
Westfield Road	A4
Wharf Road	C1
Wilton Close	E2
Windhill	A2-B2-B3-C3
Windhill Old Road	B2-B3

Hertford

Andrews Street	A2-A3-B3
Baker Street	C3
Balfour Street	A3-A4
Bell Lane	B2
Bull Plain	B3
Bullocks Lane	A1-B1
Byde Street	A4

Castle Street	B2
Cowbridge	A3-B3
Fanshawe Street	A4
Farquar Street	A4
Fore Street	B2-B3-C3
Frampton Street	B3
Gascoyne Way	A2-B2-C2-C3
George Street	A3
Green Coates	C2
Green Street	B3
Hagsdell Road	B1-C1-C2
Hale Road	B2
Hartham Lane	B3
Hertingfordbury Road	A2
Highfield Road	B1
Horns Mill Road	A1
London Road	C2-C3
Mangrove Road	C1-C2
Market Place	B2
Market Street	B2-B3
Marshgate Drive	C4
Mill Bridge	B2-B3
Mill Road	C3-C4
North Road	A2-A3
Park Road	C2
Parkhurst Road	A4
Pegs Lane	B1-B2
Port Hill	A3-A4-B4
Port Vale	A3-A4
Priory Street	B3-C3
Queens Road	B1-B2
Railway Approach	B3
Railway Street	B3-C3
Russell Street	A3-A4
St John Street	C3
South Street	C3
The Chestnuts	C2
Thornton Street	B3
Townshend Street	C3
Valley Close	C1-C2
Villiers Street	C3
Ware Road	C3
Warren Park Road	A4-B4
Wellington Street	A4
West Street	A1-A2-B2

Saffron Walden

Abbey Lane	A3
Ashdon Road	B4-C4
Audley Road	B3-C3
Birdbush Avenue	A1
Borough Lane	A2
Bridge Street	A4
Bromfield	C1
Brooke Avenue	C4
Butler Close	C2
Castle Hill	B4
Castle Street	A4-B4
Chater's Hill	C3-C4
Church Street	B4
Common Hill	B3-B4
Debden Road	A1-A2-A3
East Street	B3-C3
Emson Close	B4
Farmadine	C2-C3
Farmadine Grove	B2-C2
Four Acres	B3-C3
Freshwell Street	A4
Friarycroft Road	B3
George Street	B3

Gibson Close	A3
Gibson Gardens	A3
Gibson Way	A3
Gold Street	B3
Hanover Place	A3-A4
Highfields	C4
High Street North	A4-B4-B3-A3
High Street South	A3-B3
Hill Street	B3
Hollyhock Road	C3-C4
Hunters Way	A1
King Street	B4
Laws Close	A1
Linton Close	C1
Little Walden Road	B4
London Road	A2-A3
Long Hedges	B2
Market Place	B4
Mandeville Road	A1-A2
Mount Pleasant Road	A2-B2-B1
Museum Street	B4
New Road	B3
Newport Road	A2
Old Mill Road	B1-C1
Park Lane	A4
Peaslands Road	B1-C1
Pleasant Valley	A1
Radwinter Road	C3
Rowntree Way	A1
Saxon Way	A2-A3
Sheds Lane	C4
Shirehill	C2
South Road	B1-B2-B3
Springhill Road	A1-A2
Stanley Farm Road	C1
Station Road	A2-B2
Station Road	B2-B3
Summerhill Road	A1-A2
Thaxsted Road	C1-C2-C3
The Wayback	C4
Victoria Avenue	B2-C2
Victoria Gardens	C2
West Road	A2-B2

High Wycombe

Each year in spring, the newly elected mayor and town officials of High Wycombe are weighed outside the town's Guildhall wearing their traditional vestments, as part of an old-established 'weighing in' ceremony. Interesting old buildings as well as ceremonies have been preserved in the town, particularly around the High Street, and the Market House, known as the Pepperpot, dates from the mid-18th century. The history of the town is traced in the Guildhall Heritage Exhibition, while the Wycombe Chair and Local History Museum deals mainly with furniture manufacture — probably the best known feature of this important industrial centre today. Two miles to the west lies West Wycombe, site of the caves said to have been the meeting place for Sir Francis Dashwood's Hellfire Club during the 18th century.

Beaconsfield is the home of the Bekonscot Model Village, said to be one of the oldest in the world, and of a partly 15th-century parish church. A number of old coaching inns still stand here.

Chesham has made a name for itself with the manufacture of wooden articles such as fruit bowls, and is concerned with the leather industry. The oldest buildings in the town are mainly concentrated in the Church Street and Germain Street areas, where 16th- and 18th-century half-timbered gabled houses have been preserved.

32

Central Beaconsfield

Central Chesham

LEGEND

Town Plan
AA Recommended roads
Other roads
Restricted roads
Buildings of interest — School
Car Parks — P
Parks and open spaces
One Way Streets — →

Area Plan
A roads
B roads
Locations — Horn Hill
Urban area

Street Index with Grid Reference

High Wycombe

Abbey Way	C2-D2-D1
Abercromby Avenue	A3
Adam Close	F3-F4
Amersham Hill	D2-D3-E3
Amersham Hill Drive	E4-F4
Amersham Hill Gardens	E4
Arnison Avenue	F4
Baker Street	B3-C3
Baronsmead Road	A1-A2
Barracks Road	C1
Bassettsbury Lane	F1
Bellfield Road	C3-C4
Benjamin Road	D3
Bowerdean Road	F2
Bridge Street	C3
Brook Street	C3
Brunel Road	B4
Carrington Road	A2
Carver Hill Road	B1-B2
Castle Street	D2
Cedar Terrace	B3
Chairborough Road	A2-A3
Colville Road	A2-B2
Conifer Rise	A2
Coningsby Road	D4
Copyground Lane	A3
Crendon Street	D2
Cumbrian Way	A4-B4
Dashwood Avenue	A3
Dean Close	A1-A2
Deeds Grove	A1-A2-B1
Desborough Avenue	B1-B2-B3
Desborough Park Road	A3-A4
Desborough Road	B2-B3-C2-C3
Desborough Street	A3-B3
Dovecot Road	C3
Duke Street	E2
Easton Street	D2-E2
Fulton Close	C4
George Street	B3-C3
Gordon Road	E2-F1-F2
Green Street	A3-B3
Hamilton Road	D4
Hampden Road	D3-D4
Healey Avenue	F2-F3
Hepplewhite Close	F3-F4
High Street	D2
Hillside	F3
Hill View Road	F4
Hughenden Avenue	B4-C4
Hughenden Road	D4
Kingsley Crescent	B1
Kingston Road	A1
Kitchener Road	A3-B3-B2
Knights Hill	A1
Lilys Walk	C2
Lincoln Road	A1
Lindsay Avenue	A3
Loakes Road	C1-C2
London End	E1-E2-F1
Lucas Road	E3
Malmerswell Road	D3
Marlow Hill	C1-D1
Maybrook Gardens	E3-E4
Mayhew Crescent	F4
Mendip Way	B4
Mount Close	A1-A2
Oakridge Road	A3
Ogilvie Road	A3
Oxford Road	B3-C3
Perth Road	F4
Phillip Road	F3
Plumer Road	A2-A3-B2
Pretoria Road	E3-E4
Priory Avenue	D3
Priory Road	D2-D3
Queen Alexandra Road	C2-D2
Queens Road	E2-F1-F2
Queen Street	E2-E3
Queen Victoria Road	D2
Rectory Avenue	E3
Richardson Street	B3-C3
Roberts Road	D3-D4
Rowan Avenue	F3-F4
Rye View	E3
Saffron Road	E2
Shaftesbury Street	B3
Sharrow Vale	A2-A3
Shelly Road	B1-C1
Slater Street	E2
Suffield Road	B2-C2
The Greenway	D3
The Pastures	B3-B4
Temple End	C3-D3-D4
Temple Street	C2
Terry Road	E4
Totteridge Road	D2-E2-F2-F3
Totteridge Way	F2
Underwood Road	F3-F4

Victoria Street	B3
Wayside	F3
Wendover Street	B2-C2
Wendover Way	D1-D2
West End Street	B2-B3
West Wycombe Road	A4-B3-B4

Beaconsfield

Amersham Road	C2-C3-C4
Assheton Road	B4
Aylesbury End	B1-B2-C1
Baring Crescent	A3-A4
Baring Road	A3
Beechwood Road	A3
Burkes Crescent	A2-B2
Burkes Road	A2-A3-B3
Butlers Court Road	A1
Caledon Road	B3
Candlemas Lane	B2-C2
Candlemas Mead	B2-B3-C2
Chesterton Gardens	B3
Chiltern Hills Road	A2-A3
Curzon Avenue	A4-B4
Furzefield Road	A2-A3
Garvin Avenue	B3
Gregories Road	A3
Grenfell Road	B4
Grove Road	B2-B3
Hedgerley Lane	C1
Hyde Green	C3
Lakes Lane	C1
Ledborough Lane	A4-B4-C4
London End	C1
Malthouse Square	C1
Maxwell Road	B3-C3
Meadow Lane	C2
Mill Lane	B2
One Tree Lane	B3-C3-C4
Oxford Road	A1-B1
Park Lane	C1-C2
Penn Road	A3-A4
Reynolds Road	A3-A4
Ronald Road	C2-C3
Seelys Road	A4
Shepherds Lane	C1-C2
Station Road	A3-B3-B2
The Spinney	A1-B1
Tilsworth Road	A1
Waller Road	C3
Wattleton Road	A1-B1-B2
Warwick Road	A4-B4
Whipass Hill	C4
Wilton Crescent	B3-B4
Wilton Road	B4
Windsor End	C1
Wooster Road	A4
Wycombe Road	B1-C1
Yew Tree Close	C1-C2

Chesham

Alma Road	B4-C4
Amersham Road	B1
Amy Lane	B1

Beechcroft Road	A3-A4
Bellingdon Road	A4-B3-B4
Benham Close	C4
Berkhamsted Road	C4
Broadlands Avenue	C3
Broad Street	B3-B4
Bury Lane	B2
Cameron Road	C4
Chapmans Crescent	A4
Chartridge Lane	A3
Chessbury	A1
Church Street	B1-B2
Deansway	A4
Dellfield	A4
Dry Dell Lane	A1-A2
East Street	B2
Elm Tree Hill	A3-A4
Eskdale Avenue	C4
Essex Road	C4
Fullers Close	B1
Fullers Hill	A1-B1
George Street	C4
Germain Street	B1-B2
Gladstone Road	B3-C3
Hampden Avenue	A3
High Street	B2-B3
Hiving's Hill	A4-B4
Higham Road	B3-B4
Honeysuckle Field	B4
Kings Street	B1
Kirtle Road	C3
Lowndes Avenue	A3-B3-B4
Meades Lane	B1
Missenden Road	A1
Nalders Road	C4
Park Road	B2-B3
Pednor Road	A1-A2
Penn Avenue	A3-A4
Pond Park Road	B4
Prior Grove	C3
Red Lion Street	B1-B2
St Marys Way	B2-B3
Severals Avenue	C4
Springfield Road	C1
Stanley Avenue	B3
Sunnyside Road	B4
The Backs	B2-B3
Townsend Road	B3
Treachers Close	B3
Victoria Road	B3-C3
Wallington Road	A4-B4
Waterside	B1-C1
Wey Lane	B1
Whitehill	B3-C3
Whitehill Close	C3

Ipswich

In the Middle Ages England became rich from wool, and East Anglia in particular prospered. Ipswich shared in the wealth, being the port from which wool was exported to Europe. Twelve medieval churches survive in Ipswich, a remarkable number for a town of its size, and all of them have features of beauty and interest. Of the town's nonconformist chapels, the 17th-century Unitarian is outstanding. Unfortunately, many of Ipswich's ancient secular buildings were swept away during the 1960s fever for clearances, precincts and redevelopment; however, some of the finest survive. Best is Ancient House, dating back to 1567 and embellished on the outside with complex decorative plasterwork. Other fine buildings can be seen in Lower Brook Street and Fore Street. Christchurch Mansion dates from 1548 and now houses a museum.

Felixstowe is a seaside resort with Edwardian characteristics, a commercial centre, and a container port. Its handsome promenade is nearly two miles long.

Stowmarket has an excellent country life museum – the Museum of East Anglian Life. Among its exhibits are reconstructed buildings, agricultural machinery and domestic items. The town itself is a shopping and market centre for the rich arable farmlands of Central Suffolk.

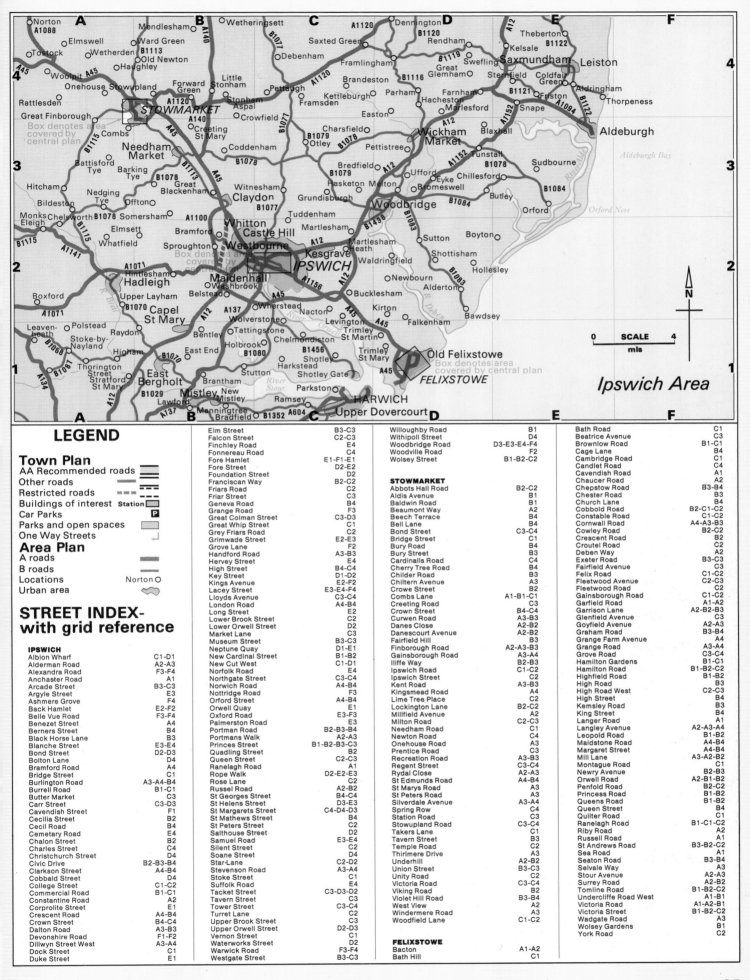

LEGEND

Town Plan
- AA Recommended roads
- Other roads
- Restricted roads
- Buildings of interest — Station
- Car Parks — P
- Parks and open spaces
- One Way Streets

Area Plan
- A roads
- B roads
- Locations — Norton ○
- Urban area

STREET INDEX- with grid reference

IPSWICH

Albion Wharf	C1-D1
Alderman Road	A2-A3
Alexandra Road	F3-F4
Anchaster Road	A1
Arcade Street	B3-C3
Argyle Street	E3
Ashmere Grove	F4
Back Hamlet	E2-F2
Belle Vue Road	F3-F4
Benezet Street	A4
Berners Street	B4
Black Horse Lane	B3
Blanche Street	E3-E4
Bond Street	D2-D3
Bolton Lane	D4
Bramford Road	A4
Bridge Street	C1
Burlington Road	A3-A4-B4
Burrell Road	B1-C1
Butter Market	C3
Carr Street	C3-D3
Cavendish Street	F1
Cecilia Street	B2
Cecil Road	B4
Cemetary Road	E4
Chalon Street	B2
Charles Street	C4
Christchurch Street	D4
Civic Drive	B2-B3-B4
Clarkson Street	A4-B4
Cobbald Street	D4
College Street	C1-C2
Commercial Road	B1-C1
Constantine Road	A2
Corprolite Street	E1
Crescent Road	A4-B4
Crown Street	B4-C4
Dalton Road	A3-B3
Devonshire Road	F1-F2
Dillwyn Street West	A3-A4
Dock Street	C1
Duke Street	E1
Elm Street	B3-C3
Falcon Street	C2-C3
Finchley Road	E4
Fonnereau Road	C4
Fore Hamlet	E1-F1-E1
Fore Street	D2-E2
Foundation Street	D2
Franciscan Way	B2-C2
Friars Road	C2
Friar Street	C3
Geneva Road	B4
Grange Road	F3
Great Colman Street	C3-D3
Great Whip Street	C1
Grey Friars Road	C2
Grimwade Street	E2-E3
Grove Lane	F2
Handford Road	A3-B3
Hervey Street	E4
High Street	B4-C4
Key Street	D1-D2
Kings Avenue	E2-F2
Lacey Street	E3-E4-F4
Lloyds Avenue	C3-C4
London Road	A4-B4
Long Street	E2
Lower Brook Street	C2
Lower Orwell Street	D2
Market Lane	C3
Museum Street	B3-C3
Neptune Quay	D1-E1
New Cardinal Street	B1-B2
New Cut West	C1-D1
Norfolk Road	E4
Northgate Street	C3-C4
Norwich Road	A4-B4
Nottridge Road	F3
Orford Street	A4-B4
Orwell Quay	E1
Oxford Road	E3-F3
Palmerston Road	E3
Portman Road	B2-B3-B4
Portmans Walk	A2-A3
Princes Street	B1-B2-B3-C3
Quadling Street	C2
Queen Street	C2-C3
Ranelagh Road	A1
Rope Walk	D2-E2-E3
Rose Lane	C2
Russel Road	A2-B2
St Georges Street	B4-C4
St Helens Street	D3-E3
St Margarets Street	C4-D4-D3
St Mathews Street	B4
St Peters Street	C2
Salthouse Street	D2
Samuel Road	E3-E4
Silent Street	C2
Soane Street	D4
Star-Lane	C2-D2
Stevenson Road	A3-A4
Stoke Street	C1
Suffolk Road	E4
Tacket Street	C3-D3-D2
Tavern Street	C3
Tower Street	C3-C4
Turret Lane	C2
Upper Brook Street	C3
Upper Orwell Street	D2-D3
Vernon Street	C1
Waterworks Street	D2
Warwick Road	F3-F4
Westgate Street	B3-C3

Willoughby Road	B1
Withipoll Street	D4
Woodbridge Road	D3-E3-E4-F4
Woodville Road	F2
Wolsey Street	B1-B2-C2

STOWMARKET

Abbots Hall Road	B2-C2
Aldis Avenue	B1
Baldwin Road	B1
Beaumont Way	A2
Beech Terrace	B4
Bell Lane	B4
Bond Street	C3-C4
Bridge Street	C1
Bury Road	B4
Bury Street	B3
Cardinalls Road	C4
Cherry Tree Road	B4
Childer Road	B3
Chiltern Avenue	A3
Crowe Street	B2
Combs Lane	A1-B1-C1
Creeting Road	C3
Crown Street	B4-C4
Curwen Road	A3-B3
Danes Close	A2-B2
Danescourt Avenue	A2-B2
Fairfield Hill	B3
Finborough Road	A2-A3-B3
Gainsborough Road	A3-A4
Iliffe Way	B2-B3
Ipswich Road	C1-C2
Ipswich Street	C2
Kent Road	A3-B3
Kingsmead Road	A4
Lime Tree Place	C2
Lockington Lane	B2-C2
Millfield Avenue	A2
Milton Road	C2-C3
Needham Road	C1
Newton Road	C4
Onehouse Road	A3
Prentice Road	C3
Recreation Road	A3-B3
Regent Street	C3-C4
Rydal Close	A2-A3
St Edmunds Road	A4-B4
St Marys Road	A3
St Peters Road	A3
Silverdale Avenue	A3-A4
Spring Row	C4
Station Road	C3
Stowupland Road	C3-C4
Takers Lane	C1
Tavern Street	B3
Temple Road	C2
Thirlmere Drive	A3
Underhill	A2-B2
Union Street	B3-C3
Unity Road	C2
Victoria Road	C3-C4
Viking Way	B1
Violet Hill Road	B3-B4
West View	A2
Windermere Road	A3
Woodfield Lane	C1-C2

FELIXSTOWE

Bacton	A1-A2
Bath Hill	C1

Bath Road	C1
Beatrice Avenue	C3
Brownlow Road	B1-C1
Cage Lane	C1
Cambridge Road	C1
Candlet Road	C4
Cavendish Road	A1
Chaucer Road	A2
Chepstow Road	B3-B4
Chester Road	B3
Church Lane	B4
Cobbold Road	B2-C1-C2
Constable Road	C1-C2
Cornwall Road	A4-A3-B3
Cowley Road	B2-C2
Crescent Road	B2
Croutel Road	C2
Deben Way	A2
Exeter Road	B3-C3
Fairfield Avenue	C3
Felix Road	C1-C2
Fleetwood Avenue	C2-C3
Fleetwood Road	C2
Gainsborough Road	C1-C2
Garfield Road	A1-A2
Garrison Lane	A2-B2-B3
Glenfield Avenue	C3
Goyfield Avenue	A2-A3
Graham Road	B3-B4
Grange Farm Avenue	A4
Grange Road	A3-A4
Grove Road	C3-C4
Hamilton Gardens	B1-C1
Hamilton Road	B1-B2-C2
Highfield Road	B1-B2
High Road	B3
High Road West	C2-C3
High Street	B4
Kemsley Road	B3
King Street	B4
Langer Road	A1
Langley Avenue	A2-A3-A4
Leopold Road	B1-B2
Maidstone Road	A4-B4
Margaret Street	A4-B4
Mill Lane	A3-A2-B2
Montague Road	C1
Newry Avenue	B2-B3
Orwell Road	A2-B1-B2
Penfold Road	B2-C2
Princess Road	B1-B2
Queens Road	B1-B2
Queen Street	B4
Quilter Road	C1
Ranelagh Road	B1-C1-C2
Riby Road	A2
Russell Road	A1
St Andrews Road	B3-B2-C2
Sea Road	A1
Seaton Road	B3-B4
Selvale Way	A3
Stour Avenue	A2-A3
Surrey Road	A2-B2
Tomline Road	B1-B2-C2
Undercliffe Road West	A1-B1
Victoria Road	A1-A2-B1
Victoria Street	B1-B2-C2
Wadgate Road	A3
Wolsey Gardens	B1
York Road	C2

35

Kidderminster

Carpets and Kidderminster have gone together since at least the 17th century, and this ancient town is also notable as the birthplace of Penny Post founder Sir Rowland Hill. A variety of historic buildings has survived here, and railway enthusiasts can now enjoy the attractions of the Severn Valley Steam Railway — it has recently been extended to Kidderminster and generally operates during the summer and on Bank Holidays. The West Midland Safari Park lies between Kidderminster and Bewdley, covering some 197 acres.

Bromsgrove prospered on nail-making before the arrival of machines in the 19th century, and today this thriving modern town attracts a variety of trades to its recently built industrial estates.

But a past which can be traced to pre-Norman times is recalled each year, when Bromsgrove holds its annual Fair at which traditional and ancient customs are displayed. Year round outdoor recreation can be found at Sanders Park.

Redditch has grown up on a rich mix of fishing tackle, cycles and springs — three of the products which have replaced its staple trade of needle-making after the mid-19th century. Set in the heart of England, Redditch today excels in the making of metal and engineering goods and boasts three sports centres, the outdoor Abbey Stadium, and 900-acre Arrow Valley Park, with its 30-acre lake.

36

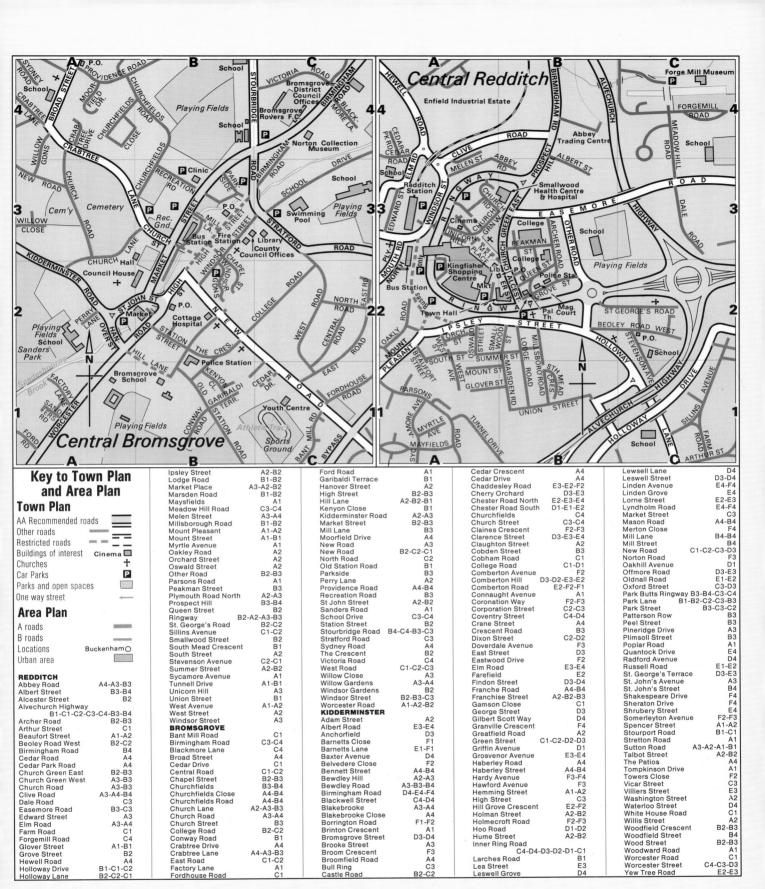

A P.O. PROVIDENCE ROAD School **B** School **C** Forge Mill Museum

Central Redditch

Enfield Industrial Estate FORGEMILL ROAD School

Central Bromsgrove

Key to Town Plan and Area Plan

Town Plan

AA Recommended roads
Other roads
Restricted roads
Buildings of interest — Cinema
Churches — †
Car Parks — P
Parks and open spaces
One way street

Area Plan

A roads
B roads
Locations — Buckenham
Urban area

REDDITCH

Abbey Road	A4-A3-B3
Albert Street	B3-B4
Alcester Street	B2
Alvechurch Highway	
	B1-C1-C2-C3-C4-B3-B4
Archer Road	B2-B3
Arthur Street	C1
Beaufort Street	A1-A2
Beoley Road West	B2-C2
Birmingham Road	B4
Cedar Road	A4
Cedar Park Road	A4
Church Green East	B2-B3
Church Green West	A3-B3
Church Road	A3-B3
Clive Road	A3-A4-B4
Dale Road	C3
Easemore Road	B3-C3
Edward Street	A3
Elm Road	A3-A4
Farm Road	C1
Forgemill Road	C4
Glover Street	A1-B1
Grove Street	B2
Hewell Road	A3
Holloway Drive	B1-C1-C2
Holloway Lane	B2-C2-C1
Ipsley Street	A2-B2
Lodge Road	B1-B2
Market Place	A3-A2-B2
Marsden Road	B1-B2
Maysfields	A1
Meadow Hill Road	C3-C4
Melen Street	A3-A4
Millsborough Road	B1-B2
Mount Pleasant	A1-A2
Mount Street	A1-B1
Myrtle Avenue	A1
Oakley Road	A2
Orchard Street	A2
Oswald Street	A2
Other Road	B2-B3
Parsons Road	A2
Peakman Street	B3
Plymouth Road North	A2-A3
Prospect Hill	B3-B4
Queen Street	B3
Ringway	B2-A2-A3-B3
St. George's Road	B2-C2
Sillins Avenue	C1-C2
Smallwood Street	B2
South Mead Crescent	B1
South Street	A2
Stevenson Avenue	C2-C1
Summer Street	A2-B2
Sycamore Avenue	A1
Tunnell Drive	A1-B1
Unicorn Hill	A3
Union Street	B1
West Avenue	A1-A2
West Street	A2
Windsor Street	A3

BROMSGROVE

Bant Mill Road	C1
Birmingham Road	C3-C4
Blackmore Lane	C4
Broad Street	C1
Cedar Drive	C1-C2
Central Road	C1-C2
Chapel Street	B2-B3
Churchfields	B3-B4
Churchfields Close	A4-B4
Churchfields Road	A4-B4
Church Lane	A2-A3-B3
Church Road	A3-A4
Church Street	B3
College Road	B2-C2
Conway Road	B1
Crabtree Drive	A4
Crabtree Lane	A4-A3-B3
East Road	C1-C2
Factory Lane	A1
Fordhouse Road	C1
Ford Road	A1
Garibaldi Terrace	B1
Hanover Street	A2
High Street	B2-B3
Hill Lane	A2-B2-B1
Kenyon Close	B1
Kidderminster Road	A2-A3
Market Street	B2-B3
Mill Lane	B3
Moorfield Drive	A4
New Road	A3
New Road	B2-C2-C1
North Road	C2
Old Station Road	B1
Parkside	B3
Perry Lane	A2
Providence Road	A4-B4
Recreation Road	B3
St John Street	A2-B2
Sanders Road	A1
School Drive	C3-C4
Station Street	B2
Stourbridge Road	B4-C4-B3-C3
Stratford Road	C3
Sydney Road	A4
The Crescent	B2
Victoria Road	C4
West Road	C1-C2-C3
Willow Close	A3
Willow Gardens	A3-A4
Windsor Gardens	B2
Windsor Street	B2-B3-C3
Worcester Road	A1-A2-B2

KIDDERMINSTER

Adam Street	A2
Albert Road	E3-E4
Anchorfield	D3
Barnetts Lane	F1
Barnetts Close	E1-F1
Baxter Avenue	D4
Belvedere Close	F2
Bennett Street	A4-B4
Bewdley Hill	A2-A3
Bewdley Road	A3-B3-B4
Birmingham Road	D4-E4-F4
Blackwell Street	C4-D4
Blakebrooke	A3-A4
Blakebrooke Close	A4
Borrington Road	F1-F2
Brinton Crescent	A1
Bromsgrove Street	D3-D4
Brooke Street	A3
Broom Crescent	F3
Broomfield Road	A4
Bull Ring	C3
Castle Road	B2-C2
Cedar Crescent	A4
Cedar Drive	A4
Chaddesley Road	E3-E2-F2
Cherry Orchard	D3-E3
Chester Road North	E2-E3-E4
Chester Road South	D1-E1-E2
Churchfields	C4
Church Street	C3-C4
Claines Crescent	F2-F3
Clarence Street	D3-E3-E4
Claughton Street	A2
Cobden Street	B3
Cobham Road	C1
College Road	C1-D1
Comberton Avenue	F2
Comberton Hill	D3-D2-E3-E2
Comberton Road	E2-F2-F1
Connaught Avenue	A1
Coronation Way	F2-F3
Corporation Street	C2-C3
Coventry Street	C4-D4
Crane Street	A4
Crescent Road	B3
Dixon Street	C2-D2
Doverdale Avenue	F3
East Street	D3
Eastwood Drive	F2
Elm Road	E3-E4
Farefield	E2
Findon Street	D3-D4
Franche Road	A4-B4
Franchise Street	A2-B2-B3
Gamson Close	C1
George Street	D3
Gilbert Scott Way	D4
Granville Crescent	F4
Greatfield Road	A4
Green Street	C1-C2-D2-D3
Griffin Avenue	D1
Grosvenor Avenue	E3-E4
Haberley Road	A4
Haberley Street	A4-B4
Hardy Avenue	F3-F4
Hawford Avenue	F3
Hemming Street	A1-A2
High Street	C3
Hill Grove Crescent	E2-F2
Holman Street	A2-B2
Holmecroft Road	F2-F3
Hoo Road	D1-D2
Hume Street	A2-B2
Inner Ring Road	
	C4-D4-D3-D2-D1-C1
Larches Road	B1
Lea Street	E3
Leswell Grove	D4
Lewsell Lane	D4
Leswell Street	D3-D4
Linden Avenue	E4-F4
Linden Grove	E4
Lorne Street	E2-E3
Lyndholm Road	E4-F4
Market Street	C3
Mason Road	A4-B4
Merton Close	F4
Mill Lane	B4-B4
Mill Street	B4
New Road	C1-C2-C3-D3
Norton Road	F3
Oakhill Avenue	D1
Offmore Road	D3-E3
Oldnall Road	E1-E2
Oxford Street	C3-D3
Park Butts Ringway	B3-B4-C3-C4
Park Lane	B1-B2-C2-C3-B3
Park Street	B3-C3-C2
Patterson Row	B3
Peel Street	B3
Pineridge Drive	A3
Plimsoll Street	B3
Poplar Road	A1
Quantock Drive	E4
Radford Avenue	D4
Russell Road	E1-E2
St. George's Terrace	D3-D4
St. John's Avenue	A3
St. John's Street	B4
Shakespeare Drive	F4
Sheraton Drive	F4
Shrubery Street	E4
Somerleyton Avenue	F2-F3
Spencer Street	A1-A2
Stourport Road	B1-C1
Stretton Road	A1
Sutton Road	A3-A2-A1-B1
Talbot Street	A2-B2
The Patios	A4
Tompkinson Drive	A1
Towers Close	F2
Vicar Street	C3
Villiers Street	E3
Washington Street	A2
Waterloo Street	D4
White House Road	C1
Willis Street	A2
Woodfield Crescent	B2-B3
Woodfield Street	B4
Wood Street	B2-B3
Woodward Road	A1
Worcester Road	C1
Worcester Street	C4-C3-D3
Yew Tree Road	E2-E3

BROMSGROVE
The 'String of Horses' at the Avoncroft Museum of Buildings is one of the many historic buildings dismantled and brought here for reconstruction, when their existence was threatened by development.

Key to Town Plan and Area Plan

Town Plan

AA Recommended roads	
Restricted roads	
Other roads	
Buildings of interest	Station ■
Car Parks	P
Parks and open spaces	
Churches	+
One Way Streets	

Area Plan

A roads	
B roads	
Locations	Midgley O
Urban area	

STREET INDEX-with grid reference

King's Lynn

Albert Avenue	B6
Albert Street	B6
Albion Street	B5
All Saints Street	A3-A4
Argyle Street	C1-C2
Austin Street	B6-C6
Baker Lane	A5
Beech Road	B1-B2
Birchwood Street	B7-C7
Blackfriars Road	C5-C6
Blackfriars Street	B5
Boal Street	A4
Bridge Street	A3-A4

Burkitt Street	C7-C8
Carmelite Terrace	A3
Chapel Street	B6
Chase Avenue	C2
Checker Street	B2-B3
Church Street	A4
Clough Lane	B5
Coburg Street	C5
Cockelshell Walk	B3-B3
County Court Road	B4
Cresswell Street	C7-C8
Cross Bank Road	A8-B8-B7
Diamond Street	A1-A2
Eastgate Street	C6
Edma Street	C7
Edward Benefer Way	B7-B8-C8
Ethel Terrace	A2-B2
Extons Road	C3
Ferry Street	A6
Friars Street	B3-A3-B3-B2
Gaywood Road	C6
George Street	C7
Gladstone Road	A2-A3-B3
Goodwins Road	C2-C3
Graham Street	C3
Guanock Terrace	B2-B3-C3
Hardwick Road	B1-B2
Harecroft Gardens	C7
Hextable Road	B7-C7
Highgate	C5-C6
High Street	A5-A6
Horsleys Chase	B1
Horsleys Fields	B1
Hospital Walk	B3
John Kennedy Road	B6-B7
John Street	B3
Kettlewell Lane	C6

King's Lynn

Pilgrims on their way to Walsingham would stop at the 15th-century Red Mount Chapel in the Walks at King's Lynn, and commercial prominence really began here as far back as the 13th century, when this Great Ouse port had connections with the German trading towns of the Hanseatic League. Prosperity continued until well into the 18th century, and although modern expansion has brought new shopping, sports and entertainment facilities to the town centre, a number of medieval buildings survive, including the Guild Hall of St George (now a theatre) and the Guild Hall of Holy Trinity. St Margaret's Church still has portions of its Norman tower. The Lynn Museum in Old Market Street looks at the history of the area, and is complemented by the Museum of Social History in King Street.

Wisbech is at the heartland of soft fruit cultivation, and is especially known for its strawberries. Set in the low-lying fens and linked to the Wash by the River Nene, it has some fine examples of Georgian architecture in the North and South Brinks which line the river on either side. Eighteenth-century Peckover House now belongs to the National Trust; also of interest is the Clarkson Memorial in Bridge Street, erected in memory of Thomas Clarkson, who campaigned for the abolition of slavery.

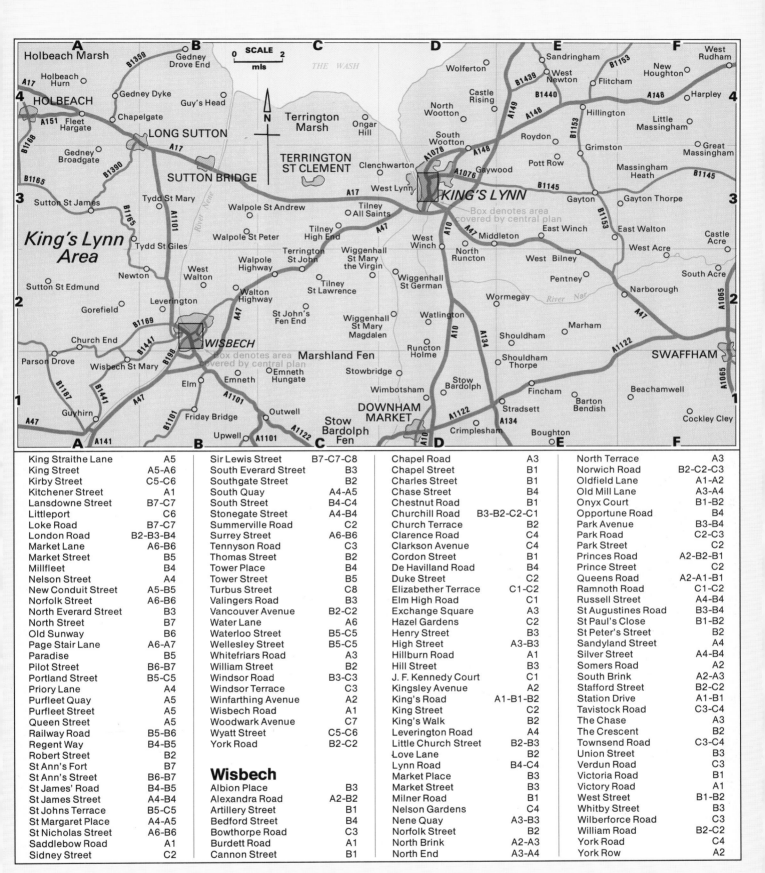

King Straithe Lane	A5	Sir Lewis Street	B7-C7-C8
King Street	A5-A6	South Everard Street	B3
Kirby Street	C5-C6	Southgate Street	B2
Kitchener Street	A1	South Quay	A4-A5
Lansdowne Street	B7-C7	South Street	B4-C4
Littleport	C6	Stonegate Street	A4-B4
Loke Road	B7-C7	Summerville Road	C2
London Road	B2-B3-B4	Surrey Street	A6-B6
Market Lane	A6-B6	Tennyson Road	C3
Market Street	B5	Thomas Street	B2
Millfleet	B4	Tower Place	B4
Nelson Street	A4	Tower Street	B5
New Conduit Street	A5-B5	Turbus Street	C8
Norfolk Street	A6-B6	Valingers Road	B3
North Everard Street	B3	Vancouver Avenue	B2-C2
North Street	B7	Water Lane	A6
Old Sunway	B6	Waterloo Street	B5-C5
Page Stair Lane	A6-A7	Wellesley Street	B5-C5
Paradise	B5	Whitefriars Road	A3
Pilot Street	B6-B7	William Street	B2
Portland Street	B5-C5	Windsor Road	B3-C3
Priory Lane	A4	Windsor Terrace	C3
Purfleet Quay	A5	Winfarthing Avenue	A2
Purfleet Street	A5	Wisbech Road	A1
Queen Street	A5	Woodwark Avenue	C7
Railway Road	B5-B6	Wyatt Street	C5-C6
Regent Way	B4-B5	York Road	B2-C2
Robert Street	B2		
St Ann's Fort	B7		
St Ann's Street	B6-B7		

Wisbech

St James' Road	B4-B5	Albion Place	B3
St James Street	A4-B4	Alexandra Road	A2-B2
St Johns Terrace	B5-C5	Artillery Street	B1
St Margaret Place	A4-A5	Bedford Street	B4
St Nicholas Street	A6-B6	Bowthorpe Road	C3
Saddlebow Road	A1	Burdett Road	A1
Sidney Street	C2	Cannon Street	B1

Chapel Road	A3	North Terrace	A3
Chapel Street	B1	Norwich Road	B2-C2-C3
Charles Street	B1	Oldfield Lane	A1-A2
Chase Street	B4	Old Mill Lane	A3-A4
Chestnut Road	B1	Onyx Court	B1-B2
Churchill Road	B3-B2-C2-C1	Opportune Road	B4
Church Terrace	B2	Park Avenue	B3-B4
Clarence Road	C4	Park Road	C2-C3
Clarkson Avenue	C4	Park Street	C2
Cordon Street	B1	Princes Road	A2-B2-B1
De Havilland Road	B4	Prince Street	C2
Duke Street	C2	Queens Road	A2-A1-B1
Elizabether Terrace	C1-C2	Ramnoth Road	C1-C2
Elm High Road	C1	Russell Street	A4-B4
Exchange Square	A3	St Augustines Road	B3-B4
Hazel Gardens	C2	St Paul's Close	B1-B2
Henry Street	B3	St Peter's Street	B2
High Street	A3-B3	Sandyland Street	A4
Hillburn Road	A1	Silver Street	A4-B4
Hill Street	B3	Somers Road	A2
J. F. Kennedy Court	C1	South Brink	A2-A3
Kingsley Avenue	A2	Stafford Street	B2-C2
King's Road	A1-B1-B2	Station Drive	A1-B1
King Street	C2	Tavistock Road	C3-C4
King's Walk	B2	The Chase	A3
Leverington Road	A4	The Crescent	B2
Little Church Street	B2-B3	Townsend Road	C3-C4
Love Lane	B2	Union Street	B3
Lynn Road	B4-C4	Verdun Road	C3
Market Place	B3	Victoria Road	B1
Market Street	B3	Victory Road	A1
Milner Road	B1	West Street	B1-B2
Nelson Gardens	C4	Whitby Street	B3
Nene Quay	A3-B3	Wilberforce Road	C3
Norfolk Street	B2	William Road	B2-C2
North Brink	A2-A3	York Road	C4
North End	A3-A4	York Row	A2

KINGS LYNN
Designed by local architect Henry Bell and dating back to 1683, the elegant Old Customs House bears witness to a longstanding importance as a trading centre serving both the Midlands (via inland waterways) and Europe.

Leicester

A regional capital in Roman times, Leicester has retained many buildings from its eventful and distinguished past. Today the city is a thriving modern place, a centre for industry and commerce, serving much of the Midlands. Among the most outstanding monuments from the past is the Jewry Wall, a great bastion of Roman masonry. Close by are remains of the Roman baths and

several other contemporary buildings. Attached is a museum covering all periods from prehistoric times to 1500. Numerous other museums include the Wygston's House Museum of Costume, with displays covering the period 1769 to 1924; Newarke House, with collections showing changing social conditions in Leicester through four hundred years; and Leicestershire Museum and Art Gallery, with collections of drawings, paintings, ceramics, geology and natural history.

The medieval Guildhall has many features of interest, including a great hall, library and police cells. Leicester's castle, although remodelled in the 17th century, retains a 12th-century great hall. The Church of St Mary de Castro, across the road from the castle, has features going back at least as far as Norman times; while St Nicholas's Church is even older, with Roman and Saxon foundations. St Martin's Cathedral dates mainly from the 13th to 15th centuries and has a notable Bishop's throne.

LEGEND

Town Plan

AA Recommended route	
Restricted roads	
Other roads	
Buildings of interest	
Car parks	P
Parks and open spaces	
One way streets	→

Area Plan

A roads	
B roads	
Locations	Creaton ○
Urban area	

Street Index with Grid Reference

Leicester

Abbey Street	D7
Albion Street	D4-D5
All Saints Road	B7
Almond Road	C1-D1
Andrewes Street	A4-A5
Aylestone Road	C1-C2
Baron Street	E5-E6
Bath Lane	B5-B6
Bay Street	C8
Bedford Street North	E8
Bedford Street South	D7
Belgrave Gate	D7-D8-E8
Bell Lane	F6-F7
Belvoir Street	D5
Bisley Street	A1-A2
Blackfriars Street	B3
Bonchurch Street	A7-A8
Bosworth Street	A6
Bowling Green Street	D5
Braunstone Gate	A4-B4-B5
Brazil Street	C1-C2
Britannia Street	E8
Briton Street	A3
Brown Street	C4
Bruce Street	A2
Brunswick Street	F7
Burgess Street	C7
Burleys Way	C7-D7-D8
Burton Street	E6
Calgary Road	E8
Campbell Street	E5
Cank Street	C6-D6

Canning Place	C8
Carlton Street	C4-D4
Castle Street	B5-C5
Celt Street	A4
Central Road	A8
Charles Street	D7-D6-D5-E5
Charter Street	D8
Chatham Street	D4-D5
Cheapside	D5-D6
Christow Street	F7-F8
Church Gate	C7-C6-D6
Clarence Street	D6-D7
Clyde Street	E6-E7
College Street	F4
Colton Street	D5-E5
Conduit Street	E4-F4-F5
Crafton Street	E7-F7
Cranmer Street	A4
Craven Street	B7-B8
Crescent Street	D4
Cuthlaxton Street	F4-F5
De Montfort Street	E3-E4
Dover Street	D4-D5
Duke Street	D4
Dunns Lane	B5
Dunton Street	A8
Dysart Way	F8
East Bond Street	C6-C7
Eastern Boulevard	B3-B4
Eastleigh Road	A2
Equity Road	A3
Filbert Street	B2-C2
Filbert Street East	C2
Fox Street	E5
Freeschool Lane	C6
Friar Lane	C5
Friday Street	B8-C8
Frog Island	B8
Gallowtree Gate	D6
Gas Street	D8
Gateway Street	B4-C4-C3
Gaul Street	A3
George Street	D8-E8
Gotham Street	F3-F4
Granby Street	D5-E5
Grange Lane	C4
Granville Road	F2-F3
Grasmere Street	B4-B3-C3-C2-C1-B1
Gravel Street	C7-D7
Great Central Street	B6-B7
Greyfriars	C5
Guildhall Lane	C6
Halford Street	D5-D6-E6
Haverlock Street	C2-C3
Haymarket	D6-D7
Hazel Street	C2
Heanor Street	B8-C8
High Cross Street	B7-B6-C6
Highfield Street	F3
High Street	C6-D6
Hinkley Road	A4
Hobart Street	F4
Horsefair Street	C5-D5
Hotel Street	C5
Humberstone Gate	D6-E6
Humberstone Road	F7
Infirmary Road	C4-C3-D3
Jarrom Street	B3-C3
Jarvis Street	B7
Kamloops Crescent	E8

Kashmir Road	F8
Kent Street	F7
King Richards Road	A5
King Street	D4
Lancaster Road	D3-E3-E2
Lee Street	D6-D7-E7
Lincoln Street	F4-F5
London Road	E5-E4-F4-F3
Madras Road	F7
Maidstone Road	F5-F6
Malabar Road	F7
Manitoba Road	E8
Mansfield Street	C7-D7
Market Place	C5-C6-D6
Market Street	D5
Marshall Street	A8
Morledge Street	E6
Montreal Road	E8-F8
Mill Hill Lane	F3
Mill Lane	B4-C4
Millstone Lane	C5
Narborough Road	A3-A4-A5
Navigation Street	D8
Nelson Street	E4
Newarke Street	C5
New Bridge Street	C5
New Park Street	A5-B5
New Road	C7
Newtown Street	D3
New Walk	D4-E4-E3-F3
Nicholas Street	E6
Noel Street	A2
Northampton Street	E5
Northgate Street	B7-B8
Norman Street	A3
Nugent Street	A7
Orchard Street	D7-D8
Ottawa Road	E7-F7
Oxford Street	C4
Paget Road	A7
Paton Street	A3
Peacock Lane	C5
Pingle Street	B7
Pocklingtons Walk	C5-D5
Prebend Street	E4-F4
Princess Road East	E3-F3
Princess Road West	D4
Queen Street	E6
Rawdykes Road	B1-C1
Regent Road	D4-D3-E3-F3-F2
Repton Street	A7-A8
Ridley Street	A4
Roman Street	A4
Rutland Street	D5-E5-E6
St George Street	E5-E6
St Georges Way	E6-F6
St John Street	D8
St Margaret's Way	B8-C8-C7
St Martins	C5
St Mathews Way	E6-E7
St Nicholas Circle	B6-B5-C5
St Peters Lane	C6
Salisbury Road	F2-F3
Samuel Stuart	F6
Sanvey Gate	B7-C7
Sawday Street	C2
Saxby Street	F4
Saxon Street	A4
Severn Street	F4
Silver Street	C6
Slater Street	B8

Soar Lane	B7
South Albion Street	E4
Southampton Street	E6
Southgates	C5
Sparkenhoe Street	F4-F5
Station Street	E5
Stuart Street	A2
Swain Street	E5-F5
Swan Street	B7
The Newarke	B4-C4
Taylor Road	E8-F8
Tewkesbury Street	A6
Thirlemere Street	B2-B3-C3
Tichbourne Street	F3-F4
Tower Street	D3
Tudor Road	A6-A7-A8
Ullswater Street	A6
Union Street	C6
University Road	E1-E2-E3-F3
Upper King Street	D3-D4
Upperton Road	A3-B3-B2
Vancouver Road	E8
Vaughan Way	C6-C7
Vaughan Street	A6
Vernon Street	A6-A7
Walnut Street	B3-B2-C2
Walton Street	A2
Warwick Street	A6
Waterloo Way	D2-D3-E3-E4
Watling Street	A6
Welford Road	D1-D2-D3-D4
Welles Street	B6
Wellington Street	D4-E4-D5
Western Boulevard	B3-B4
Western Road	A1-A2-A3-A4-B4-B5
West Street	D3-E3-E4
Wharf Street North	E7-E8
Wharf Street South	E7
Wilberforce Road	A2-A3
William Street	F6
Wimbledon Street	E6
Windermere Street	B2-B3-C3
Yeoman Street	D6
York Road	C4

Hinkley

Albert Road	B4
Alma Road	B4
Bowling Green Road	C3
Brick Kiln Street	A2
Bridge Road	B1
Brookfield Road	A1
Brookside	B1-C1
Browning Drive	A3
Brunel Road	A2-B2
Bute Close	A4
Butt Lane	C4
Canning Street	A3
Castle Street	B3-C3
Church Walk	B3
Charles Street	C2
Clarence Road	A2-B2
Clarendon Road	A3
Cleveland Road	A4
Clivesway	B2
Coley Close	B2
Council Road	B3
Coventry Lane	A2
Derby Road	B4

Druid Street	B3-B4
East Close	B1-C1
Factory Road	A4-B4
Fletcher Road	C1
Friary Close	C3
Garden Road	A4-B4
Glen Bank	C4
Granby Road	A1-A2
Granville Road	A2
Hawley Road	A1-B1
Higham Way	C1
Highfields Road	C4
Hill Street	C2-C3
Holliers Walk	B3-B4
Hollycroft	A4
Hollycroft Crescent	A4
Holt Road	C1
Hurst Road	B2-C2
John Street	C4
Lancaster Road	A2-B2
Leicester Road	C4
Linden Road	A3
Lower Bond Street	B3-B4
Mansion Lane	A3-B3
Marchant Road	A2-A3
Merevale Avenue	A1
Mill Hill Road	A3
Mount Road	B2-C2
New Buildings	B3-B4
New Street	B4
Priest Hills Road	B2-C2
Princess Road	C4
Queens Road	C2-C3
Regent Street	A2-A3-B3
Royal Court	B1
Rugby Road	A2-A1-B1
Rutland Avenue	A1
St George's Avenue	A3-A4
Shakespeare Drive	A3-A4
Southfield Road	B1-C1-C2
Spa Lane	C3-C4
Spencer Street	B4
Springfield Road	B2
Stanley Road	A4
Station Road	B1-B2
Stockwellhead	B3
The Borough	B3
The Grove	A2
The Lawns	C3
Thornfield Way	C2
Thornycroft Road	C2-C3
Trinity Lane	A2-A3-A4-B4
Trinity Vicarage Road	A3
Upper Bond Street	B4
Victoria Street	C4
West Close	B1
Westdray Drive	A4
Westfield Road	A1
Willow Bank Road	A3
Wood Street	B3-C3

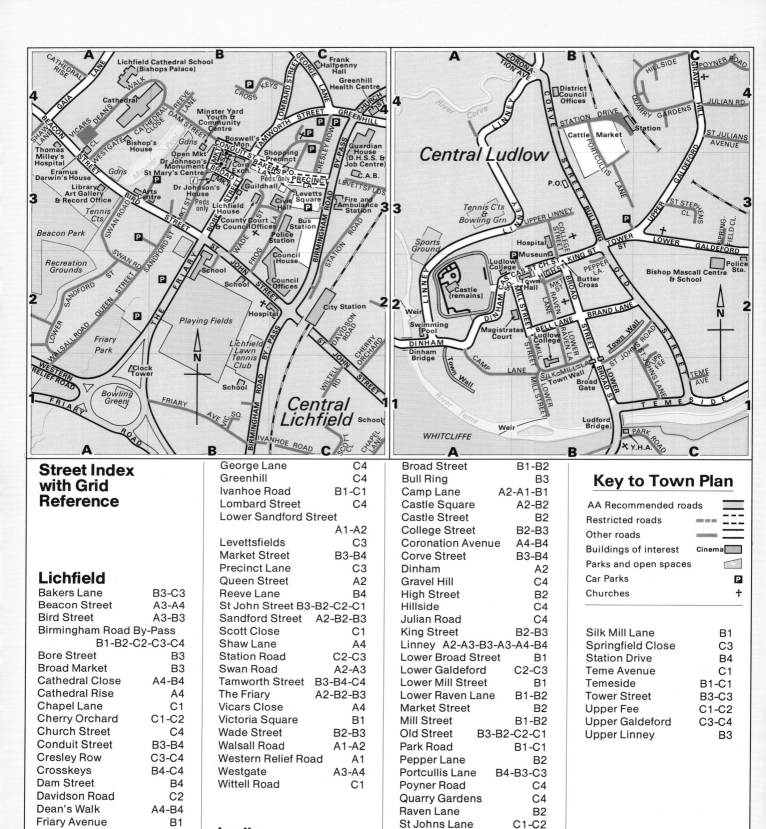

Street Index with Grid Reference

Lichfield

Bakers Lane	B3-C3
Beacon Street	A3-A4
Bird Street	A3-B3
Birmingham Road By-Pass	B1-B2-C2-C3-C4
Bore Street	B3
Broad Market	B3
Cathedral Close	A4-B4
Cathedral Rise	A4
Chapel Lane	C1
Cherry Orchard	C1-C2
Church Street	C4
Conduit Street	B3-B4
Cresley Row	C3-C4
Crosskeys	B4-C4
Dam Street	B4
Davidson Road	C2
Dean's Walk	A4-B4
Friary Avenue	B1
Friary Road	A1-B1
Frog Lane	B2-B3-C3
Gaia Lane	A4

George Lane	C4
Greenhill	C4
Ivanhoe Road	B1-C1
Lombard Street	C4
Lower Sandford Street	A1-A2
Levettsfields	C3
Market Street	B3-B4
Precinct Lane	C3
Queen Street	A2
Reeve Lane	B4
St John Street	B3-B2-C2-C1
Sandford Street	A2-B2-B3
Scott Close	C1
Shaw Lane	A4
Station Road	C2-C3
Swan Road	A2-A3
Tamworth Street	B3-B4-C4
The Friary	A2-B2-B3
Vicars Close	A4
Victoria Square	B1
Wade Street	B2-B3
Walsall Road	A1-A2
Western Relief Road	A1
Westgate	A3-A4
Wittell Road	C1

Ludlow

Bell Lane	B2
Brand Lane	B2-C2

Broad Street	B1-B2
Bull Ring	B3
Camp Lane	A2-A1-B1
Castle Square	A2-B2
Castle Street	B2
College Street	B2-B3
Coronation Avenue	A4-B4
Corve Street	B3-B4
Dinham	A2
Gravel Hill	C4
High Street	B2
Hillside	C4
Julian Road	C4
King Street	B2-B3
Linney	A2-A3-B3-A3-A4-B4
Lower Broad Street	B1
Lower Galdeford	C2-C3
Lower Mill Street	B1
Lower Raven Lane	B1-B2
Market Street	B2
Mill Street	B1-B2
Old Street	B3-B2-C2-C1
Park Road	B1-C1
Pepper Lane	B2
Portcullis Lane	B4-B3-C3
Poyner Road	C4
Quarry Gardens	C4
Raven Lane	B2
St Johns Lane	C1-C2
St Johns Road	B1-B2-C2
St Julians Avenue	C4
St Stephens Close	C3

Key to Town Plan

AA Recommended roads

Restricted roads

Other roads

Buildings of interest — Cinema

Parks and open spaces

Car Parks — P

Churches — †

Silk Mill Lane	B1
Springfield Close	C3
Station Drive	B4
Teme Avenue	C1
Temeside	B1-C1
Tower Street	B3-C3
Upper Fee	C1-C2
Upper Galdeford	C3-C4
Upper Linney	B3

Lichfield Three graceful spires known as the 'Ladies of the Vale' soar up from Lichfield's Cathedral of St Mary and St Chad. Constructed in the 13th century and combining early English and decorated Gothic styles, the Cathedral is the most outstanding feature of this attractive city, which has retained a distinctly rural appearance despite a good deal of industrial expansion.

Most distinguished son of Lichfield is Dr Samuel Johnson and his father's 18th-century house in Market Square (which served the family as a dwelling and a bookshop) has been restored and converted into a museum. Johnson's birthday (18 September) is commemorated on the nearest Saturday by a procession from the Guild Hall.

Ludlow, built on a steep hill washed on two sides by the Rivers Corve and Teme, has, since earliest times, been recognised as a strategic site, and the Normans were quick to take advantage of this. Their castle, now an impressive ruin crowning the hilltop, looks out over the Welsh Marches. The town beneath is a charming mixture of wide Georgian streets and narrow medieval alleyways where 18th-century brick and stucco rubs shoulders with half-timbered Tudor buildings with leaning walls and steeply-pitched roofs. The most famous of all the timbered buildings is the Feathers Hotel, although it has plenty of competitors, and the dignified stone Butter Cross houses the town's museum.

Lincoln

Lincoln

The striking triple-spired cathedral of Lincoln, the third largest in England, dominates the countryside for miles. Its impressive west front, decorated with many statues, is all that remains of the first cathedral the Normans built, and most of the rest dates from the 13th century. Among its treasures is one of the four extant original copies of Magna Carta.

Built on a rugged limestone plateau above the River Witham, the cobbled streets of the medieval city straggle down the sides of the hill past old houses built from the same local honey-coloured limestone as the cathedral. Modern Lincoln owes much to engineering industries, but few tentacles of change have crept into the heart of the city where the oldest inhabited house in England, Aaron's House, can be found. Other places of interest include the quaintly-named Cardinal's Hat

– thought to be named after Cardinal Wolsey who was Bishop of Lincoln for one year. Newport Arch, at the end of the picturesque street called Bailgate, is a relic from the Roman city of Lincoln – *Lindum Colonia*. It is the only Roman gateway in the country still open to traffic. Complementing the cathedral in size if not in majesty is the Norman castle. It is possible to walk along the battlements and the old prison chapel provides a grim insight into the punishment meted out in less enlightened times.

43

Lowestoft

Freshwater and sea fishing are a major attraction in this resort. Popular with families for over 100 years, it actually owes much of its prosperity to its busy port, which is the home of a major fishing fleet but is also well used today by vessels servicing the oil and gas industries.

Development has taken place within the town to improve its road system and shops, but the Maritime Museum at Sparrows Nest and Europa room collection of the Royal Naval Patrol Service Association give an insight into days gone by.

Great Yarmouth Miles of golden sand, gentle tides and the waterways of the Norfolk Broads make this a favoured holiday resort. Entertainment to suit every taste is on offer from morning till night, and children can choose from a vast selection of amenities like Pleasure Beach and Joyland. Amongst the older buildings and monuments to be seen in the town is the Nelson Column, and there are no less than eight museums, including the Maritime Museum of East Anglia. The Port (originally used by fishermen) dates at least as far back as the 16th century, and is now used by assorted vessels from Rotterdam and other European ports, and by traffic concerned with North Sea oil and gas exploration. The town's lifeboat station started in 1801, and the Royal National Lifeboat Institution base is at this point on the coast.

STREET INDEX WITH GRID REFERENCE

LOWESTOFT

Alexandra Road	D4-E4-E3
Arnold Street	E4
Avondale Road	C3-C2-D2
Battery Green Road	E3
Beach Road	E3
Beckham Road	D2-D3
Belmont Gardens	A4
Belvedere Road	E1-E2
Beresford Road	D4-D3
Bevan Street West	D2-D3-E3
Bevan Street East	E3
Bourne Road	A4
Breckland Way	A4
Broom Road	B4-C4
Burton Street	D4
Camp Road	D3
Church Road	C4-D4
Clapham Road North	D4
Clapham Road South	E3
Clemence Street	D2
Cleveland Road	E1
Clovelly Rise	A4
Commercial Road	D1-D2-E2
Crestview Drive	A4-A3
Crown Street West	D4
Denmark Road	D2-E2
Drakes Heath	B2
Eastern Way	C1-C2
El Alamein Road	A4
Elizabeth Close	A3
Esplanade	E2-E1
Essex Road	C2
Ethel Road	D3
Evans Drive	A3-B3
Evergreen Road	B3
Factory Street	D4
Ferndale Avenue	A4-B4
Field View Drive	B2
Fir Lane	A2-A3-B3
Gordon Road	E3
Granville Road	D3-D2
Grenacre Crescent	B3
Grosvenor Road	E1
Hamilton Road	E4-F4
Haven Avenue	B4
Haward Street	D3
Hervey Street	D2
Higher Drive	A2-A1
High Beech	B3
High Street	E4
Hillcrest Drive	A4-B4
Hillcrest Gardens	A4-B4
Hill Road	C3
Hollingsworth Road	B4
Horn Hill	D1-E1
June Avenue	B3
Katwijk Way	D4-D3-E3-E2
Kent Road	C2
Kirby Cane Walk	A3
Lakeland Drive	A1
Larch Road	B4
Lilac Drive	B4
London Road North	E4-E3
London Road South	E2-E1
Love Road	C3-D3-D4
Maidstone Road	D2
Malvern Rise	B4
Marham Road	C3
Marine Parade	E2-E1
Marlborough Road	A1
May Road	D3
Milton Road East	D4-E4
Mimosa Walk	B3
Minden Road	C3-D3
Monckton Avenue	A2
Monkton Crescent	A2
Mount Pleasant	E4
Newcombe Road	C3
Newsons Meadow	C2
Norfolk Street	B3
Northgate	E3
North Marina	E3
Norwich Road	C2-D2-D3
Normanston Drive	A1-A2-B2-B3-C3
Old Nelson Street	E4
Oulton Road	A3-A4-B4-C4
Parkside Drive	B2
Princes Road	C4
Princes Walk	A2-B2
Raglan Street	D4-D3-E3
Reeve Street	D4
Regent Road	E3
Riverside Road	C1-D1
Roman Road	D3
Rotterdam Road	C4-C3-C2
St John's Road	E2-E1

St Margarets Road	C4
St Peter's Street	C3-C4-D4-E4
Sandringham Road	D3-D2
Scamacre Crescent	B3-B2
Seago Street	D3
Selby Street	D2
Sharon Drive	B4
Spashett Road	A4
Stanford Street	D3-D2
Stanley Street	D3-D2
Stevens Street	C2-D2
Suffolk Road	E3
Surrey Street	E3
The Prarie	E4
Tennyson Road	E4
Thurston Road	D4
Tonning Street	D2-E2
Walberswick Way	A3
Walton Road	D3
Water Lane	E3
Waveney Roade	E2-E3
Whapload Road	E4
Wilde Street	E4-F4
Windsor Road	E1
Winnipeg Road	C4-D4
Wood's Loke East	A3
Wood's Loke West	A3
Wollaston Road	D3
Yeovil Road	C4-C3-D3
York Road	C3-C2

GREAT YARMOUTH

Acle Road	C4
Albemarle Road	E4
Albion Road	D3-E3
Alexandra Road	D3-D2
Alma Road	D1
Anson Road	B1-C1
Apsley Road	E2-E3
Audley Street	D4-E4
Blackfriars Road	D1
Bowling Green Walk	B4-C4
Breydon Road	B3
Bridge Road	B2-C2-C3
Bunns Lane	C2
Century Road	A3-B2
Cobholm Close	B3
Coronation Green	A2-B2
Coronation Road	B2
Crittens Road	B3
Crown Road	D2-E2
Dene Side	D2-D1
Devonshire Road	E1
Dorset Close	D1
East Road	D4
Elsie Road	B2
Empress Road	A2
Euston Road	E3-E4
Factory Road	D4
Ferrier Road	D4
Ferry Lane	C1
Fuller's Hill	C4
Gatacre Road	B2
George Street	C3-C4
Granville Road	A3-A2-B2
Greyfriars Way	C2
Havelock Road	D1
High Mill Road	B2
Howard Street North	C3
Howard Street South	C3-C2
Isaacs Road	B3
Jury Street	D4
King Street	D2-D1
Lancaster Road	D1-E1
Lichfield Road	B1
Manby Road	D3
Marine Parade	E1-E2-E3
Marine Parade North	E3-E4
Marsh Road	A2-B2
Middlegate	D1
Middle Market Road	D3
Mill Road	A3-B3-B2
Nelson Road Central	D1-D2-E2-D3-E3
Nelson Road North	D3-E3-D4-E4
Northgate Street	C4
North Market Road	D3
North Quay	C3-C4
Nottingham Way	C1-D1
Olive Road	B2
Paget Road	E3
Pasteur Road	B1-B2
Portland Place	C1
Princes Road	C4-D4
Priory Plain	D3-E3
Regent Road	C2-C3
Regent Street	D2-E2
Rodney Road	E2-E3
Russell Road	C3
St Francis Way	D2-E2-E1
St George's Road	C1-C2
St Marys Lane	C4-D4-D3
St Nicholas Road	D2-D1
St Peter's Place	D1-E1
St Peter's Road	D3
Sefton Lane	C1
South Market Road	B2-C2-C1
Southtown Road	C3-C2-C1-D1
South Quay	B1
Stafford Road	B3-B2-C2
Station Road	C3
Steam Mill Lane	C4-C3
Stonecutters Way	D2-D1
The Conge	D4-E4
Tolhouse Street	C4-D4
Tottenham Street	D2-E2
Town Wall Road	A3-B3
Trafalgar Road	D1-E1
Tyrell's Road	E3-E4
Victoria Road	E1
Wellesley Road	B2
Wellington Road	C3
Well Street	B2
Winifred Road	B1
Wolseley Road	C2-D2
Yarmouth Way	D2-E2-E1
York Road	

Lowestoft Area

SCALE

0   mls   2

Luton

Huge numbers of people go to Luton each year; for most the stay is very brief since it is the starting-off point for holidays on the Mediterranean and all over Europe. The airport has become Luton's best-known feature, but the town prospered for a long time before the advent of aeroplanes. Straw plaiting and straw hat making were the mainstays of its fortunes from the 19th century onwards, and even today hats are still made here. In the town's museum and art gallery, at Wardown Park, are exhibits of the hat trade, and of the pillow lace trade, another of the town's traditional industries. Also in the museum are exhibits devoted to natural history and local life, including a 'Luton Life' gallery complete with reconstructed street scene. St Mary's is the parish church. It is a huge building – one of the largest churches in England – containing much of interest. It dates principally from the 13th to 15th centuries, and has a spectacular font of Purbeck marble, along with many monuments and excellent carving in stone and wood. Just to the south of the town is Luton Hoo, a palatial mansion built to the designs of Robert Adam. It contains a notable collection of pictures and tapestries and sumptuous Faberge jewellery. The mansion is surrounded by a magnificently landscaped 1,500-acre park laid out by Capability Brown in the 18th century.

Key to Town Plan and Area Plan

Town Plan

AA Recommended roads	
Other roads	
Restricted roads	
Buildings of interest	Library
Churches	+
Car Parks	P
Parks and open spaces	
AA Service Centre	AA
One way street	→

Area Plan

A roads	
B roads	
Locations	Kensworth○
Urban area	

Street Index

Luton

Abbots Wood Road	F4
Adelaide Street	C2
Albert Road	D1-E1
Alma Street	C2-C3
Ashburnham Road	A3- 2-B2-C2
Ash Road	A4
Avondale Road	B4-B3
Beech Road	A4-B4
Belmont Road	B2-B3
Biscot Road	B4
Bolingbroke Road	A1
Bolton Road	D4
Boyle Close	D4
Brantwood Road	B2-B3
Bridge Street	D3
Brook Street	C4
Brooms Road	F3-F4
Brunswick Street	D4-E4
Burr Street	D4-D3-E4
Bury Park Road	B4
Butlin Road	A2-A3
Buxton Road	C2
Cardiff Grove	C2
Cardiff Road	C2
Cardigan Street	C3
Castle Street	D1-D2
Charles Street	E4
Chapel Street	D1-D2
Chilton Rise	C1
Church Street	D2-E2
Clifton Road	A3
Cobden Street	E4
Collingdon Street	C3
Concorde Street	E4
Corncastle Road	B1-C1
Crawley Green Road	E2-F2-F3
Crawley Road	C3-C4
Crescent Rise	E3-E4
Crescent Road	E3-F3-F2

Cromwell Road	B4-C4
Cumberland Street	D1-E1-E2
Dale Road	B2-B3
Dallow Road	A3-B3-C3
Derwent Road	F3-F4
Downs Road	B2-C2
Dudley Street	D3-D4
Duke Street	D4-E4
Dumfries Street	C2-C1-D1
Dunstable Place	C2
Dunstable Road	A4-B4-B3
Elizabeth Street	C1-D1
Farley Hill	C1
Ferndale Road	A3
Francis Street	B3-B4-C4
Frederick Street	D4
George Street	D2
George Street West	D2
Gipsy Lane	F1
Gloucester Road	E2
Gordon Street	C2-C3-D3
Granville Road	A3
Grove Road	B2-C3-C3
Guildford Street	D3
Hampton Road	A4
Hart Hill Drive	E3-F3
Hart Lane	F3-F4
Hartley Road	E3-E4
Hastings Street	C1-C2
Havelock Road	D4-E4
Hazelbury Crescent	B4
Hibbert Street	D1
Highbury Road	B4
Hightown Road	D3-D4-E4
Hilary Crescent	B1
Hillside Road	C4
Hitchin Road	E3-E4
Holly Street	D1
Hunts Close	B1
Inkerman Street	C2-C3
Ivy Road	B4
John Street	D3
Jubilee Street	E4
Kenilworth Road	B3-B4
Kimpton Road	F1
Kingsland Road	E1
King Street	D2
Langley Road	D1
Liverpool Road	C3
Lyndhurst Road	B2-B3
Malvern Road	A2-A3
Manor Road	E1-E2
Maple Road East	A4
Meyrick Avenue	A1-B1-C1
Midland Road	D3-E3
Mill Street	C3-D3
Milton Road	B1-C1
Moor Street	B3-B4-C4
Moulton Rise	E3
Napier Road	C2
Naseby Road	A2-A3
New Bedford Road	C3-C4
Newcombe Road	A2-A3-B3
Newtown Street	D1-E1
North Drift Way	A1
North Street	D4-E4
Oak Road	A4-B4
Old Bedford Road	C4-D4-D3
Osborne Road	E1-F1
Park Street	D2-E2-E1
Park Street West	D2
Pomfret Avenue	E4-F4
Poundwicks Road	E2-E3

Power Court	E2-E3
Princess Street	C2
Regent Street	C2-D2
Reginald Street	C4-D4
Ring Road	C3-C2-D2-D1-E1-E2
Rothesay Road	C2
Russel Rise	C1
Russell Street	C1
St Mary's Road	E2-E3
St Peter's Road	A2-A3
St Saviors Crescent	C1
Salisbury Road	C1-C2
Santingfield North	A1
Shaftesbury Road	A4
Shirley Road	A3
Silver Street	D2-D3
South Road	D1
Stanley Street	C1-C2
Station Road	D3-E3
Strathmore Avenue	E1
Studley Road	B4-C4
Surrey Street	E1
Tavistock Street	D1
Telford Road	C3
Tenzing Grove	B1
The Shires	C4
Tower Road	F4
Tower Way	F4
Union Street	D1
Upper George Street	C2-D2
Vernon Road	A3-B3
Vicarage Street	E2
Villa Road	C4-D4
Waldeck Road	B4
Warwick Road	A4
Wellington Street	C1-C2-D2
Wenlock Street	D4
Whipperley Ring	A1
Whipperley Way	A1
William Street	D4
Wilsden Avenue	A1-B1
Wimborne Road	A3-B3
Windmill Road	E2-F2-F1
Windsor Street	C1
Winsdon Road	C1-C2
York Street	E4

Leighton Buzzard

Albany Road	C2
Ashwell Street	B3
Atterbury Avenue	C3
Baker Street	B3
Bassett Road	A2-B2-B3
Beaudesert	B3-C3
Bedford Street	B3
Billington Road	C1
Bossington Lane	A2-A3-A4
Bridge Street	A2-B2
Brooklands Drive	A2
Broomhills Road	B4-C4
Camberton Road	A1
Church Avenue	B2
Church Road	A2
Churchill Road	C4
Church Square	B2
Church Street	B2
Clarence Road	B4-C4
Digby Street	B3

Doggett Street	B2-B3
Dudley Street	B2-C2
East Street	B3-C3
Garden Hedge	B3-B4-C4
George Street	C3
Grovebury Road	B1-C1
Grove Road	B1-B2
Harrow Road	C1
Hartwell Crescent	B2-C2
Heath Road	B3-B4
High Street	B2
Hockcliffe Road	C2-C3
Hockcliffe Street	B2-C2
King Street	B3
Lake Street	B2-B1-C1
Lammas Walk	B2-B3
Leighton Road	A2
Lime Grove	A2
Market Square	B2
Mentmore Road	A1
Miles Avenue	C3
Mill Road	B3
Nelson Road	C4
New Road	A2
North Court	B4
North Street	B2-B3
Oakley Green	C4
Old Road	A2
Pennivale Close	B3-B4
Plantation Road	B3-B4
Plumtree Lane	B3-C3
Pulford Road	B2
Queen Street	B3
Regent Street	C3
Relief Road	B2
Riverside	B4
Rothschild Road	A3
Roosevelt Avenue	C4
Ship Road	A2
South Street	C1-C2
Stanbridge Road	C1
Steppingstone Place	C2
Stoke Road	A2-A3-A4
The Martins Drive	A4
The Paddock	A3
Vandyke Road	C2-C3-C4
Vimy Road	A2
West Side	B3
West Street	A2-B2
Windsor Avenue	A3-B3
Wing Road	A1-A2
Winston Close	B4-C4
Woodman Close	C2

Dunstable

Albion Street	B3
Alfred Street	C2
Allen Close	C1
Appleby Gardens	A1-A2
Ashton Road	B4
Ashton Square	B2-B3
Beech Green	A4
Beechcroft Way	A4
Benning Avenue	A3-A4
Blows Road	C1
Borough Road	C1
Brampton Rise	A1-B1
Britain Street	B2-C2
Bull Pond Lane	B1-B2
Burr Street	A3-A2-B2

Canesworde Road	A2
Cartmel Drive	A1
Chiltern Road	A3-A4-B4
Church Street	B3-C3-C2
Clifton Road	A4-B4
Court Drive	B3-C3
Croft Green	A4
Downs Road	A2
Edward Street	B3-B4
Englands Lane	C2
Ennerdale Avenue	A2
First Avenue	A2-B2
Friars Walk	B2
Furness Avenue	B1
Garden Road	B1
George Street	B4
Grasmere Close	A1-A2
Great Northern Road	B1-C1-C2
Grove Road	C1
Half Moon Lane	C1
Hawthorn Close	B1
High Street North	B3-B4
High Street South	B3-B2-B1-C1
Hilton Avenue	A1
Howard Place	C1
Icknield Street	A1-A2
Keswick Close	A1-A2
Kingscroft Avenue	C3
Kingsway	C3
King Street	B1-C1-C2
Kirby Road	A2-A3
Kirkstone Drive	A1
Langdale Road	A1-A2
Leighton Court	A3
Loring Road	A4
Lovers Walk	B2-C2
Maidenbower Avenue	A4
Matthew Street	B3
Osborne Road	A2
Park Road	C1
Park Street	B4
Patterdale Close	A1
Penrith Avenue	A2-B2-B1
Periwinkle Lane	B1
Princes Street	A4-A3-B3
Priory Road	C2
Richard Street	C2
St Peter's Road	C2
Stavely Road	A1
Stuart Street	B4
Tarnside Close	A1
Union Street	A4-B4
Vernon Place	B3
Victoria Street	A4-B4-B3
Waterlow Road	A4-B4
Westfield Road	A4
West Parade	A3
West Street	A3-B3
Winfield Street	B4
Worthington Road	A4

47

Mansfield

Arching high over the centre of the town, Mansfield's 19th-century railway viaduct epitomises the town's involvement in industry since it developed from agricultural area to industrial centre a century ago. Crucial to the town's growth has been the productive North Nottinghamshire coalfield, but its importance as a commercial and leisure centre should not be underestimated: this is the home of one of the largest open-air markets in the country, while in contrast, the Four Seasons shopping centre offers a modern, totally enclosed and air-conditioned complex. Football League soccer can be seen at Field Mill, and the Mansfield Leisure Centre is purpose-built to seat 1,200 spectators. Places of interest include the 11th-century Parish Church of St Peter and St Paul, the Forest Stone in Sherwood Forest where swains once met to settle their debts, and Mansfield Museum and Art Gallery.

Kirkby-in-Ashfield's expansion was sparked off by the discovery of coal in Kirkby Colliery — now closed, the colliery's place is being taken by modern industrial development.

Sutton-in-Ashfield enjoys a theatre and an ice rink in the Sutton Centre, built to combine community, educational and leisure facilities for this one-time village, which grew with the textile industry from the 17th century onwards.

48

Central Kirkby-in-Ashfield

Central Sutton-in-Ashfield

Key to Town Plan and Area Plan

Town Plan
AA Recommended roads
Other roads
Restricted roads
Buildings of interest — Library
Car Parks — P
Parks and open spaces
Churches — +

Area Plan
A roads
B roads
Locations — Morton ○
Urban area

STREET INDEX WITH GRID REFERENCE

MANSFIELD

Ashfield Avenue	B3
Bancroft Lane	C1
Bath Lane	B3-C3
Bath Street	D3
Baums Lane	E3-E2-F2
Belvedere Street	C2-D2
Berryhill Road	F4
Bishop Street	F3
Blakeney Drive	E1-E2
Bridge Street	C3-C4-D4
Broxtowe Drive	D4-E4
Brunt Street	D3
Burnham Court	F3
Byron Street	B1
Cavendish Street	E4
Cedar Street	E4
Central Avenue	E3
Chaucer Street	C1
Chesterfield Road South	A1-A2-B2
Church Street	C3
Clipstone Avenue	A4-B4
Clumber Street	B2-C2-C3
Cromwell Street	E4
Crow Hill Drive	C1-D1
Dallas Street	D3
Delamere Drive	F3
Derby Street	E4
Duke Street	D2-E2
Elm Tree Street	C4-D4
Fisher Lane	E4
Forest Avenue	F3
Forest Road	F2-F3-F4
Frederick Street	F1
Garth Road	F1
Gedling Street	F2
Goldsmith Street	C1
Goodacre Street	C4
Granby Avenue	A3
Great Central Road	D3-D4-E4-E3
Grove Street	D2-E2
Harley Road	F1
Hudson Street	B1-C1

Inner Ring Road	C3-C4-D4-D3
Laurel Avenue	E4
Layton Avenue	C1
Leeming Street	C3
Lindley Street	B1
Littleworth	D3-E3-E4-F4
Lord Street	D1-D2-E2-E1
Maddon Road	A3
Meadow Avenue	E3
Midworth Street	D3
Murray Street	F2
Newgate Lane	D4
Newton Street	E3-E4
Norfolk Drive	A2-B2
Nottingham Road	D3-D2-E2-F2
Nursery Street	B3-B4
Padleyhill Road	C1
Park Avenue	A3-A4
Paulsons Drive	B2-B3
Peacock Street	C2-D2-D1
Pelham Street	C4-D4
Portland Street	D2-E2
Quaker Way	B2-C2-D2-D3
Quarry Lane	E1-E2
Queen Street	C2-D2
Radford Street	C1-D1
Ratcliffe Gate	D4
Recreation Street	C4
Regent Street	C3
Ringwood Avenue	F3
Rooth Street	D1
Rosemary Street	B1-C1
Rutland Street	F2-F3
St John Street	B1-B2
Sherringham Drive	F3
Sherwood Street	D2-E2
Stanley Road	F1-F2
Station Road	C2-D2
Station Street	D2
Stella Street	F2-F3
Stone Cross Lane	A2-A3-B3
Sutton Road	C1
Talbot Street	F2
Terrace Road	B3-B4
The Broadway	D4
The Park	A4
Thoresby Street	B1
Toothill Lane	C3
Union Street	C1-C2
Victoria Street	D1-D2
Walkden Street	C1-C2
Wallis Road	C4
Watson Avenue	B3-B4
Waverley Road	F1
Welbeck Street	B1
West Bank Avenue	A2-A3
West Bank Lea	A2-A3
West Bank Wynd	A2
Westfield Lane	B1-B2
Westgate	B2-C2
West Hill Drive	B2-B3
White Hart Street	C3-D3-D2
Windmill Lane	A4-B4
Windsor Road	F4
Wood Street	B1-B2
Woodhouse Road	A4-A3-B3

KIRKBY-IN-ASHFIELD

Abbey Road	C3
Alexandra Street	B4-C4
Alfred Street	B2

Ashwood Avenue	C4
Balfour Street	C1-C2
Beulah Road	C1
Beverley Drive	C1
Bourne Avenue	C1
Clover Street	A4-B4
Clumber Street	C2-C3-C4
Cobden Street	B2
Crocus Street	C2
Diamond Avenue	B2-C2
Ellis Street	B2-B3
Elmtree Road	A4
Erwash Street	A2
Factory Road	B2-B3
Forest Street	B2-C2
Gladstone Street	B3
Harcourt Street	A2-A3
Hazel Grove	C4
Hodgkinson Street	B2
Hoggs Lane	C2-C3
King Street	A2
Kingsley Street	B2
Kingsway	B2-B1-C1
Laurel Grove	C4
Lime Street	A2
Lindley Lane	A1-A2
Low Moor Road	B2-B3-C4
Marlborough Road	B3-C3-C4
Marshall Avenue	C1
Milton Street	B3-C3
Oak Street	C3-C4
Oxford Street	B1-C1
Pearl Avenue	C1
Pestus Street	B2
Pond Street	B3
Poplar Avenue	C4
Portland Street	B3
Precinct Road	B2-B3
Queen Street	A2
Roseberry Street	C2
Rosewood Drive	C4
St Andrews Street	C4
St John's Avenue	B1-C1-C2
St Thomas Avenue	B2-C2
Sandalwood Drive	C4
School Street	C2-C3
Scriven Road	C3
Sherwood Street	B3-C3
Spruce Grove	C4
Station Street	C2
Urban Road	A3-A2-B2
Welbeck Street	C2-C3-C4

SUTTON-IN-ASHFIELD

Aspley Road	A4
Bank Avenue	B1
Beeley Avenue	A1-A2
Bentick Street	C3
Bonser Gardens	A1-A2
Bowne Street	A4
Brierley Cottages	A2-B2-B3
Brook Street	A4-A3-B3
Carsic Lane	A4-A3-B3
Cavendish Avenue	B4
Church Avenue	A3
Church Hill	A2
Church Lane	A3
Church Street	A2-A3-B3
Coburn Street	C1
Corene Avenue	A1-B1
Coronation Street	B1-C1

Cowpasture Lane	B1-B2
Craster Street	A1-A2-B2-B1
Crown Street	B2-C2-C1
Cursham Street	C2
Davies Avenue	A4-B4
Edwin Street	B4
Firemans Row	B3
Forest Street	B3-C3
Garside Avenue	A1-A2
Grosvenor Avenue	A2
Hack Lane	A2-A3
Hardwick Lane	C1-C2
Hardwick Street	C2
Haven Close	A4
Henry Street	C1
High Pavement	B2-C2-C3
High Street	B2-B3
Jubilee Road	A4
King Street	B2
Kirkby Road	A1-A2-B2
Lammas Close	A3-B3
Lammas Road	A2-A3-B3
Langford Street	B3-B4
Langton Road	B2
Leopold Street	B1
Low Street	B3-C3
Luther Avenue	A2
Market Street	B3
Martyn Avenue	C1
Millcroft	B1
Mill Street	B2
Morven Avenue	B3
Nesbitt Street	C1
New Street	B2
Northfields Close	B4
North Street	C4
Outram Street	C3-C4
Park Street	C4
Parliament Street	C3
Penn Street	C4
Percival Crescent	A4-B4
Portland Street	C3
Priestic Road	B3-B4
Reform Street	C2
Ridge Close	A4
Silk Street	B1-B2
Spring Road	A1-A2
Station Road	C2-C3
Station Street	C2
Stevenson Crescent	A2
Stuart Street	A1-B1
The Twitchell	B1-C1
Thornton Street	C1
Titchfield Avenue	A3-A2-B2
Tudor Street	A1-B1
Union Street	C2
Welbeck Street	C3
Westbourne Road	A4
West End	A2
Willowbridge Lane	A2
Woods Hill	B2
York Street	B4

Central Milton Keynes

Central Bletchley

Key to Town Plan and Area Plan

Town Plan

AA Recommended roads	
Other roads	
Restricted roads	
Buildings of interest	Library
Parks and open spaces	
Car parks and car parking areas	P
One Way Streets	

Area Plan

A roads	
B roads	
Locations	Stanford O
Urban area	

STREET INDEX- with grid reference

Milton Keynes

Avebury Boulevard	
	A2-B2, C2-D2-E2
Bayard Avenue	F4
Boycott Avenue	C1-D1
Bradwell Common	
Boulevard	B4-C4-D4
Carlina Place	D4
Childs Way	
	B1-C1-D1-E1-F1
Cleavers Avenue	D4-E4
Clydesdale Place	F4
Coltsfoot Place	D4
Conniburrow Boulevard	
	D4-E4-F4
Cranesbill Place	E4
Elder Gate	A4-A3, B3-B2
Evans Gate	C1
Falcon Avenue	F1
Grafton Gate	B1-B2-B3
Grafton Street	B4
Gurnards Avenue	E1
Hadley Place	C4
Hampstead Gate	C4
Leys Road	A2
Mallow Gate	E4
Marlborough Gate	F2-F3
Marlborough Street	
	F1-F2-F3-F4
Midsummer Boulevard	
	B2-C2-D2-E2-F2

Milton-Keynes

The most famous of Britain's New Towns, Milton Keynes was officially opened in 1973. The new city was carefully and considerately planned to integrate with the existing towns and villages and countryside, and yet provide a self-sufficient community where industry, business and housing could develop.

Milton Keynes borough covers some 22,000 acres of North Buckinghamshire, including the towns of Bletchley, Stony Stratford and Wolverton, but the hub of the region is Central Milton Keynes. Here, one of the largest and most attractive shopping areas in Britain can be found. All the shops are under cover and are reached from tall glass-walled arcades paved with marble and lined with exotic trees and shrubs.

The variety of modern housing in Milton Keynes is another of the city's exciting attractions.

Purpose-built homes have been imaginatively planned to suit all ages, and the residential areas have generous areas of green open spaces.

Recreational facilities are also an integral part of the city's concept. Bletchley — one of three leisure centres — has a huge multi-purpose sports hall where international events are held, and an exotic free-form swimming pool. Here, beneath the tinted glass of the pyramidal building, real palm trees create a Mediterranean atmosphere.

Milton Keynes Area

SCALE: mls 0 — 2

(Map of Milton Keynes area showing towns including Towcester, Buckingham, Winslow, Stony Stratford, Wolverton, MILTON KEYNES, Bletchley, Fenny Stratford, Newport Pagnell, Olney, Bromham, Bedford, Kempston, Ampthill, Flitwick, Leighton Buzzard, Linslade, Dunstable, Luton, Hitchin, Sandy, and surrounding villages. Grid references A–F across, 1–4 vertical.)

Box denotes area covered by central map

Mitcham Place	C4
Mullen Avenue	F4
North Eighth Street	D3
North Eleventh Street	E3
North Ninth Street	D3
North Row	C3-D3-E3
North Sixth Street	C3
North Thirteenth Street	E3
North Twelfth Steet	E3
Pentewan Gate	E1
Percheron Place	F4
Plumstead Avenue	C4-D4
Portway	A4-B4-C4-D4-E4-E3-F3-F4
Ramsons Avenue	E4-F4
Saxon Gate	D1-D2-D3
Saxon Street	D1, D4
Secklow Gate	E1-E2-E3
Shackleton Place	C1
Silbury Boulevard	A3-B3, C3-D3-E3-F3
South Eighth Street	D1-D2
South Ninth Street	D1-D2
South Row	D1-E1

South Seventh Street	C1-C2
South Tenth Street	D1-D2
Speedwell Place	E4
Stonecrop Place	E4
Sutcliffe Avenue	C1-D1
Wandsworth Place	C4
Wealdstone Place	F1
Wimbledon Place	C4
Wisley Avenue	C4-D4
Witan Gate	C2-C3
Yarrow Place	F4

Bletchley

Albert Street	B2-B3
Ashfield Grove	C1
Barons Close	B3
Bedford Street	B2-B3
Bettina Grove	A1-B1

Birchfield Grove	B1-C1
Brooklands Road	B1-B2
Buckingham Road	A2
Cambridge Street	C2-C3
Cawkwell Way	B2-C2
Chestnut Crescent	C1
Clifford Avenue	B1
Dukes Drive	B3
Duncombe Street	A2-A1-B1
Eaton Avenue	C1
Findlay Way	B2-C2
Frensham Drive	B1
Hazel Grove	C1
Lennox Road	C1-C2
Leon Avenue	C1-C2
Lords Close	B3-B4
Mikern Close	B3
North Street	C3-C4
Oliver Road	B1-B2
Osborne Street	A1-B1
Oxford Street	B2-B3
Princes Way	B3-C3
Queensway	B2-C2
Regent Street	B3
St Martins Street	B3-C3

Saxon Street	A3-A2-B2-B3-B4-C4
Sherwood Drive	A2-A3-A4
Sunset Close	B1
Tavistock Street	C4
The Crescent	B4-C4
Viscount Way	B4
Water Eaton Road	A2-A1-B1-C1
Wellington Place	A1-A2
Western Road	C3
Westfield Road	B1-C1-C2
Willow Way	B1-C1
Windsor Street	B1-B2

MILTON KEYNES
Huge industrial estates and modern factories were built in Milton Keynes during the 1970s to provide employment for the people who moved to the New Town from London as a result of the capital's housing problems.

Northampton

The town's long connection with the boot and shoe trade started during the Civil War when Northampton made footwear for Cromwell's army. Now, although still internationally famous for this commodity, it is also an important light industry and distribution centre. Predictably, both the town's museums contain shoes, and include Queen Victoria's wedding shoes and Nijinsky's ballet shoes among their exhibits.

Northampton has a long and important history and its castle became a resting place for every English king from Henry I to Edward III. However, due to Charles II's destruction of the castle and the town walls, and a devastating fire in 1675, little remains of the medieval town. The vast market square – one of the largest in the country – dates from the days of the cattle drovers when Northampton was an important market centre, and many of the street names – such as Horsemarket and Mercer's Row – reflect the town's history.

Wellingborough stands in the valley of the River Nene; like Northampton, the manufacture of footwear is a well-established industry. The two churches of the town form an interesting contrast; All-Hallows retains traces of medieval workmanship and has a 17th-century house as well as a church hall, whilst St Mary's is a modern building designed by Sir Ninian Comper.

LEGEND

Town Plan

AA recommended route	
Restricted roads	
Other roads	
Buildings of interest	Library
Car parks	P
Parks and open spaces	

Area Plan

A roads	
B roads	
Locations	Winfarth ◯
Urban area	

Street Index with Grid Reference

Northampton

Abington Square	D3-E3
Abington Street	C2-D2-D3
Adams Avenue	F4
Albion Place	D1-D2
Alcombe Road	D4-E4
Alexandra Road	E2-E3
Alfred Street	F2-F3
Angel Street	C2
Artizan Avenue	F3-F4
Arundel Street	B4
Bailiff Street	C4
Barrack Road	C4
Bath Street	A3-B3
Bedford Road	D1-E1
Billing Road	E2-F2
Billington Street	F4
Black Lion Hill	A2
Bridge Street	C1-C2
Broad Street	B3-B4-C4
Byfield Road	A2
Campbell Square	C4
Campbell Street	C4
Castle Street	B3
Castillian Street	D2
Cattle Market Road	C1
Chalk Lane	B2-B3
Charles Street	C4-D4
Cheyne Walk	D1-D2
Church Lane	C3-C4
Clare Street	D4-E4
Cliftonville	E2-F2
Cliftonville Road	F1-F2
Cloutsham Street	D4-E4
College Street	C2
Commercial Street	B1-C1

Connaught Street	C4-D4
Cranstoun Street	D4
Craven Street	D4
Crispin Street	B3
Cyril Street	E2-E3
Denmark Road	E2-E3
Derngate	C2-D2-D1
Duke Street	C4-D4
Dunster Street	D3-D4-E4
Earl Street	D3-D4
Edith Street	E3
Exeter Place	E4-F4
Fetter Street	C1-C2
Free School Street	B2
Foundry Street	B1-C1
George Row	C2
Georges Street	B4-C4
Gladstone Road	A4
Gold Street	B2-C2
Grafton Street	B4-C4
Great Russell Street	D4
Greyfriars	B3-C3-D3
Grove Road	E4
Guildhall Road	C1-C2
Harding Street	B4
Hazelwood Road	D2
Henry Street	F4
Herbert Street	B3
Horsemarket	B2-B3
Horseshoe Street	B1-B2
Hunter Street	D4
Inkerman Terrace	C3
Kerr Street	C3-C4
Kettering Road	E3-E4
Kingswell	C1-C2
Lady's Lane	B3-C3-D3
Little Cross Street	B3
Lower Mounts	D3
Lower Priory Street	B4
Lower Thrift Street	F2-F3
Marefair	A2-B2
Margaret Street	D4
Market Square	C2-C3
Market Street	E4-F4
Mayor Hold	B3
Melville Street	F4
Mercers Row	C2
Newland	C3
Overstone Road	D3-D4
Palmerston Road	F3-F2
Park Street	C3
Portland Place	E3-E4
Pytchley Street	E4
Queens Road	E4
Quorn Way	B4
Regent Street	B4
Robert Street	B4
St Andrews Road	A2-A3-A4-B4
St Andrews Street	B3-B4
St Edmunds Road	D3-E3-F3
St Edmunds Street	F3
St Giles Square	C2
St Giles Street	C2-D2-D3
St James Road	A2
St James Park Road	A2-A3
St James Street	B1
St John's Street	C1
St Katherine Street	B2-C2
St Mary's Street	B2
St Michael's Road	D3-E3
St Peter's Way	A2-B2-B1-C1

Scarletwell Street	A3-B3
Sheep Street	C3-C4
Silver Street	B3-C3
Somerset Street	D4-E4
South Street	F3
Spencer Road	E4
Spencer Bridge Road	A4
Spencer Parade	D2
Spring Gardens	D2
Spring Lane	A4-B4-B3
Stockley Street	F3
Swan Street	C1-C2
The Avenue	F1
The Drapery	C2-C3
The Riding	C2-D2
Tanner Street	B1-B2
Talbot Road	E4-F4
Thenfoot Street	E2-E3
Upper Mounts	C4-C3-D3
Vernon Terrace	F2-F3
Victoria Gardens	C1
Victoria Promenade	C1-D1
Victoria Road	E2-E3
Victoria Street	C3-C4
Wellington Road	E3-F3
Wellington Street	D3
Whitworth Road	F3-F4
Woodford Street	E3-F3
Woolmonger Street	B2-C2
York Road	D3-D2

Wellingborough

Abbey Road	A1
Abbotts Way	A2
Albert Road	C3-C4
Alexandra Road	C3-C4
Alliance Terrace	B3
Alma Street	B3
Avenue Road	B4
Bedale Road	B4
Bell Court	B3-C3-C4
Broad Green	A3
Broadway	B1-C1
Brook Street East	C2
Cambridge Street	B3-C3
Cannon Street	C3-C4
Castle Lane	B2-C2
Castle Road	C1-C2
Castle Street	C2
Church Street	B3
Commercial Way	B2
Cross Road	C4
Croyland Road	A2-A1-B1
Dale Street	A2
Debdale Road	A3-A4
Doddington Road	B1-B2
Ferrestone Road	B4-C4
Finedon Road	C4
Friars Close	B1
George Street	B3-B4
Gisburne Road	B4-C4
Gold Street	A4-B4-C4
Gordon Road	C3
Grant Road	C3-C4
Great Park Street	B3-B4-C4
Hardwick Road	A3

Rushden

Adnitt Road	A2-A3
Albert Road	B3-C3
Albion Place	C1
Alfred Street	B2-B3
Allen Road	C3
Barker Close	C3
Carnegie Street	A3-B3

Harrowden Road	A3-A4
Hatton Avenue	A3-A4
Hatton Street	A4
Hatton Park Road	A4
Havelock Street	B3
Henshaw Road	A1
High Street	A3-B3-B2
Hill Street	A2
Irthlingborough Road	C1-C2
Jackson Lane	A3
Kings Street	B3
Knights Court	A4-B4
Knox Road	C2-C3
Lister Road	B4-C4
London Road	B1-B2-C2-C1
Market Street	B2-B3
Midland Road	B2-C2
Mill Road	C3
Monks Way	A1-B1-B2
Newcomen Road	C3
North Street	B3-B4
Northampton Road	A2-B2
Orient Road	C2-C3
Outlaw Lane	A3-B3
Palk Road	C2
Park Road	B3-B4
Priory Road	A1
Queen Street	B3
Ranelagh Road	C2-C3
Redwell Road	A4
Regent Street	B3-C3
Rock Street	A3
St Barnabas Street	A2
St John Street	A3-B3
Salem Court	A3-B3
Sharman Road	A2
Sheep Street	B2
Short Lane	A3
Silver Street	B2
Spring Gardens	A4
Stanley Road	C3-C4
Strode Road	C2-C3
Swanspool Parade	B1
The Avenue	B3-B4
The Drive	B1
The Pyghtle	B4
Thomas Street	C3
Tithebarn Road	B2
Upper Havelock Street	B3
Victoria Road	C2-C3
West Street	A2
Westfield Road	A3
West Villa Road	A2
Whytewell Road	A4-B4
Winstanley Road	C3
Wood Street	A2
York Road	C3

Church Street	B2
College Street	B3
Crabb Street	B1-C1
Cromwell Road	C2-C3
Dayton Street	A3
Dell Place	C2
Duck Street	B2-B3
East Grove	B4
Essex Road	C1
Fitzwilliam Street	A3-B3
Fletcher Road	A4
Glassbrook Road	A3
Griffith Street	B1-B2-C2
Grove Road	C1-C2
Hall Avenue	A1
Harborough Road	C1
High Street	B2-B3-B4
High Street South	B2-B1-C1
Higham Road	B4
John Street	B2
Kings Road	C3
Kings Place	C3
Little Street	C1
Manton Road	C2
Midland Road	A3-A4
Moor Road	A3-A4
Newton Road	C2
North Street	B4
Park Avenue	A2
Park Place	B2-C2
Park Road	C2-C1
Pemberton Street	A3-A4
Portland Road	B3-C3
Pratt Road	C3
Purvis Road	A2-A3
Queen Street	B3-C3
Quorn Road	A4
Rectory Road	B2-B3-B4
Roberts Street	C2
Robinson Road	C2-C3
St Margarets Avenue	A1-A2
St Mary's Avenue	A1-A2-B2
Shirley Road	B4-C4
Skinners Hill	B2
South Close	C1
South Park	B1
Southfields	C1
Station Approach	B4
Station Road	A3-B3-B4
Upper Queen Street	C3-C4
Victoria Road	B3-B4-C4
Washbrook Road	A4-B4
Wellingborough Road	A3-A2-B2
Wentworth Road	A3
West Street	B3
Wilson Road	A2-A3
Woodland Road	A4
Wymington Road	B1-C1
York Road	C1-C2

53

Norwich

Fortunately the heart has not been ripped out of Norwich to make way for some bland precinct, so its ancient character has been preserved. Narrow alleys run between the streets – sometimes opening out into quiet courtyards, sometimes into thoroughfares packed with people, sometimes into lanes which seem quite deserted. It is a unique place, with something of interest on every corner.

The cathedral was founded in 1096 by the city's first bishop, Herbert de Losinga. Among its most notable features are the nave, with its huge pillars, the bishop's throne (a Saxon survival unique in Europe) and the cloisters with their matchless collection of roof bosses. Across the city is the great stone keep of the castle, set on a mound and dominating all around it. It dates from Norman times, but was refaced in 1834. The keep now forms part of Norwich Castle Museum –

an extensive and fascinating collection. Other museums are Bridewell Museum – collections relating to local crafts and industries within a 14th-century building – and Strangers' Hall, a genuinely 'old world' house, rambling and full of surprises, both in its tumble of rooms and in the things which they contain. Especially picturesque parts of the city are Elm Hill – a street of ancient houses; Tombland – with two gateways into the Cathedral Close; and Pull's Ferry – a watergate by the river.

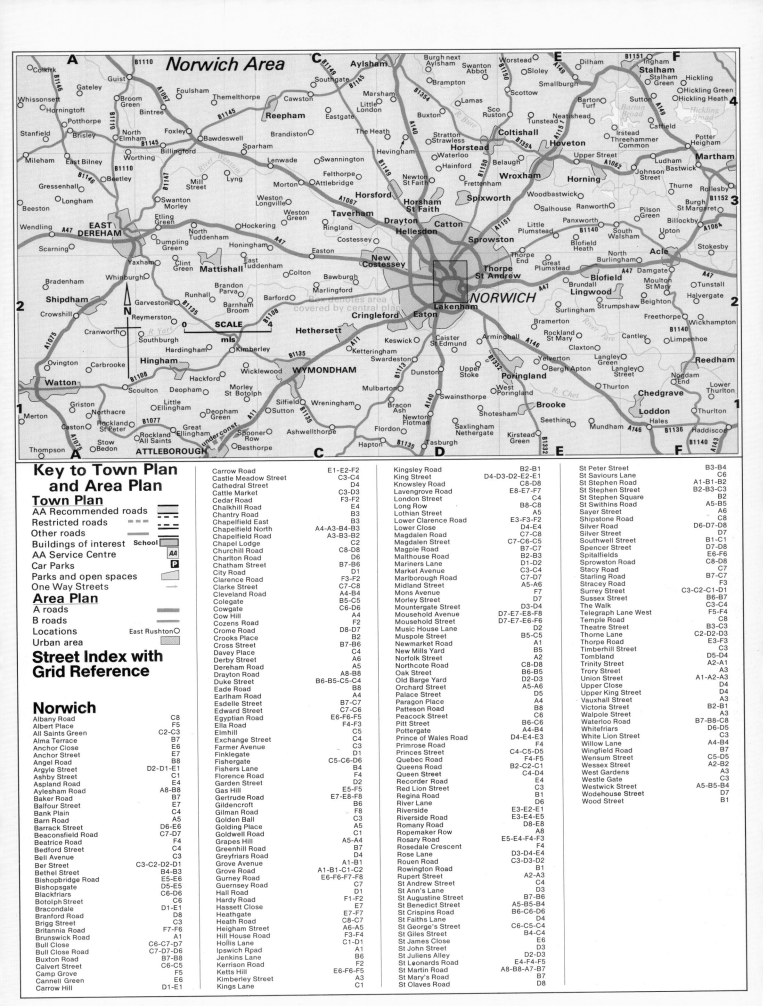

Key to Town Plan and Area Plan

Town Plan

AA Recommended roads
Restricted roads
Other roads
Buildings of interest — School
AA Service Centre — AA
Car Parks — P
Parks and open spaces
One Way Streets

Area Plan

A roads
B roads
Locations — East Rushton
Urban area

Street Index with Grid Reference

Norwich

Albany Road	C8
Albert Place	F5
All Saints Green	C2-C3
Alma Terrace	B7
Anchor Close	E6
Anchor Street	E7
Angel Road	B8
Argyle Street	D2-D1-E1
Ashby Street	C1
Aspland Road	E4
Aylesham Road	A8-B8
Baker Road	B7
Balfour Street	E7
Bank Plain	C4
Barn Road	A5
Barrack Street	D6-E6
Beaconsfield Road	C7-D7
Beatrice Road	F4
Bedford Street	C4
Bell Avenue	C3
Ber Street	C3-C2-D2-D1
Bethel Street	B4-B3
Bishopbridge Road	E5-E6
Bishopsgate	D5-E5
Blackfriars	C6-D6
Botolph Street	C6
Bracondale	D1-E1
Branford Road	D8
Brigg Street	C3
Britannia Road	F7-F6
Brunswick Road	A1
Bull Close	C6-C7-D7
Bull Close Road	C7-D7-D6
Buxton Road	B7-B8
Calvert Street	C6-C5
Camp Grove	F5
Cannell Green	E6
Carrow Hill	D1-E1

Carrow Road	E1-E2-F2
Castle Meadow Street	C3-C4
Cathedral Street	D4
Cattle Market	C3-D3
Cedar Road	F3-F2
Chalkhill Road	E4
Chantry Road	B3
Chapelfield East	B3
Chapelfield North	A4-A3-B4-B3
Chapelfield Road	A3-B3-B2
Chapel Lodge	C2
Churchill Road	C8-D8
Charlton Road	D6
Chatham Street	B7-B6
City Road	D1
Clarence Road	F3-F2
Clarke Street	C7-C8
Cleveland Road	A4-B4
Colegate	B5-C5
Cowgate	C6-D6
Cow Hill	A4
Cozens Road	F2
Crome Road	D8-D7
Crooks Place	B2
Cross Street	B7-B6
Davey Place	C4
Derby Street	A6
Dereham Road	A5
Drayton Road	A8-B8
Duke Street	B6-B5-C5-C4
Eade Road	B8
Earlham Road	A4
Esdelle Street	B7-C7
Edward Street	C7-C6
Egyptian Road	E6-F6-F5
Ella Road	F4-F3
Elmhill	C5
Exchange Street	C4
Farmer Avenue	C3
Finkelgate	C5-C6-D6
Fishergate	B4
Fishers Lane	B4
Florence Road	F4
Garden Street	D2
Gas Hill	E5-F5
Gertrude Road	E7-E8-F8
Gildencroft	B6
Gilman Road	F8
Golden Ball	C3
Golding Place	A5
Goldwell Road	C1
Grapes Hill	A5-A4
Greenhill Road	B7
Greyfriars Road	D4
Grove Avenue	A1-B1
Grove Road	A1-B1-C1-C2
Gurney Road	E6-F6-F7-F8
Guernsey Road	C7
Hall Road	D1
Hardy Road	F1-F2
Hassett Close	E7
Heathgate	E7-F7
Heath Road	C8-C7
Heigham Street	A6-A5
Hill House Road	F3-F4
Hollis Lane	C1-D1
Ipswich Road	A1
Jenkins Lane	B6
Kerrison Road	F2
Ketts Hill	E6-F6-F5
Kimberley Street	A3
Kings Lane	C1

Kingsley Road	B2-B1
King Street	D4-D3-D2-E2-E1
Knowsley Road	C8-D8
Lavengrove Road	E8-E7-F7
London Street	C4
Long Row	B8-C8
Lothian Street	A5
Lower Clarence Road	E3-F3-F2
Lower Close	D4-E4
Magdalen Road	C7-C8
Magdalen Street	C7-C6-C5
Magpie Road	B7-C7
Malthouse Road	B2-B3
Mariners Lane	D1-D2
Market Avenue	C3-C4
Marlborough Road	A5-A6
Midland Street	F7
Mons Avenue	D7
Morley Street	D3-D4
Mountergate Street	D7-E7-E8-F8
Mousehold Avenue	D7-E7-E6-F6
Mousehold Street	D7-E7-E6-F6
Music House Lane	D2
Muspole Street	B5-C5
Newmarket Road	A1
New Mills Yard	B5
Norfolk Street	A2
Northcote Road	C8-D8
Oak Street	B6-B5
Old Barge Yard	D2-D3
Orchard Street	A5-A6
Palace Street	D5
Paragon Place	A4
Patteson Road	B8
Peacock Street	C6
Pitt Street	B6-C6
Pottergate	A4-B4
Prince of Wales Road	D4-E4-E3
Primrose Road	F4
Princes Street	C4-C5-D5
Quebec Road	F4-F5
Queens Road	B2-C2-C1
Queen Street	C4-D4
Recorder Road	E4
Red Lion Street	C3
Regina Road	B1
River Lane	D6
Riverside	E3-E2-E1
Riverside Road	E3-E4-E5
Romany Road	D8-E8
Ropemaker Row	A8
Rosary Road	E5-E4-F4-F3
Rosedale Crescent	F4
Rose Lane	D3-D4-E4
Rouen Road	C3-D3-D2
Rowington Road	B1
Rupert Street	A2-A3
St Andrew Street	C4
St Ann's Lane	D3
St Augustine Street	B7-B6
St Benedict Street	A5-B5-B4
St Crispins Road	B6-C6-D6
St Faiths Lane	D4
St George's Street	C6-C5-C4
St Giles Street	B4-C4
St James Close	E6
St John Street	D3
St Juliens Alley	D2-D3
St Leonards Road	E4-F4-F5
St Martin Road	A8-B8-A7-B7
St Mary's Road	B7
St Olaves Road	D8

St Peter Street	B3-B4
St Saviours Lane	C6
St Stephen Road	A1-B1-B2
St Stephen Street	B2-B3-C3
St Stephen Square	B2
St Swithins Road	A5-B5
Sayer Street	A6
Shipstone Road	C8
Silver Road	D6-D7-D8
Silver Street	D7
Southwell Street	B1-C1
Spencer Street	D7-D8
Spitalfields	E6-F6
Sprowston Road	C8-D8
Stacy Road	C7
Starling Road	B7-C7
Stracey Road	F3
Surrey Street	C3-C2-C1-D1
Sussex Street	B6-B7
The Walk	C3-C4
Telegraph Lane West	F5-F4
Temple Road	C8
Theatre Street	B3-C3
Thorne Lane	C2-D2-D3
Thorpe Road	E3-F3
Timberhill Street	C3
Tombland	D5-D4
Trinity Street	A2-A1
Trory Street	A3
Union Street	A1-A2-A3
Upper Close	D4
Upper King Street	D4
Vauxhall Street	A3
Victoria Street	B2-B1
Walpole Street	A3
Waterloo Road	B7-B8-C8
Whitefriars	D6-D5
White Lion Street	C3
Willow Lane	A4-B4
Wingfield Road	B7
Wensum Street	C5-D5
Wessex Street	A2-B2
West Gardens	A3
Westle Gate	C3
Westwick Street	A5-B5-B4
Wodehouse Street	D7
Wood Street	B1

Nottingham

Hosiery and lace were the foundations upon which Nottingham's prosperity was built. The stockings came first – a knitting machine for these had been invented by a Nottinghamshire man as early as 1589 – but a machine called a 'tickler', which enabled simple patterns to be created in the stocking fabric, prompted the development of machine-made lace. The earliest fabric was produced in 1768, and an example from not much later than that is kept in the city's Castlegate Costume and Textile Museum. In fact, the entire history of lacemaking is beautifully explained in this converted row of Georgian terraces. The Industrial Museum at Wollaton Park has many other machines and exhibits tracing the development of the knitting industry, as well as displays on the other industries which have brought wealth to the city – tobacco, pharmaceuticals, engineering and printing. At Wollaton Hall is a natural history museum, while nearer the centre are the Canal Museum and the Brewhouse Yard Museum, a marvellous collection which shows items from daily life in the city up to the present day. Nottingham is not complete without mention of Robin Hood, the partly mythical figure whose statue is in the castle grounds. Although the castle itself has Norman foundations, the present structure is largely Victorian. It is now a museum.

Nottingham Area

Key to Town Plan and Area Plan

Town Plan

AA Recommended roads	
Restricted roads	
Other roads	
Buildings of interest	Theatre ☐
Car Parks	P
Parks and open spaces	
Churches	†
One Way Streets	→

Area Plan

A roads	
B roads	
Locations	Bagthorpe○
Urban area	

Street Index with Grid Reference

Nottingham

Abbotsford Drive	D7-D7-E7-E8
Addison Street	B7-B8
Albert Street	C4
Alfred Street	D7
Alfred Street North	C8, D7-D8
Alfreton Road	A5-A6
Angel Road	B5-B4-C4
Annesley Grove	B7-C7
Arboretum Street	A7-B7-B8
Arthur Street	A7
Ashford Street	D7-D8
Aster Road	E8-F8
Baker Street	B8
Balmoral Road	A8-B8-B7
Barker Gate	E4
Bath Gate	E5-F5
Beck Street	E5
Bellar Gate	E4
Belward Street	E4
Bluebell Hill Road	F6-F7
Bluecoat Street	C6
Bond Street	F4
Bridlesmith Gate	D4
Broad Street	D4-D5
Broadway	D4-E4
Brook Street	E5
Burns Street	A7
Burton Street	C5

Canal Street	C3-D3-E3
Canning Circus	A5
Carlton Road	F5
Carlton Street	D4
Carrington Street	D2-D3
Castle Boulevard	A2-B2-B3-C3
Castle Gate	C3-C4
Castle Market Road	E1-F1
Castle Meadow Road	B2-C2
Castle Road	C3
Cavendish Crescent South	A3
Cavendish Road East	A3-A4
Chaucer Street	B5-B6
Church Road	E8
Clarendon Street	B5-B6
Cliff Road	D3-E3
Clumber Crescent South	A3
Clumber Road East	A3-A4
Clumber Street	D4-D5
College Street	A5-B5-B4
Collin Street	C3-D3
Colville Street	B8
County Road	F1
Cranbrook Street	E4-E5
Cranmer Street	C8-D8
Crocus Street	D1-E1
Cromwell Street	A5-B6-C6
Curzon Street	D6-E6
Dakeyne Street	F5
Dane Close	D7-E7
Derby Road	A5-B5
Dryden Street	C6-C7
Fieness Crescent	A2
Fishergate	E3-E4
Fishpond Drive	A2-B2
Fletcher Gate	D4
Forest Road East	A8-B8-C8
Forest Road West	A7-A8
Friar Lane	C3-C4
Gedling Grove	A7
George Street	D4-D5
Glasshouse Street	D5-D6
Gill Street	B6-C6
Goldsmith Street	B6-C6-C5
Goose Gate	D4-E4
Great Freeman Street	D6
Hamilton Drive	B2-B3
Hampden Street	B6-C6
Handel Street	E5-F5
Haywood Street	F4-F5
High Pavement	D4-D3-E3
Hockley	E4
Holles Crescent	A3
Hollowstone	E3-E4
Hope Drive	B2-B3
Hound's Gate	C4

Howard Street	D5-D6
Hungerhill Road	E8-F8
Huntingdon Drive	A4-A3-B3
Huntingdon Drive	C8-C7-D7-D6-D5-E5
Huskisson Street	C6
Iremonger Road	E1
Kent Street	D5
King Edward Street	D5-E5
King Street	C4-C5
Lamartine Street	E6-F6
Lenton Road	A2-A3-B3
Lewis Close	E7
Lincoln Street	D5
Lister Gate	C3-C4
London Road	E1-E2-E3
Long Row	C4-D4
Lower Parliament Street	D5-E5-E4-E3
Low Pavement	C4-D4
Maid Marion Way	B4-C4-C3
Mansfield Street	C6-C7-C8
Manvers Street	F3-F4
Mapperley Road	C8
Market Street	C4-C5
Meadow Lane	F1
Meadows Road	B1-C1-D1-E1
Middle Hill	D3-D4
Milton Street	C6-C5-D5
Moorgate Street	A5
Mount Hooton Road	A8
Mount Street	B4-C4
Newark Crescent	F3
Newark Street	F3-F4
Newcastle Circus	A3
Newcastle Drive	A4-A5
Newstead Grove	B7-C7
North Street	F4-F5
North Sherwood Street	C6-C7-C8
Oliver Street	A6
Park Drive	A3-B3
Park Ravine	A2-A3
Park Row	B4
Park Terrace	A4-B4
Park Valley	A4-B4-B3
Peel Street	B6-B7-C7
Pelham Street	D4
Pennyfoot Street	E4-F4
Peveril Drive	B3
Pilcher Gate	D4
Plantagenet Street	E6
Plumptree Street	E4
Popham Street	D3
Poplar Street	E3-F3
Portland Road	A5-A6-A7
Queen's Drive	B1-C1, D1-D2
Queen's Road	D2-E2
Queen Street	C4-C5

Releigh Street	A6-A7
Regent Street	B4
Rick Street	D5
Robin Hood Street	E5-F5-F6
Russell Street	A6
St Ann's Hill Road	C8
St Ann's Valley	F7-F8
St Ann's Well Road	E5-E6-E7-F7-F8
St James Street	C4
St James Terrace	B4-B3-C3
St Mark's Street	D6
St Peters Gate	C4-D4
Shakespeare Street	B6-C6
Shelton Street	D7-D6-E6
Sherriffs Way	D1
Sneinton Road	F4
South Parade	C4-D4
South Road	A3
South Sherwood Street	C5-C6
Southwell Road	E4-F4
Station Street	D2-E2
Stony Street	D4-E4
Talbot Street	A5-B5-C5
Tattershall Drive	A4-A3-B3
Tennis Drive	A4-A5-A4
The Robewalk	A5-A4-B4
Trent Street	D2-D3
Tulip Avenue	A8
Tunnel Road	A4
Union Road	D6
Upper College Street	A5-B5
Upper Eldon Street	F4
Upper Parliament Street	B5-C5-D5
Victoria Street	D4
Villa Road	C8
Walker Street	F4-F5
Walter Street	A6-A7
Warser Gate	D4
Waterway Street	C1-D1
Watkin Street	D6-D7
Waverely Street	A8-A7-B7-B6
Wellington Street	D6-D7
West Street	F4-F5
Wheeler Gate	C4
Wilford Road	C1-C2
Wilford Street	C2-C3
Wollaton Street	A5-B5-C5
Woodborough Road	C6-C7-D7-D8
Woolpack Lane	D4-E4
York Street	C6-D6

Oxford

From Carfax (at the centre of the city) round to Magdalen Bridge stretches High Street, one of England's best and most interesting thoroughfares. Shops rub shoulders with churches and colleges, alleyways lead to ancient inns and to a large covered market, and little streets lead to views of some of the finest architecture to be seen anywhere. Catte Street, beside St Mary's Church (whose lovely tower gives a panoramic view of Oxford), opens out into Radcliffe Square, dominated by the Radcliffe Camera, a great round structure built in 1749. Close by is the Bodleian Library, one of the finest collections of books and manuscripts in the world. All around are ancient college buildings. Close to Magdalen Bridge is Magdalen College, founded in 1448 and certainly not to be missed. Across the High Street are the Botanical Gardens, founded in 1621 and the oldest such foundation in England. Footpaths lead through Christ Church Meadow to Christ Church College and the cathedral. Tom Tower is the college's most notable feature; the cathedral is actually its chapel and is the smallest cathedral in England. Among much else not to be missed in Oxford is the Ashmolean Museum, whose vast collections of precious and beautiful objects from all over the world repay many hours of study; perhaps the loveliest treasure is the 9th-century Alfred Jewel.

Central Oxford

LEGEND

Town Plan

- AA Recommended roads
- Other roads
- Restricted roads
- Buildings of interest — College
- Churches — †
- Car Parks — P
- Parks and open spaces
- One way streets

Area Plan

- A roads
- B roads
- Locations — Cumnor ○
- Urban area

OXFORD

Abbey Road	A2-A3
Adelaide Street	B5
Albert Street	A4-B4
Albion Place	C1
Alma Place	F1-F2
Arthur Street	A2
Banbury Road	C4-C5
Bath Street	F2
Bear Lane	D2
Beaumont Street	B3-C3
Becket Street	A2
Blackhall Road	C4
Blue Boar Street	C2-D2
Boulter Street	F2
Brewer Street	C2
Broad Street	C3-D3
Broad Walk	C1-D1-E1
Canal Street	A4
Cardigan Street	A4
Castle Street	B1-B2-C2
Circus Street	F1
Cornmarket Street	C2-C3
Cowley Place	F1-F2
Cowley Road	F1-F2
Cranham Street	A4-A5-B5
Cripley Road	A2-A3
Dale Close	B1
Dale Road	F1-F2
Edgeway Road	F5
Ferry Road	F5
Friars Wharf	C1
George Street	B3-C3
Gloucester Street	C3
Great Clarendon Street	A4-B4
Hart Street	A4
High Street	C2-D2-E2-F2
Hollybush Row	A4
Holywell Street	D3-E3
Hythe Bridge Street	B2-B3
Iffley Road	F1-F2
Jericho Street	A4-B4-B5
Jeune Street	F1-F2
Jowett Walk	D3-E3
Juxon Street	A4-A5
Keble Road	C4
Kingston Road	A5
Leckford Road	A5-B5
Little Clarendon Street	B4-C4
Longwall Street	E2-E3
Magdalen Street	C3
Manor Road	E4
Mansfield Road	D3-D4
Market Street	C2-C3
Merton Street	D2-E2
Mill Street	A2
Museum Road	C4
Nelson Street	A4-B4
New Inn Hall Street	C2
New Road	B2-C2
Norham Gardens	C5
Observatory Street	B5
Old Grey Friars Street	C1-C2
Oriel Street	D2
Osney Lane	A2-B2
Osney Mead	A1
Osney Street	A2
Oxpens Road	B1-B2
Paradise Square	B2
Paradise Street	B2
Park End Street	A2-B2
Parks Road	C5-C4-D4-D3
Pembroke Street	C2
Plantation Road	A5-B5
Purcell Road	F5
Pusey Street	B3-C3-C4
Queen Street	C2
Richmond Road	B4
Rewley Road	A3
Rose Lane	E2
St Aldates	C1-C2
St Bernards Road	A5-B5
St Clements	F2
St Cross Road	E3-E4
St Ebbe's Street	C1-C2
St Giles Street	C3-C4
St John Street	B4-B3-C3
St Michael's Street	C3
St Thomas Street	B2
Saville Road	D3
Ship Street	C3
Southmoor Road	A5
South Parks Road	D4
Speedwell Street	C1
Stockmore Street	F1
Temple Street	F1
Thames Street	B1-C1
Tidmarsh Lane	B2
Trinity Street	B1
Turl Street	D2-D3
Victor Street	A4
Walton Crescent	B4
Walton Street	A5-B5-B4-B3
Walton Well Road	A5
Wellington Square	B4-C4
Woodstock Road	B5-C5-C4
Worcester Place	B3-B4
Worcester Street	B2-B3

WITNEY

Ashcombe Close	A2-A3-B3
Beech Road	A3
Bridge Street	C3-C4
Burford Road	A4-B4
Burwell Drive	A1
Colwell Drive	A1
Corn Street	A2-B2
Dark Lane	B3-B4
Davenport Road	A3-A4
Dene Rise	A3
Duckington Lane	A1-A2
Farm Hill Lane	B1-C1
Gloucester Place	B3-C3

Gogges	C2
High Street	B2-B3-C3
Highworth Place	B1-B2
Holford Close	A1
Holford Road	A1
Holloway Road	B2-B3
Leys Villas	B1
Lowell Place	A2
Mill Street	B4-B3-C3
Moor Avenue	A4-A3-B3
Moorland Road	A2-A3
Newland	C3-C4
New Yatt Road	C4
Orchard Way	A2
Park Road	A3
Puck Lane	B3-B4
Queen Emmas Dyke	A2
Saxon Way	A1-A2-B2
South Lawn	A1
Spring Close	B1
Springfield Oval	A4
Springfield Park	A4
Station Lane	B1-C1-B1
The Crofts	B1-B2
Tower Hill	A2
Weavers Close	B1
Welch Way	A2-A3-B3
West End	B4-C4
Woodstock Road	C4

ABINGDON

Abbey Close	B2-C2
Abbott Road	B3-C3
Barton Lane	C3-C2-C3
Bath Street	B2-B3
Berry Croft	A4
Borough Walk	B4
Bostock Road	A4
Bowyer Road	B3-B4-C4
Boxhill Road	B3-C3
Boxhill Walk	B3
Bridge Street	B2-C2-C1
Brookside	B4
Caldecott Gardens	A1
Caldecott Road	A1-B1
Clifton Drive	B3
Conduit Road	A2-B2
Darrel Way	B4
Drayton Road	A1
East St Helens Street	B1-B2

Evelin Road	A4
Faringdon Road	A3-B3
Fieldside	A4
Fitzharrys Road	B3
Geoffrey Barbour Road	B3-C3-C4
Harcourt Way	B4
Harding Road	A3
High Street	B2
Lammas Close	B4-C4
Larkhill Place	A4
Larkhill Road	A3-A4
Lenthall Road	B3-B4
Longmead	A4
Meadowside	A1-B1
New Street	C2-C3
Norman Avenue	C4
Northcourt Lane	C4
Northcourt Road	B4-C4
Nuneham Square	B3
Ock Street	A1-A2-B2
Oxford Road	C3-C4
Park Crescent	A2-A3
Park Road	A2-B2
Radley Road	C3
St Amand Drive	A1-B1
St Helens Wharf	B1
St Johns Road	C3
St Marys Green	B4
St Nicholas	B4
Springfield Drive	A4-A3-A4
Spring Road	A1-A2-A3
Stanford Drive	A4
Station Road	B2-C2
Stert Street	B2
Stratton Way	B2
Swinburne Road	C3-C4
Tatham Road	C4
The Causeway	C1
The Motte	B2-B3
Thesiger Road	B3-C3
Thornhill Walk	A4
Tower Drive	A1
Victoria Road	A2
Vineyard	B2-C2-C3
West St Helens Street	B1-B2
Wildmoor Gate	A4
Wilsham Road	B1
Withington Court	B2-B3
Wootton Road	A4-B4-B3

Central Southend-on-Sea

Key to Town Plan and Area Plan

Town Plan
A A Recommended roads
Other roads
Restricted roads
Buildings of interest   Pavilion ▢
Car Parks   P
Parks and open spaces
Churches   ✝
One Way Streets   →

Area Plan
A roads
B roads
Locations   Parkston ○
Urban area

Street Index with Grid Reference

Southend-on-Sea

Albany Avenue	A5
Albert Road	E2
Alexandra Road	B2-C2
Alexandra Street	C2-D2
Ambleside Drive	E3-E4
Ashburnham Road	B3-C3-C2
Avenue Road	A3-A2-B2
Avenue Terrace	A2
Balmoral Road	A4
Baltic Avenue	D2-D3
Baxter Avenue	B5-B4-C4

Beresford Road	F1
Bircham Road	C6
Boscombe Road	D4-E4-F4
Boston Avenue	A5-B5-B4
Bournemouth Park Road	
	E4-E5-E6
Branksome Road	E5-F5
Brighten Road	A3-A4
Browning Avenue	D6
Burdett Avenue	A3
Burnaby Road	F1
Byron Avenue	D6-E6
Cambridge Road	A2-B2-C2
Canewdon Road	A2
Capel Terrace	C2
Carnarvon Road	B5-C5-C6
Central Avenue	D5-E5-E6-F6
Chancellor Road	D2
Chase Road	F3-F4

Chelmsford Avenue	A5-B5
Cheltenham Road	F2-F3
Chichester Road	D2-D3
Christchurch Road	F4-F5
Church Road	D1-D2
Clarence Road	C2
Clarence Street	C2-D2
Cliff Avenue	A4
Clifftown Parade	B1-C1
Clifftown Road	C2
Clifton Terrace	C1
Colchester Road	A6-B6-B5
Coleman Street	D4
Cromer Road	E2-E3
Crowborough Road	B6-C6
Devereux Road	C1-C2
Dryden Avenue	D6
Eastern Esplanade	F1
Elmer Approach	C3

Southend

The longest pleasure pier in the world and brilliant illuminations along the seafront in autumn are just two of the attractions of this thriving, immensely popular seaside resort, which offers the visitor every facet of the traditional holiday. Dance halls, theatres, amusement arcades and funfairs fill the Marine Parade area, with Peter Pan's Playground next to the pier and the

Kursall Amusement Park at the eastern end of the seafront both attracting crowds of visitors. The Pier itself offers entertainments (not least a wax museum housed in the replica of Sir Francis Drake's *Golden Hind* which lies alongside) and its 1¼ mile length is usually liberally dotted with fishermen. The most popular beaches are at Westcliffe and Thorpe Bay, while Leigh-on-Sea, linked to Southend by a lengthy promenade, makes a peaceful contrast to the main seafront area.

Places of interest include the village of Prittlewell, on the northern edge of town, with its 12th-century Priory and 13th-century church, 13th- to 14th-century Southchurch Hall (a timber-framed manor house with period furniture and beautiful grounds) and the Central Museum, which traces the history of south-east Essex back to the Romans. Good shopping and sports facilities, pleasant parks, professional cricket and football, and greyhound racing are other features of the town.

Box denotes area covered by central plan

Southend-on-Sea Area

Elmer Avenue	C3	Park Terrace	A3-B3	Tudor Road	A5-A6
Ely Road	E6	Pier Hill	D1	Tunbridge Road	B5-B6
Essex Street	D4	Pleasant Road	E1-E2	Tyler's Avenue	D2-D3
Ferndale Road	F6	Portland Avenue	D2	Tyrell Drive	D4-D3-E3
Gainsborough Drive	A6	Prince's Street	B2-B3	Vale Avenue	C6-D6
Gayton Road	C6	Prittlewell Square	C1-C2	Victoria Avenue	B6-B5-C5-C4
Gordon Place	C3	Quebec Avenue	D3	Warrior Square North	D3
Gordon Road	B3-C3	Queen Way		Warrior Square South	D3
Grainger Road	C5		B3-B4-C4-D4-D3-D2-E2	Wesley Road	E2
Great Eastern Avenue	C5	Queens Road	B3-C3	West Street	A5-A6-B6
Grove Road	D1-D2	Rayleigh Avenue	A5	Westbury Road	F6
Guildford Road	C4-D4-D5	Redstock Road	C6-D6	Westcliff Avenue	A1-A2
Hamlet Road	B2-C2	Rochford Avenue	A5	Westcliff Parade	A1-B1
Harcourt Avenue	A5-B5	Royal Mews	C1-D1-D2	Western Esplanade	
Hartington Place	E1-E2	Royal Terrace	C1-D1		A1-B1-C1-D1
Hartington Road	E1-E2	St Anns Road	C5-D5	Weston Road	C2-D2
Hastings Road	E2-E3	St Helens Road	A3	Whitegate Road	D3
Herbert Grove	D1-D2	St Johns Road	A3	Wilson Road	B1-B2
Heygate Avenue	D2	St Leonards Road	E2	Wimborne Road	D5-E5-F5
High Street	D1-D2	St Lukes Road	E6	Windermere Road	E3-F3-F4
Hillcrest Road	E3	St Vincents Road	A2-B2	Woodgrange Drive	F2
Honiton Road	F2-F3	Salisbury Avenue	A4-A5-A6	York Road	D2-E2-F2-F3
Kenway	C6	Scratton Road	B2-C2		
Kursaal Way	F1-F2	Seaway	E1		
Kilworth Avenue	E3	Selwyn Road	F6		
Lancaster Gardens	E3-E4	Shakespeare Drive	A6		
Leamington Road	F2-F3	South Avenue	D5-E5-F5-F6		
London Road	A4-A3-B3-C3	Southchurch Avenue			
Lucy Road	D1-E1		E4-E3-F3-F2-F1		
Luker Road	C3	Southchurch Road			
Lyme Road	F5		C3-C4-D4-E4-F4		
Maldon Road	C5-D5	Stadium Road	D5-D6		
Marine Avenue	A1-A2	Stanfield Road	C5-C6		
Marine Parade	D1-E1-F1	Stanley Road	E2		
Milton Road	A2-A3	Stornoway Road	F5		
Milton Street	C4-C5	Stromness Place	F4		
Napier Avenue	C3	Stromness Road	F4-F5		
Nelson Mews	C2	Summercourt Road	A3-A4		
Nelson Street	C2	Sutton Road	D4-D5-D6		
North Avenue	D6-E6-F6	Swanage Road	D5-E5		
North Road	A3-A4-A5-A6	Sweyne Avenue	A5-B5		
Oban Road	F4-F5	Sycamore Grove	D6		
Old Southend Road	E2	The Grove	E6-F6-F5		
Park Crescent	A2-A3-B3-B2	Tickfield Avenue	B6		
Park Lane	F2-F3	Toledo Road	E2-E3		
Park Road	B2-B3	Trinity Avenue	A1-A2		
Park Street	B2-B3	Trinity Road	F5		

Stevenage

This is one of the New Towns, designed shortly after World War II to provide a pleasant integration of housing, industrial estates and shopping and entertainment facilities, with an attractively landscaped park. A number of older buildings from the original town can still be seen in and around the High Street, including Alleyn's Grammar School, dating from the 16th century, and the Yorkshire Grey, an old coaching inn. The Stevenage Museum, in the undercroft of St George's Church, has an interesting collection of archaeological and historic items.

Hitchin stands on the quaintly named River Hiz, and despite a great deal of redevelopment has retained much of its medieval street plan together with a number of picturesque, half-timbered buildings. The Corn Exchange is a fine example of Italianate architecture, and the parish church offers a delightful mixture of styles, from a 12th-century tower to 17th-century wall paintings.

Letchworth The first Garden City was developed around the village of Letchworth early in the present century, and today the town is a pleasant mixture of unobtrusive industrial estates and attractive, tree-lined avenues. Places of interest include the Museum and Art Gallery and the First Garden City Museum. Norton Common, in the north, provides 63 acres of unspoilt grass and woodland.

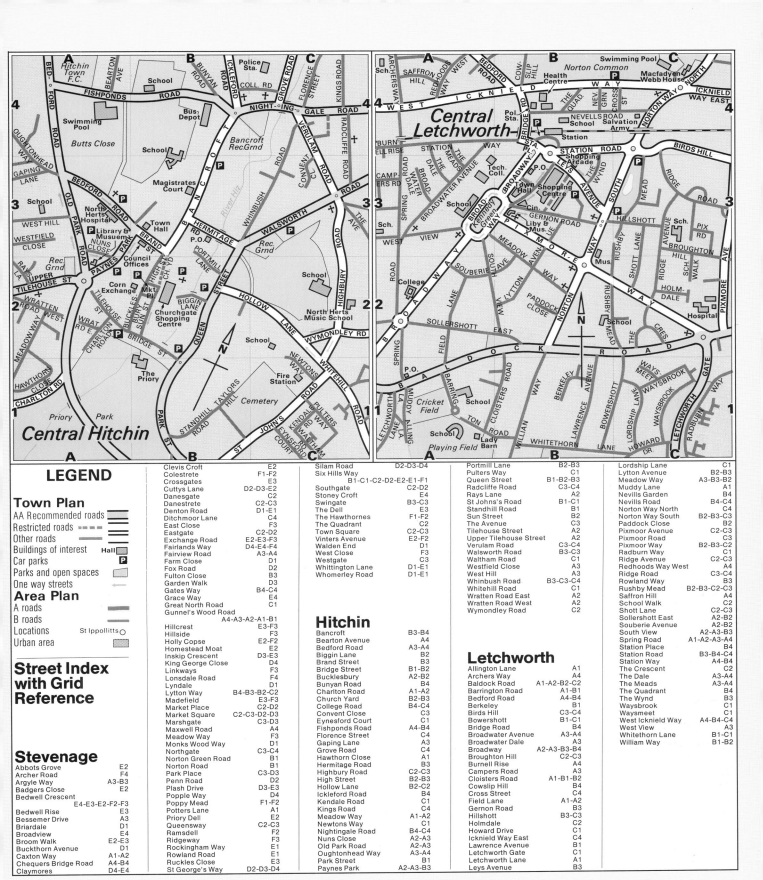

Central Hitchin

Priory Park

Central Letchworth

LEGEND

Town Plan
AA Recommended roads
Restricted roads
Other roads
Buildings of interest   Hall ▪
Car parks   P
Parks and open spaces
One way streets   ←

Area Plan
A roads
B roads
Locations   St Ippollitts ○
Urban area

Street Index with Grid Reference

Stevenage

Abbots Grove	E2
Archer Road	F4
Argyle Way	A3-B3
Badgers Close	E2
Bedwell Crescent	E4-E3-E2-F2-F3
Bedwell Rise	E3
Bessemer Drive	A3
Briardale	D1
Broadview	E4
Broom Walk	E2-E3
Buckthorn Avenue	D1
Caxton Way	A1-A2
Chequers Bridge Road	A4-B4
Claymores	D4-E4

Clevis Croft	E2
Colestrete	F1-F2
Crossgates	E3
Cuttys Lane	D2-D3-E2
Danesgate	C2
Danestrete	C2-C3
Denton Road	D1-E1
Ditchmoor Lane	C4
East Close	F3
Eastgate	C2-D2
Exchange Road	E2-E3-F3
Fairlands Way	D4-E4-F4
Fairview Road	A3-A4
Farm Close	D1
Fox Road	D2
Fulton Close	B3
Garden Walk	D3
Gates Way	B4-C4
Grace Way	E4
Great North Road	C1
Gunnel's Wood Road	A4-A3-A2-A1-B1
Hillcrest	E3-F3
Hillside	F3
Holly Copse	E2-F2
Homestead Moat	E2
Inskip Crescent	D3-E3
King George Close	D4
Linkways	F3
Lonsdale Road	F4
Lyndale	D1
Lytton Way	B4-B3-B2-C2
Madefield	E3-F3
Market Place	C2-D2
Market Square	C2-C3-D2-D3
Marshgate	C3-D3
Maxwell Road	A4
Meadow Way	F3
Monks Wood Way	D1
Northgate	C3-C4
Norton Green Road	B1
Norton Road	B1
Park Place	C3-D3
Penn Road	D2
Plash Drive	D3-E3
Popple Way	D4
Poppy Mead	F1-F2
Potters Lane	A1
Priory Dell	E2
Queensway	C2-C3
Ramsdell	F1
Ridgeway	F3
Rockingham Way	E1
Rowland Road	E1
Ruckles Close	E3
St George's Way	D2-D3-D4

Silam Road	D2-D3-D4
Six Hills Way	B1-C1-C2-D2-E2-E1-F1
Southgate	C2-D2
Stoney Croft	E4
Swingate	B3-C3
The Dell	E3
The Hawthornes	F1-F2
The Quadrant	C2
Town Square	C2-C3
Vinters Avenue	E2-F2
Walden End	D1
West Close	F3
Westgate	C3
Whittington Lane	D1-E1
Whomerley Road	D1-E1

Hitchin

Bancroft	B3-B4
Bearton Avenue	A4
Bedford Road	A3-A4
Biggin Lane	B2
Brand Street	B3
Bridge Street	B1-B2
Bucklesbury	A2-B2
Bunyan Road	B4
Charlton Road	A1-A2
Church Yard	B2-B3
College Road	B4-C4
Convent Close	C3
Eynesford Court	C1
Fishponds Road	A4-B4
Florence Street	C4
Gaping Lane	A3
Grove Road	C4
Hawthorn Close	A1
Hermitage Road	B3
Highbury Road	C2-C3
High Street	B2-B3
Hollow Lane	B2-C2
Ickleford Road	B4
Kendale Road	C1
Kings Road	C4
Meadow Way	A1-A2
Newtons Way	C1
Nightingale Road	B4-C4
Nuns Close	A2-A3
Old Park Road	A2-A3
Oughtonhead Way	A3-A4
Park Street	B1
Paynes Park	A2-A3-B3

Portmill Lane	B2-B3
Pulters Way	C1
Queen Street	B1-B2-B3
Radcliffe Road	C3-C4
Rays Lane	A2
St Johns's Road	B1-C1
Standhill Road	B1
Sun Street	B2
The Avenue	C3
Tilehouse Street	A2
Upper Tilehouse Street	A2
Verulam Road	C3-C4
Walsworth Road	B3-C3
Waltham Road	C1
Westfield Close	A3
West Hill	A3
Whinbush Road	B3-C3-C4
Whitehill Road	C1
Wratten Road East	A2
Wratten Road West	A2
Wymondley Road	C2

Letchworth

Allington Lane	A1
Archers Way	A4
Baldock Road	A1-A2-B2-C2
Barrington Road	A1-B1
Bedford Road	A4-B4
Berkeley	B1
Birds Hill	C3-C4
Bowershott	B1-C1
Bridge Road	B4
Broadwater Avenue	A3-A4
Broadwater Dale	A3
Broadway	A2-A3-B3-B4
Broughton Hill	C2-C3
Burnell Rise	A4
Campers Road	A3
Cloisters Road	A1-B1-B2
Cowslip Hill	B4
Cross Street	C4
Field Lane	A1-A2
Gernon Road	B3
Hillshott	B3-C3
Holmdale	C2
Howard Drive	C1
Icknield Way East	C4
Lawrence Avenue	B1
Letchworth Gate	C1
Letchworth Lane	A1
Leys Avenue	B3

Lordship Lane	C1
Lytton Avenue	B2-B3
Meadow Way	A3-B3-B2
Muddy Lane	A1
Nevills Garden	B4
Nevills Road	B4-C4
Norton Way North	A4
Norton Way South	B2-B3-C3
Paddock Close	B2
Pixmoor Avenue	C2-C3
Pixmoor Road	C3
Pixmoor Way	B2-B3-C2
Radburn Way	C1
Ridge Avenue	C2-C3
Redhoods Way West	A4
Ridge Road	C3-C4
Rowland Way	B3
Rushby Mead	B2-B3-C2-C3
Saffron Hill	A4
School Walk	C2
Shott Lane	C2-C3
Sollershott East	A2-B2
Souberie Avenue	A2-B2
South View	A2-A3-B3
Spring Road	A1-A2-A3-A4
Station Place	B4
Station Road	B3-B4-C4
Station Way	A4-B4
The Crescent	C2
The Dale	A3-A4
The Meads	A3-A4
The Quadrant	B4
The Wynd	B3
Waysbrook	C1
Waysmeet	C1
West Icknield Way	A4-B4-C4
West View	A3
Whitethorn Lane	B1-C1
William Way	B1-B2

STEVENAGE
East of the town centre, St George's Way provides a dramatic modern townscape, including the slender 90ft campanile of St George's Church — second largest Anglican church built in Britain since World War II.

Stoke-on-Trent

Wedgwood, Spode and Royal Doulton are among the names that spring to mind with the mention of Stoke-on-Trent. Renowned for many years as the capital of the pottery industry, the town has numerous museums dealing with the industry's history as well as with leading figures involved in it, and tours of pottery factories can be arranged. On the sporting side, Stoke City, the local football team, which plays in the Canon League, boasts Sir Stanley Matthews amongst its former players.

Hanley is the birthplace of Arnold Bennet, who immortalised the Potteries in his stories about the 'Five Towns'. Born here too was Spitfire designer Reginald Mitchell, and the town has a museum devoted to his life and work. Another great attraction of Hanley for many is the fine woodland expanse of 90-acre Central Forest Park.

Leek was once renowned for silk and dye, but now attracts visitors to its antique shops. Amongst its interesting older buildings, Brindley Mill and Museum specialises in the work of 18th-century canal builder James Brindley.

Newcastle-under-Lyme boasts a fine old Guildhall and several inns dating from the 17th and 18th centuries. Keele University, to the south-west, has contributed to the town's cultural activities in recent years.

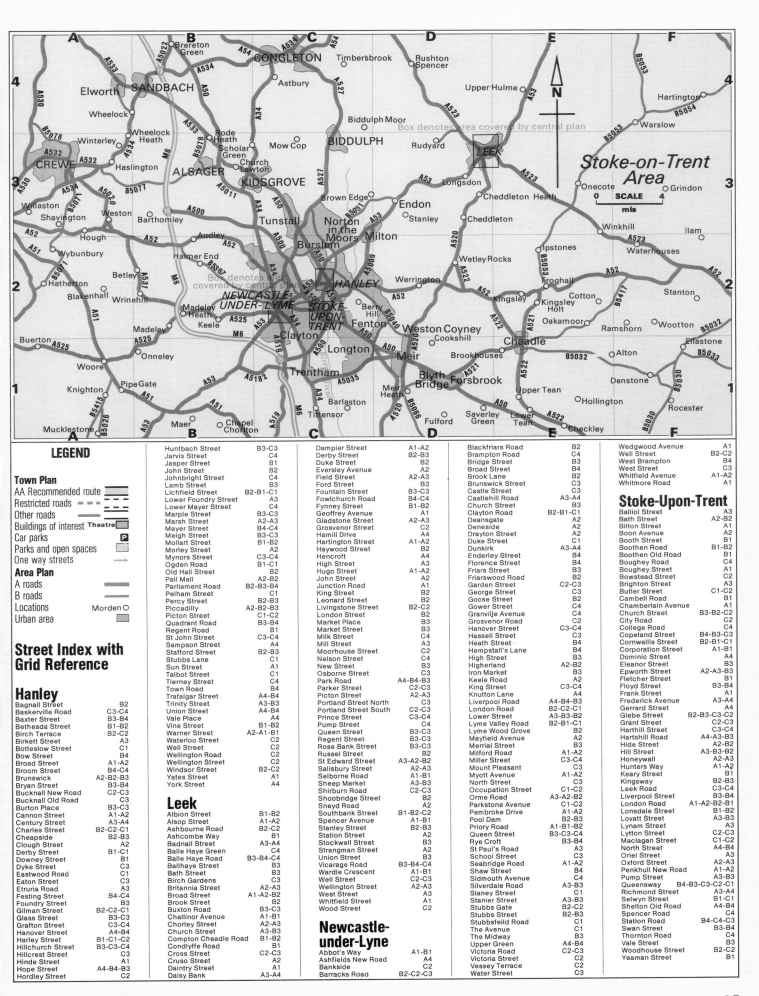

LEGEND

Town Plan
- AA Recommended route
- Restricted roads
- Other roads
- Buildings of interest — Theatre
- Car parks — P
- Parks and open spaces
- One way streets

Area Plan
- A roads
- B roads
- Locations — Morden O
- Urban area

Street Index with Grid Reference

Hanley

Street	Grid
Bagnall Street	B2
Baskerville Road	C3-C4
Baxter Street	B3-B4
Bethesda Street	B1-B2
Birch Terrace	B2-C2
Birkett Street	A3
Botteslow Street	C1
Bow Street	B4
Broad Street	A1-A2
Broom Street	B4-C4
Brunswick	A2-B2-B3
Bryan Street	B3-B4
Bucknall New Road	C2-C3
Bucknall Old Road	C3
Burton Place	B3-C3
Cannon Street	A1-A2
Century Street	A3-A4
Charles Street	B2-C2-C1
Cheapside	B2-B3
Clough Street	A2
Derby Street	B1-C1
Downey Street	B1
Dyke Street	C3
Eastwood Road	C1
Eaton Street	C3
Etruria Road	A3
Festing Street	B4-C4
Foundry Street	B3
Gilman Street	B2-C2-C1
Glass Street	B3-C3
Grafton Street	C3-C4
Hanover Street	A4-B4
Harley Street	B1-C1-C2
Hillchurch Street	B3-C3-C4
Hillcrest Street	C3
Hinde Street	A1
Hope Street	A4-B4-B3
Hordley Street	C2
Huntbach Street	B3-C3
Jarvis Street	C4
Jasper Street	B1
John Street	B2
Johnbright Street	C4
Lamb Street	B3
Lichfield Street	B2-B1-C1
Lower Foundry Street	A3
Lower Mayer Street	C4
Marple Street	B3-C3
Marsh Street	A2-A3
Mayer Street	B4-C4
Meigh Street	B3-C3
Mollart Street	B1-B2
Morley Street	A2
Mynors Street	C3-C4
Ogden Road	B1-C1
Old Hall Street	B2
Pall Mall	A2-B2
Parliament Road	B2-B3-B4
Pelham Street	C1
Percy Street	B2-B3
Piccadilly	A2-B2-B3
Picton Street	C1-C2
Quadrant Road	B3-B4
Regent Road	B1
St John Street	C3-C4
Sampson Street	A4
Stafford Street	B2-B3
Stubbs Lane	C1
Sun Street	A1
Talbot Street	C1
Tierney Street	C4
Town Road	B4
Trafalgar Street	A4-B4
Trinity Street	A3-B3
Union Street	A4-B4
Vale Place	A4
Vine Street	B1-B2
Warner Street	A2-A1-B1
Waterloo Street	C2
Well Street	C2
Wellington Road	C2
Wellington Street	C2
Windsor Street	B2-C2
Yates Street	A1
York Street	A4

Leek

Street	Grid
Albion Street	B1-B2
Alsop Street	A1-A2
Ashbourne Road	B2-C2
Ashcombe Way	B1
Badnall Street	A3-A4
Balle Haye Green	A3
Balle Haye Road	B3-B4-C4
Ballhaye Street	B3
Bath Street	B3
Birch Gardens	C3
Britannia Street	A2-A3
Broad Street	A1-A2-B2
Brook Street	B2
Buxton Road	B3-C3
Challinor Avenue	A1-B1
Chorley Street	A2-A3
Church Street	B1-B2
Compton Cheadle Road	B1-B2
Condlyffe Road	B1
Cross Street	C2-C3
Cruso Street	A2
Daintry Street	A1
Daisy Bank	A3-A4
Dampier Street	A1-A2
Derby Street	B2-B3
Duke Street	B2
Eversley Avenue	A2
Field Street	A2-A3
Ford Street	B3
Fountain Street	B3-C3
Fowlchurch Road	B4-C4
Fynney Street	B1-B2
Geoffrey Avenue	A1
Gladstone Street	A2-A3
Grosvenor Street	C2
Hamill Drive	A4
Hartington Street	A1-A2
Haywood Street	B2
Hencroft	A4
High Street	A3
Hugo Street	A1-A2
John Street	A2
Junction Road	A1
King Street	B2
Leonard Street	B2
Livingstone Street	B2-C2
London Street	B2
Market Place	B3
Market Street	B3
Milk Street	C4
Mill Street	A3
Moorhouse Street	C2
Nelson Street	C4
New Street	B3
Osborne Street	C3
Park Road	A4-B4-B3
Parker Street	C2-C3
Picton Street	A2-A3
Portland Street North	C3
Portland Street South	C2-C3
Prince Street	C3-C4
Pump Street	C4
Queen Street	B3-C3
Regent Street	B3-C3
Rose Bank Street	B3-C3
Russel Street	B2
St Edward Street	A3-A2-B2
Salisbury Street	A2-A3
Selborne Road	A1-B1
Sheep Market	A3-B3
Shirburn Road	C2-C3
Shoobridge Street	B2
Sneyd Road	A2
Southbank Street	B1-B2-C2
Spencer Avenue	A1-B1
Stanley Street	B2-B3
Station Street	A2
Stockwell Street	B3
Strangman Street	A2
Union Street	B3
Vicarage Road	B3-B4-C4
Wardle Crescent	A1-B1
Well Street	C2-C3
Wellington Street	A2-A3
West Street	A3
Whitfield Street	A1
Wood Street	C2

Newcastle-under-Lyne

Street	Grid
Abbot's Way	A1-B1
Ashfields New Road	A4
Bankside	C2
Barracks Road	B2-C2-C3
Blackfriars Road	B2
Brampton Road	C4
Bridge Street	B3
Broad Street	B4
Brook Lane	B2
Brunswick Street	C3
Castle Street	C3
Castlehill Road	A3-A4
Church Street	B3
Clayton Road	B2-B1-C1
Deansgate	A2
Deneside	A2
Drayton Street	A2
Duke Street	C1
Dunkirk	A3-A4
Enderley Street	B4
Florence Street	B4
Friars Street	B3
Friarswood Road	B2
Garden Street	C2-C3
George Street	C3
Goose Street	B2
Gower Street	C4
Granville Avenue	C4
Grosvenor Road	C2
Hanover Street	C3-C4
Hassell Street	B2
Heath Street	B4
Hempstall's Lane	B4
High Street	B3
Higherland	A2-B2
Iron Market	B3
Keele Road	A2
King Street	C3-C4
Knutton Lane	A4
Liverpool Road	A4-B4-B3
London Road	B2-C2-C1
Lower Street	A3-B3-B2
Lyme Valley Road	B2-B1-C1
Lyme Grove	B2
Mayfield Avenue	A2
Merrial Street	B3
Milford Road	A1-A2
Miller Street	C3-C4
Mount Pleasant	C3
Myott Avenue	A1-A2
North Street	C3
Occupation Street	C1-C2
Orme Road	A3-A2-B2
Parkstone Avenue	C1-C2
Pembroke Drive	A1-A2
Pool Dam	B2-B3
Priory Road	A1-B1-B2
Queen Street	B3-C3-C4
Rye Croft	B3-B4
St Paul's Road	A3
School Street	C3
Seabridge Road	A1-A2
Shaw Street	B4
Sidmouth Avenue	C4
Silverdale Road	A3-B3
Slaney Street	C1
Stanier Street	A3-B3
Stubbs Gate	B2-C2
Stubbs Street	B2-B3
Stubbsfield Road	C1
The Avenue	B3
The Midway	B3
Upper Green	A4-B4
Victoria Road	C2-C3
Victoria Street	C2
Vessey Terrace	C2
Water Street	C3

Stoke-Upon-Trent

Street	Grid
Wedgwood Avenue	A1
Well Street	B2-C2
West Brampton	B4
West Street	C3
Whitfield Avenue	A1-A2
Whitmore Road	A1
Balliol Street	A3
Bath Street	A2-B2
Bilton Street	A1
Boon Avenue	C3
Booth Street	B1
Boothen Road	B1-B2
Boothen Old Road	C4
Boughey Road	C4
Boughey Street	A1
Bowstead Street	C2
Brighton Street	A3
Butler Street	C1-C2
Cambell Road	B1
Chamberlain Avenue	A1
Church Street	B3-B2-C2
City Road	C2
College Road	C3
Copeland Street	B4-B3-C3
Cornwallis Street	B2-B1-C1
Corporation Street	A1-B1
Dominic Street	A4
Eleanor Street	B3
Epworth Street	A2-A3-B3
Fletcher Street	B1
Floyd Street	B3-B4
Frank Street	A1
Frederick Avenue	A3-A4
Gerrard Street	A4
Glebe Street	B2-B3-C3-C2
Grant Street	C2-C3
Harthill Street	C3-C4
Hartshill Road	A4-A3-B3
Hide Street	A2-B2
Hill Street	A3-B3-B2
Honeywall	A2-A3
Hunters Way	A1-A2
Keary Street	B1
Kingsway	B2-B3
Leek Road	C3-C4
Liverpool Street	B3-B4
London Road	A1-A2-B2-B1
Lonsdale Street	B1-B2
Lovatt Street	A3-B3
Lynam Street	A3
Lytton Street	C2-C3
Maclagan Street	C1-C2
North Street	A4-B4
Oriel Street	A3
Oxford Street	A2-A3
Penkhull New Road	A1-A2
Pump Street	A3-B3
Queensway	B4-B3-C3-C2-C1
Richmond Street	A3-A4
Selwyn Street	B1-C1
Shelton Old Road	A4-B4
Spencer Road	C4
Station Road	B4-C4-C3
Swan Street	B3-B4
Thornton Road	C4
Vale Street	B3
Woodhouse Street	B2-C2
Yeaman Street	B1

Map labels (Sutton Coldfield area): BLACKROOT ROAD, BEACONS FIELD RD, HALLOUGHTON ROAD, BARKER ROAD, WYVERN ROAD, EATON CT, MULROY ROAD, TUDOR HILL, ROCKINGHAM RD, RICHMOND ROAD, Sutton Park, LICHFIELD, LITTLE SUTTON LANE, Golf Course, Sports Gnd, School, BOSWELL ROAD, ALLESLEY CLO, ANCHORAGE ROAD, Fire Station, Police Station, Bishop Vesey's Grammer School, College of Further Education, Playing Fields, WEST RISE, SOUTH DRIVE, EAST RISE, PAGES CLOSE, JERRARD DRIVE, Cemy, TAMWORTH ROAD, HONEYBOURNE ROAD, MOOR MEADOW RD, BIRCH CROFT RD, Good Hope Hospital, School, RECTORY ROAD, Town Hall, Station, Peds only, UPR CLIFTON RD, CLIFTON ROAD, Wyndley Leisure Centre, Wyndley Pool, Wyndley Swimming Baths, GARRARD GDNS, Grace Church & Shop Centre, MANOR ROAD, SOMERVILLE ROAD, DIGBY ROAD, BRAEMAR RD, Cinema, Health Centre, DUKE ST, WHILE RD, Playing Fields, School, Sutton Town F.C., School, BIRMINGHAM ROAD, MANEY HILL, ELMS ROAD, MAPLE ROAD, DOUGLAS ROAD, SHIPTON ROAD, MOSS DRIVE, ROWAN ROAD, PILKINGTON AVENUE, ST BERNARDS ROAD, CONCHAR ROAD, Ebrook Adult Training Centre, Ambulance Station, EAST VIEW ROAD, School, Tennis and Squash Club, JOCKEY ROAD, MAYFIELD ROAD, GOLDIESLIE ROAD, WILKINSON CLO, HIGHBRIDGE ROAD, P.O., Rectory Park, REDDICAP TRADING EST., REDDICAP HILL, LISURES DRIVE, Plants Brook, Sutton Coldfield

Jerome Road	C2-C3
Jockey Road	A1-A2
Lichfield Road	A5-B5-B4
Little Sutton Lane	B5
Lisures Drive	C2-C3
Lower Queen Street	B3
Maney Hill Road	A2-B2-B1-C1
Manor Hill	A3
Manor Road	A3-B3
Maple Road	B2
Mayfield Road	A1
Midland Drive	B3-B4
Mill Street	B3-B4
Moor Meadow Road	C5
Moss Drive	B1-B2
Mulroy Road	A5-B5
Pages Close	B4
Park Road	A3-A4
Pilkington Avenue	A2-B2-B1-C1
Queen Street	B3
Rectory Road	B3-B4-C4
Reddicap Hill	C3
Reddicap Trading Estate	C3
Richmond Road	A4
Riland Road	C3-C4
Rockingham Road	A5-A4-B4
Rowan Road	B1-B2-C2
Royal Road	B3-C3
St Bernards Road	B1
Shipton Road	B1-B2
Somerville Road	A1-A2-A3
South Drive	B4
South Parade	B3
The Parade	A3
Tamworth Road	B5-C5
The Driffold	A2-A3
Tudor Hill	A4-A5
Tudor Road	A4
Upper Clifton Road	A4-B4
Upper Holland Road	B2-B3
Victoria Road	B3
West Rise	B4-C4
While Road	A2-B2
Wilkinson Close	A1
Wyndley Lane	A3
Wyvern Road	A5-B5

Shrewsbury

Abbey Foregate	F2-F3
Albert Street	E5-F5
Alma Street	C5
Ashton Road	A1-B1
Barker Street	C3-C4
Beacall's Lane	E5
Beeches Lane	D2
Bellstone	C3
Belmont Bank	C2-D2
Betton Street	F1
Breidden View	A5
Bridge Street	C4
Butchers Row	D3
Canonbury	B1
Castle Foregate	E5
Castlegates	D4-D5
Castle Street	D4
Chester Street	D5
Claremont Bank	B3-B4-C4
Claremont Hill	B3-C3
Claremont Street	C3
Coleham Head	E2-F2
College Hill	C3-C2-D2
Copthorne Road	A5-B5
Coton Crescent	B5
Crescent Lane	C1-C2
Cross Hill	C2-C3
Dogpole	D2-D3
English Bridge	E2-F2
Fish Street	D3
Frankwell	B5
Greyfriars	E1
Grope Lane	D3
High Street	C3-D3-D2
Hills Lane	C4
Holywell Street	F2-F3
Howard Street	E5
Kingsland Bridge	B1-B2-C2
Kingsland Bridge Approach Road	B1
Lessar Avenue	A5
Londen Coleham	D1-E1-F1
Longner Street	C5
Mardol	C3-C4
Market Street	C3
Meadow Place	D5
Milk Street	D2
Moreton Crescent	E1-F1
Mount Street	C5
Muirvance	B2-C2
Nestles Lane	B5-C5
New Street	A4-A5-B5
Old Coleham	F1
Park Avenue	A4
Pengwern Road	A4
Pride Hill	C3-D3-D4
Princess Street	C3-D3-D2
Priory Street	B4
Quarry Place	B2
Raven Meadows	C4-D4-D5
Roushill	C4

Roushill Street	C3-C4
St Austins Friars	B4
St Austins Street	B4-C4
St Chads Terrace	B2-B3
St John's Hill	B2-C2-C3
St Julian's Friars	D2-E2
St Mary's Place	D3-D4
St Mary's Street	D3
Severn Street	F5
Shoplatch	C3
Smithfield Road	C4-D4-D5
Swan Hill	C2-C3
Swan Hill Court	C2
The Dana	E5
The Mount	B5
The Square	C3-D3
Town Walls	C2-D2
Victoria Avenue	C4-B4-A4-A3-A2-B2-B1-C1-D1-D2
Victoria Street	E5-F5
Water Lane	D4-E4
Water Street	F5
Welsh Bridge	B5-C5-C4
Wyle Cop	D2

Solihull

Albany Gardens	F2
Alderbrook Road	A1-A2-B2
Alderpark Road	A1
Arley Road	B2
Ashleigh Road	B3-C3
Beaminster Road	A2-B2-B3
Beauchamp Road	C3-C4
Beaumont Grove	A3-A4
Beechnut Lane	F3-F4
Blossomfield Road	A1-B1-B2-C2
Blyth Avenue	F1
Broad Oaks Road	A4-B4-B3
Broomfields Close	E4
Brueton Avenue	F1-F2
Bryanston Road	A4
Caldwell Grove	D4-E4
Church Hill Road	D1
Cornyx Lane	E4-F4
Damson Lane	F4
Damson Parkway	F3-F4
Dorchester Road	A3-B3-B2
Dury Lane	D2
Elms Close	E4-F4
Ferndown Road	C4-D4
George Road	D2-E2
Glebe Road	E4-F4
Grove Road	D4-D3-E3
Hainfield Drive	F3-F4
Hampton Lane	E2-F2-F3
Herbert Road	C2
Hermitage Road	D4-E4
Heronfield Way	F3
High Street	D1-D2
Homer Road	C2-C2-D1
Ladbrook Road	D2
Lode Lane	C2-D2-D3-D4
Malvern Park Avenue	E1
Manor Road	C3-D3-D4
Marsh Lane	F1-F2-F3
Mells Square	D2
Milcote Road	C3
Mill Lane	D2
Muswell Close	E3
Naseby Road	C4
New Road	E1-E2
Oaken Drive	A3
Oakley Wood Drive	E1-E1
Park Avenue	E1-E1
Park Road	D1-E1
Poolfield Drive	A1
Poplar Road	D2
Princes Way	C2-C1-D1
Radford Rise	F3
Rectory Gardens	E1
Rectory Road	D1-E1
Redlands Close	E4
Redlands Road	D4-E4-F4
Rollswood Drive	A2-B2
Sandal Rise	E3-F3-F2
School Lane	B4-C4-D4
Seven Star Road	A2-A3
Sharmans Cross Road	C3
Shustoke Road	B4-B3-C3
Silhill Hall Road	F2
Silverbirch Road	D4-E4-E3-F3
Solihull By-pass	B3-B2-C2
Station Approach	C2-C2
Station Road	A3-A4
Stonor Park Road	A3-B3-C3-C2
Streetsbrook Road	C4-D4-D3
The Crescent	D3
Thornby Avenue	D2-E2-E3
Touchwood Hall Close	D2-E2-E3
Union Road	B4-C4-C3-D3-D2-E2-F2-F1
Warwick Road	A1-A2
Welcombe Grove	F4
Wherretts Well Lane	A1
White House Green	A1-B1
White House Way	A2-A3
Winterbourne Road	C4
Woodfield Road	F3-F4
Yew Tree Lane	

LEGEND

Symbol	
AA Recommended roads	
Restricted roads	
Other roads	
Buildings of interest	College
Car Parks	P
Parks and open spaces	
Churches	+
One Way Streets	→

Street Index with Grid Reference

Sutton Coldfield

Allesley Close	B5
Anchorage Road	B4-B5
Barker Road	A5-B5
Beaconsfield Road	A5
Birchcroft Road	A5
Birmingham Road	B3-A3-A2-A1-B1
Blackroot Road	A5
Boswell Road	B4-B5
Braemar Road	A1-A2
Brassington Avenue	A3-B3
Brook Road	B3-B2-C2
Broomie Close	C3
Clifton Road	A3-A4
Coles Lane	B2-C2
Coleshill Road	B3-C3
Coleshill Street	B3-B4
Conchar Road	B1-C1
Digby Road	A2
Douglas Road	B2
Duke Street	A2-B2
East Rise	C4
East View Road	C1-C2
Eaton Court	A5
Elms Road	B2
Farthing Lane	A3-B3-B2
Garrard Gardens	A3
Goldieslie Road	A1
Halloughton Road	A5
High Street	B4
Highbridge Road	A1-B1
Holland Road	A2-B2
Holland Street	B2-B3
Honeybourne Road	C5
Jerrard Drive	B4-C4

Sutton Coldfield is one of the most popular residential areas in the Birmingham region — not least because of Sutton Park, which was a royal hunting ground in the 16th century and offers 2,400 acres of heathland, lakes and woodland.

Shrewsbury is celebrated for the wealth of half-timbered black and white buildings which line its narrow streets, many of which are 16th century. Known also as the 'Town of Flowers' because of its parks and gardens, and because of the profusion of window boxes and hanging baskets to be seen in its streets, this historic market town is attractively situated in a horseshoe bend of the River Severn, and has no less than seven bridges. Charles Darwin was born and educated here, and Lord Robert Clive (Clive of India) was its Member of Parliament during the latter part of the 18th century. The Norman castle still has 12th-century features, and St Mary's Church, also 12th-century, has particularly good stained glass.

Amongst the town's many museums, 16th-century Rowley's House deals mainly with archaeology.

Solihull's fine sports facilities include an ice rink, an open air lido in Malvern Park and an athletics track and swimming pool in Tudor Grange Park. A pleasant, part-industrialised suburb lying close to Birmingham's National Exhibition Centre, it also boasts modern conference facilities and has a pedestrianised shopping precinct tucked away behind the High Street.

Central Shrewsbury

Central Solihull

Key to Town Plan and Area Plan

Town Plan

AA Recommended roads	
Other roads	
Restricted roads	
Buildings of interest	Hospital
Churches	†
Car Parks	P
Parks and open spaces	
AA Service Centre	AA
One Way Streets	→

Street Index with Grid Reference

Stafford

Stafford boasts the largest timber-framed house in England in High House, and has numerous other historic buildings. Prosperous through its wool trade long before the Industrial Revolution, Stafford became an established industrial centre through the manufacture of footwear. Today the town has fine leisure facilities in the Riverside Recreation Centre.

Stamford is thought by many to be one of England's most beautiful towns. Former Danish capital of the Fens and now a conservation area, it stands on a hilly site with fine views of three counties, and offers an admirable blend of the old with the new. Oldest building in the town is the 7th-century ruined chapel of St Leonard's Priory.

Stroud Standing on a steep hill site at the convergence of five valleys, Stroud has a distinctly country 'feel'. Running along its valleys are several early industrial buildings: this was once the most important area for broadcloth manufacture, and more recently has won world renown for its production of billiard table cloth and scarlet dye.

Tewkesbury grew up around Tewkesbury Abbey, and is one of the country's most complete medieval towns, with a wealth of ancient houses and timbered inns. Among them the Black Bear Inn is quite unique: said to date from 1308, it incorporates part of 13th-century King John's Bridge in its structure.

Central Stroud

Stratford Park, Leisure Centre, School, Convent, School, Museum & School of Art, Library, Church, School, Council Offices, Bank, Hall Gdns, Town Hall, Police, Station, Council Offices, Teachers Centre, School, *Rodborough Avenue*, *Castle Mead*, Kings Rd

Central Tewkesbury

Town Hall, P.O., Cinema, Swimming Pool, Fire Sta, Police Station, Adult Training Centre, School, Arts Centre & Clinic, Library, Mill Museum, Citadel, Museum, Sch., Hall, Hospital, Youth Centre, Sports Ground, Museum, Youth Centre, Oldfield Estate, Council Offices, Hospital, Camping Ground, Chapel, Cemetery, School

Red Lion Street	C4	Bentley Road	B4-C4	St Marys Hill
Riverway	D1-E1-E2	Blackfriar's Street	B2-C2	St Paul's Street
Rose Cottages	A3	Brazenose Lane	C3	St Peters Street
Rowley Avenue		Broad Street	B3	Scotgate
	A1-B1-B2	Brownlow Street	C2-C3	Sheep Market
Russel Street	B3	Church Lane	B1	Station Road
St John's Walk	F3	Church Street	B1	Sussex Road
Salter Street	C3	Cliff Crescent	A3-A4	Victoria Road
Sash Street	C4	Cliff Road	B3	Vine Street
South street	B2-B3	Conduit Road	B4-C4-C3	Water Street
South Walls	C3	Cornwall Road	A4	Well Court
Stafford Street	C3	Drift Road	B4-C4	West Street
Station Road	B2	East Street	B3-C3	Wharf Road
Tenter Banks	B3-B2-C2	Emlyns Street	B4	Wothorpe Road
The Oval	D1-D2	Essex Road	A4	York Road
Tipping Street	C3	Foundary Road	A2-A3	
Tithebarn Court	F4	Gloucester Road	A4-B4	
Tithebarn Road	F3-F4	High Street	B1-B2-B3	
Tixal Road	F3	Kettering Road	B1	
Victoria Road	B2	Kings Road	B4	**Stroud**
West Close	E2	Lancaster Road	A4-B4	Acre Street
Westhead Avenue	F3-F4	Maiden Lane	B2-B3	Bellevue Road
Weston Road	E2-F2-F3	New Street	B4	Beeches Green
Wolverhampton Road	C1	New Cross Road		Birches Drive
			A3-A4-B4	Brick Road
		Orchard Road	A3	Caincross Road
		Park Lane	B1-C1	Castle Meads
Stamford		Queens Street	B4	Castle Street
Adelaide Street	C2-C3	Radcliffe Road	A3-A4	Church Street
Albert Road	C2	Recreation Ground Road		Field Road
All Saints Street	A2-B2		B3-B4	Folly Lane
Austin Street	A2	Rock Road	A3	High Street
Barn Hill	A3-B3	St George's Street		Kings Road
Barnock Road	B1-C1		C2-C3	King Street
Bath Row	A2-B2	St Johns Street	B2	Lansdown
Belton Street	C2	St Leonards Street	C3	London Road
		St Martins	B1	Lower Street

St Marys Hill	B2
St Paul's Street	C3
St Peters Street	A2
Scotgate	A3-B3-B2
Sheep Market	A2-B2
Station Road	B2
Sussex Road	A4
Victoria Road	B4
Vine Street	B3-C3
Water Street	B2-C2
Well Court	C2
West Street	A2-A3
Wharf Road	B2-C2
Wothorpe Road	B1
York Road	A4

Stroud
Acre Street	C2
Bellevue Road	C3
Beeches Green	A3-B3
Birches Drive	B3
Brick Road	C3
Caincross Road	A2
Castle Meads	B1
Castle Street	C2
Church Street	B2-B3-C3
Field Road	C1
Folly Lane	B3-C3-C4
High Street	B2-B3
Kings Road	A1
King Street	B2-B3
Lansdown	B3-C3-C4
London Road	B2-C2-C1
Lower Street	C2

Merry Walks	A2-B2-B3
Middle Street	C2
Middle Street	C4
Nelson Street	C2
Painswick Road	A3-A4
Painswick Old Road	
	A4-B4
Parliament Street	C2
Park Road	C1-C2
Rodborough Avenue	A1
Rodborough Hill	A1-A2
Rowcroft	B2
Slad Road	B3-C3-C4
Stratford Road	A3
Springfield Road	C4
Spring Lane	C1-C2
Union Street	B2
Upper Leazes	C2-C3
Wallbridge	A1-A2

Tewkesbury
Abbotts Road	A1-B1
Ashchuch Road	C3
Barton Road	C3
Barton Street	B3-C3
Battle Road	A1
Bredon Road	C4
Chance Street	A3
Church Street	A3-B3
Clarence Road	B1
Cotteswold Gardens	
	C3-C4
Cotteswold Road	C3
Despenser Road	B1-B2

East Street	B3-C3
Forester's Road	A1-B1
Gander Lane	B2-B3
Gloucester Road	
	A1-A2-A3
High Street	B3-B4-C4
Hollams Road	C4
Howells Road	B3-B2-C2
Lincoln Close	A1
Lincoln Green Lane	
	A1-A2
Margaret's Road	B1
Mill Street	A3
Mythe Road	B4-C4
Neville Road	B2
Oldbury Road	B3-C3-C4
Oldfield Estate	C2-C3
Ropewalk	C3
Queen's Road	B1-B2
St Mary's Lane	A3-B3
Seymour Place	B1
Station Street	C3
Swilgate Road	B3
Tolsey Lane	B3
Walkley Road	C4
Wenlock Road	B1-B2

TEWKESBURY
The fine abbey church of St Mary was saved by the local townspeople from possible destruction during the Dissolution of the Monasteries — they found the money to buy it from Henry VIII and so kept it intact.

Walsall

Affectionately known as the 'Town of 100 Trades' because of its diversity of industries, Walsall is nevertheless a specialist in one area — leather manufacture. Saddles have been produced here since the 19th century, and all the British Army's saddles in World War I were Walsall-made.

A conservation area has been established at Church Hill, covering the Parish Church of St Matthew (which dates back to the 12th century), and part of the town centre where Italian Renaissance style Taylor's Music Shop is just one of several fine Victorian buildings to be seen. Other places of interest are the Central Library's Local History Gallery, Belsize House, the birthplace of Jerome K. Jerome (now a museum dealing with his life and work) and the Garman Ryan Collection which has art donated by Lady Kathleen Epstein, widow of sculptor Sir Jacob. The Walsall Illuminations appear each September.

Aldridge enjoys the contrasts of an industrial town set in pleasant rural surroundings. The oldest part of town, around the Parish Church, has been declared a conservation area.

Willenhall has kept its old 'Black Country' character, and the market place area is being restored in 19th-century style. A reputation for lock and key making is recalled in the local library's Lock Museum.

Key to Town Plan and Area Plan

Town Plan

AA Recommended roads	
Other roads	
Restricted roads	
Buildings of Interest	Baths
Car Parks	P
Parks and open Spaces	

Area Plan

A roads	
B roads	
Locations	Wimpstone○
Urban area	

Street Index with Grid Reference

Leamington Spa

Adelaide Road	C2-C3
Albany Terrace	B3-B4
Archery Road	B2-C2
Arley Mews	A4-B4
Augusta Place	C3
Avenue Road	B2-C2-C1
Bath Place	D1
Bath Street	D1
Beaconsfield Street	F2
Beauchamp Avenue	C4
Beauchamp Hill	B4
Bedford Street	C2-C3
Beverley Road	A4
Brandon Parade	D3-E3
Bury Road	C1-B1
Campion Terrace	E4
Chandos Street	D4
Chapel Street	D1
Chesham Street	F1
Church Hill	B3
Church Street	D1-D2
Church Terrace	D1-D2
Clapham Terrace	E1
Clarendon Avenue	C4-D4
Clarendon Crescent	B4
Clarendon Place	B3-B4-C4-C3
Clarendon Square	B4-C4
Clarendon Street	D3-D4
Clemens Street	D1
Cliffe Road	A4
Comyn Street	E4
Court Street	D1
Cross Road	A3
Cross Street	D3
Dale Street	B3-C3
Dormer Place	C2
Duke Street	E4
Earl Street	E4
Eastfield Road	E3
Eastnor Grove	F1
Euston Place	C3.D2
Fairlawn Close	A3-A4
Farley Street	E1-E2
Fernhill Drive	F3-F4
Forfield Place	D1-E1
Gaveston Road	B4
George Street	D1-D2
Gordon Street	E1-E2
Grove Street	B3
Gunnery Terrace	A3
Guy Place	C4-D4
Guy Street	C4-D4
Guys Cliffe Avenue	A4
Guys Cliffe Road	A3-A4
Hall Road	C4
Hampton Grove	E4
Heath Terrace	A3-A4-B4
High Street	D1-E1
Hill Street	D4
Holly Walk	C2-D2-D3-E3
Holly Street	E4
Hyde Place	A3-B3
John Street	C3
Kenilworth Road	C4
Kenilworth Street	D3-D4
King Street	E4
Lansdowne Circus	E3-E4
Lansdowne Crescent	D4-E4-E3
Lansdowne Street	D4
Leam Street	F2
Leam Terrace	D2-E2

Warwick

The old county town of the shire, Warwick lies in the shadow of its massive, historic castle which occupies the rocky ridge above the River Avon. Thomas Beauchamp and his son built the huge towers and curtain walls in the 14th century, but it was the Jacobean holders of the earldom, the Grevilles, who transformed the medieval stronghold into a nobleman's residence. In 1694, the heart of the town was almost completely destroyed by fire and the few medieval buildings that survived lie on the outskirts of the present 18th-century centre. Of these Oken House, now a doll museum, and Lord Leycester's Hospital, almshouses dating back to the 14th century, are particularly striking.

Stratford-upon-Avon, as the birthplace of William Shakespeare, England's most famous poet and playwright, is second only to London as a tourist attraction. This charming old market town is a living memorial to him; his plays are performed in the Royal Shakespeare Theatre which dominates the river bank, a waxwork museum specialises in scenes from his works, and his childhood home in Henley Street is a museum.

Leamington Spa, an inland spa on the River Leam, gained the prefix 'Royal' after Queen Victoria had visited it in 1838, and the town has been a fashionable health resort ever since.

Central Warwick

Central Stratford-upon-Avon

Leam Terrace East	E2-F2-F1	Thomas Street	D4-E4	Mill Street	B2	Henley Street	B2-B3

Leam Terrace East	E2-F2-F1
Leicester Street	D4-E4-F4
Lower Avenue	D1
Lower Leam Street	E2-F2
Mill Road	D2-E2
Milverton Hill	B3-C3
Milverton Terrace	B3
Morrell Street	C4-D4
Morton Street	D4
New Street	D2-E2
Newbold Street	D3
Newbold Terrace	D2-D3-E3
Newbold Terrace East	E3-F3
New Brook Street	B3
Norfolk Street	D4
Northcote Street	F1-F2
Old Warwick Road	A1-B1-C1-D1
Oswald Road	A3
Oxford Road	D4
Oxford Street	D4
Parade	C4-C3-C2-D2
Park Drive	A2-B2-B1-B2
Park Street	D3
Percy Terrace	A3
Plymouth Place	E1
Princes Drive	A1-A2
Princes Street	E4
Priory Terrace	D2
Portland Place	C2-C3
Portland Street	C3
Queen Street	E4
Radford Road	E1-F1
Regent Grove	C3-D3
Regent Street	B3-C3-D3
Rosefield Street	D2-D3-E3
Rugby Road	A3-A4-B4
Rushmore Street	E1-F1
Russell Street	C4
Russell Terrace	D1-E1-E2-F2
St Mark's Road	A4
St Mary's Crescent	E1-F1
St Mary's Road	F1-F2
St Mary's Terrace	F1
Satchwell Street	C3-D3
Smith Street	D1
Spencer Street	C1-D1-D2
Station Approach	C1
Strathearn Road	B4
Suffolk Street	D4
Tachbrook Road	D1
Tavistock Street	C4

Thomas Street	D4-E4
Union Road	B3-B4
Upper Holly Walk	E3-E4-F4
Victoria Road	B2
Victoria Street	B2
Victoria Terrace	D1-D2
Vincent Street	E4
Warwick New Road	A3-B3
Warwick Place	A3-B3
Warwick Street	B3-C3-C4-D4
Warwick Terrace	B3-B4
Waterloo Street	F1
Willes Road	E3-E2-F2-F1
Willes Terrace	F2
William Street	D3-E3
Windsor Place	C3
Windsor Street	C3
Wise Street	D1
Woodbine Street	B3
Wood Street	D3
York Road	C2

Warwick

Albert Street	A4
Banbury Road	B2-C2-C1
Barrack Street	A3
Bowling Green Street	A2
Bridge End	C1-B1-C1
Brook Street	A2
Cape Road	A3-A4
Castle Close	A1
Castle Hill	B2
Castle Lane	A1-A2-B2
Castle Street	A2
Chapel Street	B3
Cherry Street	C3-C4
Church Street	A2-A3
Coten End	C3
Coventry Road	C3-C4
Deerpark Drive	A4
Edward Street	A3-A4
Gerrard Street	B2-B3
Guys Cliffe Terrace	C4
Guy Street	C3-C4
High Street	A2
Jury Street	A2-B2
Lakin Road	C4
Market Place	A2-A3
Market Street	A2

Mill Street	B2
Myton Road	C1
New Street	A2-A3
Northgate Street	A3
North Rock	A3
Old Square	A3
Packmore Street	B4-C4
Paradise Street	B4-C4
Parkes Street	A3
Priory Road	A3-B3-C3
St Johns	C3
St Nicholas Church Street	B2-B3-C3
Saltisford	A3-A4
Smith Street	B2-B3-C3
Station Road	C4
Swan Street	A2
Theatre Street	A3
The Butts	A3-B3
Victoria Street	A3-A4
West Street	A1-A2
Woodville Road	B4

Stratford-upon-Avon

Albany Road	A2-A3
Alcester Road	A3
Arden Street	A3-A4
Arthur Road	B4
Avenue Road	C3-C4
Banbury Road	C1
Birmingham Road	A4-B4-B3
Bridgefoot	B2-C2
Bridge Street	B2
Bridgetown Road	C1
Bridgeway	C2-C3
Broad Street	A1-A2
Bull Street	A1
Chapel Lane	B2
Chapel Street	B2
Chestnut Walk	A1-A2
Church Street	A1-A2-B2
Clopton Road	B4
College Lane	A1
College Street	A1
Ely Street	A2-B2
Evesham Place	A1-A2
Great William Street	B3-B4
Greenhill Street	A3
Grove Road	A2-A3
Guild Street	B3

Henley Street	B2-B3
High Street	B2
John Street	B3
Kendall Avenue	B4
Maidenhead Road	B4-C4
Mansell Street	A3
Market Place	A3-B3
Mayfield Avenue	B4
Mulberry Street	B3
New Broad Street	A1
Old Town	A1-B1-A1
Payton Street	B3-C3
Percy Street	B4
Rother Street	A2-A3
Rowley Crescent	C4
St Gregory's Road	B4-C4-C3
St Mary's Road	B4
Sanctus Street	A1
Scholars Lane	A2-B2
Shakespeare Street	B3-B4
Sheep Street	B2
Shipston Road	C1
Southern Lane	A1-B1-B2
Swans Nest Lane	C1
Tiddington Road	C2
Tyler Street	B3
Union Street	B2-B3
Warwick Crescent	C3
Warwick Road	B3-C3-C4
Waterside	B2
Welcombe Road	C3-C4
Wellesbourne Grove	A2-A3
West Street	A1-A2
Windsor Street	A3-B3
Wood Street	B2-B3

WARWICK
These pretty brick and timbered cottages standing in the shadow of the great medieval towers of Warwick Castle are among the few buildings in the town that survived a devastating fire in the late 17th century.

73

Key to Town Plan and Area Plan

Town Plan

AA Recommended roads
Restricted roads
Other roads
Buildings of interset   Theatre 🏛
Car Parks   P
Parks and open spaces
One Way Streets

Area Plan

A roads
B roads
Locations   Wooburn O
Urban area

Street Index with grid reference

Watford

Addiscombe Road	C3
Albert Road	D4-D5
Albert Road North	D5
Alexandra Road	C5-C6
Arthur Street	F3-F4
Banbury Street	C1-C2
Beechen Grove	C5-D5-D4-E4-E3
Belgrave Avenue	B1
Benskin Road	B1-B2-C2
Brightwell Road	B1-C1-C2
Burton Avenue	B3-C3
Bushey Hall Road	F3
Canon Road	E1
Canterbury Road	D6
Cardiff Road	D1
Cassiobury Drive	A6-B6-B5-B4-C4
Cassiobury Park Avenue	A4-B4
Cassio Road	C4-C3-D3-D2
Charter Place	D3-D4-E4-E3
Chester Road	B2-C2-C3
Church Street	D3
Clarendon Road	D4-D5-D6
Clifford Street	E3
Clifton Road	D2
Clive Way	E6
Dellfield Close	B6
Denmark Street	C6
Derby Road	E3-E4
Duke Street	E4
Durban Road East	C2-C3
Durban Road West	B3-C3
Earl Street	E4
Ebury Road	E4
Elfrida Road	E1
Essex Road	C5-C6
Estcourt Road	D4-D5
Euston Avenue	A1-B1-B2
Exchange Road	D4-D3-D2-E2
Fearnley Street	C3-C2-D2
Francis Road	D3
Garden Close	A6
Gartlet Road	D4
George Street	D3
Gladstone Road	E3-E4
Golf Close	F5
Granville Road	E2-E3
Greatham Road	F3-F4
Grosvenor Road	E3-E4
Hagden Lane	A2-A1-B1-C1
Hardwoods Road	B3-B2-C2-C1
Hemstead Road	B6-B5-C5
Herga Court	B6
High Street	D4-D3-E3
Holywell Road	B1-C1-C2
Hyde Road	C5
Kemscott Crescent	B1
Kensington Avenue	A2-B2-B3
King George's Avenue	A2
Kings Avenue	A2-B2-B3
King Street	D3-E3
Lady's Close	D3-D2-E2
Lamms Road	E1
Langley Road	C6-D6
Link Road	F5-F6
Liverpool Road	D1-D2

Watford

Not the least of Watford's successes is its football club, which has reached Division One of the Canon League under the chairmanship of singer Elton John and contributed to some extent to the prosperity of the town. But Watford's present-day expansion really began with the opening of Watford Junction Railway Station in 1838, as an increasing number of commercial and industrial firms set up

premises here. Benskins Brewery had its headquarters in Watford until it was taken over in 1957, and the Mothercare chain began life in the town, where it still has a large factory. Watford has modern shopping facilities, and sports are catered for by the extensive Watford Leisure Centre and Cassiobury Park. The Watford Museum is housed in the former Benskins Brewery and has a fascinating collection of local history items.

Hemel Hempstead is a town of two faces:

the New Town, with its shopping precincts, Civic Centre and extensive Dacorum Sports Centre, and the carefully preserved older quarter, which stands on a hill to the north of its modern counterpart. A number of ancient inns can be seen in the main street of the old town, and the Old Town Hall is a fine example of Jacobean-style architecture. A collection of medieval wall paintings has been found on the walls of a 15th-century cottage at Piccotts End, on the northern outskirts.

Central Hemel Hempstead

Watford Area

Loates Lane	E3-E4	Souldern Street	C2	Anchor Lane	A1-A2-B2	Lawn Lane	B1-C1

Street	Grid
Loates Lane	E3-E4
Local Board Avenue	F2
Lower High Street	E2-F2-F1
Malden Road	C6
Market Street	D3
Marlborough Road	C3-D3
Mildred Avenue	A2-A3-B3
Muriel Avenue	E1
Nascot Road	C6
Nascot Street	C6
Neal Street	E1-E2
Occupation Road	C2-D2-D1
Orchard Close	A6-B6
Orchard Drive	A6
Orphanage Road	E5-E6
Oxford Street	C2
Park Avenue	B4-B3-C3
Park Avenue	F4-F5
Park Close	F5
Parkside Drive	A6-A5-B5
Percy Road	D3
Platts Avenue	D4-D5
Pretoria Road	C2
Prince's Avenue	A2-B2
Prince Street	E4
Queen's Avenue	A3-A2-B2-B1
Queens Road	E3-E5
Radlett Road	E4-E5-F5-F6
Rickmansworth Road	A2-A3-B3-B4-C4-C5
Rose Gardens	C1
Rosslyn Road	C4
St Albans Road	D6-D5-C5-C6
St Jame's Road	D1-D2
St John's Road	D5-E5
St Mary's Road	D2-D3
Shady Lane	D5
Shaftesbury Road	E4
Shepherd's Road	A3-A4
Smith Street	E2-E3
Sotheron Road	E4-E5

Street	Grid
Souldern Street	C2
Southsea Avenue	B2-B3
Stamford Road	C6
Stanley Road	E3-E4
Station Approach	A3-A4
Station Road	D6
Stratford Road	B6-C6
Stratford Way	A5-B5-B6
Sutton Road	E4-E5
Sydney Road	A1
Temple Close	A6
The Avenue	B6-C6-C5
The Broadway	E4
The Crescent	E2-E3
The Gardens	A5-A6-B6
The Parade	C5-C4-D4
Tolpits Lane	A1
Tucker Street	E1-E2
Upton Road	C4-D4
Vicarage Road	B1-C1-C2-D2-D3
Water Lane	E3-F3
Watermans Road	E3
Watford Field Road	E2-F2
Wellington Road	D6
Westbury Road	D5-D6
Westland Road	D5-D6
West Street	C6-D6
Whippendell Road	A2-B2-B3-C3
Wigganhall Road	D2-D1-E1
Willow Lane	C1
Woodford Road	D6-D5-E5
Woodland Drive	A6-B6-B5
York Road	E1

Hemel Hempstead

Street	Grid
Albion Hill	C2
Alexandra Road	C3-C4
Anchor Lane	A1-A2-B2
Astley Road	B3
Basil Road	C1-C2
Beaumayes Close	A2
Beechfield Road	A1-A2-A3
Bridge Street	B2
Broad Street	C4
Bury Hill	A4-B4
Bury Hill Close	B4
Bury Road	B4
Castle Mead	A1
Cedar Walk	C1
Cemetery Hill	B2
Cemmaes Court Road	B3-B4
Cemmaes Meadow	B3
Charles Street	B2
Christchurch Road	C4
Collett Road	B3
Combe Street	B3
Concorde Drive	C3-C4
Corner Hall Avenue	C1
Cornfields	A2-A3
Cotterells	B1-B2-B3
Cotterells Hill	B3
Crescent Road	C3-C4
Crouchfield	A2
Dacorum Way	B3-B4
East Street	C4
Fernville Lane	C3-C4
Gadebridge Road	A4
Glen Dale	A3
Glen View Road	A3
Hanger Close	A3
Haybourn Mead	A2
Heath Brow	B1
Heath Close	A2-B2
Heath Lane	B1-B2-B3
Hillfield Road	C3
Hillmay Drive	A2
King Harry Street	C2-C3
Lamsey Road	C1

Street	Grid
Lawn Lane	B1-C1
Leighton Buzzard Road	B1-B2-B3-B4
Lockers Park Lane	A4-A3-B3
Lower Adey-field Road	C4
Market Square	B3
Marlowes	B1-B2-C2-C3-B3-B4
Mayflower Avenue	C3-C4
Maynard Road	C2-C3
Melstead Road	A4
Midland Road	C3-C4
Moor End Road	B2
Nettlecroft	A2
Paradise Wood Lane	C2
Parkhill Road	A3
Park Lane	C1-C2
Park Road	B1-B2
Pinewood Gardens	A3-A4
Queensway	B4-C4
Reson Way	A1
St Albans Road	C1-C2
St Johns Road	A1-B1
St Pauls Road	C4
Selden Hill	C2
South Hill Road	B3
Station Road	B1
Sunnyhill Road	A3-A4
Two Waters Road	B1
Vicarage Close	B1
Warner's End Road	A4-B4
Waterhouse Street	B2-B3
Wolsley Road	C2
Woodland Avenue	A2-A3

WATFORD
Green leaves and cool water in the High Street precinct are part of a scheme to transform a traffic-congested centre into a safe and pleasant place for pedestrians.

Welwyn area

St Albans is named after the first British Christian martyr. It evolved from the Roman town of Verulamium, and, lying on Watling Street, has always been an important link with the north. The impressive Cathedral dates from the 11th century and overlooks Verulamium Park, where Roman remains and a museum can be seen. Other features are the Roman Theatre on the Gorhambury Estate, the Organ Museum and the Fighting Cocks, said to be the country's oldest licensed establishment.

Hatfield is dominated by Hatfield House, the magnificent Jacobean mansion built by Robert Cecil, Earl of Salisbury, in the early 17th century. It stands in an extensive park close to the remains of the late 15th-century Bishop's Palace, where Queen Elizabeth I is said to have held her first council. Hatfield itself grew up around the nucleus of an ancient village, and has modern shopping, sports and leisure facilities.

Welwyn Garden City was established shortly after World War I, and Welwyn remains a fine example of landscaped town planning. The overall appearance is neo-Georgian, although modern buildings have been added, such as the Campus West leisure complex and the sports centre at Gosling Stadium. Perhaps the most outstanding feature of the town is 126-acre Stansborough Park, with its swimming pool and a lake for sailing.

Key to Town Plan and Area Plan

Town Plan
A A Recommended roads
Other roads
Restricted roads
Buildings of interest   Gallery ▢
Parks and open spaces
Car Parks   P
Churches   †
One Way Streets   ←

Area Plan
A roads
B roads
Locations   Clapton ○
Urban Area

Street Index with Grid Reference

St. Albans

Abbey Mill Lane	B1-B2-C2
Abbey View Road	B2-B3
Adelaide Street	C3-D3
Albert Street	C2-D2-D1
Albion Road	F2
Alexandra Road	D2-E2
Alma Road	E1-E2
Avenue Road	D4-E4
Batchwood Drive	A4-B4
Beaconsfield Road	E2-E3
Belmont Hill	C1-D1
Bernard Street	C3-C4-D4
Blandford Road	F3
Blenheim Road	F4
Bluehouse Hill	A2-A3-A4
Brampton Road	F3
Branch Road	B3
Breakspear Avenue	F2
Bricket Road	D2-D3
Camlet Way	F2
Camp Road	F2
Cannon Street	C3-C4
Carlisle Avenue	C4-D4
Catherine Street	C3-D3
Cavendish Road	F2
Cecil Road	F2
Chequer Street	C2
Church Crescent	F2
Church Street	C3-C4-D4
Clarence Road	F2-F3-F4
Colindale Avenue	E1-F1
Cottonmill Crescent	D1
Cottonmill Lane	D1
Culver Road	E4

Dalton Street	C3-C4
Dellfield	F1
Down Edge	A4-B4
Etna Road	C3
Everlasting Lane	B2-B3
Fishpool Street	B2-B3
Flora Grove	E2-F2-F1
Folly Avenue	C4
Folly Lane	B3-C3
Fryth Mead	A3-A4
Gainsborough Avenue	E4-F4
George Street	C2
Grange Street	C4-D4
Granville Road	E2
Grimston Road	E2
Grosvenor Road	E1
Grove Road	E2
Hall Place Gardens	D4-D3-E3
Harpenden Road	D4
Hart Road	D2
Hatfield Road	D3-E3-E2-F2-F3
Heath Road	E4
High Street	C2
Hill Street	B2
Hillside Road	E3-E4
Holywell Hill	C1-C2
Inkerman Road	D2
Jennings Road	F4
Kimberley Road	C4
King Harry Lane	A1
Kings Road	B3
Kingsbury Avenue	B3
Ladies Grove	B4
Lattimore Road	E2
Lemsford Road	E3-E4
London Road	C2-D2-D1-E1
Lower Dagnall Street	C2-C3
Manor Road	E3
Marlborough Road	D2
Mount Pleasant	B3-C3
New England Street	C3
Normandy Road	C3-C4
Old London Road	D1-E1
Oswald Road	E2
Pageant Road	C2-D2-D1
Palfrey Close	D4
Park Avenue	F3-F4
Portland Street	B3
Prae Close	A3
Ramsbury Road	D1-E1
Redbourn Road	A4
Ridgemont Road	E1-E2
Riverside Road	D1-E1
Romeland Hill	B2-C2
Russel Avenue	C3
St. Michaels Street	A3-B3
St Peters Road	D3-E3
St Peters Street	C2-D2-D3-D4
Sandpit Lane	D4-E4-F4
Sandridge Road	D4-E4
Selby Avenue	C3
Shirley Road	E2-E1-F1
Sopwell Lane	C2-C1-D1
Spencer Street	C2-C3
Stanhope Road	E2-F2
Station Way	E2
Sunderland Avenue	F4
Thorpe Road	D1
Townsend Avenue	D3-D4
Upper Lattimore Road	D2-D3-E3

Upper Marlborough Road	D2-D3
Upton Avenue	C3
Vanda Crescent	F1-F2
Ver Road	B2
Verulam Road	A4-B4-B3-C3-C2
Victoria Street	C2-D2-E2
Walton Street	E4
Watsons Walk	D1-D2
Waverley Road	C4
Worley Road	C3
York Road	E3-F3

Hatfield

Aldykes	A1
Beaconsfield Road	C2-C3
Birchwood Avenue	A3-B3
Birchwood Close	A3-B3
Branch Close	C3
Briars Lane	A1
Briars Wood	A1
Cavendish Way	A1
Cecil Crescent	B3-C3
Chelwood Avenue	A3-A4-B4
Church Lane	C1
Church Street	C1-C2
Cornerfield	B4
Crawford Road	A3-B3
Crop Common	B2-B3
Dellfield Road	A1-B1
Drovers Way	B4
Ely Close	A2
French Horn Lane	B2-C2-C1
Goldings Crescent	B1-B2
Great North Road	B4-C4-C3-C2-C1
Green Lanes	A3-A4
Ground Lane	B3-C3
Hatfield By-pass	A2-A3-A4
Heathcote Avenue	A3-B3-B4
Hertford Road	C3
Hillfield	B4-C4
Homestead Road	A4-B4-B3
Howe Dell	B1-C1
Lemsford Road	A1-A2-A3
Link Drive	B1
Lockley Crescent	B3-C3-C4
Longmead	A1
Maryland	A1
Mount Pleasant Lane	C4
Northfield	B4
Old Hertford Road	C3
Old Rectory Drive	B1-B2
Park Street	C2-C3
Park View	C3
Pleasant Rise	C4
Pond Croft	A1
Queensway	A1-B1-B2
Roe Green Lane	A1
St Albans Road East	B2-C2-C3
St Albans Road West	A1
St Ethelreda's Drive	C1
Stag Green Avenue	C3-C4
Stockbreach Close	A2
Stockbreach Road	A2-B2
Stonecross Road	B2-B3
Talbot Road	A3-A4
The Common	A2-B2
The Ryde	C3-C4

Warren Close	B4
Wellfield Road	A3-A2-B2
Wood Close	B1
Woods Avenue	B1
Worcester Road	A2

Welwyn Garden City

Applecroft Road	A2
Attimore Road	A1-A2
Barleycroft Road	A2-B2
Barn Close	A2-B2
Barnfield Road	C1
Beechfield Road	C1
Bessemer Road	C3-C4
Birdcroft Road	B2
Blakemere Road	A3
Bridge Road	A3-B3-C3
Bridge Road East	C1-C2
Broadwater Crescent	C1-C2
Broadwater Road	C1-C2-C3
Brockswood Lane	A3
Chequers	C1
Digswell Road	B4
Elm Gardens	A2
Elmwood	A1-A2
Fearnley Road	B1-B2
Fordwich Road	B1-B2
Fretherne Road	B2-B3
Guessens Road	A2-B2-B3
Handside Lane	A1-A2-A3
High Oaks Road	A2-A3
Hydeway	C3
Longcroft Lane	B1-B2
Mandeville Rise	B4
Marsden Grove	A1
Marsden Road	A1-B1
Moss Green	C1
Newfields	A1
Parkway	B1-B2-B3
Peartree Lane	C2
Pentley Park	B4
Reddings	A3-A4
Rooks Hill	B1
Russellcroft Road	A3-B3
Sherrard's Park Road	A4-B4
Stanborough Road	B1
Tewin Road	C3-C4
The Campus	B3-B4-B3
Turmore Dale	A2-A1-B1
Valley Road	A1-A2-A3
Walden Road	B4
Woodhall Lane	C1
Woodland Rise	A4-B4
Youngs Rise	A2

West Bromwich

This was a small hamlet set amid a heath of broom (hence the name) until the discovery of coal and a central position in the national transport system led to the industrial development of the area. A few remaining buildings speak of the town's older history, for example the Manor House, a copybook example of a medieval timber-framed house, and Oak House, which is Tudor, and furnished in period style. Today this is a town well equipped to meet the needs of the 20th century: the Sandwell Centre is a modern, purpose-built shopping centre, the Gala Suite hosts sports events and entertainments, and top league soccer action is provided by local club West Bromwich Albion.

Wednesbury was an important fort in the Anglo-Saxon kingdom of Mercia, but the digging of coal as long ago as the 14th century developed it into a thriving industrial community. The market square is a conservation area, and dominating the town from its hill-top site is the 12th-century Parish Church of St Bartholomew, one of the Midlands' most beautiful perpendicular churches.

Smethwick means 'little village on the plain', but Smethwick itself underwent a major change when the canal system was developed in the 18th century. It is now an established industrial community, and boasts an Olympic standard running track at the Hadley Stadium.

LEGEND

Town Plan
- AA Recommended route
- Restricted roads
- Other roads
- Buildings of interest — Library
- Car parks — P
- Parks and open spaces
- One way streets

Area Plan
- A roads
- B roads

Street Index with Grid Reference

West Bromwich

Adams Street	A2
Albion Street	A1
Alfred Street	D4
Arthur Street	E1
Bache Street	D1-E1
Bagnall Street	F2
Bailey Street	A2
Baker Street	A2-B2
Barton Street	C1
Beeches Road	E3-F3-F2
Beechwood Road	A1-B1
Bell Street	D1-E1
Birmingham Road	F2
Bond Street	D1
Boulton Street	E1
Bowater Street	C2
Bratt Street	B4-C4-C2
Bridge Street	A3
Bromford Lane	C1
Brook Street	A3-B3
Bull Street	D2-D3
Burlington Road	E2-F2
Cambridge Street	B1-C1
Carters Green	A3-A4
Chapman Street	B2
Clive Street	B4
Constance Avenue	E1-F1
Cooper Street	D3-D4
Cordley Street	A3-A4
Cronehill Street	C4-D4-C4
Cronehills Linkway	C4-C3-D3
Dartmouth Street	A2-B2-B3
Devereux Road	F1
Devonshire Drive	D4-E4
Dudley Street	A4
Duke Street	B3
Earl Street	B3
Edith Street	B2
Edward Street	B3-C3-C2
Emily Street	B1-C1
Europa Avenue	F2-F3-F4
Farm Street	D1
Florence Road	F1-F2
Frederick Street	B4
Gads Lane	A1-A2
Garratt Street	A4-B4
George Street	E2
Grange Road	B2-B3
Griffin Street	C4-D4-D3
Guns Lane	A3-B3
Hall Street	D1-D2
Hambletts Road	A1
Hardware Street	C4
Harwood Street	A2-A3
Hayes Street	A3
Hazelbeech Road	B1-B2
Herbert Street	D3-E3
High Street	B3-C3-D3-D2-E2-F2
Hilton Street	A2
Hope Street	F2-F3
Horton Street	D1
Ida Road	F1
Ireland Green Road	A1-B1
Izons Road	C2
Jesson Street	F2-F3
John Street	A4-B4
Lambert Street	A2-B2
Legge Street	E1
Littleton Street	C1-D1
Lloyd Street	D4
Lodge Road	B1-B2-C2-C3
Lombard Street	C3
Lombard Street West	C3
Lyng Lane	C2-D2-D1
Margaret Street	B1
Mary Road	E1-F1
Mason Street	A3
Mill Street	B4-C4
Moor Street	C1-C2
Morris Street	D1
Mount Pleasant Street	D1
New Street	C3-D3-D4
Newhall Street	D1
Nicholls Street	E2-E3
Oak Avenue	B2
Oak Lane	B1-B2
Oak Road	A1-B1-B2-C2
Overend Street	D3-E3-E2
Oxford Road	B2
Park Crescent	D4
Pearson Street	A3
Pleasant Street	D1-D2
Poplar Avenue	E3
Queen Street	D3
Raleigh Street	B4
Railway Street	A3-B3-B2
Reform Street	D3-D4
Richard Street	A2-B2
Richard Street South	C1-C2
Roebuck Lane	F2
Rowley View	A1-B1

St Augustus Close	F3-F4
St Caroline Close	F4
St Christopher Close	F3
St Cuthberts Close	F3-F4
St Eleanors Close	F4
St Michael Street	C2-C3
Salisbury Road	F1-F2
Sams Lane	D1-E1
Sandwell Road	B3-B4-C4
Sandwell Road North	C4-D4
Seagar Street	D4
Shaftsbury Street	B3-B4
Skidmore Drive	A2
Spon Lane	D2-E2-E1
Springfield Crescent	F1
Stoney Lane	D4
Tantany Lane	B4
Tapestries Avenue	A3
Temple Street	B3-B4
The Expressway	A4-B4-C4-D4-E4-E3-F3
Thomas Street	E2
Thynne Street	E2-F2-F3
Trinity Road North	E2
Trinity Road South	E1
Trinity Street	E2
Trinity Way	E1-E2-E3
Turner Street	A2
Victoria Street	C2-C3
Walsall Street	D3-D4
Walter Street	E3
Watton Street	D1-E1
West Bromwich Ringway	C2-D2
Wheatley Street	A2
Winkle Street	A4
Wood Lane	A1-A2
Yarney Avenue	D2
Young Street	A2

Wednesbury

Albert Street	A2-B2-B1
Bilston Road	A3
Bridge Street	B1
Brunswick Park Road	C2
Brunswick Terrace	B2-B3
Camp Street	B2
Cedar Road	C1-C2
Cherry Lane	C1
Chestnut Road	C1
Church Hill	B3
Churchfields Road	B3-B4-C4
College Close	C1
Corporation Street	C2
Dale Street	A3
Darlaston Road	A3-A4
Deville Road	B3-B4
Dudley Street	A1-A2
Foley Street	C2-C3
Goldcroft Road	C4
Great Western Street	A1
Hall End	B3
Handley Street	C4
Hardy Road	C3
Hawthorne Road	A4-B4
High Street	B2-B3
High Bullen	A2-B2-B3-B2
Hobbs Road	B4-C4

Holden Road	C2
Hollies Drive	B2-B3
Holyhead Road	A3-A2-B2-B1
Hydes Road	C2
Kings Street	A2-A3
Knowles Street	C2-C3
Lilac Grove	C1
Lime Road	B4
Lloyd Street	A3
Lower High Street	B1-B2
Manor House Road	B3-B4
Mark Avenue	A3
Mark Road	A3
Market Place	B2
Meeting Street	A3
Mounts Road	B1-C1-C2
New Street	B1
Oakeswell Street	C2
Old Park Road	A3-A4
Park Lane	B4-C4
Park Street	A3-B3
Parkdale Avenue	C4
Perry Street	B1
Portway Road	C2
Potters Lane	A1-B1
Pritchard Street	C2-C3
Ridding Lane	B2-C2
Russell Street	B2
St James Street	A2
St Mary's Road	B3
Sheldon Avenue	B4-C4
Short Street	A3-A4
Spring Head	B2
Stafford Street	A2-A1-B1
Sycamore Road	C1-C2
Terrace Street	B3-C3
The Oval	B4
Trouse Lane	A3-B3
Union Street	A2-B2
Vicar Street	C3
Vicarage Road	B3-C3-C4
Victoria Street	A1-A2
Wakes Road	C1
Walsall Street	B2-C2-B3
Wellcroft Street	A3-B3
Wharfedale Street	B2-C2
Whitley Street	A3-B3
Windmill Street	C3
Wood Green	C3-C4
Woden Road South	C1
Yew Tree Lane	C1

Smethwick

Ada Road	C1
Alma Street	C4
Arden Road	A2-A3
Astbury Avenue	A1
Baldwin Street	B4-C4
Ballot Street	C3
Bearwood Road	B1-B2
Beech Way	C4
Beechfield Road	A2
Brasshouse Lane	A4
Brook Street	B4
Broom Field	A3
Buttress Way	A4-B4
Cape Hill	C2
Cemetery Road	A2

Cheshire Road	B1-B2
Church Road	A1-B1
Church Hill Street	A3-A4
Claremont Road	B2-C2
Coopers Lane	A3-B3
Corbett Street	C2-C3
Crockett's Lane	B3-B4
Cutler Street	B4
Dale Street	B1
Davison Road	A1
Dawson Street	B1
Edgbaston Road	B1-B2
Edith Road	C1-C2
Edward Road	A2-B2
Exeter Road	C3
Florence Road	C2
Gilbert Road	C1-C2
Grange Road	B1-C1
Grantham Road	A3
Green Street	A3
Hales Lane	A2
High Street	A4-A3-B3-B2-C2
Highfield Road	A3
Holly Street	A3
Hume Street	C2-C3
James Close	A3
Londonderry Lane	A2-A3
Manor Road	A2
Meadow Road	A2-B2
Messenger Road	B4-C4
New Street	B4
North Street	A3
Oakfield Road	C4
Old Chapel Road	A1
Parkes Street	A2
Pool Road	B3-B4
Portland Road	C3
Price Street	B4-C4-C3
Queens Close	A3
Rabone Lane	B4-C4
Raglan Road	C3
Regent Street	A3-A4-B4
Rolfe Street	A4-B4-C4
Roseberry Road	C2-C3
Rosefield Road	B1-B2-B3
St Mathews Road	C3
Salisbury Road	C2-C3
Selsey Road	C1
Shireland Road	C1-C2
Soho Street	C4
Soho Way	B4-C4
South Road	A3-A4
Stanhope Road	A1-B1
Stony Lane	A3-A4
Suffrage Lane	B3-C3
Sycamore Road	C1-C2
The Upland	A2
Thomas Street	C3-C4
Tiverton Road	B3-C3
Tollhouse Way	A4-B4
Trafalgar Road	C3
Valley Road	A1
Vicarage Road	A3
Victoria Park Road	B3-B4
Vince Street	A3
Waterloo Road	B1-C1-C2
Wellington Road	B1
Westbury Street	C1
Westfield Road	C2-C3-C4
Windmill Lane	C2-C3-C4

Key to Town Plan and Area Plan

Town Plan

AA Recommended roads	
Other roads	
Restricted roads	
Buildings of interest	Library
Car Parks	P
Parks and open spaces	
Churches	+
One Way Streets	

Area Plan

A roads	
B roads	
Locations	Springhill O
Urban area	

Street Index With Grid Reference

Wolverhampton

Albany Road	B3-C3
Albion Street	E3-F3
Alexandra Street	B2
Ashland Street	A1-B1
Bath Avenue	C3-C4
Bath Road	B3-C3
Bath Street	E2-F2
Bell Street	D2
Bilston Road	E2-E1-F1
Birch Street	C3
Broad Street	D3-E3-E4
Castle Street	D2-D3-E3
Chapel Ash	B3-B2-C2
Cheapside	D3
Cherry Street	B1-B2
Church Lane	C1-D1
Church Street	C1-D1
Clarence Road	C3
Clarendon Street	A3
Cleveland Road	D2-E2-E1-F1
Cleveland Street	C2-D2
Clifton Street	B2-B3
Commercial Road	F1-F2
Compton Road	A3-B3
Connaught Road	A3-A4
Corn Hill	E3-F3
Corn Hill Street	E3
Culwell Street	E4
Dale Street	B1
Darlington Street	C3-D3
Dudley Street	D2-D3
Duke Street	F1-F2
Elm Street	A2
Fryer Street	E3
Garrick Street	D2
George Street	D1
Gordon Street	E1-F1
Graiseley Street	B1-C1-B1
Great Brick Kiln Street	A1-B1-C1-C2
Great Western Street	D4-E4
Haden Hill	A3
Hallet Drive	C1
Hartley Street	A2-A3
Herrick Street	B2-C2
Horseley Field	E3-F3-F2
Humber Road	A1-A2
Jeddo Street	C1
Jenner Street	F1
Kimberley Street	A1
King Street	D3
Laburnum Street	A2-B2
Lansdowne Road	B4-C4
Larches Lane	A3-A4
Lever Street	D1-E1
Lichfield Street	D3-E3
Lime Street	A1-B1

Wolverhampton

Present-day Wolverhampton, capital of the Black Country, is a large and efficient town that belies its ancient origins. It was referred to as 'Heantun' in a 10th-century Royal charter, and the town coat of arms includes a cross ascribed to the Anglo-Saxon King Edgar.

In Victorian times Wolverhampton was widely known for its manufacture of chains, locks and nails, although the workshops were often tiny sheds in people's back yards. Today, many kinds of brass and iron products, as well as aircraft components, leave Wolverhampton's factories. Some different, but no less traditional, products of Midland craftsmen are displayed in the museum inside 19th-century Bantock House. These include japanned tin and papier-mâché articles and painted enamels, as well as early Worcester porcelain.

Pre-dating Wolverhampton's industrial history by several hundred years is the carved shaft of Dane's Cross in St Peter's churchyard. Standing 14ft high, near a holed Bargain Stone, it was supposed to commemorate the defeat of the Danes in a local battle. The church mostly dates from the 15th century, and has a panelled tower and fine stone pulpit. There was an earlier monastery on the site, refounded in 994 by Lady Wulfruna, whose charter can now be seen in the vestry.

Wolverhampton Area

SCALE 0 — 2 mls

N

Box denotes area covered by central plan

81

Worcester

County town and cathedral city, Worcester stands on the banks of the Severn in an area of rich agricultural land. Sadly, during the 1960s, the city suffered somewhat from ruthless redevelopment, but there is still much to interest the visitor, including The Commandery and the Tudor House, 15th-century buildings which both house museums. The cathedral, Worcester's oldest building, overlooks the river and the county cricket ground. It is one of the venues of the Three Choirs Festival, alternating with Gloucester and Hereford Cathedrals.

Worcester has become famous for its porcelain industry which was founded during the 18th century as an alternative to the ailing cloth trade. An exquisite collection of 'Royal Worcester' can be seen in the Dyson Perrins Museum.

Evesham is surrounded by the orchards that flourish in the fertile Vale of Evesham. It is an ancient market and light industrial town with two churches, a 16th-century bell-tower and the ruins of a Norman abbey all sharing the same grounds.

Malvern, famous for its mineral water, nestles at the foot of the Malvern Hills which are designated an Area of Outstanding Natural Beauty. Visitors have been drawn to this attractive town since Victorian times, and it retains much of the genteel elegance associated with bygone days.

Central Malvern

Central Evesham

LEGEND

Town Plan
AA Recommended roads	
Restricted roads	
Other roads	
Buildings of interest	Cinema
Car Parks	P
Parks and open spaces	
One Way Streets	→

Area Plan
A roads	
B roads	
Locations	Suckley ○
Urban area	

Street Index with Grid Reference

Worcester
All Saints Road	B2
Angel Place	C2-C3
Angel Row	B3-C3
Angel Street	C3
Arboreum Road	C4
Bank Street	C2
Black Lane South	A4-B4
Bridge Street	B2-C2
Britania Road	B4
Broad Street	C2-C3
Carden Street	D2-E2
Castle Street	B3-B4
Cecil Road	E2
Charles Street	D2
Church Street	C2
City Wall Road	D1-D2-D3
Cole Hill	E1
College Precinct	D1
College Street	D1
Copenhagen Street	C1-C2
Croft Road	B3-B2
Deans Way	C1-C2
Dolday	B2-C2
East Street	C4
Easy Row	B4
Edgar Street	D1
Farrier Street	B4-C4-C3
Foregate	C3
Foregate Street	C4-C3
Fort Royal Hill	E1
Foundry Street	E2
Friar Street	D1-D2
George Street	D3-E3
Grand Stand Road	A3-A2-B2
High Street	C2-C1-D1
Hill Street	E2-E3
Hylton Road	A3-A2-B2-B1
Love's Grove	B4
Lowesmoor	D3-D4
Lowesmoor Place	D4-E4
Lowesmoor Terrace	D4
Meal Cheapen Street	C3
Midland Road	F2-F3
Moor Street	D2-D3
New Road	B1
New Street	D2-D3
Newton Road	F3-F4
North Quay	B2
Park Street	E1-E2
Pheasant Street	D3
Pierpoint Street	C2
Powick Lane	C2
Pump Street	C2-D2
Quay Street	B2-C2-C1
Queen Street	C3-D3
Richmond Hill	E1-F1
Richmond Road	E1
Rose Terrace	E1-F1
St Martin's Gate	D3
St Mary's Street	B4-C4
St Nicholas Street	C3
St Paul's Street	D3-D2-E2
St Swithuns Street	C2-C3
St Wulstans Crescent	E1-F1
Sansome Street	C3
Sansome Walk	C4
Severn Terrace	A4-B4-B3
Shaw Street	C3
Sheriff Street	F4
Shrub Hill	E4-F4
Shrub Hill Road	E4-E3-F3
Sidbury	D1
South Field Street	C4-D4
South Parade	B2-C2-C1
South Quay	C1
Stanley Road	E2-F2
Tallow Hill	E3-F3
The Butts	B2-B3-C3
The Cross	C3
The Shambles	D2
The Tything	B4
Tolladine Road	E4-F4
Trinity Street	C3-C2
Tybridge Street	A1-A2-B2-B1
Union Street	D1
Vincent Road	E1-E2
Westbury Street	D4
Wyld's Lane	E1-F1-F2

Malvern
Abbey Road	A2-A1-B1
Albert Road South	B2-C2-C1
Albert Road North	B4-B3-B2
Avenue Road	B3-B2-C2
Back Lane	A4-A3
Barnard's Green	C3
Bellevue Terrace	A2
Broads Bank	A3-A4
Church Street	A3-A2-B2-B3
Clarence Road	B2-C2
Clerkenwell Crescent	B4-C4
College Road	B1
Como Road	A3-B3
Cookshot Road	B4
Court Road	C1
Davenham Close	B4
Edith Walk	A2-A3
Graham Road	A4-A3
Grange Road	A2-B2
Imperial Road	C2-C3
Lansdowne Crescent	C3
Lansdowne Terrace	C3
Madresfield Road	C3-C4
Orchard Road	B1-B2
Portland Road	B3
Priory Road	B3-B2-B1
Queen's Drive	A3
St Ann's Road	A2-A3
Sivan Pool Walk	A3-B3
Thorn Grove Road	C2
Tibberton Road	C3-C2
Victoria Road	A4-B4-B3
Wells Road	A2-A1
Woodshears Drive	C1
Woodshears Road	C1
Worcester Road	A4-A3-A2

Evesham
Abbey Road	A1-A2
Albert Road	A2-A3-B3
Avon Street	A2-A3-B3
Bewdley Street	A2-B2
Boat Lane	A1-A2-B2
Briar Close	A4-A3
Brick Kiln Street	B2-B3
Bridge Street	B2-C2
Burford Road	C2-C3
Cambria Road	B4
Castle Street	C2
Chapel Street	B2-B3
Church Street	C1-C2
Coopers Lane	C1
Common Road	B3-C3-C4
Conduit Hill	B3-C3
Cowl Street	B2
Coxlea Close	A3
Edward Street	A3
George Street	A3
Greenhill	A3-A4
Henry Street	A2-A3
Leicester Grove	B3
Lime Street	C2
Littleworth Street	A2-A3
Lower Leys	C2
Mansion Gardens	C1
Mill Street	B2-B3
Oat Street	B2
Owletts End	C1
Port Street	C2
Queens Road	A3
Rudge Road	A3
Rynal Place	B3
Rynal Street	B3
St Lawrence Road	A2
Swan Lane	B3
The Leys	C2
Victoria Avenue	B4
Vine Street	A2-B2
Waterside	B1-C1-C2
West Street	A2
Windsor Road	B4
Worcester Road	A4

WORCESTER
Worcester Cathedral, set high on the banks of the Severn with views across the Malvern Hills, has dominated the city for centuries. The chapter house, with its massive central column, is considered one of the finest in Britain.

North Wales

Llandudno combines Victorian charm and elegance with the modern amenities of a popular holiday destination. Lying at the foot of Great Orme and Little Orme, its varied attractions include miles of sandy beaches, the Doll Museum, the Mostyn Art Gallery, and the Cabinlift (Britain's longest cable car run). St Tudno's Church is 6th-century.

Colwyn Bay Three miles of golden sand stretch between Rhos-on-Sea and Old Colwyn at Colwyn Bay. Notable in a host of activities for visitors are the Harlequin Puppet Theatre and the extensive facilities of 50-acre Eirias Park.

Rhyl has been a resort for over a century and now attracts more visitors than ever to the glittering attractions of Suncentre, Fishing Village, Skateworld, Cyclorama and Marine Lake. Part of the shoreline is bordered by an elegant promenade edged by flower beds and lawns.

Holyhead The ruins of an ancient settlement at the summit of Holyhead mountain provide a beautiful backdrop to Holyhead, which has become a busy port for car ferry traffic to Laoghaire. The Parish Church of St Cybi is medieval. Close by Trearddur Bay is excellent for watersports.

Conwy boasts Edward I's fine 13th-century castle and Telford's magnificent suspension bridge, built over 150 years ago. The smallest house in Britain stands on the Quay.

Central Holyhead

Central Conwy

Street Index with Grid Reference

Llandudno

Abbey Road	A3-B3-B4
Albert Street	B3-C3
Anglesey Road	A3-A4
Arvon Avenue	B3-B4
Augusta Street	C2-C3
Bodnant Road	C1
Brynian Road	A2-B2-B1
Builder Street	C2
Builder Street West	B1-B2
Chapel Street	B2
Church Walks	A3-B3-B4
Clifton Road	B3
Council Street West	C2
Cwlach Road	A3-B3-B4
Cwm Road	C1-C2
Deganwy Avenue	B3
Dinas Road	B2
Fford Dewi	C1
Ffordd Penrhyn	C1-C2
Gloddaeth Avenue	A2-A3-B3
Gloddaeth Street	B3-B4
Great Ormes	A2-A3
Hill Terrace	B4-C4
Hospital Road	B1-C1
King's Avenue	B2
King's Road	B1-B2
Lloyd Street	B3-C3
Llwynon Road	A4-B4
Madoc Street	B3-C3
Maelgwn Road	B3
Maesdu Road	B1-C1
Mostyn Street	B3-C3
Mowbray Road	B1-B2
North Parade	C4
Old Road	B4
Oxford Road	C2
Plas Road	B4
St Andrews Avenue	B2
St Beuno's Road	A4
St David's Road	B2-B3
St Mary's Road	B3-B2-C2
St Seiriol's Road	B2-B3
South Parade	B4-C4-C3
The Oval	A2-A3-B3
The Parade	C3
Trinity Avenue	B1-B2-C2
Trinity Square	C3
Ty-Gwyn Road	B4
Tyn-y-Coed Road	A3-A4
Upper Mostyn Street	B4
Vaughan Street	C2-C3
West Parade	A2-A3
Winllan Avenue	A2-B2

Colwyn Bay

Abbey Drive	A4
Abbey Road	A4
Abergele Road	B2-B1-C1
Allanson Road	A3
Bay View Road	B2
Brompton Avenue	A2-A3-A4
Bryn Avenue	C1
Cayley Promenade	A3
Cherry Tree Lane	A1
Church Road	A4
Coed-Pella Road	B1-B2
Colwyn Crescent	A4
Conway Road	A2-B2
Ebberston Road East	A3
Ebberston Road West	A3
Eirias Road	C1
Elian Road	C1
Everard Road	A3-A4
Greenfield Road	B1-B2-C2-C1
Groes Road	C1
Hesketh Road	C1
Kings Drive	A1
Kings Road	A1-A2
Lansdowne Road	A2-B2
Lawson Road	B1-C1
Llannerch Road East	A3
Llannerch Road West	A3
Marine Drive	A4
Oak Drive	A2-B2
Old Highway	A1-B1-C1
Park Road	B1
Penrhyn Avenue	A4
Pen-y-Bryn Road	A1-B1
Princes Drive	A2-B2
Promenade	A3-B3-B2-C2-C1
Pwll-y-Crochan Avenue	A1-A2-B2
Queens Drive	A1-B1-B2
Rhiw Road	B1-B2
Rhos Promenade	A3-A4
Rhos Road	A3-A4
Victoria Park	A2
Whitehall Road	A3
Woodland Park	B1
York Road	B1

Rhyl

Abbey Street	B2-C2
Aled Avenue	D1
Alexandra Road	D3
Aquarium Street	B2
Barry Road	B1-C1
Bath Street	C3-C2-D2
Bedford Street	C2
Beechwood Road	D3
Bodfor Street	C2
Bridgegate Road	E2
Brighton Road	C2-D2-D3
Bro Deg	F1
Bryn Avenue	E2-E3
Brynhedydd Road	F3
Brynhyfryd Avenue	D2
Bryntirion Avenue	D3
Burns Drive	E3-E4
Butterton Road	B1-B2
Carlisle Avenue	E4-F4
Cefndy Road	D1-E1
Cheltenham Avenue	F2
Cherry Tree Walk	F2
Chester Street	D3
Church Street	C2-C3
Churton Road	D3
Clement Drive	F1
Clifton Park Road	D2-E2
Clwyd Street	C2
Conwy Street	D3
Crescent Road	C2
Dyserth Road	E2-F2-F1
East Parade	C3-D3
Eastville Avenue	E3-F3
Eaton Avenue	F4
Edgbaston Road	F3
Ellis Avenue	B1
Elm Grove	E3
Elwy Drive	D2
Elwy Street	C2
Ernest Street	C1-D1
Fairfield Avenue	C3-D3
Fford Anwyl	F2-F3
Ffordd Las	C1
Fford Elan	F2
Foryd Bridge	A1
Garford Road	F4
Garnett Avenue	B1-C1
Graham Drive	E3
Grange Road	D2-E2
Grosvenor Avenue	E1-E2
Grosvenor Road	D3
Grove Park Avenue	E3
Gwynfryn Avenue	C1
Hadley Crescent	E2
Handsworth Crescent	F1
Hardy Avenue	E3-E4
Highfield Park	D3-E3
High Street	C2
Hilton Drive	E4-F4
John Street	B2
Kinard Drive	D2-D3
Kings Avenue	C1-C2
Kingsley Avenue	D1
Kinmel Street	C2
Knowles Avenue	E3-E4-F4
Lake Avenue	B1
Larch Drive	F3
Larkmount Road	E2-F2
Llewelyn Court	F1
Llys Dedwydd	F3
Llys Gwynant	F2
Llys Helyg	F2
Lynton Walk	E3
Madryn Avenue	E1
Marine Drive	D3-D4-E4
Marsh Road	B1-C1-C2-D2
Mayfield Grove	E2
Medea Street	E3-E4
Mernal Avenue	D3
Merllyn Road	E1-F1
Mill Bank Road	D2
Molineaux Road	F3-F4
Morley Road	D2
Netley Road	C1
Oakville Avenue	E3-F3
Old Golf Road	E3-E4
Olivia Drive	E3
Palace Avenue	B1-B2
Parc Esmor	E3
Pendre Avenue	F1
Pendyffryn Road	E1-E2
Pen-y-Maes Avenue	F1
Prince Edward Avenue	D1-D2
Quay Street	A1
Queen Street	C2
Queens Walk	D3
Rees Avenue	E3
Regent Road	E3
Rhydwen Drive	C1
Rhyl Coast Road	E3-F3
Ridgway Avenue	F4
River Street	B1-B2
Russel Road	C2-D2-D3
St Asaph Street	D3
St George's Crescent	E3
St Margaret's Drive	E1
Sandringham Avenue	B1
Seabank Road	B1
Sisson Street	D1
Spruce Avenue	E3-F3
Stanley Park Avenue	E1
Sussex Street	C2
Sydenham Avenue	B1
Tarleton Street	D3
The Grove	D3
Thornley Avenue	F1
Trellewelyn Road	E1-F1
Tynewydd Road	E3-E4
Vale Park	D1
Vale Road	D1-E1
Vale Road Bridge	C2-D2-D3
Victoria Road	C1-D1
Walford Avenue	D1
Warren Road	E1
Water Street	C2
Weaver Avenue	E1
Wellington Road	A1-B1-B2-D3
Westbourne Avenue	B1
Westfield Road	D1-D2
West Kinmel Street	C1-C2
West Parade	A1-B1-B2-C2-C3
Weston Road	C1
Wood Road	B1

Holyhead

Boston Street	A3
Bryn Goleu Avenue	A4
Cambrian Street	A2-A3
Edmund Street	A2
Fford Beibio	C2
Fford Tudur	C2
Hill Street	A2
Holborn Road	A1
Llanfawr Road	B1
Longford Road	A1-A2
Maes Hyfryd Road	A1
Marine Square	B3
Market Street	A2
Morawellon Road	C1
Moreton Road	A1
Newry-Faws Street	A3-A4
Newry Street	A3
Park Road	A3-A4
Queen Park	A3
St Cybi Street	A3
Stanley Street	A2-A3
Station Road	A1
The Prince of Wales Road	A4-B4-B3
Thomas's Street	A2
Turkey Shore Road	B1-B2-C2-C3
Victoria Road	A2-A3-B3
William Street	A2
Wynne Street	A3

Conwy

Bangor Road	A4-A3-B3-B2
Benarth Road	C2
Berry Street	B3
Bryn Castell	B1
Bryn Celyn	A3
Bryn Eithin	B1
Bryn Hyfryd Park	A2
Cadnant Park	A3
Castle Square	C2
Castle Street	B2-B3
Chapel Street	B3
Church Street	B3
High Street	B2-B3
Llanrwst Road	A1-B1-B2
Lower Gate Street	B3
Maes Gweryl	A1
Mount Pleasant	A2-A3
New Bridge	C2
Old Road	A2
Quay	B3
Rosehill Street	B2
Rosemary Lane	A2-B2
St Agnes Road	A1-A2
Sychant Pass Road	A2
Town Ditch Road	B3
Ty Gwyn Gardens	A2
Uppergate Street	A2-B2

85

South Wales

Aberystwyth is both a picturesque seaside town and an important centre of learning. The National Library of Wales and several colleges and museums, are here, and by way of contrast, freshwater and sea fishing are also popular. Overlooking the southern seafront are the 1277 castle ruins; the Vale of Rheidol Steam Railway is nearby.

Carmarthen is a hive of activity of industries, colleges and schools. The River Towey offers boating and fishing; the Leisure Centre offers other sports, and St Peter's Church and the County Museum are full of interest. A Redevelopment Scheme has kept the town's old markets.

Tenby Surrounded by 13th-century walls and overlooked by medieval St Mary's church, this major resort boasts four beaches, a pretty harbour and interesting shops and streets. The Tudor Merchant's House and the Tenby Museum are worth seeing; across from Castle Beach stands St Catherine's Rock with its disused fort (closed to visitors). Three miles off the coast are the bird colonies and seals of Caldey Island, which is run by Cistercian monks skilled in producing goods such as perfume from wild flowers.

Pembroke is dominated by a magnificent Norman castle, and other attractions are Monkton Priory and the Mill Pond Walk. The town is a perfect touring centre for South Pembrokeshire.

86

Central Pembroke

Central Aberystwyth

LEGEND

A A Recommended roads
Other roads
Restricted roads
Buildings of interest   Cinema
Parks and open spaces
Churches   +
One Way Streets
Car Parks   P

Street Index with Grid Reference

Carmarthen

Abbey Mead	F4
Barn Road	D3-D4
Blue Street	C2-C3
Brewery Road	C4-D4
Bridge Street	D2
Brynhaul Street	C4
By-Pass	A1-B1-B2-C2
Cambrian Place	E4
Capel Evan Road	D3
Chapel Street	E3
Church Street	A4-A3-B3-B4
College Road	C2-D2
Coracle Way	A3
Crispin Avenue	D2-D3-E3
Dan-y-Banc	F3-F4
East Parade	C4-D3-E3
Fair Lane	B4-C4
Fountain Hall Terrace	D4
Francis Terrace	B3-B4-C4-C3
Glannant Road	D3
Hall Street	D3
Jackson's Lane	D3
John Street	D2-D3-E3
King Street	A4
Knoll Gardens	B3-C3
Lammas Street	A4-B4
Limegrove Avenue	D4-D3-E3
Little Water Street	D1-E1
Llangunoor Road	D4-E4
Long Acre Road	B4
Lon Hir	A1-A2
Maesyddernen	C3
Mansell Street	B4
Millbrook Crescent	A2
Monument Hill	B3-B2-C2
Morfa Lane	C4
Morgan Street	C3
Morley Street	B4
Myrddin Crescent	A4-B4
Nant Yr Arian	E3
North Parade	D2-E2-E1-F1
Old Llangunnor Road	E4-F4
Old Oak Lane	

Old Priory Road	F4
Old Station Road	D2-E2-E3
Orchard Street	D3-D4
Parade Road	E3
Parc Bagnell	C4
Parc Maen Street	B3
Penbryn Avenue	A3
Penlan Road	C4-D4
Pensarn Road	D1-D2
Pentrefelin Street	C4-D4
Penuel Street	E4-F4-F3
Penymorfa	E1-F1
Picton Court	B3
Picton Monument	A2
Picton Place	A2-A3
Picton Terrace	A2-B2-B3
Pond Street	C4
Priory Street	E3-E4
Quay Street	C2-D2
Queen Street	D3
Red Street	D3
Richmond Terrace	D4-E4
St Catherine Street	B3-C3
St David's Avenue	B3
St David's Street	B3-C3
St Mary Street	D2-D3
St Nons Avenue	B3
St Peter's Street	E3
Southern Terrace	D1
Spilman Street	D2-D3-E3
Station Approach	C1-D1-D2
Steele Avenue	A2-A3
Sycamore Way	A3
The Avenue	E4-E3-F3
The Parade	E3
The Quay	C2-D2
Union Street	A2-B2
Waterloo Terrace	D4
Water Street	C3
Wellfield Road	D4
Woods Row	D3

Tenby

Battery Road	C1
Bridge Street	E2
Broadwell Hayes	A4-B4
Church Park	C1-D1
Clareston Road	C2
Crackwell Street	D2-E2
Cresswell	E1-E2
Culver Park	D1
Deer Park	C3-D3-D2
Edward Street	C2
Esplanade	D1
Gas Lane	D4
Greenhill Avenue	C2-C3
Greenhill Road	C3
Gunfort Paragon	E1
Harding Street	C2
Harries Street	C1
Heywood Court	A3-A4
Heywood Lane	A4-A3-B3-B4
High Street	D2
Jones Terrace	D2
Leach Way	B4
Lexden Terrace	E2
Lower Frog Street	D2-D1-E1
Lower Park Road	C2-C3
Marsh Road	A2-B2-B3

Pembroke

Beaufort Road	B3
Belmont Terrace	C1
Bridgend Terrace	A2-A3
Bush Hill	A4
Castle View	A4
Clare Walk	B4
Coldwell Terrace	A3-A2-B2
Common Road	B4
Devon Drive	B2
East Back	B4
Elm Grove	A3-B3-B4
Golden Hill Road	B3-C3
Golden Lane	A3
Green	A4-B4
Green Meadow Avenue	C1
Grove Hill	C2
Holyland Road	C1-C2
Lower Lane	B4
Lower Row	A3-A2-B2-C2
Main Street	A1-A2
Mansell Street	A1-A2
Norgans Terrace	C2
Orchard Buildings	A2
Owen Street	B1-B2
Paynter Street	A3
Rocky Park	B3-B4
St Anne's Crescent	B1-B2
St Daniel's Hill	A2-A1-B1
South Road	C2
Station Road	A3-A2-B2
Strongbow Walk	A1-A2-B2
The Parade	B4
Thomas Street	C3-C4
Upper Row	C1-C2
Victoria Lane	A3
Well Hill	
Westgate Hill	

Narberth Road	C4
Newell Hill	B2-B3
Norton	C4-D4-D3
Park Place	C2
Park Road	C2
Park Terrace	C1-C2
Picton Road	D1-D2
Picton Terrace	D1
Queens Parade	C1
Rocky Park	C3-D3-D2
St Florence Parade	D1-D2
St Georges Street	D2-E2
St John's Hill	C3-D3
St Julian Street	E2
St Mary Street	D2-E2-E1
Serpentine Road	A4
Southcliffe Street	D1
South Parade	D2
Sutton Street	D1
The Croft	D3-D4
The Glebe	C4
The Maudlins	A4-B4
Tor Lane	E1-E2
Trafalgar Road	D2
Tudor Square	E2
Upper Frog Street	D2-D3
Upper Park Road	C2-D2
Victoria Street	D1
Warren Street	C2-D2
White Lion Street	D2-D3

West Street	A2
Whitehall Avenue	A4
Whitehall Drive	A4
Williamson Street	A1-A2
Windsor Road	B3
Woodbine Terrace	A3-B3
Woodside Avenue	A4

Aberystwyth

Alexandra Street	B2-C2
Baker Street	B3
Bath Street	B3
Bridge Street	B1-B2
Bryn Road	C4
Buarth Road	C2
Cambrian Street	B2-C2-C3
Chalybeate Street	B2
Corporation Street	B3
Custom House Street	A2
Eastgate	B2
George Street	B2
Glanrafon Terrace	B1
Glyndwr Road	B1-B2-C2
Grays Inn Road	B2
Great Darkgate Street	B2
Greenfield Street	B1-C1
High Street	A2-A3-B3
Loveden Road	C3
Maesyrafon	B1-C1
Marine Terrace	B3-B4
Market Street	B2
Mill Street	B1-B2
New Promenade	A2-A3
New Street	A2-B2
Northgate Street	C3
North Parade	B3-C3
North Road	C3-C4
Park Avenue	B2-C2-C1
Pier Street	B2-B3
Plas Crag Avenue	C1-C2
Poplar Row	C2-C3
Portland Road	C2-C3
Portland Street	B3-C3
Powell Street	B2
Prince's Street	B2
Prospect Street	A2
Quay Road	A1
Queens Avenue	B4-C4
Queens Road	B4-B3-C3
Queen Street	B2
Rheidol Terrace	A1-A2
Riverside Terrace	B1
Sea View Place	A2
South Marine Terrace	A1-A2
South Road	A2-A1-B1
Stanley Street	C2
Terrace Road	B3-B2-C2
Thespian Street	C2-C3
Trefor Road	C3-C4
Trinity Place	C2
Trinity Road	C2-C3
Union Street	B2
Vaynor Street	C3
Vulcan Street	A2
Victoria Terrace	B4

87

Cardiff

Strategically important to both the Romans and the Normans, Cardiff slipped from prominence in medieval times and remained a quiet market town in a remote area until it was transformed – almost overnight – by the effects of the Industrial Revolution. The valleys of South Wales were a principal source of iron and coal – raw materials which helped to change the shape and course of the 19th-century world. Cardiff became a teeming export centre; by the end of the 19th century it was the largest coal-exporting city in the world.

Close to the castle – an exciting place with features from Roman times to the 19th century – is the city's civic centre – a fine concourse of buildings dating largely from the early part of the 20th century. Among them is the National Museum of Wales – a superb collection of art and antiquities from Wales and around the world.

Barry has sandy beaches, landscaped gardens and parks, entertainment arcades and funfairs. Like Cardiff it grew as a result of the demand for coal and steel, but now its dock complex is involved in the petrochemical and oil industries.

Caerphilly is famous for two things – a castle and cheese. The cheese is no longer made here, but the 13th-century castle, slighted by Cromwell, still looms above its moat. No castle in Britain – except Windsor – is larger.

LEGEND

Town Plan
AA recommended route	═══
Restricted roads	━ ━ ━
Other roads	═══
Buildings of interest	Cinema ☐
Car parks	P
Parks and open spaces	◢
One way streets	㇐

Area Plan
A roads	━━━
B roads	━━━
Locations	Glyncoch ○
Urban area	◯

Street Index with Grid Reference

Cardiff

Adam Street	E1-E2-F2
Bedford Street	F4
Boulevard de Nantes	C3-D3
Bridge Street	D1-D2-E2
Brook Street	B2
Bute Street	D1-E1
Bute Terrace	D1-E1
Caroline Street	D1
Castle Street	C2
Cathedral Street	A4-A3-B3-B2-A2
Charles Street	D2-E2
Churchill Way	E2-E3
City Hall Road	C3-C4-D4
City Road	F4
Clare Street	B1
Coldstream Terrace	B2
College Road	C4
Cowbridge Road	A2
Cowbridge Road East	A2-B2-C2
Craddock Street	A1-B1
Crichton Street	D1
Custom House Street	D1
David Street	E2
Despenser Place	B1
Despenser Street	B1
Duke Street	C2-D2
Dumfries Lane	D3-E3
Dumfries Place	E3
East Grove	F4-F3
East Moor Road	F1
Fitzalan Place	F3-F2
Fitzhamon Embankment	B1-C1
Glossop Road	F3
Gloucester Street	B1

Green Street	B2
Greyfriars Road	D3
Hamilton Street	A3
Herbert Street	E1
High Street	C2-D2
King Edward VII Avenue	C4-D4-D3-C3
King's Road	A2-A3
Kingsway	C3-D3-D2
Knox Road	E3-F3-F2
Lewis Street	A2
Lower Cathedral Road	B1-B2
Machen Place	A1-B1
Mary Ann Street	E1-E2
Mill Lane	D1
Moira Place	F3
Moira Terrace	F2-F3
Museum Avenue	C4-D4
Museum Place	D4
Neville Street	A2-B2-B1
Newport Road	E3-F3-F4
Ninian Park Road	A1-B1
North Lutton Place	F2-F3
North Road	B4-C4-C3
Oxford Lane	F4
Park Grove	D4-E4
Park Lane	D3-E3
Park Place	D4-D3-E3
Park Street	C1-D1
Plantagenet Street	B1-C1
Queen Street	D2-D3
Richmond Road	E4
Richmond Terrace	E4
St Andrew's Place	D4-E4
St John Street	D2
St Mary's Street	D1-D2
St Peter's Street	E4-F4
Salisbury Road	E4
Senghenydd Road	D4-E4
South Lutton Place	F2-F3
Station Terrace	E2-E3
The Friary	D1-D2
The Hayes	D1-D2
The Parade	E3-F3-F4
The Walk	E3-E4-F4
Talbot Street	A3
Tudor Street	B1-C1
Tyndall Street	E1-F1
Wellington Street	A2
Wells Street	A1
Westgate Street	C2-D2-D1
West Grove	E4-E3-F3
Wharton Street	D2
Windsor Place	E3
Windsor Road	F2
Wood Street	C1-D1
Working Street	D2
Wyndham Place	A2
Wyndham Street	A1-A2

Barry

Aneurin Road	C3
Barry Road	A3-A4-B3-B4-C4
Bassett Street	C2-C3
Belvedere Crescent	B1-B2
Beryl Road	A1-A2
Brook Street	C2-C3
Buttrills Road	A1-A2
Caradoc Avenue	B4-C4

Castleland Street	C1-C2
Cemetery Road	A3-A4
Chesterfield Street	C4
Collard Crescent	B4
Commercial Road	C3-C4
Cora Street	B2-C2
Cornwall Rise	A3-A4
Cornwall Road	B4
Coronation Street	B1
Cross Street	B1-C1-C2
Crossways Street	C2-C3
Court Road	C2-C3-C4
Davies Street	C3-C4
Devon Avenue	B3
Dock View Road	B1-C1-C2
Dyfan Road	B4
Evans Street	A2-B2
Evelyn Street	B2-C2
Fairford Street	C4
Field View Road	C4
Fryatt Street	B1
George Street	C1-C2
Gilbert Street	C4
Gladstone Road	A1-A2-B2-B3-C3
Glebe Street	C4
Greenwood Street	A1-B1
Guthrie Street	C3-C2
Hannah Street	C4-C3
Herbert Street	C4
Holton Road	A1-B1-B2-C2
Hywel Crescent	B4-C4
Jewel Street	C1-C2
Kendrick Road	A1
Kingsland Crescent	B1-C1
Lee Road	C4
Lombard Street	A1-A2
Lower Pyke Street	C2
Maesycwm Street	B2-B3-C3
Merthyr Dyfan Road	A4
Merthyr Street	B1-B2-C2
Monmouth Way	A4
Morel Street	C2-C3
Newlands Street	B2
Orchard Drive	B3-B4
Pardoe Crescent	A3
Pyke Street	C3-C2
Regent Street	A2-B2
Richard Street	A2-B2
St Mary's Avenue	C1-C2
St Pauls Avenue	A1
St Teilo Avenue	A3-A4
Slade Road	A4
Somerset Road	A3
Somerset Road East	A3-B3
Southey Street	A2-A3
Station Street	C1
Thomson Street	B1
Tordoff Way	A3
Ty-Newydd Road	A3-B3-B2
Walker Road	A2
Warwick Way	B4
Woodlands Road	A2-B2-B3-C3
Wyndham Street	B2-C2

Caerphilly

Bartlet Street	B2-B1-C1
Bedwas Road	C3-C4
Bradford Street	B1-B2

Broomfield Street	B2
Bronrhiw Avenue	C1
Brynau Road	C3
Caenant Road	A4
Caer Bragdy	C4
Cardiff Road	B1-B2
Castle Street	C3
Celyn Avenue	B4
Celyn Grove	B4
Charles Street	C4
Claude Road	A1-A2-B2
Clive Street	B1-B2
Crescent Rod	A2-A3-B3
Danycoed	C1
Dol-y-Felen Street	B4
East View	C2
Florence Grove	A2-B2
Goodrich Street	C1-C2
Gwyn Drive	A4
Heol Fanal	A3
Heol Gledyr	A2
Heol Trecastell	A2-A3
Hillside	B1
Heol-y-Beddau	A2
Heol-yr-Owen	A3
King Edward Avenue	B1-C1
Ludlow Street	A2-B2-B1
Maes Glas	C1
Meadow Crescent	C1-C2
Mill Road	A4-B4-B3
Morgan Street	A4-B4
Mountain Road	B1
Nantgarw Road	A3-B3
North View Terrace	C2-C3
Parc-y-Felin Street	B4
Park Lane	B2
Pentrebone Street	B2
Piccadilly Square	C3
Pontygwindy Road	B4-C4
Porset Close	C3
Porset Drive	C2-C3
Prince's Avenue	C1
Railway Terrace	C1
Rectory Road	A1-B1
St Christopher's Drive	A1-A2
St Clears Close	A1
St Fagans Street	B2
St Martins Road	A1-B1
Salop Street	B2
Southern Street	C2-C3
Station Terrace	B1-C1
Stockland Street	B2
Tafwy Walk	B3-B4
Ton-y-Felen Road	C3
Underwood	C1
Van Road	C2
White Street	C2
Windsor Street	B2

Newport

When the Industrial Revolution hit South Wales Newport, on the River Usk, came into its own as a harbour for the export of the coal and iron products manufactured in the valleys. At the zenith of Newport's activity in the mid 19th century there were six miles of quays. Today it is still an important port but the range of industries using it has expanded as light industry has taken over.

The Civic Centre just to the west of the town centre is a rather striking development which is particularly well-known for a series of modern murals that illustrate the history of Monmouthshire (now part of Gwent). Further background to Newport, including the Chartist Riots of 1839, and the iron industry can be found in the town museum in John Frost Square. There is also an interesting section on the Roman history of the area, particularly concerning the nearby forts of Caerleon and Caerwent. The city is relatively short of historic buildings, but St Woolos' Cathedral, crowning Stow Hill, dates back to Norman times. Its unusual name is believed to be a corruption of Gwynllyw, a local baron who built the first church on this site.

Perhaps Newport's most remarkable structure is the Transporter Bridge which is one of just two left in Britain – the other is at Middlesbrough. The bridge consists of a suspended moveable platform which carries cars and pedestrians across the river.

90

Newport Area

LEGEND

Town Plan

AA recommended route	
Restricted roads	
Other roads	
Buildings of interest	Hall
Car parks	P
Parks and open spaces	
One way streets	→

Area Plan

A roads	
B roads	
Locations	Redwick O
Urban area	

Street Index with Grid Reference

Newport

Albert Avenue	F3-F4
Albert Terrace	B2
Allt-yr-yn Avenue	A4-A3-B3-B4
Allt-yr-yn Close	A4
Allt-yr-yn Road	A4
Archibald Street	F2-F3
Barneswell Road	C2-C3
Bedford Road	E3
Bishop Street	E4
Bishton Street	E2-F2
Blewitt Road	B2
Bond Street	D4
Bridge Street	B3-C3
Bristol Street	E4-F4
Bryngwyn Road	A2-B2
Brynhyfryd Road	B1-B2
Caerau Crescent	A1-A2
Caerau Road	A1-A2-B2
Caerleon Road	E4
Canal Parade	D1-D2
Cardiff Road	C1-D1
Caroline Street	D1-D2
Cedar Road	E3
Charles Street	C2
Chepstow Road	D3-E3-F3
Christchurch Road	F4
Church Road	E4-F4
Clarence Place	C3-D3-D4
Clifton Place	B2-B1-C1
Clifton Road	B1-C1
Clyffard Crescent	B2
Clytha Park Road	A3-B2-B1
Clytha Square	C1
Collier Street	D4
Colne Street	D2-D3
Commercial Street	C3-C2-C1-D1
Corelli Street	D4
Corporation Road	D3-E3-E2-F2-F1
Coverack Road	E1-E2-F2
Crawford Road	E4
Crown Street	F3
Cyril Street	E2
Dean Street	E4-F4
Dewsland Park Road	B1-C1
Devon Place	B3-C3
Dock Street	D2-D1-E1
Dos Road	C4
Duckpool Road	F3-F4
East Street	B2
East Usk Road	D4
Edward VII Avenue	A2-A3
Elizabeth Terrace	D1-D2
Eton Road	E2-E3
Exeter Street	E3-F3
Factory Road	C4
Fairoak Avenue	F4
Fairoak Terrace	F3
Feering Street	E2-E1-F1
Fields Avenue	A3
Fields Park Avenue	A3
Fields Park Crescent	A3
Fields Park Road	A3
Fields Road	B3-C3
Friars Road	B1
George Street	C1-D1-E1
Glebe Street	F3
Godfrey Road	B3
Gold Tops	B3
Gordon Street	F2
Grafton Road	D3
Graham Street	B1-B2
Granville Street	D1
Halstead Street	F2
Harrow Road	E3
Henry Street	C4
Hereford Street	E3-E4
Hilla Road	A2
Hill Street	C1-C2
Jeffrey Street	E2-E3
Junction Road	E4-F4
Kelvedon Street	F1
Keynsham Avenue	C1
Kingsway	C3-D3-D2
Leicester Road	D4
Lennard Street	F2
Lilleshall Street	F1
Livingstone Place	E3-F3
Llanthewy Road	A1-A2-B2
Llanvair Road	D4
Llanwern Street	E2-F2-F3
Locke Street	C4
London Street	F3-F4
Lucas Street	C4
Maindee Parade	F3-F4
Manchester Street	E4-F4

Manley Road	A2
Marlborough Road	E3-F3
Mellon Street	D1
Mill Street	C3-C4
North Street	C2
Oakfield Road	A2-A3
Park Square	C1
Phillip Street	F2
Prince Street	E3-E4
Pugsley Street	C4-D4
Riverside	D4
Rodney Road	D3
Rose Street	C4
Rudry Street	D4
Rugby Road	E2-E3
Ruperra Street	D1
St Edward Street	B1-B2
St Marks Crescent	B3-B4
St Mary Street	B2-C2
St Woollos Road	B1-B2
Serpentine Road	B3
Soho Street	F2
Spencer Road	A2
Stanley Road	B3
Stow Hill	A1-B1-C1-C2-C3
Stow Park Avenue	A1
Stow Park Circle	A1
Stow Park Crescent	A1
Summerhill Avenue	E3
Tregare Street	D4-E4
Trostrey Street	E4
Tunnel Terrace	B2
Turner Street	D4-E4
Tyllwyd Road	A2
Queens Hill Crescent	B4-C4-C3
Queensway	B3-C3
Victoria Avenue	F3
Victoria Road	C1
Vivian Road	F1-F2
Wednesbury Street	F1-F2
Westfield Road	A2-A3
West Street	B2-C2-C3
Wharf Road	F2-F3
Windsor Terrace	B2
Witham Street	F1-F2
Wyndham Street	C4
York Place	B1-B2

Cwmbran

Abbey Road	B1
Caradoc Road	B4-C4
Chapel Street	A4-B4
Clomendy Road	A3-A2-B2-B1
Commercial Road	A1-B1
Edlogan Way	C4
Forgeside	B3-B4
General Rees Square	B3
Glyndwr Road	C2-C3-C4
Grange Lane	B4
Grange Road	C1-C2-C3-C4
Greenforge Way	A3-A4
Greenhill Road	A3-A4
Green Meadow Way	A1

Hanbury Close	B4
Hill Top	A1
Isca Close	C4
Llanfrechfa Way	C1
Llantarnam Road	C1
Llywelyn Road	B3-B2-B1-C1
Long Hollow	B4
Malpas Street	B1
Meandy Way	A4-B4
Milton Close	A1
North Walk	B3
Oak Street	B1
Orchard Lane	C4
Penywaun Road	A1
Plas Graig	C4
Plas Islwyn	B4
Porth Mawr Road	B4
Prospect Place	A1
Radnor Way	B1-B2
Redbrook Way	B2-C2
St Arvans Road	C1-C2
St Davids Road	C1-C2-C3-C4
St Dials Road	A2-A1-B1
Somerset Road	C4
South Walk	B2-B3
Star Street	B1
Talgarth Close	B1
The Mall	B3
Tintern Close	B1-C1
Trelech Close	C1
Trussel Road	B4-C4
Tudor Road	B2-C2
Turberville Road	C4
Ventor Road	B1-C1
Victoria Street	B2-B1-C1
Wesley Street	A1-B1
Whitebrook Way	B2-C2
Woodside Road	A3-A4
Yew Tree Terrace	A1

Pontypool

Albion Road	A2-B2
Blaendare Road	A1-B1
Bridge Street	A2
Broadway	A2-A3-A4
Bryngwyn Road	A2
Brynwern	A3
Channel View	C3-C4
Churchwood Close	B4
Clarence Road	B2-B1-C2-C1
Clarence Street	B2
Coedcae Place	A2
College Road	C3-C4
Commercial Street	B3
Conway Road	A4
Crumlin Street	A2
Cwmyniscoy Road	C1
Davis Close	C2
Dingle Road	B1-C1
East View	A2-A3
Edward Street	A3-A4
Farm Road	B1
George Street	A4-A3-A2
Gwent Street	A2

Haden Street	A2
Hanbury Road	B2-B3
High Street	A2-A3
Hillside Drive	B1
James Street	C4
John Street	A3-A4
King Street	A3-A4
Lime Kiln Road	A2-B2
Lower Bridge Street	B2
Lower Park Gardens	B3-B4
Maesderwen Road	C1
Market Street	A3-B3
Michael Way	A4-B4
Nicholas Street	A2
North Road	A3
Old Penygarn	C4
Osbourne Road	A4-A3-B4-B3
Park Crescent	A3
Park Gardens	B3-B4
Park Road	B3-B4
Penygarn Road	B4-C4
Pen-y-Graig Terrace	B1
Penywain Road	A4
Prince Street	A3
Queen Street	A3
Riverside	B3-B4
Rockhill Road	C1
St Codac's Road	C4
St David's Close	B3-C3
St Jame's Field	B2
St Matthew's Road	B1
School Lane	A4
School View	A4
South View	A3-A4
Tranch Road	A2-A3
Trosnant Street	B2
Upper Park Terrace	A2-B2
Victoria Road	B1-C1
Wainfelin Avenue	A4
Wainfelin Road	A4

Central Swansea

Central Neath

Central Port Talbot

Swansea

Like nearly all the towns in the valleys and along the coast of Glamorgan, Swansea grew at an amazing speed during the Industrial Revolution. Ironworks, non-ferrous metal smelting works and mills and factories of every kind were built to produce the goods which were exported from the city's docks. There had been a settlement here from very early times – the city's name is derived from Sweyn's Ea – Ea means island, and Sweyn was a Viking pirate who had a base here. Heavy industry is still pre-eminent in the area, but commerce is of increasing importance and the university exerts a strong influence. Hundreds of acres of parkland and open space lie in and around the city, and just to the west is the Gower, one of the most beautiful areas of Wales. The history of Swansea is traced in the Maritime, Industrial and Royal Institution of South Wales Museums, while the Glynn Vivian Art Gallery contains notable paintings and porcelain.

Neath and **Port Talbot** are, like Swansea, dominated by heavy industry. Neath was once a Roman station, and later had a castle and an abbey, ruins of which can still be seen. Port Talbot has been an industrial centre since 1770, when a copper-smelting works was built. Steelworks and petrochemical works stretch for miles around Swansea Bay.

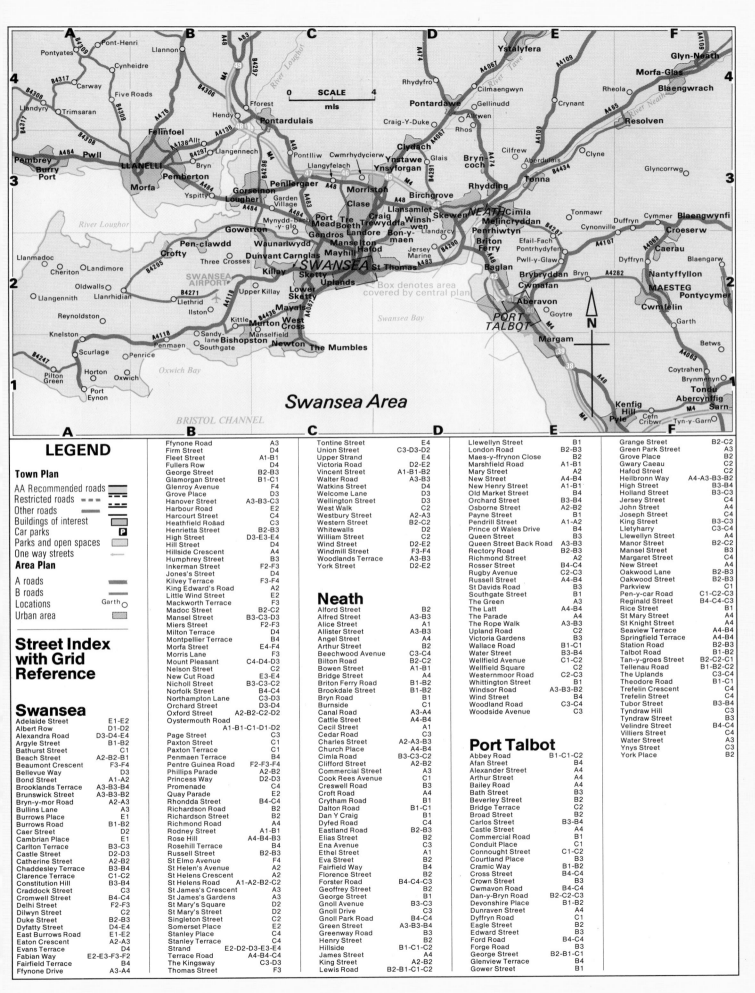

LEGEND

Town Plan

- AA Recommended roads
- Restricted roads
- Other roads
- Buildings of interest
- Car parks [P]
- Parks and open spaces
- One way streets

Area Plan

- A roads
- B roads
- Locations — Garth
- Urban area

Street Index with Grid Reference

Swansea

Adelaide Street	E1-E2
Albert Row	D1-D2
Alexandra Road	D3-D4-E4
Argyle Street	B1-B2
Bathurst Street	C1
Beach Street	A2-B2-B1
Beaumont Crescent	F3-F4
Bellevue Way	D3
Bond Street	A1-A2
Brooklands Terrace	A3-B3-B4
Brunswick Street	A3-B3-B2
Bryn-y-mor Road	A2-A3
Bullins Lane	A3
Burrows Place	E1
Burrows Road	B1-B2
Caer Street	D2
Cambrian Place	E1
Carlton Terrace	B3-C3
Castle Street	D2-D3
Catherine Street	A2-B2
Chaddesley Terrace	B3-B4
Clarence Terrace	C1-C2
Constitution Hill	B3-B4
Craddock Street	C3
Cromwell Street	B4-C4
Delhi Street	F2-F3
Dilwyn Street	C2
Duke Street	B2-B3
Dyfatty Street	D4-E4
East Burrows Road	E1-E2
Eaton Crescent	A2-A3
Evans Terrace	D4
Fabian Way	E2-E3-F3-F2
Fairfield Terrace	B4
Ffynone Drive	A3-A4
Ffynone Road	A3
Firm Street	D4
Fleet Street	A1-B1
Fullers Row	D4
George Street	B2-B3
Glamorgan Street	B1-C1
Glenroy Avenue	F4
Grove Place	D3
Hanover Street	A3-B3-C3
Harbour Road	E2
Harcourt Street	C4
Heathfield Roäad	C3
Henrietta Street	B2-B3
High Street	D3-E3-E4
Hill Street	D4
Hillside Crescent	A4
Humphrey Street	B3
Inkerman Street	F2-F3
Jones's Street	D4
Kilvey Terrace	F3-F4
King Edward's Road	A2
Little Wind Street	E2
Mackworth Terrace	F3
Madoc Street	B2-C2
Mansel Street	B3-C3-D3
Miers Street	F2-F3
Milton Terrace	D4
Montpellier Terrace	B4
Morfa Street	E4-F4
Morris Lane	F3
Mount Pleasant	C4-D4-D3
Nelson Street	C2
New Cut Road	E3-E4
Nicholl Street	B3-C3-C2
Norfolk Street	B4-C4
Northampton Lane	C3-D3
Orchard Street	D3-D4
Oxford Street	A2-B2-C2-D2
Oystermouth Road	A1-B1-C1-D1-D2
Page Street	C3
Paxton Street	C1
Paxton Terrace	C1
Penmaen Terrace	B4
Pentre Guinea Road	F2-F3-F4
Phillips Parade	A2-B2
Princess Way	D2-D3
Promenade	C4
Quay Parade	E2
Rhondda Street	B4-C4
Richardson Road	B2
Richardson Street	B2
Richmond Road	A4
Rodney Street	A1-B1
Rose Hill	A4-B4-B3
Rosehill Terrace	B4
Russell Street	B2-B3
St Elmo Avenue	F4
St Helen's Avenue	A2
St Helens Crescent	A2
St Helens Road	A1-A2-B2-C2
St James's Crescent	A3
St James's Gardens	A3
St Mary's Square	D2
St Mary's Street	D2
Singleton Street	C2
Somerset Place	E2
Stanley Place	C4
Stanley Terrace	C4
Strand	E2-D2-D3-E3-E4
Terrace Road	A4-B4-C4
The Kingsway	C3-D3
Thomas Street	F3
Tontine Street	E4
Union Street	C3-D3-D2
Upper Strand	E4
Victoria Road	D2-E2
Vincent Street	A1-B1-B2
Walter Road	A3-B3
Watkins Street	D4
Welcome Lane	D3
Wellington Street	D3
West Walk	C2
Westbury Street	A2-A3
Western Street	B2-C2
Whitewalls	D2
William Street	C2
Wind Street	D2-E2
Windmill Street	F3-F4
Woodlands Terrace	A3-B3
York Street	D2-E2

Neath

Alford Street	B2
Alfred Street	A3-B3
Alice Street	A1
Allister Street	A3-B3
Angel Street	A4
Arthur Street	B2
Beechwood Avenue	C3-C4
Bilton Road	B2-C2
Bowen Street	A1-B1
Bridge Street	A4
Briton Ferry Road	B1-B2
Brookdale Street	B1-B2
Bryn Road	B1
Burnside	C1
Canal Road	A3-A4
Cattle Street	A4-B4
Cecil Street	A1
Cedar Road	C3
Charles Street	A2-A3-B3
Church Place	A4-B4
Cimla Road	B3-C3-C2
Clifford Street	A2-B2
Commercial Street	A3
Cook Rees Avenue	C1
Creswell Road	B3
Croft Road	A4
Crytham Road	B1
Dalton Road	B1-C1
Dan Y Craig	B1
Dyfed Road	C4
Eastland Road	B2-B3
Elias Street	B2
Ena Avenue	C3
Ethel Street	A1
Eva Street	B2
Fairfield Way	B4
Florence Street	B2
Forster Road	B4-C4-C3
Geoffrey Crescent	B2
George Street	B1
Gnoll Avenue	B3-C3
Gnoll Drive	C3
Gnoll Park Road	B4-C4
Green Street	A3-B3-B4
Greenway Road	B3
Henry Street	B2
Hillside	B1-C1-C2
James Street	A4
King Street	A2-B2
Lewis Road	B2-B1-C1-C2
Llewellyn Street	B1
London Road	B2-B3
Maes-y-ffrynon Close	B2
Marshfield Road	A1-B1
Mary Street	A2
New Street	A4-B4
New Henry Street	A1-B1
Old Market Street	B4
Orchard Street	B3-B4
Osborne Street	A2-B2
Payne Street	B1
Pendrill Street	A1-A2
Prince of Wales Drive	B4
Queen Street	B3
Queen Street Back Road	A3-B3
Rectory Road	B2-B3
Richmond Street	A2
Rosser Street	B4-C4
Rugby Avenue	C2-C3
Russell Street	A4-B4
St Davids Road	B3
Southgate Street	B1
The Green	A3
The Latt	A4-B4
The Parade	A4
The Rope Walk	A3-B3
Upland Road	C2
Victoria Gardens	A4
Wallace Road	B1-C1
Water Street	B3-B4
Wellfield Avenue	C1-C2
Wellfield Square	C2
Westernmoor Road	C2-C3
Whittington Street	B1
Windsor Road	A3-B3-B2
Wind Street	B4
Woodland Road	C3-C4
Woodside Avenue	C3

Port Talbot

Abbey Road	B1-C1-C2
Afan Street	B4
Alexander Street	A4
Arthur Street	A4
Bailey Road	A4
Bath Street	B3
Beverley Street	B2
Bridge Terrace	C2
Broad Street	B2
Carlos Street	B3-B4
Castle Street	A4
Commercial Road	B1
Conduit Place	C1
Connought Street	C1-C2
Courtland Place	B3
Cramic Way	B1-B2
Cross Street	B4-C4
Crown Street	B3
Cwmavon Road	B4-C4
Dan-y-Bryn Road	B2-C2-C3
Devonshire Place	B1-B2
Dunraven Street	A4
Dyffryn Road	C1
Eagle Street	B2
Edward Street	B3
Ford Road	B4-C4
Forge Road	B3
George Street	B2-B1-C1
Glenview Terrace	B4
Gower Street	B1
Grange Street	B2-C2
Green Park Street	A3
Grove Place	B2
Gwary Caeau	C2
Hafod Street	C2
Heilbronn Way	A4-A3-B3-B2
High Street	B3-B4
Holland Street	B3-C3
Jersey Street	C4
John Street	A4
Joseph Street	C4
King Street	B3-C3
Lletyharry	C3-C4
Llewellyn Street	A4
Manor Street	B2-C2
Mansel Street	B3
Margaret Street	C4
New Street	A4
Oakwood Lane	B2-B3
Oakwood Street	B2-B3
Parkview	C1
Pen-y-car Road	C1-C2-C3
Reginald Street	B4-C4-C3
Rice Street	B1
St Mary Street	A4
St Knight Street	A4
Seaview Terrace	A4-B4
Springfield Terrace	A4-B4
Station Road	B2-B3
Talbot Road	B1-B2
Tan-y-groes Street	B2-C2-C1
Tellenau Road	B1-B2-C2
The Uplands	C3-C4
Theodore Road	B1-C1
Trefelin Crescent	C4
Trefelin Street	C4
Tubor Street	B3-B4
Tyndraw Hill	C3
Tyndraw Street	B3
Velindre Street	B4-C4
Villiers Street	C4
Water Street	A3
Ynys Street	C3
York Place	B2

LEGEND

Town Plan

AA Recommended roads	
Other roads	
Restricted roads	
Buildings of interest	H.Q.
Churches	+
Car parks	P
Parks and open spaces	
One way streets	→

Street Index with Grid Reference

Wrexham

Wrexham

Gateway to North Wales, Wrexham has emerged from a turbulent past of medieval resistance to English rule and action during the Civil War to become a more peaceable — but still active — industrial and residential centre. Kelloggs and GKN (which owns the Brymbo Steel Works) are two of the large industrial concerns which have arrived to replace the coalmining and tanning industries which were previously prevalent, and modernisation has provided pedestrian shopping areas. The development in Regent Street includes a Methodist Church at first floor level above the shops; more traditional is the Parish Church of St Giles, with its 136ft 16th-century tower, a local landmark. The main body of the church dates from the 15th century, and its churchyard contains the grave of Elihn Yale, the local boy who founded Yale University in the USA.

Places of interest within the area include Bersham Industrial Heritage, dealing with the local iron industry, and Erdigg, a late 17th-century house containing most of its original furniture. On the sporting side, Wrexham has long been the home of Association Football in Wales: the Welsh FA has its headquarters here and the Racecourse ground is regularly used for international matches, as well as by Wrexham in the Canon League.

94

Luton Airport

Opened shortly before World War II when it was used mainly by the local flying club, Luton Airport has now become one of the country's most popular take-off points for holidays in the sunshine resorts of Europe and North Africa. It is used mainly by package holiday operators, and although its heaviest period for passenger traffic is during the summer months, winter breaks are becoming increasingly popular. Catering efficiently for this special demand, Luton has sophisticated snow clearing equipment to ensure that the airport is operational in all but the most severe weather conditions. Aircraft noise is also monitored so that it can be kept to an absolute minimum.

Owned and operated by the Borough of Luton, the airport lies two miles south-east of the centre of Luton and is only 3½ miles from Junction 10 on the M1. The passenger terminal is currently undergoing reconstruction and extension, which will provide extra lounge space, refreshment services and Customs facilities in addition to those which already exist in the main concourse. These include restaurant, buffet, and bar facilities for refreshments, foreign exchange points, banking and postal services.

Space for car parking is available in a number of surface car parks: drivers are advised to go to the Terminal Building to leave passengers and luggage, and to check the car park in use for the day, before driving to the appropriate one to park. Payment is in advance, and a free mini-bus service is available to carry car drivers from the car parks to the Terminal Building. This service is also available to take drivers of cars from the Terminal Building to the appropriate car parks when they return from their flights.

In addition, a car park with spaces for 350 vehicles has been provided next to the taxiway, and gives spectators a good view of the aircraft. A small charge is made for use of this facility.

For those travelling by public transport, Luton is also well-served by express trains, as it lies on the main line from St Pancras to the Midlands and the north of England. The journey from St Pancras takes only 28 minutes by fast train, and frequent bus services operate during the day between the airport and railway station. Express bus services are operated by the National Bus Company between Luton and surrounding towns and with the London area. Regular Green Line services run between the airport and central London, and a Green Line service is also available between Luton Airport and the airports at Heathrow and Gatwick.

KEY

- = = = Authorised traffic only
- Bus stop
- Public telephone
- ⊠⊠⊠ NEC restaurant
- Maglev
- Recommended routes

SCALE

0 — 110 — 220 yds
0 — 100 — 200 mts

N

The National Exhibition Centre and Birmingham International Airport

Birmingham International Airport and NEC

Situated just nine miles east of the city, Birmingham International Airport is a short distance from the M6 and M42 motorways, and provides quick and easy access from most parts of the country. This is a popular embarkation point for charter flights to a wide range of European holiday destinations, and it also provides a comprehensive network of scheduled flights to many British and European destinations.

A special viewing area with its own shop and buffet is situated on the third level, with its own access at the front of the terminal building. The airport's choice of buffets and licensed bars also includes the 150-seater Landside Restaurant, and all of them are open to the general public as well as to passengers. Multi-storey and surface car parking is available, while Birmingham International Station offers an 80-minute rail link with London (Euston), and connections to other British cities. The airport is also the site of the Maglev transit system, which sweeps travellers in 90 seconds from the three-storey airport terminal to the Birmingham International Railway Station, and to the National Exhibition Centre. The Maglev has three unmanned cars (each taking up to 32 passengers with their luggage), suspended by magnetic levitation 15mm above guidance tracks and driven without friction by linear induction motors, along a 600 metre elevated track.

National Exhibition Centre The new centre was opened by HM the Queen in February 1976 and lies about eight miles east of Birmingham city centre. The 10 exhibition halls have an interior area of 105,085 square metres and the landscaped setting covers 310 acres. The central feature of the complex — the Piazza — has shops, banks, medical and visitor services, including the Birmingham Convention and Visitor Bureau. The International Area is a multi-purpose hall for conventions, concerts and sporting events, with seating for up to 12,000, and the Forum is designed specifically for presentations and product launches.

Northern England and Scotland

AREA MAPS ARE INDICATED IN BOLD.

Altrincham

Bonnie Prince Charlie's troops gathered in Altrincham's Old Market Place during the '45 rebellion, to demand lodgings — and Altrincham is still much in demand today as a residential area. Conveniently close to Manchester, it also has good shops, a modern sports centre, a golf course and an ice rink. Not so very long ago it stood in an agricultural district, but the coming of the railways sparked off the town's development, and it first became a cotton producing town, and later a centre for light industry.

Urmston's Davyhulme Park is one of the most attractive in the area. The town grew with the opening of the Manchester Ship Canal, and the establishment of the Trafford Park industrial estate has brought further development.

Stretford has a chilling reminder of the past in the 'Great Stone' or 'plague stone' which stands at the entrance to Gorse Hill Park. The two holes in its surface were once filled with disinfectant to purify coins which had been handled by plague victims. Stretford itself used to be a centre for the making of woollen goods, but the opening up of a way to the sea by the linking of the Bridgwater Canal and the Manchester Ship Canal began its years of greatest growth. Today it has one of the biggest shopping centres in the borough, and a modern sports centre.

Central Urmston

Central Stretford

Key to Town Plan and Area Plan

Town Plan
AA Recommended roads
Other roads
Restricted roads
Buildings of interest — Cinema
Churches — †
Car Parks — P
Parks and open spaces
One way streets — ←

Area Plan
A roads
B roads
Locations — Ibsley○
Urban area

STREET INDEX

Key to Town Plan and Area Plan

Town Plan
AA Recommended roads	
Other roads	
Restricted roads	
Buildings of interest	Hall
Car Parks	P
Parks and open spaces	
Churches	+

Area Plan
A roads	
B roads	
Locations	Jump O
Urban area	

Street Index with Grid Reference

Central Barnsley

Barnsley

Amongst the claims to fame of Barnsley must be numbered the local football club — at present in the Second Division of the Canon League. Started in 1887, it achieved fame in the early part of the present century by reaching the FA Cup Final twice, and by winning the trophy in 1911/1912. Barnsley lies in the midst of a coalmining district, and the Yorkshire area of the National

Union of Mineworkers has its headquarters in a Victorian building which is one of the many impressive features of the town. Other landmarks are the modern development of the Metropolitan Centre with its new market hall, and the tower which stands in Locke Park (on the south-eastern edge of town) which has a public viewing gallery. Leisure is catered for in the town's four sports centres, and in Worsbrough Country Park. This lies to the south and has a reservoir — popular with

both fishermen and wildlife. A working 17th-century watermill which is now a museum can also be seen here, and just north of the town centre are the remains of Monk Bretton Priory, founded in the 12th century.

Wombwell is an area of new industries, which have arrived to replace its declining local collieries. A popular place to live, it has good shops and extensive open spaces in Wombwell Park, to the south-west of the town centre.

Hopwood Street	B4	Queens Avenue	A4	Westgate	B3-C3	Margaret Road	C1
Huddersfield Road	C4	Race Common Road	B1-B2	Wharncliffe Street	B2-B3	Mellor Road	B1-C1
James Street	D4-E4	Regent Street	C3-D3	Wilson Street	D1	Newsome Avenue	A3-A4-B4-B3
John Street	D1	Regent Street South	D3	York Street	B2-C2	Park Street	C1-C2
Joseph Street	D1	St George's Road	B1-B2			Pick-Up Crescent	B1
Keik Street	B3-B4	St Mary's Place	C3			Rimington Road	C2-C3
Kendray Street	D3-E3	Sackville Street	B4-B3-C3			Roebuck Street	B1-C1
King Street	E1	Shambles Street	B2-B3-C3	**Central Wombwell**		Rutland Place	A3
Lancaster Street	A2-B2	Shaw Lane	A2-A1-B1			St Mary's Road	A2-A3
Langdale Road	E2	Shaw Street	A1-B1	Aldham House Lane	A4	Saunders Row	A2-B2-B3
Longcar Street	A1-B1	Sheffield Road	D1-E1	Bartholomew Street	B3-B4	Station Road	C2
Market Hill	C2-C3	Silver Street	C1-D1-D2	Barnsley Road	B4-B3-C3	Stubbs Road	A2-A3
Market Street	C2-D2	Southwell Street	A3-A4	Bird Avenue	A3	Summer Lane	A4-A3-B3-B2-C2
May Day Green	D2-D3	Spring Street	C1	Blythe Street	B3-B4	Thompson Road	B1
Meadow Street	E4	Springfield Street	A2	Bondfield Crescent	B2-B3	Tune Street	A3-B3
Mottram Street	D4-E4	Stanhope Street	A3	Burrow Grove	A3	Turner Avenue	A4
Nelson Street	C1-C2	Station Road	A3-B3	Cemetery Road	B3-C3	Wainwright Avenue	A4-B4
New Street	C1-D1-D2	Stocks Lane	A3-A4	Copeland Road	A2-A3-B3-B2	Washington Avenue	A2-A3
Newton Street	A3-B3	Summer Lane	A4-A3-B3-B2	Goodyear Crescent	B1-B2	Wilson Street	A4-B4
Oak Street	B2	Summer Street	B3-B4	Gower Street	C1	Windmill Road	A2-A3
Oakwell Lane	E1-F1	The Arcade	C3-D3	Hadfield Street	B1-C1	Wood Street	A2
Old Mill	C4-D4	Taylor Road	E1	Hall Street	B1-C1	Woodley Avenue	B2-B3
Park Grove	B1-C1	Thomas Street	C1-D1	Hawson Street	C2	Wright Crescent	B1-B2
Park Row	D1	Thornley Terrace	B2-C2	High Street	C2-C3	Yvonne Grove	A4
Parker Street	A2	Union Street	D1-E1	Hough Lane	A2-B2-C2		
Peel Square	C2	Vernon Street	E4	Jardine Street	B1-B2		
Peel Street	B2-C2	Victoria Crescent	B4	John Street	B4		
Pitt Street	B1-B2-C2	Victoria Crescent West	A4-B4	Jones Avenue	A4		
Pontefract Road	E2-E1-F1	Victoria Road	B4-C4	Kelvin Grove	C2		
Perserverance Street	A2-A3	Victoria Street	B4-C4	Kings Road	C1-C2		
Prince Arthur Street	A4	Walterloo Road	A1-A2	Kingsway	B2		
Princess Street	C1-C2	Waltham Street	E1	Kitchen Road	A4		
Prospect Street	B3	Welbeck Street	A3-A4	Main Street	B3-B4		
Queen Street	D2	Wellington Street	C2-D2				
Queen's Road	E3	Western Street	B4-C4				

BARNSLEY
Opened by HRH the Prince of Wales on 14 December 1933 and built at a cost of £188,000, the magnificent four-storey Town Hall has a 145ft tower of Portland stone, and is one of the town's most impressive sights.

Birkenhead

You can take the famous 'ferry across the Mersey' to reach this largest town on the Wirral Peninsula, but it also connected to Liverpool by bridges and the Mersey Tunnel. The town grew up around the Merseyside docks to become an important ship-building centre, and a number of engineering firms are still located here. Amongst Birkenhead's places of history are the remains of

a 12th-century Benedictine Priory at Monks Ferry, and the Williamson Art Gallery and Museum, which stages regular art exhibitions and also houses the Wirral Maritime Museum.

West Kirby is a place for walking and water. Lying on the estuary of the River Dee, it is well known for its Marine Lake, where boating and sailing can be enjoyed, while just offshore is the wildlife of the Hilbre Islands (accessible only to permit holders). Several pleasant parks can be

found in the town, and to the south, the Wirral Way Country Park incorporates the 12 miles of the Wirral Way footpath.

Hoylake's Windswept and world famous, the Royal Liverpool Golf Course stretches its length along the coast between Hoylake and West Kirby. Numerous parks and gardens are another attraction of this former fishing village, which lies at the north-west corner of the Wirral Peninsula and enjoys an extensive seafront.

Central West Kirby

Central Hoylake

IRISH SEA

Marine Lake

River Dee

LEGEND

Town Plan
AA recommended route
Restricted roads
Other roads
Buildings of interest — Theatre
Car parks — P
Parks and open spaces
One way streets
Area Plan
A roads
B roads
Locations — Littleney
Urban area

Street Index with Grid Reference

Birkenhead

Abbey Street	E1
Aberdeen Street	A3-A4
Adelphi Street	D2-D3
Albion Street	E3
Argyle Street	D2-D3-E3-E4
Argyle Street South	C1-D1
Arthur Street	A4
Aspinall Street	A4
Banning Close	B3
Beckingham Close	A4
Beckwith Close	A4
Beckwith Street	A4-B4-B3, C3
Bentinck Close	B2
Bentinck Place	A1-A2
Bentinck Street	B2-B3
Borough Road	B1-C1-D1
Borough Road East	D1-D2-E2
Brandon Street	E3
Bridge Street	C4-D4-E4-E3
Brook Street	B4-C4
Brook Street East	C4-C3-D3
Brookland Road	C1
Camden Street	C3
Canning Street	D4-E4
Castle Street	E3
Cathcart Street	B3-B4
Charing Cross	B1
Chester Street	E2-E3
Church Street	E3-E2-F2
Circular Road	C1
Claughton Road	A2-B2-C2-D2
Cleveland Street	B4-C4-D4-D3
Clifton Road	C1
Clwyd Street	C3
Cook Street	B1
Cole Street	A1-A2
Conway Street	B3-C3-C2
Craven Street	A2-B2-B3
Cross Street	E2
Dacre Street	C3-C2-D2
Dover Close	B3
Douglas Street	D3-E3
Duncan Street	E2-E3
East Bourne Road	A1-A2-B2
Eldon Street	C3
Elgin Way	D3
Elm Street	C2
Exmouth Street	B2-B3
Exmouth Way	B2-B3
Fearnley Road	E2
Friars Gate	D4
George Street	A1
Grange Mount	B1
Grange Road	B1-B2-C2
Grange Road East	D2
Grange Road West	A1-B1
Hamilton Lane	D3
Hamilton Square	D3-E3
Hamilton Street	D2-E2-E3
Havanley Place	A1-A2
Hazel Road	B1
Hemingford Street	C2
Henry Street	D2-D3
Henthorne Street	A1
Hind Street	D1
Hinson Street	D2
Hollybank Road	B1-C1
Hornby Street	E3
Ivy Street	E2
Jackson Street	D1
John Street	E3
Knowles Street	B3
Knox Street	E1-E2
Leta Street	C3-D3
Livingstone Street	A3-A4-B4
Lord Street	D3-D4
Lorn Street	D3
Lowwood Green	C1
Lowwood Road	B1-C1
Marcus Street	C4
Marion Street	C3-D3-D2
Market Street	C3-D3-E3-E2
Market Street West	D2-E2
Menai Street	B1
Merton Place	A1-A2
Newling Street	A4
Oliver Street	B2-C2
Oliver Street East	D2
Oxton Road	A1-B1
Park Freeman	C4
Park Road East	A2-A3-B3
Park Road North	A4-A3-B3
Park Street	C3-C4
Parkfield Avenue	C2-C3
Parkfield Place	C2-C2
Paterson Street	A2-A3-B3
Pilgrim Street	E2
Pool Street	C4
Price Street	A4-B4-C4-D3
Priory Street	E2
Prince Edward Street	A4
Quarry Bank Street	B1
Queensway Road Tunnel	C4-D4-E4-F4, E2-E3, D3-D4
Ravenscroft Road	A1
Rendel Street	C4
Rodney Street	C1
Romilly Street	C3
Rowland Street	C3
Russel Street	C4

St Anne Street	A4-B4
St Johns Square	C1-C2
St Johns Street	C2
St Mary's Gate	E2
Salisbury Street	B1
Sandford Street	D3-D4
Shore Road	D4-E4
Sidney Street	D4-E4
Simpson Street	B2-B3
Taylor Street	D4
The Woodlands	B1-C1
Thomas Street	D1
Trinity Street	A3-B3-B4
Victoria Street	B3-B4
Waterloo Place	D1-E1
Water Street	E2
Watson Street	B3-C3-C4
West Bourne Road	A1
Whetstone Lane	B1
William Street	D2

West Kirby

Abbey Road	C2-C3
Ashton Drive	A3-A2-B2
Banks Road	A3-A2-A1-B1
Beacon Drive	C2
Belmont Road	B4-C4
Black Horse Hill	C3
Boulton Avenue	C4
Bridge Road	A4-B4
Broxton Avenue	C4
Caldy Road	B1
Carpenters Lane	B2-B3
Church Road	A2-B2
Claremont Road	B4-C4
Darmonds Green	B3-B4
Dee Lane	A3
Devonshire Road	C1-C2
Dunraven Road	A3-B3
Eaton Road	A2-B2
Graham Road	A4-B4
Grange Road	B3-C3
Gresford Avenue	C4
Grosvenor Road	B3
Hilbre Road	B1-B2
Hilbreview Column Road	C2-C3
Hydro Avenue	B1
Kirby Close	C1-C2
Kirby Park	B1-C1
Lang Lane	B4-C4-C3
Leigh Road	B4-C4
Lingdale Road	A4
Ludlow Drive	B1-B2
Macdona Drive	B1
Meols Drive	A4
Monks Way	C3
Mostyn Avenue	B2
Mount Road	B1-C1
North Road	A3-B3
Orrysdale Road	B4
Park Road	A3-B3
Princes Avenue	B2-C2
Priory Road	C2-C3
Raeburn Avenue	C4
Rectory Road	B2-C2
Red House Lane	B4
Riversdale Road	A4
Riverside	B1
Salisbury Avenue	A3
Sandy Lane	A1-B1
Shrewsbury Road	A2-A3
South Parade	A1-A2-A3

South Road	A2-B2
Surrey Drive	C1
Vicarage Road	A3
Victoria Road	A2-B2
Village Road	B2-C2
Warwick Drive	B1-C1
Westbourne Grove	B3
Westbourne Road	B2-B3
Wetsone Lane	C1-C2
York Avenue	B1

Hoylake

Airlie Road	B1
Albion Road	B1
Alderley Road	A2-B2
Ashford Road	B4
Avondale Road	B2-B3
Barton Road	A1
Bertram Drive	B4-C4
Bertram Drive North	C4
Birkenhead Road	B3-B4
Cable Road	A2-B2
Carham Road	C2
Carr Lane	C1-C2
Carsthorne Road	B3
Chapel Road	B1-B2
Charles Road	A3
Clydesdale Road	A3
Courtenay Road	A1
Curzon Road	A1
Deneshay Road	A4-B4-B3
Dovedale Road	A3
Drummond Road	B1
Egbert Road	B4
Elm Grove	B3
Ferndale Road	B3
Garden Hay Road	B4
George Road	C2
Government Road	A2
Grove Road	B2
Grosvenor Road	B1-B2
Hazel Road	B3
Hoyle Road	A3-B3
Lake Place	B2
Lake Road	A2
Lee Road	B3
Manor Road	B3
Marine Road	A1-A2
Market Street	B1-B2-B3
Meols Drive	B1
Meols Parade	A3-A4
Newhall Lane	C1
Newton Road	B3
North Parade	A1-A2-A3
Proctor Road	C2
Queens Avenue	C4
Queens Road	A1-B1
Rudd Street	B2
Sandringham Avenue	B3-C3
Sandringham Close	B3
Saxon Road	A2
Sea View	A2
Stanley Road	B1
Station Road	B1
Strand Road	A2
The Kings Gap	A1-B1
Trinity Road	A2-B2-B3
Valentia Road	B1-B2
Walker Street	B2
Warren Road	A1
Waverley Road	B3
Wynstay Road	A4-B4

Key to Town Plan and Area Plan

Town Plan
AA Recommended roads
Other roads
Restricted roads
Buildings of interest — Library
Car Parks — P
Parks and open spaces
One Way Streets

Area Plan
A roads
B roads
Locations — Bourne End○
Urban area

Street Index with Grid Reference

Blackburn

Addison Street	A2-A3
Ainsworth Street	C3-C4
Alice Street	B1
Alma Street	B3
Altom Street	B4-C4
Appleby Street	E3-E4
Audley Lane	E2-E3
Audley Range	D1-E1-E2-F2
Audley Street	E2-E3
Baines Street	C1-D1
Baker Street	F2
Balaclava Street	B4-C4
Bank Top	A1
Barley Lane	A3
Barton Street	B2-B3
Bennington Street	D1
Bicknell Street	B4
Birley Street	D3-D4
Blakey Moor	B3
Bold Street	B4
Bottom Gate	E3-F3
Bridge Street	C2
Brookhouse Lane	C4-D4
Brunel Drive	D2-E2
Brunswick Street	A1
Byrom Street	B1-B2
Canterbury Street	B1-C1
Cardwell Place	B2
Carlinghurst Road	A2
Carlisle Street	C1
Chapel Street	B1-B2
Charlotte Street	C4
Cherry Street	F2-F3
Chester Street	D2-D2-E2-E1
Church Street	C2-C3
Cicely Lane	C3-D3-D2
Cicely Street	D2
Clarence Street	B4
Clayton Street	B2
Cleaver Street	D3-D4
Clifton Street	B1
Copy Nook	E3
Croft Street	D3
Culvert Street	D1
Cumberland Street	E2-F2
Daisy Lane	D4
Daisy Street	D4-E4
Darwen Street	C1-C2
Dern Street	B1
Devonport Road	A3
Dewhurst Street	E1-E2
Dock Street	D3-E3
Dombey Street	E1
Duckworth Street	A1
Duke Street	B4
Dukes Brow	A4
East Park Road	A4
Eden Street	B3
Eleanor Street	D2-D3
Elizabeth Street	D3
Feilden Street	B2-B3
Fleming Square	B2-C2
Forrest Street	D3-E3
Freckleton Street	B2-B1-C1
Further Gate	F3
Gate Street	E3
George Street	C2
George Streeet West	A1-A2
Gladstone Street	F4
Great Bolton Street	C1
Hancock Street	A1
Harrison Street	A1-B1
Harrow Drive	F1
Hart Street	D2-D3
Harwood Street	F3-F4

Blackburn

The glittering heights of championship rollerskating at the Starskate roller rink are a far cry from Blackburn's 'workshop of England' image — an image it is doing its best to change. Once the weaving centre of the world but no longer even predominantly a textile town, it has seen the redevelopment of its old industrial areas while the entire town centre is being converted into a traffic-free shopping precinct. But memories of an older Blackburn can still be seen outside the centre, and some of the stone-built terraces have been declared conservation areas. Blackburn Cathedral is an interesting mixture of old and new: it was built up around the 19th-century church which is now its nave.

Clitheroe is overlooked by a record-breaking castle keep — not only is it the smallest keep in England but it is also one of Lancashire's oldest stone structures. Little else remains of the castle, which dates back to the 12th century and was a Royalist stronghold in the Civil War. This is a very old industrial town, but one with a pleasantly rural atmosphere. St Mary Magdalene's Church is noted for its twisted spire.

Accrington's fame was built on cotton and bricks: noted for their hardness, the smooth red bricks produced in the town spread its name throughout Victorian Britain.

Helen Street	C1-D1
High Street	C2-C3
Higher Audley Street	D1-D2-D3-E3
Higher Eanam	D3-E3
Higson Street	A3
Hill Street	F3-F4
Holland Street	B4
Hope Street	A3
Houghton Street	C1
Hutton Street	E4-F4
Inkerman Street	C4
Islington	B1-C1
James Street	C3
Johnston Street	A3
Jubilee Street	C2
Kendal Street	C4
Kent Street	D1
King Street	B2
King William Street	B3-C3
Lambeth Street	E3-E2-F2-F1
Lark Hill	C4-D4
Larkhill Street	C3-D3
Limbrick	B3-B4
Lime Street	B4
Lincoln Road	F1-F2
Little Peel Street	A2-A3
Lord Street	B2-B3, C3
Lord Derby Street	C1
Lower Audley Street	C1-D1
Lucknow Street	D1
Manner Sutton Street	D3-D4
Mary Street	E2
Mayson Street	C1
Meadow Street	C1
Mill Lane	B2-C2
Mincing Lane	B2-C2
Montague Street	A4-A3-A2-B2
Mount Pleasant	D3-D4
Moss Street	E4
Nab Lane	A3-B3
Newton Street	F2-F3
New Park Street	B3-B4
Northgate	B3
Nottingham Street	E1-F1-F2
Oakenhurst Road	A2
Ordnance Street	E3-E4
Oswald Street	B4
Paradise Lane	B2
Paradise Street	B2
Pembroke Street	B1
Penny Street	C3
Park Road	C1
Preston New Road	A3-A4-B4-B3
Primrose Bank	D4
Prince's Street	B2

Pringle Street	D1-E1-F1
Pump Street	A1-A2
Queen's Road	F1
Queen's Park Road	E2-E1-F1
Railway Road	C2-C3
Randal Street	B4-C4
Regent Street	C3-C4
Richmond Terrace	B3-C3
Ripon Street	E1-F1
Roney Street	A3
St Clement's Street	F2-F3
St Paul's Avenue	B2-B3
St Paul's Street	B1-B3
St Peter Street	B1-B2
St Thomas Street	F2
Salford Eanam	C3-D3
Shakespeare Street	A1
Shaw Street	A3
Shear Bank Road	A4-B4
Shear Brow	B4
Simmon Street	B3
Stanley Street	E4-F4
Stonyhurst Road	A2-B2
Strathclyde Street	E2
Sumner Street	B1
Sussex Drive	D2-E2
Swallow Drive	C4
Temple Drive	F2
Tontine Street	B3-B4
Trinity Street	D4
Victoria Street	C3-C4
Walker Street	C1
Walpole Street	C1
Walter Street	E2-F2
Watford Street	C4
Weir Street	B2-C2
Wellington Street	B4
Wensley Road	A2
West Park Road	A4
Westwood Road	F1-F2
Whalley Banks	A1-A2-B2
Whalley Range	C4
Wharf Street	D3
Whittaker Street	A3
Windham Street	C1-D1

Clitheroe

Albemarle Street	A2
Albion Street	B3-C3
Baldwin Hill	A2
Bawdlands	A1-A2
Beech Street	A1
Brennand Street	B3

Bright Street	C3
Brook Street	C4
Brown Street	A1
Buccleugh Avenue	A2
Buccleugh Close	A2
Cardigan Avenue	A2-A3
Carlton Street	C2
Castle Gate	B2
Castle Street	B2-B3
Castle View Road	A2-A3
Chatburn Road	B4-C4
Chester Avenue	A3-A4
Church Brow	B3-B4
Church Street	B3
Cowper Avenue	A3-A4
De Lacy Street	A2
Derby Street	C2
Duck Street	C3
Eastham Street	A4
Eshton Terrace	A1-B1
Fox Street	B2
Grafton Street	C2
Greenacre Street	B1
Hawthorne Place	A4
Hayhurst Street	C1-C2
Henthorn Road	A1
Highfield Road	B2-C2-C1
Kendal Street	C4
King Lane	B3
King Street	B3
Kirkmoor Road	A3
Littlemore Road	C1
Lower Gate	B2-B3
Milton Avenue	A3-A4
Mitchell Street	A1
Montague Street	A2
New Market Street	B2-B3
North Street	C4
Peel Street	C2-C3
Park Avenue	A4-B4
Parson Lane	A2-B2
Pimlico Road	B4
Princess Avenue	B4-C4
Pump Street	A1-A2
Queen's Road	C1
Radecliffe Street	B4
Railway View Avenue	B3
Railway View Road	A3-B3
Ribblesdale Avenue	A4
St Mary's Street	B3-B4
Salford Moor Lane	B1-B2
Salthill Road	C4
Shawbridge Street	C2-C3
Station Road	B2-B3

Taylor Street	C3-C4
Thorn Street	A1
Turner Street	B1-C1
Waddington Road	A4-B4
Waterloo Road	C3-C4
Wellgate	B3-C3
Well Terrace	B4
West View	B1
Wilson Street	B1
Woone Lane	B1
York Road	B3-B4-C4

Accrington

Abbey Street	C1-C2-C3
Addison Street	C3-C4
Aitken Street	C4
Albion Street	A3
Argyle Street	A4-B4
Arnold Street	C3-C4
Avenue Parade	C2-C3
Back Wellington Street	B2
Bank Street	B1-B2
Barnes Street	C2
Beech Street	C1
Birtwistle Street	C1
Black Abbey Street	B1-C1
Blackburn Road	A3-A2-B2-C2
Blake Street	A3
Bradshaw Street	C3
Bramley Street	B4
Bridge Street	C1
Broadway	B2-B3
Bold Street	C2
Burnley Road	C3
Cannon Street	A2-B2
Castle Street	B3
Chapel Street	C1
Church Street	B1-B2
Cobden Street	B3
Cobham Street	C1
Cotton Street	A1-B1
Crawshaw Street	B2-B3
Croft Street	B3-B4
Cross Street	B1-B2
Derby Street	B4-B3-C3
Dowry Street	B3-C3-C4
Dutton Street	B2
Edgar Street	A3-B3
Ellison Street	A2-A3
Fort Street	A3
Fox Street	A3
Gillies Street	C1-C2
Grange Lane	B1

Grange Street	B1
Hargreaves Street	C1
Haywood Road	C4
Hindle Street	A3
Holme Street	B2
Hood Street	C3-C4
Horne Street	C3-C4
Hyndburn Road	A4-A3-B3
Infant Street	B2-C2
Jacob Street	B1
Kenyon Street	B3
King Street	A3-B3
Knowlmere Street	B4
Lee Street	C1-C2
Malt Street	B4
Marlborough Road	C1
Maudsley Street	B3-C3-C4
Meadow Street	B3-C3-C4
Melbourne Street	C2-C3
Midland Street	C1
Moore Street	C3
Napier Street	B1
Nutter Road	C4
Oak Street	B2-B1-C1
Ormerod Street	A1
Oswald Street	C2
Owen Street	B4-C4
Oxford Street	A3-A4
Paradise Street	A2-B2-B1
Park Street	C1-C2-C3
Paxton Street	A3
Peel Street	B2-C2
Pitt Street	C1-C2
Plantation Street	C1
Pleck Road	B2
Pollard Street	C4
St James Street	A1-A2-B2
Sandy Lane	C1
Scaitcliffe Street	A1-A2
Stanley Street	C2
Sydney Street	C3
Taylor Street West	A3
Union Street	B2-B3
Victoria Street	A1
Warner Street	B2-C2-C1
Water Street	C3
Wellington Street	B1
Whalley Road	B4-B3-C3
Willow Street	A2-B2
York Street	A4-B4

BLACKBURN
A central sanctuary and altar allow everyone to see the service at the Cathedral, which has a Gothic revival church of Longridge stone for its nave. A church has stood on this site since at least the 10th century.

Central Blackpool

Central Fleetwood

Central Lytham

Blackpool

No seaside resort is regarded with greater affection than Blackpool. It is still the place where millions of North Country folk spend their holidays; its famous illuminations draw visitors from all over the world. It provides every conceivable kind of traditional holiday entertainment, and in greater abundance than any other seaside resort in Britain. The famous tower – built in the 1890s as a replica of the Eiffel Tower – the three piers, seven miles of promenade, five miles of illuminations, countless guesthouses, huge numbers of pubs, shops, restaurants and cafes play host to eight million visitors a year.

At the base of the tower is a huge entertainment complex that includes a ballroom, a circus and an aquarium. Other 19th-century landmarks are North Pier and Central Pier, the great Winter Gardens and Opera House and the famous trams that still run along the promenade – the only electric trams still operating in Britain. The most glittering part of modern Blackpool is the famous Golden Mile, packed with amusements, novelty shops and snack stalls. Every autumn it becomes part of the country's most extravagant light show – the illuminations – when the promenade is ablaze with neon representations of anything and everything from moon rockets to the Muppets. Autumn is also the time when Blackpool is a traditional venue for political party conferences.

Blackpool Area

Box denotes area covered by central plan

SCALE 0 — 4 mls

Box denotes area covered by central plan

Box denotes area covered by central plan

LEGEND

Town Plan
- AA recommended route
- Restricted roads
- Other roads
- Buildings of interest — School
- Car parks — P
- Parks and open spaces
- One way streets

Area Plan
- A roads
- B roads
- Locations — Wrea Green ○
- Urban area

Street Index with Grid Reference

Blackpool

Street	Grid
Abingdon Street	B7
Adelaide Street	B6-B7-C7
Albert Road	B6-C6
Alexandra Road	B2
Alfred Street	B7-C7-C6
Ashton Road	C4-C5
Bank Hey Street	B6-B7
Banks Street	B8
Bloomfield Road	B3-C3
Blundell Street	B4
Bolton Street	B2-B3-B4
Bond Street	B1-B2
Bonny Street	B5-B6
Buchanan Street	C7-C8
Caunce Street	C7-C8
Central Drive	B6-B5-C5-C4-C3-C2
Chapel Street	B5
Charles Street	C7-C8
Charnley Road	B6-C6
Church Street	B7-C7
Clifton Street	B7
Clinton Avenue	C5
Cocker Street	B8
Cookson Street	B8-B7-C7
Coop Street	B5
Coronation Street	B5-B6-B7
Corporation Street	B7
Crystal Road	B2
Dale Street	B4-B5
Deansgate	B7-C7
Dean Street	B1
Dickson Road	B7-B8
Erdington Road	B5-C5-C4
Elizabeth Street	C7-C8
Falmouth Road	C2-C3
Field Street	C3
General Street	B8
George Street	C7-C8
Gorton Street	C8
Grasmere Road	C4
Grosvenor Street	C7
Haig Road	B2
Harrison Street	C5
Henry Street	C3
High Street	B8
Hornby Road	B6-C6
Hull Road	B6
Kay Street	B5
Kent Road	B5-C5-C4
Keswick Road	C4-C5
King Street	C7
Larkhill Street	C8
Leamington Road	C7
Leopold Grove	B7-B6-C6
Lincoln Road	C6-C7
Livingstone Road	C5-C6
Lonsdale Road	B3
Lord Street	B8
Lunedale Avenue	C2
Lune Grove	C4
Lytham Road	B1-B2-B3-B4
Market Street	B7
Milbourne Street	C7-C8
Osbourne Road	B1
Palatine Road	B5-C5-C6
Palmer Avenue	C3
Park Road	C5-C6-C7
Princess Parade	A7-A8-B8-B7
Princess Street	B4-B5-C5
Promenade	B1-B2-B3-B4-B5-B6-A6-A7-B7-B8
Queen Street	B7-B8
Queen Victoria Road	C3-C4
Raikes Parade	C6-C7
Rawcliffe Street	B1
Reads Avenue	B5-C5-C6
Regent Road	C6-C7
Ribble Road	C5
Rigby Road	B4-C4
Rydal Avenue	C5
St Annes Road	C1-C2
St Chad's Road	B3
St Heliers Road	C2-C3
Salthouse Avenue	C4
Saville Road	C2-C3
Shannon Street	B5
Shaw Road	B2
Sheppard Street	B6
Shetland Road	C2-C3
South King Street	C6-C7
Springfield Road	B8
Station Road	B1
Station Terrace	B1
Talbot Road	B7-B8-C8
Topping Street	B7
Tyldesley Road	B4
Vance Road	B6
Victoria Street	B6
Victory Road	C8
Waterloo Road	B2-C2
Wellington Road	B3
Westmorland Avenue	C4
Woodfield Road	B3
Woolman Road	C5
Yorkshire Street	B5

Fleetwood

Street	Grid
Abbotts Walk	A3
Adelaide Street	B3-C3-C2
Addison Road	A1
Albert Street	C2-C3
Ash Street	A1-A2
Aughton Street	C3
Balmoral Terrace	B4
Belmont Road	A1
Blakiston Street	A2-B2-B3
Bold Street	B4-C4
Burns Road	A3
Byron Street	A3

Street	Grid
Chaucer Road	A2
Church Street	C2
Cop Lane	A1-B1-B2
Copse Road	A1
Custom House Lane	C3
Dock Road	A1
Dock Street	B1-B2-C2
Dryder Road	A2-A3
Elm Street	A1-A2
Harris Street	A2-A3-B3
Hesketh Place	B3
Kemp Street	B2-B3
Kent Street	B3-C3
London Street	B2-B3
Lord Street	A1-A2-B2-C2-C3
Lower Lune Street	C3
Milton Street	A2-A3
Mount Road	A3-B3
Mount Street	A2-B2
North Albert Street	C3-C4
North Albion Street	A1-A2
North Church Street	B3-B4
North Street	B3
Oak Street	A1-A2
Outer Promenade	A4-B4
Pharos Street	B3-C3-C4
Poulton Road	A2
Poulton Street	A2
Preston Street	B2
Promenade Road	A3-A4
Queen's Terrace	C3-C4
Radcliffe Road	A1
Rhyl Street	B3
St Peters Place	B2-B3
Siding Road	A1
Station Road	A1
Styan Street	A2-A1-B1
Tennyson Road	A2
The Esplanade	A3-A4-B4
Upper Lune Street	C4
Victoria Street	B3-C3
Walmsley Street	A3-A2-B2
Warrenhurst Road	A1
Warren Street	B3-B2-C2
Willow Road	A1
Windsor Terrace	B4

Lytham

Street	Grid
Agnew Street	B2-B3
Alder Grove	A3-B3
Ballam Road	B2-B3-B4-C4
Bannister Street	C2
Bath Street	B2
Beach Street	B2
Bellingham Road	C4
Bleasdale Road	C3
Brook Road	C3
Cecil Street	A2-A3
Central Beach	B2-C2
Church Road	A2-B2
Cleveland Road	B3-C3
Clifton Street	B2-C2
East Beach	C2
Forest Drive	A3-B3
Hastings Place	B2-B3
Henry Street	B2
Lilac Avenue	B4
Longacre Place	A3
Lowther Terrace	A2
Market Square	B2
Moorfield Drive	B3
Mythop Avenue	C3
Mythop Road	C3
Norfolk Road	C4
North Clifton Street	B2-C2
North Warton Street	C2
Park Street	C2
Parkview Road	C2-C3-C4
Queen Street	B2
Ring Dyke Way	A3
Rogerly Close	A3
South Clifton Street	B2-C2
Southolme	C3
South Park	A3-B3
South Warton Street	C2
Station Road	C2
Upper Westby Street	A2-B2
Warton Street	C2
West Beach	A2-B2
Westby Street	B2-C2
Westwood Road	A2
Woodville Terrace	A2
Wykeham Road	C3-C4

BLACKPOOL
Three piers, seven miles of promenade packed with entertainments galore and seemingly endless sandy beaches spread out beneath Blackpool's unmistakable tower which stands 518ft high in Britain's busiest and biggest holiday resort.

11

Key to Town Plan and Area Plan

Town Plan
A.A. Recommended roads
Other roads
Restricted roads
Buildings of interest   Theatre
Car Parks   P
Parks and open spaces
One way streets

Area Plan
A roads
B roads
Locations   Summers O
Urban area

Street Index with Grid Reference

Central Bolton

All Saints Street	C4-D4
Ashbourne Avenue	F1
Ashburner Street	B2-C2
Bark Street	B4-C4
Blackhorse Street	B3-C3-C2
Bow Street	C4-D4
Bradford Street	E2-E3-F3
Bradshawgate	D2-D3-D4

Breightmet Street	D2
Bridge Street	C3-C4
Bridgeman Place	D2-E2
Bridgeman Street	C1
Bromwich Street	E2-E1-F1
Bury New Road	D4-E4-E3-F3
Bury Old Road	E3-E4
Cannon Street	A1-A2
Castle Street	E3-E2-F2
Chadwick Street	E2-F2
Chorley New Road	A4
Chorley Street	B3-B4
Church Bank	D3
Clive Street	D2-D3
College Way	A1-B1
Crown Street	D3-D4
Dawes Street	C2
Dawson Lane	B4
Deane Road	A1-B1-B2
Deansgate	B3-C3-D3
Derby Street	B1
Devon Street	E3
Dorset Street	E2-E3
Ellesmere Street	A2
Fletcher Street	B1-C1
Folds Road	D4-E4
Gas Street	B3
Gibraltar Street	A2
Goodwin Street	E4
Great Moor Street	C2-D2
Grosvenor Street	D1-E1
Halstead Street	E2-E3
Hanover Street	B3
Hilden Street	E2
John Brown Street	B4
Kay Street	D4
Kestor Street	E4-F4-F3

Knowsley Street	C3-C4
Le Mans Crescent	C2-C3
Lower Bridgeman Street	D1-D2
Manchester Road	D1-D2
Marsden Road	B3-B4
Mayor Street	A2-A3
Mill Street	E4
Mill Hill Street	E4
Moncrieffe Street	D1
Moor Lane	B2-B3
Mule Street	E3-E4
Nelson Square	C3-D3
New Holder Street	B3
Newport Street	C1-C2-C3
Orlando Street	D1-E1
Ormrod Street	B2-C2
Radcliffe Road	F1-F2-F3
Rashbottom Street	A1-B1
River Street	D2-E2
St George's Road	A4-B4-C4
St George's Street	C4-D4
St Peter's Way	D4-D3-E3-E2-E1
Salop Street	D2
Shiffnall Street	D2
Silverwell Street	D3
Soho Street	C1-C2
Spa Road	A2-A3-B3
Trinity Street	B2-C2-C1-D1-D2
Vernon Street	B4
Victoria Square	C2-C3
West Brook Street	E1

BOLTON

public buildings and places of interest

Civic Centre (Town Hall and Tourist Information Centre)	C3
Institute of Technology	B1
Library and Museum	C2-C3
Market Hall	C4
New Octagon Theatre	C3
Old Man and Scythe Inn	D3

An historic old inn, where Lord Derby, executed in 1651, is said to have spent his last night

Technical College	D1

Situated in Tonge Moor Road, 1m north-east of the town centre, is the Textile Machinery Museum containing Arkwright's water frame of 1768, Crompton's spinning mule (1799) and Hargreave's original spinning jenny.

2m north, is Hall i'the'Wood, a picturesque, 16th-century, half-timbered house, now a museum. It is associated with William Crompton, 2m north-west is Smithils Hall, a half-timbered 15th-century and later house, noted for its old hall. It is now a museum.

Bolton

This was one of Lancashire's great cotton centres, and a fitting birthplace for revolutioniser of the textile industry Samuel Crompton, whose invention the 'spinning mule' is on display at the Tonge Moor Textile Machinery Museum. Born in 1753, Crompton lived in the picturesque 15th-century house Hall I' Th' Wood, which lies to the north of the town at Firwood Fold.

The town boasts another celebrated son in William Hesketh Lever, born in 1851, who not only founded Lever Brothers (later the giant Unilever Group), but also invented Sunlight Soap. Lever, who became Lord Leverhulme, gave Bolton a school, a church and a park.

Bolton today has become more concerned with engineering than with the textiles for which it was famous, but reminders of the past live on in the town's older monuments. The Victorian Town

Hall and Civic Centre stand prominently amidst the 20th-century development in the middle of town, and nearby is The Old Man and Scythe, a medieval inn. Lord Derby spent his last night here before he was executed by Cromwell in retaliation for a massacre by the Royalists in the Civil War.
Popular with both locals and outsiders is Bolton's Octagon Theatre, and another attraction for some is Bolton Wanderers Football Club, providing league football at Burnden Park.

Spinning gold — the machines that made a landscape

It was called a mule because it was a hybrid of two existing machines — and together with a handful of other inventions, it transformed forever the face of northern England. Not overnight and not singlehanded: without the workers and a huge, insatiable demand for cotton, the spinning mule and other 18th-century innovations would have sunk without trace. But coming as they did, when they did, they shaped irrevocably the towns of the industrial north — and most of were the inspiration of local men.

In 1733, **Bury's** John Kay thought up the flying shuttle for faster handloom weaving. Meeting the demand it created for faster spinning of yarn, James Hargreaves of **Blackburn** brought out the 1763 spinning jenny, named after his wife and able to spin six threads at once. Mechanisation came in 1769 with **Preston**-born Richard Arkwright's water-powered spinning frame, and improving on both frame and jenny came the 1770s spinning mule, which could spin fine, strong threads 400 at a time. The frame and the mule took spinning out of the home and into mills — often sited in remote parts of the Pennines to be near water power and probably to keep out radical influences.

For the handloom weavers this was a golden age — but two developments were to make them some of the most pitiable victims of industrialisation. Steam power became the great driving force of the factories when James Watt of **Greenock** added a separate condenser to the steam engine in the 1770s and turned it for the first time into a really effective tool. And in the 1780's the power loom was invented, by Melton Mowbray clergyman Edmund Cartwright who had never even seen the hand driven variety.

Steam needed coal; the new factories needed space, and they moved down from the Pennine streams to the canals and coalfields. And so began the explosive growth of towns like **Manchester,** king of them all, **Burnley, Bolton, Wigan, Rochdale, Oldham** and **Blackburn** — the once-mighty textile centres of the world.

Samuel Crompton's spinning mule made a fortune for the mill owners of Manchester and Bolton — but the inventor gained only a meagre £60, and died a poor and embittered man.

Street Index with Grid Reference

Bradford

Adolphus Street	E1-E2
Ann Place	B1
Ash Grove	A1
Balme Street	D4
Bank Street	C3-D3
Barkerend Road	E4-F4
Barry Street	B3-B4
Bolling Road	E1
Bolton Road	D4-D5-E5
Bridge Street	C3-D3-D2
Britannia Street	D1
Broadway	D3
Buck Street	F1-F2
Burnett Street	E3
Burrow Street	C1
Butler Street	F5
Caledonian Street	E1
Canal Road	D4-D5
Carlton Street	A2-A3
Chain Street	A4-B4
Channing Way	C2
Chapel Street	E3
Charles Street	D3
Cheapside	C4-D4-D3
Chester Street	B2
Church Bank	D3-E3-E4
City Road	A5
Claremont	A1-A2
Croft Street	C1-D1-D2
Dale Street	C4-D4
Darley Street	C3-C4
Diamond Street	E2-F2

Drake Street	D2-D3
Drewton Road	B4-B5
Dryden Street	E1-F1
Duke Street	C4
Eastbrooke Lane	E2
East Parade	E3-E4-F4
Edmund Street	B1
Edward Street	D1
Filey Street	E2-F2
Forster Square	D3-D4
Fullerton Street	F2
George Street	E2-E3
Godwin Street	C3-C4
Grattan Road	A4-B4
Great Cross Street	E2-E3
Great Horton Road	A1-A2-B2
Grove Terrace	B2
Hallfield Road	A5-B5
Hall Ings	C2-D2-D3
Hall Lane	E1
Hammerton Street	F2-F3
Harris Street	F3-F4
Henry Street	B1-C1
Holdsworth Street	D5
Howard Street	B1
Humboldt Street	F3-F4
Hustlergate	C3-D3
Ivegate	C3
James Street	B4-C4
John Street	B4-C4
Joseph Street	F3
Kirkgate	C3-C4-D4
Lansdowne Place	B1
Leeds Road	E3-F3
Lister Hills Road	A3
Little Horton Lane	B1-B2-C2
Longside Lane	A3
Lumb Lane	A5-B5
Malvern Street	F3

Bradford

Wool and Bradford are almost synonymous, such was its importance in the 19th century as a central market after the Industrial Revolution brought steam power to the trade. Like many small market towns that exploded into industrial cities almost overnight, Bradford's architecture is a mish-mash of grand civic buildings, factories and crowded housing. Among the former, the Wool Exchange is

impressive, with its ornate tower adorned with stone busts of 13 famous men, and the massive town hall, also topped by a tower, 200ft high. Few traces remain of the town's past but one obvious exception is the cathedral. Set on a rise, its detailed carvings – particularly the 20 angels that support the nave roof – catch the eye.

Bradford boasts several parks – notably Lister Park where there is a boating lake, an open-air swimming pool, a botanical garden and a scented

garden for the blind – and Bowling Park, on the other side of town. Cartwright Hall, named after the inventor of the power loom, stands in Lister Park. It now houses Bradford's permanent art collection.

Keighley The Brontë sisters used to walk from Haworth to this pleasant 19th-century town for their shopping sprees. Nowadays, the restored Keighley and Worth Valley Railway is a great attraction and passengers can travel to Oxenhope.

Bradford Area

SCALE 0 mls 2

Box denotes area covered by CentralPlan

Manchester Road	C1-C2	The Tyrls	C2-C3
Manningham Lane	B5	Thornton Road	A4-A3-B3-C3
Mannville Terrace	A2-B2-B1	Trafalgar Street	B5
Manor Row	C4-C5	Tumbling Hill Street	A2-A3
Market Street	C3-D3	Tyrrel Street	C3
Melbourne Place	A1-B1	Upper Piccadilly	C4
Merton Road	A1	Valley Road	D4-D5
Mill Street	D4-D5	Vicar Lane	D2-E2-E3
Morley Street	A1-B1-B2-C2	Wakefield Road	E2-E1-F1
Neal Street	B1-C1	Wapping Road	E5
Nelson Street	C2-C1-D1	Well Street	D3-E3
Northgate	C4-C5	Westgate	B4-C4-C3
North Parade	C4-C5	West Street	E3
North Wing	E4-E5	White Abbey Road	A5-B5-B4
Otley New Road	F4-F5	Wigan Street	A4-B4
Otley Road	E4-F4-F5	William Street	B1-C1
Peckover Street	E4-E3-F3	Wilton Street	B1-B2
Peel Street	E2-E3		
Pemberton Drive	A1	**Keighley**	
Petergate	D3	Aireworth Street	A1-B1
Piccadilly	C3-C4	Alice Street	B3-C3
Portland Street	C1-D1	Alkincote Street	B1
Priestley Street	E1	Beck Street	B1
Princes View	C1	Becks Road	A1-A2
Princes Way	C2	Belgrave Road	A2-A3
Quebec Street	B3-B2-C2	Berry Lane	B1
Rawson Road	B4-C4	Bradford Road	C2-C3
Rawson Square	C4	Bradford Street	C3
Richmond Road	A2	Caledonia Road	C3
Richmond Street		Cark Road	B3
Salem Street	C5	Cartmel Road	A2-A3
Sawrey Place	B1	Cashmere Street	A2
School Street	C4-D4-D5	Castle Road	B3
Sharpe Street	C1	Cavendish Street	B2-C2
Smith Street	A3	Church Street	B1-B2
Southgate	B3	Cliffe Street	A3-B3
Stone Street	C5	Coney Lane	C1-C2
Stott Hill	D4-E4	Croft Street	A1
Sunbridge Road	A4-A3-B3-C3	Damside	B1
Swan Street	B1-C1		

Dean Road	A2	South Street	B1
Devonshire Street	A2-B2	Spencer Street	A2-B2
Drewery Road	A2-A3	Spring Gardens Lane	B3
Earl Street	B3	Springfield Gardens	A3
East Avenue	B3, C3	Starkie Street	B1
East Parade	C2	Strawberry Street	B3
Edenser Street	A2	Sun Street	B1-C1
Goulbourne Street	A1-B1	Vernon Street	B3
Greengate Road	B1	View Road	A3
Hanover Street	C2	Victoria Road	A1
High Street	B2	Waterside Lane	B1
Highfield Lane	A3-A2-B2	West Lane	A2-B2
Holker Street	B3	Woodville Road	A3-B3
Ivy Street	A3-B3	Worth Way	C1-C2
Kendal Street	C1		
Kensington Street	A1-B1		
Lawkholme Lane	B2-C2-C3		
Long Croft	B1-C1		
Lord Street	B2		
Low Mill Lane	C2		
Luton Street	A2-B2		
Malsis Road	A1		
Market Street	B1-B2		
Marlborough Street	C3		
Marley Street	B1		
Marriner Road	B1		
Mayfield Road	A3-B3		
Mornington Street	A3-B3		
North Street	B2-B3		
Oakworth Road	A1-B1-B2		
Otley Street	B1		
Park Lane	C1		
Park Wood Street	C1-C2		
Parker Street	B1		
Parson Street	C3		
Plover Street	C3		
Richmond Street	A3		
Russell Street	B2		
Scott Street	B2-B3		

LEGEND

Town Plan

AA Recommended Route	▬▬
Other roads	═══
Restricted roads	▬ ▬ ▬
Buildings of interest	Market
Car parks	P
Parks and open spaces	
One Way Streets	←

Area Plan

A roads	▬▬
B roads	▬▬
Urban area	
Locations	Richmond ○

BRADFORD
St George's, built with the profits of the wool trade, is one of Bradford's imposing Victorian buildings. It is once again being used for the purpose for which it was intended – a concert hall – and has exceptionally good acoustics.

15

Burnley

International fame was brought to Burnley in the 1960s by its local football team, which can still be seen playing at Turf Moor. An old mill town lying in a bend of the Leeds and Liverpool Canal, Burnley's prosperity is reflected in the fine new developments it has seen, particularly since the opening of the M65. Half a mile south-east of the town stands Towneley Hall, a restored house dating back to the 14th century, which houses an art gallery and museum with an interesting local history collection.

Rawtenstall has made its name in the manufacture of felt, and now enjoys the luxury of an artificial ski-slope in Haslingden Old Road among its many good sports facilities.

Nelson was named after a pub, called Nelson's Inn (in honour of the hero of Trafalgar). It once stood alone here, but a burgeoning cotton town sprang up around it during the 19th century, and eventually took its name. Not far off looms the dark mass of Pendle Hill — the notorious haunt of Lancashire witches.

Colne's 18th-century wool trading prosperity is remembered in the fine Cloth Hall, which dates from this period. With a past traceable back to Roman times, Colne is also the site of the British in India Museum, which stands in Sun Street and can be visited at weekends in summer.

16

Central Nelson

Central Colne

Key to Town Plan and Area Plan

Town Plan

AA Recommended roads
Other roads
Restricted roads
Buildings of interest — Mill
One way street
Car Parks — P
Parks and open spaces — P

Area Plan

A roads
B roads
Locations — Hawkshaw O
Urban area

STREET INDEX

BURNLEY

Accrington Road	A2-B2-B3
Adlington Street	E3
Airdrie Crescent	B1
Albert Street	E3-F3
Albion Street	B1-C1-C2
Arch Street	D4-D3
Ashfield Road	C3-C4-D4
Athol Street	B1
Athol Street North	A1
Bank House Road	D3-D4
Bank Parade	D4-D3-E3
Barracks Road	A3-A2-B2
Belvedere Road	F3-F4
Berkeley Street	C4-D4
Berry Street	D1
Bivel Street	A3
Blakey Street	E3-F3
Blannel Street	B2-B3
Bread Street	A3
Brown's Square	E3-E4
Brown Street	D3
Brownsholme Avenue	F3
Brunshaw Road	F2-F3
Brunswick Street	E1-F1
Burdett Street	A2
Burnham Gate	B2-C2
Calder Street	D3
Calder Vale Road	C3
Carlton Road	C1-C2
Cavalry Way	A3
Centenary Way	D1-D2-E2-E3
Chichester Close	F3
Church Street	E3-E4
Clark Street	B3-B4
Clevelands Road	C1
Clifton Street	C3-C4
Coal Clough Lane	B1-B2
Cog Lane	A1-A2
Cog Street	A2
Colin Street	A2-B2
Colne Road	D4-E4
Cotton Street	A3-B3-B4
Cow Lane	D2-D3
Croft Street	D2-E2-E3
Crowther Street	E1
Crow Wood Avenue	A4-B4
Cuerden Street	D4
Curzon Street	D3
Dunoon Street	A1
Durban Grove	B1
Elgin Crescent	A1
Eliza Street	E1
Faraday Street	A4
Fielden Street	A2
Finsley Gate	D2-D1-E1
Forest Street	E4
Grosvenor Street	C4
Hammerton Road	D2-D3
Hargher Street	A1-A2
Hargreaves Street	D2-D3
Hargrove Avenue	A4-B4
Harold Avenue	A1
Harold Street	A1-B1
Harriet Street	C1
Hart Street	E3
Healey Mount	C1
Hemeldon Approach	A2
Herbert Street	B1-C1
Higgin Street	F2
Hirst Street	E1-F1
Holcombe Drive	F3
Hollingreave Road	E2
Holmes Street	E2-F2
Howard Street	A2-B2
Hull Street	E2
Ighten Road	A4
Jockey Street	A2
Junction Street	B3, B4
Keppel Place	B2
King Street	C2-C3
Kingsway	D3
Kinross Street	A1-B1
Kirkgate	E1-F1
Laithe Street	D1
Lanark Street	B1
Lansdowne Close	C1
Leven Street	A2
Leyland Road	E3-F3-F4
Lindsay Street	E3
Lyall Street	F1
Lyndhurst Road	B2-A1-B1
Manchester Road	C1-D1-D2-D3
Marlborough Street	D1-E1
May Street	E1
Melrose Avenue	A1
Mitella Street	F3
Montague Road	B2-C2-C1
Nairne Street	B1-B2
Naples Avenue	A1
Nelson Square	D2
Netherby Street	B1
Newton Street	A4
Nicholas Street	D2
Ormerod Road	E3-E4-F4
Oxford Road	E2-F2-F1
Padiham Road	A3-A4
Paisley Street	A2-A1-B1
Palatine Square	C1-C2
Parker Lane	D2-D3
Parkwood Avenue	A4
Parliament Street	E1-F1-F2
Pendle Way	A3-B3-B4
Perth Street	A2

Piccadilly Road	B2-C2-C1
Plumbe Street	E1-E2
Powell Street	B1-C1
Princess Way	C4-D4
Pritchard Street	B1
Queensberry Road	B2-B1-C1
Raglan Road	B1-B2-C2
Railway Street	D4
Rectory Road	C4-D4
Richard Street	E2
Royle Road	C4-D4-D3
St James Street	C3-D3-E3
St John's Street	B4
St Matthews Street	B1-C1
Sandy Gate	C2-C3
Scarlett Street	B1-B2
Scott Park Road	B1-C1
Scott's Terrace	A2
Serpentine Road	C1-D1
Springfield Road	E1
Spring Hill Road	C1-D1
Standish Street	D3
Swindon Street	B2
Tabor Street	A3-A4
Tartleton Street	F1
Tay Street	A2-B2
Temple Street	E2-F2
Thursfield Road	F2
Thurston Street	E4-F4-F3
Todmorden Road	F1-F2
Trafalgar Street	B3-C3-C2-D2
Tunnel Street	A3-B3
Ulster Street	B1-B2
Venice Street	A1-A2
Villiers Street	A2
Ward Street	C3
Waterloo Road	E1-F1
Wellfield Drive	A4
Westgate	B3-C3
Whittam Street	C2-D2
Wiseman Street	C3
Woodgrove Road	F1
Yorkshire Street	E3

RAWTENSTALL

Almond Crescent	A1
Andrew Avenue	A1
Bacup Road	B2-C2
Bank Street	B3
Barnes Avenue	A3
Barrit Road	A3
Beech Street	A3
Bocholt Way	B2-C2
Burnley Road	B4
Bury Road	A1-B1-B2
Carr Lane	B1
Cherry Crescent	A1
Daisy Hill	B3-C3
Elm Street	B4
Fall Barn Crescent	A1-B1-B2-C2
Fallbarn Road	C2
Grange Road	A1
Grange Walk	B3-C3
Greenbank Park	C2
Hall Carr Road	B1-B2
Hanworth Avenue	A3
Hardman Avenue	B1-B2-C2
Hargreaves Drive	A3-B3
Haslingden Road	A2-B2
Haslingden Old Road	A3-B3

Henry Street	B3
Holland Avenue	A4-B4
Hurst Lane	B3-B4-C4
Ivy Grove	B4
Lavender Hill	A1
Lomas Lane	A1-B1
Mill Gate	B3-C3
Musbury Grove	B1-B2-B1
Newchurch Road	B3-C3
New Hall Hey Road	A1-A2
Oakley Road	A2-A3
Rawtenstall-Edenfield By-Pass	A2-B2
St James Street	B4
St Mary's Way	B3
Schofield Road	A3-B3-B1
Union Street	C3-C4
Waingate Close	C3
Waingate Road	C3-C4
Whittle Street	B3-B4

NELSON

Albert Street	A2-B2
Albion Street	B3
Ann Street	B3-C3
Arthur Street	C3
Arundel Street	A3
Ball Street	A4
Bank House Road	C4
Beaufort Street	B1
Bishop Street	A1-A2
Bond Street	A1
Bradley Road	B3-C3
Bradshaw Street	B1-C1
Broad Street	B2
Broadway	B2
Brook Street	C2
Brunswick Street	C1
Burns Street	B4
Calder Street	B4
Carlton Street	B1
Carr Street	A3-B3-B2
Chatham Street	A4-B4
Chapel House Road	C1
Chapel Street	C2-C3
Clayton Street	A2-A3-B3-B4
Cliffe Street	C4
Clifford Street	C1
Cobden Street	B1
Commercial Road	C1-C2
Conduit Street	A3-A4
Cooper Street	B4-C4
Craven Street	A2
Crawford Street	C4
Cross Street	B2-B3
Dalton Street	C4
Derby Street	B2
Ellen Street	B3-C3
Elizabeth Street	B4-C4
Elm Street	C3
Essex Street	B4-C4
Every Street	A1-A2-B2-B3-B4
Fleet Street	B4
Forest Street	B3-B4
Fountain Street	B4
Garden Street	C1-C2
Giles Street	C3-C4
Gill Street	A4
Gordon Road	A3
Gott Side	C3
Hargreaves Street	A1

Hartley Street	C1
Henry Street	A4
Hibson Road	B1
Hibson Road	B2-C2
High Street	B1
Holme Street	C2-C3
Hope Street	A1
Howard Street	A3
John Street	B1-C1, C2
Jude Street	B2-B3
Kendall Street	A3-A4
Kiln Street	B1-B2
Leonard Street	C1
Lomeshaye	A1-B1
Lomeshaye Road	A1-A2
Lowther Street	A2-A3
Macleod Street	A2
Manchester Road	A1-A2-B2-C2-C3
Market Street	B2-B3
Maurice Street	A1-A2
Milton Street	A3-A4
Mosley Street	A2-B2
Netherfield Road	B1-B2-C2
Nile Street	B3-B4
Norfolk Street	A2-A3-A4
North Street	B3
Oakland Street	C3
Pendle Street	A4-B4-B3
Percy Street	B1
Pollard Street	B3-C3
Princess Street	B1-C1
Raglan Street	B1
Regent Street	C4
Ripon Street	B1
Rook Street	B4-C4
St Mary's Street	A1-A2
Sagar Street	C2
Scotland Road	B2-B3-B4
Scott Street	A4-B4
Stanley Street	A3-A2-B2
Stanworth Road	B1-B2
Surrey Road	A4
Swaine Street	A4
Thomas Street	B1-C1
Vernon Street	C1
Victoria Street	A2
Water Street	B1-C1-C2
Wellington Street	B3
West Moreland Street	A2
Wilkinson Street	B1-C1
William Street	C2

COLNE

Albert Road	A1-A2
Argyle Street	A2-B2
Belgrave Road	A3-B3
Birtwistle Avenue	A3-A4-B4
Bold Street	C4
Boundary Street	A1-B1
Buck Street	B2
Byron Road	C3
Carr Road	B4
Carry Lane	C1-C2
Casserley Road	B4-C4
Castle Road	C4
Chapel Street	A1
Charles Street	B2
Chatham Street	B3-C3
Church Street	B2
Clayton Street	B1
Colne Lane	B1-B2

Cook House Road	B4
Craddock Road	B2-C2
Cragg Street	A1-A2
Cross Street	C2
Curzon Street	B1-C1
Derby Street	A1-A2
Dickson Street	B3
Dockray Street	B2
Doughty Street	A1-B1
Duke Street	A1
Earl Street	A1
Elm Street	C3
Exchange Street	A1-B1
Fern Street	C3
Glenroy Avenue	A3-B3-B4
Glen Street	B3
Gordon Street	C3
Granville Street	C3
Grosvenor Street	C1-C2
Hall Street	A1
Hanover Street	A3-B3
Harrison Drive	A2
High Street	A3
Hill Street	A1
Ivegate	B2
Judge Fields	A3
Keats Close	A3
Keighley Avenue	A3-B3
Keighley Road	C2
King Street	B2
Langroyd Road	B3-B4
Lilac Street	C3
Linden Road	A1-A2
Market Street	B2-C2
Midgley Street	B2
Milton Road	A2-A3
Montague Road	B3-B4
New Market Street	C2
Norfolk Street	C2
North Street	B3-C3
North Valley Road	A2
Oak Street	C3
Peter Street	C1
Portland Street	C2
Red Lane	A4-B4
River Street	A1
Rook Street	A2-B2
Ruskin Avenue	A2-A3-A4
Russell Avenue	B4-C4
Rutland Street	C2-C3
Salisbury Street	B2-C2
Seldon Street	B1
Shaw Street	A1-B1
Skelton Street	B2
Skipton Road	B4-C4-C3-C2
Slater Avenue	A3
Snell Grove	C4
Spring Lane	A1-A2
Stanley Street	A2
Stone Bridge	B2
Talbot Street	A3-A4-B4
Temple Street	B3-C3
Tennyson Road	A2-A3
The Crescent	B3
Thorn Grove	C3-C4
Varley Street	C3-C4
Walton Street	B1
West Street	B1
Windsor Street	B3-C3
Windy Bank	B2
York Street	B1
Zion Street	B1

17

Bury / Rochdale

Bury has been celebrated for its black pudding for over a century, and this special delicacy is still an important attraction of Bury Market. The market has been chartered since 1440 and nearby is Bury's oldest building — the Two Tubs, said to have been built around two giant oak trees in the reign of Charles II. Celebrated sons of Bury include 'flying shuttle' inventor John Kay who was born here. His invention helped to transform 18th-century weaving, and the town remembers him by the John Kay Gardens, where his statue stands.

Rochdale Gracie Fields came from Rochdale — a town which saw dramatic changes in the early 19th century. This was when the textile mills arrived and brought with them a whole new lifestyle for local people. They rose to the challenge with innovations like the now worldwide co-operative movement, the brainchild of the 'Rochdale Pioneers' whose original shop has become a museum in the Toad Lane Conservation Area. More radical ideas came from Rochdale-born John Bright, campaigner for the repeal of the Corn Laws in 1846. His statue is one of many in the town, which also has the unusual Lancashire Dialect Writers Memorial. The town centre is dominated by a magnificent Victorian Gothic Town Hall, set in parks and gardens with the medieval Parish Church of St Chad nearby.

Central Rochdale

Key to Town Plan and Area Plan

Town Plan

AA Recommended roads	
Restricted roads	
Other roads	
Buildings of interest	Hospital
Car parks	P
Churches	+
Parks and open spaces	

Area Plan

A roads	
B roads	
Locations	Bottoms
Urban area	

Street Index with Grid Reference

Bury

Albert Street	F2-F3
Albion Street	A2-A3
Alfred Street	E1-F1-F2
Andrew Street	E2-F2
Angouleme Way	D1-D2
Ash Street	F3
Arthur Street	A2
Audlum Street	F3
Back Foundry Street	D2-E2
Back Princess Street	D2-E2-E1
Badger Street	E4
Baker Street	A2
Bambury Street	E3-E4
Bank Street	C2
Barcroft Street	D4
Barlow Street	D3-E3
Baron Street	B1-C1
Barrett Street	F2-F3
Bazaar Street	D4
Bell Lane	E4-F4
Belle Vue Terrace	B1-C1
Benson Street	E2-E1-F1
Birch Street	D4
Bold Street	E4
Bolton Road	A2-A3
Bolton Street	A3-B3-C3-C2
Bond Street	F2-F3
Boundary Street	D4
Brandlesholme Road	A3-A4
Brick Street	E3-F3-F4
Bridge Road	B1-B2
Bridge Street	E4
Bright Street	F4
Brighton Street	F4
Broad Street	C2
Brook Street	E4
Buckley Street	D4-E4
Butcher Lane	D3
Buxton Street	A2
Castle Street	C3
Castle Croft Road	B3-C3-C4
Cecil Street	D1
Cedar Street	F3-F4
Chamberhill Street	C4
Chapel Row	D3
Charles Street	D4
Chesham Crescent	F4
Church Street	E4-F4-F3
Clerke Street	D2-D3
Cobden Street	E4-F4
Cook Street	E2
Cork Street	F3
Croft Street	E3-F3
Cross Street	D2-D3
Crostons Road	A3
Derby Street	E3
Doctors Lane	B2-B3
East Street	D1-E1
Eden Street	D3
Edward Street	D1
Ely Drive	A4
Fern Street	D4
Fletcher Street	E3
Flint Street	D4
Fir Street	F3
Fold Street	B2
Foundry Street	D2-E2
Fountain Street	F2
Fountain Street North	E3
Frank Street	D1-E1
Franklin Street	D4
George Street	D2-E2
Georgiana Street	C2-D2
Georgiana Street	D1
Gladstone Street	F3-F4
Gordon Street	C4
Hacking Street	E2
Harper Street	D4
Haymarket	C2
Heys Street	A2

Heywood Street	E1-E2
Hinds Street	A1
Holly Street	F3
Hornby Street	D4
Hulme Street	A4
Hurst Street	E2-F2
Ingham Street	E1-E2
Irwell Street	B2
James Street	F1
John Street	D3
Jubilee Way	B3-B2-C2
Kershaw Street	F2
Knowsley Street	C1-C2
Laurel Street	F3
Lodge Street	E4-F4
Lord Street	D2-E2
Lower Woodhill Road	A3-B3
Lucas Street	F4
Manchester Road	C1
Manor Street	E3-F3
Market Parade	D2
Market Place	C2-C3
Market Street	C2-D2-D1
Mason Street	C2
Mausley Street	B1-C1
Maxwell Street	F4
Merton Street	A4
Mill Yard	E4
Millett Street	B2-B3
Milton Street	A4
Minden Parade	D2
Moor Street	D4
Moorgate Crescent	E4
Moss Street	F4
Murray Road	D2
Myrtle Street	F2-F3
North Street	D4
Nuttall Street	E1-F1
Olive Street	A2-A3
Openshaw Street	E1
Orell Street	A3-A4
Ormond Street	E3
Ormrod Street	E2-F2
Oxford Street	E1-F1
Paradise Street	D3
Parker Street	E2
Parks Yard	C2
Parkside Walk	D1
Parsonage Street	F3-F4
Parsons Lane	D3
Peel Way	B3-C3-D3-D4-E4
Percy Street	F4
Peter Street	E4
Phoenix Street	B2-B3
Pimhole Fold	F1-F2
Pimhole Road	F2
Pine Street	F2-F3
Princess Parade	D2
Princess Street	D2-D3
Queen Street	E2
Raby Street	F3
Revers Street	A4
Richard Burch Street	E4
Rochdale Road	D3-E3-E2-F2
St Mary's Place	C2
St Pauls Street	F3-F4
Samuel Street	E4-F4
Sankey Street	B2
School Street	F1-F2
Shaw Street	F4
Shepherd Street	E1-E2
Silver Street	C2

South Cross Street	D2-E2-E1
Spring Street	D2-D1-E1
Taylor Street	E4
Tenterden Street	B2
The Haymarket	C2-D2
The Rock	C3-D3-E3-E4
The Square	D2
The Wylde	C3
Tile Street	D4
Tinune Street	F2
Tithe Barn Street	D3
Topping Street	D2
Tottington Road	A3-A4
Townside Row	D1
Trinity Street	D1
Union Arcade	D2
Union Street	D2-D3
Victoria Row	A1-A2
Victoria Street	A2-A3
Villiers Street	F4
Walmersley Road	E4
Walshaw Road	A3-A4
Wash Lane	E4-E3-F3
Webb Street	A3-B3
Wellington Street	A1-A2
White Street	A4
Wike Street	A3
Wilson Street	E1-F1
Wood Street	A3
Woodfield Terrace	D4
Woodhill Road	A4-B4
York Street	E3

Rochdale

Acker Street	D3
Albion Road	B1-B2
Ann Street	D1-D2
Arthington Street	F3
Arthur Street	B3-B4
Ashworth Street	B4-C4-C3
Baillie Street	D3-E3
Ball Street	E4
Barlow Street	E2
Baron Street	D2-E2
Beech Street	B2
Bell Street	D3
Bilberry Street	E1-F1
Bradshaw Street	E4-F4
Briar Street	B2
Bridgefield Street	B2
Bridgefold Road	A3-A4
Bulwer Street	F3-F4
Bunyan Street	E4
Bury Road	A2-B2-B3
Castle Avenue	B1-C1
Castlemere Street	C1
Chaseley Road	B4-C4
Church Lane	D2-D3
Church Road	F1
Church Stile	D1-D2
Church Street	B1-B2
Cinnamon Street	B4
Clarke's Lane	B4
Clement Royds Street	B3-C3-C4
Clover Street	C3
Clyde Street	F1
College Road	B3-C3
Copenhagen Street	F3
Corbett Street	F4
Corporation Road	A1-B1-B2

Crimble Street	B3-C3
Dane Street	B2-C2
Devon Street	D1
Dowling Street	D1
Drake Street	C1-D1-D2-E2
Duke Street	D4
East Street	E4
Eastgate Street	D3-D4-E4
Edmund Street	B4-C4
Edward Street	F4
Elbow Lane	E1-E2
Elliott Street	E4
Emma Street	C4
Entwisle Road	E3-F3-F4
Essex Street	D1
Falinge Road	C4
Falkland Avenue	A4
Fishwick Street	E1
Fitton Street	E4-F4
Fleece Street	D3
Fox Street	F4
Further Pits	A3
Garden Street	F1
Geneva Terrace	A4
George Street	E3-E4
Great George Street	D2
Halliwell Street	C3
Hamer Lane	F4
Haynes Street	E4
Heath Street	B1-B2
Heights Lane	C4
Henry Street	D1
High Street	E3
High Level Road	D1-E1
Hill Street	E2
Holland Street	C3
Holmes Street	B3
Hope Street	D4
Hovingham Street	F3
Howard Street	D4
Hugh Street	E3
Hunters Lane	D3
Jermyn Street	E4
John Street	E3
Jutland Avenue	A4
Kathleen Street	B3
Kenion Street	E2
Key Street	F3
Kitchen Street	E3
Knowsley Street	C4
Leach Street	F1
Liley Street	E2-F2
Littledale Street	C3-C4
Livsey Street	E2
Longfield Road	A4
Lower Tweedale Street	D1
Maclure Road	D1
Manchester Road	C1-C2
March Street	E2
Marne Crescent	A3-A4
May Street	F4
Meanwood Brow	A4-B4
Mellor Street	C2-B2-B3-B4-A4
Mere Street	C1-D1
Miall Street	D1-E1
Milkstone Road	D1
Mill Street	B2
Milnrow Road	E2-E1-F1
Milton Street	E2
Mitchell Street	B3-B4
Molesworth Street	E2-E3
Molyneux Street	B4
Mons Avenue	A4

Moore Street	D2
Morley Street	F4
Moss Lane	E1
Moss Street	F1
Mount Street	C3-C4
Nelson Street	D2
Newgate	C3-D3
Nile Street	E3-F3
Norfolk Street	C1
Norman Road	B1-B2
North Street	E4
Oakenrod Hill	A2
Oakfield Terrace	A4
Oldham Road	E1-E2
Oswald Street	F4
Peel Street	C4
Pilling Street	B4
Pits Farm Avenue	A3
Primrose Street	B4
Pym Street	B3
Ramsay Street	E3-F3
Red Cross Street	D4
Regent Street	E4
Richard Street	D1-E1
River Street	D2-D3
Roach Place	E3
Robert Street	E3
Robinson Street	E2
Rope Street	E4
Rugby Road	E4-F4
St Albans Street	C1-C2-D2
St John Street	F1
St Mary's Gate	C2-C3-D3-D4
St Peter's Street	F1
School Lane	D4
Selby Street	F4
Sherriff Street	C4
Silver Street	B4
Slack Street	D3-E3
Smith Street	D3-E3
South Parade	D3
South Street	E3-E4-F4
Sparrow Hill	C2-D2
Sparth Bottoms Road	B1-C1
Spodden Street	B4
Spotland Road	B4-C4-C3-D3
Stanley Street	C4
Station Road	D1
Stuart Street	E1
Summer Street	E2
Sussex Street	C1-D1
Tell Street	B3
The Butts	D3
The Esplanade	C2-D2-D3
Toad Lane	D4
Town Hall Square	D2
Trafalgar Street	F3-F4
Tweedale Street	C1-D1
Vavasour Street	F1
Vicars Drive	D1-D2
Walker Street	E2
Water Street	D2-E2-E3
Waterhouse Street	D4
Watts Street	D4
West Street	E3-E4
Whitehall Street	D4
Whitworth Road	D4
William Street	C1-D1
Wood Street	D3
Yorkshire Street	D3-E3-E4-F4

19

Chester

Chester is the only English city to have preserved the complete circuit of its Roman and medieval walls. On the west side, the top of the walls is now at pavement level, but on the other three sides the walk along the ramparts is remarkable. Two of the old watchtowers contain small museums: the Water Tower, built to protect the old river port, displays relics of medieval Chester; King Charles's Tower, from which Charles I watched the defeat of the Royalist army at the Battle of Rowton Moor in 1645, portrays Chester's role in the Civil War.

Looking down from the top of the Eastgate, crowned with the ornate and gaily-coloured Jubilee Clock erected in 1897, the view down the main street, the old Roman *Via Principalis,* reveals a dazzling display of the black-and-white timbered buildings for which Chester is famous. One of these, Providence House, bears the inscription 'God's Providence is Mine Inheritance', carved in thanks for sparing the survivors of the plague of 1647 that ravaged the city.

On either side of Eastgate, Watergate and Bridge Street are the Rows, a feature unique to Chester, and dating back at least to the 13th century. These covered galleries of shops, raised up at first-floor level, protected pedestrians from weather and traffic. Chester's magnificent cathedral has beautifully carved choir stalls.

Central Northwich

Central Middlewich

Key to Town Plan and Area Plan

Town Plan

AA Recommended roads
Other roads
Restricted roads
Buildings of interest — College
One Way Streets
Car Parks — P
Parks and open spaces
Churches — +

Area Plan

A roads
B roads
Locations — DuddonO
Urban area

Street Index with Grid Reference

Chester

Albion Street	D2
Andrews Crescent	E1
Anne's Way	E2-E1
Beaconsfield Street	E3
Black Friars	C1-C2
Bottom's Lane	E1-F1
Boughton	E3-F3
Bouverie Street	B4
Bridge Street	C2
Brook Street	D4
Cambrian Road	A4-B4
Canal Street	B3-C3
Castle Drive	C1
Castle Street	C1
Catherine Street	A3-B3
Chichester Street	B4-C4
City Road	E3-E4
City Walls Road	B3-B2
Commonhall Street	C2
Crewe Street	D4-E4
Crook Street	C2
Cross Heys	E1
Cuppin Street	C2
Curzon Park North	A1
Dee Hills Park	E3
Dee Lane	E3
Delamere Street	C4
Denbigh Street	B4
Duke Street	D1-D2
Eastern Path	D1-E1
Edinburgh Way	E1
Egerton Street	D4
Elizabeth Crescent	E1-E2
Finchetts Drive	A4
Foregate Street	D3
Forest Street	D3-E3
Francis Street	D4
Frodsham Street	D3
Garden Lane	A4-B4
Garden Terrace	B3-B4
George Street	C3-C4
Gladstone Avenue	A3-A4
Gladstone Road	A4
Goss Street	C2
Gorse Stacks	C4-C3-D3
Granville Road	A4
Grey Friars	C2
Grosvenor Park Road	E3
Grosvenor Road	C1
Grosvenor Street	C1-C2
Groves Road	D2-E2
Handbridge	D1
Henshall Street	B4
Hoole Lane	F3-F4
Hoole Way	D4
Hunter Street	B3-C3
King Street	B3-C3
Lightfoot Street	E4-F4
Lord Street	F3
Lorne Street	B4
Lower Bridge Street	C2-C1-D1
Lower Park Road	D2-E2
Love Street	D3
Lyon Street	D4
Meadows Lane	E1
Milton Street	D4
New Crane Street	A3-B3-B2
Newgate Street	D2
Nicholas Street	C2-C1
Northgate Street	C3-C2
North Lorne Street	B4
Nuns Road	B2-B1-C1
Pepper Street	C2-D2
Princess Street	C3
Prince's Avenue	E4
Queen's Drive	E1-E2
Queen's Park Road	D1-E1
Queen's Road	E4
Queen Street	D3
Raymond Street	B3-B4
Richmond Terrace	F4
St Anne Street	C4-D4
St George's Crescent	E1
St Johns Road	E1
St Johns Street	D2
St John Street	D3-D2
St Martins Way	B4-B3-C3-B2-C2
St Oswalds Way	C4-D4-D3
Sealand Road	A3
Seller Street	D3
Souters Lane	D2
South Crescent Road	D2-E2-E1
South View Road	A3-B3
Spital Walk	F4-F3
Stadium Way	A4
Stanley Street	B2
Station Road	D4-E4
Station View	F4
The Bars	D2-E2
The Groves	C2
The Rows	C2
Tower Road	B3
Trafford Street	C4-D4
Union Street	D2-D3-E3
Upper Cambrian Road	A4-B4-B3
Upper Northgate Street	B4-C4-C3
Vernon Road	A3-B3-B4
Vicars Lane	D2
Victoria Crescent	D1-E1
Victoria Path	C4
Victoria Road	B3-B2
Walls Avenue	B4
Walpole Street	B2-C2
Watergate Street	C2
Water Tower Street	B3-C3
Weaver Street	C2
West Lorne Street	B4
White Friars	C2
Whipcord Lane	A4-B4
York Street	D3

Northwich

Albion Road	B3
Apple Market	A3
Ash Street	B4-C4
Barons Quay Road	A4-B4
Beswicks Road	A4
Binney Road	C2
Brockhurst Street	B3
Brook Street	B3-C3-C4
Carlton Road	C2-C1
Castle Street	A2-A3
Chester Way	A2-B2-B3-C3
Chester Way Spur	B3
Church Road	C2-C1
Danebank Road	C2
Danefield Road	C2
Dane Street	A3-A2
Forest Street	C3
Greenall Road	C2-C3
Hayhurst Close	A2
Highfield Road	A2
High Street	A3
Jubilee Street	A2
Kingsway	C3
Leicester Street	B3-B4
Lock Street	A3
London Road	A1-A2-B2
Manora Road	C2
Meadow Street	B3
Navigation Road	A1-A2
Neumann Street	C3
New Warrington Street	C3-C4
Oak Street	B4-C4
Old Warrington Road	C4-C3
Orchard Street	C3
Paradise Street	C3
Percy Street	B3
Post Office Place	B4-B3
Princes Avenue	C3
Priory Street	B2-B3
School Way	B3
Sheath Street	B3
Station Road	C3
The Crescent	A1
Tabley Street	B4-B3
Timber Lane	B3
Town Bridge	A3
Vicarage Road	C2
Vicarage Walk	C2
Victoria Road	C2-C3
Water Street	A3-B3
Watling Street	A3-B3-B4
Weaver Way	A3-B3-B4
Weir Street	A1

Middlewich

Wesley Place	C3
Westfield Road	C2
Whalley Road	B3-B2
Winnington Street	A3
Witton Street	B3-C3
Ashfield Street	C2
Beech Street	B2-B3
Beta Road	C2-C1
Booth Lane	C1
Brooks Lane	C3-C2
Canal Terrace	C2
Chester Road	A4-A3
Croxton Lane	A4
Darlington Street	A3-B3
Dawe Street	C4
Dierdene Terrace	B3
East Road	A3
Elm Road	C1
Finney's Lane	A4-B4
Flea Lane	A1
Garfitt Street	B4-C4
Glastonbury Drive	A3
Hannah's Walk	A2-B2
Hayhurst Avenue	A1-B1
High Town	B3
Holmes Chapel Road	C3-C4
Hubert Drive	B1
Kinderton Street	B3-C3
King Edward Street	B2
King's Crescent	B4-C4
King Street	B4-C4-C3
Kitfield Avenue	B1-C1
Lewin Street	B3-B2-C2-C1
Lichfield Street	C4
Long Lane	B2
Longwood Close	B2
Lower Street	B3
Manor Fields	B1
Manor Lane	A2-B2
Mill Lane	A2
Nantwich Road	A1-A2-A3
New King Street	B4-C4
Newton Bank	A4-A3
Newton Heath	A3
Orchard Close	C1
Park Road	A2-B2
Pepper Street	B4-B3
Prosperity Way	C3
Queen Street	B2-B3
Rolt Crescent	A1-B1
Roy Lance Drive	B2
St Anne's Avenue	B1-C1
St Anne's Road	A3-B3-B2-B1
St Michaels Way	A3-B3
School Walk	B2
Seddon Street	B4
Southway	B3
Sutton Lane	B1-B2-C2
The Crescent	A3
Walker Drive	B1
Wavertree Drive	A1
Webbs Lane	B4
West Avenue	B4
Westlands Road	A3-A2
West Street	B3
Wheelock Street	A3-B3
White Horse Alley	B2
Wych House Lane	B3-C3

Darlington

Railways and Darlington have gone together since 1825, when George Stephenson's *Locomotion*, the world's first public steam train, passed through on its historic journey from Witton Park to Stockton-on-Tees. The *Locomotion* is now on show with other rolling stock at the Darlington Railway Museum. Appropriately, this is at North Road Station, which is one of the country's earliest.

The town became a major industrial centre during the industrial revolution, and a number of Georgian houses can be seen in the Market Square area. Bennet House, a former merchant's residence, is used by community service organisations, and it stands side by side with the new Dolphin Centre, the most recent addition to the town's leisure facilities. The Parish Church of St Cuthbert is 12th-century, and the Edwardian style of the 1907 Civic Theatre has been carefully preserved.

Bishop Auckland's castle has been the seat of the Bishops of Durham since the 12th century, and stands in an extensive park which is now owned by the local council.

Crook lies between the twin peaks of Mount Pleasant and Dowfold Hill, and has the unusual feature of the 'Blue Stone' or 'Devil's Stone'. Preserved in the Market Place, the stone is thought to have come from Borrowdale in the Lake District, during the Ice Age.

Key to Town Plan and Area Plan

Town Plan
AA Recommended roads
Restricted roads
Other roads
Buildings of interest — Town Hall
AA Centre — AA
Car Parks — P
Parks and open spaces
Churches — †

Area Plan
A roads
B roads
Locations — Mount Pleasant ○
Urban area

Street Index with Grid Reference

Darlington

Abbey Road	A2-B2-C2
Adelaide Street	F1-F2
Albert Street	F1
Ashcroft Road	B1
Beaconsfield Street	C4
Beaumont Street	D1-E1
Beck Street	E4
Bedford Street	E1
Beechwood Avenue	D2
Blackwellgate	B4-C4
Bloomfield Road	D2-D3
Bondgate	D2-D3
Borough Road	E2-F2-F3
Bracken Road	B4
Branksome Terrace	D4
Breck Road	A2
Brunswick Street	E2-F2
Carmel Gardens	A1
Carmel Road North	A1-A2-A3-A4
Chestnut Street	E4
Clareville Road	A3
Cleveland Avenue	B3-B2-B1-C1
Cleveland Terrace	A1-B1-C1
Clifton Road	E1
Commercial Street	D3-E3
Coniscliffe Road	B1-C1-D1-D2
Corporation Road	E2-E3
Crown Street	E3
Cuthbert's Way	B3
Dale Road	A2-A3
Danesmoor Crescent	A2-A3
Dene Grove	B4
Dodd's Street	D4
Duke Street	C2-D2
Dundee Street	F4
Easson Road	D3-D4
East Mount Road	E4-F4-F3
East Raby Street	D2
East Street	E3
Elmfield Terrace	D4-E4
Elms Road	C3
Elton Grove	B1
Elton Parade	B1
Elton Road	B1-B2-A2-B2-B3
Eskdale Street	C3-D3
Fife Road	C1-C2
Feethams	E1-E2
Flora Avenue	B1
Four Riggs	D3
Garden Street	E3
Gladstone Street	D3-E3
Grange Road	C1-D1-D2
Greenbank Crescent	C4-D4
Greenbank Road	D3-D4
Greenbank Road North	C4
Green Street	F2
Hargreave Terrace	E1-F1-F2
Haughton Road	E3-F3-F4
Highbury Road	A4
High Northgate	E4
High Row	D2
Hollyhurst Road	B4-C4
Houndgate	D2-E2
Hummersknott Avenue	A2
Kendrew Street	D3
Kingston Street	D4
Langholm Crescent	B1-C1-C2
Larchfield Street	D2-D3
Linden Avenue	A1
Lodge Street	E3-F3
Market Place	D2-E2
Marshall Street	D4
Maude Street	D3
Melland Street	F2
Milbank Road	A3-B3-C3
Montrose Street	F4
Mowden Terrace	D4-E4
Neasham Road	F1-F2
Neville Road	A1-A2-A3-B3
Northgate	D2-D3-E3-E4
North Lodge Terrace	D3-D4
Nunnery Lane	A3
Oak Dene Avenue	C1
Outram Street	C2-C3
Oxford Street	E4
Parkgate	E2-F2
Park Lane	E1-F1
Park Place	E1-E2
Peel Street	F2
Pendower Street	D4
Pensbury Street	F1-F2
Pierremont Crescent	B3-B4
Pierremont Drive	B4
Pierremont Gardens	B3-B4
Pierremont Road	B4
Polam Lane	D1
Polam Road	D1
Post House Wynd	D2
Powlett Street	C2-D2
Prebend Row	D2
Priestgate	D2-E2
Raby Street West	C2-D2
Russell Street	E3
St Augustines Way	D3-E3
St Cuthbert's Way	E1-E2
St Johns Crescent	D4
Salisbury Terrace	F1
Salt Yard	D2-D3
Selbourne Road	D3-D4
Skinnergate	D2-D3
Southend Avenue	C1-D1
South Terrace	D1-E1
Staindrop Road	A4
Stanhope Road	C3-C2-D2
Swinburne Road	C1-C2
Sun Street	D3
Thornbury Rise	A3-A4
Thornfield Road	A3
Thornton Street	D3-D4
Tower Road	B4
Trinity Road	B3-C3
Tubwell Row	D2-E2
Uplands Road	B2-C2
Valley Street North	E3-E4
Vane Terrace	C2-C3
Victoria Embankment	E1
Victoria Road	D1-E1
Waverley Terrace	E1
Westbourne Grove	B2
Westcliffe Court	C1-D1
West Crescent	C3-C4
Witbank Road	C4
Woodland Road	A4-B4-C4-C3-D3
Woodland Terrace	A3-A4
Wycombe Street	C3-D3
Yarm Road	F1-F2

Crook

Addison Street	B4-C4
Alexandra Terrace	C3
Arthur Street	C3-C4
Bell Street	B3
Bladeside	C2
Blencathra Crescent	B1-C1
Brookside Avenue	A1
Broom Avenue	A4
Buttermere Grove	B1
Church Hill	C3-C4
Church Street	B3-C3
Coniston Crescent	B1-B2-C2
Croft Avenue	B3
Croft Street	B3
Dawson Street	B2-B3-C3
Derwent Avenue	C1-C2
East Bridge Street	C3
Ennerdale Drive	C1-C2
Esk Gardens	C1
Foundry Fields	A4-A3-B3
George Terrace	C3
Gladstone Street	B3-B4
Grey Street	B3-B4
Hartside	A4
High Hope Street	B4
Hollowdene	A1-B1
Holly Terrace	A4
Hope Street	B3-B4
Laburnum Avenue	A4
Langdale Avenue	C1-C2
Lishman Avenue	A4
Maple Crescent	A4
Milburn Street	B4-C4
Mill Street	C3
Nelson Street	B3
New Road	A2-B2-B3
North Terrace	B3-C3
Osborne Gardens	C2
Roseberry Crescent	A4
Rydale Drive	C1
St Mary's Avenue	A4-B4
Scafell Gardens	C1
Southend Villas	A2-B2
South Street	B3

Bishop Auckland

Acacia Road	B1-C1
Albion Terrace	B1-C1
Ashcroft Gardens	B1
Batts Terrace	C4
Berkeley Grove	A1
Bowser Street	B1
Bridge Road	A3-A4-B4
Bridge Street	B4
Chester Street	B2-C2
Clarence Street	A3-B3
Clayton Street	B4
Cleveland Avenue	B1
Cockton Hill Road	B1-B2
Craddock Street	B1-C1
Deerness Road	A1
Dial Stob Hill	C4
Durham Road	C3-C4
Durham Street	B3
Eastlea Avenue	C1
Edward Street	B3
Escomb Road	A1-B1
Etherley Lane	A1-A2-A3-B3
Fleet Street	B1
Fore Bondgate	B4-C4
Gib Chare	C3
Gibbon Street	B3
Granvill Road	A1
Grey Street	B2-B3
High Bondgate	B4
James Street	B1
Kings Way	C3
Market Place	C4
May Street	B2-B3
Newgate Street	B2-C2-C3-C4
Newlands Avenue	B1
Newton Cap Bank	B4
North Bondgate	B4-C4
Northumberland Avenue	A1-B1
Oak Terrace	C1
Peel Street	C2
Princes Street	B3
Queen's Road	C2
Railway Street	B2-C2
Sadler Street	B3
Salisbury Place	C2
South Church Road	C1-C2-C3
South Terrace	C2-C3
Sun Street	C1
Surtees Street	B3
Tenters Street	B3-C3
Union Street	B2-C2
Vickers Street	B3
Waldon Street	B3
Warwick Road	A1
Wearchase	C4
Westfield Road	A1-B1
Westgate Road	B3-C3
Westlea Avenue	C1
West Road	B3-B4
Woodlands Road	C2

Sycamore Gardens	A3-A4
Ullswater Crescent	B1-C1
Victoria Avenue	C2-C3
Victoria Street	B3-B4
West Bridge Street	C3
West End Villas	A3
West Road	A3-B3
Wheatbottom	C2-C3
Wilson Street	B4-C4

Key to Town Plan and Area Plan

Town Plan
A A Recommended roads
Other roads
Restricted roads
Buildings of interest
Car Parks
AA Service Centre
Parks and open spaces
One way streets

Area Plan
A roads
B roads
Locations   Ashton O
Urban area

Street Index — with grid reference

Central Doncaster

Alderson Drive	D2-E2-E3
Apley Road	C2
Ardeen Road	E4-F4
Avondale Road	F3
Bawtry Road	F1-F2
Belle Vue Avenue	E1-F1-F2
Bennetthorpe	D2-E2
Broxholme Lane	C4
Buckingham Road	E4
Carr House Road	C1-D1-E1-E2
Chequer Avenue	C1-D1-E1
Chequer Road	C1-C2-C3
Christchurch Road	B4-C4-C3
Church View	A4-B4
Church Way	B4-C4
Cleveland Street	A1-A2-B2-B3
Clumber Road	E1
College Road	B2-C2
Copley Road	B4-C4
Craithie Road	E4-F4-F3
Cunningham Road	C1-C2
Danum Road	D1-E1-E2
Dockin Hill Road	B4-C4
Dublin Road	F4
Duke Street	A3-B3-B2
East Laithe Gate	B3-C3
Elmfield Road	C1-C2
Firbeck Road	D2-E2
Franklin Crescent	E2-E3
Glamis Road	F3
Glyn Avenue	C4
Goldsborough Road	E3-F3
Granby Crescent	E2
Greendyke Road	A1-B1
Grey Friar's Road	A4-B4
Hallgate	B3-C3
Hamilton Road	D1
Hampton Road	E3-E4
Harewood Road	F3
High Street	B3
Highfield Road	C4-D4
Holyrood Road	E4-E3-F3
Imperial Crescent	E4
Jarratt Street	B1-C1
King's Road	C4
Lakeen Road	F4
Lawn Avenue	C3-D3
Lawn Road	C3-D3
Leger Way	F2-F3
Leicester Avenue	F3
Limetree Avenue	D1-E1
Low Fisher Gate	B4
Neterhall Road	B4-C4
North Bridge Road	A4
Manor Drive	E2-E3
Marlborough Road	E4
Milton Walk	B1-B2
Osborne Road	E4
Oxford Street	B1
Palmer Street	C1
Park Road	C3-C4
Queens Road	C4-D4
Rainton Road	C1
Regent Square	C3
Roberts Road	A1
Roman Road	D1-D2
Rufford Road	E1
St Anne's Road	F1-F2
St Cecilia's Road	E1-F1
St Helen's Road	E1-F1
St Hilda's Road	E1-F1
St James Street	A1-A2-B2
St Mary's Road	D4
St Sepulchre Gate West	A1-A2
St Ursula's Road	F1
Sandy Lane	E1
Sandbeck Road	E1-E2
Sandringham Road	E3-F3-F4
Shaftesbury Avenue	F3
Silver Street	B3
South Parade	C3-C2-D2
South Street	C1
Stockil Road	D1
Theobald Avenue	D1
Thoresby Avenue	E1
Thorne Road	C3-C4-D4
Trafford Way	A3-A2-B2-B1-C1
Town Moor Avenue	D4-E4-E3-F3-F2
Tudor Road	F4
Waterdale	B2-B3-C3
Welbeck Road	D2-E2
Whitburn Road	C2
Windsor Road	D4-E4
Wood Street	B3
Zetland Road	E4-F4-F3

Mexborough

Adwick Road	C2-C3-C4-B4
Albert Road	B3-B4
Alexandra Road	B3-C3
Argyle Road	B3
Auckland Road	B3
Bank Street	B2-B1-C1
Carlyle Road	B2-B3
Cemetery Road	A4-B4
Church Street	C1
College Road	B2-C2
Cromwell Road	B2
Dolcliff Road	A2-A3-A2-B2
Garden Street	A2-B2
Genoa Street	C2-C3

Doncaster

Diana Rigg, Kevin Keegan and Freddie Trueman are just a few of the popular figures of fame who come from Doncaster, a busy commercial and industrial town which is set in a predominantly coalmining area and happens to be the birthplace of a good many celebrities. The town is also notable for its racecourse, which has been the site of the St Leger since the late 18th century, and it is well provided with professional football from Doncaster Rovers, who play in the Canon League.

Amongst the town's interesting older buildings, the 19th-century Church of St George was designed by Sir Gilbert Scott, and one of the few surviving Victorian Mansion Houses can also be seen here. The local Museum and Art Gallery offers displays of geology, natural history and the past of the Doncaster area. A museum of social history is housed in the attractive setting of Cusworth Hall, a fine 18th-century Palladian mansion which stands on the outskirts of the town.

Mexborough was a small village until the changes of the early 19th century fostered its expansion into an industrial town. The modern developments of streets and housing in more recent years have left Mexborough very little in the way of older buildings, but the Parish Church of St John the Baptist has retained vestiges of its Norman origins.

Greenfell Avenue	C4	
Hall Avenue	C3	
Hampden Road	B2	
Harlington	C2-C3-C4	
Helena Street	A3-B3	
High Street	A2-B2	
Kelvin Street	B3	
King's Road	B3-C3	
Kirby Street	A3-B3	
Lorna Road	B3	
Market Street	B2-B1-C1	
Milton Road	B2-B3	
Park Road	A2-A3-A4	
Princess Road	C4	
Pym Road	B3	
Station Road	B1	
Swinton Road	A2	
Ruskin Avenue	C4	
Tennyson Road	C4	
Victoria Road	B4-C4	
Washington Street	C3	
Wellington Street	B3	
West View Road	B2	

DONCASTER

public buildings and places of interest

AA Road Service Centre	**B4**
Central Library and Tourist Information Centre, Waterdale Shopping Centre	**B2**
Corn Exchange and Market Hall	**B3-B4**
Doncaster Grammar School	**C3**
Mansion House. An impressive building of 1748 containing several finely decorated public rooms. Adjacent are the Metropolitan Borough Council Offices	**B3**
Museum and Art Gallery	**C2**
St George's Church Designed by Sir Gilbert Scott and completed in 1858, it stands on the site of a Norman church destroyed by fire in 1853. The pinnacled tower rises to 170 feet.	**B4**
Technical College	**B2-C2**

DONCASTER
Britain's oldest racecourse has long been a mecca for punters — amongst its better known visitors is Charles Dickens, who in 1875 watched the 110th St Leger from the ornate and still-used 18th-century grandstand.

Central Durham

Durham

The castle and the cathedral stand side by side high above the city like sentinels, dramatically symbolising the military and religious power Durham wielded in the past. Its origins date from about 995 when the remains of St Cuthbert arrived from Lindisfarne and his shrine was a popular centre of pilgrimage. Soon after that early fortifications were built, later replaced by a stone

castle which became the residence of the Prince-Bishops of Durham – powerful feudal rulers appointed by the King. Today the city's university, the oldest in England after Oxford and Cambridge, occupies the castle and most of the buildings around peaceful, secluded Palace Green. The splendid Norman cathedral, sited on the other side of the Green, is considered to be one of the finest in Europe. Its combination of strength and size, tempered with grace and beauty, is awe-inspiring.

Under the shadow of these giants the old city streets, known as vennels, ramble down the bluff past the 17th-century Bishop Cosin's House and the old grammar school, to the thickly-wooded banks of the Wear. Here three historic bridges link the city's heart with the pleasant Georgian suburbs on the other side of the river.

Although Durham is not an industrial city, it has become the venue for the North-East miners' annual Gala Day in July.

Durham Area

SCALE 0 — 4 mls

N

Magdalene Street	F4
Margery Lane	B1-B2
Market Place	C3-D3
May Street	A2-B2
Milburngate	C3
Mistletoe Street	B2
New Elvet	D2
New Street	B3
Neville Street	C2-C3
North Bailey	D2-D3
North Road	B4-B3-C3-C2
Obelisk Lane	B4
Old Elvet	D2-E2
Owengate	C2-D2
Percy Terrace	A1
Pimlico	C1
Princes Street	B4-B3
Providence Row	D3-D4
Quarry Heads Lane	C1
Ravensworth Terrace	D3-E3
Red Hills Lane	A2-B2
St Hild's Lane	E3-F3
St John's Road	A1
St Monica Grove	A2
Saddler Street	D3
Sidegate	C4
Silver Street	C2-C3
South Bailey	C1-D1-D2
South Street	C1-C2
Springwell	A4
Sutton Street	B3-B2
The Avenue	A1-B1-B2
Tinklers Lane	D3
Waddington Street	B3
Waterside	C4
Wearside Road	D4
West View	F4

Western Hill	B4-B3
Whinney Hill	E1-E2

Chester-le-Street

Allen Street	A1-B1
Ashley Terrace	B4
Avondale Terrace	A2-B2
Baden Street	B1
Bede Terrace	A3
Benson Street	B1
Blands Opening	B3-C3
Broadwood View	B1
Bullion Lane	A3-A2
Cheviot Road	A1
Church Chare	B2-B3-C3
Clarence Terrace	B2
Clifford Terrace	A1-B1
Cookson Terrace	A3
Co-operative Street	B3
Cone Terrace	B4-B3-C3
Cumbrian Avenue	A1
Eardulph Avenue	C2
Eighth Avenue	A4
Ernest Terrace	A1-A2
Fell Road	A4-B4
Fife Avenue	A3
Finchdale Terrace	A2
Foundry Lane	B3
Front Street	B1-B2-B3-B4
George Street	B1
Grasmere Avenue	A1
Greenbank Street	C4-C3
High Chare	B2
Hillside	B4

Holmlands Park	C1-C2
Hopgarth	B4-C4-C3
Hopgarth Gardens	C4-C3
Jacques Terrace	A3-A4
Lambton Street	B1
Lancaster Terrace	C1
Lindisfarne Avenue	B2-C2
Lindom Avenue	C2
Low Chare	B3-C3
Lumley Terrace	B1
Mains Park Road	B2
Melville Street	A1
Mendip Avenue	A1-A2
Middle Chare	B3
Moorfoot Avenue	A1-A2
Murray Place	A4
Murray Road	A3
Newcastle Road	B4-C4
Newker Crescent	A2
Ninth Avenue	A4-A3
North Burns	B4
Osborne Road	B2-B3
Park Road Central	C3-C2-C1
Park Road North	C3-C4
Park Road South	C1
Pelaw Bank	B4
Pennine Avenue	A1-A2
Picktree Lane	B4-C4
Plantagenet Avenue	C1
Poplar Street	B2
Poplar Terrace	C3
Prospect Street	B4
Queens Park	C1
Ramsey Street	B1
Relton Terrace	A1-B1
Roman Avenue	B2-C2
Ropery Lane	B1-C1

Rydal Road	A1
St Cuthbert Avenue	C2
Seventh Avenue	A4
South Approach	A3-A2
South Burns	B4
Station Road	A3-B3
Station View	A2-A3
The Avenue	A3
The Green	A3-A4
The Parade	B1
Tuart Street	B3
Twelfth Avenue	A4
Viador	B4
Victor Street	B2-B3
Waldridge Road	A2
Weldon Terrace	B1
Wesley Terrace	B3
West Lane	A2-B2
York Terrace	B1

DURHAM
High above the wooded banks of the River Wear, Durham's castle and cathedral crown the steep hill on which the city is built. They share the site with several of the university's attractive old buildings.

27

Central Bridlington

Central Grimsby

Central Cleethorpes

East coast towns

Scarborough is a classic seaside resort. It has good beaches and all the amusements required of a popular holiday destination, and it also shares in the grandeur of the impressive 12th-century castle ruins which stand on a headland between its two principal beaches.

Bridlington has thrived and flourished as a resort, with fine beaches sheltered by towering Flamborough Head. The older part of the town has several Georgian buildings, and the Bayle Gate (part of former priory) is now a museum. Nearby Sewerby Hall is a Georgian country house set in extensive parkland, and includes a small zoo.

Grimsby was little more than a village not so very long ago, but in the 19th century it rapidly expanded into a major River Humber port. The medieval Parish Church of St James still has some 14th-century features, and also worth seeing are the Welholme Galleries' museum and art gallery.

Cleethorpes has dealt effectively with the vagaries of tide and weather by installing an artificial beach and wave machine in its seafront Leisure Centre pool. Succulent oysters were the pride of the town in its fishing village days, but now visitors prefer to come for the sandy beaches and the entertainments which have made it such a popular resort. Sidney Park is noted for its aviaries and an arch made from a whale's jawbone.

LEGEND

Town Plan
AA Recommended roads
Other roads
Restricted roads
Buildings of interest Hall
Churches +
Car parks P
Parks and open spaces
One way streets

Street Index with Grid Reference

Bridlington

Albion Terrace	E3
Alexandra Promenade	E3-E4
Belgrave Road	B1-C1
Bessingby Road	A2-B2
Bessingby Way	A1-A2
Borough Road	B4-B3
Brett Street	A4-B4
Bridge Street	D2
Bright Crescent	D3
Brookland Road	A4
Cambridge Street	B3-B2
Cardigan Road	B1-B2
Carlisle Road	E3
Carlton Street	B3-C3
Chapel Street	D2
Clarence Road	D2-D3
Cliff Street	D2
Dale Road	C4
East Road	B1-C1
Eighth Avenue	E4
Elma Avenue	B2-B3
Esplanade	D2-E2
First Avenue	E4
Flamborough Road	E4-E3
Fort Terrace	D2
Garrison Street	D2
George Street	B1
Gypsey Road	A4
Hamilton Road	C1-C2
Havelock Place	B4
Havelock Street	B3
Hermitage Road	A4-B4
Hilderthorpe Road	B2-C2
Holyrood Avenue	D3
Horsforth Avenue	B1-C1
Jameson Road	A4
Kingsgate	B1-B2
King Street	D2
Lamplugh Road	E4
Lamplugh Square	E4
Lansdowne Road	D3
Lawson Road	B4
Manor Street	D2
Marshall Avenue	D2-D3
Medina Avenue	B3
Midway Avenue	B3
Milner Road	B4-C4
Moorfield Road	C2
Nelson Street	C2
Neptune Street	C1
New Burlington Road	C2
North Marine Drive	E4-F4
North Street	D2-D3
Oxford Street	C1-C2
Palanza Terrace	C1-C2
Park Avenue	D4
Prince Street	D2
Princess Street	D2
Promenade	D2-D3-E3
Prospect Street	D2
Quay Road	B3-C3
Queensgate	B4-C4
Queensgate Square	B4-C4
Queen Street	D2
Regent Terrace	D2
Richmond Street	B1-C1
Rosebery Avenue	B1
Roundhay Road	B1
Royal Crescent	D3
St Andrew Road	D4
St Annes Road	E4
St Chad Road	D4
St Georges Avenue	D3
St Hilda Street	C2
St James Road	B1-B2
St Johns Avenue	A2-B3
St John Street	B4
St Johns Walk	A4-A3-B3
St Stephen Road	C4-D4
St Thomas Road	C4-D4
St Wilfred Road	D4
Sands Lane	E4
Savage Road	B1-B2
South Cliff Road	C1-D1-D2
South Marine Drive	C1
Springfield Avenue	C3-C2
Station Road	B2-B3
Tennyson Avenue	D3
The Spa	C1
Trinity Road	D3-E3
Turner Avenue	D4
Vernon Road	D3-E3
Victoria Road	C3-D3

Grimsby

Abbey Park Road	A1
Abbey Road	A1-B1
Adam Smith Street	A4
Ainsley Street	B1
Albert Street	C4-C3
Albion Street	C3-C4
Alexandra Road	A2-A3-A4
Armstrong Street	A3
Baxtergate	A2-B2
Bradley Street	B2-C2
Brighowgate	A1
Buller Street	C2
Cartergate	A2
Charlton Street	A4-A3
Church Street	A1-A2
Church Lane	A1-A2
Church Street	B4-C4
Cleethorpes Road	B4-C4
Convamore Road	C1-C2-C3
Corporation Road	A3-B3
Deansgate	A2
Doughty Road	B1-B2
Dudley Street	C3
Duncombe Street	A1
Earl Street	A2
Edward Street	C2
Eleanor Street	C2
Frederick Street	A3
Freeman Street	C3-C4
Garden Street	B2-B1
Garibaldi Street	C3
Granville Street	A1
Hainton Avenue	C1-C2
Hare Street	C2
Heneage Road	C1-C2
Holles Street	B2-B3
Jackson Street	A3
Kent Street	A1
King Edward Street	B3-B4
Ladysmith Road	C1-C2
Lambert Road	A1-B1
Legsby Avenue	B1
Lord Street	A2
Manor Avenue	A1
Nelson Street	C3
Newmarket Street	B3-C3
Orwell Street	C4
Osborne Street	A2-B2
Oxford Street	C3
Pasture Street	B2-C2
Patrick Street	C1
Railway Street	B3-B4
Rendel Street	A4-A3
Riby Street	C4
Ropery Street	C1-C2
Sheepfold Street	B2
Sixhills Street	B2-C2
Strand Street	A4
Victor Street	B2
Victoria Street North	B3-B4
Victoria Street South	B3-B2
Welholme Road	B1-C1
Wellington Street	C3
Wellowgate	A1
Wintringham Road	B1
Wood Street	B3-C3

Cleethorpes

Alexandra Road	B3-B2-C2
Bark Street	C1-C2
Beacon Avenue	A2-A1
Bentley Street	A2-A3
Bradford Avenue	C1
Brereton Avenue	A3
Brooklands Avenue	C1
Bursar Street	A2
Cambridge Street	B2
Campden Crescent	A3
Chapman Road	A4
Claremont Road	A2
Clee Road	A2-A3
College Street	B3
Crowhill Avenue	B2
Curzon Avenue	A1
Elm Road	B2
Fairview Avenue	A2-B2
George Street	B1-B2
Glebe Road	B2
Grant Street	B3
Grimsby Road	A4-A3
Hardy's Road	B1
High Cliff Road	C2-C1
Highgate	B1-B2
High Street	B2-B3
Isaac's Hill	B3-B2
Kew Road	B2
Kingsway	C1
Lindsey Road	B1
Lindum Road	C1
Market Street	B2
Mill Road	B1-B2
Neptune Street	B3
Normandy Road	A2
Oxford Street	C1
Parker Street	B2
Pelham Road	A3-A4
Penshurst Road	A1
Poplar Road	A3-B3
Prince's Road	B3
Queens Parade	C1
Reynolds Street	A3
Richmond Road	B1

Grimsby (continued, top)

Wellington Road	D3
West Street	C1
Windsor Crescent	C2-C1
York Road	E3

Central Scarborough

Robson Road	A3
St Hughs Avenue	A2
St Peter's Avenue	B2
Sea Road	B3
Sea View Street	C2
Sherburn Street	B1
Sign Hills Avenue	C1
Suggitt's Lane	A4
Taylor's Avenue	B1
Tennyson Road	A3
Thruscoe Road	B1
Trinity Road	B1
Warwick Road	A1
White's Road	C1
William Street	B2-B1
Wollaston Road	A2
Woodsley Avenue	B1
Yarra Road	B2

Scarborough

Aberdeen Walk	B3-C3
Albion Road	C2
Avenue Road	A2-B2
Avenue Victoria	C1-C2-D2-D1
Bar Street	C3
Bellevue Street	B3
Belvedere Place	C1-D1
Belvedere Road	C1-D1
Blenheim Terrace	B4-C4
Cambridge Street	B3
Candler Street	A2-A3-B3
Castlegate	D4
Castle Road	B3-B4-C4
Columbus Ravine	A4-B4-B3-A3-B3
Commercial Street	A2-B2
Cromwell Road	B2
Cross Street	C3-C4
Crown Terrace	C2
Dean Road	A3-B3-B4
Durham Street	B3
Eastborough	C3-C4-D4
Esplanade	C2-D2-D1
Esplanade Gardens	C1-C2
Esplanade Road	C1-C2
Falsgrave Road	A2-B2
Filey Road	C2-C1-D1
Fore Shore Road	C3-C4-D4
Garfield Road	A3
Gladstone Road	A2-B2-B3

Glen Bridge	A3-A4
Gordon Street	A3
Hampton Road	A2
Hibernia Street	A2-A3
Highfield	A1-A2
Holbeck Avenue	D1
Holbeck Hill	D1
Holbeck Road	D1
Hope Street	B4
Hoxton Road	A3-B3
James Street	B3-B4
King Street	C3
Lonesborough Road	B2
Long Westgate	C4-D4
Lowdale Avenue	A4
Manor Road	A2-A3
Marine Drive	D4
Moorland Road	B4
Mountside	C1
Nares Street	A3
Nelson Street	B3
Newborough	C3
North Marine Road	B4-C4
North Street	B3-C3
Northstead Manor Drive	A4
Northway	B3
Oak Road	A1-A2
Oliver's Mount Road	B1-C1
Oriel Crescent	B1
Paradise	C4-D4
Park Avenue	A1-A2
Park Street	A2
Peasholm Drive	A3-A4
Princess Street	D4
Prince of Wales Terrace	C2
Prospect Road	A3-B3
Queen Margaret's Road	B1-C1
Queens Parade	B4
Queen Street	C3-C4
Raleigh Street	A3
Ramsey Street	A3
Ramshill Road	C2-C3
Roscoe Street	B2
Rosebery Avenue	A1
Rothbury Street	A3-B3
Royal Albert Drive	B4-C4
Royal Avenue	B2-C2
Ryndleside	A4
St Johns Road	A2
St Martins Avenue	C2
St Sepulchre Street	C4-D4
St Thomas Street	C3-C4
Sandside	D4
Scalby Road	A2
Sea Cliff Road	D1
Seamer Road	A2-A1-B1

Spring Bank	A1
Spring Hill Road	A1
Stepney Avenue	A2
Stepney Road	A2
The Garlands	B1-C1
The Glade	B1-C1
Tindall Street	B3
Tollergate	C4
Trafalgar Road	B4
Trafalgar Square	B4
Trinity Road	B1-C1
Valley Bridge	C2
Valley Bridge Road	B3-C3
Valey Road	A1-A2-B1-B2-C2-C3
Vernon Road	C3
Victoria Park Mount	A4
Victoria Road	B2-B3
Victoria Street	B3
Weaponness Drive	C1
Westborough	B2-B3-B3
Westbourne Grove	B1-B2-C2-C1
Westover Road	B2
West Street	C2-C1-D1
Westwood	B2-B3
Westwood Road	B2
Wrea Lane	B3-B4
Wykeham Street	A2-B2
York Place	B3-C3

29

Gateshead

Seven bridges make the link across the Tyne to Newcastle from Gateshead, which is largely a modern town: a disastrous fire in the 19th century destroyed most of its older buildings. One notable escape from the fire was St Mary's Church, which has been heavily restored but still has some of its 12th-century features, and serves as a reminder that this is in fact an ancient Tyneside settlement. The town has suffered in this century too, with the decline of its dock area, but light engineering has come to take the place of its older industries, and the town has world renown today as a venue for national and international events at its celebrated athletics stadium.

South Shields has safe, sandy beaches and a good selection of entertainments and amusements for visitors, and another of its attractions is the South Tyneside Leisure and Gymnastics Centre, where the extensive swimming complex includes a wave machine. Overlooking the market square is the fine 18th-century Old Town Hall — irreverently known by locals as the Pepperpot. The Metal Arts Precinct features the work of local artists, and the Arbeia Roman Fort and Museum can be visited in Baring Street.

Consett was once a steel producing town, and has a pleasant Derwentside setting with a number of attractive parks.

Street	Grid Ref
High West Street	B1-B2-B3
Hillgate	B6
Hills Street	B5
Hopper Street	B4-C4-B4
Jackson Street	B4
Langton Street	C1
Lincoln Street	A1
Lindisfarne Drive	C2-C3
Melbourne Court	A5
Milton Square	C1
Mulgrave Terrace	A4-A5
Nelson Street	B5
Nuns Lane	B4-C4
Oakwell Gate	B5-B6
Old Ham Road	B1
Park Lane	C3
Pipewell Gate	A6
Prince Consort Road	A1-A2-A3-A4-A5-B5
Princess Street	A3-B3
Quarryfield Road	C5-C6
Queens Terrace	A3-B3
Regent Terrace	A3-B3
St Cuthberts Road	A4
Shakespeare Street	C2
South Shore Road	B6-C6
Sunderland Road	B1-C1-C2-C1
Swan Street	B4-C4
Swinburne Street	B5
Trinity Square	B4
Tyne Bridge	B6
Wellington Street	A6-A5-B5
West Street	B3-B4-B5
Worcester Green	A1-A2
Wordsworth Street	C1
Wylam Street	A4-B4

Consett

Street	Grid Ref
Albert Road	B1-B2
Ashdale Avenue	B3-C3
Ashdale Road	C2
Aynsley Terrace	B2-B3
Balfour Street	B3
Barr House Avenue	B3
Berry Edge Street	A1-B1
Bertha Street	B2
Bright Street	B4
Clarence Gardens	B4
Cleadon Street	B2-B3
Constance Road	A1-A2-B2
Cyril Street	B4-C4
Delves Lane	B1-C1
Dixon Street	A3-A4
Durham Road	A4-B4
East Parade	B1
Edith Street	A1-B1-B2
Elmfield Road	B4
Front Street	B1
George Street	B2
Gladstone Road	C2
Green Street	B2
Hartington Street	B2-C2
Hope Street	A4
John Street	B2
Knitsley Lane	B1
Laburnum Avenue	A3-A4
Medomsley	B2-B3-B4-C4
Middle Street	B1-B2
Morley Street	B4
Oakdale Road	C2-C3
Palmerston Street	B1
Park Avenue	C2
Park Road	A3-B3-B2-A2
Park Street	A4
Parliament Street	A2-B2
Railway Street	B1
Sherburn Terrace	B2-C2
Spencer Street	A2-B2
Stanley Street	B2
Steel Street	A2-A3
The Crescent	B4
The Promenade	B3-B4
Taylor Street	B1

Victoria Road	B1-B2
Victoria Street	A2-B2
Villa Real Road	C3-C4

South Shields

Street	Grid Ref
Albion Court	A3
Anderson Street	B1-B2
Baring Road	B3-B4
Beach Road	B1-B2-C2
Bright Street	C2
Broughton Road	B1-C1-C2
Candlish Street	B1-C1
Chapter Row	A2
Church Way	A2
Commercial Road	A1-A2
Coronation Street	A2
Coston Drive	B3
Crossgate	A1-B1
Derby Terrace	B1
Erskine Road	B1-C1-C2
Fairles Street	B3-C3
Ferry Street	A2
Flagg Court	B2-B3-C3
Fort Square	B3-B4
Fowler Street	B1-B2
Garden Lane	B1-B2
Greens Place	A4-B4
Handel Street	C1
Harbour Drive	C3-C4
Hedley Court	A3-B3
Henry Nelson Street	C3
Heron Drive	A3
Hyde Street	B1-C1
James Mather Street	B3
Julian Avenue	B3-C3
Julian Street	B3
Keppel Street	A2-B2
King Street	A2-B2
Lady's Walk	A3-A4
Ladysmith Street	C1
Lawe Road	B4-C4-C3
Market Place	A2
Marine Approach	C2
Marine Drive	C2
Maxwell Street	A1-B1
Mile End Road	A4-A3-B3-B2
Milldam	A1
Morton Walk	B3
Mount Terrace	B2
Ocean Road	B2-B3-C3
Palatine Street	A3
Pearsons Street	B4
Pier Parade	C3
River Drive	A2-A3-A4-B4-C4
Roman Road	B4-B3-C3
St Aidens Road	B3-C3
St Hilda Street	B1
Salem Street	A2
Salisbury Place	C2
Salmon Street	B3
Scott Road	C3
Sea Road	C3
Sea Way	C2
Seafield Terrace	C2-C3
Seaview Terrace	C2
South Woodbine Street	C1-C2
Station Road	A1-A2
Thomas Street	B2
Trajan Avenue	B4
Trajan Street	B3-B4
Union Alley	A2-B2
Wapping Street	A4
Westoe Road	B1
Wharton Street	B1-C1
Woodbine Street	B2-C2
Wouldhaye Court	C2

Key to Town Plan and Area Plan

Town Plan
AA Recommended roads
Other roads
Restricted roads
Buildings of interest — Cinema
One Way Streets
Parks and open spaces
Car Parks — P
Churches — +
Metro Stations — M

Area Plan
A roads
B roads
Locations — Ripley O
Urban area

Street Index with Grid Reference

Gateshead

Street	Grid Ref
Abbots Road	B6-C6
Alexandra Road	A1-A2-A3
Anne Street	B3
Arthur Street	A2-B2
Askew Road	A4-A5
Bank Road	B6
Bedes Drive	B2-B3
Bensham Road	A3-A4-B4
Bewick Road	A1-B1
Bottle Bank	B5-B6
Bridge Street	A6-B6
Camilla Street	B1
Canon Street	B6
Cemetery Road	B1-C1
Charles Street	A3-B3-C3
Chaucer Street	C2
Chichester Close	A2
Church Street	B5-B6
Coburg Street	A2-B2
Coulthards Lane	C5
Denmark Street	A1-B1-B2
East Street	C5
Ellison Street	A4-B4
Gateshead Highway	B1-B2-C2-C3-C4-C5-B5-B6
Gladstone Terrace	A1-B1
Granville Street	A1-B1
Half Moon Lane	A5-B5
Hawks Road	B5-C5-C6
Hector Street	A4-B4
High Level Road	A5-A6
High Street	B2-B3-B4-B5

Halifax Area

Central Brighouse

Key to Town Plan and Area Plan

Town Plan
AA Recommended roads
Restricted roads
Other roads
Buildings of interest — Station ▣
Car Parks — P
Parks and open spaces
One Way Streets

Area Plan
A roads
B roads
Locations — Dalmellington ○
Urban area

STREET INDEX WITH GRID REFERENCE

HALIFAX

Aked's Road	C3
Albert Street	C4-C5
Allerton Place	A4
Arden Road	B2-B3
Backsmith Street	E6
Bailey Hall Road	F2-F3-F4
Balmoral Place	C3-D3
Bank Bottom	F4
Battinson Road	A5
Beacon Hill Road	E5-E6-F5
Bedford Street	C4
Bedford Street North	C4-C5
Bell Hall Terrace	B1
Berry Lane	F4
Blackwall	C3-D3
Broad Street	D4-D5
Bull Close Lane	C3-D3-D4
Bull Green	D3-D4
Burdock Way	C3-C4-C5-D5
Carlton Street	D3
Charleston Road	E5-E6-F4-F5
Cheapside	D4
Church Street	E3-E4-F4
Clare Road	D3-E2-E3
Claremount Road	E6-F6
Clover Hill Road	C1
Colin Street	C5
Commercial Street	D3-D4
Cow Green	D4
Crossley Street	D4
Crossley Terrace	B5
Crown Street	D4
Dean Clough	D5-D6
Eldroth Road	A1-B1
Elmfield Terrace	B1
Emscote Street South	B1-B2
Fenton Road	A2
Fountain Street	D3-D4
Francis Street	B3-B4
Free School Lane	A1-B1-C1-D1
Gaukroger Lane	E1-E2
George Street	D4
Gerrard Street	C4
Gibbett Street	A4-B4-C4-D4
Gladstone Road	B4-B5
Godley Road	F5-F6
Great Albion Street	D5
Haley Hill	D6
Hampden Place	B4-C4
Hanson Lane	A5-B5-C5
Hare Street	A3-A4
Harrison Road	D3-D4
Haugh Shaw Road	A2-B2
Heath Road	D1
High Grove Road	F1-F2
High Level Way	A5-A6
Hope Street	C4-C5
Hopwood Lane	A3-B3-B4-C3-C4-D4
Horley Green Road	F5-F6
Horton Street	E3-E4
Huddersfield Road	D1-E1
Hunger Hill	D2-E2
Hyde Park	B2
Hyde Park Road	A2-B2
Ingram Street	A1
King Street	E4-F4
King Cross Road	A1-A2-B2-B3
King Cross Street	B3-C3
Lee Bridge	C6-D6
Lightowler Road	B4-B5
Lister Lane	A4-B4-C4-D4
Listers Road	F5
Lord Street	D4
Love Lane	C2-D2
Lucy Street	E6-F6
Market Street	D4-E4
Mayfield Avenue	B2-B3
Milton Place	B4-C4

Halifax

Rising up from the eastern edge of the Pennine Hills, this old industrial town occupies a magnificent setting and offers an unexpected wealth of fine buildings. Jewel in the crown is Piece Hall, a unique 18th-century cloth hall built around a quadrangle, which serves as a fitting testimony to the town's long history of textile manufacture. The Perpendicular style Parish Church is 15th-century; the Town Hall was designed by the same architect as the Houses of Parliament, and is thought by some to be one of the finest in the country. Most eccentric of the town's monuments must be Wainhouse Tower, designed as a chimney, but never used as such. It is now an ornamental tower and viewpoint. Halifax also has no less than three model villages: purpose-built to house textile workers these would have been ahead of their time when first constructed. Not content with the history to be seen in its buildings, the town also offers the insights into the past of Bankfield Museum and Shibbden Hall.

Brighouse is the reputed burial place of Robin Hood, who might have fared far worse than this friendly and welcoming town nestling in the valley of the River Calder. An industrial centre with a charming setting, it has several pleasant open spaces, and country walks can be enjoyed only a short distance from the town centre.

32

Central Halifax

Moorfield Street	B1-B2	South Parade	E2-E3	Birds Royd Lane	B1-B2-C1-C2	Lister Street	A3
Mulcture Hall Road	E4-E5	South Street	C3	Bonegate Road	B3-B4	Longroyd Road	A1
Navigation Road	F3-F4	Southgate	D3-D4	Bradford Road	B3-B4	Lords Lane	B1-C1
New Bank	E6-F6	Southowram Bank	F3-F4	Bramston Street	A1-B1	Lower Newlands	C1
New Road	D3-E3	Spring Edge	A1	Bridge End	B1-B2	Manley Street	B3
New Bond Street	C4	Square Road	E4	Bridge Lane	B4	Marion Street	A4-B4
North Gate	D4-D5-D6-E4-E5-E6	Stead Street	C4-D4	Briggate	B2	Mary Street	B4
Old Lane	C6-D6	Swan Bank Lane	E2-F2	Brighousewood Lane	A3	Mill Lane	B2-C2
Ovenden Road	C6-D5-D6	Swires Road	B3-C2-C3	Brook Street	A1-B1	Millroyd Street	B2
Oxford Road	D2-D3	The Gardens	D1	Bryan Street	A1-A2	New Street	A4-B4
Park Road	B3-C3	Thomas Street West	A1	Camm Street	B4	Oak Hill Road	C3
Parkinson Lane	A2-A3-B3	Trinity Road	D3	Castle Avenue	A1	Oaklands	A1
Pellon Lane	A6-B5-B6-C5-D4-D5	Trooper Lane	F2	Church Lane	B3	Old Lane	B3-B4
Portland Place	E6	Union Street	E3-E4	Churchfields Street	B3-B4	Owlerings Road	A2-B2
Portland Road	E6	Union Street South	E2-E3	Clifton Road	C2-C3	Parsonage Lane	B3
Prescott Street	D3-E3	Victoria Road	A4-A5	Close Lea	A1	Pheonix Street	C2-C3
Prospect Road	E6	Victoria Street East	E5	Commercial Street	B2-B3	Piggott Street	A4
Queen's Road	A2-A3-A4-A5-A6	Violet Street	A5-A6	Cookson Street	A4	Raines Row	B2-C2
Raglan Street	B5	Wade Street	E4-E5	Crown Street	A4	Rastrick Commor	A1-B1
Range Bank	E6	Walnut Street	A3-A4	Crossley Street	C1	Raynor Road	A4-B4
Rhodes Street	C4	Wardsend	D3-E3	Daisy Street	B2	Richard Street	B4
Richmond Road	C5-D5	Water Lane	E2	Dyehouse Lane	C1-C2	St John Street	B1-B2
Richmond Street	D5	Waterside	E2-E3	East Street	B1-B2	Spring Street	B2
Rothwell Drive	C2	Wellington Street West	C3	Elland Road	A2-A3	Stoney Hill	A1-A2
Rothwell Road	B1-B2-C2	Well Head Drive	D2	Firth Street	A1	Sunnybank Road	A3
St James Road	D4-D5	Well Head Lane	D2-D3	Foundry Street	C1	Thornhill Road	A1-A2
St John's Road	D3	West Parade	C3	Frances Street	A3-A4	Thornhills Bridge Lane	B4
St Thomas Street	F5-F6	Westfield Street	C2-C3	Garden Road	A4-B4	Upper Bonegate	B3
Savile Crescent	C2-C3-D3	Westgate	D4-E4	George Street	A1-A2-B1	Victoria Street	B1
Savile Drive	C1	Whitegate Road	E1	George Street	C2	Wakefield Road	C2-C3
Savile Parade	C1	Winding Road	E5	Gooder Lane	B1	Waterloo Road	A3-A4-B4
Savile Road	C2-D2-D3	Wood Street	D6	Grove Street	C2	Wharf Street	C2
Savile Park Road	B1-B2-C1-C2-C3	Woodside Road	C6-D6	Halifax Road	A3-A4-B3	William Street	B1
Savile Park Street	B1			Hardy Street	B4	Wood Street	C2
Shaw Hill	E1-E2			Harriet Street	B4	Woodvale Road	B4-C4
Shaw Lane	E1	**BRIGHOUSE**		Healeywood Road	B1		
Shay Syke	E2	Aire Street	B1	Hey Street	B4		
Shroggs Road	B6-C6	Anvil Street	B4	High Street	B3		
Siddal New Road	E1-E2-F1-F2	Armytage Road	C2	Huddersfield Road	B1-B2		
Silver Street	D4	Arthur Street	C2	Illands Lane	A2-B2		
Simmonds Lane	E1	Atlas Mill Road	A2-B2	King Street	B3-C3		
Skircoat Road	D1-D2-D3	Bank Street	A2-A3-B2	Lawson Road	B2-C2-C3		
Skircoat Moor Road	A1	Bethel Street	B2	Laura Street	B1		
Smithy Street	E4-E5			Lee Street	B4		
				Lightcliffe Road	A3-A4		

33

Harrogate

Dignified Victorian stone buildings and lovely gardens reflect Harrogate's 19th-century popularity as a spa town and its Royal Baths, opened in 1897, became one of the largest hydrotherapy establishments in the world. More recently the town has become a busy conference centre, the main venues being the Royal Hall and the elegant old Assembly Rooms. A glass-covered walkway in Valley Gardens leads to the Sun Pavilion and part of the lovely Harlow Car Gardens is used for experimental horticulture.

Ripon, known as the Gateway to the Dales, stands at the junction of three rivers; the Ure, the Skell and the Laver. Its small cathedral, a delightful 12th-century building occupying the site of an Anglo-Saxon church, has a small museum of church treasures in the original crypt. One corner of the town's rectangular market square is marked by the medieval Wakeman's house, now a local museum and tourist information centre.

Knaresborough Here buildings scramble higgledy-piggledy up a rocky outcrop from the banks of the River Nidd to the town's ruined 14th-century castle. The keep, two baileys and two gatehouses have survived, and there is a museum in the grounds. The town is able to claim two records; it has the oldest linen-mill and the oldest chemist's shop in England.

LEGEND

Town Plan

AA recommended route
Restricted roads
Other roads
Buildings of interest — Station
Car parks — P
Parks and open spaces
One way streets

Area Plan

A roads
B roads
Locations — Nidd ○
Urban area

Street Index with Grid Reference

Harrogate

Albert Street	C2
Alexandra Road	C4
Ansty Road	E4-F4
Arthington Avenue	D2
Ashfield Road	D4
Avondale Road	F4
BackEast Park Road	D1
Beech Grove	B1-C1
Belford Road	C1
Belmont Road	B1
Beulah Street	C2
Bower Road	C3-D3
Bower Street	C3-D3
Brunswick Drive	A2
Cambridge Road	C2
Cambridge Street	C2
Chelmsford Road	D2-D3
Cheltenham Crescent	B3-C3
Cheltenham Mount	C3
Cheltenham Parade	C3
Christchurch Oval	E2-E3
Chudleigh Road	D3
Clarence Drive	A2-A3
Claro Road	E3-E4
Cold Bath Road	A1-B1-B2
Commercial Street	C3
Coppice Drive	B4-C4

Cornwall Road	A2-B2-C2
Crescent Gardens	B3
Crescent Road	B2-B3
Devonshire Place	E3
Devonshire Way	E4
Dragon Avenue	D3-D4
Dragon Parade	D3-D4
Dragon Road	D3-D4
Dragon Terrace	D4
Duchy Road	A3-A4-B4
East Parade	D2-D3-E3-E4
East Park Road	D1-D2
Esplanade	B2
Franklin Mount	C4
Franklin Road	C3-C4
Franklins Square	C4
Gascoigne Crescent	E4-F4
Glebe Avenue	B1
Glebe Road	A1-B1
Granby Road	F3
Granville Road	C3
Grove Park Terrace	D4-E4
Harcourt Drive	D2-D3
Harcourt Road	D3
Hayward Street	C3-D3
Heywood Road	B1
Hollins Crescent	B4
Hollins Road	B4
Homestead Road	D1-D2
Hyde Park Road	D3
James Street	C2
John Street	C2
Kent Avenue	A3
Kent Road	A3-A4-B4
King's Road	B3-C3-C2
Kingsway Drive	D2-D3
Knaresborough Road	E1-E2-F2-F3
Lime Grove	E3-E4
Lime Street	E4
Mayfield Grove	C3-C4
Mayfield Terrace	C4-D4
Montpellier Road	B2
Montpellier Street	B2
Moor Drive	A1
Mornington Crescent	D4-E4
Mornington Terrace	D3-D4
Mount Parade	C3
Mowbray Square	D3-E3
Myrtle Square	C3
North Park Road	D2-E2
Nyddvale Road	C3-C4-D4
Oakdale Rise	A4
Oak Kent Drive	A4
Oatlands Drive	E1
Oxford Street	B2-C2-C3
Park Chase	E3
Park Parade	E1-E2-E3
Park View	D3
Parliament Street	B3-B2-C2
Princes Square	C1-C2
Princes Street	C2
Princes Villa Road	D1
Prospect Place	C1-C2
Providence Terrace	C4
Queen Parade	D2-D1-E1
Raglan Street	C1-C2
Regent Avenue	E4
Regent Grove	D4-E4
Regent Parade	E3-E4
Regent Street	E4

Regent Terrace	E4
Ripon Road	B3-B4
Robert Street	C1
Roseville Avenue	F3
Roseville Drive	F3
Rutland Road	A2
St Catherine's Road	F1
St Marys Avenue	B1
St Mary's Walk	B1-B2
St Winifreds Avenue	F1-F2
St Winifreds Avenue West	F1-F2
St Winifreds Road	F1
School Court	C2
Silverfields Road	F3
Skipton Road	D4-E4-E3-F3
Somerset Road	A1-B1
South Park Road	D1
Springfield Avenue	B4-B3-C3-C4
Spring Grove	B4
Spring Mount	B4
Station Avenue	D2
Station Bridge	C2
Station Parade	C3-C2-C1-D1
Station Square	C2
Stoke Lake Road	D3
Strawberry Dale Road	C3
Studley Road	C4
Swan Road	B2-B3
The Ginnel	B2
The Grove	D3-E3
The Parade	C2-D2
Tower Street	C1
Union Street	B2
Valley Drive	A1-A2-B2
Valley Mount	A1-B1-B2
Valley Road	B2
Victoria Avenue	C1-D1-D2
Victoria Road	B1-B2
West Park	C1-C2
Wetherby Road	F2
Woodside	D2-D3
Wood View	A4
York Place	D1-E1
York Road	A3-A2-A3-B3

Ripon

Agnesgate	B2-C2
Ailcey Road	C3
Allhallowgate	B3-C3
Alma Gardens	C2
Barefoot Street	A2-B2
Bedern Bank	B2
Blossomgate	A3
Bondgate	B1
Bondgate Green	B2-C2-C1
Bondgate Green Lane	C1-C2
Borrage Green Lane	A1
Borrage Lane	A2
Brewery Lane	B3
Canal Road	C1-C2
Church Lane	A3
Claro Road	B1
College Road	A4
Coltsgate Hill	A4-B4
Crescent Back Road	A4-B4
Crescent Parade	A4-B4

Finkle Street	B3
Firby Lane	A2-A3
Fishergate	B3
Friars Avenue	C1-C2
Harrogate Road	A1-A2
Heckler Lane	B1-B2
High Skellgate	A3-A2-B2-B3
High Street	B2
King Street	B1-B2
Kirkby Road	A3-A4
Kirkgate	B2-B3
Lickley Street	C3-C4
Locker Lane	A1-B1
Low Mill Lane	C2
Lowskellgate	A2
Low Street	C2-C3
Magdalen's Road	C4
Mawson Lane	B1
Minster Road	B2-B3-C3
Newby Street	C1
North Street	B3-B4
Park Street	A3
Priest Lane	C2-C3
Princess Close	B4-C4
Princes Road	B4-C4
Queen Street	B2
Rayner Street	A3-A4
Residence Lane	C3
St Agnesgate	C2
St Marygate	C3
Shirley Avenue	A1
Skell Bank	A2
Skellgarths	B2
Somerset Row	A2
South Crescent	A1-A2
Southgate	B1
Southgate Lane	B1
Stonebridgegate	C3-C4
Tower Road	B4
Trinity Lane	A3-A4
Victoria Avenue	C2
Victoria Grove	B3
Vyner Street	C1
Waterskellgate	A2-B2
Wellington Street	B2
Westbourne Grove	A3
Westgate	A3-B3
Whitcliffe Avenue	A1

Knaresborough

Abbey Road	A1-B1
Bland's Hill	A1
Bond End	B4
Boroughbridge Road	B4-C4
Brewerton Road	B2
Briggate	A1-B1-B2
Castleings Road	A1-B1-B2
Charlton Court	C2
Charlton Drive	C2
Charlton Grove	C2
Cheapside	B2
Church Lane	B3-B4
Finkle Street	B3
Fisher Gardens	B2
Gracious Street	B2
Hambleton Grove	C2-C3

High Bond End	B4
High Bridge	A3
High Street	B2-B3-B4
Hilton Lane	B3
Holly Court	C2
Iles Lane	B1-C1
Jockey Lane	B2-B3
King James Road	B1-C1
Kirkgate	B2-B3
Knaresborough and Harrogate Road	A3
Low Bond End	A3-A4-B4
Manor Gardens	C2
Manor Road	C2
Market Place	B2
Park Drive	C2
Park Place	B2-C2
Park Row	C2
Princess Avenue	C1
St Margaret's Close	B3-B4
St Margaret's Gardens	B3-C3
St Margaret's Road	B3-C3
Silver Street	B2
Station Road	B3
Stockdale Walk	B1
Stockwell Avenue	C4
Stockwell Crescent	C4
Stockwell Drive	C4
Stockwell Grove	C4
Stockwell Lane	C4
Stockwell Road	C2-C3-C4
Tentergate Avenue	B4-C4
Tentergate Road	B4-C4
The Avenue	C4
Vicarage Lane	B2
Waterside	A1-A2-B2-B3-A3
Whincup Avenue	C3
Whincup Grove	C2-C3
Windsor Lane	B1-B2
York Lane	C1
York Place	B2-C2-C1
York Road	C1

Key to Town Plan and Area Plan

Town Plan

AA Recommended roads	
Restricted roads	
Other roads	
Buildings of interest	Cinema
One Way Streets	
Car Parks	P
Parks and open spaces	

Area Plan

A roads	
B roads	
Locations	Cockersdale○
Urban area	

STREET INDEX WITH GRID REFERENCE

HUDDERSFIELD

Albion Street	C1-C2
Alfred Street	D1
Anohor Street	E3-E4
Bankfield Road	B1-C1
Bath Street	C4
Beaumont Street	D4-E4
Belmont Street	B4-C4
Bow Street	B1-B2
Byram Street	D3
Cambridge Road	C4
Carr Pitt Road	F1-F2
Castlegate	C1-C2-C3-C4
Cecil Street	B2-C2
Cedar Avenue	A4
Cedar Mount	A4
Cedar Street	A4
Chapel Street	C1-D1
Clare Hill	C4
Claremont Street	C4
Cloth Hall Street	C2-D2
Colne Street	E1
Commercial Street	D1-E1
Cross Church Street	D2
Dundas Street	C2
Elmwood Avenue	B4-C4
Firth Street	E1
Fitzwilliam Street	B3-C3-C4
Gasworks Street	E4
Gledholt Bank	A1-A2
Greenhead Road	A2-B2-C2
Grove Street	B1-C1
Half Moon Street	C2
Henry Street	C2
Highfields Road	B4
High Street	C2-D2
Ivy Street	F2
John's Road	C4
John William Street	D3
Kilner Bank	F2-F3-F4
King's Mill Lane	E1-F1
King Street	D2-E2

Huddersfield

With a long history of textile making and a more recent involvement in chemicals and engineering, Huddersfield has for many years been a busy industrial and commercial centre. But another aspect of the town is its fine old buildings: the best area for these is around St George's Square, where the railway station's mid-19th-century colonnaded facade is thought by

some to be one of the finest in the country.

Yet another side to Huddersfield is its role as a venue for local choirs and bands, who regularly come here for performances at the Town Hall. A good collection of English watercolours can be seen in the art gallery in Princess Alexandra Walk, and the Tolson Memorial Museum in Ravensknowle Park deals with geology, natural history and the area's own rich past. Near the village of Almondsbury to the south stands Castle

Hill, an ancient hill fort topped with a 19th-century tower.

Dewsbury is one of the main towns of the West Yorkshire Heavy Woollen District, and is well known for its manufacture of blankets and carpets. Lying on the River Calder, this is a popular market and shopping centre, and has its own museum and art gallery. Places of interest include the parish church, which has retained some 12th-century features.

Huddersfield Area

Kirkgate	D2-D3	St Andrew's Road	E2-E3-E4	Ashworth Gardens	A3	Northgate	B3

Kirkgate — D2-D3
Leeds Road — D3-D4-E4
Lincoln Street — E2-F2-F3
Lord Street — D3
Lower Fitzwilliam Street — D4-E4
Lynton Avenue — B2
Manchester Road — A1-B1-C1
Maple Street — F1
Market Street — C2
Merton Street — B2-B1-C1-C2
Mountjoy Road — A4-B4
Mulberry Street — F1
New Street — C1-D1-D2
New North Parade — C3
New North Road — A4-B4-B3-C3
Northgate — D4
Northumberland Street — D3
Oastler Avenue — B1-B2-A2
Oldgate — E2-D2-D3
Old Leeds Road — E3-E4
Outcote Bank — C1
Oxford Street — D4
Park Avenue — B2-B3
Park Drive — A4-A3-B3
Park Drive South — A3-A2-A3-B3
Park Grove — B2
Pine Street — D3-E3
Portland Street — B3
Princess Street — D1
Prospect Street — B1-C1
Quay Street — E3
Queensgate — D1-D2-E2
Queen Street — D1-D2
Railway Street — C3
Ramsden Street — D1-D2
Rook Street — C4

St Andrew's Road — E2-E3-E4
St Peter's Street — D3
Seed Hill Road — E2
Silver Street — F1-F2
Somerset Road — F1
Southgate — D3-D2-E3-E2
South Street — C1-C2
Spring Street — B2-C2
Spring Grove Street — B1-C1
Springwood Avenue — B2
Springwood Hall Gardens — A1-A2
Springwood Street — B2-C2
Threadneedle Street — C2
Trinity Street — A4-A3-B3-C3-C2
Turnbridge Road — E3
Union Street — D4
Upperhead Row — C2
Vernon Avenue — A4-B4
Venn Street — D2
Viaduct Street — D3-D4
Victoria Lane — D2
Wakefield Road — E2-E1-F1
Water Street — B1-B2
Waverley Road — B3
Wentworth Street — B3-B4
Trinity Westgate — C3-C2-D2-D3
William Street — D4
Wood Street — D3
Zetland Street — D2

DEWSBURY

Albion Street — A4-B4
Aldhams Road — A2-A1-B1-B2
Ashworth Gardens — A3
Ashworth Road — A2-A3
Bank Street — C2-C3
Bath Street — A4
Battye Street — C3
Bond Street — B2-B3
Bradford Road — B3-B4
Camroyd Street — C3
Carlton Road — A4
Church Street — B2
Cliffe Street — B3-C3-C4
Cloth Hall Street — B3
Commercial Road — A4-B4
Crackenedge Lane — B3-B4-C2-C3
Daisy Hill — B2
East Ward Street — B4
Eightlands Road — A3-B3
Foundry Street — B3-C3-C2
Greaves Road — B4
Grove Street — B2
Halifax Road — A4-A3-B3
Halliley Street — A2
Highgate Road — C2-C3
Hirst Road — A4-B4
Leeds Road — C2-C3
Long Causeway — B2-C2-C1
Low Street — A4
Manor Street — C2-C3
Market Place — B2-C2
Mill Street East — B1-C1
Mill Street West — A1-B1
Moorlands Avenue — A3-A4
Moorlands Road — A3
Northfield Place — A4
Northfield Street — A4

Northgate — B3
Old Westgate — A2-B2
Park Street — B4
Pyrah Street — A4
Railway Street — C1-C2
Rishworth Road — C2
Sands Lane — C1
Saville Bridge — B1
Scargill Street — A2-A3
Sharp Street — C3
South Street — B2
Springfield Street — A3-B3
Springfield Terrace — A3
Stonefield Street — A4
Union Street — B2-B3
Upper Camroyd Street — C3-C4
Vicarage Road — B2-C2
Victoria Road — A4-B4
Vulcan Road — A2-A3
Wakefield Road — C2
Webster Hill — A1-A2
Wellington Road — A2-B2-B3
Westgate — B2
Willan's Road — A3-B3
Wilton Street — B1-B2
Wood Street — B4-B3-C3
Wormald Street — A2

HUDDERSFIELD
Designed by J. P. Pritchett and built in the 1840s, the splendid railway station is one of the earlier ones, but is quite outstanding with its Corinthian columns and pediment flanked by fine colonnades.

Key to Town Plan and Area Plan

Town Plan
A A Recommended roads
Other roads
Restricted roads
Buildings of interest — Hall
Car Parks — P
Parks and open spaces
One Way Streets — ←
Churches — +

Area Plan
A roads
B roads
Locations — Swine ○
Urban area

Street Index with grid reference

Hull

Adelaide Street	B1-C1
Albion Street	C3
Alfred Gelder Street	D2-D3-E3
Anlaby Road	A2-B2-C2
Anne Street	C2
Arlington Street	A2
Baker Street	C3
Beverley Road	B4
Blackfriargate	D1-E1
Blanket Row	D1
Blenkin Street	F4
Bond Street	C3
Bourne Street	D3-D4
Brisbane Street	B1
Brook Street	B3-C3
Cambridge Street	B2
Canning Street	B3
Caroline Street	D4
Carr Lane	C2
Castle Street	C1-C2-D2-D1
Charles Street	C3-C4
Church Street	F3-F4
Clarendon Street	A3-A4
Clarence Street	E3-F3-F4
Colliers Street	B2-B3
Colonial Street	B3-B4
Commercial Road	C1
Dagger Lane	D2
Danson Lane	F4
De La Pole Street	F3
Dock Office Row	E3-E4
Dock Street	C3-D3
Ferensway	B4-B3-C3-C2-C1
Fountain Street	A2-A3
Francis Street	C4-D4
Freehold Street	A4
Garrison Road	E2-F2
George Street	C3-D3-D4-E4-E3
Great Thornton Street	A1-A2-B2-B1
Great Union Street	E4-E3-F3
Grey Street	A4-B4
Grimston Street	D3
Guildhall Road	D2-D3
Hall Street	B4
Hedon Road	F3
Hessle Road	B1-C1
High Street	E2-E3
Hobart Street	B1-B2
Hodgson Street	E4
Holborn Street	F4
Holderness Road	F4
Humber Street	D1-E1
Humber Dock Street	D1

Hull

Officially Kingston-upon-Hull, this ancient port was specially laid out with new docks in 1293, on the decree of Edward I, and echoes of the town's past can be seen in the Town Docks Museum. The docks and the fishing industry are synonymous with Hull – it has Britain's busiest deep-sea fishing port – although flour-milling, vegetable oil extraction and petrochemical production are also important. The centre of Hull consists of broad streets and spacious squares and parks, such as Queen's Gardens, laid out on the site of what used to be Queen's Dock. The older part of the town which lies south-east of here between the docks and the River Hull is full of character, with a number of Georgian buildings and places of interest.

Beverley is one of England's most distinguished towns. Between its two principal buildings – the famous Minster and St Mary's Church – are medieval streets and pleasing market squares graced by redbrick Georgian houses built by the landed gentry of the East Riding during the town's heyday as a fashionable resort. The Minster's twin towers soar above the rooftops of the town as a constant reminder that here is one of the most beautiful pieces of Gothic architecture in Europe. The wealth of beauty and detail throughout is immense, but carving in both stone and wood is one of its most outstanding features.

Hull Area

Hutt Street	A4
Hyperion Street	E3-E4-F4
Jameson Street	C2-C3
Jarrett Street	C3-D3
John Street	C4-D4
King Street	C4-D4
King Street	D2
King Edward Street	C3-C2-D2
Kingston Street	C1-D1
Liddel Street	C4
Lime Street	D4-E4
Lombard Street	B3
Linnaes Street	A1-A2
Londesborough Street	A3
Lowgate	D2-D3
Manor Street	D2
Market Place	D2
Marvel Street	F3-F4
Mason Street	D4
Midland Street	B2
Mill Street	C3
Morpeth Street	A4
Myton Bridge	E1-E2
Myton Street	C2
Nelson Street	D1
New Cleveland Street	E4
New George Street	D4
Norfolk Street	B4-C4
North Street	B3
North Walls	B3
Osborne Street	B2-C2
Paragon Street	C2
Park Street	B2-B3-A3-A4
Pease Street	B2
Peel Street	A4
Pemberton Street	F4
Percy Street	C3-C4
Pier Street	D1
Popple Street	F3
Porter Street	B1-B2
Portland Street	B3
Posterngate	D2
Princess Street	D4

Princes Dock Street	D2
Prospect Place	B4-B3-C3
Pryme Street	B4-C4
Queen Street	D1
Queens Dock Avenue	D3
Railway Street	C1-D1
Raywell Street	C4
Reform Street	C4-D4
Rodney Close	C4
Roper Street	C2
Russell Street	C4
St Lukes Street	B2
St Peter Street	E3-F3
St Stephens Street	B3
Salthouse Lane	E3
Saville Street	C2-C3
Scale Lane	D2-E2
Scott Street	D4
Spring Bank	A4-B4
Spring Street	B3-B4
Spyvee Street	E4-F4
Strawberry Street	F4
Sykes Street	D4
Thomas Street	F3-F4
Tower Street	E2-E3
Union Street	C3
Upper Union Street	B2-C2-C1
Vane Street	B4
Walker Street	A1-B1-B2
Walmesley Street	B4
Waterhouse Lane	C1-C2
Waverley Street	B1
Wellington Street	C1-D1
Wenlock Street	A3-A4
West Parade	A2-A3
West Street	C3
Whitefriar Gate	D2
Wilberforce Drive	D3
Wilberforce Street	A2
William Street	B1-C1
Williamson Street	F4
Wilton Street	F4
Wincolmlee	D4-E4

Witham	E4-F4
Worship Street	D3-D4
Wright Street	C3-C4

Beverley

Admiral Walker Road	A1-B1-B2
Albert Terrace	A2
Athelston Road	C4
Bishops Croft	A2-B2
Cartwright Lane	A1
Central Avenue	A1-A2-B2
Champney Road	A2-B2
Chantry Lane	C2
Cherrytree Lane	C3-C4
Cooper Street	C4
Corporation Road	B4-B3-C3
Cross Street	B2
Dog and Duck Lane	B3
Eastgate	C2
Ellerker Road	A1-A2
Flemingate	C1-C2
Fisher Square	A2-B2
George Street	C3
Goths Lane	C4
Grayburn Lane	A2-B2
Greyfriars Crescent	A1
Hengate	A3-B3
Highgate	C2
Holderness Crescent	C3
Keldgate	B1-C1
Keldgate Road	A1
Kings Square	B3-B4-C4-C3
Kitchen Lane	B1
Ladygate	B3
Lairgate	B1-B2-B3-A3
Landress Lane	B2
Long Lane	C1
Lord Roberts Road	B2-C2
Manor Close	A4-B4
Manor Road	A4-B4-B3

Mill Lane	C3-C4
Minster Avenue	C1
Minster Moorgate	B2-C2
Morton Lane	B3-C3
Napier Close	A4
New Walkergate	B3-C3-C2
Newbegin	A2-A3-B3
Nolloth Crescent	C3-C4
North Bar Within	A3
North Bar Without	A3-A4
Norwood	B3-B4-C4
Park Avenue	A4
Pasture Terrace	A3
Quaker Lane	A3
Queensgate	A1-B1
Railway Street	C2
St Andrew's Street	C1-C2
St Gile's Croft	A2
St John Street	C1-C2
St Mary's Walk	A4
Sample Avenue	C4
Sole Lane	A1
The Causeway	C3-C4
The Leases	A1-A2
Thurstan Road	A1
Tiger Lane	A3
Toll Gavel	B2-B3
Trinity Grove	C2-C3
Trinity Lane	C2-C3
Walkergate	B2-B3
Watts Road	C4
Well Lane	B2
Wellington Road	B4-C4
Westwood Road	A2
Wilbert Grove	C3
Wilbert Grove	C3
Wilbert Lane	B2-B3-C3
Willow Avenue	A3
Woodlands Wood Lane	A2-A3
Wylie's Road	A3-A4-B4
York Road	A3

HULL
Schemes to cross the Humber estuary were first discussed over 100 years ago, but it was not until 1981 that the mammoth project was sucessfully completed. At 4626ft, the Humber Bridge has the longest main span in the world.

Lake District

Keswick With the River Greta running through it and Skiddaw looming above, this is a charming, quiet market town set amid beautiful scenery at the southern end of Derwentwater. The Fitz Park Museum and Art Gallery houses a collection of manuscripts by the numerous authors and poets who took their inspiration from the Lakeland.

Windermere has remained unspoiled despite the enormous popularity it has won as a holiday resort. Centred around its extensive lake, it stands in a setting which has been exalted by poets and artists for years. Windermere's architecture is mainly Victorian, as a result of the railway coming in the mid-19th century and bringing prosperity to the town. But conservationists campaigned to stop the railway going any further, and so the natural peace of the area was preserved.

Lancaster Dominating the city from its hilltop site, Lancaster Castle was once the headquarters of the Duchy and is still in use today — as a prison. Its late Georgian courtrooms and the beautiful Shire Hall are open to visitors. Close by stands the Priory, an architectural gem, and also of interest is the early 17th-century Judge's Lodgings house, which provided accommodation for assize judges for 150 years. The building now houses a display of dolls, with beautiful

Central Bowness-on-Windermere

LEGEND

AA Recommended roads	▬▬
Restricted roads	-- --
Other roads	▬▬
Buildings of interest	Library ◻
Car Parks	P
Parks and open spaces	◻
One Way Streets	←
Churches	✝

Street Index with Grid Reference

Carlisle

Abbey Street	A2-A3
Annetwell Street	A3
Bank Street	B2-C2
Blackfriars Street	B1-B2
Botchergate	C1
Bridge Street	A3
Brunswick Street	C1-C2
Castle Street	A3-A2-B2
Castle Way	A3-B3-B4
Cecil Street	C1
Chapel Street	C3
Charlotte Street	A1
Chatsworth Square	C2
Chiswick Street	C2
City Walls	A3
Compton Street	C3
Corporation Road	B3-B4
Crosby Street	C1-C2
Dacre Road	A3-A4
Drovers Lane	B3
Duke's Road	B4-C4
East Tower Street	B3
Eden Bridge	B4
English Damside	B1-B2
English Street	B2
Finkle Street	A3
Fisher Street	A3-B3
Georgian Way	B4-B3-C3
Junction Street	A1
Lonsdale Street	C2
Lorne Crescent	A1
Lowther Street	B3-B2-C2
Market Street	B3
Mary Street	C1
Milbourne Crescent	A1
Millbourne Street	A1-A2
Newark Terrace	C4
Paternoster Row	A2-A3
Peter Street	B3
Portland Place	C1
Rickergate	B3
St Mary's Gate	B2-B3
Scotch Street	B2-B3
Spencer Street	C2
Strand Road	C3
Tait Street	C2
Viaduct Estate Road	A2-A1-B1
Victoria Place	C2-C3
Victoria Viaduct	B1
Warwick Road	C1-C2
Warwick Street	B3
West Tower Street	B3
West Walls	A2-B2-B1

Kendall

All Hallows Lane	A2-A3
Anchorite Fields	A1
Ann Street	C4
Aynam Road	B1-B2-B3
Beast Banks	A2
Beezon Road	B4
Blackhall Road	A4-B4-B3
Bridge Street	B3
Captain French Lane	A1
Castle Crescent	C3-C4
Castle Garth	C3-C4
Castle Road	C3-C4
Castle Street	B4-C4
Finkle Street	A3
Gilling Gate	A1
Highgate	A1-A2
Kirkbarrow	A1
Kirkland	A1
Little Aynam	B2-B3
Longpool	C4
Low Fellside	A3
Lowther Street	A3-B3
Market Place	A3
Maude Street	A4
New Road	B3
Parr Street	B1-B2
Sandes Avenue	A4-B4
Station Road	B4
Stramongate	B3
Stricklandgate	A3-A4
Sunnyside	B1-C1
Thorny Hills	B3-C3
Westgate	C4
Wildman Street	B4
Windermere Road	A4

Keswick

Acorn Street	C1
Ambleside Road	C1
Bank Street	B2
Blencathra Street	C2
Borrowdale Road	B1
Briar Rigg	A4-B4-C4
Brundholme Road	C3-C4
Castlehead Close	C1
Church Street	C1
Crosthwaite Road	A3-A4
Derwent Close	B2
Eskin Street	C1-C2
Glebe Close	A4
Greta Bridge	A2-A3
Greta Side	B2
Greta Street	C2
Heads Road	A2-B2-B1
Helvellyn Street	C2
High Hill	A3
Keswick By Pass	C4
Lake Road	B1-B2
Lime Pots Road	A3-A4
Main Street	B2
Manor Park	C1
Market Place	B2
Penrith Road	C2
St Herbert Street	C1-C2
St John Street	B2-B1-C1
Southey Street	C1-C2
Spring Road	C1
Stanger Street	B2-B3
Station Road	C2-C3
Station Street	B2
The Crescent	A2
The Headlands	A1-A2
The Heads	A1-B1
Tithebarn Street	A2
Vicarage Hill	A4
Victoria Street	B2
Wordsworth Street	C1

Lancaster

Aberdeen Road	C1
Albert Road	B3-B4
Alfred Street	C2-C3
Balmoral Road	C1
Black Caton Road	C3-C4
Blades Street	A1
Brewary Lane	C2
Bridge Lane	A2-B2-B3
Brock Street	B1
Bulk Road	C3-C4
Bulk Street	C1-C2
Cable Street	B2-B3
Castle Hill	A2
Castle Park	A2
Caton Road	C4
Chapel Street	B2
Cheapside	B2
China Street	A2
Church Street	B2
Dale Street	C1
Dallas Road	A1-A2
Dalton Square	B1-B2
Damside Street	A3-B3-B2
Derby Road	B3-B4
De Vitre Street	C3
East Road	C1
Edward Street	C2
Elgin Street	C1
Fenton Street	A1-A2
George Street	B1-C1
Great John Street	B2
Green Street	C3
High Street	A1
King Street	A2-B2-B1
Lindow Street	A1-B1
Lodge Street	C2
Long Marsh Lane	A2
Lune Street	B3-B4
Main Way	C4
Market Street	B2
Meeting House Lane	A2
Middle Street	A1-B1
Moorgate	C2
Moor Lane	B2-C2
Morecambe Road	A4-B4
Nelson Street	B1-C1
North Road	B2-B3
Owen Road	B4-C4
Parliament Street	C3-C4
Penny Street	B1-B2
Quarry Road	C1
Queen Street	B1
Regent Street	A1
Ridge Lane	C3
St George's Quay	A3-A4
St Leonard's Gate	B2-C2-C3
St Peter's Road	C1-C2
Sibsey Street	A1
Stirling Road	C1
Stonewell	B2
Sulyard Street	B2-C2
Thurnham Street	B1
Wheatfield Street	A1-A2
Williamson Road	C2
Wolseley Street	C2-C3
Woodville Street	C2

Bowness-on-Windermere

Beresford Road	B3-B4
Birkett Hill	A2-B2-B1
Biskey Howe Road	B3-C3
Brakenfield	B2
Brantfell Road	B2
Brow Crescent	C4
Church Street	A2-A3-B3
Craig Way	B4-C4-B4-B3
Crook Road	C1
Fallbarrow Road	A2-A3
Glebe Road	A2-A1-B1
Helm Road	B3
Kendall Road	B1-B2
Lake Road	B3-B4
Langridge Drive	B2-B3
Longlands Road	B3-B4
Meadow Road	C4
Promenade	A2-B2
Rayrigg Road	A4-A3-B3
Rectory Road	A1-A2
Smithy Lane	B1
Thornbarrow Road	B4-C4
Windermere Park	C4

furniture from Gillows and other cabinet makers.

Kendal's motto is "Wool Is My Bread" — a constant reminder that wool was the town's staple trade for over 600 years and brought it the prosperity which it still enjoys today. Flemish weavers started the industry when they settled here in the 14th century, and the town is now a centre for the production of such different products as turbines, carpets, shoes, socks and hornware — although its best known product must be the sustaining Kendal Mint Cake. An interesting local feature are the numerous named and numbered yards which lie tucked away through Kendal's archways and down alleyways, and were once a focus of small industry.

Carlisle Bonnie Prince Charlie proclaimed his father King of England from the steps of Carlisle Cross before marching south to be taken prisoner by the Duke of Cumberland, and Carlisle Castle was the centre of turbulent scenes between English and Scots from Norman times to the Jacobite rebellion. This is the 'Border City', capital of the Border area between England and Scotland. But as well as a past of conflict it can also claim to have some beautiful buildings. Finest of all perhaps is the cathedral; other places of interest are the Guildhall, which is 15th-century, Tullie House (a fine Jacobean building with Victorian extensions), and the city's museum and art gallery, which has a good collection of artefacts from its past.

Leeds

In the centre of Leeds is its town hall – a monumental piece of architecture with a 225ft clock-tower. It was opened by Queen Victoria in 1858, and has been a kind of mascot for the city ever since. It exudes civic pride; such buildings could only have been created in the heyday of Victorian prosperity and confidence. Leeds' staple industry has always been the wool trade, but it only became a boom town towards the end of the 18th century, when textile mills were introduced. Today, the wool trade and ready-made clothing (Mr Hepworth and Mr Burton began their work here) are still important, though industries like paper, leather, furniture and electrical equipment are prominent.

Across Calverley Street from the town hall is the City Art Gallery, Library and Museum. Its collections include sculpture by Henry Moore, who was a student at Leeds School of Art. Nearby is the Headrow, Leeds' foremost shopping thoroughfare. On it is the City Varieties Theatre, venue for many years of the famous television programme 'The Good Old Days'. Off the Headrow are several shopping arcades, of which Leeds has many handsome examples. Leeds has a good number of interesting churches; perhaps the finest is St John's, unusual in that it dates from 1634, a time when few churches were built.

Leeds District

SCALE
mls 0

LEGEND

Town Plan

AA Recommended roads	▬▬
Other roads	▬ ▬
Restricted roads	▪▪▪
Buildings of interset	Museum
AA Service Centre	AA
Parks and open spaces	
Car Parks	P
Churches	†
One way streets	←

District Plan

A roads	▬
B roads	▬
Stations	Kirkgate ●
Urban area	
Buildings of interest	Hospital

Street Index with Grid Reference

Leeds

Aire Street	C3
Albion Place	D4
Albion Street	D3-D4-D5
Archery Road	C7-C8
Argyle Road	F5
Barrack Road	E8-F8
Barrack Street	B1-B2
Bath Road	C4
Bedford Street	D5-E5
Belgrave Street	A5
Belle Vue Road	E7-F7
Benson Street	F1-F2-F3
Black Bull Street	C7-C8
Blackman Lane	C8-C7-D7
Blenheim Grove	C8
Blenheim View	B8-C8-C7
Blenheim Walk	D3-D4
Boar Lane	C4-D4
Bond Street	

Bowman Lane	E3-F3
Bridge End	D3-E3
Bridge Road	B1
Bridge Street	E5-E6
Briggate	D3-D4-D5
Burley Street	A4-A5
Butterley Street	E1-E2
Byron Street	E6-F6
Call Lane	E3
Calverley Street	C5-C6
Carlton Carr	D7
Carlton Gate	D7
Carlton Street	D7-D8
Castle Street	B3-B4
Chadwick Street	F2
Chapletown Road	E8
Cherry Row	F7
City Square	C3-C4-D4-D3
Clarence Road	F2-F3
Clarendon Road	A8-A7-A6-A5-B5
Clay Pit Lane	D6
Commercial Street	D4
Cookbridge Street	C5-C6-D6
Cross Stamford Street	F6-F7
Crown Street	E3-E4
Crown Point Road	E2-F2-F3
David Street	C1-C2
Devon Road	C8
Dock Street	E3
Dyer Street	E4-F4
East Parade	C4-C5
East Street	F3
Eastgate	E5-F5
Edward Street	E5
Elmwood Road	D6
Enfield Street	F8
Enfield Terrace	F8
George Street	C5
George Street	E4
Globe Road	A2-B2-C2
Gower Street	E5-F5
Grafton Street	E6
Great George Street	C5-D5
Great Portland Street	B5-C5
Great Wilson Street	D2-E2
Greek Street	C4-D4
Hanover Square	A5
Hanover Way	A5-B5
High Court	E3
Holbeck Lane	A1-B1
Holmes Street	D1-E1
Hope Road	F5-F6
Hunslett Road	E3-E2-E1-F1-F2
Hyde Street	A6

Hyde Terrace	A6
Infirmary Street	C4-D4
Inner Ring Road	B5-B6-C6-C7-D7-D6-E6-E5-F5
Junction Street	E1-E2
Kendal Lane	A5-A6
Kendal Lane	E3
Kidacre Street	E1
King Street	C3-C4
King Edward Street	D4-E4
Kirkgate	E4-E3-F3-F4
Kirkstall Road	A4
Lady Lane	E5
Lands Lane	D4-D5
Leicester Place	C8
Leylands Road	F6
Lisbon Street	B3-B4
Little Queen Street	B3-B4
Little Woodhouse Street	B6
Lofthouse Place	C7-D7
Lovell Park Hill	E7
Lovell Park Road	D6-E6-E7
Lower Basinghall Street	D3-D4
Mabgate	F6
Manor Road	C1-D1
Manor Street	E8-F8
Mark Lane	D5
Marlborough Street	A4
Marsh Lane	F4
Marshall Street	C1-C2
Meadow Lane	D1-D2-E2-E3
Meanwood Road	D8-E8
Melbourne Street	D5-E5
Merrion Street	D6
Merrion Way	D3
Mill Hill	D4
Mill Street	F4
Moorland Road	A7-A8
Mushroom Street	F6-F7
Neville Street	D2-D3
New Briggate	D5-E5
New Station Street	D3
New York Road	F5
New York Street	E4-F4
North Street	E5-E6-E7
Northern Street	B3
Oatland Lane	D8-D7-E7
Oatland Road	D8
Oxford Row	C5
Park Cross Street	C4-C5
Park Lane	A5-B5-B4
Park Place	B4-C4
Park Row	C4-C5-D5-D4
Park Square East	C4

Park Square North	B4-C4
Park Square South	C4
Park Square West	B4
Park Street	B5-C5
Portland Crescent	C5-C6
Portland Way	C6
Quebec Street	C3-C4
Queen Street	B3-B4
Queen Square	C6-D6
Queen Victoria Street	D4-E4
Regent Street	F5-F6
Roseville Road	F7-F8
Rossington Street	C5-D5
Roundhay Road	E8-F8
St Ann Street	C5-D5
St Mark's Spur	B8-C8
St Paul's Street	B4-C4
St Peter's Street	E4-F4
Servia Hill	C8-D8
Servia Road	C8-D8
Sheepscar Link Road	E7-E8
Sheepscar Street North	E8
Sheepscar Street South	E8-E7-F7
Skinner Lane	E6-F6
South Brook Street	E2
South Parade	C4
Sovereign Street	D2-D3-E3
Springwell Road	A1-B1
Springwell Street	A1
Sweet Street	C1-D1
Sweet Street West	B1-C1
Swinegate	D3
The Calls	E3-F3
The Headrow	C5-D5
Templar Lane	E5
Templar Street	E5
Thoresby Place	B5-B6
Trinity Street	D4
Upper Basinghall Street	D4-D5
Vicar Lane	E4-E5
Victoria Road	D1-D2
Wade Lane	D5-D6
Water Lane	B1-B2-C2-D2
Waterloo Street	E2-E3
Well Close View	D8
Wellington Road	A3
Wellington Street	A3-B3-C3
Westgate	B4-B5-C5-C4
Wharf Street	E3-E4
Whitehall Road	A1-A2-B2-B3-C3
Whitelock Street	E7-F7
Woodhouse Lane	A8-B8-B7-C7-C6-D6-D5
York Place	B4-C4
York Street	F4

LEEDS
Offices now occupy the handsome twin-towered Civic Hall which stands in Calverley Street in front of the new buildings of Leeds Polytechnic. This area of the city – the commercial centre – has been extensively redeveloped

43

Central Liverpool

Liverpool

Although its dock area has been much reduced, Liverpool was at one time second only to London in pre-eminence as a port. Formerly the centrepiece of the docks area are three monumental buildings – the Dock Board Offices, built in 1907 with a huge copper-covered dome; the Cunard Building, dating from 1912 and decorated with an abundance of ornamental carving; and best-known of all, the world-famous Royal Liver Building, with the two 'liver birds' crowning its twin cupolas.

Some of the city's best industrial buildings have fallen into disuse in recent years, and have been preserved as monuments of the industrial age. One has become a maritime museum housing full-sized craft and a workshop where maritime crafts are demonstrated. Other museums and galleries include the Walker Art Gallery, with excellent collections of European painting and sculpture; Liverpool City Libraries, one of the oldest and largest public libraries in Britain, with a vast collection of books and manuscripts; and Bluecoat Chambers, a Queen Anne building now used as a gallery and concert hall. Liverpool has two outstanding cathedrals: the Roman Catholic, completed in 1967 in an uncompromising controversial style; and the Protestant, constructed in the great tradition of Gothic architecture, but begun in 1904 and only recently completed.

LEGEND

Town Plan
- AA recommended route
- Restricted roads
- Other roads
- Buildings of interest — Castle
- Car parks — P
- Parks and open spaces
- One way streets

District Plan
- A roads
- B roads
- Locations — Sefton O

Street Index with Grid Reference

Liverpool

Addison Street	C6-D6
Arrad Street	F3-F4-F3
Barton Street	B6
Bath Street	A6-B6-B5
Bedford Street South	F2-F3
Berry Street	E3
Birkett Street	D6-E6-E7
Blackburn Place	E3-F3
Blackstock Street	C7-D7
Blenheim Street	C8-D8
Blundell Street	C2-D2
Bold Street	D4-D3-E3
Breck Road	F8
Brick Street	D2
Brook Street	B5
Brownlow Hill	D4-E4-F4
Brow Side	E7-F7
Brunswick Road	F6
Brunswick Street	B4-C4
Burlington Street	B7-C7-C8
Byrom Street	D6
Cambridge Street	F3
Canning Place	C3-C4
Canning Street	E2-F2
Carlton Street	A8-B8-B7
Carter Street	F1
Carver Street	E6-F6
Caryl Street	D1
Castle Street	C4-C5
Catherine Street	F2-F3
Chadwick Street	B7
Chaloner Street	C2-C1-D1-D2
Chatham Street	F3
Chapel Street	B5
Cheapside	C5
Chisenhale Street	B7-C7
Christian Street	D6
Christian Street	D6-D7
Churchill Way North	C6-D6-D5
Church Street	C4-D4
Clarence Street	E4
Colquitt Street	D3-E3
Cook Street	C4
Cooper Street	D4
Copperas Hill	D4-E4-E5
Cornhill	C2-C3
Cotton Street	A8-B8
Cresswell Street	F7
Crown Street	F4-F5
Dale Street	C5
Daulby Street	F5
Dawson Street	D5-D4
Derby Square	C4
Devon Street	E6-F6
Dexter Street	E1
Dickson Street	A8-B8
Dryden Street	D8
Dublin Street	A8-B8
Duke Street	C3-D3-E3
Dundee Street	B6
Earle Street	B5
Eaton Street	B6-C6
Eldon Street	C7
Elliot Street	D4
Erskine Street	F6
Everton Brow	E7
Everton Road	F7-F8
Everton Terrace	E8-E7-F7
Exchange Street East	B5-C5
Falkner Street	F2-F3
Falkner Street	F2-F3
Fleet Street	D3-D4
Flint Street	D1
Fontenoy Street	D6

Ford Street	C7-D7
Formby Street	B7-B6
Fox Street	D7-E7
Fraser Street	E5
Freemasons' Row	C6-D6
Gascoyne Street	B6-C6
Gibson Street	F1
Gilbert Street	D3
Gill Street	E4-E5
Goree Piazza	B4
Grafton Street	D1
Great Crosshall Street	C6
Great George Street	E1-E2-E3
Great Homer Street	D7-D8
Great Howard Street	B6-B7-B8
Great Newton Street	E5-E4-F4
Greenland Street	D1
Green Street	C8-D8
Hampton Street	E1-F1
Hanover Street	C3-C4-D4
Hardman Street	E3
Hatton Garden	C5-C6
Henry Street	D3
Heyworth Street	F8
Hill Street	D1-E1
Hood Street	D5
Hope Street	E2-E3-F3-F4
Hurst Street	C2-C3
Huskisson Street	F2
Islington	E6-F6
Jamaica Street	D1-D2
James Street	B4-C4
Jordan Street	D1-D2
Juvenal Street	D7
Kempston Street	E5-F5-F6
Kent Street	D2-D3
Kepler Street	E8-F8
Kings Dock Street	C2-D2
King Edward Street	B5-B6
Kingsway (Tunnel)	A6-A7-B7-C7
Kitchen Street	C2-D2
Landseer Road	F8
Langsdale Street	E6-F6
Leece Street	E3
Leeds Street	B6-C6
Limekiln Lane	C7-D7-D8
Lime Street	D4-D5
London Road	D5-E5-F5
Lord Nelson Street	D5-E5
Lord Street	C4
Love Lane	B7-B8
Lydia Ann Street	D3
Mansfield Street	E6
Mann Island	B4
Mathews Street	C4

Mill Street	E1
Moss Street	F5-F6
Mount Pleasant	F4
Mount Street	E3
Myrtle Street	E3-F3
Naylor Street	C6-D6
Nelson Street	D2-D3-E3
Neptune Street	B6
Netherfield Road South	E8-E7
Netherfield Road South	E7-E8
New Bird Street	D1-D2
New Islington	E6-F6
New Quay	B5
North John Street	C4-C5
Norton Street	E5
Oil Street	A7-B7
Old Hall Street	B5-B6
Oriel Street	C6-C7-D7
Oxford Street	F3-F4
Pall Mall	B7-B6-C6-B5-C5
Paradise Street	C3-C4
Parker Street	D4
Park Lane	C3-D3-D2
Park Way	F1-F2
Parliament Street	D1-E1-E2
Paul Street	C7-D7
Pembroke Place	E5-F5
Percy Street	E2-F2
Porter Street	A7-B7
Prescot Street	F5-F6
Prince Edwin Street	E7-E8
Prince's Road	F1-F2
Queensway (Tunnel)	A3-A4-B4-C4-C5
Ranelagh Street	D4
Regent Street	A7-B7
Renshaw Street	D4-E4-E3
Richmond Row	D7-E7
Roberts Street	B6
Rodney Street	E3-E4
Roe Street	D5
Roscoe Street	E3-E4
Roscommon Street	D8-E8
Rose Place	D7-E7
Rose Vale	E8
Russell Street	E4-E5
St Anne Street	D7-D6-E6
St James's Place	E1
St James Road	E2-E1
St James's Street	D2-D1-E1
Salisbury Street	E7-E6-F6
Saltney Street	A8-B8
Sandon Street	F2
School Lane	C4-D4
Scotland Road	D6-D7-D8

Seel Street	D4-D3-E3
Sefton Street	D1
Seymour Street	E5
Shaw Street	E7-F7-F6
Silvester Street	C8-D8
Simpson Street	D1-D2
Slater Street	D3-D4
Soho Street	E6-E7
South John Street	C4
Sparling Street	C2-D2
Spencer Street	F7
Stanhope Street	D1-E1
Stone Street	B8
Strand Street	B4-C4-C3
Tabley Street	C2-C3-D3
Tatlock Street	C7
Titchfield Street	C7-C8
Tithebarn Street	B5-C5-C6
The Strand	B4
Upper Duke Street	E3
Upper Hampton Street	F2
Upper Hill Street	E1-F1
Upper Parliament Street	F2
Upper Pitt Street	D2
Upper Stanhope Street	E1
Upper Stanhope Street	E1-F1
Vauxhall Road	C6-C7-C8
Victoria Street	C4-C5-D5
Village Street	F7
Vine Street	F3
Vulcan Street	A7-A8
Wapping	C2-C3
Waterloo Road	A8-A7-B7-A6-B6
Water Street	B4-B5-C5
Whitechapel	C4-C5-D5
Wilbraham Street	D8
William Brown Street	D5
William Henry Street	E6-E7-F7
Windsor Street	E1-F1
Wood Street	D4-D3-E3
York Street	C3-D3

LIVERPOOL
The Metropolitan Cathedral of Christ the King is one of Liverpool's most striking landmarks. Crowning the conical roof is a tower of stained glass which throws a pool of coloured light on to the altar below.

Macclesfield

One hundred and eight steps rise up to the Church of St Michael, which makes a striking and dramatic backdrop to the town that rises to meet it. The church can also be entered on the level from the market place, and its large monuments are amongst the best in Cheshire. The church is the finest reminder of the town's medieval origins, and other buildings of architectural interest include some early mills and Georgian houses. Once the centre of the English silk industry, Macclesfield today concentrates on the production of man-made fibres, and still remains a pleasant market town. Amongst its open spaces, West Park is one of the oldest public parks in the country, and has at its entrance the Macclesfield Museum and Art Gallery, where a fine Egyptian collection can be seen.

Congleton Stone Age man is thought to have built the chambered tomb known as Bridestones

which stands on the road to Leek, so Congleton can claim to date from Neolithic times. The town's medieval street plan is still intact, and it has some fine Tudor buildings — a legacy to its prosperity at this time. Now an important cattle market and textile town, its focal point is the fine Venetian-Gothic style Victorian Town Hall.

Wilmslow nestles in the valleys of the Bollin and Dean. With one of the area's most picturesque positions, this is a pleasant dormitory town.

Central Congleton

Central Wilmslow

LEGEND

Town Plan
- AA recommended route
- Restricted roads
- Other roads
- Buildings of interest — Hall
- Car parks — P
- Parks and open spaces

Area Plan
- A roads
- B roads
- Locations — Littleton ○
- Urban area

Street Index with Grid Reference

Macclesfield

Albert Place	D2-D3
Albert Street	B3-B4
Alton Drive	F4
Armitt Street	B2-B1
Athey Street	B3
Baker Street	A2
Bank Street	D1-E1
Barton Street	B1
Bedford Road	A3-A2
Beswick Street	A3
Black Lane	E3-E4
Black Road	E1
Boden Street	D2-D3
Bond Street	A1-B2-B3
Bread Street	A2
Bridge Street	B2-C2-C3
Brock Street	D4
Brocklehurst Avenue	E3-E4-F4
Brook Street	D2-D1-E1
Brookfield Lane	E1
Brooklands Avenue	A3-A2
Brough Street	A2-B2
Brown Street	B2-B1
Brunswick Street	D3
Buckley Street	B2-B1-C1-C2
Buxton Road	D3-D2-E2-E1-F1
Cambridge Road	A2
Canal Street	D2
Canterbury Court	D3
Carisbrook Avenue	F4
Castle Street	C3
Catherine Street	B3-C3
Chadwick Terrace	E4-F4
Chapel Street	C1-D1
Charlotte Street	D2
Chestergate	C4-C3
Chester Road	A4-B4-B3-C4
Churchill Way	C2-C3
Clegg Street	D2
Clowes Road	A3-A4
Coare Street	C4-D4
Commercial Road	D3-E3
Conway Crescent	F4
Cottage Lane	F1
Cottage Street	A3-B3
Cranford Avenue	F1
Crew Avenue	E4
Crompton Road	A2-B2-B3
Crossall Street	B2-C2
Crown Street West	B3
Cumberland Street	B4-C4
Dale Street	E2
Davenport Street	D1-D2-D3
Duke Street	C2
Eden Drive	F3
Elizabeth Street	C2
Exchange Street	C3-C2
Fence Avenue	E2-E3
Fieldbank Road	A4
Flint Street	E2
Fountain Street	D2
Fowler Street	D4
Garden Street	E3-E4
Gas Road	D3
George Street	D2
Grange Road	B1
Great King Street	B3-C3
Green Street	D1-D2
Grosvenor Street	B4-C4
Hallefield Road	D1-D2
Hall Street	C4-D4
Hatton Street	B2
Henderson Street	B3-B2
Hibel Road	D4-D3
High Street	C1
Higher Fence Road	F1-F2
Hobson Street	C1
Hope Street	B4
Hurdsfield Road	E3-F3
James Street	C1
Jodrell Street	D1-E1
Jordangate	D3-D4
King Street	D3
King Edward Street	C4-C3-D3
Knight Street	D1
Lakelands Close	F1
Lansdowne Street	E3-F3
Lime Grove	E2
Loney Street	B2
Longacre Street	B4
Longden Street	E2
Lord Street	C1
Lowe Street	C1
Lower Bank Street	D2-D1
Lower Exchange Street	C2-D2
Lower Field Road	E4
Lyon Street	C1
Mill Lane	B3
Mill Street	C2-C3
Moran Crescent	A2
Moran Road	A2
Newton Street	B1-B2
Nicholson Avenue	E4-F4
Nicholson Close	E4
Old Park Lane	C1-C2
Oxford Road	A2-A3-B3-B4
Paradise Street	B2-C2
Park Green	B1
Park Lane	A2-A1-B1-C1
Park Street	C1
Park View	E3
Parker Street	D1-E1
Park Vale Road	A1-B1
Parr Street	B3
Parsonage Street	C1-C2
Pearl Street	C4-D4
Peel Street	C1
Peter Street	A1-A2-B2
Pickford Street	C2-D2
Pierce Street	B3-C3
Poplar Road	B1
Pownall Street	C2
Prestbury Road	B4-C4
Queens Avenue	E4-E3
Riseley Street	B4
Rodney Street	C1
Roe Street	B3-C2
Ryle Street	B1-C1
Ryle's Park Road	A1
St George's Street	C1
Samuel Street	C2
Sandringham Road	F3
Shaw Street	B3-C3
South Park Road	B1-B2
Statham Street	B2-C2
Station Street	D4
Sunderland Street	C1-C2-D2
Swettenham Street	E1
Turnock Street	D1
Union Street	B2-C2
Union Street	E1-E2
Victoria Street	C2-C3-D3
Victoria Walk	E3
Vincent Street	B1-C1-C2
Waterside	D1
Water Street	C2-C3
Water's Green	D3
West Bond Street	B3-B2
Westminster Road	C4
Whalley Hayes	C4
Withyfold Drive	E4
Wood Street	C2
York Street	E2

Congleton

Antrobus Street	B3
Astbury Street	A3
Bank Street	C2
Belgrave Avenue	B4-B3
Berkshire Drive	B4-C4
Booth Street	A2-A3
Bridge Street	B2
Broadhurst Lane	A4
By-Pass	A3-A4-B4
Canal Street	C2-C1
Chapel Street	B4
Crescent Road	A3-A2
Dane Street	A3-A4
Derby Street	B4
Eardley Crescent	C4
Elizabeth Street	A3
Fountain Street	B2
Harper Grove	C4
High Street	B2-C2
Hillfields	C4
Hillfields Close	C4
Howey Lane	B2-B1
Howey Hill	A1-B1
John Street	A3
Jubilee Road	C1
Kinsey Street	C2
Lawton Street	C2
Lime Street	A2
Lion Street	A2-B2
Lowe Avenue	C1
Lower Park Street	C2
Market Street	B2-C2-C3
Milk Street	B4-C4
Mill Green	C4-C3
Mill Street	B3-C3
Moody Street	B2
Moor Street	C2
Mountbatten Way	C3-C2
New Street	C1
North Street	B3
Overton Close	A3-A3
Park Road	C3
Park Street	C2
Park View	C3
Pear Tree Bank	C1
Priestyfields	B1-B2
Princess Street	B2-B3
Queen Street	A3
River Street	B3
Rood Hill	B4-C4
Rood Lane	B4-C4
Rope Walk	B3
Royle Street	B3-B4-C4
Silk Street	A3
South Street	B3
Springfields Drive	B4
Stonehouse Green	C3
Swan Street	A1-A2-B2
The Crescent	A2
Townsend Road	C1
Union Street	B4
Victoria Street	B2-B3
Wagg Street	B2
Waggs Road	A1-A2-B2
Wallworths Bank	C1
West Street	A3-B3-B2
Wood Street	C4
Woodland Park	A3-A4
Woodlands Avenue	B4-C4
Worral Street	C3-C2

Wilmslow

Albert Street	B2
Alderley Road	B1-B2-B3-C3
Alma Lane	A2
Alton Road	A3
Altrincham Road	A2-A3-B3
Bedells Lane	B2-B1
Beech Grove	A2
Beech Lane	A2
Birch Avenue	A2-A1
Bollin Hill	B4
Bollin Walk	C3
Bourne Street	A2
Briarwood	C4
Broad Walk	A3
Broadway	B3-B2-C2
Buckingham Road	A2-A1
Cambridge Road	A2
Carwood Road	A4-A3
Chancel Lane	B4
Chapel Lane	A1-A2-B2
Church Street	B3
Cliff Road	B4
Cliff Side	B4
Clifford Road	A2-A1
Cow Lane	C4
Dave Hall Avenue	A3
Donkey Lane	B1
Eastwood Road	A2
Fulshaw Avenue	B2-B1
Granville Road	A1
Gravel Lane	A1
Green Lane	B3
Greenway	B2
Grove Avenue	B3
Grove Street	B3
Hall Road	B3
Hawthorn Grove	A3-B3
Hawthorn Lane	A3-B3
Hawthorn Street	A2-B2-B3
Hawthorn Walk	A3
Hill Top Avenue	B4-C4
Holly Road North	B2-C2
Holly Road South	B1-B2
Kennerleys Lane	B3
Kings Close	B2-B3
Knutsford Road	A1-B1
Ladyfield Street	C3
Lindfield Estate South	A2
Longmeade Gardens	C3-C2
Macclesfield Road	C3
Manchester Road	B3-C3-C4-B4
Mill Road	B3
Mill Street	B4-B3
Moor Lane	A1
Northward Road	A2-A1
Nursery Lane	A1-B1
Oak Lane	A2-A1
Old Brow	B4
Park Avenue	A4
Park Road	A3
Parkway	B3-B2
Pownall Road	A3
Race Course Road	A2
South Oak Lane	A1
Station Road	C3
Stoney Lane	A1
Strawberry Lane	A1
Styal Road	A4-B4
The Meade	C2
Thorngrove Drive	C2
Thorngrove Road	C3-C2
Victoria Road	B2
Wates Lane	B3
Westward Road	A2
Wilmslow Park Road	C3-C4
Windsor Avenue	A2
Wyecliffe Avenue	B2-B3

Manchester

The gigantic conurbation called Greater Manchester covers a staggering 60 square miles, reinforcing Manchester's claim to be Britain's second city. Commerce and industry are vital aspects of the city's character, but it is also an important cultural centre – the Halle Orchestra has its home at the Free Trade Hall (a venue for many concerts besides classical music), there are several theatres, a library (the John Rylands) which houses one of the most important collections of books in the world, and a number of museums and galleries, including the Whitworth Gallery with its lovely watercolours.

Like many great cities it suffered badly during the bombing raids of World War II, but some older buildings remain, including the town hall, a huge building designed in Gothic style by Alfred Waterhouse and opened in 1877. Manchester Cathedral dates mainly from the 15th century and is noted for its fine tower and outstanding carved woodwork. Nearby is Chetham's Hospital, also 15th-century and now housing a music school. Much new development has taken place, and more is planned. Shopping precincts cater for the vast population, and huge hotels have provided services up to international standards. On the edge of the city is the Belle Vue centre, a large entertainments complex including concert and exhibition facilities, and a speedway stadium.

48

Key to Town Plan and Area Plan

Town Plan

AA Recommended roads	
Other roads	
Restricted roads	
Buildings of interest	Baths
Car parks	P
Parks and open spaces	
Churches	+
AA Centre	AA
One Way Streets	

District Plan

A roads	
B roads	

STREET INDEX
-with grid reference

Manchester

Addington Street	E7-E6-F6
Albert Square	C4-D4
Albion Street	C2-C3
Angel Street	E7
Aytoun Street	E4-F4-F3-E3
Back Piccadilly	E5-F5-F4
Balloon Street	D6-E6
Barrack Street	A1
Blackfriars Road	A8-A7-B7-B6-C6
Blackfriars Street	C5-C6-D6
Bloom Street	B6
Blossom Street	F6
Booth Street	E1-F1
Bootle Street	C4
Brazennose Street	C4-D4
Brewery Street	A6-B6
Bridge Street	B5-C5
Bridgewater Street	B3
Brook Street	E2
Broughton Road	A8
Brown Street	B6-C6-C5
Brown Street	D4-D5
Bury Street	B6-C6

Byrom Street	B4
Cambridge Street	D2
Camp Street	B4-C4-C3
Cannon Street	A7
Cannon Street	D6-D5-E5
Carnarvon Street	D8
Chapel Street	A6-A5-B5-B6-C6-D6
Charles Street	E2
Charlotte Street	D4-E4
Cheetham Hill Road	D7-D8
Chepstow Street	D3
Chester Road	A1-A2-B2-C2-C3
Chester Street	D2-E2
Chorlton Road	B2-A2-A1-B1
Chorlton Street	E3-E4
Church Street	A6-B6
Church Street	E5
City Road	C2
Cleminson Street	A6
Cooper Street	D4
Cornel Street	F6
Corporation Street	D6-D7-E7
Cottenham Drive	B8
Cross Street	D4-D5-D6
Dale Street	E5-F5-F4
Dantzig Street	D6-E6-E7-E8-F8
Dawson Street	A3
Deansgate	C3-C4-C5
Downing Street	F2
Dulcie Street	F4
Dutton Street	D7-D8
East Ordsall Lane	A5
Egerton Street	A2
Ellesmere Street	A2
Elton Street	A8-B2
Fairfield Street	F3
Faulkner Street	D4-E4
Fennel Street	D6
Fountain Street	D4-D5
Garden Lane	B6-B7
Gartside Street	B4-B5
George Street	A5
George Street	D3-D4-E4
Goadsby Street	E6
Gore Street	B5
Gould Street	E8-E7-F7
Granby Road	E3-F3
Gravel Lane	C6-C7
Great Ancoats Street	F5-F6
Great Bridgewater Street	C3-D3
Great Ducie Street	C8-C7-D7
Great Jackson Street	B2-C2
Greengate	B7-C7
Grosvenor Street	E1-E2-F2
Hampson Street	A4

Hanover Street	D7-D6-E6
Hardman Street	C4
Henry Street	F5-F6
High Street	E5-E6
Higher Cambridge Street	D1
Hilton Street	E5-F5
Hulme Street	D2
Humberstone Avenue	C1
Hunmaby Avenue	C1
Hunt's Bank	D6-D7
Irwell Street	A5-B5
Jackson Crescent	B1-C1
Jackson's Row	C4
John Dalton Street	C5-C4-D4-D5
Julia Street	C8-D8
Jutland Street	F4
Kincardine Road	F1-F2
King Street	A7-B7-B6-C6
King Street	C5-D5
King St West	C5
Leaf Street	C1
Lever Street	E5-F5-F6
Little Peter Street	B2-C2
Liverpool Road	A4-A3-B4-B3-C3
Lloyd Street	C4
London Road	F3-F4
Long Millgate	D6-D7
Lord Street	D8-E8
Lordsmead Street	A1
Lower Byrom Street	B3-B4
Lower Mosley Street	C3-D3-D4
Lower Ormond Street	D2
Loxford Street	D1
Mancunian Way	B2-B1-C2-C1-D1-D2-E2-F2
Market Street	D5-E5
Mary Street	C7-C8
Medlock Street	C2
Miller Street	D7-E7-E6
Minshull Street	E4
Mosley Street	D4-D5-E4-E5
Mount Street	A6-A7-B7
Newton Street	F5
New Bailey Street	B5
New Bridge Street	C7-D7
North George Street	A6-A7
New Quay Street	B4-B5
Oak Street	E6
Oldham Road	F6-F7
Oldham Street	E5-E6-F6
Oxford Road	D2-E2-E1
Oxford Street	D4-D3-D2
Pall Mall	D4-D5
Park Street	D8
Parker Street	E4-E5

Peru Street	A6
Peter Street	C4-D4
Piccadilly	E5-E4-F4
Port Street	F5
Portland Street	D3-D4-E4-E5
Princess Road	C1-D1
Princess Street	D4-E4-D3-E3-E2
Quay Street	B4-C4
Queenby Street	A1
Red Bank	E7-E8
River Street	C2
Robert Street	D8
Rochdale Road	E7-F7-F8
Roger Street	E8
St Ann Street	C5-D5
St Mary's Gate	C5-C6-D5-D6
St Mary's Parsonage	C5-C6
St James Street	D3-D4
St John Street	B4-C4
St Peter Square	D4
St Stephen Street	A6-B6-B7
Sackville Street	E2-E3-E4
Sherrat Street	F6
Sherborn Street	B8-C8
Shudehill	D6-E6
Silk Street	A7
Southall Street	C8-D8
Southmill Street	C4
Spring Gardens	D4-D5
Springfield Lane	C7-C8
Store Street	F4
Style Street	E7-E8
Sudell Street	F7-F8
Sussex Street	A8
Swan Street	E6-F6
Tatton Street	A1
Tariff Street	F5
Thomas Street	E5-E6
Thompson Street	F6-F7
Tib Street	E5-E6-F6
Travis Street	F3
Upper Brook Street	E2-E1-F1
Viaduct Street	C6
Victoria Bridge Street	C6-D6
Victoria Street	C6-D6
Wadeson Road	F2
Water Street	A3-A4-B4
Watson Street	C3-C4
Wersley Street	A2
Whitworth Street	D3-E3
Whitworth Street West	B3-C3-C2-D2-D3
William Street	B6
Windmill Street	C4-C3-D3
Withy Green	D6
York Street	D5-D4-E4

MANCHESTER
The Barton Swing Bridge carries the Bridgewater Canal over the Manchester Ship Canal, which links Manchester with the sea nearly 40 miles away. Completed in 1894, the canal is navigable by vessels up to 15,000 tons.

49

Middlesbrough

Heavy industry dominates Middlesbrough. It has been a centre of iron and steel manufacture since the 1840s although much of the steel-making has moved eastwards to a new works near Redcar. Its rise had begun ten years before, when the Stockton and Darlington Railway purchased land here and turned what had been a quiet riverside village into a busy coal exporting town. Middlesbrough's most notable structure is the Transporter Bridge, built across the Tees in 1911. It is one of only two bridges of its type left in Britain. The town centre is modern with spacious shopping areas and new public buildings. The Dorman Museum covers the region's history and there are two major art galleries.

Stockton has a place in transport history; it was here, on 27 September 1825, that the world's first steam passenger railway service began. The town, also situated on the River Tees, became an engineering and shipbuilding centre and is still an important industrial centre today. It has a town hall of 1763 standing in the middle of one of the widest main streets in England.

Billingham also stands on the Tees, and the river was one of the factors which encouraged various chemical industries to become established here. North Sea oil has given a boost to that industry, and the town centre has been completely rebuilt with every facility.

Central Stockton-on-Tees

Central Billingham

Key to Town Plan and Area Plan

Town Plan

AA Recommended roads
Other roads
Restricted roads
Buildings of interest
Car Parks
Parks and open spaces
One way street

Area Plan

A roads
B roads
Locations   Aycliffe ○
Urban area

Street Index with Grid Reference

Middlesbrough

Abingdon Road	D2-E2-E3
Acklam Road	A1-B1
Aire Street	B1-B2-C2
Albert Road	D3-D4
Albert Terrace	C2-D2
Aske Road	C2
Ayresome Green Lane	A2-B2-B1
Ayresome Park Road	C1
Ayresom Road	A2
Ayresome Street	B1-C1
Barnaby Avenue	A1
Bilsdale Road	E1-F1
Blake Road	D4-E4-E3
Borough Road	C3-D3-E3
Bradhope Road	F1
Bridge Street West	C4-D4
Bright Street	E3
Bush Street	C1
Cannon Park Road	B3-C3
Cannon Park Way	B3-C3
Cannon Street	B3
Cargo Fleet Road	E3-F3-F4
Charles Street	E3
Clairville Road	E1-E2
Clarendon Road	D2-D3
Clifton Street	C2
Clive Road	B1-C1
Connaught Road	A1-A2
Corporation Road	D4-D3-E3
Craggs Street	E3
Crescent Road	B2-C2-C1
Derwent Street	B2-B3
Diamond Road	C2-C3
Dock Street	E4
Egmont Road	E2
Falmouth Street	E2
Florence Street	E2
Forty Foot Road	B4-C4
Glebe Road	B3-B2-C2
Grange Road	D3-E3
Grange Road West	C3-D3
Granville Road	C2-D2
Gray Street	D4-E4
Gresham Road	C2
Hartford Street	B1-B2
Hartinton Road	C3
Heywood Street	A2-B2
Highfield Road	E1-F1
Hutton Road	F1
Ingram Road	F1
James Street	F2-F3
Kensington Road	C1
Kings Road	F2-F3
Lansdowne Road	E1
Laycock Street	B2
Lees Road	B3
Linthorpe Road	C1-C2-C3-D3-D4
Liverton Avenue	A1-B1
Lloyd Street	C4
Longford Street	B1-B2
Longlands Road	E1-F1-F2
Lothian Road	E1-E2
Lower East Street	D4-E4
Lower Feversham Street	D4
Maldon Road	A1
Manor Street	C2-C3
Maple Street	D2-D3
Marsh Street	B3
Marton Road	D4-D3-E3-E2-E1
Meath Street	B2
Newlands Road	E2-E3
Newport Road	B2-B3-C3-C4-D4-D3
Newstead Road	E1
North Road	B4-C4
North Ormesby Road	E3-F3
Nut Lane	E1
Park Lane	D2-E2
Park Road North	C1-C2-D2-E2
Park Road South	C1-D1-E1
Park Vale Road	D1-E1-E2
Parliament Road	B2-C2
Portman Street	C2-C3
Princes Road	C2
Roman Road	B1
Roseberry Road	E1-F1
Ruby Street	C3
Russell Street	D3-E3
St Barnabas' Road	B1-C1
St Douglas Street	E1-E2
St Paul's Road	E3-E2-F2
Saltwells Road	C2-D2-E2
Smeaton Street	F3
Snowdon Road	C4
Southfield Road	C2-D2-D3
Stockton Street	C1
Surrey Street	B1-B2
Trinity Crescent	F2-F3
Ulla Street	D2
Union Street	B2-C2-C3
Victoria Road	C2-D2-E2
Victoria Street	B2-B3
Waterloo Road	D2-E2
Wellesley Road	E2
West Lane	A1-A2
Westbourne Grove	F2-F3
Westminster Road	C1-D1
Wicklow Street	B1-B2
Wilson Street	C4-D4
Wilton Road	C2-D2
Woodlands Road	D2-D3
Wood Street	D4
Worcester Street	C1-C2
Zetland Street	D4

Stockton-on-Tees

Alma Street	B3-B4
Bath Lane	C3
Bishopton Lane	A3-B3
Bishopton Road	A4-A3
Bridge Road	B2-B1-C1
Buchanan Street	A1-A2
Church Road	B3-C3
Church Yard Road	B1
Cromwell Avenue	C3
Dean Street	A2
Dixon Street	B2
Dovecot Street	A2-B2
Dunmail Road	A3
Durham Road	A4
Edwards Street	A1-B1
Ford Street	B4
Gayles Street	A2
Haffron Avenue	C3-C4
Hartington Road	B1-B2
High Street	B2-B3
Hind Street	A1
Hutchinson Street	B3
John Street	B3
King Street	C3
Light Pipe Hall Road	A1-A2
Lucan Street	B4
Manfield Street	A1-A2
Maritime Road	C3-C4
Mill Street	B3
Nelson Terrace	B2-B3
Norton Road	B3-B4-C4
Oxbridge Lane	A1
Oxford Street	B4-C4
Park Road	A1
Parliament Street	B1
Portrack Lane	C4
Prince Regent Street	B1-B2
Princes Avenue	C4
Riverside	C1-C2-C3
St Paul's Street	A3-A4
Silver Street	B2-C2
Skinner Street	B1-B2
Spring Street	A1
Station Street	C4
Thompson Street	B4
Thorpe Street	C3
Vicarage Street	A4
Wellington Street	B3
Westbourne Street	A1-B1
Westgate	B3-B4
West Row	B2
Wren's Field Road	A3-A4
Yarm Lane	A1-B1-B2
Yarm Road	A1

Billingham

Allendale Road	A2
Bedford Terrace	C2-C3
Belasis Avenue	B1-C1
Billingham Station By-pass	A1-A2
Braid Crescent	B3
Brendon Crescent	C3
Central Avenue	A2-B2-B1-C1-C2
Chapel Road	A1-B1
Cheviot Crescent	A3-B3
Conifer Crescent	A2
Cotswold Crescent	A3-A2-B2-B3-C3
Cowpen Lane	C1-C2-C3
Cumberland Crescent	B1
Easby Road	C3-C4
Finchale Avenue	B4
Gainford Road	C4
Grampian Road	B3
Hatfield Road	C4
Kenilworth Road	B4-C4
Kingsway	A4-A3-B4-B3
Knole Road	C4
Leeholme Road	C3-C4
Lomond Avenue	B3-C3
Lunedale Road	A2-B2
Malvern Road	A3-B3
Marsh House Avenue	C4
Melrose Avenue	B4
Mendip Road	A3
Ochil Terrace	B3
Parklands Avenue	A1-B1
Pentland Avenue	A3-B3-B4-C3-C4
Roseberry Road	A4
Sidlaw Road	A4
Station Crescent	A2
Station Road	A3-A2-A1-B1
Stokesley Crescent	B2-C2
Swaledale Crescent	B2
Teesdale Avenue	A2-B2-C2
Tintern Avenue	B4
The Causeway	A4-B4-C4
The Linkway	C4
Weardale Crescent	A2-A1-B2-B1-C1
Wharfdale Avenue	B1-B2
Wolviston Road	A2-A3-A4
York Crescent	B1-C1

MIDDLESBROUGH
In 1911 the Transporter Bridge was built to replace the river ferry between Port Clarence and Middlesbrough. It is still used today and a special viewing platform has been built to enable visitors to watch the bridge in operation.

Newcastle

Six bridges span the Tyne at Newcastle; they all help to create a striking scene, but the most impressive is the High Level Bridge, built by Robert Stephenson in 1845-49 and consisting of two levels, one for the railway and one for the road. It is from the river that some of the best views of the city can be obtained. Grey Street is Newcastle's most handsome thoroughfare. It dates from the time, between 1835 and 1840, when much of this part of the city was replanned and rebuilt. Elegant façades curve up to Grey's Monument. Close to the Monument is the Eldon Centre, combining sports facilities and shopping centre to form an integrated complex which is one of the largest of its kind in Europe. Newcastle has many museums. The industrial background of the city is traced in the Museum of Science and Engineering, while the Laing Art Gallery and Museum covers painting, costumes and local domestic history. The Hancock Museum has an exceptional natural history collection and the John George Joicey Museum has period displays in a 17th-century almshouse. In Black Gate is one of Britain's most unusual museums – a collection of over 100 sets of bagpipes. Within the University precincts are three further museums. Of the city's open spaces, Town Moor is the largest. At nearly 1,000 acres it is big enough to feel genuinely wild.

Newcastle Area

Map labels (selected): Belsay, Ogle, Stannington, BLYTH, Newsham, East Hartford, Nelson Village, New Hartley, Cramlington, East Cramlington, Seaton Sluice, Berwick Hill, Seghill, SEATON DELAVEL, Milbourne, Dinnington, Seaton Burn, WIDE OPEN, Burradon, Earsdon, WHITLEY BAY, Fenwick, Heugh, Ponteland, Prestwick, Hazlerigg, Backworth, Shiremoor, Cullercoats, Dalton, Stamfordham, Darras Hall, High Callerton, Woolsington, New York, TYNEMOUTH, Harlow Hill, Black Callerton, LONGBENTON, Willington, NORTH SHIELDS, Throckley, GOSFORTH, Heaton, WALLSEND, SOUTH SHIELDS, Horsley, Heddon on-the-Wall, NEWBURN, Byker, Walker, JARROW, Harton, Ovington, Wylam, RYTON, NEWCASTLE UPON TYNE, HEBBURN, Monkton, Boldon Colliery, Cleadon, Whitburn, Ovingham, Crawcrook, BLAYDON, FELLING, Mickley Square, Greenside, Barlow, WHICKHAM, GATESHEAD, Wrekenton, BOLDON, Painshawfield, High Spen, Rowlands Gill, Sunniside, Springwell, Southwick, Roker, Hedley-on-the-Hill, Highfield, Lamesley, WASHINGTON, Chopwell, Whittonstall, Hamsterley, Burnopfield, Kibblesworth, Birtley, South Hylton, SUNDERLAND

N

mls 0 SCALE 2

LEGEND

Town Plan

AA recommended route
Restricted roads
Other roads
Buildings of interest — Hall
Car parks — P
Parks and open spaces
Metro stations — M
One way streets

Area Plan

A roads
B roads
Locations — Craghead○
Urban area

Street Index with Grid Reference

Newcastle

Abinger Street	A2
Argyle Street	E2
Avison Street	A3
Barrack Road	A4-B4-B3
Barras Bridge	D4
Bath Lane	B2-C2
Bigg Market Street	C2-D2
Blackett Street	C3-D3-D2
Blandford Street	B1-B2
Blenheim Street	B1-B2
Breamish Street	F2
Buckingham Street	A2-B2-B3
Byker Bridge	F2-F3
Byran Street	E3-E4
Central Motorway	E1-D1-D2-E2-E3-E4
Chester Street	E4
City Road	E1-E2-F2
Clarance Street	F2-F3
Clayton Street	C2
Clayton Street West	B1-C1-C2
Clothmarket	D2
College Street	D3-D4
Colliery Lane	B3
Collingwood Street	C1-D1
Cookson Close	A3
Copland Terrace	E3-F3
Coppice Way	F3

Corporation Street	B2-B3
Cotten Street	A2
Crawhill Road	F2
Croft Street	D2
Darn Crook	C2-C3
Dean Street	D1-D2
Derby Street	A3-A4
Diana Street	A2-A3-B3
Dinsdale Place	F4
Doncaster Road	F4
Douglas Terrace	A3-B3
Edward Place	A3
Ellison Place	D3-E3
Elswick Road	A2
Elswick Row	A2
Falconer Street	E3
Forth Street	C1-D1
Gallowgate	B3-C3
George Street	A1-B1
Gibson Street	F2
Gladstone Place	E4
Grainger Street	C1-C2-D2
Grantham Road	F4
Grey Street	D2
Great Market	D1-D2
Harrison Place	E4
Haymarket	D3-D4
Helmsley Road	F4
High Bridge	D2
High Villa	A2
Hillgate	E1
Howard Street	F2
John Dobson Street	D3-D4
Leazes Lane	C3
Leazes Park Road	C3-C4
Leazes Terrace	C3-C4
Maple Terrace	A1
Market Street	D2
Marlborough Crescent	B1
Melbourne Street	E2-F2
Morden Street	C3
Moseley Street	D1-D2
Neville Street	C1
New Bridge Road	F2-F3
New Bridge Street	D3-E3-E2-F2
Newgate Street	C2-C3
New Mills	A4
Northumberland Street	D4-D3-E4
Nun Street	C2
Oakes Place	A2-B2-B3
Perry Street	C3-D3-D4
Pilgrim Street	D2
Pitt Street	B3
Portland Road	F3-F4
Pudding Chape	C1-C2
Quayside	D1-E1-F1-F2
Queen Victoria Road	C4
Rock Terrace	E3
Rosedale Terrace	F4
Rye Hill	A1-A2
St James Street	C3
St Mary's Place	D4
St Nicholas Square	D1-D2
St Thomas Street	C3-C4
Sandford Road	D4-E4
Sandhill	D1
Shield Street	E3-F3-F4
Sheildfield Lane	F3
Side	D1
Simpson Terrace	E3
South Shore Road	E1-F1
Stanhope Street	A3-B3

Stepney Lane	E2-F2
Stoddart Street	F3
Stone Street	A3
Stowell Street	B2-C2
Strawberry Place	B3-C3
Summerhill Grove	A2-B2-B1
Tindall Street	A2
Tower Street	E2
Union Street	F3
Vallum Way	A3
Victoria Square	E4
Walter Terrace	A4
Warwick Street	F4
Waterloo Street	B1-B2-C2
Wellington Street	B3
Westgate Road	A2-B2-C2-C1-D1
Westmorland Road	A1-B1
West Blandford Street	B1-B2
Worswick Street	D2
Wreatham Place	E3-F3

North Shields

Addison Street	B1
Albion Road	B3-C3
Albion Road West	A2-B2-B3
Alma Place	B3
Ayre's Terrace	B3
Bedford Street	B3-B2-C2
Belford Terrace	B4-C4
Borough Road	B2-B1-C1
Brightman Road	A3-B3
Brighton Grove	A3
Camden Street	C2-C3
Camp Terrace	B4
Campville	A4-B4
Cecil Street	B2
Charlotte Street	C2-C3
Chirton Green	A2
Chirton West View	A1-A2
Cleveland Avenue	A4
Cleveland Road	A4-B4
Cleveland Terrace	A3-A4
Clive Street	C1-C2
Coach Lane	A2-B2-B1
Collingwood View	A3
Drummond Terrace	C3-C4
Fontbarn Terrace	C4
Grey Street	C3-C4
Grosvenor Place	A3-B3
Hawkey's Lane	A2-A3-A4
Hopper Street	A2
Howard Street	C2-C3
Howdon Road	B1
Hylton Street	A1-B1
Jackson Street	C3
Laet Street	C1
Lansdowne Terrace	A3
Liddell Street	C2
Linskill Terrace	C3-C4
Lovaine Place	B2
Lovaine Terrace	B3
Military Road	C3-C4
Milton Terrace	A4
Nile Street	B3
Norfolk Street	C2-C3
North King Street	C3-C4

Northumberland Place	B3-C3
Park Crescent	C4
Preston Road	B3-B4
Prudhoe Street	B1-B2
Queen Street	C3
Rudyard Street	B2-C2-C1
Russell Street	B2
Sackville Street West	B2-C2
Saville Street	C2
Scorer Street	A2-A3
Seymour Street	B1
Sibthorne Street	C1-C2
Sidney Street	B2-B3
Spring Gardens	A2-A3
Spring Terrace	B3
Stanley Street	B1-B2
Stephenson Street	C2-C3
Stormont Street	A1-A2-B2
The Nook	A2
Trevor Terrace	B4-C4
Trinity Street	B1
Tyne Street	C2
Tynemouth Road	C3
Union Street	C2
Upper Elsdon Street	A1-B1
Vicarage Street	B1
Waldo Street	C1
Waterville Road	A1-B1
Waterville Terrace	B2
West Percy Road	A1-A2
West Percy Street	A2-B2-B3
William Street	B2-C2
Yeoman Street	C1-C2

Whitley Bay

Algernon Place	B2
Alma Place	B1
Alnwick Avenue	A3
Amble Avenue	A1-B1
Beach Avenue	A3-B3-B4
Beech Grove	A4
Belsay Avenue	A1-B1
Brook Street	B3-B4
Burfoot Crescent	B1
Burnside Road	A1-B1
Cambridge Avenue	B3-B4
Charles Avenue	B3-B4
Cheviot View	B2-C2
Chollerford Avenue	A1-B1
Clifton Terrace	B2-B3
Coquet Avenue	A4-B4
Countess Avenue	A4
Delaval Road	B2-C2-C1
Dilston Avenue	A2-B2
Duchess Avenue	A4
East Parade	B3-B4
Edwards Road	B2-C2
Egremont Place	B2
Esplanade	B2-B3-C3
Esplanade Place	B3-B4-C3
Etal Avenue	A2-B2
Felton Avenue	A2-B2
Gordon Square	A3
Grafton Road	C1
Grosvenor Drive	A3
Hawthorne Gardens	A4

Helena Avenue	B2-C2
Hill Heads Road	A2-A3-A2
Holly Avenue	A4-B4
Holystone Avenue	A1-A2
Jesmond Terrace	A2-B2
Kings Drive	A3
Lish Avenue	B1
Lovaine Avenue	A2
Marden Road	A2-A3-B3
Marden Road South	A1-A2
Margaret Road	C1
Marine Avenue	A4-B4
Marine Gardens	A4-B4
Mason Avenue	B3
Norham Road	A3
North Parade	B3
North View	B1
Ocean View	B3
Oxford Street	B3-B4
Park Avenue	B3-B4
Park Parade	A3-B3
Park Road	B4
Park View	A3-A4
Percy Avenue	A3-A4
Percy Gardens	A2
Percy Road	B2-C2-C3
Plessey Crescent	A2-B2-B1
Promenade	C1-C2-C3
Queens Drive	A3
Rockcliffe Street	C1-C2
Roxburgh Terrace	A3-B3
Shaftesbury Crescent	A1
Shorestone Avenue	A1-B1
South Parade	B3
Station Road	B2
Studley Gardens	A1-A2
The Broadway	A1
Trewit Road	B2
Victoria Avenue	B2-C2
Victoria Terrace	B2-B3
Warkworth Avenue	A3
Waters Street	C1
Whitley Road	B1-B2-B3
Windsor Crescent	C1
Windsor Terrace	C1
York Road	B3

Oldham

Snooker championships are a feature of Oldham's Queen Elizabeth Hall, which is also in frequent use by the BBC for recording concerts. This ex-mill town has prospered with the coming of the M62, and as well as the Civic Centre, which is the site of the hall, it also has a fine modern Town Square Shopping Centre. In a pleasant combination of the old and new, it stands proudly alongside the old-established Tommyfield Market, said to be one of the country's largest permanent markets. The Local Interest Centre traces Oldham's past.

Ashton-under-Lyne Pride of Ashton-under-Lyne is the Parish Church of St Michael, noted for its fine 16th-century stained glass.

Glossop Cobbled streets, 17th-century stone houses and easy access to the Dark Peak moors are among the attractions of this High Peaks town. A popular touring centre, it also draws railway enthusiasts: nearby Dinting Railway Centre has a fine collection of steam locomotives offering rides most Sundays and Bank Holidays, while Manor Park is noted for its miniature steam railway. The park also draws the crowds for the annual local festival, which is held here each July.

Hyde lies in the Tame Valley and was once a centre for cotton manufacturing and for coal mining. Good shops and sports facilities can be found in the town.

Key to Town Plan and Area Plan

Town Plan

AA Recommended roads	
Restricted roads	
Other roads	
Buildings of interest	Theatre
Car Parks	P
Parks and open spaces	

Area Plan

A roads	
B roads	
Locations	Dobcross ○
Urban area	

STREET INDEX WITH GRID REFERENCE

OLDHAM

Acre Lane	F4
Albion Street	D2
Alfred Street	A1
Allen Street	B1
Arkwright Street	A2
Arnold Street	F4
Ashley Street	A3-A4
Ashton Road	C1
Bar Gap Road	D4
Barlow Street	E1-F1
Beever Street	E2-E3
Bell Street	E3-F3
Belmont Street	C4-C3-D3
Ben Brierley Way	D3
Bolton Street	F1
Bow Street	D2-E2
Bower Street	F3
Bowden Street	F1
Brackley Street	E3
Bradshaw Street	D2-D3
Brook Street	F2-F3
Brunswick Street	C1
Busk Road	A4
Cardinal Street	E2
Castle Mill Street	F3
Chadderton Way	B4-B3-C3
Chadwick Street	B3
Chaucer Street	C1
Cheapside Street	C2-C3
Churchill Street	E1
Clegg Street	D1-D2
Coldhurst Street	C4-D4-D3
Colwyn Street	B1
Congreave Street	C4
Coppice Street	A1-B1
Cromford Street	F4
Cromwell Street	C1-D1
Cross Street	F2-F3
Crossbank Street	C1
Daisy Street	A3-B3
Davies Street	B4
Derker Street	F3-F4
Eden Street	C3
Edward Street	A1
Egerton Street	D3-E3-E4
Eleanor Street	B4
Ellen Street	A4-B4
Featherstall Road North	A3-A4-B4
Featherstall Road South	A1-A2-A3
Fletcher Close	B2
Franklin Street	C4
Gas Street	E1-E2
George Street	C2
Glodwick Road	F1-F2
Godson Street	C4
Gould Street	F3-F4
Grange Street	B3-C3
Greaves Street	D1-D2
Green Street	B1
Greengate Street	E1-F1
Hamilton Street	F2
Hardy Street	E1-F1
Hebson Street	D1-D2
Henshaw Street	C2-C3-D3-D4
High Street	D2
Highfield Street	B2-B3
Higginshaw Road	E3-E4
Hilda Street	B3
Hill Street	E1-F1
Hooper Street	F1
Horsedge Street	D4-D3-E3-E2
Huddersfield Road	F2-F3
Jespearson Street	F1
John Street	C1-C2
Kersley Street	C4
King Street	C1-C2
Kirkbank Street	B3-B4
Kranj Way	D3
Lane Road	E4
Latimer Street	F1
Lee Street	B1
Lees Road	F2
Lemnos Street	E2-E3
Lord Street	D2-D3
Main Road	A2-A3-A4
Malby Street	D4
Malton Street	B1
Manchester Street	A1-B1-B2-C2

Market Place	C2
Marlborough Street	E1
Mars Street	A3-A4
Middleton Road	A3-B3-B2-C2
Mitchell Street	B4-C4
Mortimer Street	E4
Mumps	E2
Napier Street East	A1-B1
New Radcliffe Street	C3
Nugget Street	F1
Oldham Way	B4-B3-B2-B1-C1-D1-E1-E2-F2
Osborne Street	A4
Park Road	C1-D1
Park Street	C1
Peter Street	D2
Pitt Street	F1
Plato Street	B3
Plough Street	A1
Prospect Road	A3
Quebec Street	A4
Queen Street	D2
Radcliffe Street	D4
Railway Road	A1-B1
Regent Street	E2-E3
Rhodes Street	E2
Rifle Street	D3-D4
Rochdale Road	C2-C3-C4
Rock Street	D2-D3-E3
Roscoe Street	E2
Ruskin Street	B4
Ruth Street	D3-D4
St James's Street	F3
St John's Street	A1
St Mary's Way	C3-D3-D2
St Stephen's Street	E4
Shaw Road	E4-F4-F3
Shaw Street	D3-E3-E4
Spencer Street	B4
Spinks Street	F1
Stirling Street	A3
Sunfield Road	D4
Suthers Street	A1
Sylvan Street	A3
Thames Street	E4
Tilbury Street	B4-C4
Tin Street	B4
Trafalgar Street	C4
Trinity Street	C4
Union Street	C1-C2-D2-E2-E3
Union Street West	B1-C1
Vale Drive	A2-B2-B1
Villiers Street	B1-C1
Waddington Street	A4
Ward Street	B4-C4
Washington Street	A3
Waterloo Street	D2-E2-E1
West Street	B2-C2
West End Street	B3-B4
Widdop Street	B3
Willow Street	B3
Willow Street	E3-F3
Winterbottom Street	D1-E1
Woodstock Street	B1
Worthington Street	B1
York Street	B2
Yorkshire Street	D2-E2

ASHTON-UNDER-LYNE

Adam Street	C3
Alexandra Road	B3-B4-C4
Bentinck Street	A2-A3

Blandford Street	A2-A3-B3
Boodle Street	B3-B4
Brook Street East	A2
Burlington Street	A2-A3-B3
Buttermere Road	A4
Canterbury Street	C4
Coniston Grove	A4
Cooper Street	B1-C1
Cotton Street	A2-B2
Cowhill Lane	C3
Crescent Road	C1
Cricket's Lane	C3
Currier Lane	C2
Dale Street	A2
Dean Street	A2-A3-B3
Egerton Street	B3
Elgin Street	A4-B4
Elizabeth Street	C4
Fleet Street	B2-C2
Fletcher Street	C3
Furnace Street	B1-C1
Haser Street	B2
Henrietta Street	B4-C4-C3
Hill Street	A1-B1-B2
Holden Street	C4
John Street East	A1
Junction Street	C3-C4
Katherine Street	A2-B2-B3
Kenyon Street	A3
Knowle Avenue	A4
Lees Square	B4
Lees Street	B4
Leicester Street	B4
Lennox Street	C3
Lord Street	B4
Lower Wharf Street	B2-C2
Margaret Street	A1-A2
Minto Street	A4-B4
Mount Pleasant Street	B2
Newman Street	A3-B3
Old Street	B2-B3-C3-C2
Old Cross Street	C3
Oldham Road	A4-A3-B3-B2
Park Road	C1
Penny Meadow	C3
Portland Street South	A1
Riverside	C3-C4
Romney Street	C3-C4
Stamford Street	A1-A2-B2-C2
Stockport Road	A1
Taunton Road	A4
Texas Street	C1
Turner Lane	B3-B4
Turner Street	B4
Union Road	C4
Union Street	B4-B3-C3
Uxbridge Street	A3
Victoria Street	A1
Warrington Street	B2-B3
Water Street	B3
Welbeck Street	A1
Wellington Road	A3-B3-C3
Wellington Street	B2-C2
Westbury Street	B1-C1
Wharf Street	C2
Whitelands	C1-C2
Whitelands Road	C1-C2
Winton Street	B3-B4

HYDE

Albert Road	A1
Albion Street	A2-B2

Alexandra Street	A1
Ashton Road	C4
Bedford Avenue	C3-C4
Beech Street	B3
Boston Street	C2
Brook Street	C3
Chapel Street	A1-B1-B2
Church Street	B1
Clarendon Place	B2
Clarendon Road	B3-B4-C4
Clarendon Street	B3
Commercial Brow	C3-C4
Commercial Street	C3
Corporation Street	A2-B2
Croft Street	A1-A2-B2
Crook Street	B2
Cross Street	A2-B2-B3
Dawson Street	C1
Douglas Street	C1-C2
Dowson Road	B1
Dunkinfield Road	A3-A4
Edna Street	A1-B1
Fleet Street	C3-C4
Furnace Street	A4
Gair Street	A4
Grafton Street	A3-B3
Great Norbury Street	A3-A4-A1-B1
Greenfield Street	A2-B2
Haughton Street	B1-C1
Henry Street	B1
Higher Henry Street	B1
Holme Street	C3
Hoviley Street	C3
Hyde By-pass	A3-B3-C3
John Street	B2-B3
Lewis Street	C2-C3
Lodge Lane	B4
Lumn Road	C1-C2
Manchester Road	A3
Mansfield Road	C1
Market Place	B2
Market Street	B3-B2-B1-C1
Mary Street	A3
Mona Street	B1-C1
Mottram Road	C2
Nelson Street	B1-C1-C2
Newton Street	A3-A4
Norfolk Street	B1-B2
Oldham Street	B3
Orchard Street	C2
Park Drive	B4
Park Road	B3-B4
Peel Street	C1
Perrin Street	B1-B2
Queen Street	C1
Raglan Street	A2
Railway Street	A1-A2
Ridling Lane	B2-C2
Repton Avenue	C3-C4
St Pauls Street	C3-C4
Spring Gardens	A4
Syddal Street	B1
Tanner Street	B3
The Mall	B2
Throstle Bank	A4
Tom Shepley Street	C2
Travis Street	B2-C2
Union Street	C4
Victoria Street	C1-C2
Walker Street	B2-C2
Ward Street	B2-C2
Water Street	A3-A2-B2

Well Meadow	A4
Woodend Lane	A1-B1

GLOSSOP

Arundel Street	B3
Ashleigh Avenue	A4-B4-C4
Ashton Street	B1
Bernard Street	B3
Chapel Street	B3
Charles Street	C3-C4
Charlestown Road	B1
Derby Street	B2-C2
Dinting Road	A4
Duke Street	B1-B2
Ebenezer Street	C1
Edward Street	B3
Ellison Street	C3
Fauvel Road	B4-C4
Fitzalan Street	C4
Freetown	B1-C1
George Street	B2-B3
Gladstone Street	B2-C2-C1
Hadfield Place	B1-B2
Hadfield Road	B1-B2
Henry Street	B3-C3
High Street East	C3
High Street West	A3-B3-C3
Highfield Road	B3
Hollins Cross	A1-B1
Howard Street	B4-B3-C3
James Street	B1
John Street	C3
Kershaw Street	B1-C1-C2
King Street	C2
King Edward Avenue	C3-C4
Lord Street	C4
Market Street	B2-B3
Mount Street	B2
Norfolk Street	C3-C4
North Road	B4
Philip Howard Road	B2
Pike's Lane	A1-A2
Primrose Lane	A1-A2
Princess Street	A2-B2
Queen Street	C4
Royle Avenue	C4
St Mary's Road	B2-B3
Shaw Street	A2-B2
Simmondley New Road	A1
Slatelands Road	A1
Shrewsbury Street	B3-B4
Spire Hollin	B4
Sumner Street	A2-B2
Sunlaws Street	A2-A3
Surrey Street	A4-B4-B3
Talbot Street	B3-C3-C4
Tredcroft Street	A2-B2
Turnlee Road	A1-B1
Union Street	C2
Unity Street	B1-C1
Uplands Road	C1
Victoria Street	B2-C2-C3
Whitfield Avenue	B1-C1
Whitfield Cross	C1
Wood Street	B1-C1-C2

Preston

The decline of the cotton trade after World War I hit Preston badly: this was one of the most important centres in the 19th century.
But today the town is once again an important industrial centre, and one which is well-served by the motorway network.

By way of contrast, Preston also offers a generous number of parks and open spaces, and the River Ribble offers pleasant riverside walks. It has an impressive Market Square, where the neo-classical Harris Museum and Art Gallery houses an extensive collection of decorative and fine art, and displays on social history and archaeology can also be seen here.

Leyland was transformed by the setting up in 1892 of Leyland Motors, which later became Leyland Vehicles. Less well known is the town's restored 16th-century grammar school, now the home of the Museum and Exhibition Centre. Another attractive feature is Worden Park, which offers 160 acres of natural beauty and is also the venue of the Leyland Festival.

Chorley Fast expanding Chorley was once a major cotton centre and it's still a flourishing industrial town, although now its interests are more widely based. Close to the centre the wooded park and 16th-century house of Astley Hall are situated.

LEGEND

Town Plan

- AA Recommended roads
- Other roads
- Restricted roads
- Buildings of interest   Station
- Churches   +
- Car parks   P
- Parks and open spaces
- One way streets

Area Plan

- A roads
- B roads
- Locations   Warehorne ○
- Urban area

STREET INDEX
Preston

Adelaide Street	F2
Adelphi Street	B4-B3
Albyn Street	F1-F2
Arthur Street	A2-B2
Aspden Street	F3-F2
Astley Street	D4
Avenham Lane	D1-E1
Avenham Road	C1-D1
Avenham Street	D2-D1
Bairstow Street	C1
Bentinck Street	A3-A4
Birley Street	C2-D2
Bleasdale Street East	F4
Bolton's Court	D2-D1
Bow Lane	A2-A1
Brixton Road	F1
Brook Street	A4-B4
Butler Street	B1
Campbell Street	F3
Cannon Street	C2-C1
Carlisle Street	D3
Catherine Street	F3
Chaddock Street	C1
Chapel Street	C1
Christ Church Street	A1
Christian Road	B1
Church Row	D2
Church Street	D2-E2
Cobden Street	A4
Coronation Crescent	F1
Corporation Street	B3-B2-B1
Cragg's Row	C4
Croft Street	A3-A2
Crook Street	F3
Cross Street	C1-D1
Crown Street	C4
Curwen Street	F4
Deepdale Mill Street	F4
Deepdale Road	E4-E3
Derby Street	D3-D2
East Street	D3-E3
East View	E4-E3
Edward Street	B2-B3

Egan Street	D4-D3
Elizabeth Street	C3
Euston Street	A2-A1
Fishergate	B1-C1-C2
Fishergate Hill	A1
Fisher Street	F3-F4
Fitzroy Street	A2-A1
Fleet Street	B2-C2
Fletcher Road	E3-E4-F4
Fox Street	C2-C1
Friargate	B3-B2-C2-C3
Fylde Road	A4-B4
Fylde Street	B3
Garden Street	B1-C1
George Street	F1
Glover's Court	C2-C1
Glover Street	D1
Great Georges Street	C4-D4
Great Shaw Street	B3-C3
Greenbank Street	A4
Grimshaw Street	D2-E2-E1
Guildhall Street	C2-C1
Harrington Street	B4
Hartington Road	A1
Hawkins Street	A4
Heatley Street	B2
Holstien Street	E4-E3
Hope Street	B3
James Street	F1
Jutland Street	D3-E3
Kent Street	D4
Ladyman Street	A2-A1
Ladywell Street	B3
Langton Street	A1
Lancaster Road South	A1
Larkhill Road	E1
Larkhill Street	E1-F1
Laurel Street	D2-D1
Lawson Street	C4-C3
Leighton Street	A3-A2
Livesley Street	F1
Lodge Street	A2
London Road	F2-F1
Lord Street	D2
Lune Street	C2
Manchester Road	D2-E2-E1
Market Street	C2
Market Street West	C3
Marsh Lane	A2-B2-B3
Maudland Bank	A4-A3
Maudland Road	A3-B3
Meadow Street	D3-D4-E4
Miller Street	F2
Moor Lane	B3-B4-C4
Moore Street	C1
Mount Street	C1
New Hall Lane	F2-F3
North Road	C4-D4-D3
North Street	C3
Oak Street	D1-E1
Old Vicarage	D3
Orchard Street	C2
Ormskirk Road	C3-D3
Oxford Street	D1
Peel Hall Street	E4
Peel Street West	A4
Pedder Street	A3
Percy Street	D2-E2-E3
Pitt Street	A2-B2-B1
Plevna Road	F3
Pole Street	D3-D2
Primrose Hill	D2-F2
Pump Street	D3

Queen Street	E1-E2-F2
Ribble Bank Street	A2-A1
Ribbleton Lane	E3-F3-F4
Ribbleton Street	E3
Ringway	B2-C2-C3-D3-E3
River Street	A1-A2
Roman Road	F1
Rose Street	D2
St Austin's Road	D1-E1
St Ignatius Square	D4-D3
St Mary's Street	F3-F2
St Mary's Street North	E3
St Paul's Road	D4-D3
St Paul's Square	D3-E3
St Peter's Square	B3
St Peter's Street	B4
Salmon Street	F1-F2
Savoy Street	A2
Sedgwick Street	C4-D4
Selbourne Street	E1-F1
Shepherd Street	D1-D2
Silver Street	E1
Sizer Street	B4
Slade Street	A2
Snow Street	C3
Spritwield	C2-D2-C1-D1
Stanleyfield Road	D4-E4
Stanley Place	A1
Stanley Street	E2-F2
Stoney Gate	D2-D1
Syke Street	C1-D1
Swan Street	F4-F3
Theatre Street	B1
Thomas Street	F1
Tiber Street	E1
Tithebarn Street	D3-D2
Trout Street	F1
Tuson Street	A3-A2
Victoria Street	A4-B4
Walburges	A4-A3
Walker Street	B3-C3
Waltons Parade	A1
Warwick Street	B4-B3-C3
Wilfred Street	B2-C2
Winckley Square	C1
Winckley Street	C1

Leyland

Balcarres Road	B2-C2-C3
Balshaw Road	A4-B4
Bannister Drive	A3-A4
Beech Avenue	B1-B2
Borrowdale Road	C2
Broadfield Drive	B2-A2-A3-A4
Broadfield Walk	A2-A3
Broadway	C2
Brownhill Road	A3
Canberra Road	C2-C3
Carlton Road	B3
Cedarwood Drive	A2
Chapel Brow	C3-C4
Churchill Way	C2
Church Road	B2-C2
Clifton Avenue	C2
Crawford Avenue	C2
Cumberland Avenue	A1
Dalehead Road	B1-C1
Denford Avenue	C2
East Street	C3
Eden Street	B2
Ennerdale Close	B1-C1
Fox Lane	A2-B2

Golden Hill Lane	A4-B4-C4
Gorsewood Road	A3
Goulding Avenue	C3
Haig Avenue	A3-B3
Hall Lane	B4
Hastings Road	C4
Headley Road	A3
Hillbrook Road	A4-B4
Hough Lane	B3-C3
King Street	B3
Kingsway	A1
Lancaster Gate	B2
Larchwood Crescent	A3
Lindsey Avenue	C3
Mead Avenue	C2
Moss Lane	C1
Nelson Avenue	C3
Newsome Street	B2
Northbrook Road	A3-A4
Northgate	A1
Parkgate Drive	A1-A2
Park Road	B1
Preston Road	C4
Quin Street	B3
Regent Road	B3
Royal Avenue	A1-A2
Sandy Lane	B2-C2
School Lane	B3-B4
Southbrook Road	A3
Spring Gardens	B2
Tomlinson Road	A3
Towngate	B1-B2-B3
Turpin Green Lane	C3
Vevey Street	B3
Vicarsfield Road	B1-C1
Westfield Drive	A3
Westgate	B2-B3
West Paddock	A2
Whelton Lane	B4
Winsor Avenue	C2
Wood Green	A4
Woodlands Drive	A3-B3
Woodlea	A2
Worden Lane	B1
Wyrsdale Drive	C1
Yewlands Avenue	B3

Chorley

Albert Street	B3-C3
Alker Street	A2
Anderton Street	B2-C2
Ashby Street	B1-C1
Ashfield Road	A2-A3
Avondale Road	A2-B2
Bengal Street	B4
Bolton Road	B2-B1-C1
Bowland Avenue	C3-C4
Brierchiffe Road	C4
Brindle Street	B1
Brooke Street	C2
Brock Road	B4-C4
Brown Street	C3
Burlington Street	B2-B2
Carrington Road	A2-B2
Chapel Street	B3-C3
Charnock Street	C2
Cheam Avenue	C1
Chelmsford Place	A2
Church Brow	B4
Claremont Avenue	A1-A2
Clarence Street	C2
Clifford Street	B4-B3-C3

Colliery Street	B1-B2
Collison Avenue	A3
Cranbourne Grove	C1-C2
Crown Street	A3
Cuncliffe Street	B2-C2
Devonshire Road	A1-A2-A3
Duke Street	B1
Fellery Street	B3-B4
Fleet Street	B2
Friday Street	C3-C4
George Street	B2-C2
Gillibrand Street	A3-A2-B2
Gillibrand Walk	A1-A2-B2
Goulding Street	C1
Grime Street	C1
Halliwell Street	B3
Hamilton Road	A3-A2-B2
Harington Road	A3-A4
Highfield Road	B4
High Street	B3
Hill Street	B3
Hindley Street	A1
Hollinshead	B4
Isleworth Drive	A2
Jackson Street	B1-C1
Kensington Road	A3
King Street	B1-C1
Lawrence Road	A2
Leigh Street	B2
Letchworth Drive	A1
Lyons Lane	C2
Lyons Lane South	B1-C1-C2
Market Street	B2-B3
Maud Street	A1
Mayfield Road	C4
Nelson Road	A2
New Market Street	B3
Pall Mall	A1-B1-B2
Parker Street	B4
Park Road	B4
Parkside Avenue	A3-A4
Poplar Street	C1
Primrose Street	C4
Princess Street	C1
Queens Road	A3-B3-B4
Queen Street	C1
Railway Street	C2-C3
Rawcliffe Road	A1-A2-B2-B1
Regent Road	A2-A3
Rotherwick Avenue	A2
Russell Square West	C4
Rydal Place	A1
Rylands Road	A2
St George's Street	B3
St Peter Street	A3-B3
St Thomas's Road	A3-B3
Seymour Street	C3
Shaftesbury Place	A3
South Avenue	C1
Spring Road	A3
Standish Street	B2-C2
Steeley Lane	C2-C3
Stratford Road	C4
Stump Lane	B4-C4
Townley Street	C2
Union Street	B3
Ventnor Place	A1
Victoria Street	B2-B3
Walgarth Drive	A2
Water Street	B4
Westbourne Road	A1
West Street	A3-B3
Windsor Road	A3

Rotherham

Evidence of Rotherham's industry goes back at least as far as the Romans, whose ironworking artefacts have been found here. They were followed by a group of 12th-century monks who established a mining site, and in the 18th century came the beginnings of Rotherham as a major industrial centre with iron smelting on a large scale. Today this is a pleasant town with broad, largely 19th- and 20th-century streets, and offering a pleasant blend of architectural styles. Outstanding in both senses is the large, Norman Perpendicular Church of All Saints with its majestic spire and interior, and another cause for pride is the medieval chapel on Rotherham Bridge. Typical of its time, this is now one of only three perfect examples surviving in the country.

Swinton Rich coal seams beneath the town are chiefly responsible for modern Swinton, but its name is more widely associated with Rockingham pottery which is much sought-after today. Just one kiln from the original pottery remains, and can be seen off the A633 Swinton to High Haugh road.

Maltby's coalfields only began to be worked about half a century ago, and more recent developments give it the feel of a bright modern town. But a pre-coal, pre-industrial Maltby still exists, and can be reached by steps and steep slopes from the main centre.

Central Swinton

Central Maltby

LEGEND

Town Plan
AA Recommended roads	
Other roads	
Restricted roads	
Buildings of interest	Station
Car Parks	P
Parks and open spaces	
One Way Streets	→

Area Plan
A roads	
B roads	
Locations	Nutwell O
Urban area	

Street Index with Grid Reference

Central Rotherham

Albany Road	E1-F1
Albert Street	B1-B2
Albion Road	E1
Bedes Road	B1-B2
Bridge Street	C2-D2
Bridgegate	D2
Brinsworth Street	B1
Carlisle Street	E2-E3
Central Road	C1-C2
Clifton Lane	E2-F2-F1
Clifton Mount	E1-F1
Clifton Terrace	E1
Clough Road	A2, A3-A4-B4
Clough Street	A3-B3
College Road	A2-B2-C2
College Street	D2
Coronation Bridge	A1-A2
Corporation Street	D1-D2
Cottenham Road	F3-F4
Denham Street	F4
Doncaster Road	D2-E2-F2-F3
Douglas Street	D1-E1
Drummond Street	D3-E3-E2
Effingham Street	D2, E3-E4

Fitzwilliam Road	E3-E4-F4
Frederick Street	D2-D3
Garden Street	A2-A3
Greasbrough Road	C4-D4-D3
Greasbrough Street	C3-C4
Grosvenor Road	F4
Hatherley Road	E4-F4
High Street	D1-D2
Holmes Lane	A1
Howard Street	D2-E2-D2
James Street	B2-B3
Lindley Street	E4-F4
Main Street	B1-C1-D1
Mansfield Road	D1-E1
Market Street	D1-D2
Masborough Street	A1-B1
Midland Road	A2
Mill Moor Lane	A1-B1
Milton Road	F4
Moorgate	D1
Moorgate Street	D1-D2
Morpeth Street	E2
Nelson Street	E2-E3
Nottingham Street	E3
Park Street	A3
Percy Street	E2
Princes Street	A1-A2
Rawmarsh Road	D3-D4
Ridge Road	F3
Roger Street	A4-A3-B3
St Ann's Road	E4-E3-F3-F2
St Leonards Road	E3-F3
Selbourne Street	E4-F4
Ship Hill	D1
Snail Hill	D1-D2
Stanley Street	D1
Station Road	A2-A1-B1
Tenter Street	B3-C3
The Crofts	D1
Union Street	A1-A2
Victoria Street	A2-B2
Walter Street	B3
Wellgate	D2-D1-E1
Wellgate Mount	E1
Westgate	D1
Wharncliffe Street	E2
Wilfred Street	D1
William Street	E1
Winifred Street	B2
York Road	E3-F3-F4

Central Maltby

Alexandra Street	C1
Ash Grove	C4
Bevan Crescent	A4

Blyth Road	B2-B1-C1
Braithwell Road	A3-A4
Burns Street	B2
Byron Road	B2-C2
Carlye Road	B2
Charnwell Avenue	B3-C3
Cheetham Drive	B4
Clarence Place	B4-C4
Cripps Close	C1
Cross Street	B3
Davy Drive	A4-B4
Devonshire Road	B4-B3-C3
Duke Avenue	C1
Dunns Dale	C3
Earl Avenue	B2-B1-C1
Farquhar Road	C2-C3
Firth Crescent	B1-C1
Grange Lane	C3-C4
Hamilton Road	C2
Haslam Place	C4
Hayhurst Crescent	B1
High Street	A2-B2-B3-C3
Highfield Park	C4
Hoyland Street	C2
King Avenue	C1-C2
Lansbury Avenue	C1
Limesway	A3
Lilly Hall Road	A3
Lincoln Street	C2
Little Hay Wooking Lane	A3-A4
Makins Hill	A2-B2
Manor Road	B3-B4
Millindale	B2-B3
Morrell Street	B1-B2-C2
Muglet Lane	C1-C2-C3
Nelson Road	C2
Newland Avenue	A4
Norwood Avenue	A3-A4
Park View	C3-C4
Portland Place	B3
Queen Avenue	B1-C1
Rosston Road	C3
Rotherham Road	A2
Russel Place	B4
Salisbury Road	A4-B4-C4
Scarborough Crescent	B1-B2-C2
Scholfield Crescent	C1
School Walk	A3-B3
Tickhill Road	C2-C3
Victoria Street	B1-C1
Walters Road	C3

Central Swinton

Albert Street	C3-C4
Birkdale Rise	C1

Bolton Road	A3
Bower Road	B4-C4
Bramfield Road	A2
Brookfield Avenue	B1-C1-C2
Broome Avenue	B3
Central Avenue	A1-A2
Charles Street	C2
Charnwood Street	C3
Church Street	A3-A2-B2
Cliffefield Road	C2
Creswell Road	B4
Crossland Street	C2
Duke Street	B3-C3
East Avenue	A1
Edward Street	B3-C3
Fitzwilliam Street	B2-B1-C1
Golden Smithies Lane	A3-A4-B4
Goodwin Crescent	B3-B4
Grange Road	A1
Greno Road	B1
Griffin Road	A2
Hatherley Road	B4-C4
Highcliffe Drive	C2-C3
Highfield Road	A2
Hoylake Drive	C1
Landsdowne Crescent	C1
Lime Grove	C1-C2
Manor Road	B1-B2-C2
Marys Crescent	B3
Milton Road	B2
Muirfield Avenue	C1
North Street	C2-C3
Park Road	A1-A2
Picadilly Road	B1
Queen Street	B2-B3-C3-C4
Queens Avenue	C3-C4
Racecourse Road	A2-A3
Rookery Road	A1-A2
St Georges Avenue	A3
St Johns Road	B2-B3
St Michaels Avenue	B4-C4
Sidney Street	C2-C3
Slade Road	B2
South Avenue	A1
Station Street	B2-C2
Storey Street	B3
Temporence Street	B2-C2
The Croft	A1
Thomas Street	B3-B4-C4
Toll Bar Road	A2
Valley Road	A1
Wood Street	C2

ROTHERHAM
Begun in 1483 and used after the Reformation as an almshouse, town prison, plague isolation hospital and tobacconist's shop, the Chapel of Our Lady on Chantry Bridge was restored and rededicated in 1924.

St Helens

Pilkington Glass have been manufacturing glassware here for over 150 years, and today there is a fascinating museum attached to the company's Prescot Road works. A town of fine sporting facilities, St Helens also offers the attractions of its noted Rugby League team and of horse racing at Haydock Park Racecourse, which lies to the north-east of the town.

Wigan is known to millions through George Orwell's book *The Road to Wigan Pier*, but has seen radical changes in recent years. Not least of these has been the development of the area around the Leeds and Liverpool Canal, where the original pier, or wharf, is being turned into a Leisure and Recreation Centre. Several old warehouses have been renovated and a working mill engine is on display, while providing visitors with food and drink is a new pub — the Orwell.

Skelmersdale's once-important coal mining has declined in recent years, but the establishment in the 1960s of a New Town offering all the appropriate facilities has helped to attract new industries. A history dating back to the Romans can be traced here.

Leigh stands on the Leeds and Liverpool Canal. Familiar to Rugby enthusiasts for its Rugby League team, it's also popular with anglers and sailors for 1,000-acre Pennington Flash Country Park.

LEGEND

Town Plan

AA recommended route
Restricted roads
Other roads
Buildings of interest   Station ▣
Car parks   Ⓟ
Parks and open spaces ▢
One way streets →

Area Plan

A roads
B roads
Locations   West Toppings○
Urban area ▢

Street index with Grid Reference

St Helens

Alfred Street	C3-C4
Argyle Street	A4
Baldwin Street	A2-A3
Barrow Street	B2
Bickerstaffe Street	B2-C2
Birchley Street	B2
Bridge Street	A1-B1-B2
Brynn Street	B3-B4-C4
Canal Street	A1
Cansfield Street	B3-C3
Central Street	B3-C4
Chalon Way	A1-B1-C1
Chapel Street	A4
Charles Street	C2-C3-C4
Church Square	B1
Church Street	B2-B1-C1
Claughton Street	A3-B3-B2
Clifton Street	B4-C4-C3
College Street	A3-B3-B4
Corporation Street	B2-C2
Cotham Street	B2
Crab Street	A4-B4
Duke Street	A3-B3
George Street	C1-C2
Gleave Street	A4
Halefield Street	C1-C2-C3
Hall Street	C1-C2-C3
Hardshaw Street	B2-B3-C3-C4
Henry Street	A3
Hospital Street	C4
King Street	A2-A3
Lagrange Arcade	B1
Liverpool Road	A1
Mill Street	A3-A4
New Cross Street	A3-A4
North Road	A3-A4
Ormskirk Street	A3-A2-B2
Parade Street	B3-B2-C2
Rigby Street	A3

St Mary's Arcade	B1-C1
Shaw Street	C1-C2-C3
Standish Street	C4
Stanhope Street	A4
Tolver Street	B3-C3-C2
Vincent Street	B2-C2-C3-C4
Volunteer Street	A3
Ward Street	A4-B4-B3
Waterloo Street	A1-A2-B2
Water Street	A1-B2
Westfield Street	A2
Woodville Street	C3-C4

Wigan

Acton Street	C4
Appleton Street	A2
Arcade Street	C1
Ascroft Street	E1-E2
Baldwin Street	E3
Bankes Street	D2-E2
Baron Street	E4
Birkett Bank	F2
Birkett Street	F2-F3
Bishop Gate	B2
Bolton Street	E4
Brideman Terrace	B4
Brookhouse Street	D1-D2
Brown Street	B1-B2
Butler Street	D3
Cambridge Street	E2
Caroline Street	B1
Catherine Terrace	B1
Caunce Road	E4-E3-F3-F4
Cecil Street	F3
Chapel Lane	C1
Chapel Street	B1-C1
Chat Street	F2
Clarington Grove	F1-F2
Clayton Street	A2-B2
Coop Street	E4
Crompton Street	C3
Crook Street	A3
Darlington Street	C1-D1-E1-E2-F2
Dawber Street	A3-A2-B2
Dean Street	E2
Derby Terrace	D3
Dicconson Street	B4-C4
Dicconson Terrace	C4
Dorning Street	B2-B3
Durham Street	F4
Essex Street	E4
Florence Street	F3
Frog Lane	A3-B3
Gidlow Lane	A1
Gilroy Street	E3
Gordon Street	F2
Great George Street	A2-B2-B1
Greenough Street	D4-D3-E3
Haig Street	B3
Hallgate	B2-B3
Hardy Butts	D2-E2-F2
Harper Street	E2-F2
Harrogate Street	C2-D2-D1
Henry Park Street	F1-F2
Herbert Street	A3
Hey Street	A3
Hill Street	A4
Hilton Street	C4-D4
Hodson Street	B1
Hope Street	B4-B3-B2
Hunt Street	E2

Ivy Street	A2-A3
Johnson Street	E1
Kearsley Street	A4
Kendal Street	A3-A4
Kent Street	E1
King Street	C1-C2
King Street West	B2
Kirkless Street	F2-F3
Land Street	A3
Leader Street	F3
Leeds Street	A1-A2
Leigh Street	E1-E2
Library Street	C2
Lime Street	D3
Lorne Street	E3-F3
Lyon Street	B1-B2
Market Place	C2-C3
Market Street	B3-C3-C2
Markland Street	F2
Marton Street	C4
Mason Street	A1
Mesnes Street	B4-C4-C3
Millgate	C2-D2
Mill Meadow	D1-D2
Mill Street	B1-B2
Miry Lane	A1
Morris Street	D3
New Market Street	B3-B4
Northumberland Street	F4
Orchard Street	D3
Orrell Street	D1
Parsons Walk	A4-B4-B3
Peppermill Lane	D1
Pitt Street	B1
Platt Lane	A4
Prescott Street	A2-A3
Princess Street	B1-C1
Pottery Road	A1-B1
Powell Street	C4
Queen Street	B1-C1
Richmond Street	B3
River Way	D2-C2-C3-C4-D4
Rodney Street	C2
Rupert Street	E2
Scholes	D2-D3-E3-E4
Scholefield Lane	E3-E2-F2
School Lane	D2-D3
School Street	D3-D4
Scott Street	A3-A4
Sharp Street	A1
Silver Street	D2-E2
Soverign Road	D1
Spring Street	D2-E2-E1
Standishgate	C2-C3
Station Road	C2-C3
Sullivan Way	D4-E4
Swann Street	A1-A2
Taylor Street	A2
Teck Street	E2
Tic Street	A1
Turner Street	D4
Upper Dicconson Street	E2-E3
Vauxhall Road	E2-E3
Wallgate	A1-B1-B2-C2
Warrington Lane	D2-D1-E1
Water Street	C3-C4
Watkin Street	C3
Wellington Street	D3-D2-E2
Wells Place	F4
Wiend	C2
Windermere Street	E4-F4
Windmill Close	D3
Woodcock Street	B3-C3

Wray Street	F2-F3
York Street	A2

Skelmersdale

Abbeystead	C1
Abbeywood	C1
Berry Street	A3
Birch Green Road	B4-C4
Church Road	A2-A3
Daniels Lane	C1-C2
Digmoor Road	C2
Elmers Green	C4
Elswick	C3
Eskbrook	C3
Eskbank	C2-C3
Eskdale	C2-C3
Findon	B4-C4
Firbeck	B3-C3-C4
Flamstead	C3-C4
Flaxton	C4
Flimby	C4
Flordon	C4
Garnett Place	B1
Gillibrands Road	A2-A1-B1-C1
Glebe Road	B1-B2
Glenburn Road	A1-B1-B2-A2-A3-A4
Greenhey Place	A2
Greetby Place	B1-B2
Grimrod Place	B1-B2
Grimshaw Road	B2-C2
Harsnips	C4
Hartshead	C4
Heathbrook	B4-C4
Helmsdale	C4
Heversham	C4
High Street	A2
Houghtons Road	A4-B4
Inglewhite	A4-B4
Inskip	A4-B4
Irwell	A4-B4
Ivydale	B4
Mill Lane	A3
Northway	B4-B3-C3
Ormskirk Road	C2
Railway Road	A1-A2
Southway	B2-B3-C3
Spencers Lane	C1-C2
Tanfields	A3
Tanhouse Road	C2-C3
Tarlswood	A2-A3
Tawd Road	C2
White Ledge Road	B2-C2-C1
White Moss Road	A1
Wigan Road	A2
Willow Hey	A2
Windrows	A2
Yewdale	A3-A2-B2-B3

Leigh

Abbey Street	B3
Albion Street	B1-B2
Arthur Street	A1
Bengal Street	A2-B2
Bold Street	B2-C2-C3
Bond Street	B2-C2
Boughey Street	B4
Boydell Street	A2
Bradshawgate	B2-C2
Brakley Street	B1
Brookfield Street	C4

Brown Street	C1-C2
Brunswick Street	C1
Canal Street	A1
Catherine Street	B4-C4
Chadwick Street	A4-B4
Chapel Street	C1
Charles Street	C2-C3-C4
Chester Street	B3-C3
Church Street	B2-C2
Coniston Street	A2-A3
Cook Street	A1-B1-B2
Coral Grove	A1
Derby Street	B1-C1
Diamond Street	A1
Dorothy Grove	A1
Earl Street	C1-C2
Ellesmere Street	B1-B2
Etherstone	A1
Eyet Street	A2-A3
Fairhurst Street	A2
Farnham Close	B3-B4-C4-B4
Gas Streets	B2-C2-C1
Glebe Street	A3-A4
Gordon Street	A3-B3-B4
Hanover Street	C3-C4
Henrietta Street	B3-C3-C2
Henry Street	C1
High Street	C1-C2
Holden Road	B3-C3
Hope Street	B2-B3-B4
Irvine Street	B3
King Street	B1-B2
Langdale Street	A2-A3
Ledbury Street	B4
Leigh Road	B2-B3-B4
Lilford Street	A1
Lord Street	B2-C2
Market Street	B2
Mather Lane	C1
Milton Street	A2
Opal Grove	A1
Organ Street	A2
Oxford Street	B3-B4
Peel Street	A3
Platfold Street	C2-C3
Platt Street	B3
Poets Nook	A1
Prescott Street	A3-B3
Princess Street	C2
Railway Road	A2-B2
Ramsey Street	C1
Reeves Street	B4
Romford Avenue	C4
Ruby Grove	A1
Rydal Street	A1-A2
St Helens Road	A1-B1
Sefton Street	B3
Selwyn Street	B3-B4
Silk Street	B2
Smithy Street	A1-B1
Stringer Street	A2-B2
The Avenue	B3-C3-C4
Thirlmere Street	A2
Twist Lane	A2-A1-B1
Ulleswater Street	A4
Union Street	B2-B3
Vernon Street	B2-C3
Victoria Street	A4
Walmesley Road	A3-A2-B2
West Bridgewater Street	A1-B1
Wilkinson Street	A1-A2
Windermere Road	A3-B3

61

Central Swinton

Central Salford

Central Eccles

Key to Town Plan and Area Plan

Town Plan

AA Recommended roads
Other roads
Restricted roads
Buildings of interest
Car Parks   P
Parks and open spaces
One Way Streets

Area Plan

A roads
B roads
Locations   Kenyon ○
Urban area

Street Index with Grid Reference

Salford

Adelphi Street	B2-B3
Arlington Street	B3-B4
Atherton Street	C1
Bank Place	B3
Bank Street	B3
Barrow Street	B2
Blackburn Street	B4
Blackfriars Road	C3-C4
Bloom Street	C3
Brewery Street	B3-C3
Bridge Water Street	C4
Briggs Street	B3-B4-C4
Bury Street	C3
Calder Street	B1
Cannon Street	B3-B4-C4
Chapel Street	B2-C2-C3
Cleminson Street	B3-C3
Clowes Street	B4-C4
Cook Street	C3
Coronation Street	A1
Corporation Street	B3
Duncan Street	A1
East Market Street	C3
East Ordsall Lane	B1-B2-C2
Flax Street	B4
Frederick Street	C3
George Street	B2
Gore Street	C2
Grape Street	C1
Graythorn Street	B2
Great George Street	B3
Greengate	C4
Hampson Street	B1-B2
Hardman Street	C2
Hope Street	A2-B2
Hulme Street	A2-B2
Irwell Street	C2
Islington Street	B2
James Street	B2
King Street	C3
Liam Street	C3
Liverpool Road	C1
Liverpool Street	A1-A2

Salford

Salford exploded into phenomenal growth with the Industrial Revolution — it was one of the fastest expanding places in the country, with vast areas of mills and poor quality housing. Much of this old Salford has disappeared, and the city now offers an interesting and lively blend of the industrial, commercial, rural and even maritime. It also boasts a fine university, and has been recorded for posterity in the paintings of L. S. Lowry, who knew it well. The Museum and Art Gallery has a collection of his work, and also of interest here is a Victorian street reconstruction. The Museum of Mining has two reproduction coalmines, and recalling a far older Salford is timber-framed Ordsall Hall's museum.

Swinton is said to owe its name to the unglamourous occupation of rearing pigs, but its more recent background is coal. An industrial area and residential district of Manchester, it has its own Civic Centre and a shopping precinct flanked by the attractive Victorian church of St Peter.

Eccles cakes first came from a shop in Church Street, where they are still being made to the original recipe. A busy area squeezed between the Manchester Ship Canal and the M62, this was once a group of medieval villages. Monk's Hall is Tudor and houses a museum. The Church of St Mary the Virgin dates from the 12th century.

62

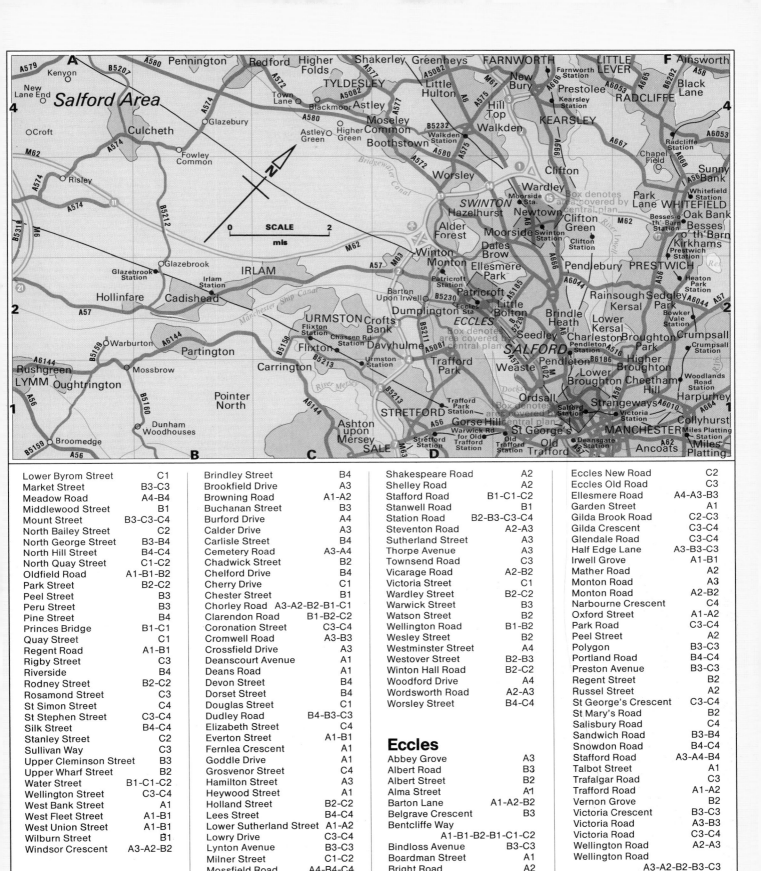

Lower Byrom Street	C1	Brindley Street	B4	Shakespeare Road	A2	Eccles New Road	C2
Market Street	B3-C3	Brookfield Drive	A3	Shelley Road	A2	Eccles Old Road	C3
Meadow Road	A4-B4	Browning Road	A1-A2	Stafford Road	B1-C1-C2	Ellesmere Road	A4-A3-B3
Middlewood Street	B1	Buchanan Street	B3	Stanwell Road	B1	Garden Street	A1
Mount Street	B3-C3-C4	Burford Drive	A4	Station Road	B2-B3-C3-C4	Gilda Brook Road	C2-C3
North Bailey Street	C2	Calder Drive	A3	Steventon Road	A2-A3	Gilda Crescent	C3-C4
North George Street	B3-B4	Carlisle Street	B4	Sutherland Street	A3	Glendale Road	C3-C4
North Hill Street	B4-C4	Cemetery Road	A3-A4	Thorpe Avenue	A3	Half Edge Lane	A3-B3-C3
North Quay Street	C1-C2	Chadwick Street	B2	Townsend Road	C3	Irwell Grove	A1-B1
Oldfield Road	A1-B1-B2	Chelford Drive	B4	Vicarage Road	A2-B2	Mather Road	A2
Park Street	B2-C2	Cherry Drive	C1	Victoria Street	C1	Monton Road	A3
Peel Street	B3	Chester Street	B1	Wardley Street	B2-C2	Monton Road	A2-B2
Peru Street	B3	Chorley Road	A3-A2-B2-B1-C1	Warwick Street	B3	Narbourne Crescent	C4
Pine Street	B4	Clarendon Road	B1-B2-C2	Watson Street	B2	Oxford Street	A1-A2
Princes Bridge	B1-C1	Coronation Street	C3-C4	Wellington Road	B1-B2	Park Road	C3-C4
Quay Street	C1	Cromwell Road	A3-B3	Wesley Street	B2	Peel Street	A2
Regent Road	A1-B1	Crossfield Drive	A3	Westminster Street	A4	Polygon	B3-C3
Rigby Street	C3	Deanscourt Avenue	A1	Westover Street	B2-B3	Portland Road	B4-C4
Riverside	B4	Deans Road	A1	Winton Hall Road	B2-C2	Preston Avenue	B3-C3
Rodney Street	B2-C2	Devon Street	B4	Woodford Drive	A4	Regent Street	B2
Rosamond Street	C3	Dorset Street	B4	Wordsworth Road	A2-A3	Russel Street	A2
St Simon Street	C4	Douglas Street	C1	Worsley Street	B4-C4	St George's Crescent	C3-C4
St Stephen Street	C3-C4	Dudley Road	B4-B3-C3			St Mary's Road	B2
Silk Street	B4-C4	Elizabeth Street	C4			Salisbury Road	C4
Stanley Street	C2	Everton Street	A1-B1	**Eccles**		Sandwich Road	B3-B4
Sullivan Way	C3	Fernlea Crescent	A1	Abbey Grove	A3	Snowdon Road	B4-C4
Upper Cleminson Street	B3	Goddle Drive	A1	Albert Road	B3	Stafford Road	A3-A4-B4
Upper Wharf Street	B2	Grosvenor Street	C4	Albert Street	B2	Talbot Street	A1
Water Street	B1-C1-C2	Hamilton Street	A3	Alma Street	A1	Trafalgar Road	C3
Wellington Street	C3-C4	Heywood Street	A1	Barton Lane	A1-A2-B2	Trafford Road	A1-A2
West Bank Street	A1	Holland Street	B2-C2	Belgrave Crescent	B3	Vernon Grove	B2
West Fleet Street	A1-B1	Lees Street	B4-C4	Bentcliffe Way		Victoria Crescent	B3-C3
West Union Street	A1-B1	Lower Sutherland Street	A1-A2		A1-B1-B2-B1-C1-C2	Victoria Road	A3-B3
Wilburn Street	B1	Lowry Drive	C3-C4	Bindloss Avenue	B3-C3	Victoria Road	C3-C4
Windsor Crescent	A3-A2-B2	Lynton Avenue	B3-C3	Boardman Street	A1	Wellington Road	A2-A3
		Milner Street	C1-C2	Bright Road	A2	Wellington Road	
		Mossfield Road	A4-B4-C4	Cavendish Road	A3-A4		A3-A2-B2-B3-C3
Swinton		New Cross Street	C1	Chadwick Road	A2	Wentworth Road	B4-C4
Abbey Drive	A2-A3-B3	Normanby Street	A3-A4	Chatsworth Road	B4	Westminster Road	A3-A4-B4
Ackworth Road	A4-B4	Partington Lane	A1-B1-B2	Church Road	B2		
Bain Street	B1-C1	Pendlebury Road	C1-C2-C3	Church Street	A2-B2		
Bancroft Road	A4-B4	Priory Road	A3-B3-B2	Clarendon Crescent	B3-B4-B3		
Beech Street	B1-C1	Queensway Lane	C4	Clarendon Road	B3		
Bingham Street	C1	Raymond Street	B3	Corporation Road	A1-A2		
Bolton Road	B1-C1	Rutland Street	B4-C4	Davis Street	A1		
Boundary Road	B3-B2-C2	Rutland Street	A3	Devonshire Road	C2-C3		
Brierley Road	A4-B4	St Peter's Road	A1-A2	Eccles By-pass	A3-A2-B2-C2		
		Sefton Road	B3-B4				

63

Sheffield

Cutlery – which has made the name of Sheffield famous throughout the world – has been manufactured here since at least as early as the time of Chaucer. The god of blacksmiths, Vulcan, is the symbol of the city's industry, and he crowns the town hall, which was opened in 1897 by Queen Victoria. At the centre of the industry, however, is Cutlers' Hall, the headquarters of the Company of Cutlers. This society was founded in 1624 and has the right to grant trade marks to articles of a sufficiently high standard. In the hall is the company's collection of silver, with examples of craftsmanship dating back every year to 1773. A really large collection of cutlery is kept in the city museum. Steel production, a vital component of the industry, was greatly improved when the crucible process was invented here in 1740. At Abbeydale Industrial Hamlet, 3½ miles south-west of the city centre, is a complete restored site open as a museum and showing 18th-century methods of steel production. Sheffield's centre, transformed since World War II, is one of the finest and most modern in Europe. There are no soot-grimed industrial eyesores here, for the city has stringent pollution controls and its buildings are carefully planned and set within excellent landscaping projects. Many parks are set in and around the city, and the Pennines are within easy reach.

LEGEND

Town Plan

AA Recommended roads	
Other roads	
Restricted roads	
Buildings of interest	
One Way Streets	←
Car Parks	P
Parks and open spaces	

Area Plan

A roads	
B roads	
Locations	Oakworth ○
Urban area	

Street Index with grid reference

Sheffield

Street	Grid
Addey Street	A7-A8
Albert Terrace	A8
Alma Street	C7-D7
Andrew Street	E7
Angel Street	D5-D6
Arundel Gate	D4-D5
Arundel Street	C2-D2-D3-D4
Bailey Street	C5
Ball Street	C8
Balm Green	C4-C5
Bank Street	D6
Bard Street	F5
Barker's Pool	C4-C5-D5
Bedford Street	B8
Beet Street	B5
Bernard Street	F4-F5-F6
Blonk Street	E6
Bolsover Street	A5
Boston Street	C1-C2
Bower Street	C7-D7
Bowling Green	C7
Bramall Lane	C1-C2
Bridge Street	D7-D6-E6
Broad Lane	B5-C5-C6
Broad Street	E6.F5-F6
Brocco Street	B6
Brook Hill	A5-B5
Broomhall Place	A2
Broomhall Road	A2
Broomhall Street	A2-A3,B4
Broomspring Lane	A4-B4
Brown Street	D3
Brunswick Street	A3-A4
Brunswick Road	E7-E8
Burgess Street	C4
Cambridge Street	C4
Campo Lane	C5-D5-D6
Carlisle Street	F8
Carver Street	C4-C5
Castle Street	D6-E6
Castlegate	E6
Cavendish Street	B4
Cemetery Road	A1-B1-B2
Charles Street	D3-D4
Charlotte Road	C2-D2-D1-E1
Charter Row	C3-C4
Chatham Street	D5-E5-E6
Church Street	C5-D5
Clarke Street	A3
Cliff Street	B1
Clough Road	C1-D1-D2
Club Garden Road	B1
Collegiate Crescent	A3
Commercial Street	E5
Corporation Street	D6-D7
Countess Road	C2-D2-D1
Cricket Inn Road	F6
Cumberland Way	C3
Daniel Hill	A8
Denby Street	C1
Devonshire Street	B4-C4
Division Street	C4
Duchess Road	D2-E2
Duke Street	F4-F5
Earl Street	C3
Earl Way	C3
East Bank Road	E1-E2
Ecclesall Road	A1-A2-B2
Edmund Road	D1-D2
Edward Street	B6
Effingham Street	F7
Egerton Street	B3
Eldon Street	B4
Ellin Street	C2
Eyre Street	C2-C3-D3-D4
Exchange Street	E6
Fargate	D5
Farm Road	E1-F1
Fitzwilliam Street	B4-B3-C3
Flat Street	E5
Fornham Street	E3
Furnival Gate	C3-C4-D3-D4
Furnival Road	E6-F6-F7
Furnival Street	D3
Garden Street	B6-C6-C5
Gell Street	A4-A5
Gibraltar Street	C7-C6-D6
Glencoe Road	F3-F4
Glossop Road	A4-B4
Granville Road	E2-F2
Granville Street	E3-E4
Green Lane	B8-C8-C7
Hanover Way	A3-B3-B2
Harmer Lane	E4
Hartshead	D6
Harwood Street	C1
Harvest Lane	C8
Hawley Street	C5
Haymarket	E5-E6
Henry Street	B7
Hereford Street	C2
High Street	D5-E5
Hill Street	B1-C1
Hollis Croft	B6-C6
Holly Street	C4-C5
Hounsfield Road	A4-A5
Howard Street	D4-E4
Hoyle Street	B7
Infirmary Road	A8-B8 B7
Jessop Street	C2
John Street	C1-D1
Johnson Street	D7-E7
King Street	D5-E5-E6
Leadmill Road	D2-D3-E3
Leavy Greave Road	C5-C6
Lee Croft	C5-D5
Leopold Street	C4-D4-D5
London Road	C1-B1-B2-C2
Maltravers Street	F6
Mappin Street	B4-B5
Margaret Street	D2
Matilda Street	C3-D3-D2
Matilda Way	C3
Meadow Street	B6-B7
Mitchell Street	A5-A6
Montgomery Terrace Road	A7-B7-B8
Moorfields	C7
Moore Street	B2-B3-C3
Mowbray Street	C8-D8-D7
Napier Street	A1-B1-B2
Neepsend Lane	B8-C8
Netherthorpe Road	A5-A6-B6-B7
Norfolk Park Road	E1-E2-F2
Norfolk Road	F3-F4
Norfolk Row	D5
Norfolk Street	D4-D5
North Church Street	D6
Nottingham Street	E8
Nursery Street	D7-E7-E6
Old Street	F5-F6
Orchard Lane	C5
Oxford Road	A7-A8
Park Grange Road	E1-F1
Park Square	E5-E6-F6-F5
Paternoster Row	D3-D4-E4
Pear Street	A1
Penistone Road	B7-B8
Pinfold Street	C2
Pinstone Street	C4-D4-D5
Pitsmoor Road	D8
Pond Hill	E5
Pond Street	E4-E5
Portobello Street	B5-C5
Priestley Street	D1-E1-E2
Queen Street	C6-D6
Queen's Road	E1-E2
Randall Street	C1
Red Hill	B5-B6
Regent Street	B4-B5
Rock Street	D8
Rockingham Street	B5-C5-C4
Russell Street	C7
Rutland Road	B8
Rye Bank Road	D8
St Mary's Gate	C2
St Mary's Road	C2-D2-E2-E3
St Philip's Road	A6-A7-B7-B8
Savile Street	E7-F7-F8
Scotland Street	B6-C6
Shales Moor	B7-C7
Sheaf Gardens	D2-E2
Sheaf Street	E4-E5
Sheffield Parkway	F6
Shepherd Street	B6-B7-C7
Shoreham Street	D1-D2-D3-E3
Shrewsbury Road	E3-E4-F3-F4
Shude Lane	E5
Shude Hill	E5-E6
Sidney Street	D3
Silver Street	C6
Snig Hill	D6
Solly Street	B5-B6-C6
South Lane	C2
South Street	E4-E5
Spital Hill	E7-E8-F8
Spital Street	E8-F8
Spitalfields	D7-E7
Spring Street	D6-D7
Stanley Street	E7
Suffolk Road	E3
Summerfield Street	A2-A1-B1
Sunny Bank	A2
Surrey Place	D4
Surrey Street	D4-D5
Sussex Street	F7
Sylvester Street	C2-D2
Talbot Place	F4
Talbot Street	F4
Tenter Street	C6
The Moor	C3-C4
Townhead Street	C5
Trippet Lane	C5
Tudor Street	D4-D5
Tudor Way	D5
Union Street	C4-D4
Upper Allen Street	B6
Upper Hanover Street	A3-A4-A5
Upperthorpe Road	A7-A8
Verdon Street	D8-E8
Vicar Lane	C5-D5
Victoria Station Road	E6-E7-F7
Waingate	E6
Walker Street	E7
Washington Road	B1
Watery Street	B7-B8
Wellington Street	B4-C4
West Bar	D6
West Bar Green	C6-D6
West Street	B4-B5-C5
Weston Street	A5-A6
Wheel Hill	E5
Wicker	E6-E7
Wilkinson Street	A4
William Street	A2-A3
York Street	D5-D6
Young Street	B2-C2

Southport

Seven miles of firm beaches and a ¾-mile long pier are just two of the attractions of Southport, which has been a popular resort since the 18th century. The elegant Victorian buildings of Lord Street run parallel with the Promenade, designated a conservation area, and in Lord Street itself, Atkinson Gallery houses a collection of 19th- and 20th-century art. The town also enjoys the distinction of having its own Botanic Gardens, and here the exhibits of the Botanic Gardens Museum include a collection of 18th- and 19th-century china. By way of contrast, Southport also offers the delights of such different areas of interest as the Steam Transport Museum, a model village and a model railway. Also to be seen are the birds and animals of Southport Zoo, which stretches over 1 ½ acres of land.

Formby people were farmers and seafarers right up until the 19th century. Unsuccessful attempts were made then to turn the town into a resort, and the National Trust now controls some 400 acres of the foreshore and sand dunes that lie to the west.

Ormskirk Granted a Royal Charter in 1670, Ormskirk's market has been the focal point of the town ever since. Standing at the junction of two trunk roads, this is still very much a market town, even though it has seen expansion in its industries and its residential areas.

Southport Area

(Map showing Southport Area with locations including Longton, Walmer Bridge, Much Hoole, Hesketh Bank, Becconsall, Tarleton, Bretherton, Croston, Banks, Marshide, Churchtown, High Park, SOUTHPORT, Birkdale, Hillside, Ainsdale, Scarisbrick, Shirdley Hill, Bescar, Mere Brow, Holmeswood, Rufford, Mawdesley, Burscough Bridge, Burscough, Parbold, Newburgh, Ring o' Bells, Pinfold, Halsall, Haskayne, Great Altcar, FORMBY, Downholland Cross, ORMSKIRK, Westhead, Blaguegate, SKELMERSDALE, Stanley Gate, Aughton, Hightown, Ince Blundell, Lydiate, Bickerstaffe, Barrow Nook, Rainford Junction, Rainford, MAGHULL, Blundellsands, Netherton, Melling, Brighton le Sands, Great Crosby, Waddicar, Aintree, KIRKBY, CROSBY, Litherland)

Box denotes area covered by central plan

Key to Town Plan and Area Plan

Town Plan
- AA Recommended roads
- Other roads
- Restricted roads
- Buildings of inter — University
- Car Parks — P
- Parks and open spaces
- One Way Streets

Area Plan
- A roads
- B roads
- Locations — Brasted ○
- Urban area

Street Index with Grid Reference

Southport

Albany Road	D3-D4
Albert Road	D2-D3-E3
Alexandra Road	D1-D2-D3
Allerton Road	F2
Alma Road	A1
Arbour Street	C1
Argyle Road	E3-F3
Arnside Road	C2-D2
Aughton Road	A1-A2
Avondale Road	D3-E3
Bath Street	C3
Beach Road	A2-A3
Belmont Street	A1-A2
Bold Street	C2-C3
Booth Street	C3
Bridge Street	B1
Brocklebank Road	F2
Cambridge Road	F2
Castle Street	C2
Castle Walk	A2
Chapel Street	B2-C2
Chester Avenue	E1-F1
Churchgate	F1
Church Street	C1-C2
Cliff Road	E3
Coastal Road	A3-A4
Coronation Walk	B2-B3
Coudray Road	F2
Court Road	D2-E2
Cross Street	B1
Derby Road	C1
Duke Street	A1-A2-A3
East Street	D1
Eastbank Street	B1-B2
Esplanade	A3-B3
Fearnley Road	A1
Fleetwood Road	E3-F3
Gloucester Road	A1-A2
Gordon Avenue	D3
Gordon Street	C3-D3
Grange Road	E1
Hall Street	C1-D1
Hartwood Road	D1-E1
Hawkshead Street	D1-D2
Hawkside Street	C1-C2
Hesketh Drive	F1-F2
Hesketh Road	F2-F3-F4
Hill Street	C2
Hollybrook Road	A2
Hope Street	D1
Houghton Street	C2-D2
Irton Road	E1
Kensington Road	C1-D1
King Street	A2-B2
Kingsway	B2-B3
Knowsley Road	D3-E3
Lathom Road	D3-E3
Leicester Street	D3
Leyland Road	D4-D3-E3-E2-E1
Linaker Street	B1-C1
London Street	C1-C2
Lord Street	B2-C2-D2
Lord Street West	A2
Lulworth Road	A2
Lyons Road	A1
Manchester Road	D2-D1-E1
Marine Drive	A4-B4-C4-D4-E4-F4
Marine Parade	B4-C4-C3
Market Street	B2
Marlborough Road	C2-D2
Marlborough Street	C2-D2
Melling Road	E1
Morley Road	E1-E2
Mornington Road	C1-C2
Mount Street	D1
Nevill Street	C2-C3
Park Avenue	E1-E2-F2
Park Crescent	E2-F2-F3-E3
Park Road	E1-E2-E3
Park Road West	E3-E4
Part Street	A1-B1
Portland Street	B1-B2
Preston Road	E1
Princes Street	A2-B2
Promenade	B3-C3-D3-D4-E4
Queen's Road	D2-E2
Railway Street	A1-B1
Railway Terrace	A1-B1
Rawlinson Road	E2-F2
Riding Street	B1
Roe Lane	E1-F1
Rookery Road	F1
Rotten Row	A3
St James Street	B1
St Luke's Road	D1
St Paul's Street	A2
Saunders Street	D3
Scarisbrick Avenue	B2-B3
Scarisbrick Street	B2-B3
Seabank Street	C2-C3
Shakespeare Street	A1-B1
South Bank Street	B1
Stanley Street	C3
Sussex Road	C1-D1
Talbot Street	A2-B2
Tulketh Street	B1-B2-C2
Union Street	C2
Upper Aughton Road	A1
Victa Street	C3
Virginia Street	B1-C1
Vulcan Street	C2
Westcliffe Road	A2
West Street	B2-B3-C3
Windsor Road	D1
Wright Street	C2
York Avenue	A1
York Road	A1
Zetland Street	C1-D1

Formby

Abbots Way	C1
Alderson Crescent	B3-B4
Alt Road	C1-C2
Altcar Road	C2
Andrews Lane	A1-A2
Ashcroft Road	B1
Barkfield Avenue	A3-A4
Barkfield Lane	A4
Bill's Lane	B1-C1
Birkey Lane	B1
Brows Lane	A2-B2
Bull Cop	C3
Cable Street	C4
Castle Drive	A1-B1
Chapel Lane	B2-B3
Cheapside	B1
Church Road	C2-C3-B3-B4-C4
College Avenue	A2-A3-A4
Coronation Avenue	B1-C1
Cropton Road	B2
Crossgreen	B2-C2
Crown Close	C1
Davenham Road	B3-C3
Derby Road	A4-B4
Dickinson Road	B1-B2
Ditchfield	C2
Dobbs Drive	C4
Dobbs Gutter	C3
Duke Street	A2-B2
Dukes Way	A2
Elbow Lane	B2
Ennerdale Road	A2
Flaxfield Road	C2-C3
Formby Fields	C1-C2
Formby Lane	C2
Formby Street	A1-A2
Fountains Way	C1
Freshfield Road	A2-A3-A4
Gardener Road	C3
Graburn Road	B4
Granton Close	A2
Halsall Lane	B3-B4
Hampton Road	A1
Kent Road	B1-C1
Kenyon's Lane	C3
Kings Road	A1-A2
Kirklake Road	A2
Liverpool Road	B2-B1-C1
Long Lane	A3-B3
Lonsdale Road	A3-B3
Lytles Close	B2-C2
Michaels Close	A2-A3
Mittens Lane	C3
Old Mill Lane	B4
Old Town Lane	A4-B4
Orms Way	A2-A3
Park Avenue	A1-B1
Park Road	A1-B1
Phillip's Lane	A1-A2-B2
Piercefield Road	B4
Priesthouse Lane	C2-C3
Priory Close	C1
Queen's Road	A1
Raven Meols Lane	A1-B1-C1
Red Gate	C1-C2
Rosemary Lane	A3-B3-B2
Royal Crescent	C1
St George's Road	A4-B4
Sandringham Road	A1
School Lane	B3-C3
Three Tuns Lane	B2-B3
Tyrers Close	B1-B2
Watchyard Lane	C3-C4
Whalley Close	C2
Whitehouse Lane	C3
Wick's Lane	A3
Willow Grove	B4
Windsor Road	B4
York Road	B2-C2

Ormskirk

Abbotsford	C2-C3
Ashcroft Avenue	B4
Aughton Street	A1-A2-B2
Bath Springs	C3
Bridge Avenue	A2-B2
Bridge Street	A2-A1-B1
Brook Lane	A1-B1
Burscough Road	B3-B4-C4
Burscough Street	B2-B3-B4
Calder Avenue	A1
Chapel Street	B1-B2
Church Fields	A3
Church Street	A3-B3-B2
Clucas Gardens	B4
County Road	A3-A4
Derby Street	A3-B3-C3
Dyers Lane	A1
Farrington Drive	B4
Green Lane	A3-A4-B4
Greetby Hill	C3
Hants Lane	A3-B3
Hardacre Street	B3
Jubilee Avenue	B4
Knowsley Road	B1-B2
Leyland Way	B2-B3
Mill Street	C1-C2
Moor Gate	A1-B1-B2
Moor Street	B2
Moss View	B1
Norfield	C2-C3
Owen Avenue	B4
Park Avenue	A2
Park Road	A2-A3
Pennington Avenue	A4-B4
Queen Street	A1-A2
Railway Road	B2-B3
Ravenscroft Avenue	B1
Rosecroft Close	A3
Ruff Lane	B2-B1-C1
Ryburn Road	A1
St Helens Road	B2-B1-C1
Scarisbrick Street	A4-B4
Small Lane	B1
Southport Road	A3-A4
South Terrace	A1
Stanley Street	B2-C2-C3
Station Road	B3
Town End	A1
Vicarage Road	A3
Weldon Drive	C1
West View	B2
Wigan Road	B2-C2
Windmill Avenue	C2
Yew Tree Road	B4-C4

SOUTHPORT
Retreating seas and a growing expanse of sands inspired the creation in the late 19th century of the 86-acre Marine Lake — a boating lake spanned by Princes Park Bridge and flanked by attractive gardens.

Stockport

The cafes, bandstand and open air travelators of the Merseyway Shopping Precinct stand in direct contrast with the narrow cobbled streets that run close to Stockport's old established traditional market, and the lively mixture must have contributed to making the town the popular destination for shoppers that it is today. Standing on the River Mersey, this was once a textile town, and today its good road and rail connections with the rest of the country have helped to keep it busy in its new role as commercial and industrial centre. It has a museum at Vernon Park and professional football is provided by Stockport County, currently in the Fourth Division of the Canon League.

Cheadle Hulme has become a popular place to live, with its good facilities for shopping and for recreation. It can also boast the lovely Bramhall Hall among its places of interest: this black and white half-timbered mansion dates from the 14th century and lies to the south-east in a pleasantly landscaped park.

Hazel Grove is a relatively new name for this settlement. In its old days as a village, it was called simply Bullock Smithy, and only switched to the less earthy Hazel Grove in the mid-19th century. Today it can offer a wide variety of water sports at extensive Torkington Park.

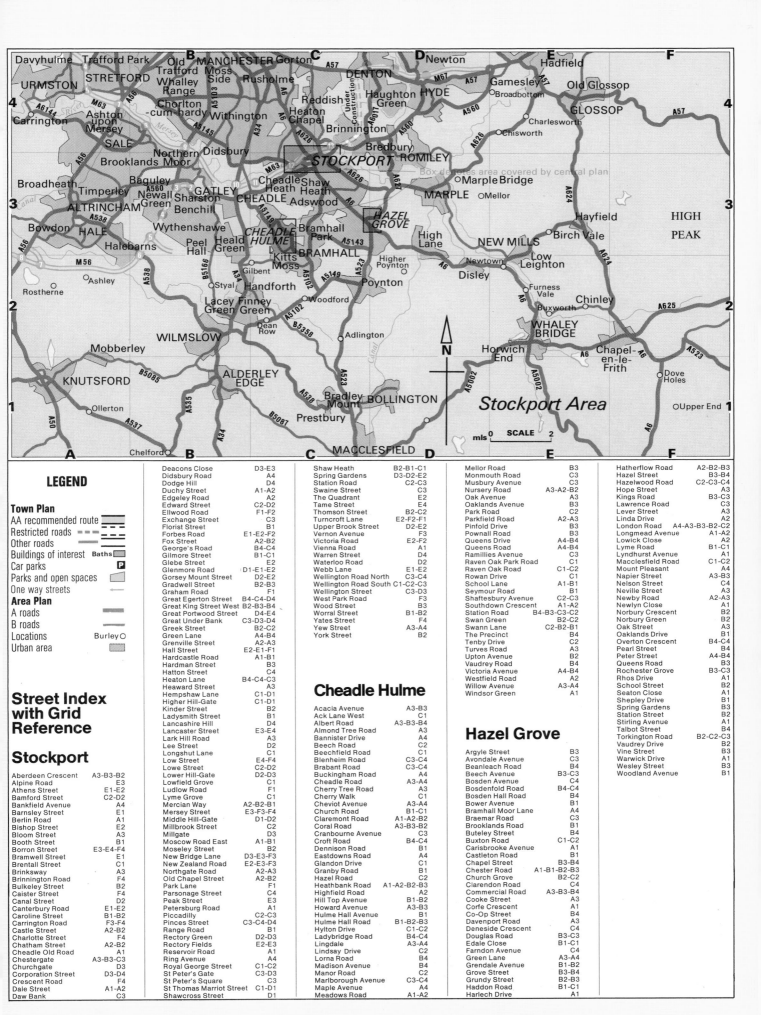

LEGEND

Town Plan

AA recommended route
Restricted roads
Other roads
Buildings of interest — Baths
Car parks — P
Parks and open spaces
One way streets

Area Plan

A roads
B roads
Locations — Burley ○
Urban area

Street Index with Grid Reference

Stockport

Aberdeen Crescent	A3-B3-B2
Alpine Road	E3
Athens Street	E1-E2
Bamford Street	C2-D2
Bankfield Avenue	A4
Barnsley Street	E1
Berlin Road	A1
Bishop Street	E2
Bloom Street	A3
Booth Street	B1
Borron Street	E3-E4-F4
Bramwell Street	E1
Brentall Street	C1
Brinksway	A3
Brinnington Road	F4
Bulkeley Street	B2
Caister Street	F4
Canal Street	D2
Canterbury Road	E1-E2
Caroline Street	B1-B2
Carrington Road	F3-F4
Castle Street	A2-B2
Charlotte Street	F4
Chatham Street	A2-B2
Cheadle Old Road	A1
Chestergate	A3-B3-C3
Churchgate	D3
Corporation Street	D3-D4
Crescent Road	F4
Dale Street	A1-A2
Daw Bank	C3
Deacons Close	D3-E3
Didsbury Road	A4
Dodge Hill	D4
Duchy Street	A1-A2
Edgeley Road	A2
Edward Street	C2-D2
Ellwood Road	F1-F2
Exchange Street	C3
Florist Street	B1
Forbes Road	E1-E2-F2
Fox Street	A2-B2
George's Road	B4-C4
Gilmore Street	B1-C1
Glebe Street	E2
Glenmore Road	D1-E1-E2
Gorsey Mount Street	D2-E2
Gradwell Street	B2-B3
Graham Road	F1
Great Egerton Street	B4-C4-D4
Great King Street West	B2-B3-B4
Great Portwood Street	D4-E4
Great Under Bank	C3-D3-D4
Greek Street	B2-C2
Green Lane	A4-B4
Grenville Street	A2-A3
Hall Street	A1-B1
Hardcastle Road	B3
Hardman Street	B3
Hatton Street	C4
Heaton Lane	B4-C4-C3
Heaward Street	F1
Hempshaw Lane	C1-D1
Higher Hill-Gate	C1-D1
Kinder Street	B2
Ladysmith Street	B1
Lancashire Hill	D4
Lancaster Street	E3-E4
Lark Hill Road	A3
Lee Street	D2
Longshut Lane	C1
Low Street	E4-F4
Lowe Street	C2-D2
Lower Hill-Gate	D2-D3
Lowfield Grove	C1
Ludlow Road	F1
Lyme Grove	C1
Mercian Way	A2-B2-B1
Mersey Street	E3-F3-F4
Middle Hill-Gate	D1-D2
Millbrook Street	C2
Millgate	D3
Moscow Road East	A1-B1
Moseley Street	B2
New Bridge Lane	D3-E3-F3
New Zealand Road	E2-E3-F3
Northgate Road	A2-A3
Old Chapel Street	A2-B2
Park Lane	F1
Parsonage Street	C4
Peak Street	E3
Petersburg Road	A1
Piccadilly	C2-C3
Pinces Street	C3-C4-D4
Range Road	B1
Rectory Green	D2-D3
Rectory Fields	E2-E3
Reservoir Road	A1
Ring Avenue	A4
Royal George Street	C1-C2
St Peter's Gate	C3-D3
St Peter's Square	C3
St Thomas Marriot Street	C1-D1
Shawcross Street	D1

Shaw Heath	B2-B1-C1
Spring Gardens	D3-D2-E2
Station Road	C2-C3
Swaine Street	C3
Tame Street	E4
The Quadrant	E2
Thomson Street	B2-C2
Turncroft Lane	E2-F2-F1
Upper Brook Street	D2-E2
Vernon Avenue	F3
Victoria Road	E2-F2
Vienna Road	A1
Warren Street	D4
Waterloo Road	D2
Webb Lane	E1-E2
Wellington Road North	C3-C4
Wellington Road South	C1-C2-C3
Wellington Street	C3-D3
West Park Road	F3
Wood Street	B3
Worral Street	B1-B2
Yates Street	F4
Yew Street	A3-A4
York Street	B2

Cheadle Hulme

Acacia Avenue	A3-B3
Ack Lane West	C1
Albert Road	A3-B3-B4
Almond Tree Road	A3
Bannister Drive	A4
Beech Road	C2
Beechfield Road	C1
Blenheim Road	C3-C4
Brabant Road	C3-C4
Buckingham Road	A4
Cheadle Road	A3-A4
Cherry Tree Road	A3
Cherry Walk	C1
Cheviot Avenue	A3-A4
Church Road	B1-C1
Claremont Road	A1-A2-B2
Coral Road	A3-B3-B2
Cranbourne Avenue	C3
Croft Road	B4-C4
Dennison Road	B1
Eastdowns Road	A4
Glandon Drive	C1
Granby Road	B1
Hazel Road	C2
Heathbank Road	A1-A2-B2-B3
Highfield Road	A2
Hill Top Avenue	B1-B2
Howard Avenue	A3-B3
Hulme Hall Avenue	B1
Hulme Hall Road	B1-B2-B3
Hylton Drive	C1-C2
Ladybridge Road	B4-C4
Lindale	A3-A4
Lindsay Drive	C2
Lorna Road	B4
Madison Avenue	B4
Manor Road	C2
Marlborough Avenue	C3-C4
Maple Avenue	A4
Meadows Road	A1-A2

Mellor Road	B3
Monmouth Road	C3
Musbury Avenue	C3
Nursery Road	A3-A2-B2
Oak Avenue	A3
Oaklands Avenue	B3
Park Road	C2
Parkfield Road	A2-A3
Pinfold Drive	B3
Pownall Road	B3
Queens Drive	A4-B4
Queens Road	A4-B4
Ramillies Avenue	C3
Raven Oak Park Road	C1
Raven Oak Road	C1-C2
Rowan Drive	C1
School Lane	A1-B1
Seymour Road	B1
Shaftesbury Avenue	C2-C3
Southdown Crescent	A1-A2
Station Road	B4-B3-C3-C2
Swan Green	B2-C2
Swann Lane	C2-B2-B1
The Precinct	B4
Tenby Drive	C2
Turves Road	A3
Upton Avenue	B2
Vaudrey Road	B4
Victoria Avenue	A4-B4
Westfield Road	A2
Willow Avenue	A3-A4
Windsor Green	A1

Hazel Grove

Argyle Street	B3
Avondale Avenue	C3
Beanleach Road	B4
Beech Avenue	B3-C3
Bosden Avenue	C4
Bosdenfold Road	B4-C4
Bosden Hall Road	B4
Bower Avenue	B1
Bramhall Moor Lane	A4
Braemar Road	C3
Brooklands Road	B1
Buteley Street	B4
Buxton Road	C1-C2
Carisbrooke Avenue	A1
Castleton Road	A4
Chapel Street	B3-B4
Chester Road	A1-B1-B2-B3
Church Grove	B2-C2
Clarendon Road	C4
Commercial Road	A3-B3-B4
Cooke Street	A3
Corfe Crescent	A1
Co-Op Street	B4
Davenport Road	A3
Deneside Crescent	C4
Douglas Road	B3-C3
Edale Close	B1-C1
Farndon Avenue	C4
Green Lane	A3-A4
Grendale Avenue	B1-B2
Grove Street	B3-B4
Grundy Street	B2-B3
Haddon Road	B1-C1
Harlech Drive	A1

Hatherflow Road	A2-B2-B3
Hazel Street	B3-B4
Hazelwood Road	C2-C3-C4
Hope Street	A3
Kings Road	B3-C3
Lawrence Road	A3
Lever Street	A3
Linda Drive	A3
London Road	A4-A3-B3-B2-C2
Longmead Avenue	A1-A2
Lowick Close	A2
Lyme Road	B1-C1
Lyndhurst Avenue	A1
Macclesfield Road	C1-C2
Mount Pleasant	A4
Napier Street	A3-B3
Nelson Street	C4
Neville Street	A3
Newby Road	A2-A3
Newlyn Close	A1
Norbury Crescent	B2
Norbury Green	B2
Oak Street	A3
Oaklands Drive	B1
Overton Crescent	B4-C4
Pearl Street	B4
Peter Street	A4-B4
Queens Road	B3
Rochester Grove	B3-C3
Rhos Drive	A1
School Street	B2
Seaton Close	A1
Shepley Drive	B1
Spring Gardens	B3
Station Street	B2
Stirling Avenue	A1
Talbot Street	B4
Torkington Road	B2-C2-C3
Vaudrey Drive	B2
Vine Street	B3
Warwick Drive	A1
Wesley Street	B3
Woodland Avenue	B1

69

Sunderland

Renowned for its shipbuilding industry, Sunderland is also an important coal port. Its name is derived from the fact that it was 'sundered' from a monastery founded on the far bank of the River Wear in 674. Wearmouth Bridge, originally built in 1796, but replaced in 1929, was one of the first cast-iron bridges in the country. A modern Civic Centre and three museums feature among the town's amenities. Nearby are the fine beaches of Roker and Seaburn.

Peterlee, built to attract industry in the 1950s, is one of Durham's most successful New Towns. It is named after Peter Lee, who started work down the mines at the age of ten, and rose to become president of the Miners' Union. An unexpected but welcome feature of the town is Castle Eden Dene – a three-mile stretch of natural woodland kept as a nature reserve.

Washington is another New Town burgeoning in this industrial corner of north-east England. In the original village stands 17th-century Washington Old Hall, the former home of George Washington's ancestors. Now in the care of the National Trust, it has been fully restored in period style. Another far cry from industry is the Wildfowl Trust's 103-acre park on the north bank of the Wear, where visitors can observe a comprehensive collection of the world's waterfowl in landscaped surroundings.

Central Houghton-le-Spring

Industrial Estate

Sunderland Area

SCALE mls 2

LEGEND

Town Plan

AA recommended route	
Restricted roads	
Other roads	
Buildings of interest	Cinema
Car parks	P
Parks and open spaces	
One way streets	←

Area Plan

A roads	
B roads	
Locations	Haswell O
Urban area	

Street Index with Grid Reference

Sunderland

Addison Street	E2-F2
Adelaide Place	E3
Amberley Street	D1
Argyle Street	B1-C1
Ashwood Road	A1-B1-B2
Ashwood Terrace	A1
Athenaeum	C3-D3
Avon Street	E2
Azalea Terrace South	B1-C1
Beach Road	A4
Beechwood Terrace	A1-B1
Bedford Street	C3-C4
Belvedere Road	B1-C1
Beresford Park North	A1-B1
Borough Road	C2-D2-D3-E3
Bridge Street	C3-C4
Brougham Street	C3
Burdon Road	C1-C2
Burlington Road	E1
Burn Park Road	A1-A2
Chester Road	A2-B2
Chester Terrace	A2
Church Street East	E3-E4
Cleft Street	A2
Commercial Road	E1-F1
Cork Street	D3-D4
Coronation Street	D3-E3
Cousin Street	E3
Cowan Terrace	C2
Crowtree Road	B3-C3-C2
D'Arcy Road	D2-E2
Deptford Road	A3-A4
Derby Street	B2
Derwent Street	B2-C2
Durham Road	A1-A2
East Back Parade	F1
East Hendon Road	F2-F3
Eden House Road	A1
Elmwood Street	A1
Farringdon Row	A3-A4-B4
Fawcett Street	C2-C3
Ferguson Street	F2
Fern Street	A4
Fontaine Road	B4
Fox Street	A1
Gill Bridge Avenue	B3-B4
Gill Road	B4-C4
Glebe Street	A2
Gorse Road	C1
Gray Road	D1-E1
Hartley Street	E4
Havelock Terrace	A2-A1-B1
Hendon Road	E1-E2-E3
Hendon Street	E2-F2
Henry Street East	F2
High Street East	D3-D4-E4
High Street West	B3-C3-D3
Hind Street	B2-B3
Holmeside	C2
Hope Street	A3-B3
Hudson Road	D3
Hylton Road	A3
J. A. Williams Street	E3-E4
John Street	C2-C3
Lawrence Street	E3
Lily Street	A4
Livingstone Road	B3
Lorne Terrace	C1
Low Road	B2-B3
Matamba Terrace	A3
Marlborough Street	A3-B3
Matlock Street	C4
May Street	A3-A4
Milburn Street	A3-A4
Moor Terrace	E3-F3
Mowbray Road	D1-E1
Murton Street	D2
Nelson Street	D1
New Durham Road	A2-B2
Noble Street	E1
Norfolk Street	D3
North Bridge Street	C4
Olive Street	B2-C2
Otto Terrace	A1
Paley Street	B3
Park Lane	C2
Park Road	C1-D1
Park Place	D1
Peel Street	D1
Prospect Row	E4-F4
Railway Row	A3
Ravensworth Street	A3-A4
Ridley Street	E1
Rosedale Street	A2-A3
Rose Street	A3
St Bedes Terrace	C1-D1
St George's Way	C1
St Mary's Way	C3-C4
Salisbury Street	D2
Sans Street	D3-D4
Salem Road	D1-D2
Salem Street	D1
Silksworth Row	A3-B3
Silver Street	E4-F4
Stockton Road	B2-C2-C1
Suffolk Street	D1-E1
Tatham Street	D2-D3
Thelma Street	A1-A2
Thornhill Park	B1
Thornholme Road	B1
Toward Road	D1-D2
Tower Street	E1
Trimdon Street	A3-A4
Tunstall Road	B1
Tunstall Terrace	B2-C2
The Parade	F1
The Royalty	A2
The Quadrant	E3-F3-F4-E4
Vane Terrace	F1
Villiers Street	D3
Vine Place	B2-C2
Walton Lane	E3-E4
Wear Street	E3
Westbourne Street	A2-A3
West Lawrence Street	D3-E3
West Sunniside	D3
West Wear Street	C4-D4
Wharncliffe Street	A2-A3
White House Court	D1
White House Road	D1-E1-E2
Woodbine Street	E2-E3-F3

Houghton-le-Spring

Alamein Avenue	C2-C3
Balfour Street	B4
Balmoral Crescent	C2
Brinkburn Crescent	A4
Broadway	B3
Burn Park Road	A3
Burns Avenue	B2
Church Street	B3
Dairy Lane	A3-B3
Dene Gardens	C2
Dunkirk Avenue	C2
Durham Road	A1-B1-B2
Earsdon Road	C2
Edwin Street	B4-B3-C3
Elizabeth Street	B3-B4
Fairburn Avenue	B1
Gillas Lane	A1-B1-C1-C2
Gilpin Street	A3
Hall Lane	B3-B2-C2
Hetton Road	B2-B1-C1
Holly Avenue	B3-C3
Houghtonside	A4-B4
Ironside Street	B4
John Street	C3
Kingsway	B2-C3
Kirklea Road	C2-C3
Lawnswood	C2
Market Place	C3
Meadow Close	C1-C2
Mill Hill	A1
Milton Avenue	B1-C1
Moore Crescent	B2
Mount Pleasant	C3
Nesham Place	B3-C3
Newbottle Street	A4-A3-B3
Normandy Crescent	B2-C2
Outram Street	B4
Queensway	B2-C2-C3
Ryhope Street	C3
Seaham Road	C3
Shakespeare Street	B1-B2
Station Road	A4
Sunderland Street	B4
The Green	C3-C4
Wallace Street	A3
Waller Terrace	B2-C2
Warwick Drive	B1

Windsor Crescent	C3
Windsor Drive	B1
Wordsworth Avenue	B2-B1-C1

Washington

Abbey Road	C2
Albany Way	B3-B4
Arklecrag	B3
Ashgill	A2
Bamborough Close	A2
Barrington Drive	A1
Bede Crescent	B3-B2-C2
Blue House Lane	A4-B4
Boston Avenue	B2-B3
Bracken Way	A4
Brancepeth Road	A1
Brandy Lane	A3
Brindley Road	C3
Burn Way	A4-B4
Castle Road	A1-A2
Dryburgh	B2-C2
Dunstanburgh Close	A1
Durham Avenue	A4
Eastern Highway	A2
Fatfield Road	C1
Fell Close	A3-A4
Fountains Close	C1
Front Street	C4
Glebe Crescent	C2
Glendale Avenue	B4
Havannah Road	A3-A4
Hertburn Gardens	C3
Hill Rise	C3
Hollin Hill Road	C3-C4
Industrial Road	C3-C4
Lanercost	B2
Langdale	B3
Lingmell	A3
Lumley Close	A2
Manor Park	C4
Manor Road	C4
Mitford Road	A1
Moorway	A3-A2-B2-B3
Oxclose Road	C1
Parkway	B1-B2-C2-C1
Parsons Road	A3-A4
Richmond Avenue	B2-B3-C3
Roche Court	B1
Rose Close	A4
Rosegill	A3
Spout Lane	C2-C3-C4
Station Road	C1
Stridingedge	A2
Sunderland Highway	A2-B2-B3-C3
The Avenue	C1-C2
The Terraces	C1
Thirlmoor	A3
Titchfield	B1
Urban Gardens	C3
Vermont	B4-C4
Victoria Road	B4-C4
Village Lane	B2-C2
Warkworth Close	A1
Washington Highway	A1-A2-A3-A4
Wharfedale Avenue	A4-B4
Windlass Lane	B3
Woburn	B1

Peterlee

Acre Rigg Road	A4

Ashton Rise	C3
Avon Road	A1
Bailey Rise	B4
Basingstoke Road	A3-A4
Bede Way	B2, B1-C1
Beverley Way	A3-A4
Brandlings Way	B3
Burnhope Way	A2-A3-B2
Cambridge Road	A4
Cann Road	B4
Chapel Hill Road	C1-C2-C3
Crawford Avenue	B4
Cumbrian Way	B2-C2-C1
Dart Road	A1
Derwent Road	B3
Dunelm Walk	B3-B4
Dunn Road	B3-B4
Edenhill Road	C2-C3
Eden Lane	B4-C4-C3
Elliot Road	B3
Ellison Road	C3
Essington Way	A4-B4-A3-B3-B2
Fairbairn Road	B4
Franklyn Road	A4
Fullwell Road	C1
Galloway Road	B4-B3-C3
Gilbert Road	A3
Granville Road	C1
Grisedale Road	C2
Helford Road	A1
Howletch Lane	A3-B3
Jarvis Road	B4
Jude Place	B4
Keswick Road	C2-C3
Kirkstone Avenue	C2
Little Eden	B3
Mabon Road	B4
Manor Way	B1-C1
Morton Square	A4
Nesbit Road	B1-C1
Neville Road	A2-A3
Passfield Road	A1-A2
Robson Avenue	B4-B3-C3
Rydal Crescent	C2
St Cuthberts Road	B1-B2
Smith Crescent	B4
Southway	A1
Staveley Road	C2
Surtees Road	B2
Thames Road	A1
Thirlmere Road	C2-C3
Tweed Close	A2
Weston View	A3
Windermere Road	C3
Yoden Road	B3-B4
Yoden Way	B2-C2-C1
York Road	A4

Wakefield

Towers and turrets unfolding over the hillsides greet the visitor to Wakefield, and the 247-ft spire of the Cathedral Church of All Saints has been a landmark for over 500 years. Today the spire looms over the Bull Ring pedestrian precinct which is part of a town centre development, and even older is the stone-built, nine-arched Old Bridge, site of the 14th-century Chapel of St Mary. This was among the finest of the bridge chapels — perhaps because even in the 13th century, Wakefield was an important weaving and dyeing centre (coal mining and a growing reputation as an international industrial centre are more important today). The excellent art gallery has an enterprising collection of modern sculpture and paintings.

Castleford Birthplace of Henry Moore in 1898, this mining and bottlemaking town is on the site of a Roman station. The Castleford Library Museum Room shows late 18th-century Castleford pottery.

Pontefract has been making Pontefract cakes for over 200 years, although today imported, not home-grown, liquorice is used. Its castle was one of the strongest in the north in medieval times and a bloody place of execution in the Wars of the Roses; of Pontefract's 18th- and 19th-century buildings, the Town Hall has the plaster casts used for the panel's at Nelson's Column's base.

Wakefield Area

Map labels (area plan): MORLEY, Middleton, ROTHWELL, Allerton Bywater, Fairburn, Burton Salmon, Birkin, Topcliffe, Carlton, Mickletown, New Fryston, Upper Batley, Ardsley East, Tingley, Ouzlewell Green, Methley, Brotherton, Beal, Lofthouse, Lee Moor, Lower Altofts, Whitwood, CASTLEFORD, Ferrybridge, Kellingley, BATLEY, Lower Soothill, Upper Green, Haigh Moor, Lofthouse Gate, Stanley, Altofts, New Town, KNOTTINGLEY, Mount Pleasant, Hanging Heaton, Gawthorpe, Kirkhamgate, Outwood, NORMANTON, North Featherstone, PONTEFRACT, Cridling Stubbs, Dewsbury Moor, DEWSBURY, Earlsheaton, Wrenthorpe, Kirkthorpe, Warmfield, Streethouse, FEATHERSTONE, Purston Jaglin, Darrington, Saville Town, OSSETT, WAKEFIELD, Belle Vue, Sharlston Common, High Ackworth, East Hardwick, Carleton, Wolmerley, Thornhill Lee, HORBURY, Lupset, Sandal Magna, Crofton, Ackworth Moor Top, Wentbridge, Little Sheaton, Overthorpe, Thornhill, Durkar, Walton, Fitzwilliam, Thorpe Audlin, Middlestown, Netherton, Crigglestone, Winterset Reservoir, Ryhill, Kinsley, Upton, North Elmsall, Flockton, Woolley Edge, Woolley, Notton, South Heindley, HEMSWORTH, South Elmsall, Clayton West, Kexbrough, DARTON, Staincross, Carlton, ROYSTON, Shafton, CUDWORTH, Brierley, South Kirkby, Hampol, Skellow, Skelmanthorpe, West Bretton

SCALE 0 — 4 mls

N

Warrington

This industrial town, situated near the Manchester Ship Canal, has been designated a New Town and is therefore expanding rapidly. Its traditional industry was clock-making, but in recent years this has given way to light industry, chemical production, metal casting and engineering. A few old houses can still be seen in the town, including the half-timbered Barley Mow inn.

Runcorn, on the River Mersey, is another industrial centre and has extensive petrochemical works. However, Norton Priory on the eastern edge of the town is of particular interest. Set in seven acres of landscaped woodland, the remains of the priory include a 12th-century undercroft notable for its beautiful carved passage. Excavation of the site in 1978 won the National Archaeological Award and the museum here, as well as containing various finds from the priory, has one of the best

exhibitions on medieval monastic life in Britain.

Widnes was just a collection of scattered villages before the Runcorn Gap and St Helen's Railway Company built the world's first railway, canal and dock complex here in the mid-19th century. Chemical and alkali works began to develop and the area rapidly grew into an industrial town with large housing estates. Today Widnes is linked to Runcorn by the railway bridge of 1868 and a road bridge which was built in 1961.

Central Warrington

Central Widnes

LEGEND

Town Plan

AA recommended route

Restricted roads

Other roads

Buildings of interest Club

Car parks P

Parks and open spaces

One way streets

Area Plan

A roads

B roads

Locations Grittleton ○

Urban area

Street Index with Grid Reference

Warrington

Academy Street	B2-C2
Academy Way	B2
Allen Street	A3-B3
Arpley Street	A1-A2
Arthur Street	A3
Ashton Street	B3
Austins Lane	B2
Bank Street	B2
Battersby Lane	C3-C4
Bewsey Road	A3-A4
Bewsey Street	A3-B3
Brick Street	C3
Bridge Street	B2
Buckley Street	B4
Buttermarket Street	B2-C2
Cairo Street	B2
Catherine Street	A4
Chester Road	B1
Church Street	C2-C3
Clegge Street	B4-C4
Cobden Street	B4-C4
Cockhedge Lane	B3-C3
Crossfield Street	A2-A3
Crown Street	B3
Dallem Lane	A4-B4-B3
Ellesmere Street	C2
Eustace Street	A3

Fairclough's Avenue	C1-C2
Fennel Street	C2-C3
Forshaw Street	C4
Foundry Street	B3
Fountain Street	C1
Froghall Lane	A3
Golborne Street	B2-B3
Half Street	C2
Haydock Street	B3-B4
Horse Market	B2-B3
Hopwood Street	C3
John Street	B3
Kendrick Street	A3
Kent Street	C1
Knutsford Road	B1-C1
Leigh Street	A3-A2-B2
Lilford Street	A4
Lord Nelson Street	C2
Lythgoes Lane	B4-B3-C3
Marbury Street	C1
Mersey Street	B1-B2-C2
Museum Street	A2-B2
Napier Street	C2
New Road	C1
Nicholson Street	A3
Norman Street	B4-C4
Old Road	B1
Oliver Street	B4
Orford Lane	B4-C4
Orford Street	B2-B3
Owen Street	A4-B4
Palmyra Square	A2-B2
Parker Street	A1-A2
Parr Street	C2
Paul Street	A3
Pinners Brow	B4
Pitt Street	A4
Richard Street	C3
St Mary's Street	C1
Sankey Street	A2-B2
School Brow	C3
Scotland Road	B2-B3
Scott Street	C4
Sharp Street	C4
Slutchers Lane	A1
Suez Street	B2
Tanners Lane	A3-B3
Thynne Street	A2
Vernon Street	C1-C2
Wellington Street	C2
Wharf Street	B1-B2-C2-C1
Wilson Patten Street	A1-B1-B2
Winmarleigh Street	A1-A2
Winwick Road	B4
Winwick Street	B3
York Street	C1

Runcorn

Ascot Avenue	C1-D1
Ashbourne Road	C1
Astmoor Road	C4-D4-E4
Banke's Lane	A2-A1-B1
Beechwood Avenue	D1-E1
Birch Road	C3-D3

Boston Avenue	C3-D3-E3
Bridge Street	C4
Bridgewater Expressway	E4-F4
Brindley Road	E4
Brindley Street	B4
Brookfield Avenue	E4
Calvers	E3
Canal Street	C4-D4
Castner Avenue	A2
Castle Rise	D4-D3-E3
Castlefields Avenue	E3-F3
Castlefields Avenue East	F3-F4
Castlefields Avenue North	
	E3-E4-F4
Cavendish Farm Road	B1-C1
Central Expressway	E1-C2-D1
Clifton Road	C2-C1-D1
Crofton Road	B3
Davy Road	E4
Dudley Avenue	D4
East Lane	E2
Eddison Road	E4
Festival Way	D2-D3
First Avenue	E2-E3
Gaunts Square	E1-E2
Grangeway	D1-D2
Greenway Road	B3-C3-C4
Hallwood Link Road	E1-E2
Halton Brook Avenue	D3-E3
Halton Brow	E3
Halton Lodge Avenue	D2
Halton Road	C4-D4-E4
Heath Road	C2-C3-C4
Heath Road South	B1-B2-C2
High Street	B4-C4
Highlands Road	B2-B3
Hollow Way	B3-B4
Ivy Street	C3
Kenilworth Avenue	C2
King James Square	E2
Lambsickle Lane	B1-C1
Langdale Road	C3
Latham Avenue	C3-D3
Linkway	D2
Lydiate Lane	A2-B2
Main Street	E3-F3-F2
Malpas Road	C1-C2-D2-D1
Maple Avenue	D2-D3
Masseyfield Road	F1
Mather Avenue	A2
Mersey Road	B4-C4
Morval Crescent	D3
Moughland Lane	B3-C3
Norleane Crescent	C2-C3
Norman Road	C3
Norton View	F2-F3
Oxford Road	B3-C3-C2
Palacefields Avenue	F1-F2
Park Road	B2-C2
Penn Lane	B3
Percival Lane	B4
Picow Farm Road	A2-A3-B3-B4
Picton Avenue	C3-C4-B4
Post Office Lane	A2
Runcorn Bridge Approach	B4
Runcorn Expressway	C4-D4-E4
Runcorn Spur Road	
	B4-C4-C3-D3-E3-E2
Russell Road	B2-B3

Sandy Lane	A2-B2
Saxon Road	C4-D4
School Lane	E3-F3
Sea Lane	D4
South Parade	A2
Southern Expressway	E1-F1
Spark Lane	E3-F3
Stockham Lane	F2-F3
Sycamore Road	D2-D3
The Butts	E4
The Glen	E1-F1
Thorn Road	D2
Trentham Street	B4
Union Street	C4-D4-D3
Victoria Road	C3-C4
Vista Road	C2-C3
Walpole Road	C2-C1-D1
West Lane	E2
West Road	A2
Westfield Road	A3-B3
Weston Road	B1-B2-B3
Weston Point Expressway	
	B4-B3-A3-B3-B2-B1-C1-D1
Westway	E2
Wicksten Drive	C4-D4
Woodhatch Road	F1
York Street	C3-C4

Widnes

Albert Road	C4
Alexandra Street	A1-B1
Alforde Street	B1-B2
Alfred Street	C2
Ann Street East	C1
Ann Street West	C1
Appleton Street	C1
Brynn Street	C2
Caldwell Road	A2-B2
Cambridge Street	C2
Cameron Road	A2-A3
Carlton Street	B3
Catherine Street	B1-C1
Charles Street	B3
Chester Street	C4
Croft Street	B1-C1
Deacon Road	C4
Deidre Avenue	B4
Dickson Street	B4-C4-C3
Ditton Road	A1-B1
Egypt Street	A2
Eleanor Street	B1
Ellis Street	A1
Finlan Road	A1-B1
Frederick Street	C3-C4
Gerrard Street	C3
Henderson Road	A3-A4-B4
Hood Road	A4
Keble Street	B2-C2
Kingsway	B2-B3-B4
Lacey Street	B1-C1
Leigh Avenue	A4-B4-C4
Liverpool Road	A4
Lower House Lane	A2-A3-A4
Lugsdale Road	B2-C2-C1-C2

Luton Street	B1
Major Cross Street	B2-B1-C1
Market Street	B1-B2
Masefield Avenue	A2-A3
Milton Avenue	A2
Milton Road	A2-B2-B3-C3
Moor Lane	A1-A2-B2-B1
Moon Street	C3-C4
Mottershead Road	A3-B3-B4
Ollier Street	B1
Oxford Street	C2
Princess Street	C3
Quinn Street	C2
Rose Street	A2
Ross Street	C4
Saxon Terrace	C4
Sayce Street	C4
Scott Avenue	A3
Sharp Street	B3-C3
Shelagh Avenue	B4
Sinclair Avenue	A3-B3
Smith Road	A2
Squires Avenue	A4-B4
Stewards Avenue	A3-A4
Sutton Lane	C1
Travis Street	C3
Vicarage Road	B2
Victoria Road	B2
Victoria Square	B1-B2
Victoria Street	C1-C2
Village Close	C4
Vine Street	C2
Violet Street	B1
Wallace Street	B3-C3
Wavertree Avenue	A3-B3
Widnes Road	B2-C2-C3
Witt Road	B1

75

York

York Minster, unquestionably the city's outstanding glory, is considered to be one of the greatest cathedral churches in Europe. It is especially famous for its lovely windows which contain more than half the medieval stained glass in England.

Great medieval walls enclose the historic city centre and their three-mile circuit offers magnificent views of the Minster, York's numerous fine buildings, churches and the River Ouse. The ancient streets consist of a maze of alleys and lanes, some of them so narrow that the overhanging upper storeys of the houses almost touch. The most famous of these picturesque streets is The Shambles, formerly the butchers' quarter of the city, but now colonised by antique and tourist shops. York flourished throughout Tudor, Georgian and Victorian times and handsome buildings from these periods also feature throughout the city.

The Castle Museum gives a fascinating picture of York as it used to be and the Heritage Centre interprets the social and architectural history of the city. Other places of exceptional note in this city of riches include the Merchant Adventurer's Hall; the Treasurer's House, now owned by the National Trust and filled with fine paintings and furniture; the Jorvik Viking Centre, where there is an exciting restoration of the original Viking settlement at York, and the National Railway Museum.

Key to Town Plan and Area Plan

Town Plan

AA Recommended roads
Other roads
Restricted roads
Buildings of interest **Station**
Churches
Car Parks
Parks and open spaces
AA Service Centre
One Way Streets

Area Plan

A roads
B roads
Locations Fangfoss ○
Urban area

Street Index with Grid Reference

York

Abbey Street	A8
Albermarle Road	A2-A1-B1
Aldwark	D5-E5
Alne Terrace	F2
Amber Street	E8
Ann Street	D1
Asylum Lane	C8-C7-D7
Avenue Road	B8
Avenue Terrace	A7-A8-B8
Baile Hill Terrace	C2-C3-D3
Baker Street	C8
Barbican Road	E2-F2-F3-E3
Belle Vue Street	F2
Belle Vue Terrace	F2
Bewlay Street	C1-D1
Bishopgate Street	C2-D2-D3
Bishophill Junior	C3
Bishophill Senior	C3
Bishop Thorpe Road	C1-C2
Blake Street	C5
Blossom Street	B2-B3
Blue Boar Lane	E2
Bootham	B6-C6
Bootham Crescent	B7-C7-C8
Bootham Row	C6

Bootham Terrace	B6
Bridge Street	C4-D4
Brook Street	D7
Brownlow Street	D7-E7-E8
Buckingham Street	C3
Burton Stone Lane	B7-B8
Cambridge Street	A2-A3
Carmelite Street	D4-E4
Castlegate	D3-D4
Cemetery Road	E1-E2
Charlton Street	C1-D1
Cherry Street	D2
Church Street	D5
Cinder Lane	A4
Claremont Terrace	C6-C7
Clarence Street	C6-C7-D7
Clementhorpe	C2-D2
Clifford Street	D3-D4
Clifton	A8-A7-B7
Clifton Dale	A7-A8
Colliergate	D4-D5
Compton Street	A7-A8
Coppergate	D4
Cromwell Road	C3-D3
Dale Street	B2-B3
Dalton Terrace	A2
Darnborough Street	C2-D2
Daygate	C5-C4-D4-D5
Deangate	D5
Dennison Street	E7
Dewsbury Terrace	B3-C3
Diamond Street	E8
Dodsworth Avenue	E8-F8-F7
Driffield Terrace	A2
Dudley Street	D7-E7
Duncombe Place	C5
Dundas Street	E4-E5
East Parade	F6-F7
East Mount Road	B2
Ebor Street	C2-D2
Edgware Road	F1
Eldon Terrace	D8-E8
Elvington Terrace	F3
Emerald Street	E7-E8
Escrick Street	E2
Faber Street	F6
Fairfax Street	C3
Farndale Street	E1
Farrar Street	F2-F3
Fawcett Street	E2-E3
Fenwick Street	C1-D1
Fetter Lane	C3-C4
Fifth Avenue	F5-F6
Filey Terrace	C8
Fishergate	E2-E3
Foss Bank	E5-E6
Fossgate	D4
Foss Islands Road	E4-E5-F5-F4
Frederick Street	B5
Fulford Road	E1-E2
Garden Street	D7
George Hudson Street	C4
George Street	E3-E4
Gillygate	C5
Glen Avenue	F6
Goodramgate	D5-D6
Gordon Street	F2
Grange Croft	E1
Grange Garth	E1
Grange Street	E1

Greencliffe Way	A7-A8
Grosvenor Road	B8-C8
Grosvenor Terrace	B6-B7-C7-C8
Grove Terrace Lane	E7-E8
Grove View	A7
Hallfield Road	F5-F6
Hampden Street	C3
Harcourt Street	F6
Harloft Street	E1
Hawthorne Green	F6
Hawthorn Street	F6
Haxby Road	D7-D8
Heslington Road	E2-F2
Heworth Green	E6-E7-F7
High Ousegate	D4
High Petergate	C5-C6
Holgate Road	A2-A3-B3
Hope Street	E3
Horsman Avenue	E2-F2
Howard Road	E1
Hudson Street	C8
Huntington Road	E6-E7-E8
Hyrst Grove	F7
Irwin Avenue	F7-F8
Jackson Street	D7-E7
James Street	E1
James Street	F3-F4
Jewbury	E5
Kensal Rise	E1
Kent Street	E2
Kilburn Road	E1-F1
Kings Straithe	C4-D4-D3
King Street	C4-D4
Knavesmire Road	A1
Kyme Street	C3
Lawrence Street	F3
Layerthorpe	E5-E6-F6
Lead Mill Lane	E3
Leake Street	F3
Leeman Road	A5-A4-B5-B4
Lendal Coney Street	C5-C4-D4
Lewisham Street	E1
Little Hallford Road	F5
Long Close Lane	E3-F3
Longfield Terrace	B5-B6
Lord Mayors Walk	C6-D6
Lumley Road	B8
Love Lane	A1-A2
Lower Petergate	D5
Lower Priory Street	C3
Lowther Street	D7-E7
Lowther Terrace	A3
Maida Grove	E1
March Street	D7
Margaret Street	E3
Market Street	D4
Markham Crescent	D7-D8
Markham Street	D7-D8
Marlborough Grove	E2
Marygate	B5-B6-C6
Melbourne Street	E2
Micklegate	B3-B4-C4
Millfield Road	C1-C2
Mill Lane	F7
Mill Mount Lane	A2-B2
Minster Yard	C5-D5
Monkgate	D6-E6
Moss Street	B2-B3
Mount Vale	A1
Museum Street	C5

Navigation Road	E4-E3-F3
Nelson Street	D8-E8
Neville Street	D8
Neville Terrace	D8-E8
Newborough Street	C8
New Street	C4-C5
Newton Terrace	C2-C3
New Walk Terrace	E1
Norfolk Street	C1-D1
North Parade	B6
North Street	C4
Nunmill Street	C1-C2
Nunnery Lane	B3-C3-C2
Nunthorpe Avenue	B1-B2
Nunthorpe Grove	C1
Nunthorpe Road	B2-C2
Paragon Street	E3-F3
Park Crescent	E7
Park Grove	E7-E8
Park Street	B2
Parliament Street	D4-D5
Peasholme Green	E5
Pembroke Street	B8
Penley's Grove Street	D7-E7-E6
Peters Way	A7-B7-B8
Piccadilly	D4-D3-E3-E4
Portland Street	C6
Pottery Lane	F8
Prices Lane	C2
Priory Street	B3-C3
Queen Annes Road	B6
Queen Street	B3
Railway Terrace	A3
Redness Street	F5-F6
Regent Street	F2-F3
Richardson Street	C1-D1
Rosslyn Street	A7
Rougier Street	C4
Russel Street	C1-C2
St Andrewgate	D5
St Aubyns Place	A1
St Denys Road	E3-E4
St Johns Street	D6-D7
St Leonards Place	D5-D6
St Lukes Grove	B8
St Marys	B6
St Maurices	D6-D5-E5
St Olaves Road	B7-B8
St Pauls Terrace	A3
St Peters Grove	B7
St Saviourgate	D4-D5-E5
Sandringham Street	E1
Saxon Place	E8-F8
Scarborough Terrace	C8
Scarcroft Hill	B1-B2
Scarcroft Road	A2-B2-C2-C1
Scott Street	C1-C2
Shambles	D4-D5
Shaw Terrace	B2-B3
Shipton Road	A8
Shipton Street	B8-C8
Skeldergate	C4-C3-D3
Skeldergate Bridge	D3
South Esplanade	D3
Southlands Road	C1
South Parade	B2-B3
Stanley Street	D8
Station Avenue	B4
Station Rise	B4
Station Road	B3-B4-C4-C5

Stonegate	C5-D5
Swinegate	D5
Sycamore Place	B6
Sycamore Terrace	A5-B5-B6
Tanner Row	B4-C4
Telford Terrace	B1
The Avenue	A7
The Crescent	B3
The Mount	A1-A2-B2
The Stonebow	D4-E4-E5
Thomas Street	F3-F4
Thorpe Street	C1-C2
Toft Green	B3-B4
Tower Street	D4-D3-E3
Townend Street	D7
Trent Holme Drive	A1
Trinity Lane	C3-C4
Union Terrace	C7
Upper Price Street	B2-C2
Victor Street	C3
Vine Street	C2-D2
Walmgate	D4-E4-E3-F3
Walpole Street	D8-E8
Water Lane	A8
Watson Street	A2-A3
Wellington Row	C4
Wellington Street	F2-F3
Westminster Road	A7
William Street	D1
Willis Street	F2-F3
Winterscale Street	E2
Wolseley Street	F2

LEGEND

Town Plan

AA Recommended roads	
Restricted roads	
Other roads	
Buildings of interest	Hospital 🏥
Car Parks	🅿
Parks and open spaces	▢
One Way Streets	→
Churches	+

STREET INDEX- with grid reference

Dundee

Airlie Place	B1-B2
Albert Street	F4
Allan Street	E2-E3
Ann Street	D4
Arbroath Road	F4
Arthur-Stone Terrace	E4-F4
Ash Street	A4-B4
Bank Street	C2
Barrack Road	B4-C4
Barrack Street	C2-C3
Bellfield Street	A2-A3
Bell Street	C3-D3
Blackness Road	A3-B3
Blackscroft	E3-F3
Blinshall Street	B3-B4

Brook Street	A3-B3-B2
Brown Street	B2-B3-B4
Camperdown Street	E2-F2-F3
Candle Lane	D3-D2-E2
Castle Street	D2
Commercial Street	D2-D3
Constable Street	E3-F3
Constitution Road	C3-C4
Cotton Road	E4
Cowgate	D3-E3
Crescent Street	E3-E4-F4
Dock Street	D2
Douglas Street	A3-B3
Dunhope Street	C4-D4
East Dock Street	E2-E3-F3
Edward Street	A3-A4
Erskine Street	F4
Euclid Crescent	C3
Forebank Road	D4
Foundry Lane	E3-F3
Gellatly Street	D2
Greenfield Place	A1
Guthrie Street	B3
Hendersons West Wynd	B3-B4
High Street	C2-D2
Hilltown	D4
Kemback Street	F4
King Street	D3-E3
Ladywell Lane	D4-E4
Larch Street	A3
Laurel Bank	C4
Lindsay Street	C2-C3
Lochee Road	A4-B4
Lower Pleasance	A3-A4
Lyon Street	E4-F4
Market Gait	D3-C3-C4-B4-B3-B2-C2

Mary Ann Lane	E2-E3
Meadowside	C3-D3
Millers Wynd	A2
Milners East Wynd	E3
Miln Street	B3
Murraygate	D3
Nelson Street	D4-E4
Nethergate	B1-C1-C2
Old Hawkhill	A2-B2
Panmure Street	C3-D3
Park Place	B1-B2
Park Street	A3-A4
Peep O'Day Lane	F3
Perth Road	A2-A1-B1
Polepark Road	A3-A4
Prince's Street	E3-E4-F4
Prospect Place	C4
Raglan Street	F4
Reform Street	C3-C2-D2
Riverside Drive	C2-D2
Roseangle	A1-B1
Rosebank Road	C4
Rosebank Street	C4-D4
St Andrews Street	D3
St Mary Street	A4
Seagate	D2-D3-E3
Smalls Wynd	B2
South George Street	D4-E4
South Tay	B2-C2-C1
South Ward Road	B3-C3-C2-C3
Springfield	A1-A2
Tay Bridge Road	D2-D1-E1
Trades Lane	D3-D2-E2
Union Street	C2
Union Terrace	C4
Victoria Road	D3-D4-E4
Victoria Street	E4-F4

Walton Street	A3
Ward Road	B3-C3
Wellington Street	E4
West Bell Street	B3-C3
Westfield Place	A1
Westport	B2
Whitehall Street	C2-D2
William Street	E4
Willison Street	C2

Inverness

Abban Street	A3
Academy Street	B3-B2-C2
Anderson Street	A4-B4
Annfield Road	C1-D1
Ardconnel Street	C1-C2
Ardross Street	B1
Ardross Terrace	B1-B2
Argyle Street	C1
Bank Street	B2-B3
Beaufort Road	D2
Bishop's Road	A1-B1
Bridge Street	B2-C2
Broadstone Park	D1-D2
Bruce Gardens	A1
Burnett Road	C3-C4
Carse Road	A3
Castle Road	B1-B2
Castle Street	C1
Cawdor Road	D2
Chapel Street	B3
Charles Street	C2
Church Street	B2-B3
Coronation Park	A4
Cromwell Road	B4
Crown Avenue	C2-D2

Crown Circus	D2	Barrack Street	B3
Crown Drive	D2-D3	Bellwood Park	D2
Crown Road	C2-C3-D3	Bowerswell Road	D3
Crown Street	C2	Brompton Terrace	D2-D3
Culduthel	C1	Caledonian Road	B2-B3
Darnaway Road	D1	Canal Street	C2
Dochfour Drive	A1-A2	Cavendish Avenue	
Douglas Row	B3		A1-B1
Duncraig Street	A2-B2	County Place	B2
Eastgate	C2-C3-D3	Crieff Road	A4
Fairfield Road	A2	Darnhall Drive	A1
Forth Street	C2	Dupplin Road	A4
Friar's Lane	B3	Dundee Road	D1-D2
George Street	B3	Dunkeld Road	A4-B4-B3
Gilbert Street	A3-A4	Edinburgh Road	C1
Glebe Street	B3	Feus Road	A3-A4
Glenur Road	A1-B1	Florence Place	A4-B4
Grant Street	A4	Friar Street	B1
Greig Street	B2	Gannochy Road	D3-D4
Harbour Road	B4-C4-D4	Glasgow Road	A1-A2
Harrowden Road	A2-A3	Glover Road	A2-B2-B1
Haugh Road	B1	Gowrie Street	D2-D3
High Street	C2	Gray Street	A2-B2-B1
Hill Street	C2	Hay Street	B3-B4
Huntly Place	A3	High Street	
Huntly Street	A3-B3-B2		B3-B2-C2-C3
Innes Street	B3-C3	Isla Road	C4-D4
Kenneth Street	A3-A2-B2	Jeanfield Road	A3
Kingsmill's Road		King's Place	B1-C1
	C2-D2-D1	King Street	C2
Kings Street	A3-B3-B2	Kinnoull Street	C3
Leys Drive	D1	Leonard Street	B2
Lochalsh Road	A2-A3-A4	Long Causeway	A3-B3
Longman Road	C3-C4	Main Street	D3-D4
Lovat Road	C2	Manse Road	D2
Macewan Drive	D1-D2	Marshall Place	C1
Mayfield Road	C1	Mill Street	C3
Midmills Road	D2	Muirhall Road	D3
Milburn Road	D3	Muirhall Terrace	D3
Montague Row	A1-A2	Muirton Place	A4-B4
Muirtown Street	A3	Murray Crescent	A1
Ness Bank	B1	Needless Road	A1-B1
Old Edinburgh Road	C1	North Methven Street	B2
Park Road	A1	Park Place	A1
Planefield Road		Perth Bridge	C3-D3
	A2-A1-B1	Pickletullum Road	A1-A2
Rangemore Road	A2	Pitcullen Terrace	D4
Riverside Street	B3	Pithealis Terrace	A1
Rose Street	B3-C3	Princes Street	C2
Ross Avenue	A2	Priory Place	B1
Seafield Road	C4-D4	Queens Bridge	D2
Shore Street	B3-B4	Rigg's Road	A2-A3
Smith Avenue	A1	Rose Crescent	A1
Southside Place	C1-D1	St Catherines Road	B3
Telford Road	A3-A4	St Leonards Bank	B1
Telford Street	A3	Scott Street	C2
Thornbush Road	A4	Shore Road	C1-D1
Tomnahurich Street		South Methven Street	
	A1-B1-B2		B3-B2-C2
Union Road	C2-D2	South Street	C2
Union Street	B2-C2	Stanley Crescent	A4
Victoria Drive	D3	Stuart Avenue	A1
Walker Road	B4-C4	Tay Street	C2-D2-C2-C3
Waterloo Place	B3	Unity Terrace	A3-A4
Wells Street	A3	Victoria Street	C2
Wyvis Place	A4	Wilson Street	A1-B1
		York Place	B2

Perth

Abbot Street	B1
Albany Terrace	A4
Annat Road	D4
Atholl Street	B3-C3
Balhousie Street	B3-B4
Barossa Place	B3-C3

Central Inverness

Central Perth

INVERNESS
Crowding the skyline with its battlements and towers, Inverness Castle commands an imposing site above the town — but was only built in the last century.

79

Central St Andrews

Central Dumfries

St Andrews is synonymous with golf. There are no less than 15 golf courses in the vicinity, and the Royal and Ancient Golf Club, founded in the 18th century, has come to be regarded as the international headquarters of the game. But the town's links with the past go back even further: it has a distinguished university which was founded in 1411, its castle is 13th-century and the cathedral dates from the 12th century.

Stirling lies just north of Bannockburn, where

Robert the Bruce inflicted a swingeing defeat on the armies of England in 1314, and twelve years later he held his first parliament in the town's Cambuskenneth Abbey, which can still be seen. The castle dates back to the 13th century and its Landmark Centre provides an exciting audio-visual display. The Wallace Memorial offers fine views.

Oban has been a popular desination for tourists since the 19th century, not least because of its ferry links with the Hebrides. Visitors

can see paperweights being made at the local glassworks, and other attractions are the fine views of the town and its surroundings to be seen from McCaig's Tower and Pulpit Hill.

Dumfries is Walter Scott's 'Queen of the South': a fine country town and market centre of old sandstone and spacious parks. Robert Burns spent the last years of his life here, and Burns House, where he died in 1796, is now a museum. His Mausoleum stands in St Michael's Churchyard.

Aberdeen

Granite gives Aberdeen its especial character; but this is not to say that the city is a grim or a grey place, the granites used are of many hues – white, blue, pink and grey. Although the most imposing buildings date from the 19th century, granite has been used to dramatic effect since at least as early as the 15th century. From that time dates St Machar's Cathedral, originally founded in AD580,

but rebuilt several times, especially after a devasting fire started on the orders of Edward III of England in 1336. St Machar's is in Old Aberdeen, traditionally the ecclesiastical and educational hub of the city, while 'New' Aberdeen (actually no newer) has always been the commercial centre. Even that definition is deceptive, for although Old Aberdeen has King's College, founded in 1494, New Aberdeen has Marischal College, founded almost exactly a century later (but rebuilt in 1844)

and every bit as distinguished as a seat of learning. Both establishments functioned as independent universities until they were merged in 1860 to form Aberdeen University. The North Sea oil boom has brought many changes to the city, some of which threatened its character. But even though high-rise buildings are now common, the stately façades, towers and pillars of granite still reign supreme and Union Street remains one of the best thoroughfares in Britain.

Aberdeen Area

Key to Town Plan and Area Plan

Town Plan

A A Recommended roads	
Other roads	
Restricted roads	
Buildings of interest	Cinema
Car Parks	P
Parks and open spaces	
One Way Streets	→
Churches	†

Area Plan

A roads	
B roads	
Locations	Hattoncrook O
Urban area	

Street Index with Grid Reference

Aberdeen

Abbotsford Lane	C2-D2
Academy Street	C4-D4
Advocates Road	E8
Affleck Street	D3
Albert Quay	E3-F3
Albert Place	A5-A6
Albert Street	A4-A5
Albert Terrace	B2-C2
Albury Place	B2-C2-C3
Albury Road	A4
Albyn Grove	A4-A3-B3-B4
Albyn Lane	A4-B4
Albyn Place	B4
Alford Place	A1-A2
Allan Street	C7-C8
Ann Street	A3-B3
Ashvale Place	A4
Back Wyndd	D5
Baker Street	B6-C6
Balmoral Place	A1
Balmoral Road	A1-B1
Bank Street	D2
Beach Boulevard	F6
Belgrave Terrace	A6
Belmont Street	D5
Belvidere Street	B8-C8
Berryden Road	B2
Bethany Gardens	D6
Blackfriars Street	A2-A1-B1
Bloomfield Place	A1-B1
Bloomfield Road	B4-C4-C3
Bon-Accord Crescent	B4-C4-C3
Bon-Accord Crescent Lane	C3-C4
Bon-Accord Square	C2-C3-C4
Bon-Accord Street	C2-C3-C4
Bridge Place	D4

Broad Street	E5-E6
Broomhill Road	A1-A2
Caledonian Lane	C2
Caledonian Place	C2-C3
Canal Road	D8
Canal Street	D8-E8
Carden Place	A5
Carmelite Street	D4
Caroline Place	B8-B7-C7-C8
Castle Street	E5-F5
Castle Terrace	F5
Causeway End	D8
Chapel Street	B4-B5
Charles Street	C8-D8
Charlotte Street	C7-D7-D6
Claremont Street	A3
College Street	D3-D4
Commerce Street	F4-F5
Commercial Quay	E3-F3
Constitution Street	F6
Cornhill Road	A8
Craibstone Lane	C3-C4
Craigie Loanings	A5-A6
Craigie Street	D7
Crimon Street	C5
Crombie Place	F1-F2
Crombie Road	F1
Crown Street	D2-D3-D4-C4
Crown Terrace	D3-D4
Cuparstone Row	A3-B3
Dee Place	C3-D3
Dee Street	C3-C4
Deemont road	C1-D1
Denburn Road	D5
Devanha Gardens	C1
Devanha Terrace	D1-D2
Diamond Street	C4-D4-C5
Duff Street	F6-F7
East North Street	E6-F6
Errol Street	F8
Esslemont Avenue	A6-B6-B5
Exchange Street	E4-E5
Farmers Hill	C6-C7
Ferryhill Place	C2
Ferryhill Road	C2-D2
Ferryhill Terrace	C2-D2
Fonthill Road	A2-B2-C2
Fonthill Terrace	B1-B2
Forbes Street	B7-C7
Fraser Place	C8-D8
Fraser Road	C8
Fraser Street	C8
Frederick Street	E6-F6
Gallowgate	D7-E7-E6
George Street	C8-D8-D7-D6-D5
Gerrard Street	D7
Gilcomston Park	C6
Glenbervie Road	F1
Golden Square	C5
Gordon Street	C3-C4
Grampian Road	E1-F1
Great Southern Road	A1-B2-B1
Great Western Place	A1-B1
Great Western Road	A2-A3
Grosvenor Place	A6
Guild Street	D4-E4
Hanover Street	F5-F6
Hardgate	A1-A2-B2-B3-B4
Hill Street	C7
Holburn Road	A2
Holburn Street	A1-A2-A3-B3-B4
Holland Street	C8

Hollybank Place	A3-B3
Howburn Place	A3-B3-B2
Huntly Street	B5-C5-C4
Hutcheon Street	B8-C8-D8
Innes Street	D7-E7
Irvine Place	A2
James Street	F7
Jasmine Place	F4-F5
Jasmine Terrace	E7-F7
John Street	C6-D6-D7
Jopp's Lane	D6-D7
Justice Street	E5-F5-F6
Justice Mill Lane	B3-B4
Jute Street	D8-E8
Kidd Street	B5-C5
King Street	E5-E6-E7-E8-F8
Kintore Place	B6-B7-C7
Langstone Place	C4
Leadside Road	B6
Lemon Street	F6
Little John Street	E6
Loanhead Place	A7-A8-B8
Loanhead Terrace	A7
Loch Street	D6-D7
Maberley Street	C7-D7
Marischal Street	E5-F5-F4
Market Street	E3-E4-E5
Marywell Street	D3
Meal Market Street	E6
Mearns Street	F4-F5
Menzies Road	E1-E2-F2
Millburn Street	D2
Minster Holly	B5-C5
Mount Holly	E7-E8
Mount Street	B7-B8
Nellfield Place	A2
Nelson Street	E7-E8
North Esplanade East	E3-F3
North Esplanade West	D1-D2-E2-E3
North Silver Street	C5
Northfield Place	B6
Old Ford Road	D2
Osborne Place	A5
Oscar Road	F1
Palmerston Place	D2
Palmerston Road	D2-D3-E3
Park Place	F6
Park Road	F7
Park Street	F6-F7
Polmuir Road	C1-C2
Portland Street	D2-D3
Poynernook Road	D2-E2-E3
Princes Street	E6-F6
Prospect Terrace	D1-D2
Queen Street	E5-E6
Raeburn Place	C6
Raik Road	E2-E3
Regent Road	F3-F4
Regent Quay	E5-F5
Rennies Wyndd	D4
Richmond Street	B6-B7
Richmond Terrace	B7
Riverside Drive	D1
Rose Street	B4-B5
Rosebank Place	B3
Rosebank Terrace	C3-D3
Rosemount Place	A7-A6-B6-B7-C7
Rosemount Terrace	B7-B8
Rosemount Viaduct	B6-C6-C5
Roslin Street	F7-F8
Roslin Terrace	E7-F7
Rubislaw Terrace	A4

Russell Road	E2
St Andrew Street	C6-D6
St Clair Street	E7
St John's Place	D4
St Mary's Place	D3
St Nicholas Street	D5-E5
St Paul Street	D6-E6
School Hill	D5
Seaforth Road	F8
Ship Row	E4-E5
Short Loanings	B6
Sinclair Road	F2
Skene Square	C6-C7
Skene Street	A5-B5-C5
Skene Terrace	C5
South College Street	D2-D3
South Crown Street	C1-D1-D2
South Esplanade East	F2
South Esplanade West	E1-E2
South Mount Street	B6-B7
Spa Street	C6
Spital Kings Crescent	E8
Spring Garden	D7
Spring Bank Street	C3-D3
Spring Bank Terrace	C3-D3
Stell Road	E3
Stirling Street	D4-E4
Summer Street	B4-B5-C5
Summerfield Terrace	E6-F6
Sycamore Place	B1-C1
The Green	D4-D5
Thistle Lane	B4-B5
Thistle Street	B4
Thomson Street	A7
Trinity Quay	
Upper Denburn	B6-C6
Upper Kirkgate	D5-D6-E5-E6
Urquhart Lane	F7-F8
Urquhart Place	F7
Urquhart Road	F7
Urquhart Street	F7-F8
Union Bridge	D4-D5
Union Glen	B3
Union Grove	A3-B3
Union Row	B4-C4
Union Street	B4-C4-D4-D5-E5
Union Terrace	C5-D5
Victoria Bridge	E3-E2-F2
Victoria Road	F1-F2
Victoria Street	A5-B4-B5
View Terrace	B7
Virginia Street	E5-F5
Wales Street	F6
Walker Road	E1-F1
Wallfield Crescent	A6
Wallfield Place	A6-A7
Watson Street	A7-A8
Waverley Lane	A4-A5
Waverley Place	A4-B4
Wellington Place	D3
West Mount Street	B7
West North Street	E6-E7-E8
Westburn Road	A8-B8
Whinhill Road	B1-C1-C2
Whitehall Place	A5-A6-B6
Willow Bank Road	B3-C3
Willowdale Place	E7
Windmill Brae	C4-D4
Woolmanhill	C6-D6-D5

83

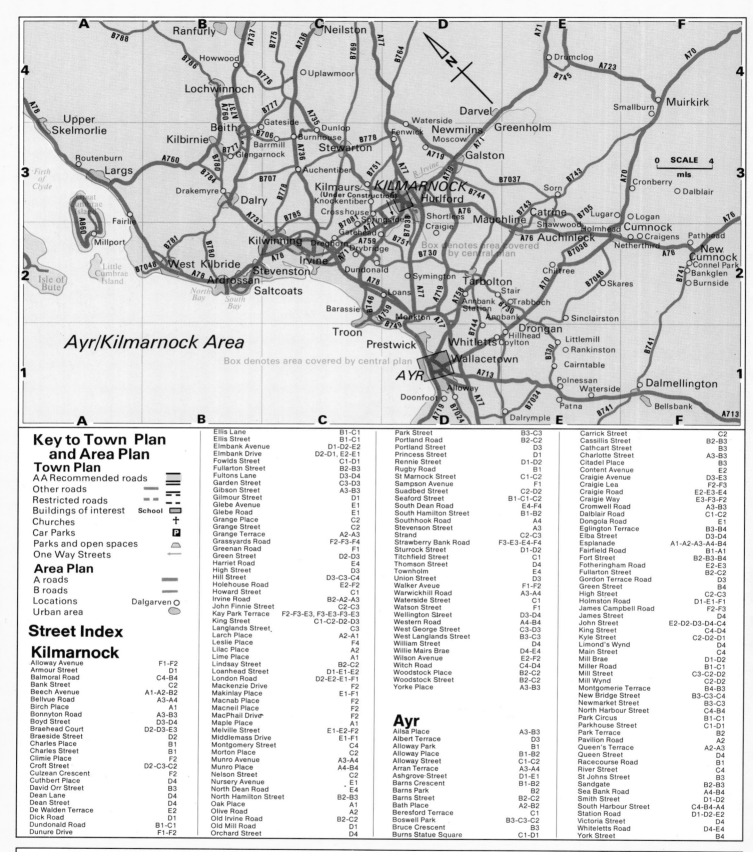

Ayr/Kilmarnock Area

Key to Town Plan and Area Plan

Town Plan

AA Recommended roads	▬▬▬
Other roads	▬ ▬
Restricted roads	▬ ▬
Buildings of interest	School ▭
Churches	+
Car Parks	P
Parks and open spaces	△
One Way Streets	←

Area Plan

A roads	▬▬▬
B roads	▬
Locations	Dalgarven ○
Urban area	⬭

Street Index

Kilmarnock

Alloway Avenue	F1-F2
Armour Street	D1
Balmoral Road	C4-B4
Bank Street	C2
Beech Avenue	A1-A2-B2
Bellvue Road	A3-A4
Birch Place	A1
Bonnyton Road	A3-B3
Boyd Street	D3-D4
Braehead Court	D2-D3-E3
Braeside Street	D2
Charles Place	B1
Charles Street	B1
Climie Place	F2
Croft Street	D2-C3-C2
Culzean Crescent	F2
Cuthbert Place	D4
David Orr Street	B3
Dean Lane	D4
Dean Street	D4
De Walden Terrace	E2
Dick Road	D1
Dundonald Road	B1-C1
Dunure Drive	F1-F2
Ellis Lane	B1-C1
Ellis Street	B1-C1
Elmbank Avenue	D1-D2-E2
Elmbank Drive	D2-D1, E2-E1
Fowlds Street	C1-D1
Fullarton Street	B2-B3
Fultons Lane	D3-D4
Garden Street	C3-D3
Gibson Street	A3-B3
Gilmour Street	D1
Glebe Avenue	E1
Glebe Road	E1
Grange Place	C2
Grange Street	C2
Grange Terrace	A2-A3
Grassyards Road	F2-F3-F4
Greenan Road	F1
Green Street	D2-D3
Harriet Road	E4
High Street	D3
Hill Street	D3-C3-C4
Holehouse Road	E2-F2
Howard Street	C1
Irvine Road	B2-A2-A3
John Finnie Street	C2-C3
Kay Park Terrace	F2-F3-E3, F3-E3-F3-E3
King Street	C1-C2-D2-D3
Langlands Street	C3
Larch Place	A2-A1
Leslie Place	F4
Lilac Place	A2
Lime Place	A1
Lindsay Street	B2-C2
Loanhead Street	D1-E1-E2
London Road	D2-E2-E1-F1
Mackenzie Drive	F2
Makinlay Place	E1-F1
Macnab Place	F2
Macneil Place	F2
MacPhail Drive	F2
Maple Drive	A1
Melville Street	E1-E2-F2
Middlemass Drive	E1-F1
Montgomery Street	C4
Morton Place	C2
Munro Avenue	A3-A4
Munro Place	A4-B4
Nelson Street	C2
Nursery Avenue	E1
North Dean Road	E4
North Hamilton Street	B2-B3
Oak Place	A1
Olive Road	A2
Old Irvine Road	B2-C2
Old Mill Road	D1
Orchard Street	D4
Park Street	B3-C3
Portland Road	B2-C2
Portland Street	D3
Princess Street	D1
Rennie Street	D1-D2
Rugby Road	B1
St Marnock Street	C1-C2
Sampson Avenue	F1
Suadbed Street	C2-D2
Seaford Street	B1-C1-C2
South Dean Road	E4-F4
South Hamilton Street	B1-B2
Southhook Road	A4
Stevenson Street	A3
Strand	C2-C3
Strawberry Bank Road	F3-E3-E4-F4
Sturrock Street	D1-D2
Titchfield Street	C1
Thomson Street	D4
Townholm	E4
Union Street	D3
Walker Aveue	F1-F2
Warwickhill Road	A3-A4
Waterside Street	C1
Watson Street	F1
Wellington Street	D3-D4
Western Road	A4-B4
West George Street	C3-D3
West Langlands Street	B3-C3
William Street	D4
Willie Mairs Brae	D4-E4
Wilson Avenue	E2-F2
Witch Road	C4-D4
Woodstock Place	B2-C2
Woodstock Street	B2-C2
Yorke Place	A3-B3

Ayr

Ailsa Place	A3-B3
Albert Terrace	D3
Alloway Park	B1
Alloway Place	B1-B2
Alloway Street	C1-C2
Arran Terrace	A3-A4
Ashgrove Street	D1-E1
Barns Crescent	B1-B2
Barns Park	B2
Barns Street	B2-C2
Bath Place	A2-B2
Beresford Terrace	C1
Boswell Park	B3-C3-C2
Bruce Crescent	B3
Burns Statue Square	C1-D1
Carrick Street	C2
Cassillis Street	B2-B3
Cathcart Street	B3
Charlotte Street	A3-B3
Citadel Place	B3
Content Avenue	E2
Craigie Avenue	D3-E3
Craigie Lea	F2-F3
Craigie Road	E2-E3-E4
Craigie Way	E3-F3-F2
Cromwell Road	A3-B3
Dalblair Road	C1-C2
Dongola Road	E1
Eglinton Terrace	B3-B4
Elba Street	D3-D4
Esplanade	A1-A2-A3-A4-B4
Fairfield Road	B1-A1
Fort Street	B2-B3-B4
Fotheringham Road	E2-E3
Fullarton Street	B2-C2
Gordon Terrace Road	D3
Green Street	B4
High Street	C2-C3
Holmston Road	D1-E1-F1
James Campbell Road	F2-F3
James Street	D4
John Street	E2-D2-D3-D4-C4
King Street	C4-D4
Kyle Street	C2-D2-D1
Limond's Wynd	D4
Main Street	C4
Mill Brae	D1-D2
Miller Road	B1-C1
Mill Street	C3-C2-D2
Mill Wynd	C2-D2
Montgomerie Terrace	B4-B3
New Bridge Street	B3-C3-C4
Newmarket Street	B3-C3
North Harbour Street	C4-B4
Park Circus	B1-C1
Parkhouse Street	C1-D1
Park Terrace	B2
Pavilion Road	A2
Queen's Terrace	A2-A3
Queen Street	D4
Racecourse Road	B1
River Street	C4
St Johns Street	B3
Sandgate	B2-B3
Sea Bank Road	A4-B4
Smith Street	D1-D2
South Harbour Street	C4-B4-A4
Station Road	D1-D2-E2
Victoria Street	B3
Whiteletts Road	D4-E4
York Street	B4

Ayr

Set on the lovely coastline of the Firth of Clyde, Ayr enjoys a well-deserved reputation as one of Scotland's most attractive seaside resorts. Its fine natural assets of sandy beaches and pastoral river scenery have been augmented by extensive parks and gardens, as well as a host of leisure amenities.

However, some of Ayr's visitors are drawn to the town by its associations with Scotland's beloved national poet – Robert Burns. He was born at the nearby village of Alloway and many of the places immortalised in his poems can be seen in Ayr. These include the medieval Auld Brig, one of the famous 'twa brigs' that span the River Ayr. The thatched Tam O'Shanter Inn in the High Street, now a museum devoted to Burns, and an imposing statue, are further reminders that this was 'Rabbie's' town.

Ayr has been a prosperous fishing port for centuries and its harbour provides a particularly charming focal point to the town. Surprisingly, few buildings pre-date the 19th century, but one exception is Loudon Hall – a fine 16th-century town house now open to the public. Several handsome Georgian edifaces surround Wellington Square, overlooked by the soaring steeple of the Town Buildings. A statue here commemorates another son of Ayr, John Macadam, who invented the road surface that bears his name.

84

AYR
The town has been an important fishing port on the Firth of Clyde for several hundred years. Today, Ayr is a major seaside resort and tourist centre and the harbour is as busy as ever, with yachts and leisure craft.

Coatbridge

Six villages went into the making of Coatbridge, a town whose iron and coal mining made it the centre of the Scottish iron industry. Scotland's first railway was here, but today Coatbridge achieves industrial prominence via its waterway, which gives it the largest inland port in Britain and is part of a major project to revitalise the entire town. Drumpellier Country Park nearby stands in fine wood and loch surroundings.

Airdrie Few industrial towns make such a pleasant first impression on the visitor as Airdrie, which, for all its industrial past, still has the air of a country market centre.

Motherwell Heartland of Scottish steelmaking, the place where the metal for the hulls of the *Queen Mary* and *Queen Elizabeth* was forged, Motherwell is a town where industry is heard and felt. But the town's name has gentler origins: it

comes from a well — or pool — dedicated to the Virgin Mary, the site of which is marked by a plaque in Ladywell Road.

Hamilton's most notable landmark is the beautiful dome construction of Hamilton Mausoleum, noted for the six-second echo it produces. An industrial centre set in attractive surroundings, the town also enjoys a race course and an ice-rink, and in Strathclyde Park, it has excellent land and water sports facilities.

Map labels (Coatbridge Area): A891, B822, Lennoxtown, Queenszieburn, Banton, KILSYTH, A803, Milton of Campsie, Auchinstarry, Dullatur, Castlecarry, Croy, Twechar, B8048, Torrance, B803, A803, CUMBERNAULD, Banknock, FALKIRK, Redding, Maddiston, Shieldhill, Wallacestone, Brightons, California, Avonbridge, Slamannan, B8022, Standburn, Westfield, KIRKINTILLOCH, Condorrat, Mollinsburn, Riggend, Greengairs, High Limerigg, B825, Armadale, Balmore, Bishopbriggs, Boghead, Lenzie, Muirhead, Marnock, Wattston, Block Loch, Blackridge, A89, Springburn, Balornock, Stepps, Garnkirk, Glenboig, Glenmavis, Caldercruix, Plains, Hillend Res., M8, Barmulloch, Garthamlock, Gartsherrie, AIRDRIE, Drumgelloch, Harthill, Port Garngad, Easterhouse, COATBRIDGE, Coatdyke, Gartlea, Eastfield, Whitburn, GLASGOW, Carntyne, Baillieston, A8, Chapelhall, Kirk of Shotts, Fauldhouse, Bridgeton, Calderbank, Salsburgh, B7010, Gorbals, Parkhead, Muirhead, Birkenshaw, Calderbank, Shotts, Dalmarnock, Carmyle, Kylepark, Mossend, Holytown, B718, Stane, Outlands, Tannochside, New, Newarthill, Dykehead, Rutherglen, Uddingston, Bellshill, Stevenston, B7011, Netherlee, Flemington, Bothwell, Carfin, Hareshaw, Cleland, Hartwood, Allanton, B715, Castlemilk, Nerston, Stonefield, MOTHERWELL, Craigneuk, Wishaw, New mains, Carmunnock, Burnbank, Sheildmuir, Forth, East Mains, Udston, HAMILTON, Muirhouse, Wildmanbridge, West Mains, EAST KILBRIDE, Laighstonehall, Low, Allanton, A72, The Murray, Fairhill, Waters, Limekilnburn, Larkhall, B7056, B7011, Yieldshields, Millheugh, Machan, Ashgill, CARLUKE, A721, Chapelton, Glassford, River Clyde, Carstairs, STONEHOUSE, M74, LANARK, A706, A70, STRATHAVEN, Kirkmuirhill, Kirkfieldbank, New Lanark, Avon Water, Drumclog, A723, Lesmahagow, Coatbridge Area, SCALE, N, A71

Boxes denote area covered by central plan

Key to Town Plan and Area Plan

Town Plan
A A Recommended roads
Other roads
Restricted roads
Buildings of interest Mill
Car Parks P
Parks and open spaces

Area Plan
A roads
B roads
Locations Banton
Urban Area

Street Index with Grid Reference

Coatbridge

Academy Street	B2-B3
Albert Street	B3
Albion Street	C2
Alexander Street	B3-C3
Alston Avenue	B4-C4
Baird Street	B3
Bank Street	A2
Blairhill Street	A2
Bowling Street	A2
Buchanan Street	A2
Burnbank Street	B4-C4
Cameron Street	C4
Cecil Street	B1
Chassels Street	B4
Chisholm Street	C4
Church Street	B2-B3
Clyde Street	C2
Coatbank Street	C1-C2
Coats Street	C2
Colt Place	B3
Colt Terrace	B3
Coltswood Road	B4
Cornhill Drive	A3-A4
Corsewall Street	A2-A3
Crichton Street	B3
Dunbeth Avenue	B3-C3
Dunbeth Road	B2-B3
Dundyvan Road	A1-A2
Eglinton Street	C3
Gartgill Road	A4
Gartsherrie Road	A4-B3-B4
Henderson Street	A1-A2
Hillcrest Avenue	A4
Hollandhurst Road	A4
Hutchinson Place	A1
Inveresk Place	B4
Jackson Street	C2
Kelso Quadrant	A3
Kildonan Street	C3
King Street	A2
Kirk Street	A1-A2
Laird Street	B3-C3
Laurelbank	A4-B4
Lefroy Street	A2
Lugar Street	B3-C3
Main Street	B2-C2
Manse Street	A1-A2
Miller Street	C1
Montgomery Avenue	A3
Morton Street	B4
Muiryhall Street	B2-B3-C2-C3
Oxford Street	A1-A2
Park Street	C2-C3
Portland Street	C3
Reid Street	B4
Russel Colt Street	B3-B4
St John Street	B2-B3
South Circular Road	B2
Stewart Street	B3-B4
Stobcross Street	A2-B1-B2
Summerlee Street	A2-A3
Sunnyside Road	A3-B3
Tennent Street	C1
Turner Street	A1
Waverley Street	C4
Weir Street	B3
West Canal Street	A2
West George Street	A4-B4

Airdrie

Aitchison Street	A3
Aitken Street	B4-C4
Albert Place	C3
Alexander Street	A2-A3
Arran Drive	A4
Arthur Avenue	A2-B2
Ballochney Street	A4
Bank Street	B3
Bell Street	A3
Bellsdyke Road	A1-A2-B1
Broomfield Street	B2-C2
Broomknoll Street	B2-B3
Bore Road	C3-C4
Burnbank Street	A3
Burns Crescent	C1-C2
Cairnhill Crescent	A1-B2
Cairnhill Road	A1-B1-B2
Cairnview	A1
Central Park Avenue	B3-C3-C4
Chapel Street	B4
Clark Street	C3
Commonhead Street	A4
Craig Street	A2
Davidson Street	A3
Devonview Street	A1-A2
Douglas Street	B1-B2
Drumbathie Road	C3
Faskine Avenue	A1
Firhill Avenue	A1
Flowerhill Street	C3
Forsyth Street	C3
Frew Street	B4-C4
Gartfield Street	B1
Gartlea Road	B1-B2-B3
Gartleahill	B1-C1-C2
Graham Street	B3
Hallcraig Street	B3-C3

Henderson Street	C3
High Street	A3
High Street East	B3
Hillfoot Road	C1
Hillhead Drive	B1-C1
Hogg Street	B2
Hunter Street	A4-B4
Hyslop Street	A3
Imperial Drive	A1
Johnston Street	C3
Kelvin Drive	C4
Kennedy Drive	A2
Kirkness Street	B3-B4-C4
Knox Street	C3
Lady Ann Crescent	C1-C2
Lady Wilson Street	C2
Lingley Avenue	B1
Livingstone Place	C2
Mavis Bank Street	A3-A4
Mill Road	B4
Milton Street	B3
Mitchel Street	A3
Monkland Street	B2-C2
Mossview Crescent	B1
North Biggar Road	C3
North Bridge Street	A3-A4-B3
Old Union Street	C2
Park Street	A3
Parkhead Lane	B3
Parnell Street	A1
Queen Victoria Street	A3
Reid Street	C4
Robertson Street	A3
Scotts Place	C3
Shanks Street	B4
South Biggar Road	C2-C3
South Bridge Street	B3
South Commonhead Avenue	A4-B4
Stirling Street	A3-B3
Stonefield Street	B4-C4
Strain Street	C2
Sword Street	A3
Target Road	C1-C2
Thomson Drive	A1-A2
Thistle Street	C4
Tinto Road	C1
Tollbrae Avenue	C2
Victoria Crescent	A2
Victoria Place	A2-B2
Waddell Street	B4-C4
Waverley Drive	C4
Wellington Street	B4
Wellwynd	A3-B3
Wesley Street	A3
West Kirk Street	A3
Western Mavisbank Avenue	A4
Wheatholm Street	C4
Whinhall Avenue	A4
Wilson Street	A3-A4
Woodburn Avenue	A1-A2

Hamilton

Abercorn Crescent	C2
Abercorn Drive	C1
Almada Street	A4
Alness Street	A1
Arthur Street	A4
Aspen Way	B1
Auchincampbell Road	A2
Auchingramont Road	A3-B3
Avon Street	B2
Avonside Grove	C2
Barncluith Road	C1-C2
Barrack Street	A4
Beckford Street	A4
Bent Road	A2
Blackswell Lane	C3
Bothwell Road	A4
Brandon Street	B2
Burnblea Gardens	A1-B1
Burnblea Street	A1-B1
Burns Street	A1-A2
Burnside Lane	B2
Cadzow Street	B3-C3
Campbell Street	B3-C3
Carlisle Road	C2
Castle Street	C3
Chestnut Crescent	B1-C1
Cheviot Road	C1-C2
Church Street	B3-C3
Duke Street	B2-C2
Dixon Street	A2
Edward Street	A1
Gateside Street	B2
Glebe Street	A1-A2
Graham Street	B2
Guthrie Street	A4
Haddow Street	B2
High Patrick Street	B2-C2
Hillside Crescent	A1
Hope Street	B2-B3
John Street	B2
Johnstone Road	B1
Keith Street	C3
Kemp Street	A2-B2
Laburnum Lea	B1
Lamb Street	B2-B3
Larch Grove	B1-C1
Leechlee Road	B2-B3
Lilac Hill	C1
Low Patrick Street	C2
Maple Bank	C1
Miller Street	C2
Montrose Crescent	A3
Morgan Street	A1
Mote Hill	C4
Motherwell Road	C3
Muir Street	B4-C4
Noyar Street	A1
Orchard Place	A2
Orchard Street	B2
Park Road	A2
Portland Park	B1
Portland Place	B1
Quarry Street	A2-B2
Regent Way	C2
Saffronhall Crescent	A3-A4
Scott Grove	A1

Scott Street	A1
Silvertonhill Avenue	B1
Station Road	B2
Strathmore Road	B3
South Park Road	A1-A2
Sycamore Drive	C1
Townhead Street	C2
Tuphall Road	A1-B2
Union Street	A2-A3
Windmill Road	A3-B4
Woodland Gardens	C1
Woodside Walk	B1-B2

Motherwell

Addie Street	B4-C4
Adele Street	C1
Airbles Drive	A1
Airbles Road	A1-B1-C1
Airbles Street	B2
Albert Street	B3-C3
Albion Street	C4
Allan Street	B2
Anderson Street	B1
Aster Gardens	A1-A2-B2-B3-A3
Avon Street	A4
Bellshill Road	B2-B3-C2
Brandon Street	B4-C4
Brown Street	A3-A4
Bruce Street	A2
Cadzow Street	B2
Cairn Street	B4
Calder Grove	B4
Cameron Street	B1-B2-C2
Camp Street	B4
Cassels Street	B1
Catherine Street	C3
Coursington Gardens	B3-C3-C4
Coursington Road	A2
Crawford Street	C2
Cross Hill Street	A2-A3
Cunningham Street	B3-B4
Dalziel Street	C1
Dellburn Street	A3
Douglas Street	C4
Draffen Court	B4
Duke Street	A3
Elm Street	A3
Elvan Street	C1
Farm Street	B1
Firpark Street	B1-C1
Freesia Court	B1
Gavin Street	B2-C2-C1
George Street	A2-A3-B3
Glencairn Street	A3-B3
Hamilton Road	A3-A4
High Road	A4
High Street	B4
James Street	A4
Kilnwell Quad	C1
Kirk Street	A3
Kirkland Street	C3-C4
Knowetop Avenue	B1
Ladywell Road	C1
Leslie Street	B2
Leven Street	B2-B3
Manse Street	C2
Mason Lane	B3-B4
Mason Street	B4-C4
Meadow Road	B4
Menteith Road	B4
Merry Street	A4-B3
Mill Road	A2
Millburn Street	C4
Milton Street	A3-A4
Morton Street	B2
Muir Street	A2
Muirhead Terrace	C4
Nigel Street	B2-C2
North Street	A3
North Orchard Street	B3-C3
Oakfield Road	B2-C2
Orbiston Street	A4-B4
Orchard Street	B3
Park Street	A4-B4
Parkhead Street	C2
Parkneuk Street	A3-A4
Paterson Street	B3
Pollock Street	C1
Roman road	B4
Rose Street	B2-B3
Scotia Street	A3
Scott Street	C1
Toll Street	B4
Vulcan Street	B2
Watson Street	A3
Wellview Drive	B2-B3
West Hamilton Street	C4
Wilson Street	C1-C2
Windmill Hill Street	B4
Woodburn Street	

Key to Town Plan and Area Plan

Town Plan
- A A Recommended roads
- Other roads
- Restricted roads
- Buildings of interest — Gallery
- Car Parks — P
- Parks and open spaces
- One Way Streets
- Churches — +

Area Plan
- A roads
- B roads
- Locations — Newcraighall O
- Urban area

Street Index with Grid Reference

Edinburgh

Abercromby Place	C6-D6
Adam Street	F3
Ainslie Place	B5
Albany Street	D6-E6
Alva Street	A4-B4
Ann Street	A6
Argyle Place	D1
Athol Crescent	A3-A4-B4
Bank Street	D4
Belford Road	A5
Belgrave Crescent	A5
Bells Brae	A5
Bernard Terrace	F1
Blackfriars Street	E4

Bread Street	B3-C3
Bristo Place	D3-E3
Brougham Street	C2
Broughton Street	E6
Bruntsfield Place	B1-C1
Buccleuch Place	E2
Buccleuch Street	E2-F2-F1
Buckingham Terrace	A5-A6
Caledonian Crescent	A2
Caledonian Road	A2
Calton Road	E5-F5
Candlemaker Row	D3
Canongate	E4-F4-F5
Canning Street	A3-B3-B4
Castle Hill	D4
Castle Street	C5
Castle Terrace	B4-B3-C3
Chalmers Street	C2-D2
Chambers Street	D3-E3
Charlotte Square	B4-B5

Chapel Street	E2
Chester Street	A4
Clerk Street	F1-F2
Clyde Street	D6-E6
Coates Crescent	A4-B4
Cockburn Street	D4-E4
Comely Bank Avenue	A6
Cowgate	D4-E4-F4
Dalry Road	A3
Dean Bridge	A5
Dean Park Crescent	A6
Dean Terrace	B6
Dewar Place	A3-B3
Doune Terrace	B6
Drummond Street	E3-F3-F4
Drumsheugh Gardens	A4-A5
Dublin Street	D6
Dumbiedykes Road	F3-F4
Dundas Street	C6
Dundee Street	A1-A2

Edinburgh

Scotland's ancient capital, dubbed the "Athens of the North", is one of the most splendid cities in the whole of Europe. Its buildings, its history and its cultural life give it an international importance which is celebrated every year in its world-famous festival. The whole city is overshadowed by the craggy castle which seems to grow out of the rock itself. There has been a fortress here since the 7th century and most of the great figures of Scottish history have been associated with it. The old town grew up around the base of Castle Rock within the boundaries of the defensive King's Wall and, unable to spread outwards, grew upwards in a maze of tenements. However, during the 18th century new prosperity from the shipping trade resulted in the building of the New Town and the regular, spacious layout of the Georgian development makes a striking contrast with the old hotch-potch of streets. Princes Street is the main east-west thoroughfare with excellent shops on one side and Princes Street Gardens with their famous floral clock on the south side.

As befits such a splendid capital city there are numerous museums and art galleries packed with priceless treasures. Among these are the famous picture gallery in 16th-century Holyroodhouse, the present Royal Palace, and the fascinating and unusual Museum of Childhood.

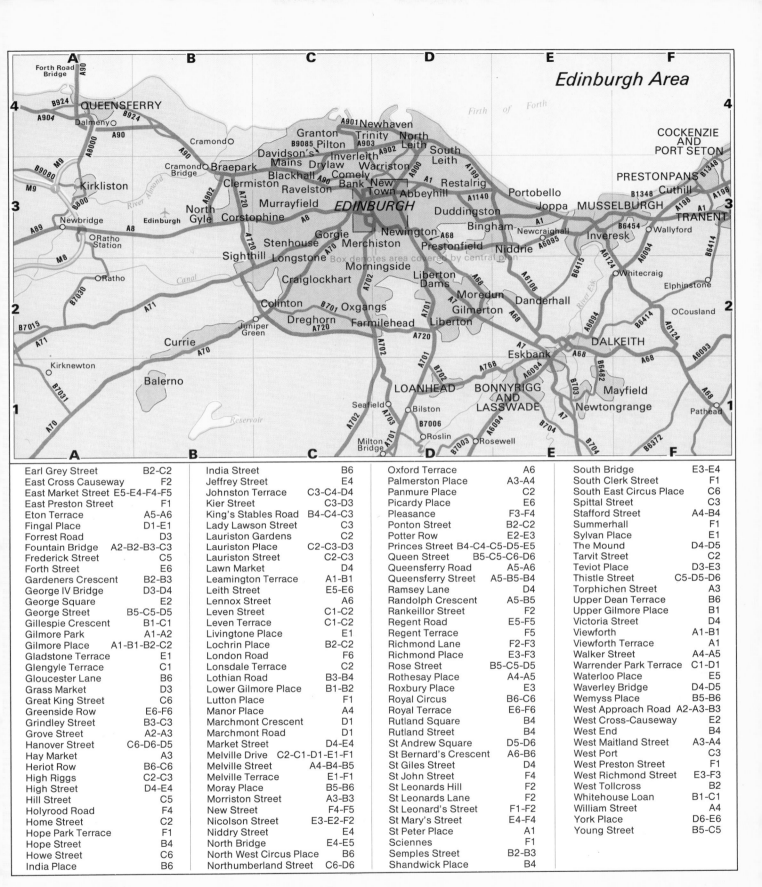

Edinburgh Area

Earl Grey Street	B2-C2	India Street	B6
East Cross Causeway	F2	Jeffrey Street	E4
East Market Street	E5-E4-F4-F5	Johnston Terrace	C3-C4-D4
East Preston Street	F1	Kier Street	C3-D3
Eton Terrace	A5-A6	King's Stables Road	B4-C4-C3
Fingal Place	D1-E1	Lady Lawson Street	C3
Forrest Road	D3	Lauriston Gardens	C2
Fountain Bridge	A2-B2-B3-C3	Lauriston Place	C2-C3-D3
Frederick Street	C5	Lauriston Street	C2-C3
Forth Street	E6	Lawn Market	D4
Gardeners Crescent	B2-B3	Leamington Terrace	A1-B1
George IV Bridge	D3-D4	Leith Street	E5-E6
George Square	E2	Lennox Street	A6
George Street	B5-C5-D5	Leven Street	C1-C2
Gillespie Crescent	B1-C1	Leven Terrace	C1-C2
Gilmore Park	A1-A2	Livingstone Place	E1
Gilmore Place	A1-B1-B2-C2	Lochrin Place	B2-C2
Gladstone Terrace	E1	London Road	F6
Glengyle Terrace	C1	Lonsdale Terrace	C2
Gloucester Lane	B6	Lothian Road	B3-B4
Grass Market	D3	Lower Gilmore Place	B1-B2
Great King Street	C6	Lutton Place	F1
Greenside Row	E6-F6	Manor Place	A4
Grindley Street	B3-C3	Marchmont Crescent	D1
Grove Street	A2-A3	Marchmont Road	D1
Hanover Street	C6-D6-D5	Market Street	D4-E4
Hay Market	A3	Melville Drive	C2-C1-D1-E1-F1
Heriot Row	B6-C6	Melville Street	A4-B4-B5
High Riggs	C2-C3	Melville Terrace	E1-F1
High Street	D4-E4	Moray Place	B5-B6
Hill Street	C5	Morrison Street	A3-B3
Holyrood Road	F4	New Street	F4-F5
Home Street	C2	Nicolson Street	E3-E2-F2
Hope Park Terrace	F1	Niddry Street	E4
Hope Street	B4	North Bridge	E4-E5
Howe Street	C6	North West Circus Place	B6
India Place	B6	Northumberland Street	C6-D6

Oxford Terrace	A6	South Bridge	E3-E4
Palmerston Place	A3-A4	South Clerk Street	F1
Panmure Place	C2	South East Circus Place	C6
Picardy Place	E6	Spittal Street	C3
Pleasance	F3-F4	Stafford Street	A4-B4
Ponton Street	B2-C2	Summerhall	F1
Potter Row	E2-E3	Sylvan Place	E1
Princes Street	B4-C4-C5-D5-E5	The Mound	D4-D5
Queen Street	B5-C5-C6-D6	Tarvit Street	C2
Queensferry Road	A5-A6	Teviot Place	D3-E3
Queensferry Street	A5-B5-B4	Thistle Street	C5-D5-D6
Ramsey Lane	D4	Torphichen Street	A3
Randolph Crescent	A5-B5	Upper Dean Terrace	B6
Rankeillor Street	F2	Upper Gilmore Place	B1
Regent Road	E5-F5	Victoria Street	D4
Regent Terrace	F5	Viewforth	A1-B1
Richmond Lane	F2-F3	Viewforth Terrace	A1
Richmond Place	E3-F3	Walker Street	A4-A5
Rose Street	B5-C5-D5	Warrender Park Terrace	C1-D1
Rothesay Place	A4-A5	Waterloo Place	E5
Roxburgh Place	E3	Waverley Bridge	D4-D5
Royal Circus	B6-C6	Wemyss Place	B5-B6
Royal Terrace	E6-F6	West Approach Road	A2-A3-B3
Rutland Square	B4	West Cross-Causeway	E2
Rutland Street	B4	West End	B4
St Andrew Square	D5-D6	West Maitland Street	A3-A4
St Bernard's Crescent	A6-B6	West Port	C3
St Giles Street	D4	West Preston Street	F1
St John Street	F4	West Richmond Street	E3-F3
St Leonards Hill	F2	West Tollcross	B2
St Leonards Lane	F2	Whitehouse Loan	B1-C1
St Leonard's Street	F1-F2	William Street	A4
St Mary's Street	E4-F4	York Place	D6-E6
St Peter Place	A1	Young Street	B5-C5
Sciennes	F1		
Semples Street	B2-B3		
Shandwick Place	B4		

EDINBURGH
Holyrood Palace orginated as a guest house for the Abbey of Holyrood in the 16th century, but most of the present building was built for Charles II. Mary Queen of Scots was one of its most famous inhabitants.

Glasgow

Although much of Glasgow is distinctly Victorian in character, its roots go back very many centuries. Best link with the past is the cathedral; founded in the 6th century, it has features from many succeeding centuries, including an exceptional 13th-century crypt. Nearby is Provand's Lordship, the city's oldest house. It dates from 1471 and is now a museum. Two much larger museums are to be found a little out of the centre – the Art Gallery and Museum contains one of the finest collections of paintings in Britain, while the Hunterian Museum, attached to the University, covers geology, archaeology, ethnography and more general subjects. On Glasgow Green is People's Palace – a museum of city life. Most imposing of the Victorian buildings are the City Chambers and City Hall which was built in 1841 as a concert hall but now houses the Scottish National Orchestra.

Paisley is famous for the lovely fabric pattern to which it gives its name. It was taken from fabrics brought from the Near East in the early 19th century, and its manufacture, along with the production of thread, is still important.

Greenock has been an important port and shipbuilding centre since as early as the 16th century. Its most famous son is James Watt, the inventor of steam power, born here in 1736. The town has numerous memorials to the great man.

LEGEND

Town Plan

AA recommended route
Restricted roads
Other roads
Buildings of interest Station
Car parks
Parks and open spaces
One way streets

Area Plan

A roads
B roads
Locations Garvock O
Urban area

Street Index with grid reference

Glasgow

Paisley

Greenock

Glasgow environs

Cumbernauld is a New Town — built during the 1950s and '60s, it was specially designed to provide easy access for both motorists and pedestrians. A multi-level shopping area, a sports centre and a thriving local theatre are some of the amenities it enjoys, and amongst the many parks and open spaces in the area, Palacerigg Country Park (1½ miles to the south-east) covers over 600 acres.

Bearsden is noted for its public parks and woodland areas. It became established as a residential area in the 19th century, but a number of Georgian buildings are used by the community: Kilmardinny House, for instance, is an Arts Centre with a small theatre.

East Kilbride was well-known for its shoemaking and weaving in the 18th century. Its designation as a New Town shortly after the end of World War I boosted its expansion, and today, it is noted for

the good integration of new buildings with old. Popular attractions among the modern buildings are the arcaded shopping precinct and the Dollan Swimming Pool, lying beneath an unusually deep roof within the town's central park.

Kirkintilloch Once a station on the old Roman wall, Kirkintilloch in recent years has suffered from the decline of a good many local industries. The former Parish Church of St Mary has been converted into a local history museum.

92

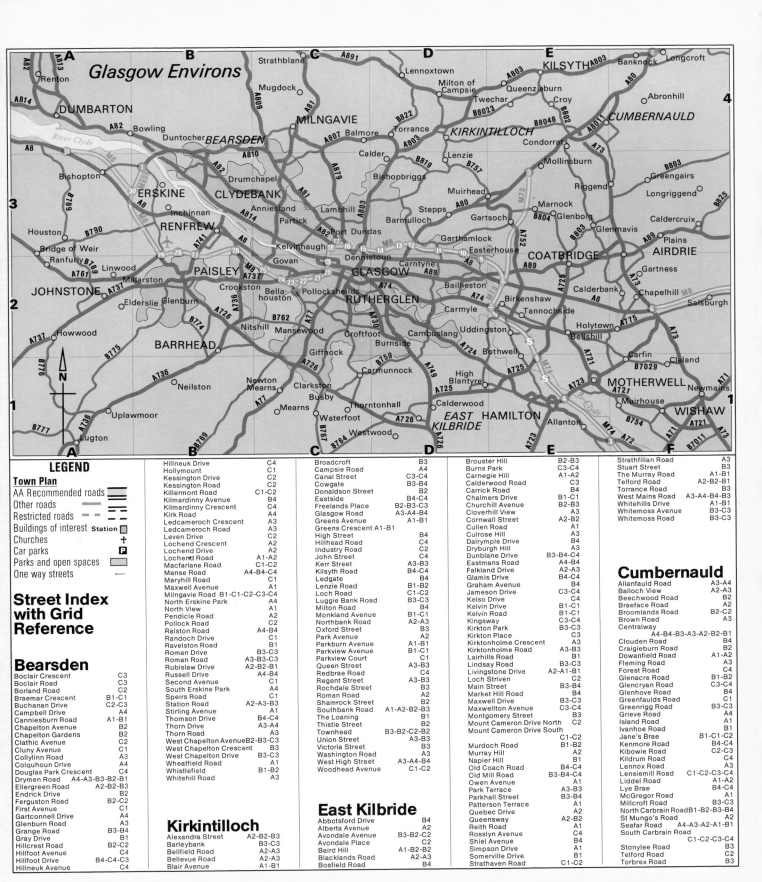

Glasgow Environs

(Map showing Glasgow and surrounding areas including Dumbarton, Bearsden, Milngavie, Kirkintilloch, Kilsyth, Cumbernauld, Clydebank, Renfrew, Paisley, Johnstone, Barrhead, Glasgow, Rutherglen, Coatbridge, Airdrie, Motherwell, Wishaw, Hamilton, East Kilbride, etc.)

A 4

LEGEND

Town Plan
AA Recommended roads	▬▬
Other roads	
Restricted roads	‒ ‒ ‒
Buildings of interest	Station ▣
Churches	+
Car parks	ℙ
Parks and open spaces	▭
One way streets	←

Street Index with Grid Reference

Bearsden

Boclair Crescent	C3
Boclair Road	C3
Borland Road	C2
Braemar Crescent	B1-C1
Buchanan Drive	C2-C3
Campbell Drive	A4
Canniesburn Road	A1-B1
Chapelton Avenue	B2
Chapelton Gardens	B2
Clathic Avenue	C2
Cluny Avenue	C1
Collylinn Road	A3
Colquhoun Drive	A4
Douglas Park Crescent	C4
Drymen Road	A4-A3-B3-B2-B1
Ellergreen Road	A2-B2-B3
Endrick Drive	B2
Ferguston Road	B2-C2
First Avenue	C1
Gartconnell Drive	A4
Glenburn Road	A3
Grange Road	B3-B4
Gray Drive	B1
Hillcrest Road	B2-C2
Hillfoot Avenue	C4
Hillfoot Drive	B4-C4-C3
Hillneuk Avenue	C4
Hillneuk Drive	C4
Hollymount	C1
Kessington Drive	C2
Kessington Road	C2
Killermont Road	C1-C2
Kilmardinny Avenue	B4
Kilmardinny Crescent	C4
Kirk Road	A4
Ledcameroch Crescent	A3
Ledcameroch Road	A3
Leven Drive	C2
Lochend Crescent	A2
Lochend Drive	A2
Lochend Road	A1-A2
Macfarlane Road	C1-C2
Manse Road	A4-B4-C4
Maryhill Road	C1
Maxwell Avenue	A1
Milngavie Road	B1-C1-C2-C3-C4
North Erskine Park	A4
North View	A1
Pendicle Road	A2
Pollock Road	C2
Ralston Road	A4-B4
Randoch Drive	C1
Ravelston Road	B1
Roman Drive	B3-C3
Roman Road	A3-B3-C3
Rubislaw Drive	A2-B2-B1
Russell Drive	A4-B4
Second Avenue	C1
South Erskine Park	A4
Speirs Road	A1
Station Road	A2-A3-B3
Stirling Avenue	A1
Thomson Drive	B4-C4
Thorn Drive	A3-A4
Thorn Road	A3
West Chapelton Avenue	B2-B3-C3
West Chapelton Crescent	B3
West Chapelton Drive	B3-C3
Wheatfield Road	A1
Whistlefield	B1-B2
Whitehill Road	A3

Kirkintilloch

Alexandra Street	A2-B2-B3
Barleybank	B3-C3
Bellfield Road	A2-A3
Bellevue Road	A2-A3
Blair Avenue	A1-B1
Broadcroft	B3
Campsie Road	A4
Canal Street	C3-C4
Cowgate	B3-B4
Donaldson Street	B2
Eastside	B4-C4
Freelands Place	B2-B3-C3
Glasgow Road	A3-A4-B4
Greens Avenue	A1-B1
Greens Crescent	A1-B1
High Street	B4
Hillhead Road	C4
Industry Road	C2
John Street	C4
Kerr Street	A3-B3
Kilsyth Road	B4-C4
Ledgate	B4
Lenzie Road	B1-B2
Loch Road	C1-C2
Luggie Bank Road	B3-C3
Milton Road	B4
Monkland Avenue	B1-C1
Northbank Road	A2-A3
Oxford Street	B3
Park Avenue	A2
Parkburn Avenue	A1-B1
Parkview Avenue	B1-C1
Parkview Court	C1
Queen Street	A3-B3
Redbrae Road	C4
Regent Street	A3-B3
Rochdale Street	B3
Roman Road	A2
Shamrock Street	B2
Southbank Road	A1-A2-B2-B3
The Loaning	B1
Thistle Street	B2
Townhead	B3-B2-C2-B2
Union Street	A3-B3
Victoria Street	B3
Washington Road	A3
West High Street	A3-A4-B4
Woodhead Avenue	C1-C2

East Kilbride

Abbotsford Drive	B4
Alberta Avenue	A2
Avondale Avenue	B3-B2-C2
Avondale Place	C2
Baird Hill	A1-B2-B2
Blacklands Road	A2-A3
Bosfield Road	B4
Brouster Hill	B2-B3
Burns Park	C3-C4
Carnegie Hill	A1-A2
Calderwood Road	C3
Carrick Road	B4
Chalmers Drive	B1-C1
Churchill Avenue	B2-B3
Cloverhill View	A3
Cornwall Street	A2-B2
Cullen Road	A1
Culrose Hill	A3
Dalrymple Drive	B4
Dryburgh Hill	A3
Dunblane Drive	B3-B4-C4
Eastmans Road	A4-B4
Falkland Road	A2-A3
Glamis Drive	B4-C4
Graham Avenue	B3
Jameson Drive	C3-C4
Kelso Drive	C4
Kelvin Drive	B1-C1
Kelvin Road	B1-C1
Kingsway	C3-C4
Kirkton Park	B3-C3
Kirkton Place	C3
Kirktonholme Crescent	A3
Kirktonholme Road	A3-B3
Lairhills Road	B1
Lindsay Road	B3-C3
Livingstone Drive	A2-A1-B1
Loch Striven	C2
Main Street	B3-B4
Market Hill Road	B4
Maxwell Drive	B3-C3
Maxwellton Avenue	C3-C4
Montgomery Street	B3
Mount Cameron Drive North	C2
Mount Cameron Drive South	C1-C2
Murdoch Road	B1-B2
Murray Hill	A2
Napier Hill	B1
Old Coach Road	B4-C4
Old Mill Road	B3-B4-C4
Owen Avenue	A1
Park Terrace	A3-B3
Parkhall Street	B3-B4
Patterson Terrace	A1
Quebec Drive	A2
Queensway	A2-B2
Reith Road	A1
Rosslyn Avenue	C4
Shiel Avenue	B4
Simpson Drive	A1
Somerville Drive	B1
Strathaven Road	C1-C2
Strathfillan Road	A3
Stuart Street	B3
The Murray Road	A1-B1
Telford Road	A2-B2-B1
Torrance Road	B3
West Mains Road	A3-A4-B4-B3
Whitehills Drive	A1-B1
Whitemoss Avenue	B3-B4
Whitemoss Road	B3-C3

Cumbernauld

Allanfauld Road	A3-A4
Balloch View	A2-A3
Beechwood Road	B2
Braeface Road	A2
Broomlands Road	B2-C2
Brown Road	A3
Centralway	A4-B4-B3-A3-A2-B2-B1
Clouden Road	B2
Craigieburn Road	A1-A2
Downanfield Road	A3
Fleming Road	C4
Forest Road	C4
Glenacre Road	B1-B2
Glencryan Road	C3-C4
Glenhove Road	B4
Greenfaulds Road	C1
Greenrigg Road	B3-C3
Grieve Road	A4
Island Road	B1
Ivanhoe Road	B1
Jane's Brae	B1-C1-C2
Kenmore Road	B4-C4
Kibowie Road	C2-C3
Kildrum Road	C4
Lennox Road	A3
Lensiemill Road	C1-C2-C3-C4
Liddel Road	A1-A2
Lye Brae	B4-C4
McGregor Road	A1
Millcroft Road	B3-C3
North Carbrain Road	B1-B2-B3-B4
St Mungo's Road	A2
Seafar Road	A4-A3-A2-A1-B1
South Carbrain Road	C1-C2-C3-C4
Stonylee Road	B3
Telford Road	C2
Torbrex Road	B3

EAST KILBRIDE
A fine modern Civic Centre symbolises the forward-looking approach of East Kilbride — an agricultural town of just 2,400 people in 1946, but now one of Britain's biggest new towns.

TERMINAL
BUILDING

JUBILEE ROAD

CAR PARK

Car Hire
Return

POL

Airport Administration
Offices

Car Hire

Port Royal
Golf Range

ROYAL HIGHLAND
SHOWGROUND (INGLISTON)

Exhibition
Hall

Parade
Ring

Agricultural
Musuem

R.H. Ag.
S. of Scot.
Offices

INGLISTON ROAD

A8

Security
Gate

EASTFIELD ROAD

General Aviation
Terminal

RUNWAY

RUNWAY

Cargo
Terminal

CAMMO ROAD

TURNHOUSE ROAD

RAF
TURNHOUSE

TURNHOUSE FARM ROAD

River Almond

N

GLASGOW — ROAD — A8

Edinburgh Airport

SCALE

0   200 yds

0   220 mtrs

Forth Road
Bridge

A90

QUEENSFERRY

B924

Dalmeny

A904

A8000

A90

B9080 M9

Kirkliston

B800

M9

A89

Newbridge

A8

Ratho
Station

M8

Ratho

B7030

A71

Canal

River Almond

Cramond

Braepark

Cramond
Bridge

A902

A720

North Gyle

Edinburgh
Airport

Sighthill

N

Edinburgh Airport

Charter flights to international holiday
destinations such as Spain, Italy, Corsica and
Portugal, business flights to Paris, Amsterdam
and Frankfurt and commuter links with the Leeds,
Humberside, East Midlands and Norwich Airports are
among the services offered by Edinburgh Airport.

Originally known as Turnhouse Aerodrome, it
was used by the Royal Flying Corps in World War I,
because its closeness to the railway allowed for
the delivery of aircraft by rail. The airport
remained under military control and in World War
II was a fighter station — a period commemorated
by the vintage Spitfire which is on display near
the cargo terminal.

Next came the very different years of
redevelopment, and the British Airports Authority
took control in 1971. A new runway and terminal
building had been added by 1977, the year in which
HM the Queen honoured Edinburgh Airport by coming
here to open the new building.

Available for the convenience of passengers and
other visitors to the airport today is the
Aerogrill on the first floor. Refreshments are
also supplied by the buffet on the ground floor.
Alongside each of these is a bar, and to
complement the service they provide, the
International Departure Lounge also offers the
facilities of a bar and buffet.

Ready to deal with any enquiries or problems
that arise is the Airport Information Desk, which
is situated on the main concourse of the Terminal,
and is open from 7am to 11pm.

For those wishing to watch the aeroplanes and
the airport at work, a spectators' viewing terrace
has been provided. This is accessible by lift and
is open to visitors during daylight hours. The
terrace runs along the northern side of the second
floor of the Terminal.

The airport can be reached by car via the A8
from Edinburgh, and open air car parking is
available for 1,025 vehicles. A regular coach
service operates between Edinburgh (Waverley
Bridge) and the airport, and the journey takes 25
minutes. There is also a coach service to link it
with Glasgow Airport, with a pick-up point on the A8
outside the airport.

Glasgow Airport

(map labels) Glasgow Airport · A726 · BARNSFORD ROAD · Black Cart Water · SCALE · 0 220 440 yds · 0 200 400 mtrs · N · RUNWAY · Control Tower · DOMESTIC PIER · INTERNATIONAL PIER · TERMINAL BUILDING · McAlpine Helicopters Ltd · Loganair · MULTI-STOREY CAR PARK · SHORT TERM CAR PARK · Cargo Area · Flying Clubs · BUTE ROAD · CAR PARK · CAR PARK · ANDREW'S ST · DRIVE · CALEDONIA WAY · POL · Administration Building · CAMPSIE DRIVE · ABBOTSINCH · White Cart Water · Swan National Car Hire · Exits · CAR PARK · Excelsior Hotel · ST ANDREWS DRIVE · Hertz & Avis (Return Cars) · M8 · A726 · A726 ROAD · BARNSFORD ROAD · M8 · A726 · 29 · Footbridge · Playing Fields · St James Park (Playing Fields) · 28 · Sauderling Service Station (07.00-22.00) · Swan National (Return Cars) and Budget Rent a Car · MARCHFIELD AVENUE · Godfrey Davis Car Hire · INCHINNAN ROAD · NEW INCHINNAN ROAD · MOSSLANDS ROAD · M8 · A740 · McFARLANE STREET · A726 · RUSSELL ST · GOCKLYN ROAD · FULLERTON STREET · A741 RENFREW RD.

Glasgow Airport

Crucial as the fast link between Scotland's business community and the financial centre of London, this is Scotland's busiest international airport. Business flights have been calculated to make up approximately 40 per cent of Glasgow Airport's traffic, but it is also popular with other travellers — both scheduled and holiday flights are operated from here and go to a wide variety of destinations around the world.

The original site was known as Abbotsinch, and was used as an aerodrome by 602 Squadron of the Royal Auxiliary Air Force. During World War II it was converted into an RAF station, and was an important base at this time for the Fleet Air Arm. With the coming of peace and up until 1963, the airport became essentially a centre for repairs and for the fitting and testing of new aircraft.

By the early 1960s, however, it had been decided that the runway facilities at nearby Renfrew Airport were inadequate. Abbotsinch was selected as a more suitable site, and over the next three years the old aerodrome was to see a period of major redevelopment. Finally, it was renamed Glasgow Airport, and was officially opened as such by HM the Queen in 1966. Military connections of the past were remembered by the hanging in the main terminal of the crest and ship's bell of *HMS Sanderling,* which had operated from here during the war years.

In 1975, the ownership of the airport passed to the British Airports Authority. For car drivers, it lies eight miles west of Glasgow off the M8 at Junction 28. The airport is also accessible from the A8 west of Renfrew. Two car parks provide parking spaces under cover for 712 vehicles, and open air parking is provided for a further 1,164.

There are regular coach services direct from Central Glasgow, and coach services also operate between the airport and Edinburgh. Local buses run from Renfrew and Paisley.

For travellers and other visitors to the airport coming by British Rail, the nearest station is Paisley (Gilmour Street), which stands approximately one mile from the airport. Train connections are available to Ayrshire, Gourock, Glasgow and Wemyss Bay.

(inset map labels) Mugdock · A81 · KILPATRICK HILLS · MILNGAVIE · A809 · B8050 · A807 · A807 · Bowling · A810 · B8049 · Bardowie · Duntocher · BEARSDEN · A879 · ERSKINE · Drumchapel · A82 · N · M898 · A814 · CLYDEBANK · Temple · Inchinnan · River Clyde · A739 · A81 · A82 · A8 · RENFREW · A814 · Partick · A82 · M8 · Glasgow Airport · A741 · M8 · Govan · GLASGOW · A726 · 29 · 28 · 26 · 25 · 23 · 22 · PAISLEY · A740 · A737 · Eldersie · A736 · B766 · Cathcart · B775 · Glenburn · B774 · B771 · B762 · Nitshill · Pollokshaws · A77 · B766

95

Manchester International Airport

Nine miles south of the city of Manchester lies Manchester International Airport, operating flights to and from the Midlands, the north west, north east, Yorkshire and Wales. As well as flights within Britain, there are regular scheduled services operating to all the major business centres in Europe, the Far East and Australia. Charter and inclusive tour flights also operate from here to destinations world-wide.

The airport has been in use since just before World War II, and enjoys the distinction that its main buildings were opened by HRH Prince Philip. This was not until 1962, when the Prince became the first pilot to park an aircraft alongside the arrivals pier, and the first passenger to use the airport's facilities.

Today Manchester International has a spacious concourse area on the first floor of the terminal.

A bank, post office, bookstall, tobacconist and pharmacy are situated here. At the apron end of the concourse (and lying adjacent to the observation windows) is the Concourse Cafe, a self-service restaurant and bar. Also offering refreshments for travellers and other visitors to the airport is the 200-seat Lancaster restaurant and cocktail lounge, which overlooks International Pier B, and within just two minutes walk the Excelsior Hotel offers 300 bedrooms, a restaurant, a coffee shop and a bar.

The airport is well placed for passengers coming here by both road and rail. It offers easy access to the M56 and to the national motorway network. Greater Manchester Transport buses link the airport to Manchester and to Stockport all the year round, and also make a link to most towns in Greater Manchester during the summer months. Coach services also run to Birmingham, Liverpool, Lancaster, Leeds and Sheffield.

For railway travellers, the nearest station to the airport is Heald Green, which is about two miles away and has two bus services. Frequent trains go to Manchester (Piccadilly) and to Crewe.